Lecture Notes in Artificial Intelligence   2167

Subseries of Lecture Notes in Computer Science
Edited by J. G. Carbonell and J. Siekmann

Lecture Notes in Computer Science

Edited by G. Goos, J. Hartmanis, and J. van Leeuwen

Springer
Berlin
Heidelberg
New York
Barcelona
Hong Kong
London
Milan
Paris
Tokyo

Luc De Raedt Peter Flach (Eds.)

Machine Learning: ECML 2001

12th European Conference on Machine Learning
Freiburg, Germany, September 5-7, 2001
Proceedings

Springer

Series Editors

Jaime G. Carbonell,Carnegie Mellon University, Pittsburgh, PA, USA
Jörg Siekmann, University of Saarland, Saarbrücken, Germany

Volume Editors

Luc De Raedt
Albert-Ludwigs University Freiburg
Department of Computer Science
Georges Köhler-Allee, Geb. 079, 79110 Freiburg, Germany
E-mail: deraedt@informatik.uni-freiburg.de

Peter Flach
University of Bristol, Department of Computer Science
Merchant Ventures Bldg., Woodland Road
Bristol BS8 1UB, United Kingdom
E-mail: peter.flach@bristol.ac.uk

Cataloging-in-Publication Data applied for

Die Deutsche Bibliothek - CIP-Einheitsaufnahme

Machine learning : proceedings / ECML 2001, 12th European Conference on
Machine Learning, Freiburg, Germany, September 5 - 7, 2001. Luc de Raedt ;
Peter Flach (ed.). - Berlin ; Heidelberg ; New York ; Barcelona ; Hong Kong ;
London ; Milan ; Paris ; Tokyo : Springer, 2001
    (Lecture notes in computer science ; Vol. 2167 : Lecture notes in
    artificial intelligence)
    ISBN 3-540-42536-5

CR Subject Classification (1998): I.2, F.2.2, F.4.1

ISBN 3-540-42536-5 Springer-Verlag Berlin Heidelberg New York

This work is subject to copyright. All rights are reserved, whether the whole or part of the material is
concerned, specifically the rights of translation, reprinting, re-use of illustrations, recitation, broadcasting,
reproduction on microfilms or in any other way, and storage in data banks. Duplication of this publication
or parts thereof is permitted only under the provisions of the German Copyright Law of September 9, 1965,
in its current version, and permission for use must always be obtained from Springer-Verlag. Violations are
liable for prosecution under the German Copyright Law.

Springer-Verlag Berlin Heidelberg New York
a member of BertelsmannSpringer Science+Business Media GmbH

http://www.springer.de

© Springer-Verlag Berlin Heidelberg 2001
Printed in Germany

Typesetting: Camera-ready by author, data conversion by PTP Berlin, Stefan Sossna
Printed on acid-free paper   SPIN 10840363   06/3142   5 4 3 2 1 0

Preface

It is our pleasure to present the proceedings of the 12th European Conference on Machine Learning (this volume) and the 5th European Conference on Principles and Practice of Knowledge Discovery in Databases (*Lecture Notes in Artificial Intelligence 2168*). These two conferences were held September 3–7, 2001 in Freiburg, Germany, marking the first time – world-wide – that a data mining conference has been co-located with a machine learning conference.

As Program Committee co-chairs of the two conferences, our goal was to co-ordinate the submission and reviewing process as much as possible. Here are some statistics: a total of 117 papers was submitted to ECML 2001, 78 papers were submitted to PKDD 2001, and 45 papers were submitted as joint papers. Each paper was carefully reviewed by 3 (in exceptional circumstances 2 or 4) members of the Program Committees. Out of the 240 submitted papers, 40 were accepted after the first reviewing round, and 54 were accepted on the condition that the final paper would meet the requirements of the reviewers. In the end, 90 papers were accepted for the proceedings (50 for ECML 2001 and 40 for PKDD 2001).

We were also aiming at putting together a 5-day program that would be attractive, in its entirety, to both communities. This would encourage participants to stay the whole week and thus foster interaction and cross-fertilization. The PKDD 2001 conference ran from Monday to Wednesday, and the ECML 2001 conference from Wednesday to Friday, with the Wednesday program carefully selected to be of interest to a mixed audience. On each day there was an invited talk by an internationally renowned scientist. Tom Dietterich spoke on *Support Vector Machines for Reinforcement Learning*; Heikki Mannila on *Combining Discrete Algorithmic and Probabilistic Approaches in Data Mining*; Antony Unwin on *Statistification or Mystification, the Need for Statistical Thought in Visual Data Mining*; Gerhard Widmer on *The Musical Expression Project: A Challenge for Machine Learning and Knowledge Discovery*; and Stefan Wrobel on *Scalability, Search, and Sampling: From Smart Algorithms to Active Discovery*. In addition, there was an extensive parallel program of 11 workshops and 8 tutorials. Two workshops were devoted to results achieved by the participants in the two learning and mining challenges that were set prior to the conferences.

It has been a great pleasure for us to prepare and organize such a prestigious event, but of course we could not have done it without the help of many colleagues. We would like to thank all the authors who submitted papers to ECML 2001 and PKDD 2001, the program committee members of both conferences, the other reviewers, the invited speakers, the workshop organizers, and the tutorial speakers. We are particularly grateful to the workshop chairs Johannes Fürnkranz and Stefan Wrobel; the tutorial chairs Michèle Sebag and Hannu Toivonen; and the challenge chairs Petr Berka and Christoph Helma for their assisstance in putting together an exciting scientific program. Many thanks to Michael Keser for his technical support in setting up the CyberChair website, to Richard van de Stadt for developing CyberChair, and to the local team at Freiburg for the organizational support provided. We would also like to thank Alfred

Hofmann of Springer-Verlag for his co-operation in publishing these proceedings. Finally, we gratefully acknowledge the financial support provided by the sponsors; EU Network of Excellence MLnet II, National Institute of Environmental Health Sciences (US), SICK AG, the city of Freiburg, and the Albert-Ludwigs University Freiburg and its Lab for Machine Learning.

Although at the time of writing the event is yet to take place, we are confident that history will cast a favourable eye, and we are looking forward to continued and intensified integration of the European machine learning and data mining communities that we hope has been set in motion with this event.

July 2001   Luc De Raedt
                                                                Peter Flach
                                                                Arno Siebes

Executive Commitees

Program Chairs ECML-2001: Peter Flach (University of Bristol)
Luc De Raedt (Albert-Ludwigs University)
Program Chairs PKDD-2001: Arno Siebes (Utrecht University)
Luc De Raedt (Albert-Ludwigs University)
Tutorial Chairs: Michèle Sebag (Ecole Polytechnique)
Hannu Toivonen (Nokia)
Workshop Chairs: Johannes Fürnkranz (Austrian Research Institute for Artificial Intelligence)
Stefan Wrobel (University of Magdeburg)
Challenge Chairs: Petr Berka (University of Economics Prague)
Cristoph Helma (Albert-Ludwigs University)
Local Chairs: Luc De Raedt (Albert-Ludwigs University)
Stefan Kramer (Albert-Ludwigs University)
Local Organization: Catherine Blocher (K&K Freiburg)
Susanne Bourjaillat (Albert-Ludwigs University)
Dirk Hähnel (Albert-Ludwigs University)
Cristoph Helma (Albert-Ludwigs University)
Michael Keser (Albert-Ludwigs University)
Kristian Kersting (Albert-Ludwigs University)
Walter Koch (K&K Freiburg)
Andrea Kricheldorf (K&K Freiburg)
Advisory Committee : Ramon Lopez de Mantaras (IIIA-CSIC Artificial Intelligence Research Institute)
Heikki Mannila (Nokia and Helsinki University of Technology)
Jan Rauch (University of Economics Prague)
Maarten van Someren (University Amsterdam)
Stefan Wrobel (University of Magdeburg)
Djamel Zighed (University of Lyon 2)

ECML Program Committee

A. Aamodt (Norway)
H. Blockeel (Belgium)
H. Bostrom (Sweden)
I. Bratko (Slovenia)
P. Brazdil (Portugal)
W. Burgard (Germany)
J. Cussens (UK)
W. Daelemans (Belgium)
L. De Raedt (Germany)
M. Dorigo (Belgium)
S. Džeroski (Slovenia)
F. Esposito (Italy)
D. Fisher (USA)
P. Flach (UK)
J. Fürnkranz (Austria)
J.-G. Ganascia (France)
Y. Kodratoff (France)
S. Kramer (Germany)
N. Lavrač (Slovenia)
R. Lopez de Mantaras (Spain)
D. Malerba (Italy)
B. Manderick (Belgium)

S. Matwin (Canada)
K. Morik (Germany)
H. Motoda (Japan)
V. Moustakis (Greece)
S. Muggleton (UK)
C. Nedelec (France)
E. Plaza (Spain)
G. Paliouras (Greece)
C. Rouveirol (France)
L. Saitta (Italy)
M. Sebag (France)
A. Siebes (The Netherlands)
M. van Someren (The Netherlands)
D. Sleeman (UK)
P. Stone (USA)
P. Turney (Canada)
P. Vitanyi (The Netherlands)
G. Widmer (Austria)
R. Wirth (Germany)
S. Wrobel (Germany)

PKDD Program Committee

E. Baralis (Italy)
P. Berka (Czech Republic)
J.-F. Boulicaut (France)
H. Briand (France)
L. Carbonara (UK)
L. De Raedt (Germany)
L. Dehaspe (Belgium)
S. Džeroski (Slovenia)
A. Feelders (The Netherlands)
P. Flach (UK)
A. Flexer (Austria)
E. Frank (New Zealand)
A. Freitas (Brasil)
J. Fürnkranz (Austria)
P. Gallinari (France)
M.-S. Hacid (France)
H.J. Hamilton (Canada)
J. Han (Canada)
D.J. Hand (UK)
J. Keller (Germany)
J.-U. Kietz (Switzerland)
J. Kok (The Netherlands)
R. King (UK)
M. Klemettinen (Finland)
W. Klösgen (Germany)
Y. Kodratoff (France)
J. Koronacki (Poland)
S. Kramer (Germany)
G. Lausen (Germany)
H. Mannila (Finland)

S. Matwin (Canada)
H. Motoda (Japan)
W. Pedrycz (Canada)
R. Rakotomalala (France)
Z.W. Ras (USA)
J. Rauch (Czech Republic)
G. Ritschard (Switzerland)
C. Rouveirol (France)
S. Schulze-Kremer (Germany)
M. Sebag (France)
A. Siebes (The Netherlands)
A. Skowron (Poland)
M. van Someren (The Netherlands)
M. Spiliopoulou (Germany)
N. Spyratos (France)
E. Suzuki (Japan)
L. Todorovski (Slovenia)
S. Tsumoto (Japan)
A. Unwin (Germany)
J. Van den Bussche (Belgium)
G. Venturini (France)
L. Wehenkel (Belgium)
D. Wettschereck (Germany)
G. Widmer (Austria)
W. Winiwarter (Austria)
R. Wirth (Germany)
S. Wrobel (Germany)
D.A. Zighed (France)

Referees

F. Abbattista
E. Alphonse
I. Androutsopoulos
J. Azé
B. Bakker
M. Bernadet
A. Bianchetti-Jacques
G. Bisson
K. Bo
O. Bousquet
O. Brevik
P. Brockhausen
J. Cassens
G. Castellano
L-P. Castillo
J-H. Chauchat
R. Cicchetti
J. Costa
A. Cournuejols
E. de Jong
M. de Jong
J. Demšar
M. deRougemont
K. Driessens
C. Drummond
N. Fanizzi
S. Ferrili
R. Fried
J. Gama
W. Gersten
P. Geurts
A. Giacometti
B. Goethals
C. Green
M. Grobelnik

F. Guillet
S. Haustein
S. Hoche
T. Hrycej
M. Imhoff
N. Jacobs
A. Jakulin
B. Jeudy
A. Jorge
P. Juvan
N. Kabachi
D. Kalles
V. Karkaletsis
K. Kersting
F. Kirchner
M. Kirsten
R. Kosala
W. Kosters
M-A. Krogel
P. Kuntz
A. Lüthje
N. Labroche
L. Lakhal
C. Lanquillon
A. Lanza
D. Laurent
F. Lisi
P. Marcel
D. McAllester
N. Meuleau
R. Munos
C. Olaru
A. Oliver
J. Pei
G. Petasis

J-M. Petit
B. Pfahringer
O. Pivert
K. Pohle
T. Poibeau
S. Rüping
J. Ramon
O. Ritthof
M. Robnik-Šikonja
T. Scheffer
A. Seewald
C. Soares
F. Sormo
D. Suc
R. Sutton
I. Tellier
S. ten Hagen
A. Termier
G. Theocharous
N. Theocharous
M. Tommasi
L. Torgo
F. Torre
F. Toumani
Y. Tzitzikas
V. Ventos
M. Vetah
D. Vladusic
M. Wiering
K. Winkler
J. Wyatt
T. Yoshida
R. Zücker
B. Zupan

Tutorials

Development and Applications of Ontologies
Alexander Maedche

Bayesian Intelligent Decision Support
Kevin Korb

Support Vector Machines
Thorsten Joachims

Co-training and Learning from Labeled Data and Unlabeled Data
Francois Denis and Rémi Gilleron

KDD for Personalization
Bamshad Mobasher, Bettina Berendt, and Myra Spiliopoulou

Web Mining for E-Commerce: Concepts and Case Studies
Jaideep Srivastava and Robert Cooley

Text Mining: What If Your Data Is Made of Words?
Dunja Mladeníc and Marko Grobelnik

Visual Data Mining and Exploration of Large Databases
Daniel A. Keim and Mihael Ankerst

Workshops

Semantic Web Mining
  Gerd Stumme, Andreas Hotho, and Bettina Berendt

Machine Learning as Experimental Philosphy of Science
  Kevin Korb and Hilan Bensusan

Visual Data Mining
  Simeon J. Simoff, Monique Noirhomme-Fraiture, and Michael H. Böhlen

Integrating Aspects of Data Mining, Decision Support, and Meta-Learning
  Christophe Giraud-Carrier, Nada Lavrač, and Stephen Moyle

Active Learning, Database Sampling, Experiment Design: Views on Instance Selection
  Tobias Scheffer and Stefan Wrobel

Multi-relational Data Mining
  Arno Knobbe and Daniël van der Wallen

The Discovery Challenge on Thrombosis Data
  Petr Berka, Shusaku Tsumoto, Katsuhiko Takabayashi, and Shishir Gupta

The Predictive Toxicology Challenge for 2000-2001
  Christoph Helma, Ross D. King, Stefan Kramer, and Ashwin Srinivasan

Database Support for KDD
  Gunter Saake, Daniel Keim, Kai-Uwe Sattler, and Alexander Hinneburg

Data Mining for Marketing Applications
  Wendy Gersten and Koen Vanhoof

Ubiquitous Data Mining: Technology for Mobile and Distributed KDD
  Hillol Kargupta, Krishnamoorthy Sivakumar, and Ruediger Wirth

Contents

Invited Papers

An Axiomatic Approach to Feature Term Generalization

Hassan Aït-Kaci[1] and Yutaka Sasaki[2]

[1] Simon Fraser University
Burnaby, BC, Canada V5A 1S6, Canada
hak@sfu.ca

[2] NTT Communication Science Laboratories, NTT Corporation
2-4 Hikaridai, Seika-cho, Soraku-gun, Kyoto 619-0237, Japan
sasaki@cslab.kecl.ntt.co.jp

Abstract. This paper presents a missing link between Plotkin's least general generalization formalism and generalization on the *Order Sorted Feature (OSF)* foundation. A *feature term* (or ψ-*term*) is an extended logic term based on *ordered sorts* and is a normal form of an OSF-term. An *axiomatic* definition of ψ-term generalization is given as a set of OSF clause generalization rules and the least generality of the axiomatic definition is proven in the sense of Plotkin's least general generalization (lgg). The correctness of the definition is given on the basis of the axiomatic foundation. An operational definition of the least general generalization of clauses based on ψ-terms is also shown as a realization of the axiomatic definition.

1 Introduction

A *feature term* (or ψ-*term*) is an *order-sorted logic term*, *i.e.*, an extended form of a logic term where functor symbols are *ordered sorts*. In addition, *features* (or attribute labels) are added to a sort as argument indicators. [1,2,3]

For example, the following two ψ-terms describe George and his mother as having the same last name "Bush" and Al and his mother as having the same last name "Gore":

$$George(\ last \quad \Rightarrow Y_1 : Bush,$$
$$mother \Rightarrow Barbara(last \Rightarrow Y_1)),$$

$$Al(\ last \quad \Rightarrow Y_2 : Gore,$$
$$mother \Rightarrow Pauline(last \Rightarrow Y_2)).$$

In this example, *George, Barbara, Bush, Al, Pauline,* and *Gore* are sort symbols, while *last* and *mother* are feature symbols. The variables Y_1 and Y_2 link George's and Al's last names to their mother's last names.

A goal of a ψ-*term generalization* is to calculate (or *induce*) the following generic knowledge from the two examples:

$$person(\ last \quad \Rightarrow Y : name,$$
$$mother \Rightarrow person(last \Rightarrow Y))$$

L. De Raedt and P. Flach (Eds.): ECML 2001, LNAI 2167, pp. 1–12, 2001.
© Springer-Verlag Berlin Heidelberg 2001

Formally, without syntax sugaring, the schema is represented as

$$X : person(\; last \quad \Rightarrow Y : name,$$
$$mother \Rightarrow Z : person(last \Rightarrow Y : \top))$$

where $\top$ is the *universal*—*i.e.*, the most general—sort, and variable tags are systematically used for each sort.

The ψ-term is useful in many subjects of Artificial Intelligence (AI), most notably in Natural Language Processing (NLP). For instance, the feature term [5], equivalent to the ψ-term, is used to represent the syntax and semantics of natural language sentences. In case-based reasoning, feature terms are used as the data structures of cases [9] and the generalization of cases is a key towards the reuse of cases. Inductive Logic Programming (ILP) was extended to an induction (*i.e.*, generalization) of logic programs based on ψ-terms [11,12].

While feature terms play an essential role in AI and NLP, there is a missing link between Plotkin's least general generalization formalism of classic logic terms and the generalization of ψ-terms on the basis of the OSF foundation. This paper presents the missing link.

2   Preliminaries on ψ-Terms

This section introduces ψ-terms on the basis of the *Order-Sorted Feature (OSF)* formalism [2,3].

2.1   Syntax

Definition 1 (OSF Signature) *An OSF Signature is given by*

$$\Sigma_{OSF} = \langle \mathcal{S}, \preceq, \sqcap, \sqcup, \mathcal{F} \rangle, \; s.t. :$$

- *$\mathcal{S}$ is a set of sort symbols with the sorts $\top$ and $\bot$;*
- *$\preceq$ is a partial order on $\mathcal{S}$ such that $\top$ is the greatest element and $\bot$ is the least element;*
- *$\langle \mathcal{S}, \preceq, \sqcap, \sqcup \rangle$ is a lattice, where $s \sqcap t$ is defined as the infimum (or glb) of sorts s and t and $s \sqcup t$ is the supremum (or lub) of sorts s and t;*
- *$\mathcal{F}$ is a set of feature symbols.*

For sorts $s_1, s_2 \in \mathcal{S}$, we denote $s_1 \prec s_2$ iff $s_1 \preceq s_2$ and $s_1 \neq s_2$.
Let $\mathcal{V}$ be a countable infinite set of variables.

Definition 2 (OSF-terms) *Given $\Sigma_{OSF} = \langle \mathcal{S}, \preceq, \sqcap, \sqcup, \mathcal{F} \rangle$, if $s \in \mathcal{S}$, $l_1, \ldots, l_n \in \mathcal{F}$, $X \in \mathcal{V}$, $n \geq 0$, and $t_1, ..., t_n$ are OSF-terms, then an OSF-term has the form*

$$X : s(l_1 \Rightarrow t_1, ..., l_n \Rightarrow t_n).$$

Let $\psi = X : s(l_1 \Rightarrow t_1, ..., l_n \Rightarrow t_n)$. X is called the root variable of ψ, which is described as $Root(\psi)$, and s is called the root sort of ψ, which is described as $Sort(\psi)$.

For a lighter notation, hereafter we omit variables that are not shared and the sort of a variable when it is $\top$.

Definition 3 (ψ-terms) *An OSF-term*

$$\psi = X : s(l_1 \Rightarrow \psi_1, \ldots, l_n \Rightarrow \psi_n)$$

is in a normal form (and is called a ψ-term) if:

- *For any variable V_i in ψ, V_i is the root variable of at most one non-top ψ-term, i.e., one whose root sort is not $\top$;*
- *s is a nonbottom sort in $\mathcal{S}$;*
- *$l_1, \ldots, l_n$ are pairwise distinct feature symbols in $\mathcal{F}$;*
- *$\psi_1, \ldots, \psi_n$ are ψ-terms.*

We will see that OSF-terms can be normalized to ψ-terms by OSF clause normalization rules, which are given in Section 2.3, or are otherwise proven to be inconsistent by being reduced to $\bot$.

Let $\psi = X : s(l_1 \Rightarrow \psi_1, ..., l_n \Rightarrow \psi_n)$. $s(l_1 \Rightarrow \psi_1, ..., l_n \Rightarrow \psi_n)$ is called an *untagged ψ-term*.

Definition 4 (Feature Projection) *Given a ψ-term $t = X : s(l_1 \Rightarrow t_1, \ldots, l_n \Rightarrow t_n)$, the l_i projection of t (written as $t.l_i$) is defined as $t.l_i = t_i$.*

The definitions of atoms, literals, clauses, Horn clauses, and definite clauses are as usual with the difference being that terms are ψ-terms. If a feature is a non-zero integer $1, \ldots, n$, then a ψ-term $X : s(1 \Rightarrow t_1, 2 \Rightarrow t_2, \ldots, n \Rightarrow t_n)$ can be abbreviated to $X : s(t_1, t_2, \ldots, t_n)$.

2.2   Semantics

Definition 5 (OSF Algebras) *An OSF Algebra is a structure*
$\mathcal{A} = \langle D^{\mathcal{A}}, (s^{\mathcal{A}})_{s \in \mathcal{S}}, (l^{\mathcal{A}})_{l \in \mathcal{F}} \rangle$ *s.t. :*

- *$D^{\mathcal{A}}$ is a non-empty set, called a domain of $\mathcal{A}$;*
- *for each sort symbol $s \in \mathcal{S}$, $s^{\mathcal{A}} \subseteq D^{\mathcal{A}}$; in particular, $\top^{\mathcal{A}} = D^{\mathcal{A}}$ and $\bot^{\mathcal{A}} = \emptyset$;*
- *$(s \sqcap s')^{\mathcal{A}} = s^{\mathcal{A}} \cap s'^{\mathcal{A}}$ for two sorts $s, s' \in \mathcal{S}$;*
- *$(s \sqcup s')^{\mathcal{A}} = s^{\mathcal{A}} \cup s'^{\mathcal{A}}$ for two sorts $s, s' \in \mathcal{S}$;*
- *for each feature symbol $l \in \mathcal{F}$, $l^{\mathcal{A}} : D^{\mathcal{A}} \to D^{\mathcal{A}}$.*

Definition 6 ($\mathcal{A}$-Valuation) *Given $\Sigma_{OSF} = \langle \mathcal{S}, \preceq, \sqcap, \sqcup, \mathcal{F} \rangle$, an $\mathcal{A}$-valuation is a function $\alpha : \mathcal{V} \to D^{\mathcal{A}}$.*

Definition 7 (Term Denotation) *Let t be a ψ-term of the form*

$$t = X : s(l_1 \Rightarrow t_1, \ldots, l_n \Rightarrow t_n).$$

Given an OSF Algebra $\mathcal{A}$ and an $\mathcal{A}$-valuation α, the term denotation of t is given by

$$[\![\, t \,]\!]^{\mathcal{A},\alpha} = \{\alpha(X)\} \cap s^{\mathcal{A}} \cap \bigcap_{1 \le i \le n} (l_i^{\mathcal{A}})^{-1}([\![\, t_i \,]\!]^{\mathcal{A},\alpha}).$$

$$[\![\, t \,]\!]^{\mathcal{A}} = \bigcup_{\alpha: \mathcal{V} \to D^{\mathcal{A}}} [\![\, t \,]\!]^{\mathcal{A},\alpha}.$$

2.3   Unification of ψ-Terms

An alternative syntactic presentation of the information conveyed by OSF-terms can be translated into a constraint clause [2].

Definition 8 (OSF-Constraints) *An order-sorted feature constraint (OSF-constraint) has one of the following forms:*

- $X : s$
- $X \doteq Y$
- $X.l \doteq Y$

where X and Y are variables in $\mathcal{V}$, s is a sort in $\mathcal{S}$, and l is a feature in $\mathcal{F}$.

Definition 9 (OSF-clauses) *An OSF-clause ϕ_1 & ... & ϕ_n is a finite, possibly empty conjunction of OSF-constraints $\phi_1, \ldots, \phi_n (n \ge 0)$.* [1]

We can associate an OSF-term with a corresponding OSF-clause.
Let ψ be a ψ-term of the form

$$\psi = X : s(l_1 \Rightarrow \psi_1, ..., l_n \Rightarrow \psi_n).$$

An OSF-clause $\phi(\psi)$ corresponding to an OSF-term ψ has the following form:

$$\phi(\psi) = X : s \ \& \ X.l_1 \doteq X'_1 \ \& \ldots \& \ X.l_n \doteq X'_n$$
$$\& \ \phi(\psi_1) \qquad \& \ldots \& \ \phi(\psi_n),$$

where $X, X'_1, \ldots, X'_n$ are the root variables of $\psi, \psi_1, \ldots, \psi_n$, respectively. We say $\phi(\psi)$ is dissolved from the OSF-term ψ.

Example 1 *Let $\psi = X : s(l_1 \Rightarrow Y : t, l_2 \Rightarrow Y : \top))$. The OSF-clause of ψ is:*
$\phi(\psi) = X : s \ \& \ X.l_1 \doteq Y \ \& \ Y : t \ \& \ X.l_2 \doteq Y \ \& \ Y : \top$

---

[1] We sometimes regard an OSF-clause as a set of OSF constraints.

Sort Intersection:

$$\frac{\phi \ \& \ X : s \ \& \ X : s'}{\phi \ \& \ X : s \sqcap s'}$$

Inconsistent Sort:

$$\frac{\phi \ \& \ X : \bot}{X : \bot}$$

Variable Elimination:

$$\frac{\phi \ \& \ X \doteq X'}{\phi[X/X'] \ \& \ X \doteq X'}$$

$$if \ X \neq X' \ and \ X \in Var(\phi)$$

Feature Decomposition:

$$\frac{\phi \ \& \ X.l \doteq X' \ \& \ X.l \doteq X''}{\phi \ \& \ X.l \doteq X' \ \& \ X' \doteq X''}$$

Fig. 1. OSF Clause Normalization Rules

On the other hand, an OSF-clause ϕ can be converted to an OSF-term $\psi(\phi)$ as follows: first complete it by adding as many $V:\top$ constraints as needed so that there is exactly one sort constraint for every occurrence of a variable V in an $X.l=V$ constraint, where X is a variable and l is a feature symbol; then convert it by the following ψ transform:

$$\psi(\phi) = X : s(l_1 \Rightarrow \psi(\phi(Y_1)), \ldots, l_n \Rightarrow \psi(\phi(Y_n)))$$

where X is a root variable of ϕ, ϕ contains $X : s$, and $X.l_1 \doteq Y_1, \ldots, X.l_n \doteq Y_n$ are all of the other constraints in ϕ with an occurrence of variable X on the left-hand side. $\phi(Y)$ denotes the maximal subclause of ϕ rooted by Y.

Definition 10 (Solved OSF-Constraint) *An OSF-clause ϕ is called solved if for every variable X, ϕ contains:*

- *at most one sort constraint of the form $X : s$, with $\bot \prec s$;*
- *at most one feature constraint of the form $X.l \doteq Y$ for each $X.l$;*
- *no equality constraint of the form $X \doteq Y$.*

Given ϕ in a normal form, we will refer to its part in a solved form as $Solved(\phi)$.

Example 2 *Let $\phi = X : s \ \& \ X.l_1 \doteq Y \ \& \ Y : t \ \& \ X.l_2 \doteq Y \ \& \ Y : \top$. The solved normal form of ϕ is :*
$Solved(\phi) = X : s \ \& \ X.l_1 \doteq Y \ \& \ Y : t \ \& \ X.l_2 \doteq Y.$

Theorem 1 *[2] The rules of Fig. 1 are solution-preserving, finite-terminating, and confluent (modulo variable renaming). Furthermore, they always result in a normal form that is either an inconsistent OSF clause or an OSF clause in a solved form together with a conjunction of equality constraints.*

Note that $Var(\phi)$ is the set of variables occurring in an OSF-clause ϕ and $\phi[X/Y]$ stands for the OSF-clause obtained from ϕ after replacing all occurrences of Y by X.

Sort Induction (SI):

$$\frac{\{X_1\backslash X\} \cup \Gamma_1, \{X_2\backslash X\} \cup \Gamma_2 \vdash \phi \ \& \ ((X_1\!:\!s_1 \ \& \ \phi_1) \ \lor \ (X_2\!:\!s_2 \ \& \ \phi_2))}{\{X_1\backslash X\} \cup \Gamma_1, \{X_2\backslash X\} \cup \Gamma_2 \vdash \phi \ \& \ (X\!:\!s_1 \sqcup s_2) \ \& \ ((X_1\!:\!s_1 \ \& \ \phi_1) \ \lor \ (X_2\!:\!s_2 \ \& \ \phi_2))}$$

$$if \ \neg\exists s \ (X\!:\!s \in \phi)$$

Feature Induction (FI):

$$\frac{\{X_1\backslash X\} \cup \Gamma_1, \{X_2\backslash X\} \cup \Gamma_2 \vdash \phi \& ((X_1.l \doteq Y_1 \& \phi_1) \lor (X_2.l \doteq Y_2 \& \phi_2))}{\{X_1\backslash X, Y_1\backslash Y\} \cup \Gamma_1, \{X_2\backslash X, Y_2\backslash Y\} \cup \Gamma_2 \vdash \phi \& X.l \doteq Y \& ((X_1.l \doteq Y_1 \& \phi_1) \lor (X_2.l \doteq Y_2 \& \phi_2))}$$

$$if \ \neg\exists \ y \ (Y_1\backslash y \in \{X_1\backslash X\} \cup \Gamma_1 \ and \ Y_2\backslash y \in \{X_2\backslash X\} \cup \Gamma_2)$$

Coreference Induction (CI):

$$\frac{\{X_1\backslash X, Y_1\backslash Y\} \cup \Gamma_1, \{X_2\backslash X, Y_2\backslash Y\} \cup \Gamma_2 \vdash \phi \& ((X_1.l \doteq Y_1 \& \phi_1) \lor (X_2.l \doteq Y_2 \& \phi_2))}{\{X_1\backslash X, Y_1\backslash Y\} \cup \Gamma_1, \{X_2\backslash X, Y_2\backslash Y\} \cup \Gamma_2 \vdash \phi \& X.l \doteq Y \& ((X_1.l \doteq Y_1 \& \phi_1) \lor (X_2.l \doteq Y_2 \& \phi_2))}$$

$$if \ X.l \doteq Y \notin \phi$$

Fig. 2. OSF Clause Generalization Rules

Theorem 2 (ψ-term Unification) *[2] Let ψ_1 and ψ_2 be two ψ-terms. Let ϕ be the normal form of the OSF-clause $\phi(\psi_1)$ & $\phi(\psi_2)$ & $X_1 \doteq X_2$, where X_1 and X_2 are the root variables of ψ_1 and ψ_2, respectively. Then, ϕ is an inconsistent clause iff the glb of the two ψ-terms is $\bot$. If ϕ is not an inconsistent clause, then the glb $\psi_1 \sqcap \psi_2$ is given by the normal OSF-term ψ (Solved(ϕ)).*

3 Axiomatic ψ-Term Generalization

As a dual of ψ-term unification, ψ-term generalization (or anti-unification) can be defined as OSF clause generalization rules.

To define the generalization, we introduce a new constraint symbol $\lor$, where $A \lor B$ denotes the generalization of two OSF clauses A and B.

A ψ-term generalization rule is of the form:

$$\frac{\Gamma_1, \Gamma_2 \vdash \phi \ \& \ (\phi_1 \ \lor \ \phi_2)}{\Gamma_1', \Gamma_2' \vdash \phi' \ \& \ (\phi_1 \ \lor \ \phi_2)}$$

where Γ_1 and Γ_2 are sets of substitutions of the form $\{X_1\backslash X_1', \ldots, X_n\backslash X_n'\}^2$, ϕ and ϕ' are OSF-clauses, and ϕ_1 and ϕ_2 are solved normal forms of OSF-clauses of target ψ-terms ψ_1 and ψ_2, respectively.

Definition 11 (Axiomatic Generalization) *Let ϕ_1 and ϕ_2 be solved normal forms of ψ_1 and ψ_2, respectively, and Γ_1 and Γ_2 be variable substitutions. Then, a generalized OSF-clause ϕ of*

$$\Gamma_1, \Gamma_2 \vdash \phi \ \& \ (\phi_1 \lor \phi_2)$$

---

[2] This means that X_i is substituted by X_i.

is obtained by applying OSF clause generalization rules (Fig. 2) until no rule is applicable, initiated with

$$\{X_1 \backslash X\}, \{X_2 \backslash X\} \vdash (\phi_1 \vee \phi_2)$$

where $X_1 = Root(\psi_2)$, $X_2 = Root(\psi_2)$, and X is a fresh variable.

A generalized ψ-term is given as $\psi(\phi)$.

Proposition 1 *The result of the axiomatic generalization is an OSF-clause in the normal form.*

Proposition 2 *The OSF clause generalization is finite terminating.*

Proof. Termination follows from the fact that the number of variables in ϕ_1 is finite because OSF-clauses are finite, and each of the three rules SI, FI, and CI strictly decreases the number of combinations of variables in ϕ_1 and ϕ_2 that satisfy the preconditions of the OSF generalization rules.

From the definition of $\phi(\cdot)$ and OSF clause normalization rules (Fig. 1), the number of variables in ϕ_i is finite since ψ_i is finite by the definition of OSF-terms. The Sort Induction (SI) strictly decreases the number of variable pairs that satisfy the conditions of the generalization rules. That is, the variable pair X_1 of $X_1 : s_1$ and X_2 of $X_2 : s_2$ does not satisfy the precondition of SI after its application. The Feature Induction (FI) strictly decreases the number of pairs of variable pairs that satisfy the rule conditions. The pair of variable pairs $\langle X_1, Y_1 \rangle$ and $\langle X_2, Y_2 \rangle$ does not satisfy the precondition of FI after its application. Since FI is only applicable a finite number of times, FI increases the finite number of pairs applicable to the SI and CI rules. Like FI, the Coreference Induction (CI) strictly decreases the number of pairs of variable pairs that satisfy the rule conditions. The pair of variable pairs $\langle X_1, Y_1 \rangle$ and $\langle X_2, Y_2 \rangle$ does not satisfy the precondition of CI after its application.

3.1   Least General Generalization

This section newly introduces the *least general generalization of ψ-terms* along the line of Plotkin's *least general generalization (lgg)* [10].

Definition 12 (Sorted Substitution) *A sorted substitution has the form $\{X_1{:}s_1/Y_1{:}t_1, \ldots, X_n{:}s_n/Y_n{:}t_n\}$, where $X_1, \ldots, X_n$ are pairwise distinct variables and $Y_1, \ldots, Y_n$ are variables in $\mathcal{V}$, $s_1, \ldots, s_n$ and $t_1, \ldots, t_n$ are sort symbols with $\bot \prec s_i \preceq t_i$ for every i. If expression E is a term, a literal, or a clause, $E\theta$ is the result of replacing all occurrences of $Y_i{:}t_i$ by $X_i{:}s_i$ and Y_i by X_i simultaneously for every i.*

Note that the sorted substitution changes only variable names and sorts; it does not add or remove constraints of the form $X.l \doteq Y$. This means that the sorted substitution preserves the structure of an original expression.

Definition 13 (Sorted Ordering of ψ-terms) *Let ψ_1 and ψ_2 be two ψ-terms. Let ϕ_1 and ϕ_2 be solved normal forms of OSF clauses of ψ_1 and ψ_2, respectively. $\psi_1 \leq \psi_2$ iff there exists a sorted substitution θ such that $\phi_1\theta \subseteq \phi_2$ [3] and $(Root(\psi_2) : Sort(\psi_2)/Root(\psi_1) : Sort(\psi_1)) \in \theta$.*

We read $\psi_1 \leq \psi_2$ as meaning that ψ_1 *is more general than* ψ_2.

Example 3 $(X:s) \leq Y:t(l \Rightarrow Z:u)$ *with $t \preceq s$ because for $\theta = \{Y:t/X:s\}$, $(X:s)\theta = \{Y:t\} \subseteq (Y:t \And Y.l \doteq Z \And Z:u)$.*

Proposition 3 *If ϕ is the result of the ψ-term generalization of the OSF-clauses of ψ-terms ψ_1 and ψ_2 and $\psi = \psi(\phi)$, then $\psi \leq \psi_1$ and $\psi \leq \psi_2$ in terms of sorted ordering $\leq$.*

Proof. Prove $\psi \leq \psi_1$. Let ϕ_1 be a solved normal form of ψ_1. Let the final result of the ψ-term generalization be $\Gamma_1, \Gamma_2 \vdash \phi \And (\phi_1 \vee \phi_2)$ with $\Gamma_1 = \{X_1'\backslash X_1, \ldots, X_n'\backslash X_n\}$. Let s_i' be the sort of $X_i':s_i' \in \phi(\psi_1)$ and s_i be the sort of $X_i:s_i \in \phi(\psi)$. A sorted substitution $\theta = \{X_1':s_1'/X_1:s_1, \ldots, X_n':s_n'/X_n:s_n\}$ clearly satisfies the relation $\phi\theta \subseteq \phi_1$ according to the OSF generalization rules. The proof of $\psi \leq \psi_2$ is the same.

Definition 14 (Least General Generalization) *Let ψ_1 and ψ_2 be ψ-terms. ψ is the least general generalization (lgg) of ψ_1 and ψ_2 iff*

(1) $\psi \leq \psi_1$ and $\psi \leq \psi_2$.
(2) If $\psi' \leq \psi_1$ and $\psi' \leq \psi_2$, then $\psi' \leq \psi$.

Theorem 3 (Least Generality of Generalization) *The axiomatic ψ-term generalization is a least general generalization with respect to the sorted ordering of ψ-terms.*

Proof. (1) $\psi \leq \psi_1$ and $\psi \leq \psi_2$ are immediate from Proposition 3. (2) Let ψ_1 and ψ_2 be ψ-terms and ψ be the result of the ψ-term generalization of ψ_1 and ψ_2. Also assume that there exists a ψ-term ψ' such that $\psi' \leq \psi_1$, $\psi' \leq \psi_2$, and $\psi < \psi'$, i.e., ψ is strictly more general than ψ'. Let ϕ, ϕ_1, ϕ_2, and ϕ' be solved normal forms of ψ, ψ_1, ψ_2, and ψ', respectively. The assumption $\psi < \psi'$ requires that there be an OSF constraint C' in ϕ' such that no sorted substitution θ satisfies $C'\theta \in \phi$ and $\phi'\theta \subseteq \phi$. There are two cases to be considered: (case 1) C' is of the form $X' : s'$ and (case 2) C' is of the form $X'.l \doteq Y'$.

Case 1: From the assumptions $\psi' \leq \psi_1$ and $\psi' \leq \psi_2$, $X' : s'$ can be substituted to $X_1 : s_1$ in ϕ_1 and $X_2 : s_2$ in ϕ_2. Therefore, $s_1 \preceq s'$ and $s_2 \preceq s'$. Since sorted substitutions preserve the structures of ψ-terms, according to ψ-term generalization rules, if $X_1 : s_1$ and $X_2 : s_2$ correspond to the same constraint $X' : s$, then $X : s$ should be included in ϕ. By SI, sort s in ψ is the least upper

---

[3] We regard a clause as a set of constraints here.

bound (lub) of a sort s_1 in ψ_1 and a sort s_2 in ψ_2. This contradicts $s_1 \preceq s'$, $s_2 \preceq s'$, and $s' \prec s$.

Case 2: Similarly, from the assumptions of $\psi' \leq \psi_1$ and $\psi' \leq \psi_2$, $X'.l \doteq Y'$ can be substituted to $X_1.1 \doteq Y_1$ in ϕ_1 and $X_2.l \doteq Y_2$ in ϕ_2. Since sorted substitutions preserve the structures of ψ-terms, if $X_1.l \doteq Y_1$ and $X_2.l \doteq Y_2$ correspond to the same constraint $X'.l \doteq Y'$, then $X.l \doteq Y$ should be in ϕ. This is a contradiction.

4   Operational ψ-Term Generalization

On the other hand, an operational definition of ψ-term generalization [11] has been defined as an extension of Plotkin's *least general generalization (lgg)* using the following notations. a and b represent untagged ψ-terms. s, t, and u represent ψ-terms. f, g, and h represent sorts. X, Y, and Z represent variables in $\mathcal{V}$.

Definition 15 (lgg of ψ-terms)   *Let ψ_1 and ψ_2 be ψ-terms. $lgg(\psi_1,\psi_2)$ is defined as follows with the initial history $Hist = \{\}$.*

1. $lgg(X : a, X : a) = X : a$.
2. $lgg(X : a, Y : b) = Z : \top$, *where $X \neq Y$ and the tuple (X,Y,Z) is already in the history $Hist$.*
3. *If $s = X{:}f(l_1^s \Rightarrow s_1, \ldots, l_n^s \Rightarrow s_n)$ and $t = Y{:}g(l_1^t \Rightarrow t_1, \ldots, l_m^t \Rightarrow t_m)$, then $lgg(s,t)=Z{:}(f \sqcup g)(l_1 \Rightarrow lgg(s \rightarrow l_1, t \rightarrow l_1), \ldots, l_{|L|} \Rightarrow lgg(s \rightarrow l_{|L|}, t \rightarrow l_{|L|}))$, where $l_i \in L = \{l_1^s, \ldots, l_n^s\} \cap \{l_1^t, \ldots, l_m^t\}$. Then, (X,Y,Z) is added to Hist.*

Note that in this definition $s \rightarrow l$ is defined as $s \rightarrow l = X : a$ if $s.l = X : \top$ and $X : a \in \psi_1$ with $a \neq \top$ else $s \rightarrow l = s.l$. $t \rightarrow l$ is defined similarly.

For example, the lgg of $X{:}passenger(of{\Rightarrow}X'{:}10)$ and $Y{:}man(of{\Rightarrow}Y'{:}2)$ is $Z : person(of \Rightarrow Z' : number)$, if $passenger \sqcup man = person$ and $10 \sqcup 2 = number$.

Theorem 4 (Correctness) *The result of the operational ψ-term generalization ψ is the least general generalization of ψ-terms ψ_1 and ψ_2 in terms of the sorted ordering.*

Proof. (Sketch) Each step of the operational definition can be translated into OSF generalization rules. Step 1 is a special case of Sort Induction.

Step 2 is Coreference Induction where tuple (X,Y,Z) in $Hist$ corresponds to $X \backslash Z$ in Γ_1 and $Y \backslash Z$ in Γ_2.

Step 3 is Sort Induction of $X : f \sqcup g$ and Feature Induction, where tuple (X, Y, Z) added to $Hist$ corresponds to $X \backslash Z$ and $Y \backslash Z$ which are added to variable substitutions. All of the steps of the operational definition are realizations of the OSF clause generalization. Therefore, the result of the operational generalization is a least general generalization of ψ-terms.

5   Generalization of Clauses Based on ψ-Terms

This section presents the least general generalization of logic programs based on ψ-terms along the line of Plotkin's lgg of atoms and clauses [10].

Definition 16 (Ordering of Atoms) *Let $A_1 = p(\psi_1, \ldots, \psi_n)$ and $A_2 = q(\psi'_1, \ldots, \psi'_n)$ be atomic formulae based on ψ-terms. $A_1 \leq A_2$ iff $A_1\theta = A_2$ for some sorted substitution θ which includes a substitution replacing the root variable of ψ_i by the root variable of ψ'_i.*

Definition 17 (Ordering of Clauses) *Let C_1 and C_2 be clauses based on ψ-terms. $C_1 \leq C_2$ iff $C_1\theta \subseteq C_2$ for some sorted substitution θ which includes substitutions replacing the root variables of ψ-terms in C_1 by the corresponding root variables of ψ-terms in C_2.*

Definition 18 (Lgg of Atoms) *Given a signature $\Sigma_{OSF} = \langle S, \preceq, \sqcap, \sqcup, \mathcal{F} \rangle$ and a set of predicate symbols $\mathcal{P}$, let P and Q be atomic formulae. An operational definition of a function $lgg(P, Q)$ that computes the least general generalization of P and Q is as follows:*

1. *If $P = p(s_1, \ldots, s_n)$ and $Q = p(t_1, \ldots, t_n)$,*
   $lgg(P, Q) = p(lgg(s_1, t_1), \ldots, lgg(s_n, t_n))$ with the sharing of history Hist.
2. *Otherwise, $lgg(P, Q)$ is undefined.*

Definition 19 (Lgg of Literals) *Let P and Q be atoms and L_1 and L_2 be literals. The lgg of the literals is defined as follows [8].*

1. *If L_1 and L_2 are atoms, then $lgg(L_1, L_2)$ is the lgg of the atoms.*
2. *If L_1 and L_2 are of the forms $\neg P$ and $\neg Q$, respectively, then $lgg(L_1, L_2) = lgg(\neg P, \neg Q) = \neg lgg(P, Q)$.*
3. *Otherwise, $lgg(L_1, L_2)$ is undefined.*

Definition 20 (Lgg of Clauses) *Let clauses $C = \{L_1, \ldots, L_n\}$ and $D = \{K_1, \ldots, K_m\}$. Then $lgg(C, D) = \{ lgg(L_i, K_j) \mid L_i \in C, K_j \in D$ and $lgg(L_i, K_j)$ is not undefined$\}$.*

The least general generality of lggs of atoms, literals, and clauses is conservative extension of Plotkin's lgg since the operational ψ-term generalization is an lgg of terms.

6   Related Works

The definition of the *least general generalization (lgg)* was first investigated in [10]. The lgg of ψ-terms has already been illustrated [1]; however, axiomatic and operational definitions have been left untouched. The lgg of a subset of *description logics*, called the *least common subsumer (LCS)*, was studied in [4]. The lgg of *feature terms*, which are equivalent to ψ-terms, can be found in [9]. The generalization for *Sorted First Order Predicate Calculus (SFOPC)* [7] is presented in [6].

7   Conclusion and Remarks

Two generalization approaches have been presented and related. An *axiomatic* definition of ψ-term generalization was presented as ψ-term generalization rules. The definition was proven to be a *least general generalization (lgg)* in terms of Plotkin's lgg on the OSF foundation. The correctness of an *operational* definition of ψ-term generalization was provided on the basis of the generalization rules. The operational definition was shown to be one realization of the axiomatic generalization. An lgg of clauses based on ψ-terms was presented, and a fundamental bridge between ψ-term generalization and the lgg useful for inductive logic programming was given. The main benefit of this paper is that it expresses generalization (and hence induction) as an OSF constraint *construction* process. This approach may lead to other axiomatic constraint systems provided with inductive algorithms.

Acknowledgment. This paper is based on the research results done during the first author's stay at the NTT Communication Science Laboratories, Kyoto, Japan, in April, 1999.

References

1. Hassan Aït-Kaci and Roger Nasr. LOGIN: A logic programming language with built-in inheritance. *Journal of Logic Programming*, 3:185–215, 1986.
2. Hassan Aït-Kaci and Andreas Podelski. Towards a meaning of LIFE. *Logic Program.*, 16(3-4):195–234, July-August 1993.
3. Hassan Aït-Kaci, Andreas Podelski, and Seth Copen Goldstein. Order-sorted feature theory unification. *Journal of Logic Programming*, 30(2):99–124, 1997.
4. Franz Baader, Ralf Küsters and Ralf Molitor. Computing Least Common Subsumers in Description Logics with Existential Restrictions. *Proccedings of the Sixteenth International Joint Conference on Artificial Intelligence*, pages 96–101, 1999.
5. Bob Carpenter. *The Logic of Typed Feature Structures*, volume 32 of *Cambridge Tracts in Theoretical Computer Science*. Cambridge University Press, Cambridge, UK, 1992.
6. Alan M. Frisch and C. David Page Jr. Generalization with taxonomic information. In *Proceedings of the 8th National Conference on Artificial Intelligence*, pages 755–761, Boston, MA, 1990. AAAI-90.
7. Alan M. Frisch. A general framework for sorted deduction: Fundamental results on hybrid reasoning. In *Proceedings of the 1st International Conference on Principles of Knowledge Representation and Reasoning*, pages 126–136, 1989.
8. Nada Lavrač and Sašo Džeroski. *Inductive Logic Programming: Techniques and Applications*. Ellis Horwood, 1994.
9. Enric Plaza. Cases as terms: A feature term approach to the structured representation of cases. In *Proceedings of the 1st International Conference on Case-Based Reasoning*, pages 263–27, 1995.
10. Gordon Plotkin. A note on inductive generalization. In *Machine Intelligence*, pages 153–163. Edinburgh University Press, 1969.

11. Yutaka Sasaki. Induction of logic programs based on ψ-terms. In *Proceedings of the 10th International Conference on Algorithmic Learning Theory*, pages 169–181, Tokyo, Japan, 1999. ALT-99, Springer-Verlag LNAI 1720.
12. Yutaka Sasaki. *Hierarchically Sorted Inductive Logic Programming and Its Application to Information Extraction*. Ph.D thesis, Graduate School of Systems and Information Engineering, University of Tsukuba, Japan, September 2000.

Appendix (Example of Axiomatic ψ-Term Generalization)

Suppose that we have two ψ-terms ψ_1 and ψ_2, and $u = s \sqcup t$.

$$\psi_1 = X : s(a \Rightarrow Z : s, b \Rightarrow Z)$$
$$\psi_2 = Y : t(a \Rightarrow W : t, b \Rightarrow U : t)$$

The normal form of OSF clauses of these ψ-terms are:

$$\phi(\psi_1) = X : s \ \& \ X.a \doteq Z \ \& \ Z : s \ \& \ X.b \doteq Z,$$
$$\phi(\psi_2) = Y : t \ \& \ Y.a \doteq W \ \& \ W : t \ \& \ Y.b \doteq U \ \& \ U : t.$$

A generalization of these two OSF clauses is obtained by applying generalization rules to the OSF clause $C = \phi(\psi_1) \vee \phi(\psi_2)$. The following steps show the process to achieve a generalization.

$\{X\backslash V\}, \{Y\backslash V\} \vdash$
  $((\underline{X : s} \ \& \ X.a \doteq Z \ \& \ Z : s \ \& \ X.b \doteq Z) \vee$
  $(\underline{Y : t} \ \& \ Y.a \doteq W \ \& \ W : t \ \& \ Y.b \doteq U \ \& \ U : t))$
$\{X\backslash V\}, \{Y\backslash V\} \vdash \quad (V : u)$
  $\& \ ((X : s \ \& \ \underline{X.a \doteq Z} \ \& \ Z : s \ \& \ X.b \doteq Z) \vee$
  $(Y : t \ \& \ \underline{Y.a \doteq W} \ \& \ W : t \ \& \ Y.b \doteq U \ \& \ U : t)) \ (\text{by SI})$
$\{X\backslash V, Z\backslash V'\}, \{Y\backslash V, W\backslash V'\} \vdash \quad (V : u \ \& \ V.a \doteq V')$
  $\& \ ((X : s \ \& \ X.a \doteq Z \ \& \ \underline{Z : s} \ \& \ X.b \doteq Z) \vee$
  $(Y : t \ \& \ Y.a \doteq W \ \& \ \underline{W : t} \ \& \ Y.b \doteq U \ \& \ U : t)) \ (\text{by FI})$
$\{X\backslash V, Z\backslash V'\}, \{Y\backslash V, W\backslash V'\} \vdash \quad (V : u \ \& \ V.a \doteq V' \ \& \ V' : u)$
  $\& \ ((X : s \ \& \ X.a \doteq Z \ \& \ Z : s \ \& \ \underline{X.b \doteq Z}) \vee$
  $(Y : t \ \& \ Y.a \doteq W \ \& \ W : t \ \& \ \underline{Y.b \doteq U} \ \& \ U : t)) \ (\text{by SI})$
$\{X\backslash V, Z\backslash V', Z\backslash V''\}, \{Y\backslash V, W\backslash V', U\backslash V''\} \vdash (V : u \& V.a \doteq V' \& V' : u \& V.b \doteq V'')$
  $\& \ ((\underline{X : s} \ \& \ X.a \doteq Z \ \& \ Z : s \ \& \ X.b \doteq Z) \vee$
  $(Y : t \ \& \ Y.a \doteq W \ \& \ W : t \ \& \ Y.b \doteq U \ \& \ \underline{U : t})) \ (\text{by FI})$
$\{X\backslash V, Z\backslash V', Z\backslash V''\}, \{Y\backslash V, W\backslash V', U\backslash V''\} \vdash$
$\underline{(V : u \ \& \ V.a \doteq V' \ \& \ V' : u \ \& \ V.b \doteq V'' \ \& \ V'' : u)}$
  $\& \ ((X : s \ \& \ X.a \doteq Z \ \& \ Z : s \ \& \ X.b \doteq Z) \vee$
  $(Y : t \ \& \ Y.a \doteq W \ \& \ W : t \ \& \ Y.b \doteq U \ \& \ U : t)) \ (\text{by SI})$

Therefore, an OSF clause ψ_3 of a ψ-term generalization of ψ_1 and ψ_2 is:

$$\phi_3 = V : u \ \& \ V.a \doteq V' \ \& \ V' : u \ \& \ V.b \doteq V'' \ \& \ V'' : u$$

The ψ-term of ψ_3 is: $\psi(\phi_3) = V : u(a \Rightarrow V' : u, b \Rightarrow V'' : u)$.

Lazy Induction of Descriptions for Relational Case-Based Learning

Eva Armengol and Enric Plaza

IIIA - Artificial Intelligence Research Institute,
CSIC - Spanish Council for Scientific Research,
Campus UAB, 08193 Bellaterra, Catalonia (Spain).
{eva, enric}@iiia.csic.es,

Abstract. Reasoning and learning from cases are based on the concept of similarity often estimated by a distance. This paper presents LID, a learning technique adequate for domains where cases are best represented by relations among entities. LID is able to 1) define a *similitude term*, a symbolic description of what is shared between a problem and precedent cases; and 2) assess the importance of the relations involved in a similitude term with respect to the purpose of correctly classifying the problem. The paper describes two application domains of relational case-based learning with LID: marine sponges identification and diabetes risk assessment.

1 Introduction

Reasoning and learning from cases is based on the concept of similarity. Often similarity is estimated by a distance (a metric) or a pseudo-metric. In addition to this, an assessment of which properties are "important" or "relevant" in the similarity is needed. This approach proceeds by a pairwise similarity comparison of a *problem* with every *precedent case* available in a case base; then one case (or k cases) with biggest (bigger) similarity is (are) selected. This process is called the *retrieval* phase in Case-based Reasoning (CBR), and also plays a pivotal role in lazy learning techniques like Instance-based Learning (IBL) and k-nearest neighbor. In classification tasks, the solution class of the *problem* is inferred from the solution class of the precedent case(s) selected.

However, distance-based approaches to case retrieval are mainly used for propositional cases, i.e. cases represented as attribute-value vectors. We are interested in this paper in learning tasks where cases are best represented in a scheme that uses relations among entities. We will call this setting *relational case-based learning*. One option to achieve case-based learning in a relational setting is to adapt the process of pairwise similarity comparison by defining a distance that works upon relational instances. This approach is taken in "relational IBL" [5] where cases are represented as collections of Horn clauses (see related work on §6).

The approach taken in this paper is different from pairwise similarity comparison based on metrics or pseudometrics. Basically, in our approach, similarity

L. De Raedt and P. Flach (Eds.): ECML 2001, LNAI 2167, pp. 13–24, 2001.
© Springer-Verlag Berlin Heidelberg 2001

between two cases is understood as that which they "share". In addition, we need to be able to evaluate if what they share is what is important (or to which degree they share what is important). This paper presents a technique called LID for relational case-based learning. LID is based on two main notions: 1) similarity is constructed as a symbolic description of what is shared between precedent cases and a specific *problem* to be classified, and 2) there is some assessment function to help the system decide which relations among entities are "important" or "relevant" to be shared with the precedent cases.

The representation formalism used to represent cases, feature terms, is presented in §2. Then, §3 introduces the framework of relational case-based learning and the main building blocks that we will use in §4 to describe the LID method. In §5 two application domains of relational case-based learning with LID are described: diabetes risk assessment and marine sponges identification. The paper closes with the sections on related work and conclusions.

2   Representation of the Cases

LID handles cases represented as feature terms. *Feature terms* (also called feature structures or ψ-terms) are a generalization of first order terms [2,8]. The main difference is that first order terms parameters are identified by position, e.g. $f(x, y, g(x, y))$ can be formally described as a tree and a fixed tree-traversal order. The intuition behind a feature term is that it can be described as a labelled graph where arcs are labelled with feature symbols and nodes stand for sorted variables.

Given a signature $\Sigma = \langle \mathcal{S}, \mathcal{F}, \leq \rangle$ (where $\mathcal{S}$ is a set of sort symbols that includes $\perp$; $\mathcal{F}$ is a set of feature symbols; and $\leq$ is a decidable partial order on $\mathcal{S}$ such that $\perp$ is the least element) and a set ϑ of variables, we define *feature terms* as an expression of the form:

$$\psi ::= X : s[f_1 \doteq \Psi_1 \ldots f_n \doteq \Psi_n] \tag{1}$$

where X is a variable in ϑ called the *root* of the feature term, s is a sort in $\mathcal{S}$, $f_1 \ldots f_n$ are features in $\mathcal{F}$, $0 \leq n$, and each Ψ_i is a set of feature terms and variables. When $n = 0$ we are defining a variable without features. The set of variables occurring in ψ is noted as ϑ_ψ.

Sorts have an informational order relation ($\leq$) among them, where $s \leq s'$ means that s has less information than s' Ñor equivalently that s is more general than s'. The minimal element ($\perp$) is called *any* and it represents the minimum information. When a feature has unknown value it is represented as having the value *any*. All other sorts are more specific than *any*.

A *path* $\pi(X, f_i)$ is defined as a sequence of features going from the variable X to the feature f_i. When two paths $\pi(X, f_i)$ and $\pi(Y, f_j)$ point to the same value we say that there is a *path equality*.

The function $root(\psi)$ returns the sort of the root of ψ. We note F_ψ the set of features $\{f_1 \ldots f_n\}$ of the root of ψ.

$$X_1 = \begin{bmatrix} person \\ address \doteq A_2 \\ spouse \doteq Z = \begin{bmatrix} person \\ address \doteq A_2 \end{bmatrix} \end{bmatrix} \qquad X_2 = \begin{bmatrix} person \\ address \doteq A_3 \\ spouse \doteq P_1 = \begin{bmatrix} person \\ address \doteq A_3 \end{bmatrix} \\ children \doteq \begin{matrix} P_2 \\ P_3 \end{matrix} \end{bmatrix}$$

a)   b)

Fig. 1. Examples of feature terms.

The *depth* of a feature f in a feature term ψ with root X is the number of features that compose the path from the root X to f, including f, with no repeated nodes.

Given a particular maximum feature depth k, a *leaf feature* of a feature term is a feature f_i such that either 1) the depth of f_i is k or 2) the depth of f_i is less than k and the value of f_i is a term without features.

The semantic interpretation of feature terms brings an ordering relation among feature terms that we call *subsumption*. Intuitively, a feature term ψ subsumes another feature term ψ' ($\psi \sqsubseteq \psi'$) when all information in ψ is also contained in ψ'. In other words, a feature term ψ subsumes another feature term ψ' when the following conditions are satisfied: 1) the sort of $root(\psi')$ is either the same or a subsort of $root(\psi)$, 2) if F_ψ is the set of features of ψ and $F_{\psi'}$ is the set of features of ψ' then $F_\psi \subseteq F_{\psi'}$ and 3) the values of the features in F_ψ and $F_{\psi'}$ satisfy the two conditions above.

For instance, the feature term X_1 in Figure 1a represents a person that is married with a person Z and both live at the address A_2 (i.e. there is a path equality since $X_1.address = X_1.spouse.address$). Because all the information in X_1 is also present in X_2 (Figure 1b), X_1 subsumes X_2 ($X_1 \sqsubseteq X_2$). However X_2 does not subsume X_1 —since X_1 has not the feature *children*.

A more detailed explanation about the feature terms and the subsumption relation can be found in [3]. In this reference there is also a detailed explanation of how feature terms can be translated to clause and graph representations.

3   Relational Case-Based Learning

There are three aspects that we need to define in order to perform CBR on relational cases: 1) to define a *case* from a constellation of relations, 2) to define a way to assess similarity between cases, and 3) to establish a degree of importance for the relations involved in the similarity.

A *case base* contains a constellation of relations between objects. The first step is to determine which of these relations constitute a case. A *case* (in feature terms) is specified from a relational case base using two parameters: a *root sort* and a *depth*. Assuming a *case base* expressed as a collection of feature terms, a case is a feature term whose root node is subsumed by the *root sort* and whose depth is at most *depth*. Examples of case specification are $case[\text{root-sort} \doteq$

patient, depth $\doteq$ 5] in the diabetes domain and *case*[root-sort $\doteq$ *sponge*, depth $\doteq$ 4] in the marine sponges domain (see §5).

The estimation of the similitude between cases is one of the key issues of the lazy learning algorithms. Those techniques (such as IBL [1] and *k*-nearest neighbor) that use cases represented as attribute-value vectors define the *similitude* of two cases by means of a distance measure. The LID method (§4) uses a symbolic estimation of the similitude between cases. The intuition of a symbolic similitude is that of a description containing the features shared by the two cases. In feature terms this intuition is formalized using the subsumption.

We say that a term s is a *similitude term* of two cases c_1 and c_2 if and only if $s \sqsubseteq c_1$ and $s \sqsubseteq c_2$ i.e. the similitude term of two cases subsumes both cases. In this framework, the task of similarity assessment is a search process over the space of similarity descriptions determined by the subsumption relation.

The next subsection explains a technique to assess the importance of a feature using the cases present in the case base. This technique is a heuristic measure based on the López de Mántaras (RLM) distance. Then, §4 explains how LID incrementally builds a similitude term based on the RLM heuristic.

3.1   Relevance of Attributes

Given a new example to be classified, the goal is to determine those features that are most relevant for the task. The relevance of a feature is heuristically determined using the RLM distance [11] that assesses how similar are two partitions (in the sense that the lesser the distance the more similar they are). Each feature $f_i \in \mathcal{F}$ induces a partition P_i of the case-base, namely a partition whose sets are formed by those cases that have the same value for feature f_i. The *correct partition* is a partition $P_c = \{C_1 \ldots C_m\}$ where all the cases contained into a set C_i belong to the same solution class. For each partition P_i induced by a feature f_i, LID computes the RLM distance to the correct partition P_c. The proximity to P_c of a partition P_i estimates the relevance of feature f_i.

Let P_i and P_j the partitions induced by features f_i and f_j respectively. We say that the feature f_i is *more discriminatory than* the feature f_j iff $RLM(P_i, P_c) < RLM(P_j, P_c)$, i.e. when the partition induced by f_i is closer to the correct partition P_c than the partition induced by f_j. Intuitively, the most discriminatory feature classifies the cases in a more similar way to the correct classification. LID uses the *more discriminatory than* relationship to estimate the features that are more relevant for the purpose of classifying a current problem.

4   Lazy Induction of Descriptions

In this section we introduce a new method called Lazy Induction of Descriptions (LID). The goal of LID is to classify a problem as belonging to one of the solution classes. The main idea of LID is to determine which are the more relevant features of the problem and to search in the case base for cases sharing these relevant

Function LID (S_D, p, D, C)
    if stopping-condition(S_D)
      then return $class(S_D)$
      else $f_d :=$ Select-leaf (p, S_D, C)
          $D :=$ Add-path$(\pi(root(p), f_d), D)$
          $S_{D'} :=$ Discriminatory-set (D, S_D)
          LID $(S_{D'}, p, D, C)$
    end-if
end-function

Fig. 2. The LID algorithm. D is the similitude term, S_D is the discriminatory set of D, C is the set of solution classes, $class(S_D)$ is the class $C_i \in C$ to which all elements in S_D belong.

features. The problem is classified when LID finds a set of relevant features shared by a subset of cases belonging all of them to the same solution class. Then, the problem is classified into that solution class.

Given a case base B containing cases classified into one of the solution classes $C = \{C_1 \ldots C_m\}$ and a problem p, the goal of LID is to classify p as belonging to one of the solution classes. The problem and the cases in the case base are represented as feature terms (see §2). We call *discriminatory set* the set $S_D = \{b \in B | D \sqsubseteq b\}$ that contains the cases of B subsumed by the similitude term D.

The main steps of the LID algorithm are shown in Figure 2. In the first call $LID(S_D, p, D, C)$ parameter S_D is initialized to B (the whole case base) and parameter D can be initialized to *any* or to a value $D = D^0$ (where $D^0 \neq any$) based on domain knowledge we may have (see an example in §5.1).

The specialization of a similitude term D is achieved by adding features to it. In principle, any of the features used to describe the cases could be a good candidate. Nevertheless, LID uses two biases to obtain the set F_l of features candidate to specialize D. First, of all possible features in $\mathcal{F}$, LID will consider only those features present in the problem p to be classified. As a consequence, any feature that is not present in p will not be considered as candidate to specialize D. The second bias is to consider as candidates for specializing D only those features that are leaf features of p (see §2). This bias is similar to that of the *relational pathfinding* method [16] in that it favours the selection of relations chained together in the examples.

The next step of LID is the selection of a leaf feature $f_d \in F_l$ to specialize the similitude term D. Selecting the most discriminatory leaf feature in the set F_l is heuristically done using the RLM distance of §3.1 over the features in F_l. Let us call f_d the most discriminatory feature in F_l.

The feature f_d is the leaf feature of path $\pi(root(p), f_d)$ in problem p. The specialization step of LID defines a new similitude term D' by adding to the current similitude term D the sequence of features specified by $\pi(root(p), f_d)$. After this addition D' has a new path $\pi(root(D'), f_d)$ with all the features in the path taking the same value that they take in p. After adding the path π to D, the new similitude term $D' = D + \pi$ subsumes a subset of cases in S_D, namely the discriminatory set $S_{D'}$ (the subset of cases subsumed by D').

Next, LID is recursively called with the discriminatory set $S_{D'}$ and the similitude term D'. The recursive call of LID has $S_{D'}$ as first parameter (instead of S_D) because the cases that are not subsumed by D' will not be subsumed by any further specialization. The process of specialization reduces the discriminatory set $S_D^n \subseteq S_D^{n-1} \subseteq \ldots \subseteq S_D^0$ at each step.

The stopping condition of LID, given the current similitude term D, is that all the cases in its discriminatory set S_D belong to only one solution class $C_k \in C$. LID gives D as an explanation of classifying p in C_k and S_D as the cases justifying that result. The similitude term D can be viewed as a *partial* description of C_k because it contains a subset of features that are discriminant enough to classify a case as belonging to C_k. Notice that D is not the most general generalization of C_k since in general D does not subsume all the cases belonging to C_k but only a subset of them (those sharing the features of D with the new problem). The similitude term D depends on the new problem, for this reason there are several partial descriptions (i.e. similitude terms) for the same class.

5   Experiments

In this section we describe two applications developed usimg LID: diabetes risk assessment (5.1) and identification of marine sponges (5.2).

5.1   Complications Risk Assessment in Diabetes

Diabetes mellitus is one of the most frequent human chronic diseases. There are two major types of diabetes: diabetes type I (or insulin-dependent) usually found in people younger than 40 years, and diabetes type II (or non insulin-dependent) often developed in people over this age. Both forms of diabetes produce the same short-term symptoms (i.e. increase of thirst, and high blood glucose values) and long-term complications (i.e. blindness, renal failure, gangrene and amputation, coronary heart disease and stroke).

The main concern in the management of the diabetes is reducing the individual risks of patients in developing new long-term complications and reducing risk of progression in the complications already present. In fact, the expected risks are different whether the patient has diabetes type I than he has diabetes type II. Moreover, the risk is also different whether the patient has no complications (*development risk*) or he has developed some complication (*progression risk*). We have developed a case base of 370 patients in collaboration with an expert.

The goal of LID in this domain is to assess the individual risks of complications for diabetic patients. Specifically, LID has to classify a patient in one of the following risk classes: *low risk, moderate risk, high risk,* and *very high risk*. We will focus on three macro-vascular complications: infarct, stroke and amputations. Each of these tasks requires LID to independently classify a problem using

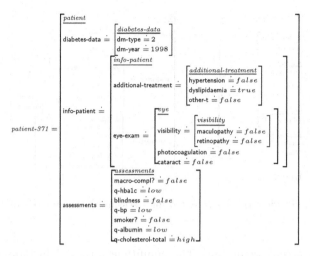

Fig. 3. Partial description of a diabetic patient. Here only 15 leaves are shown out of a total of more than 50 leaves present in the complete description of the patient.

the patients available in the case base. In order to illustrate the performance of LID in the diabetes domain we will focus on the assessment of the infarct risk. For this task the correct partition P_C is formed by the sets of patients that have the same risk class for the infarct complication.

Let us suppose that LID is used to assess the risk of infarct for the *patient-371* described in Figure 3. The search of LID can be constrained using domain knowledge. In this domain, we are only interested in considering patients in the case base that share with our current patient the same type of diabetes and the fact of whether or not the patient has macro-complications. Specifically, LID is initialized with D^0 (Figure 4a) having features *dm-type* with value 2 and *macro-compl?* with value *false* as in *patient-371*. The discriminatory set S_D^0 contains 144 cases having different infarct risk. Therefore the similitude term D^0 has to be specialized. The first step is to select the most discriminatory leaf feature using the RLM distance where the correct partition P_C is the classification of the cases according to their infarct risk degree.

LID finds the leaf feature *q-albumin* as the most discriminatory and builds the similitude term D^1 by adding to D^0 the path $\pi(patient, q\text{-}albumin)$ with *q-albumin* taking value *low* as in the *patient-371* (see Figure 4b). The discriminatory set S_D^1 contains 99 cases with different infarct risk. Therefore the similitude term D^1 has to be specialized by adding a new leaf feature. LID finds now the leaf feature *maculopathy* as the most discriminatory. The similitude term D^2 is obtained by adding the path $\pi(patient, maculopathy)$ to D^1 with value *false* as in *patient-371*.

The discriminatory set S_D^2 contains 66 cases with different infarct risk therefore D^2 has to be specialized. Now LID finds *other-t* as the most discriminant leaf feature. The similitude term D^3 subsumes 57 cases with different infarct risk. This means that D^3 has to be specialized. The next more discriminant

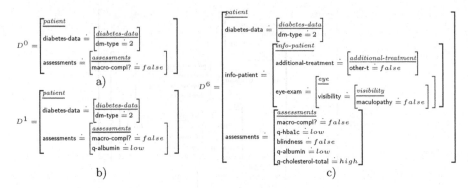

Fig. 4. Three similitude terms constructed for assessing the infarct risk of *Patient-371*.

leaf feature is *q-cholesterol-total*. The similitude term D^4 including the path $\pi(patient, q\text{-}cholesterol\text{-}total)$ with value *high* subsumes 16 cases that also have different infarct risk. The similitude term D^5 is obtained by adding to D^4 the path $\pi(patient, blindness)$ with value *false*. The discriminatory set S_D^5 still contains cases having either *high* or *moderate* infarct risk. Finally, the similitude term D^6 (Figure 4c) is obtained by adding to D^5 the path $\pi(patient, q\text{-}hba1c)$ with value *low*. The discriminatory set S_D^6 contains two cases with *moderate* risk of infarct. Therefore LID concludes that *patient-371* has a *moderate risk* of infarct. LID explains this classification with the similitude term D^6 of Figure 4c and justifies this result with the 2 cases of S_D^6.

LID has been evaluated in the following way. An expert diabetologist constructed a gold standard consisting of a risk pattern for macro-complications for the 370 cases of the base. This gold standard gives a unique "correct" risk value for each complication and considers all other risk estimations "incorrect". In fact, this assumption is too strong because often the expert assesses a range of risks (e.g. *very high* or *high*).

The experimental evaluation has been performed with this definition of correctness for the tasks of assessing the risk of stroke, infarct and amputation. For each task, we have built 15 test sets with the 370 patients case base, where each test set has 300 cases randomly chosen as training set. The results of LID upon the remaining 70 cases for each test set where compared with the gold standard and averaged for each task. The accuracy of LID is the following: 100% correct in assessing the stroke risk, 90% correct in assessing amputation risk, and 72.45% correct in assessing the infarct risk. In fact, the incorrect assessment of the infarct risk fail only by one degree (e.g. high risk vs. very-high risk) in 81.69% of the cases. We are currently analyzing those cases with the support of the expert since often he assesses a range of risks that includes the answer of LID.

In addition to estimate the accuracy of LID we have also analyzed the justifications (similitude terms) in order to determine whether the risk has been obtained based on correct assumptions or, conversely, whether it has been obtained from assumptions that the expert considers irrelevant for estimating a risk. Let

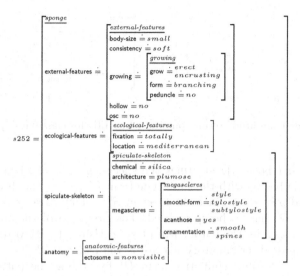

Fig. 5. Partial representation of a sponge using feature terms.

us consider assessing the stroke risk where LID always obtains a similitude term containing only one feature: the blood pressure. The expert confirms that the blood pressure is the determining factor for the risk of stroke. When assessing the risk of amputation, the justification contains the feature *polyneuropathy* that is one of the most important factors according to the expert criteria. Concerning the assessment of the infarct risk, the LID explanations also use among others features such as diabetes duration, cholesterol or haemoglobin that the expert considers as determinant factors for assessing the infarct risk.

Notice that LID explanations are not generalizations describing a class, they are symbolic descriptions of the (important) aspects shared between the problem and similar cases.

5.2   Identification of Marine Sponges

Marine sponges are relatively little studied and most of the existing species are not yet fully described. The main problems in sponge identification are due to the morphological plasticity of the species, to the incomplete knowledge of many of their biological and cytological features and to the frequent description of new taxa. Moreover, there is no agreement around the species delimitation since it is not clear how the different taxa can be characterized. The application of LID to this domain allows the classification of new specimens based on their similarity to specimens clearly classified in some taxa. This similarity, in turn, is based on the relevant features of the specimen that has to be classified.

With the support of two experts, we have developed a case base with the descriptions of 280 sponges belonging to the orders: $C = \{astrophorida,\ hadromerida,\ axinellida\}$. LID has been used to identify the order of new specimens.

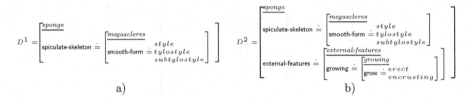

Fig. 6. Sequence of similitude terms constructed by LID for classifying sponge $s252$.

Let us consider how LID identifies the specimen $s252$ of Figure 5 given a case base B. LID begins with the similitude term $D^0 = any$, the discriminatory set $S_D^0 = B$ and $p = s252$. Since the cases in S_D^0 belong to several orders, the similitude term D^0 has to be specialized. The first step of the specialization is to select the most discriminatory leaf of $s252$. Using the RLM distance LID finds that the most discriminatory feature is the leaf *smooth-form*. Then LID specializes D^0 to the new similarity term D^1 by adding the path $\pi(sponge, smooth\text{-}form)$ taking as value the set $\{style, tylostyle, subtylostyle\}$ (Fig. 6a).

The discriminatory set S_D^1 contains 25 cases subsumed by the similitude term D^1. Since these cases belong to several orders D^1 has to be specialized. Now LID finds that the most relevant leaf feature is *grow*. Then D^1 is specialized to D^2 adding the path $\pi(sponge, grow)$ with value the set $\{erect, encrusting\}$ (see Figure 6b). The discriminatory set S_D^2 contains 10 cases belonging to the *axinellida* order. Therefore LID classifies the sponge $s252$ in the *axinellida* order. The explanation of this classification is the similitude term D^2 of Figure 6b stating that the sponge $s252$ is *axinellida* because 1) has megascleres of form *style, tylostyle* and *subtylostyle*, and 2) grows *erect* and *encrusting*.

We evaluated LID in the marine sponges domain with the goal of identifying the order of specimens. We performed six ten-fold crossvalidation runs on the case base containing 280 descriptions of marine sponges. The average accuracy of LID is 89.998% with a standard deviation of 5.827.

6   Related Work

There are two main lines of research closely related to our approach on similarity assessment in relational representations. On the one hand, there is research about similarity assessment of structured and complex cases in CBR; and, on the other hand, there is research on relational IBL.

Although a lot of work in similarity assessment of cases in CBR is focused on weighted distances among attribute value vectors there is also active research in establishing similarity estimates among structured representation of cases [6, 7,15]. Some approaches share the idea of building a "structural similarity" (as our "similitude term" approach) but they use techniques subtree-isomorphism or subgraph isomorphism detection for building the description of this "structural similarity" [7]. In [6] the "structural similarity" is used to guide adaptation phase of CBR [6] and not for the retrieval phase. Another way to construct a similitude term is using antiunification (computing the most specific generalization of two cases) [15], and later having a measure to assess which similitude term is better (e.g. using an entropy measure [14]) to select the best precedent in the case-base.

A related approach to feature terms as case representation formalism is that of using Description Logics for this purpose; antiunification can also be used but some assessment measure is also needed, as shown in [12] where a probabilistic interpretation of the "least common subsumer" is used. LID does not use antiunification to build the similitude term; instead it constructs the similitude term guided by an example-driven heuristic to assess the relevance of the features to be added to the similitude term. Finally, some research work on case retrieval use inductive techniques involving the construction of decision trees (as in [4]) and only for cases that are attribute-value vectors.

Relevant work is being carried on for transferring IBL techniques to relational learning, mainly in the ILP framework of a Horn clause representation of cases and background knowledge. An approach in ILP using a concept closed to similitude terms [15,14] is that of Progol's Analogical Prediction [13]. Progol's AP is a lazy induction technique capable of binary classification. For each problem, AP tries to build an hypothesis using the Progol engine. If this hypothesis is found the problem is classified as *true*, otherwise the problem is classified as *false*. LID builds a similitude term ("hypothesis") but can deal with multiple classes. The RIBL system [9,10] first generates cases out of Horn clauses in a knowledge base, then calculates the distance among cases by estimating the relevance of predicates and attributes. RIBL 2.0 [10] uses an "edit distance" to estimate the distance between cases (that can contain lists and terms). Instead of the notion of "distance" among cases LID uses a distance in the heuristic assessment of the importance of features to be included in the similitude term. Moreover, our assessment is not based on a pairwise comparison of "problem vs. case" similarity but takes into account all cases that share a particular "structural similarity" embodied by those cases subsumed by the similitude term that LID builds.

7 Conclusions

We have developed a technique for case-based learning where cases are best represented as collection of relations among entities. The LID approach is based on a similarity assessment used by a heuristic search in a space of symbolic descriptions of similitude. Moreover, the symbolic description of similitude provides an explanation of the grounds on which a precedent case is selected from the case base as most relevant (or "similar") to the current problem. The symbolic similitude that classifies a problem subsumes a subset of the elements in a class, and as such it is just a partial description of that class. Indeed, this is the main difference between a lazy learning approach like LID and an eager approach as that of induction (see the INDIE inductive method in [3]).

As for future work, we intend to explore a variation of LID that adaptively chooses a middle ground between the extreme points of lazy and eager approaches. Our assumption is that it is unlikely that a lazy (or eager) approach is always the best suited for all application domains. Thus, our aim will be to investigate in which situations it is useful to store (memorize) the partial class descriptions provided by LID an use them to solve new problems and in which situations is better to keep a purely lazy approach.

Acknowledgements. This work has been supported by Projects SMASH (CI-CYT TIC96-1038-C04-01) and IBROW (IST-1999-19005). The authors thank Dr. Marta Domingo and physician Albert Palaudàries for their assistance in developing the marine sponges and diabetes applications.

References

[1] D. Aha, editor. *Lazy Learning*. Kluwer Academic Publishers, 1997.
[2] Hassan Aït-Kaci and Andreas Podelski. Towards a meaning of LIFE. *J. Logic Programming*, 16:195–234, 1993.
[3] E. Armengol and E. Plaza. Bottom-up induction of feature terms. *Machine Learning*, 41(1):259–294, 2000.
[4] E. Auriol, S. Wess, M. Manago, K.-D. Althoff, and R. Traphöner. Inreca: A seamless integrated system based on inductive inference and case-based reasoning. In *CBR Reseacrh and Development*, number 1010 in Lecture Notes in Artificial Intelligence, pages 371–380. Springer-Verlag, 1995.
[5] U. Bohnebeck, T. Horváth, and S. Wrobel. Term comparisons in first-order similarity measures. In D. Page, editor, *Proc. of the 8th International Workshop on ILP*, volume 1446 of *LNAI*, pages 65–79. Springer Verlag, 1998.
[6] K Börner. Structural similarity as a guidance in case-based design. In *Topics in Case-Based Reasoning: EWCBR'94*, pages 197–208, 1994.
[7] H Bunke and B T Messmer. Similarity measures for structured representations. In *Topics in Case-Based Reasoning: EWCBR'94*, pages 106–118, 1994.
[8] B. Carpenter. *The Logic of typed Feature Structures*. Tracts in theoretical Computer Science. Cambridge University Press, Cambridge, UK, 1992.
[9] W. Emde and D. Wettschereck. Relational instance based learning. In Lorenza Saitta, editor, *Machine Learning - Proceedings 13th ICML*, pages 122 – 130. Morgan Kaufmann Publishers, 1996.
[10] Tamas Horvath, Stefan Wrobel, and Uta Bohnebeck. Relational instance-based learning with lists and terms. *Machine Learning*, 43(1):53–80, 2001.
[11] Ramon López de Mántaras. A distance-based attribute selection measure for decision tree induction. *Machine Learning*, 6:81–92, 1991.
[12] T. Mantay and R. Moller. Content-based information retrieval by computing least common subsumers in a probabilistic description logic. In *Proceedings of the ECAI Workshop Intelligent Information Integration*, 1998.
[13] Stephen Muggleton and Michael Bain. Analogical prediction. In *Proc. ILP*, 1999.
[14] E. Plaza, R. López de Mántaras, and E. Armengol. On the importance of similitude: An entropy-based assessment. In I. Smith and B. Saltings, editors, *Advances in Case-based reasoning*, number 1168 in Lecture Notes in Artificial Intelligence, pages 324–338. Springer-Verlag, 1996.
[15] Enric Plaza. Cases as terms: A feature term approach to the structured representation of cases. In M. Veloso and A. Aamodt, editors, *Case-Based Reasoning, ICCBR-95*, number 1010 in Lecture Notes in Artificial Intelligence, pages 265–276. Springer-Verlag, 1995.
[16] B. L. Richards and R. J. Mooney. Learning relations by pathfinding. In *proceedings of AAAI-92*, pages 50–55, 1992.

Estimating the Predictive Accuracy of a Classifier

Hilan Bensusan[1] and Alexandros Kalousis[2]

[1] Department of Computer Science, University of Bristol
The Merchant Venturers Building, Woodland Road
Bristol, BS8 1UB, England
hilanb@cs.bris.ac.uk
[2] CSD University of Geneva,
CH-1211 Geneva 4, Switzerland
kalousis@cui.unige.ch

Abstract. This paper investigates the use of meta-learning to estimate the predictive accuracy of a classifier. We present a scenario where meta-learning is seen as a regression task and consider its potential in connection with three strategies of dataset characterization. We show that it is possible to estimate classifier performance with a high degree of confidence and gain knowledge about the classifier through the regression models generated. We exploit the results of the models to predict the ranking of the inducers. We also show that the best strategy for performance estimation is not necessarily the best one for ranking generation.

1   Introduction

The practice of machine learning often involves the estimation of how well a classification learning algorithm would perform in a dataset. There is no classifier that can be predictively successful in every dataset. In addition, any device that selects the most appropriate classifier for a dataset based on its properties is bound to fail in some area of the dataset space [23]. However, there may exist a sub-area of the dataset space that is small enough for such a device to have high performance, compensated by bad performance elsewhere, and yet large enough to include all the datasets we are actually interested [22,17]. Machine learning is possible only if this sub-area exists. Within this sub-area it is possible to estimate the performance of different learners according to the nature of the dataset.

Currently, this estimation is done through the expertise of the machine learning practitioner. The practitioner, of course, brings her previous experience with classifiers as well as her preferences to the estimation process. As a consequence, the estimation is often vague, in many cases unprincipled and always relying on the human expert. Often, the practitioner can appeal to a well established technique in the field, cross-validation, to help the estimation or at least to establish which classifiers are likely to work best. Cross-validation is a priori justifiable because it works for a large enough area of the dataset space [22]. It is, however, too costly. Moreover, it provides no insight concerning the relations between

L. De Raedt and P. Flach (Eds.): ECML 2001, LNAI 2167, pp. 25–36, 2001.
© Springer-Verlag Berlin Heidelberg 2001

the performance of a classifier and the properties of the domain. In this sense it provides no principled basis for an analysis of what lies behind successful performance estimations.

Meta-learning is the endeavour to learn something about the expected performance of a classifier from previous applications. In any scenario, it depends heavily on the way we choose to characterize the datasets. Meta-learning has often concentrated on predicting whether a classifier is suitable for a dataset [11] and on selection of the best option from a pool of classifiers[1,13]. In the former, we ask whether a good performance is to be expected from a classifier given the properties of a dataset. In the latter, given a pool of classifiers, we attempt to establish which ones are the best. In both cases meta-learning is constructed as a classification task. Little work has been reported on direct estimation of the performances of classifiers.

In this paper we propose and examine an approach to the direct estimation of classifiers' performances via meta-learning. We face meta-learning tasks as regression tasks whereby we look for relationships between the properties of a dataset and the performance of the classifier. This direct approach is more flexible than meta-learning for model selection since the estimations are not relative to a specific pool of classifiers.

2   How Can We Predict Accuracies

The idea of using regression to predict the performance of learning algorithms was first used by Gama and Brazdil in [7], were they continued on the framework adopted in STATLOG. They tried to directly predict the error of an algorithm for a specific dataset based on the characteristics of the dataset, as these were defined in the STATLOG project. For each of the learners they evaluated various regression models like linear regression, instance based regression and rule based regression. They report poor results in terms of the Normalised Mean Squared Error (NMSE).

Sohn in [19] uses the results of STATLOG (i.e. same data characterization, same learning algorithms and same datasets) and constructs linear regression models that predict the errors of the learning algorithms on unseen datasets. As she is using the results of STATLOG, the study is limited to 19 datasets To overcome the small number of datasets she used bootstraping resampling to estimate the parameters of the regression models. The models were used to provide a ranking of the available learning algorithms. The results show that the statistical models produced, exhibit high performance. However they must be interpreted cautiously because of the limited number of datasets used in the study.

A recent paper provided some initial results related to the use of estimated performances for model selection [10]. It shows that estimating performances leads to a better result in selecting a learner from a pool than learning through a repository of datasets classified in terms of the best performing algorithm in the pool. Using a pool composed by three classifiers, the paper indicates that regression (by M6), when used to estimate the error of the three classifiers, selects the classifier with least error with better performance than using classification (with C5.0) to decide the best algorithm for a dataset. The experiments, however, were preliminary and concentrated only on one strategy of dataset characterization, on only three classifiers and were performed on artificially generated datasets.

A work on a similar direction is that of instance-based ranking of classifiers through meta-learning, also called zooming[18]. The goal there is to determine a preference order over a pool of classifiers, based on predictive accuracy and computational cost. The ranking for a new dataset is built by inspecting a number of k-nearest neighbours in a collection of reference datasets, that form a meta-dataset. The produced ranking is based on a preference function that weights cost and accuracy. This approach cannot be used as it is to estimate accuracies of learners, but only to provide a relative ranking of them.

Our goal was to broaden this research by considering a greater number of classifiers and different strategies of dataset characterization. We therefore concentrate primarily on performance estimation. Our approach was to construct meta-datasets for regression so that any technique could then be used for performance estimation. A meta-dataset is constructed for each classifier. In order to do that, each dataset needs to be characterised by a dataset characterization stategy that produces meta-attributes. The meta-attributes produced are then the attributes for the meta-learning problem where each data-point corresponds to a dataset. Each data-point contains the description of the dataset by the meta-attributes and the performance of the classifier in the dataset. The meta-dataset can then be treated as an ordinary regression dataset.

In this paper we concentrate on 8 classifiers: two decision tree learning methods (Ltree [6] and C5.0tree [14]), Naive Bayes [4], two rule methods (Ripper [3] and c5.0rules [14]), linear discriminant, nearest neighbor [4] and a combination method, c5.0boost [15,5]. These classifiers are representative of different types of induction procedures and are among the most popular non-parametric classifiers in machine learning.

3   Strategies of Dataset Characterization

The characterization of datasets is the touchstone of meta-learning. Its success depends on how well can the meta-attributes support generalization. We aim at dataset characteristics that produce accurate estimates and insightful regression models. We will make use of three different strategies of dataset characterization:

- A set of information-theoretical and statistical features of the datasets that were developed as a sequel to the work done in STATLOG [11]. We refer to this strategy as DCT. We used the extended set of characteristics given in [20].
- A finer grained development of the STATLOG characteristics, where histograms were used to describe the distributions of features that are computed for each attribute of a dataset, thus preserving more information than

the initial mean based approach of STATLOG. We refer to this strategy as HISTO. A detailed description of the histograms can be found in [9].

- Landmarking, a characterization technique where the performance of simple, bare-bone learners in the dataset is used to characterise it [13]. In this paper we use seven landmarkers: *Decision node, Worst node, Randomly chosen node, Naive Bayes, 1-Nearest Neighbour, Elite 1-Nearest Neighbour* and *Linear Discriminant*. We refer to this dataset characterisation strategy as LAND. Obviously, when we want to predict the error of an algorithm that is also a landmarker, this landmarker is omited from the description of the dataset.

Of the three approaches landmarking has a completely different philosophy since it is using the performance of simple learners to characterize datasets. DCT and HISTO are both based on a description of datasets in terms of their statistical and information based properties although using a different set of characteristics, with HISTO trying to exploit the full information contained in the distribution of these characteristics.

4   Regression on Accuracies

Regression was used to estimate the performance of classifiers using the different strategies of dataset characterization. Since the quality of the estimate depends on its closeness to the actual accuracy achieved by the classifier, the meta-learning performance is measured by the Mean Absolute Deviation (MAD). MAD is defined as the sum of the absolute differences between real and predicted values divided by the number of test items. It can be seen as measure of the distance between the actual values and the predicted ones.

In order to compare the estimation capabilities of the three strategies of dataset characterization we used Cubist [16] and a kernel method [21] to perform regression on the meta-dataset. Kernel methods work in an instance-based principle and they fit a linear regression model to a neighborhood around the selected instance. It is straightforward to alter their distance metric in order to make better use of the semantics of the non-applicable values that occur in meta-attributes of DCT and HISTO. The drawback of kernel methods is that they do not produce a model that can be used to improve our knowledge of the relationships between performance and dataset. Cubist, on the other side, produces models in the form of rulesets and therefore is more suitable for our analysis of the insight gained about a classifier by the process of estimating its accuracy. The disadvantage of Cubist, on the other hand, is that it can make no direct use of the non-applicable values found in the meta-features of DCT and HISTO. To be able to use the algorithm we had to recode those values to new ones that lie outside the domain of definition of the dataset characteristics we use. Since at least one of these limitations would apply to every existing regression system, we remedy the situation by applying both the kernel method and Cubist to all meta-datasets. We do that while bearing in mind that the kernel methods

Table 1. Kernel on estimating performance.

CLASSIFIER	DCT	HISTO	LAND	DMAD
C50BOOST	0.112	0.123	0.050	0.134
C50RULES	0.110	0.121	0.051	0.133
C50TREE	0.110	0.123	0.054	0.137
LINDISCR	0.118	0.129	0.063	0.137
LTREE	0.105	0.113	0.041	0.132
MLCIB1	0.120	0.138	0.081	0.153
MLCNB	0.121	0.143	0.064	0.146
RIPPER	0.113	0.128	0.056	0.145

are more likely to produce good results for DCT and HISTO meta-datasets while Cubist is being run for the rulesets it produces.

Experiments were done with 65 datasets from the UCI repository [2] and from the METAL project [8]. For each classifier meta-dataset, we run a 10-fold cross-validation to assess the quality of performance estimations. The quality of the estimation is assessed by the MAD in the 10 folds, and it is compared with the default MAD (dMAD). The latter is the MAD obtained by predicting that the error of a classifier in a test dataset is the mean of the error obtained in the training datasets. dMAD is a benchmark for comparison. We expect regression to produce a smaller MAD than the dMAD. We have to note here that, in the case of landmarkers, when ever we build a model to predict the performance of a classifier that is a member of the set of landmarkers the corresponding landmarker is removed.

The quality of the estimation with the kernel method using different dataset characterization strategies is shown in table 1. The table presents the MAD in the 10 folds for every regression problem and the dMAD. Using the three dataset characterization strategies, the MAD obtained by the kernel method is smaller than the dMAD, showing that regression is worth trying. Landmarking outperforms the other two strategies by far and produces estimated accuracies with a MAD smaller than 0.081 for every classifier. This means that the average error of the estimated accuracy in unseen datasets will be in the worst case (that of mlcib1) 8.1%. The table shows that a great deal of meta-learning is taking place. HISTO and DCT do not produce estimates as good as the ones produced by landmarking. One could suspect that this is because the meta-dataset is relatively small when compared to the large number of meta-attributes used by these two strategies of dataset characterization. To check whether reducing the dimensionality of the problem would significantly improve the estimates, we performed feature selection through wrapping in the DCT and the HISTO meta-dataset. The estimates, however, were not greatly improved. We conclude that landmarking performs best in performance estimation using kernel.

With Cubist, the situation is similar. Table 2 shows that LAND still performs better than DCT and HISTO. The table also gives figures for LAND-, a strategy

Table 2. Cubist on estimating performance.

CLASSIFIER	DCT	HISTO	LAND	LAND-	DMAD
C50BOOST	0.103	0.128	0.033	0.079	0.134
C50RULES	0.121	0.126	0.036	0.077	0.133
C50TREE	0.114	0.130	0.044	0.078	0.137
LINDISCR	0.118	0.140	0.054	0.127	0.137
LTREE	0.114	0.121	0.032	0.054	0.132
MLCIB1	0.150	0.149	0.067	0.077	0.153
MLCNB	0.126	0.149	0.044	0.052	0.146
RIPPER	0.128	0.131	0.041	0.061	0.145

Table 3. P-values of paired T-tests of significance comparing with the dMAD (Kernel).

CLASSIFIER	DCT	HISTO	LAND
C50BOOST	*tie* (0.112)	*tie* (0.361)	+ (0.00)
C50RULES	*tie* (0.075)	*tie* (0.319)	+ (0.00)
C50TREE	+ (0.045)	*tie* (0.242)	+ (0.00)
LINDISCR	*tie* (0.110)	*tie* (0.548)	+ (0.00)
LTREE	+ (0.030)	*tie* (0.115)	+ (0.00)
MLCIB1	+ (0.037)	*tie* (0.269)	+ (0.00)
MLCNB	+ (0.036)	*tie* (0.807)	+ (0.00)
RIPPER	+ (0.024)	*tie* (0.217)	+ (0.00)

of dataset description where only decision node, random node, worst node, elite nearest neighbour and linear discriminants are used as landmarkers. The reason for this is that with less landmarkers we obtain more insightful models. Also, the loss in MAD is not extreme and LAND- still performs well when compared to the dMAD.

To examine whether the results presented are significant we performed t-paired tests of significance. In Table 3 we give the results of the t-paired test between each model and the dMAD. We present results only for the kernel based models, but the situation is similar for the cubist based ones. In this table and in the following ones, "+" indicates that the method is significantly better than the default, *tie* signifies that there is no difference, "−" that the method is significantly worse then the default. The table shows that the performance of landmarkers is always significantly better then the default. DCT is significantly better in 5 out of the 8 cases, and HISTO performance is not statistically different than the default. Furthermore, landmarking is always significantly better than DCT and HISTO for all the eight different learning algorithms. Between DCT and HISTO the differences are not significant for any of the 8 learners.

Concluding we can say that the use of landmarkers to perform accuracy estimation is a method with very good performance and low estimation error, significantly better from HISTO and DCT. The reason for that is: landmark based

Table 4. Average Spearman's Correlation Coefficients with the True Ranking

	MODELS		
RANKINGS	KERNEL	CUBIST	ZOOMING
DEFAULT	0.330	0.330	0.330
DCT	0.435	0.083	0.341
HISTO	0.405	0.174	0.371
LAND	0.180	0.185	
LAND-		0.090	0.190

characteristics are better suited for that type of task. They provide a direct estimation of the hardness of the problem since they are themselves performance estimations. On the other side DCT and HISTO, give an indirect description of the hardness of the problem, through the use of characteristics like attributes correlations, which are more difficult to directly associate with accuracy.

5 Using Estimates to Rank Learners

An obvious way to use the accuracies predicted by regression is to provide a ranking of the learners based on these predictions. In this section we give results for various ways of predicting rankings. We validate their usefulness by comparing them with the true ranking, and the performance of a default ranking.

To evaluate the different approaches, the rankings produced for a dataset are compared to the true ranking of the learners on this dataset. The true ranking is known since we know the accuracies of all the learners on the 65 datasets that we are using. As a measure of similarity of the rankings, we used Spearman's rank correlation coefficient [12]. We also compare our method with zooming [18]. The results in terms of the average Spearman rank correlation coefficient are given in table 4. Zooming cannot be applied to the full set of landmarkers, since that will mean using the performance of lindiscr, mlcib and mlcnb to predict their ranking. This is why the corresponding combination, (zooming+land) is not included in the table. We also give the average Spearman's rank correlation coefficient of the *default ranking* with the true ranking. The default ranking is a ranking that remains the same no matter what the dataset under examination is. It is computed on the basis of the mean accuracies that the learners achieve over all the datasets. The default ranking, starting from the best learner, is : c50boost, c50rules, c50tree, ltree, ripper, mlcib1, mlcnb, lindiscr. A ranking method is interesting if it performs significantly better than this default ranking: in this case it is worth applying the meta-learning method to discover a suitable ranking for a given dataset. Table 5 gives the results of the statistical significance tests, between the different models and the default ranking. We concentrate on kernel since the rankings produced by cubist perform always worse than the default.

Surprisingly enough the only case that a model is significantly better than the default ranking is the combination of Kernel and DCT, even ranking with zoom-

Table 5. P-values of paired t-tests, between the rank correlation coefficients of the models and the rank correlation coefficient of the default ranking

DATASET	MODELS	
CHARACTERIZATION	KERNEL	ZOOMING
DCT	$+(0.05)$	$tie(0.862)$
HISTO	$tie(0.147)$	$tie(0.482)$
LAND	$-(0.010)$	
LAND-		$-(0.018)$

ing a method specifically created to provide rankings is not significantly better then the default. Although landmarking constructs regression models that have a very low MAD error, it fails to provide a good ranking of the classifiers. The predictions provided by Kernel and DCT, while worse than the ones provided by landmarking based models, systematically keep the relative order of the accuracies of the classifiers. So although they do not estimate the performances accurately, they do rank the classifiers well. A reason for the poor performance of landmarking in ranking is that landmarking based regression models give the error as a function of the error of simple learners. This can lead to models where the error of an inducer is proportional to the error of another inducer resulting in a more or less fixed ranking of the available inducers, a fact that explains the poor performance of landmarkers when it comes to ranking inducers.

6   What Regression Models Can Tell Us about Classifiers

An advantage of using regression for meta-learning is that we can extract useful knowledge about the classifiers whose performance we are trying to estimate. The generated models refer to a specific classifier. They associate characteristics of the datasets, classifier error. Examining them will give us an idea of what are the dataset characteristics that affect the performance of classifiers.

The main motivation behind the application of Cubist, was the construction of a set of rules in order to see how datasets characteristics associate with learners' performances, and more important, whether the associations that pop up make sense. Below we can see typical examples of rules constructed by Cubist to estimate the error of Naive Bayes. For each rule, we give the number of the cases (i.e. datasets) that are covered by the rule, and the mean error of Naive Bayes on the cases covered by the rule. Every rule consists of two parts, an *IF* and a *THEN* part. The *IF* part specifies the precondictions that must hold in order for the rule to apply, these preconditions are conditions on specific dataset characteristics which are determined by cubist. The *THEN* part of a rule is the regression model constructed by cubist to predict the error of Naive Bayes on the datasets covered by the preconditions of the rule. Below we are going to review the produced rules in terms of their agreement with expert knowledge.

*DCT rules:
```
a)7 cases, mean error 0.06           b)17 cases, mean error 0.10
   IF MAXAttr_Gini_sym > 0.245          IF MAXAttr_Gini_sym <= 0.245
      AVGAttr_gFunction > -0.91            AVGAttr_gFunction > -0.91
   THEN mlcnb_error = -0.0748          THEN mlcnb_error = -0.0965
      - 0.1528 Cancor                     - 0.252 AVGAttr_gFunction
      + 0.1479 Frac                       - 0.1706 Cancor
      - 0.1179 AVGAttr_gFunction          + 0.1613 Fract
```

* HISTO rules:
```
a)29 cases, mean error 0.22          b)11 cases, mean error 0.46
   IF conc_hist_4 <= 0.0032 AND         IF num_attributes > 7
   conc_hist_with_class_0 <= 0.68      con_histo_4 <= 0.0032
   THEN mlcnb error = 0.2074            conc_histo_class_0 > 0.68
      - 0.25 correl_hist_4             THEN mlcnb_error = 0.4235
      + 0.21 correl_hist_5               - 0.25 correl_hist_4
      + 0.04 correl_hist_2               + 0.21 correl_hist_5
      + 0.02 conc_hist_class_0           + 0.04 correl_hist_2
      - 0.01 conc_hist_class_1           + 0.026 conc_histo_class_0
      - 0.01 con_histo_4                 - 0.021 con_histo_4
                                         - 0.016 conc_histo_class_1
```

* LAND rules:
```
a)34 cases, mean error 0.218         b)16 cases, mean error 0.385
   IF Rand_Node <= 0.57                IF Rand_Node > 0.57
      Elite_Node > 0.084               THEN mlcnb = 0.339
   THEN mlcnb = 0.167                     - 1.099 Worst_Node
      + 0.239 Rand_Node                  + 0.792 Dec_Node
      - 0.18 Worst_Node                  + 0.292 Rand_Node
      + 0.105 Elite_Node                 + 0.105 Elite_Node
```

If we examine the two rules of DCT, we see that they define two sets of datasets based on the MAXAttr_Gini_Sym. The first one containing seven datasets, with the mean error of Naive Bayes on these to be 6%, and the second set containing seventeen datasets, with a mean error of 10%. MAXAttr_Gini_Sym is the maximum gini index, that we compute between one attribute and the class variable. If this characteristic has a high value, this means that there exists one attribute on the dataset that has high information content for the class attribute. The higher the value of this characteristic is, the easier the prediction of the class. By examining the two rules we can see that on the datasets with a smaller value of MAXAttr_Gini_Sym, Naive Bayes has higher mean error. Examining now the regression models constructed for the two rules we see that they are quite similar, they have the same set of dataset characteristics and the same signs on coefficients, with just a slight difference on the magnitude of the coefficients. Cancor is the first canonical correlation between the attributes and the class. As this increases we expect the error to decrease and this is indeed the case, since on the regression models it has a negative sign. Frac is the proportion of total class variation explained by the first canonical discriminant. It seems that this feature has a negative effect on the error of Naive Bayes, since the corresponding regression coefficient has a positive sign. The gFunction is a measurement for the probability of finding the joint distribution of classes and attribute values for a specific attribute. AVGAttr_gFunction is the average overall the attributes, the higher the value of the characteristic the easier the problem it is, and indeed the error of Naive Bayes decreases when AVGAttr_gFunction increases.

In HISTO, datasets separated according to the value of con_histo_with_class_0. This characteristic gives the percentage of attributes that have a concentration coefficient with the class attribute, between 0 and 0.1, (the concentration coefficient is a measure of association between two discrete characteristics, with 0 for no association at all, and 1 for the highest association). A high value of it implies low association between the attributes and the class attribute, thus one would expect a high error, for the datasets that exhibit that property. The two rules comply with this expectation. Datasets covered by the first rule (i.e. datasets were less than 68% of the attributes have a concentration coefficient with the class variable smaller than 0.1) have lower error, 0.22, than the datasets covered by the complementary rule, 0.46.

In the case of landmarking, we used the smaller set of landmarkers to generate the regression model with Cubist (that is, LAND-). In the two rules given above using landmarking, two disjoint sets of datasets are established based on the value of the Rand_Node. Rand_Node is the error of a single decision node created from a randomly chosen attribute. If this node exhibits a high error, chances are that the attributes have poor discriminating power. This situation is indeed captured by the rules. As we may see the datasets covered from the first rule (lower error of Rand_Node), exhibit a lower mean error from the datasets covered from the second rule.

7   Computational Cost

Setting up the different regression models, is a task that is performed only once. After that the produced models can be used on new unseen cases. The main cost of the method comes on the exploitation phase, from the characterization of a new dataset. DCT and HISTO are information and statistical based approaches. Their main cost is on the construction of the contigency tables and the covariance matrixes of the datasets. These have a complexity of $O(n)$, where n is the number of examples of a dataset. Some of the characteristics used require the computation of eigen values of the covariance matrixes, this has a complexity of $O(p^3)$, where p is the number of attributes, so the computational complexity of DCT and HISTO is $O(n + p^3)$ which is much smaller of that of cross validation. In the case of landmarking the computational complexity is that of the cross validation of the landmarkers. The most expensive landmarker used here is the 1-nearest neighbor, whose complexity is $O(n^2)$. We can reduce this complexity, obtaining similar results, if we omit the nearest neighbor landmarker. In this case the complexity is determined by linear discriminants that have a complexity of $O(n + p^3)$.

8   Conclusions

In this paper we invistigated the use of regression learners in order to directly estimate the errors of classification inducers on specific datasets through the use of three different ways of characterizing the datasets. Landmarking provided by far the best predictions among the three different approaches. Using these predictions we were able to provide a ranking of the inducers, with the results being acceptable, on the limit, in only one of the examined cases.

Two are the main prerequisites for meta-learning to be effective, first a good characterization of the datasets and second the morphological similarity of new datasets to the ones used to construct the meta-models. This is not different from the fact that in order, for learned models to be useful, the examples on which they are applied should come from the same distribution as the training examples. The ideal environment for successfull utilisation of the approach is one where the analyst normally faces datasets of similar nature.

This is still an initial study and there is lot of work that has to be done, especially in the area of datasets characterization, possibly with the use of new characteristics, or with the combination of the existing ones to a single characterization.

Acknowledgements. This work is part of the METAL project supported by an ESPRIT Framework IV LTR Grant (Nr 26.357). Thanks to Carlos Soares for providing with the results on zooming.

Appendix Datasets Used

abalone, acetylation, agaricus-lepiota, allbp, allhyper, allhypo, allrep, australian, balance-scale, bands, breast-cancer-wisc,breast-cancer-wisc_nominal, bupa, car, contraceptive, crx, dermatology, dis, ecoli, flag_language, flag_religion, flare_c, flare_c_er, flare_m, flare_m_er, flare_x, flare_x_er, fluid, german, glass, glass2, heart, hepatitis, hypothyroid, ionosphere, iris, kp, led24, led7, lymphography, monk1, monk2, monk3-full, mushrooms, new-thyroid, parity5_5, pima-indians-diabetes, proc-cleveland-2, proc-cleveland-4, proc-hungarian-2, proc - hungarian-4, proc-switzerland-2, proc-switzerland-4, quisclas, sick-euthyroid, soybean-large, tic-tac-toe, titanic, tumor-LOI, vote, vowel, waveform40, wdbc, wpbc, yeast.

References

1. H. Bensusan. God doesn't always shave with Occam's Razor – learning when and how to prune. In *Proceedings of the 10th European Conference on Machine Learning*, pages 119–124, 1998.
2. C. Blake and C. Merz. UCI repository of machine learning databases, 1998. http://www.ics.uci.edu/.
3. W. Cohen. Fast effective rule induction. In *Proceedings of the 12th International Conference on Machine Learning*, pages 115–123. Morgan Kaufmann, 1995.

4. R. O. Duda and P. E. Hart. *Pattern classification and scene analysis*. John Wiley, 1973.
5. Y. Freund and R. E. Schapire. Experiments with a new boosting algorithm. In *Proceedings 13th International Conference on Machine Learning*, pages 148–146, 1996.
6. J. Gama. Discriminant trees. In *Proceedings of the 16th International Machine Learning Conference (ICML'99)*, pages 134–142, 1999.
7. J. Gama and P. Brazdil. Characterization of classification algorithms. In *Proceedings of the 7th Portugese Conference in AI, EPIA 95*, pages 83–102, 1995.
8. C. Giraud-Carrier et al. A meta-learning assistant for providing user support in data mining and machine learning, 1999-2001. http://www.metal-kdd.org.
9. A. Kalousis and T. Theoharis. Noemon: Design, implementation and performance results of an intelligent assistant for classifier selection. *Intelligent Data Analysis*, 3(5):319–337, 1999.
10. C. Köpf, C. Taylor, and J. Keller. Meta-analysis: from data characterisation for meta-learning to meta-regression. In P. Brazdil and A. Jorge, editors, *PKDD'2000 Workshop on Data Mining, Decision Support, Meta-Learning and ILP*, 2000.
11. D. Michie, D. J. Spiegelhalter, and C. C. Taylor, editors. *Machine Learning, Neural and Statistical Classification*. Ellis Horwood, 1994.
12. H. Neave and Worthington P. *Distribution Free Tests*. Unwin Hyman, London, UK, 1992.
13. B. Pfahringer, H. Bensusan, and C. Giraud-Carrier. Meta-learning by landmarking various learning algorithms. In *Proceedings of the Seventeenth International Conference on Machine Learning*, pages 743–750, 2000.
14. J. R. Quinlan. *C4.5: Programs for Machine Learning*. Morgan Kaufmann, 1993.
15. J. R. Quinlan. Bagging, boosting, and C4. 5. In *Proceedings of the Thirteenth National Conference on Artificial Intelligence and the Eighth Innovative Applications of Artificial Intelligence Conference*, pages 725–730, 1996.
16. R. Quinlan. An overview of cubist. Rulequest Research, November 2000. http://www.rulequest.com/.
17. R.B. Rao, D. Gordon, and W. Spears. For every generalization action, is there really an equal and opposite reaction? In *Proceedings of the 12th International Conference on Machine Learning*, 1995.
18. C. Soares and P. Brazdil. Zoomed ranking: Selection of classification algrorithms based on relevant performance information. In *Proceedings of the 4th European Conference on Principles of Data Mining and Knowledge Discovery*, pages 126–135. Springer, 2000.
19. S. Y. Sohn. Meta analysis of classification algorithms for pattern recognition. *IEEE Transactions on Pattern Analysis and Machine Intelligence*, 21(11), 1999.
20. L. Todorovski, P. Brazdil, and C. Soares. Report on the experiments with feature selection in meta-level learning. In *Proceedings of the Workshop on Data Mining, Decision Support, Meta-learning and ILP at PKDD'2000*, pages 27–39, 2000.
21. L. Torgo. *Inductive Learning of Tree-based Regression Models*. PhD thesis, Department of Computer Science, Faculty of Sciences, University of Porto, Porto, Portugal, September 1999.
22. D Wolpert. The existence of a priori distinctions between learning algorithms. *Neural Computation*, 8:1391–1420, 1996.
23. D Wolpert. The lack of a priori distinctions between learning algorithms. *Neural Computation*, 8:1341–1390, 1996.

Improving the Robustness and Encoding Complexity of Behavioural Clones

Rui Camacho[1,2] and Pavel Brazdil[1,3]

[1] LIACC, Rua do Campo Alegre, 823, 4150 Porto, Portugal
[2] FEUP, Rua Dr Roberto Frias, 4200-465 Porto, Portugal
rcamacho@fe.up.pt
http://www.ncc.up.pt/ tau
[3] FEP, Rua Dr Roberto Frias, 4200-464 Porto, Portugal
pbrazdil@ncc.up.pt
http://www.ncc.up.pt/ pbrazdil

Abstract. The aim of behavioural cloning is to synthesize artificial controllers that are robust and comprehensible to human understanding. To attain the two objectives we propose the use of the Incremental Correction model that is based on a closed-loop control strategy to model the reactive aspects of human control skills. We have investigated the use of three different representations to encode the artificial controllers: univariate decision trees as induced by C4.5; multivariate decision and regression trees as induced by CART and; clausal theories induced by an Inductive Logic Programming (ILP) system.
We obtained an increase in robustness and a lower complexity of the controllers when compared with results using other models. The controllers synthesized by CART revealed to be the most robust. The ILP system produced the simpler encodings.

Keywords: cognitive modeling, behavioural cloning, decision trees

1 Introduction

Two important issues in behavioural cloning concern the robustness and comprehensibility of the models constructed. For a successful application of the methodology it is required that the controllers constructed by the ML algorithm should be intelligible to human understanding and should replicate the robustness features of the human subject being modeled. It is further desirable that the model be constructed as automatically as possible.

An automatic process of reverse engineering human control skills offers a useful process of fast construction of controllers, specially in tasks where traditional Control Theory is not applicable. As pointed out by Sammut *et al.* (1992) it is also a very useful tool for training student pilots, particularly with regard to determining the aptitude of a candidate at an early stage of training. Hamm 92 ([5]) refers that Westland Helicopters Ltd uses helicopter engineering simulations, controlled by pilot models, for rotor loads and performance prediction studies. Because a human pilot is not included in the control loop, it is not

L. De Raedt and P. Flach (Eds.): ECML 2001, LNAI 2167, pp. 37–48, 2001.
© Springer-Verlag Berlin Heidelberg 2001

necessary for the helicopter simulation to run in real time — performance models may be run faster than real time for chart data production, and complex models may be run at less than real time, in cheap workstations. As Hamm points out, an accurate model of a human pilot is an important issue in this application. Urbančič *et al.*([18]) describe the application of the reverse engineering methodology to the control of a crane simulation in loading/unloading ships in a harbor.

Experiments reported in Sammut 92 and Michie and Camacho 94 revealed a lack in robustness and high complexity in the synthesised controllers. We made a first extension to the model used in those experiments introducing goals (*Goals model*) which allowed an increase in diversity in the datasets (the traces could be collected from different task plans). However, the robustness and comprehensibility objectives were not attained satisfactorily as shown in the Camacho 98 experiments. In Camacho 98 the IC model was introduced and the experimental results showed a significant improvement in robustness and complexity of the induced controllers. In those experiments C4.5 was used as the ML tool. C4.5 is not designed to take advantage of numerical classes and is restricted to univariate trees. In this paper we investigate how the previous results concerning robustness and complexity can be further improved using more powerful representation schemes. In the current study we compare the univariate trees results with multivariate decision and regression trees and also with clausal theories. Sammut *et al.* (1992) already suggested the use of First Order Logic to establish a set of operators with which the controllers should be composed. ILP systems offer a more natural way of providing background knowledge to the learning task than propositional learners. In the current study we profit also from the possibility of specifying constraints on the hypothesis language and therefore discarding "uninteresting" rules.

The experimental results indicate a significant improvement over the C4.5 results.

Although Reinforcement Learning algorithms and Neural Networks have achieved successful applications in control (see [21] and [10]) we did not consider in the current study approaches that, alone, do not produce symbolic and comprehensible descriptions. Comprehensibility is an important issue in applications we address. The use of such algorithms would require an approach similar to the one by Sammut (1988) where a decision tree learning algorithm was applied to extract the strategy produced by BOXES system (Michie and Chambers, 1968) after training to achieved to control the pole and cart. This line of research is currently pursued by Ryan and Reid ([11]) using hierarchical RL.

Application of predictive fuzzy control was already successfully done by Yasunobu and Hasegawa (1986) to the crane problem. However their approach is very time consuming and therefore there is place for the automatic synthesis of control rules from recorded performance of well trained operators. A classical automatic controller by Sakawa and Shinido (1982) was reported to be vulnerable to wind and other unpredictable factors.

Suč and Bratko (1997) applied a novel approach whereby and ML algorithm induces an approximate model of the controlled system that enables the identification of subgoals the operator is said to pursue at various stages of the execution trace. They based their approach on the theory of Linear Quadratic regulator (LQ) controllers. The constructed clones are essentially LQ controllers. The controller is goal directed and takes into account the systems dynamics resulting in a high degree of robustness. The system is able to automatically identify the stages in a complete trace sequence.

Experimental results show that the LQ clones have no difficulty in controlling the rope swing doing better than regression tree clones of Urbančič and Bratko (1995).

The GRAIL methodology by Bain and Sammut (1999) was intended as an extension of the behavioural cloning methodology to handle goals and overcome robustness problems. It is in a prliminary stage but results show that it produces theories more compact than those of the Sammut *et al.* (1992) study and learns with much less traces. Bain and Sammut (1999) stress that the extension of GRAIL to use structured theories and background knowledge via first-order learning is most likely to further improve the performance of behavioural cloning.

The rest of the paper is structured as follows. In Section 2 we describe the methodology for reverse engineering human control skills together with some improvements on the original methodology. Section 3 discusses the models of Human Control Skills and describes our Incremental Correction model in detail. The experiments and the results obtained are reported in Section 4. In this section we present the comparative experimental results of using the different controller's encoding schemes. The last section presents the conclusions.

2   Reverse Engineering Human Control Skills

The methodology for reverse engineering human control skills, as described in [15], consists in the following six steps.

(1) Characterisation of the system being controlled as a set of state and control variables, representing the system status and decisions made by the human controller. (2) Definition of a task plan as a temporal sequence of stages. (3) Execution of the control task by the human controller according to the task plan. While performing the control task the system's state and control variables are recorded at regular intervals (the behavioural traces). (4) Pre-processing of the trace files to produce the ML tool datasets. (5) Induction of the decision trees using the ML tool. One tree for each control variable and for each stage. (6) Post-processing procedure by assembling all parts into an artificial controller. Apart from the induced code for determining the value

of each control variable, there is a hand-coded part that is responsible for switching the set of trees whenever there is a stage change in the task plan. The artificial controller replaces the human subject in the control cycle.

In the pre-processing phase (step 4) the data undergoes a series of filtering operations. The first filter splits the trace data into stages. A dataset is then created for each control variable and for each stage. Each dataset is then subject to another filtering operation that transforms samples into ML cases. In each sample, the value of the control variable is associated with the state variables and the other control variables of a sample recorded some time before. The time lag accounts for the human perceive-act delay. The control variable of the data set constitutes the class and the state, and the other control variables constitute the attributes. When the synthesised controller is run as an auto-pilot the perceive-act delay is introduced in the control cycle.

In the study of this paper we introduced two changes into the original methodology. First we require that in step 2 each stage corresponds to a *basic control manoeuvre* characterised by two kinds of goals discussed below. The second improvement includes the use of a *wrapper* ([6]) to facilitate the controller construction process by tuning the ML and model parameters (step 5).

The two kinds of goals, *Achievable goals* and *Homeostatic goals*, used here are imported from the work on AI planning by [4]. *Achievable goals* have a well-defined set of start and final states in the state space; arriving at anyone of the final state marks the achievement and termination of such a goal. These goals are the most common type in AI systems. *Homeostatic goals* are being achieved continuously. They do not terminate when the system is in one of the final states; when changes occur, and the state has changed, activity to re-achieve the final state is re-initiated. *Homeostatic goals* are like tracking certain required values.

A set of basic operations needs to be defined using the two kinds of goals defined above. During a basic operation the homeostatic and achievable goals remain constant. The task plan is then defined as a sequence of basic operations. In the flight domain, for example, the basic control operations are manoeuvres such as straight and level flight, levelled left turn, etc. In a levelled turn, for example, the homeostatic goals are the bank angle, the altitude and the climb rate and the achievable goal is the final heading. A flight plan is then a sequence of manoeuvres: straight climb, levelled left turn, levelled right turn, etc. We found that including more than a basic manoeuvre into a plan stage would increase the complexity of the control modules for that stage.

3   Models of Human Control Skills

The artificial controllers used in the experiments of [15], [8], [18] and [16] employ a two-level hierarchy of control: a high level module and a low-level one. The high-level module is intended to model the cognitive activity of human control skills. Such activity includes planning and monitoring. The low-level module includes the models for the reactive aspects of the human control skills. In the work of Stirling ([16]) the high-level module involves traditional knowledge acquisition (the influence matrix) whereas the low-level module was hand-coded using control theory PD controllers.

In [15], [8] and in the current study the high-level module is hand coded and its only role is to sequence the stages of the task plan. Here the high-level module is also responsible for establishing the context for the low-level module. It switches the low-level modules according to the stage of the task plan. The context is further specified by defining the goal values for the new stage. The low-level module has been implemented as a set of decision trees[1], one for each aircraft control and for each stage. At each stage only the trees constructed for that stage are active. This module is the only one induced from the behavioural traces and will be referred as the "model" from now on. We were only considering models for the reactive aspects of human control skills.

Sammut and Cribb (1990) and Whitley (1995) already pointed out the necessity of data diversity in order to produce robust controllers. However the model used in [15] and in [8] did not allow a great diversity of contexts in the behavioural traces. The *Goals model* (Camacho 98) improved matters allowing the traces to be collected under different task plans. Although there was an increase in robustness of the *Goals model* controllers the results were far from the behavioural cloning objectives. It was conjectured in [2] that the models in [15] and in [8] were not a plausible cognitive model. A controller induced within that framework acts as a mapping from a situation (or range of situations) to a control value. This model, therefore requires that the control values have to be memorised for each situation or range of situations. We conjecture that, for complex control tasks, humans do not use such strategy. All these supported the use of the Incremental Correction Model that we now describe.

3.1 The Incremental Correction Model

The Incremental Correction (IC) model is based on a closed-loop or feedback control strategy. There is a acceptable situation in which the controlled system is most of the time. The acceptable situation is characterised by a very small or non existing deviation from the homeostatic goal values. An acceptable situation requires no control change. Action is taken whenever the goal variables values deviate from the goal value. Usually a reasonable "wild guess" is used to make the first correction, specially if the deviation is large. After the first change, a sequence of three basic steps — (re)evaluation, corrections and waiting for the effects of the correction to become perceivable — takes place until the acceptability of the situation is restored. The amount of waiting time involved in real-time control is usually very small. The control strategy is adaptive, in the sense that the direction and magnitude of the correction is directly affected

---

[1] In some experiments we have used an ILP system (IndLog) that generated Prolog-like rules

by the previous change. If the previous change produces a too small reduction in the deviation then the direction of the next change is maintained and the magnitude of change increased. On the other hand, if the deviation is reduced too much or an overshooting is expected, then the direction is changed in the next cycle.

Human expert controllers would make a much more educated guess at the first corrective action than would a novice controller. An unexperienced controller would require a longer sequence of corrective actions than the expert. An expert may even anticipate the system response and dispense the feedback information.

The equations to compute the control values within the IC model are:

$$\Delta \ control = \begin{cases} 0, & situation \ ok \\ \mathbf{f}(state \ vars, \ goals, \ other \ controls), & situation \ not \ ok \end{cases}$$

The IC model implements the equation by means of two modules. One module (Coarse Decision) is used to determine if the situation requires a change in the controls. If a change in the controls is required (*situation not ok*), then another module computes the values of the increment/decrement of the control variables. This module is referred to as Refined Decision module. Whenever a change to a control is made the controller uses a waiting time for the effects of the change to become perceivable (feedback). The IC model inherits the goals and the perceive-act delay from the Goals model. Both modules are induced using ML methods from the behavioural traces of the human subject.

The IC model assumes that a required state can be achieved using corrective actions in the form of increments on the current position of the control value device. This avoids memorisation of the magnitude of the control value for each undesirable situations. In consequence, this model is not only easier to implement, but also provides a more plausible model of human control behaviour.

4   The Experiments

4.1   Experimental Settings

The control task chosen for the experimental evaluation of the models consists in the control of a simulation of an F-16 aircraft performing a levelled left turn. A levelled turn is a nontrivial manoeuvre requiring a close coordination among the controls. The experiments were carried out using ACM 2.4 public domain flight simulator running on a HP Apollo *Series* 735 workstation. The author played the role of the human pilot necessary for this study. A detailed description of the empirical evaluation of the models can be found in Camacho (2000).

The data used in the experiments are traces of 90 levelled left turn missions performed by the author. Aircraft state and control variables were sampled every 0.1 second. For the levelled left turn the achievable goal is the *final heading*. The homeostatic goals are the *bank angle*, the *altitude* and the *climb rate*. For each mission the achievable and homeostatic goals (except climb rate) were randomly generated from a range of admissible values. In all missions and at all times the aircraft was kept within the security envelope (see below). The missions were flown by instruments only, the landscape was not rendered, reducing the possibility of the pilot to use features not measured by the aircraft instruments.

The 90 missions were split into two halves, one for constructing the model and the other to estimate the predictive accuracy of the constructed model. The 90 missions contain approximately 481 000 samples.

The attributes used in the construction of the controller's *ailerons* trees were: bank angle; bank angle derivative; bank angle acceleration; pitch and; pitch rate. The attributes used in the construction of the controller's *elevators* trees were: altitude deviation; climb rate; climb rate derivative; bank angle; bank angle derivative and climb rate acceleration.

The *wrapper* is a simple cycle that generates combinations of parameters values, synthesises the controller's components with such parameters values and estimates the performance of the controller with the constructed components. In the current study the wrapper was applied to the synthesis of each controller component (i.e. a decision tree) separately, estimating its performance on an independent test set (at induction time). Although we are including model parameters such as the perceive-act human delay in the *wrapper* we have no guarantee the component will behave well at deployment-time. At deployment-time there are interactions among controls that are not taken into account by the estimates on independent test sets when a single component is constructed at a time. To overcome such limitation of our current study we envisage to include in the *wrapper* the simulator where the controllers are evaluated. Doing that we may synthesise and test the deployment performance of the whole controller and generate the best combination of parameters for the full set of controller components.

4.2   Performance Evaluation

The following error measures give an indication on how close the model is to the original system, the human controller. The Error Rate (ER) and the Root Mean Square Error (RMSE) were measured on an independent test set and defined as

$$ \mathbf{ER} = 100 \times \frac{\displaystyle\sum_{i=1}^{N} \begin{cases} 0 & if\ cls_i = cls_i \\ 1 & otherwise \end{cases}}{N} \qquad \mathbf{RMSE} = \sqrt{\frac{\displaystyle\sum_{i=1}^{N}(cls_i - cls_i)^2}{N}} $$

where cls_i is the actual class and cls'_i is the predicted value. Since the Coarse Decision module of the IC model outputs an action/no action decision, that is, a non numerical decision, only the Error Rate is used in this case.

Complexity of the induced trees was estimated using the tree size.

The *robustness* of the controllers is estimated by the number of successful missions within the total used. A mission is successful if there is no crash between the initial and final points.

The flight *smoothness* is evaluated using a deviation measure associated with each of the three homeostatic attributes. For each homeostatic attribute the Mean Absolute Deviation (MAD) is measured using the definition

$$MAD = \frac{\sum_{i=1}^{N}|att_i - goal|}{N}$$

Associated with each homeostatic goal there is a maximum acceptable deviation for that variable values. The frontier of the n-dimensional region containing the maximum acceptable values for the homeostatic variables is called the *security envelope*. All missions flown by the human subject that produce the behavioural traces were flown within the security envelope. The boundary for the altitude deviation is 100 ft, for the climb rate is 1000 ft/min and for the bank angle is 3°. The performance is evaluated by measuring the flight time percentage spent outside the envelope.

4.3   Evaluating the IC Model

For the IC model all samples are initially considered. The target definitions to learn within the IC model are: "change the control or not" and if the previous decision is favorable to change the control then the next decision is "what is the increment/decrement value to use". However the samples with no change in the control value largely outnumber the samples with "events" (the ratio is 36:1). The unbalance of such a dataset affects the results and needs to be corrected. The adopted procedure is as follows. In the first decision (action/no action) consider all the "events" as belonging to the same class (action) and all non-event samples as the other class (noaction). Build a data set with two classes equally represented by sampling from the noaction cases a number of cases equal to the action cases. The tree constructed with such dataset is then used to filter the "events" and produce the dataset for the Refined Decision module. In such a filtering procedure an event case is retained if it is predicted as "action" by the tree of the Coarse Decision module, otherwise is discarded. In the dataset of the Refined Decision module the increment of the control variable is restored as the class value.

Results with Univariate Trees

In the first set of experiments we used C4.5 as the ML algorithm. The induced controller successfully flew all the 90 missions. As the smoothness results, are concerned the MAD values (see Table 1) are very close to the human performance and even surpass the human performance in two of the measurements (climb rate and bank angle). There is also an improvement in Error rate (see Table 2) that is nearly half of the values obtained with previous models (*Goals model*). When comparing with previous models, the tree size is substantially smaller.

Table 1. Deployment-time performance. The results for altitude, climb rate and bank angle represent the average of the MAD values weighted with flight time.

Model	altitude (ft)		climb (ft/min)		bank angle ( )	
	train	test	train	test	train	test
IC (C4.5)	36	34	95	94	0.5	0.5
IC (CART)	15	14	105	104	0.4	0.4
Human	22	21	194	194	0.70	0.71

Table 2. Independent test set results for tree learners. *CD* stands for Coarse Decision module. *RD* stands for Refined Decision module.

tool	module	ailerons			elevators		
		tree size	Error Rate	RMSE	tree size	Error Rate	RMSE
		nodes	(%)	x1e4	nodes	(%)	x1e3
C4.5	CD	83	38.6	-	65	42.4	-
	RD	663	-	4.0	143	-	2.1
CART	CD	47	37.3	-	21	37.5	-
	RD	75	-	1.8	15	-	1.5

Results with Multivariate Trees

The Refined Decision control has to predict a numerical quantity and therefore we expected that CART would do better than C4.5 on those datasets since CART induces regression trees that minimise the RMSE. There was in fact an improvement of the CART trees over the C4.5 ones. The CART results on RMSE are nearly half the C4.5 results (Table 1). The controllers constructed with CART have smaller tree size than the ones constructed with C4.5 (Table 2) (compare the tree size of the CART controller — 15 nodes — with the C4.5 tree for the elevators control — 143 nodes). However the complexity of the internal nodes in the CART trees are higher since CART trees may have linear combination of attributes in the internal nodes. The internal nodes of CART's trees are much more difficult to interpret than the simple $>$ and $\leq$ tests used in the C4.5 trees.

The results with both univariate and multivariate trees were confirmed by repeating the experiments using four extra partitions of the train/test set.

Comparison with Human Controller Performance

The results of Table 1 show that the IC model controller constructed with CART outperformed the human controller in all of the three deviation measures whereas the C4.5 surpasses the human subject in two (climb rate and bank angle). The climb rate MAD of the controller constructed with CART is 54% the MAD of the human subject. The bank angle MAD value is 57% of the human subject and the altitude MAD value is 71%. These results represent a significant evidence of the "clean-up effect" (Michie *et al.*, 1990).

Results with Clausal Theories

The third set of experiments aims at further reducing the complexity of the induced controllers. For that purpose we used and Inductive Logic Programming (ILP) system called IndLog (Camacho 2000) and encode the controller components as clausal theories.

The IndLog system was provided with background knowledge that included the < and > relations available to C4.5 and CART and also linear discriminants capable of producing equations similar to CART trees internal nodes. IndLog was further provided with multivariate linear regression equations to predict numerical control values in the Refined Decision module. We expected that this latter facility would increase controller robustness. A linear equation would allow the controller to extrapolate from the training conditions and produce control values for large deviations not seen during the training. An ILP system like IndLog is able to use almost any kind of bakground knowledge (statistical models, geometrical models etc..). Furthermore the user may easily specify restriction to the hypothesis language that avoid "uninteresting" rules to be produced. Both of these features revealed important in the current study.

Table 3. Independent test set results for ILP system. *CD* stands for Coarse Decision module. *RD* stands for Refined Decision module.

module	ailerons			elevators		
	theory size clauses	Error Rate (%)	RMSE x1e4	theory size clauses	Error Rate (%)	RMSE x1e3
CD	6	37.3	-	9	37.1	-
RD	5	-	1.6	4	-	1.4

The induction-time results are very close to the ones obtained with CART as can be seen in Table 3.

So far we haven't been able to successfully fly the 90 missions with the controller induced by the ILP system. The main reason is due to the linear equations that may very easily produce instability in the control since they may extrapolate to large control values. We are considering imposing a limit in maximum and minimum control values.

5   Conclusions

The use of goals and attributes that measure deviations from the defined goals brings a significant improvement in the models. It makes possible to use data from different task plans when constructing the controllers and it enables to use the same controller in different circumstances. Being able to increase the diversity of the training data is an important issue when trying to construct robust controllers.

The main contribution of the IC model is a substantial increase in robustness of the new controllers. The flight simulation performance values surpassed those of the human subject performance on the same missions (clean-up effect).

The trees constructed within the IC model exhibit a smaller size than the ones from previous experiments in reverse engineering human control skills. Intelligibility of the models is an essential point in the success criteria and the small tree sizes are a good step towards their comprehensibility.

Multivariate trees and clausal theories evaluated in the study revealed a significant improvement over the univariate trees. ILP system allowed the specification of background knowledge and language constraints that improves comphensibility of controllers.

As future work we intend to include the flight simulator in the *wrapper* cycle in order to account for control interactions at deployment-time.

Acknowledgments. Thanks are due to Universidade do Porto and JNICT for the financial support during the PhD. The authors thank the Programa PRAXIS and FEDER and the Programa de Financiamento Plurianual de Unidades de I&D da JNICT.

References

1. M. Bain and C. Sammut. A framework for behavioural cloning. In *Machine Intelligence 15*. Oxford University Press, Oxford, U.K., 1999. (to appear).
2. R. Camacho. Inducing models of human control skills. In *Proceedings of the European Conference on Machine Learning – ECML-98*, Germany, April 1998.
3. R. Camacho. *Inducing Models of Human Control Skills using Machine Learning Algorithms*. PhD thesis, Universidade do Porto, July 2000.
4. A. A. Covrigaru and R. K. Lindsay. Deterministic autonomous systems. *AI Magazine*, 12(3):110–117, fall 1991.
5. J. C. Hamm. The use of pilot models in dynamic performance and rotor load prediction studies. In *Proceedings of the Eighteenth European Rotorcraft Forum*, pages 15–18, Avignon, France, September 1992. Association Aeronautique et Astronautique de France.
6. H. G. John, R. Kohavi, and K. Pfleger. Irrelevant features and the subset selection problem. In W. W. Cohen and H. Hirsh, editors, *Machine Learning: Proceedings of the Eleventh International Conference*, pages 121–129, San Francisco, California, June 1994. Morgan Kaufmann.
7. D. Michie, M. Bain, and J. Hayes-Michie. Cognitive models from subcognitive skills. In M. G. J. McGhee and P. Mowforth, editors, *Knowledge-Based Systems for Industrial Control*, pages 71–99. Peter Peregrinus for IEE, London, UK, 1990.
8. D. Michie and R. Camacho. Building symbolic representations of intuitive real-time skills from performance data. In D. M. eds. K. Furukawa and S. Muggleton, editors, *Machine Intelligence 13*, pages 385–418. Oxford University Press, Oxford, United Kingdom, 1994.
9. D. Michie and R. A. Chambers. Boxes: an experiment in adaptive control. In *Machine Intelligence 2*, pages 137–152. Oliver and Boyd, Edinburgh, 1968. eds. Dale, E. and Michie, Donald.

10. J. Randlov and P. Alstrom. Learning to drive a bicycle using reinforcement learning and shaping. In *Proceedings of the International Conference on Machine Learning – ICML-98*, pages 463–471, Madison, Wisconsin USA, July 1998.

11. M. Ryan and M. Reid. Learning to fly: An application of hierarchical reinforcement learning. In P. e. Langley, editor, *Proceedings of the Seventeenth International Machine Learning Conference, ICML-2000*, pages 807–814, San Francisco, CA., 2000. Morgan Kaufmann Publishers.

12. Y. Sakawa and Y. Shinido. Optimal control of container cranes. *Automatica*, 18:257–266, 1982.

13. C. Sammut. Experimental results from an evaluation of algorithms that learn to control dynamic systems. In *Proceedings of the Fifth International Workshop of Machine Learning 88*, pages 437–443, Ann Arbor, Univ of Michigan, June 1988. editor John Laird.

14. C. Sammut and J. Cribb. Is learning rate a good performance criterion for learning? In *Proceedings of the Seventh International Workshop of Machine Learning 90*, pages 170–178, Texas, June 1990.

15. C. Sammut, S. Hurst, D. Kedzier, and D. Michie. Learning to fly. In *Proceedings of the Ninth International Workshop of Machine Learning 92*, pages 385–393, Aberdeen, U.K., 1992.

16. D. Stirling. *CHURPs: Compressed Heuristic Reaction Planners*. PhD thesis, University of Sydney, 1995.

17. D. Šuc and I. Bratko. Skill reconstruction as induction of lq controllers with subgoals. In *Proceedings of the Fifteenth International Joint Conference on Artificial Intelligence – IJCAI-97*, volume 2, pages 914–920, Nagoya, Japan, 1997.

18. T. Urbančič and I. Bratko. Reconstructing human skill with machine learning. In *The Eleventh European Conference on Artificial Intelligence*, pages 498 – 502, Amsterdam, Netherlands, 1994. ed. A. Chon.

19. T. Urbančič and I. Bratko. Controlling container cranes: A case-study in reconstruction of human skill. In *The Second International Workshop on Artificial Intelligence Techniques– AIT95*, pages 113–126, Brno, Czech Republic, 1995.

20. D. Whitley. Genetic algorithms and neural networks. In *Genetic Algorithms in Engineering and Computer Science*, chapter 11. John Wiley & Sons Ltd, 1995. Eds. J. Periaux and G. Winter.

21. B. Widrow, D. E. Rumelhart, and M. A. Lehr. Neural networks: Applications in industry, business and science. *Communications of the ACM*, 37(3):93–105, 1994.

22. S. Yasunobu and T. Hasegawa. Evaluation of an automatic container crane operation system based on predictive fuzzy control. *Control-Theory and Advanced Technology*, 2:419–432, 1986.

A Framework for Learning Rules from Multiple Instance Data

Yann Chevaleyre and Jean-Daniel Zucker

LIP6-CNRS, University Paris VI,
4, place Jussieu,
F-75252 Paris Cedex 05, France
{Yann.Chevaleyre,Jean-Daniel.Zucker}@lip6.fr

Abstract. This paper proposes a generic extension to propositional rule learn-ers to handle multiple-instance data. In a multiple-instance representation, each learning example is represented by a \bag" of fixed-length \feature vectors". Such a representation, lying somewhere between propositional and first-order representa-tion, offers a tradeoff between the two. NAIVE-RIPPERMI is one implementation of this extension on the rule learning algorithm RIPPER. Several pitfalls encountered by this naive extension during induction are explained. A new multiple-instance search bias based on decision tree techniques is then used to avoid these pitfalls. Experimental results show the benefits of this approach for solving proposition-alized relational problems in terms of speed and accuracy.

1 Introduction

In most ML applications, the choice of knowledge representation for a learning example is between a fixed-length "feature vector" and a first-order representation. The motiva-tion for using first-order representation is that it is the natural extension to propositional representation. However, a known drawback of using first-order logic is that its expres-sivity is so high that in order to learn efficiently, strong biases such as *determinacy*, are often required on the hypothesis space. Giordana *et al.* have recently shown that there is a phase transition in relational learning [10] linked to the exponential complexity of matching. They argued that relational learners could hardly search in practice for target concepts having more than four non-determinate variables. The difficulty of learning re-lations has stimulated attempts towards extending Attribute/Value representation rather than directly using first-order logic based representation. Multiple-instance representa-tion, where each example is represented by a "bag" of fixed-length "feature vectors" [8], is an extension that offers a good tradeoff between the expressivity of relational learning and the low complexity of propositional learning. Data represented as bags of vectors may either be found naturally in chemical domains [8], in images classification tasks [12], or be produced after multiple-instance propositionalization of first-order data [17, 1].

Much work has been done on multiple-instance learning. Unfortunately, available learners are not able to efficiently generate easily interpretable rule sets or decision trees. Also, the generated models cannot be reformulated into first-order theories; these

L. De Raedt and P. Flach (Eds.): ECML 2001, LNAI 2167, pp. 49–60, 2001.
© Springer-Verlag Berlin Heidelberg 2001

learners can therefor not be used to solve relational learning problems with multiple-instance propositionalized data. Because propositionalization based relational learners (such as STILL [14]) often outperform classical relational learners, relational learning based on multiple-instance propositionalization (which is much more adapted to non-determinate domains than standard propositionalization [17]) is a promising field for which efficient multiple-instance rule learners will be needed.

This paper proposes a framework for extending propositional rule learners to handle multiple-instance data. A first extension is presented and implementated in the RIPPER rule learning algorithm. The resulting algorithm, called NAIVE-RIPPERMI, is evaluated and analysed on artificial datasets. Several pitfalls encountered by this naive extension are then characterized before showing that a modification of the refinement procedure implemented in RIPPERMI avoid these pitfalls. Experiments on artificial datasets are used to validate these improvements. The last section presents experiments on relational data and shows the benefits of a multiple-instance learner for relational learning. As our algorithms generate rule sets, it is possible to use them on relational learning problems reformulated into multiple-instance learning tasks, to generate first-order rules. NAIVE-RIPPERMI and RIPPERMI are compared against three popular relational learners on the mutagenesis prediction problem.

2   The Multiple Instance Learning Problem

2.1   Deﬁnition and Notation

In the traditional setting of machine learning, an object is represented by a feature vector x, to which is associated a label $f(x)$. Let $\mathcal{X}$ be a feature vector space, and $\mathcal{Y}$ the finite set of labels or classes. For the sake of simplicity, we will restrict ourselves to the two-class case, i.e. $\mathcal{Y} = \{\oplus, \ominus\}$. The goal then, typically, is to find a classifier $h : \mathcal{X} \to \mathcal{Y}$ which minimizes the probability that $f(x) \neq h(x)$ on a newly observed example $(x, f(x))$.

Within the multiple instance framework, objects are represented by *bags of vectors* of variable size. Vectors are also called *instances*. As in the traditional setting, they can contain numeric as well as symbolic features. The size of a bag b is noted $\sigma(b)$. Its instances are noted $b_1 \ldots b_{\sigma(b)}$. The multiple instance induction task consists of finding a classifier $H : 2^{\mathcal{X}} \to \mathcal{Y}$, which accurately predicts the label $F(b)$[1].

The multiple instance learning problem has been associated to a bias introduced by [8], which will here be refered to as the *single-tuple bias*, as opposed to the multi-tuple bias proposed by [13]. It can be formally defined as follows:

Deﬁnition 1 *The single-tuple bias is a restriction on the set of functions* $H :$ $2^{\mathcal{X}} \to \{\oplus, \ominus\}$ *to those for which there exists a function* $h : \mathcal{X} \to \{\oplus, \ominus\}$ *such that* $H(b) \equiv \exists i, h(b_i)$.

The underlying idea is that for certain learning tasks, if a bag is labeled positively, then at least one of its instances must be responsible for this.

---

[1] Note that functions on the instance space (resp. bag space) will be noted lower case (resp. upper case).

This idea can be particularly well illustrated in an example on which this bias has been extensively used: the task of predicting whether molecules smell musky or not [8]. Dieterich chooses to represent molecules as bags of vectors, each vector describing a steric configuration of the molecule. It is well known by chemists that a molecule is musky iff at least one of its configurations has given properties, which make the entire molecule smell musky. Thus, there exists a function h representing these properties, such that the function $H(b)$ - which is derived from h as shown earlier - is an accurate classification function for this learning task.

2.2 Related Work

Previous work on learning from multiple-instance examples has focused on the problem of learning axis-parallel rectangles (APR) under the single-tuple bias. In particular, Dietterich *et al.* [8] have designed APR algorithms to solve the task of predicting whether a molecule is musky or not. Other APR algorithms such MULTIINST [3] have been tested on this learning task, and many interesting learnability results have been obtained [5, 2]. More recently, Maron *et al.* proposed a new multiple-instance algorithm called *Diverse Density* [12], which they applied to image classification. Finally, the lazy learning approach to multiple-instance learning has been investigated by Jun *et al.* [16].

The algorithms mentioned here do not generate interpretable hypotheses such as rule sets, which is our purpose. In the following, a method for inducing multiple-instance rules with a modified traditional rule learner will be presented. Note that Blockeel and De Raedt [4] already presented a method for extending propositional learners to handle relational data. The extension of a propositional learner to the multiple-instance case is less complex, and yields specific multiple-instance issues, as will be shown in the following.

3 Extending a Propositional Learner

3.1 Motivation

This section presents a method for the extension of a propositional learner to handle multiple-instance data using the single-tuple bias. Our choice to adapt a propositional learner instead of designing new multiple-instance algorithms is justified by the three following points. First, the two learning problems are very similar. In fact, multiple-instance data can easily be represented by a single set of vectors, and under the single-tuple bias, the multiple-instance and the single-instance search spaces are identical. Thus, the extension may be simple. Secondly, the existing multiple-instance learners [8,3,12] do not generate interpretable rules or decision trees. Note that an MI learner able to generate rule sets can be used to solve relational learning problem with an appropriate reformulation algorithm such as REPART [17]. This will be detailed in the final section. Finally, propositional learning is a mature field, and many of the available algorithms can efficiently handle large databases, while achieving low error rates. The extension of such a learner to the multiple-instance case will thus benefit from this maturity.

Extending a decision tree induction algorithm to the multiple-instance case raises several algorithmic problems, due to the *divide-and-conquer* aspect of the learner. These issues are beyond the scope of this paper and will be addressed elsewhere. Fortunately, these problems are not encountered in the rule learning coverage algorithms. We have therefore chosen to propose an extension of propositional rule learners using a coverage algorithm.

3.2   A Single-Tuple Naive Extension of RIPPER

Let us now study the modifications needed by a single-instance (i.e. traditional) rule learning algorithm in order to incorporate the single-tuple bias. Let us consider a generic single-instance rule learner using a coverage algorithm. It can be seen as an algorithm iteratively searching for a function h under a given bias, such that this function will minimize a given criterion related to the prediction error of h on the training dataset D. This criterion varies from one algorithm to another. RIPPER [7] and C4.5 both use a criterion based on the information gain. To compute the value of this criterion, the learners first evaluate $count(h, D, \oplus)$ and $count(h, D, \ominus)$, which denote the number of positive (resp. negative) examples from D covered by h.

In order to adapt a single-instance learner to the multiple instance case, we first need to transcribe a multiple instance bag set into a simple set of vectors, without any loss of information. This can be done by adding to each instance two attributes, the first one named $bagid$ identifying the bag it belongs to and the second one named $bagclass$ encoding the class of its bag.

After having done this, we must now modify the evaluation criterion, such that $H(b) = \exists i, h(b_i)$ is evaluated instead of h. To do so, we will replace the function $count(h, D, c)$ by $count_{single-tuple}(h, D, c)$ evaluating the number of bags of class c encoded in D covered by H. Note that because of the single-tuple bias, if h covers a single vector x, then the bag identified by $bagid(x)$ will be considered as covered by H. Thus, we have:

$$count_{single-tuple}(h, D, c) =$$
$$|\{bagidx(x); \ x \in D \wedge h(x) \wedge bagclass(x) = c\}|$$

We have chosen to implement these modifications in RIPPER, a fast efficient rule learner designed by Cohen [7] which has been shown to be as accurate as C4.5 on classical datasets. In addition, the rule sets induced by RIPPER are usually very short, thus being easily interpretable. RIPPER includes several functionalities such as pruning and rule optimization, which also had to be adapted to handle single-tuple hypotheses. The rule refinement strategy of RIPPER consists in greedily adding the best literal without any backtracking. The optimization phases are thus important to improve the accuracy of the rules induced. The resulting algorithm, which we call NAIVE-RIPPERMI, inherits most of RIPPER's qualities, such as the ability to efficiently handle large datasets in nearly linear time with the number of examples and the number of features.

3.3   Evaluating NAIVE-RIPPERMI

In order to compare NAIVE-RIPPERMI to the other multiple-instance learners, we chose to run experiments on the musk datasets, already presented in section 2.2. For a detailed description of these datasets, see [8]. Table 1 presents the results of NAIVE-RIPPERMI measured using a tenfold cross-validation on the data.

On the musk1 dataset, the hypotheses generated by NAIVE-RIPPERMI contain an average of seven literals. This is primarily due to efficient pre-pruning and post-pruning techniques implemented in RIPPER. In addition, the average induction time is less than sixty seconds on a Sun SparcStation 4 computer. The two algorithms which are here more accurate than NAIVE-RIPPERMI on musk1 generate models which are not directly interpretable. Both ITERATED-DISCRIM-APR and ALL-POS-APR have been specifically designed for this learning task [8]. In contrast, the ILP algorithms such as TILDE which give comprehensible theories are slower than our learner on this specific task.

On the musk2 dataset, NAIVE-RIPPERMI obtains an accuracy of 77%, which is far from the results on the musk1 dataset. In the former, the average number of instances per bag is much bigger than in the latter. More precisely, during cross-validations, NAIVE-RIPPERMI generates from the musk2 dataset concise hypotheses achieving low error rates on the training data, but whose error rates on the test data are significantly higher. This may be due to the large number instances and attributes, which causes some non predictive hypotheses to be consistent with the training data. Instance selection algorithms based on prototype selection techniques are currently under investigation by the authors to overcome this problem. Finally, note that because the musk datasets only contain numerical attributes, we do not expect our algorithms to compete with fully numerical methods such as APR learners.

In the following, the relation between consistency on training data and predictive power will not be addressed. Hence, our goal will not be to improve the accuracy of our learner on the musk datasets. Instead, we will focus on the ability of NAIVE-RIPPERMI to find consistent hypotheses. Considering that NAIVE-RIPPERMI is a simple MI extension of an optimized single-instance algorithm, it is likely to be sub-optimal. For example the greedy search procedure of RIPPER may not be adapted to finding consistent MI hypotheses on datasets containing many instances. In the following section, the behavior of our algorithm will be analyzed carefully on artificial datasets, in order to design improvements.

Table 1. Compared accuracy of MI learners on both musk datasets.

Learner	Musk1	Musk2	Model
ITERATED-DISCRIM-APR [8]	0.92	0.89	Axis-parallel Rectangle
CITATION-κNN [16]	0.92	0.86	k-nearest neighbour
DIVERSE DENSITY [12]	0.89	0.82	Points in $\mathcal{X}$
RIPPERMI	0.88	0.77	rule set
NAIVE-RIPPERMI	0.88	0.77	rule set
TILDE [4]	0.87	0.79	horn clauses
ALL-POS-APR [8]	0.80	0.73	APR
MULTIINST [3]	0.77	0.84	APR

4   Analysis of RIPPERMI Algorithms

The purpose of this section is to analyze and to understand the behavior of the algorithm presented earlier as NAIVE-RIPPERMI. This analysis will enable us to discover potential drawbacks, which we will try to solve. The following questions will guide our research. When the number of instances is equal to one, NAIVE-RIPPERMI is equivalent to RIPPER; how, therefore, does the algorithm react when the number of instances increases? Is the search procedure of NAIVE-RIPPERMI adapted to large numbers of instances? When does the algorithm fail to induce a theory? Considering that a multiple-instance learner can be viewed as a biased ILP learner [13], how well does an ILP algorithm compare to ours?

To answer these question, we need datasets on which all is known, in order to run several experiments. We have therefore decided to design a simple artificial dataset generator. The following subsection presents the generation of these datasets and their use.

4.1   Validation Protocol Using Arti□cial Datasets

In order to test and validate the multiple instance abilities of NAIVE-RIPPERMI, we constructed an artificial dataset generator which builds MI datasets according to parameters provided by the user[2]. As stated above, we were primarily interested in understanding the behavior of our algorithm as the number of instances per bag increases. For this reason, we measured the accuracy of our algorithms on several randomly generated datasets having a given number of instances per bag.

Each artificial dataset contains 200 bags, a given number of instances, and 12 boolean attributes. The target concept is a boolean conjunction of three literals combining 3 attributes out of 12. The distribution of the values of each attribute is chosen randomly by the artificial dataset generator. The bags are then built by drawing a given number of instances independently from this distribution, and labeled according to the target concept chosen by the generator. The decision to use a conjunction of boolean attributes, and a static number of instances per bag was intended to focus only on the multiple instance aspect of NAIVE-RIPPERMI, without taking into account its capability of handling numerical attributes or bags of variable size. Note that in the single-instance case this class of target concepts is PAC-learnable, whereas in the multiple-instances case, it is not. In the latter case, if viewed in the ILP setting, these concepts are *12-nondeterminate linked horn clauses*, which were proven not to be PAC-learnable [11]. Thus, the complexity shift from one to more than one instances is very large.

NAIVE-RIPPERMI will finally be tested on the mutagenesis dataset containing both numerical attributes and bags of variable size in the last section.

The different MI extensions of RIPPER described in this paper were run on these datasets with the default parameters, which consist of two optimization passes each followed by a pruning phase. Hundreds of datasets containing a given number k of instances per bag were generated; then, the accuracy of each algorithm was measured

---

[2] the source code and further experimentation details can be found on
http://www-poleia.lip6.fr/~chevaley/ART_DAT_GEN/

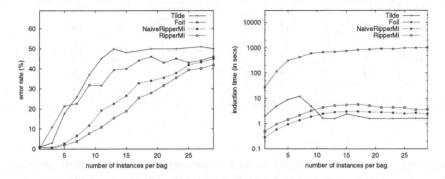

Fig. 1. Classification error rate (left figure) and induction time (right figure) of FOIL, TILDE, NAIVE-RIPPERMI, RIPPERMI (see section 4.3), on artificial datasets with various numbers of instances per bag

by averaging two-fold cross-validations over these datasets. The average classification error is ploted on figure 1, as well as the corresponding learning time using a log-scale. For example, on datasets containing 15 instances per bag, NAIVE-RIPPERMI obtains an average classification error rate of 26.5%, and the induction phase lasts less than a three seconds on a Sun SparcStation 4 computer.

The ILP learners FOIL and TILDE [4] were also run on these datasets in order to evaluate the ability of ILP tools on multiple-instance data. The top curve on the left part of figure 1 shows their accuracy with various numbers of instances per bag. On this particular task, they are outperformed by NAIVE-RIPPERMI in terms of accuracy. However, TILDE's induction time is very low, due to the "learning from interpretation" framework it implements.

4.2 Pitfalls during Induction

In this section, NAIVE-RIPPERMI will be analyzed, its pitfalls will be described, and the next section will propose algorithmic modifications to overcome them.

Let $x_j(b_i)$ denote the jth attribute of the instance b_i. For the sake of simplicity, multiple-instance rules $H(b)$ of the form $\exists i, x_1(b_i) = 0 \wedge x_2(b_i) = 1 \wedge \ldots \wedge x_j(b_i) = 0$ will be noted   as $(x1 = 0) \wedge (x2 = 1) \wedge \ldots \wedge (x_j = 0)$. A careful examination of the theories induced on the artificial datasets revealed three pitfalls of NAIVE-RIPPERMI. To illustrate these pitfalls, let us consider the four bags shown in table 2. The target concept is $(x1 = 1) \wedge (x2 = 0) \wedge (x3 = 1)$. NAIVE-RIPPERMI's strategy to refine a rule will be to examine each possible literal, and to add the one which brings the highest gain. Here, starting with an empty rule, the candidate rules $(x1 = 1)$, $(x2 = 0)$, and $(x3 = 1)$ each cover all four bags, $(x1 = 0)$ and $(x3 = 0)$ both cover one positive and two negative bags, and $(x2 = 1)$ covers two positive and one negative. Thus the best literal to start with, in terms of information gain, is $(x2 = 1)$. This literal is *misleading* w.r.t. target concept. Given a target concept $F(b) \equiv \exists i, f(b_i)$, a literal ℓ will be said *misleading* iff $\ell \Rightarrow \neg f$. We can easily show that with the artificial data sets used here,

bag	class	x_1	x_2	x_3
$bag1$	$\oplus$	1	0	1
		1	1	0
$bag2$	$\oplus$	0	1	1
		1	0	1

bag	class	x_1	x_2	x_3
$bag3$	$\ominus$	0	0	0
		1	1	1
$bag4$	$\ominus$	0	0	1
		1	0	0

Fig. 2. Two positive bags and two negative bag, with two instances each. Target: $(x_1 = 1) \wedge (x_2 = 0) \wedge (x_3 = 1)$

rules containing misleading literals have the following property: whatever their empirical error rate[3] is, their true error rate is higher than that of the default rule. In addition, when the number of instances per bag increases, the probability of having misleading literals correlated with the target concept on the dataset also increases, so does the probability that the induction algorithm chooses a misleading literal. Note that misleading literals is a typical multiple-instance phenomenon which cannot appear in the single-instance case. In the latter case, any rule containing a misleading literal would have an empirical error rate of 100%. Thus, empty rules would always be preferred to rules with misleading literals. In the following section, an algorithmic modification will be proposed to cope with this pitfall. The second pitfall can again be observed on the examples of table 2. From the six candidate rules proposed by NAIVE-RIPPERMI three rules cover the four bags. These three rules are thus *indistinguishable* for the learner. To avoid this pitfall, a new coverage measure has been developed. Due to space limitations, this measure which is based on counting the number of instances per bag covered by a rule will be described in a forthcoming paper. The last pitfall described in this paper consists in *irrelevant literals* added to rules. Irrelevant literals are literals which do not belong to the target concept, but which are not misleading. In single-instance rule learning, irrelevant literals are generally added at the end of rules because of overfitting. In multiple-instance learning, irrelevant literals may appear anywhere in a rule because candidate literals are often *indistinguishable*, as explained earlier. Although this phenomenon appears very often with multiple-instances, it can also appear with single-instance data.

4.3 Avoiding Pitfalls

Algorithmic modifications of NAIVE-RIPPERMI's search procedure to avoid misleading and irrelevant literals are now described. Suppose we are refining a rule R which is known not to contain any misleading literal yet. Let ℓ be the best literal to add to R, according to NAIVE-RIPPERMI's greedy strategy. Of course, we cannot be sure that ℓ is not a misleading literal. Yet, it is clear that at least one of the two literals ℓ and $\neg\ell$ is not misleading. Hence, by considering both $R \cup \ell$ and $R \cup \neg\ell$, at least one of the two rules will not contain any misleading literal. The induction process thus undoubtedly avoids this pitfall. Note that the process of examining two rules at each refinement step can be seen as building a binary decision tree from which a single rule is extracted. In such a tree, each node corresponds to a literal and paths from the root node to the leaves corresponds to the candidate rules.

---

[3] the empirical error rate of a rule is generally defined as $\frac{fp}{fp+tp}$ with tp and fp being the number of covered examples which label is (resp. is not) that predicted by the rule

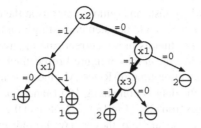

Fig. 3. Decision tree induced from bags in table 2

Our new refinement procedure builds such a decision tree, starting with a root node. Let $\{s_i\}$ be the set of leaves of the current tree, and r_i, the rule associated with the path from the root node to the leaf s_i. Let $gain(r, r*)$, the gain function used by NAIVE-RIPPERMI to evaluate the benefit of replacing the rule r by $r*$. Let ℓ_i be the literal which maximizes the gain $g_i = gain(r_i, r_i \cup \ell_i)$ for each rule r_i. The leaf s_j which has the highest gain g_j is chosen for expansion: the leaves corresponding to literals ℓ_j and $\neg\ell_j$ are added to s_j, which is now an internal node. This refinement process stops when all gains g_i are null. At last, the rule r_i which brings the highest value of $gain(\{\}, r_i)$ is extracted from the tree.

Considering the worst case, the storage requirement of this algorithm is linear with the total number of instances in the training set. In practice, small trees are generated by this algorithm, as all gains g_i become null rather quickly. This is due to the fact that often in multiple-instance learning tasks, large parts of the instance space are of no use to separate positive bags from negative ones. Note that the complexity of building this tree is similar to building a single-instance decision tree, which is $O(ma \log m)$ where m is the number of examples in the single-instance case and a the number of attributes. In the multiple-instance setting, m represents the total number of instances. Assuming as in [7,9] that the number of generated rules is approximately constant, the complexity of RIPPERMI is thus $O(ma \log m)$. Further experiments conducted on the artificial datasets confirmed that the algorithm's runtime was approximately linear with the number of bags. Due to lack of space, these experiments will be detailed elsewhere.

When running this algorithm on the small dataset described in table 2, it explores the decision tree as shown in figure 3. The leaves of the tree indicate how many positive and negative bags are covered by the corresponding rule. Here, the rule $(x2 = 0) \wedge (x1 = 1) \wedge (x3 = 1)$ covers two positive bags ($2\oplus$) and no negative one. This rule will thus be extracted from the tree, and the pitfall will be avoided. Much work has been done recently on the use of decision trees as a temporary representation for single-instance rule induction. Nevertheless, as stated by Frank and Witten [9], in the single-instance case, decision trees are used as a substitute to a global optimization on rule sets. Thus they do not provide a qualitative algorithmic improvement, unlike in the multiple instance case for which they enable pitfalls to be avoided.

In addition to misleading literals, induced theories may contain irrelevant literals anywhere in the rules. In the single-instance case, irrelevant literals usually appear at the end of the rule, because of overfitting. To avoid this, RIPPER implements a *reduced error pruning technique* which tests and removes literals at the end of rules. We therefore added after this pruning step another step consisting in a modified reduced error pruning algorithm examining literals in the current rule in any order. Using the same validation procedure as earlier, the graphs of figure 1 respectively show the average classification error rate and induction time of RIPPERMI, the new algorithm implementing both improvements. With the dataset containing 15 instances per bag, for example, the classification error decreases from 26.5% to 18.9%. Note that these algorithmic improvements, aimed at inducing consistant hypotheses, have no impact on the musk learning task, as NAIVE-RIPPERMI was already consistant on these data.

5   Experiments on Relational Data

It has been shown that under various biases, the problem of learning from first-order data can be converted to a lower-order learning problem, in particular to attribute-value learning tasks. This process, called *propositionalization*, has already been investigated within the multiple-instance framework in [17]. In this section NAIVE-RIPPERMI and RIPPERMI will be used in association with REPART [17] to solve a traditional ILP problem : the mutagenesis prediction task [15].

5.1   Solving the Mutagenesis Problem with a Multiple-Instance Learner

The mutagenesis prediction problem [15] consists in inducing a theory which can be used to predict whether a molecule is mutagenic or not. To achieve this, a dataset describing 188 molecules with prolog facts is used. Several relational descriptions of the domain are available. We will use the description termed B_2 [15] where atoms and bonds are described, and B_3 which includes B_2 as well as two global molecular properties.

The algorithm REPART [17] has been used to generate several propositionalizations. After each propositionalizations, the MI learner is launched on the reformulated data, and it outputs an hypothesis and its accuracy on the training set. The process stops if this accuracy is sufficiently high. If not, another more complex reformulation is chosen, and so forth. Using the description B_2, REPART first represents molecules as bags of atoms. Thus, each instance contains the three attributes describing a single atom. As expected, this reformulation did not yield good results. During the second step, REPART represented molecules as bags of pairs of bonded atoms. The following subsection describes the results using this reformulation. With the B_3 description level, the first reformulation

Table 2. Compared accuracy of RipperMi with ILP learners on the mutagenesis dataset.

	B_2	B_3
RIPPERMI	0.82	0.91
NAIVERIPPERMI	0.78	0.91
TILDE	0.77	0.86
PROGOL	0.76	0.86
FOIL	0.61	0.83

chosen by REPART has shown to be sufficient. This reformulation consisted in representing each molecule as a bag of atoms each to which was added global molecular properties.

5.2 Experiments and Results

The results of NAIVE-RIPPERMI and RIPPERMI are compared to those of state of the art ILP learners able to generate comprehensible hypotheses PROGOL [15], TILDE [4], and FOIL. Table 2 shows the accuracy of these learners measured with a tenfold cross-validation . Both NAIVE-RIPPERMI and RIPPERMI perform equally well on the B_3 description, which is not surprising, because most literals added to the induced theories are global literals. Therefore, their multiple-instance ability is not challenged here. On the other hand, the reformulation using the B_2 description level does not contain any global attributes. This explains the higher accuracy obtained by RIPPERMI compared to that of NAIVERIPPERMI. The following is an example of rule generated by our learner: active ← (type1 = 1) ∧ (ch1 < 0.288) ∧ (ch2 < -0.404) It indicates that if a molecule has a pair of bonded atoms such that the first one is of type 1 and has a partial charge lower than 0.288 and that the second one has a partial charge lower than -0.404, then the molecule is mutagenic. Both MI learners are faster than ILP algorithms. For example, on the B_2 description level, NAIVE-RIPPERMI induces an hypothesis less than 150 seconds on a Sun SparcStation 4. In comparison, PROGOL requires 117039 seconds, TILDE requires 539 seconds, and FOIL requires 4950 seconds.

6 Conclusion

The problem of supervised multiple-instance learning is a recent learning problem which has raised interest in the machine learning community. This problem is encountered in contexts where an object may have several alternative vectors to describe its different possible configurations. Solving multiple-instance problems using propositional algorithms raises subtle issues that are related to the notion of bags of instances whose coverage is by essence different from that of mono-instance problems. We have proposed an method to extend a propositional rule learning algorithm to the multiple-instance case. Some drawbacks of this method have been detected and a better search procedure was developed. Each refinement has been validated on artificial datasets.

With the help of the REPART [17] algorithm, which reformulates first-order examples into bags of instances, our algorithm has been tested on the well known mutagenesis relational dataset. RIPPERMI yielded good results compared to those of FOIL TILDE and PROGOL on this problem. It also showed to be significantly faster. We therefore argue that the multiple instance paradigm may be very useful for solving a wide range of relational problems. Relational data mining tasks may also be addressed by multiple-instance learners, in particular when it is possible to create bags of instances making sense by joining tables together [6]. Finally, a future application of our learner will be to embed it in a mobile robot to recognize real-world objects from segmented images.

Many questions remain opened. The pitfalls described here appear more often when instances are independantly drawn from a distribution $\mathcal{D}$. How often do they appear if this does not hold any more ? In fact, most theoretical studies were made under this statistical assumption which was shown to be reasonable in many cases. An interesting research issue would be to develop weaker assumptions which would be more realistic.

Acknowledgments. We would like to thank the anonymous reviewers for their helpful suggestions, comments, and pointers to relevant literature.

References

1. Erick Alphonse and Celine Rouveirol. Lazy propositionalization for relational learning. In *ECAI*, 2000.
2. P. Auer, P. Long, and Ashwin Srinivasan. Approximating hyper-rectangles: Learning and pseudo-random sets. In *Annual ACM Symposium on Theory of Computing*, 1997.
3. Peter Auer. On learning from multi-instance examples: Empirical evaluation of a theoretical approach. In *Proc. 14th International Conference on Machine Learning*, 1997.
4. Hendrik Blockeel, Luc De Raedt, Nico Jacobs, and Bart Demoen. Scaling up inductive logic programming by learning from interpretations. *Data Mining and Knowledge Discovery*, 3(1):59–93, 1999.
5. Avrim Blum and Adam Kalai. A note on learning from multiple-instance examples. *Machine Learning*, 30, 1998.
6. Yann Chevaleyre and J.D. Zucker. Noise tolerant rule induction for multiple-instance data and potential data mining application. Tech. Rep. University of Paris 6, available at http://www-poleia.lip6.fr/~chevaley/michurning.ps, 2001.
7. William W. Cohen. Fast effective rule induction. In *Proc. 12th International Conference on Machine Learning*. Morgan Kaufmann, 1995.
8. Thomas G. Dietterich, Richard H. Lathrop, and Tomás Lozano-Pérez. Solving the multiple-instance problem with axis-parallel rectangles. *Artificial Intelligence*, 89(1-2), 1997.
9. Eibe Frank and Ian H. Witten. Generating accurate rule sets without global optimization. In *Proc. 15th ICML*, 1998.
10. Attilio Giordana, Lorenza Saitta, Michele Sebag, and Marco Botta. Analyzing relational learning in the phase transition framework. In *Proc. 17th ICML*, 2000.
11. J.U. Kietz. Some lower bounds for the computational complexity of inductive logic programming. In *ECML*, 1993.
12. Oded Maron and Aparna Lakshmi Ratan. Multiple-instance learning for natural scene classification. In *Proc. 15th ICML*, pages 341–349, 1998.
13. Luc De Raedt. Attribute-value learning versus inductive logic programming: The missing links. In *Proc. 8th International Conference on ILP*, 1998.
14. Michele Sebag and Celine Rouveirol. Tractable induction and classification in first order logic. In *IJCAI*, Nagoya, Japan, 1997.
15. A. Srinivasan and S. Muggleton. Comparing the use of background knowledge by two ilp systems. In L. de Raedt, editor, *ILP-95.*, Katholieke Universiteit Leuven, 1995.
16. Jun Wang and Jean-Daniel Zucker. Solving multiple-instance problem: a lazy learning approach. In *Proc. 17th ICML*, 2000.
17. Jean-Daniel Zucker and Jean-Gabriel Ganascia. Learning structurally indeterminate clauses. In *Proc. 8th International Conference on ILP*. Springer-Verlag, 1998.

Wrapping Web Information Providers by Transducer Induction

Boris Chidlovskii

Xerox Research Centre Europe, Grenoble Laboratory, France
6, Chemin de Maupertuis, F–38240 Meylan
childovskii@xrce.xerox.com

Abstract. Modern agent and mediator systems communicate to a multitude of
Web information providers to better satisfy user requests. They use wrappers to
extract relevant information from HTML responses and to annotate it with user-
defined labels. A number of approaches exploit the methods of machine learning
to induce instances of certain wrapper classes, by assuming the tabular structure
of HTML responses and by observing the regularity of extracted fragments in the
HTML structure. In this work, we propose a general approach and consider the
information extraction conducted by wrappers as a special form of transduction.
We make no assumption about the HTML response structure and profit from
the advanced methods of transducer induction, in order to develop two powerful
wrapper classes, for samples with and without ambiguous translations. We test the
proposed induction methods on a set of general-purpose and bibliographic data
providers and report the results of experiments.

1 Introduction

The World Wide Web has become an enormous information resource and a bunch of
new applications rely on Web search engines, news, weather or shopping sites, in order
to find and deliver information relevant to user needs. The communication with Web
information providers is done by retrieving Web pages or sending cgi-requests; in either
case, an application faces the problem of understanding a provider response in HTML
and extracting and labeling relevant information fragments; special software components
dedicated to this task are conventionally called *wrappers* [5,12].

The manual generation of wrappers is a time-consuming and error-prone task and a
number of methods have addressed the automatic wrapper generation [4,8,9,10,11,13,
14]. These methods invoke the machine learning techniques and define the problem of
wrapper generation as induction of instances of a certain wrapper class from labeled
samples.

While wrapping one-value or one-slot HTML responses, such as stock values or
weather forecast rarely poses serious problems to any learning program, wrapping pages
with complex structure often unveils its limitations. As an example, most approaches
to wrapping search engines assume the tabular form of answers and provide special
treatment for different variations, like missing or multi-valued attributes. However, the

L. De Raedt and P. Flach (Eds.): ECML 2001, LNAI 2167, pp. 61–72, 2001.
© Springer-Verlag Berlin Heidelberg 2001

assumption does not hold for search engines with sophisticated responce structure like Medline or Cora [1].

The power of a wrapper class is crucial as more powerful classes allows one to successfully wrap more sites. In this work, we propose a general approach which makes no assumption about the response structure and consider the information extraction conducted by wrappers as a special form of transduction. Our approach is inspired by the OSTIA transducer induction method [15] which learns transducers from positive samples and pushes back the output labels to postpone translation conflicts. By analogy, in our methods we learn accurate wrapper extraction rules from positive samples which may have ambiguous labeling.

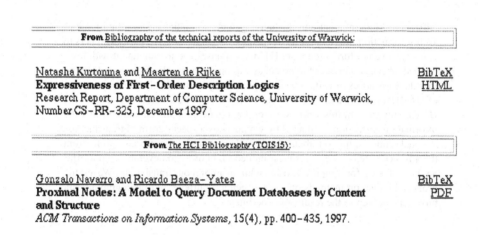

Fig. 1. Sample fragment from CSBiblio site.

In HTML pages with complex structure, extracted information can be complex and thus labels that annotate extracted fragments may have a path-like form. The result of information extraction is *semistructured data*, represented as a tree where each node is labeled and may have a value [5]. The extracted semistructured data can be similar, poor or richer than the structure of original HTML file; its complexity is actually driven by the user's perception and needs. The semistructured data model has a highly expressive power, it permits one to cope with all possible variations in the page structure. Figure 1 shows a sample fragment from the Computer Science Bibliography site.[2] The extracted data is shown in Figure 2; it has a nested structure where each tuple groups coherent information and tuples are grouped by bibliographic collections.

HTML and XML. The problem of wrapping HTML pages may disappear with the wide use of XML for data exchange. However, the current expansion of XML remains essentially limited to business-to-business solutions, therefore HTML interface will remain,

---

[1] http://www.medportal.com, http://cora.whizbang.com.

[2] http://liinwww.ira.uka.de/bibliography/index.html.

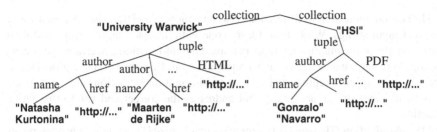

Fig. 2. Extracted semistructured data.

at least for some time in future, the principal way of interaction with thousands of Web information providers.

Determinism in wrappers. Applications relying on Web data require from wrappers the delivery of reliable and accurate data. For this reason, the determinism is of the prime interest in the wrapper induction. While the induction methods can be nondeterministic or stochastic, the deterministic information extraction remains a must in the wrapper generation.

2 Transducers

Wrappers parse input HTML strings, extract some tokens and annotate them with user labels. Thus, the information extraction conducted by a wrapper appears similar to trans-duction of strings of an input alphabet into strings of output alphabet [9]. Below we we remind some notions from the formal language theory and discuss the difference between transducers and wrappers.

For any string x over an alphabet Σ, x^r denotes the reverse of x. The concatenation of two strings x and u is denoted xu. The string v is a *prefix* of the string x if and only if there exists a string u such that $vu = x$. A *language* is any subset of Σ^*. $Pr(L)$ denotes all prefixes of L. A *positive sample set* of the language L is a finite set of strings from L.

A *transducer* T is a 6-tuple $T = (\Sigma, H, Q, q_0, F, \delta)$, where Σ and H are input and output alphabets, Q, q_0, F are sets of all, initial and final states, and δ is a map from $Q \times \Sigma$ to $Q \times H$ [7]. Transducer T is deterministic, iff there is at most one rule for any pair (q, a) in δ: if $\delta(q, a) = (q', h')$ and $\delta(q, a) = (q'', h'')$, then $q' = q''$ and $h' = h''$, where $a \in \Sigma$, $h', h'' \in H$, $q, q', q'' \in Q$. For an accepted string $x \in \Sigma^*$, transducer T translates x into an output $y = T[x] \in H^*$.

Wrappers and transducers. There are two main difference between wrappers and trans-ducers. The first, obvious one is in the way they produce the output. When a transducer consumes an input token a and executes the transition $\delta(q', a) = (q, h)$, it emits an output symbol h. A wrapper instead outputs the value of token a labeled with h, denoted $a(h)$. In other words, *translation* in transducers corresponds to *labeling* in wrappers. One can easily establish a one-to-one mapping between outputs produced by transduc-ers and wrappers, in the following we will use the notions of translation and labeling interchangeably.

The second, more serious difference between wrappers and transducers is in the way they treat input strings. While transducers cope with accepted input strings and their translation, the prime interest in wrappers remain the information extraction and correct labeling. As result, we develop a wrapper representation alternative to conventional transducers. Any wrapper is represented as a set of information extraction rules; it neglects the issue of input strings acceptance but addresses the correct and valid information extraction.

HTML tokenization. There are different ways to tokenize HTML files, where elements use opening and closing tags to group element contents and sub-elements. Unfortunately, unlike XML, the HTML standard does not require the proper tag nesting; as consequence, the majority of real-world HTML files are not well-formed. For this reason, we consider a *simple* tokenization of HTML, where alphabet Σ contains all HTML tags (both opening and closing ones) and a special token C for element contents, $\Sigma = \{C, \texttt{<html>}, \texttt{</html>}, \texttt{<title>}, \ldots\}$; any HTML file is considered as a string over Σ. For example, an HTML fragment $\texttt{<title>}$Home Page$\texttt{</title>}$ is a sequence of three tokens, $\texttt{<title>}$, C and $\texttt{</title>}$, where C's value is 'Home Page'.

Elementary information extracted from a tokenized HTML file can be one token or a part of token, like $\texttt{href}$ attribute in an $\texttt{<a>}$ element or $\texttt{src}$ attribute in an $\texttt{<img>}$ element. However, in the following, we assume that only element contents (denoted by C) are extracted from a file, that is, labeled with user-defined labels, like $\texttt{Author}$ or $\texttt{Title}$, while all other tokens are labeled with a dummy label $\lambda \in H$.[3] This assumption is made only for the sake of simplicity; in the general case, the algorithms can be directly extended to allowing user-defined labels on any tokens from Σ [3].

Example 1. Assume an information provider I generates HTML pages using the following regular structure: $\texttt{<hr>} (C(\texttt{Author})\texttt{<p>}(C(\texttt{Title})\texttt{<hr>}|\texttt{
}))*$. The corresponding transducer T_1 is given by $(\Sigma, H, Q, q_0, F, \delta)$, where $\Sigma = \{\texttt{<hr>}, \texttt{<p>}, \texttt{
}, C\}$, $O = \{\texttt{Author}, \texttt{Title}, \lambda\}$, $Q = \{q_0, \ldots, q_4\}$, $F = \{q_1\}$ and $\delta = \{$
$\delta(q_0, \texttt{<hr>}) = (q_1, \lambda)$, $\delta(q_1, C) = (q_2, \texttt{Author})$, $\delta(q_2, \texttt{<p>}) = (q_3, \lambda)$,
$\delta(q_3, C) = (q_4, \texttt{Title})$, $\delta(q_3, \texttt{
}) = (q_4, \lambda)$, $\delta(q_4, \texttt{<hr>}) = (q_1, \lambda)\}$.
The transducer is shown in Figure 3; for transparency we omit all occurrences of λ.

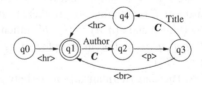

Fig. 3. Transducer T_1.

---

[3] Those element contents which are not extracted from a file are equally labeled with λ.

3 Induction from Positive Samples

To induce a wrapper for an information provider, one has to collect sample HTML pages generated by the provider; such pages form a positive sample set denoted S, from which the transducer should be induced [15]. Any element $s \in S$ is a couple (x, y), $x \in \Sigma^*$, $y \in H^*$. In the case of HTML samples, s is a tokenised HTML file, pre-processed by annotating all occurences of C with labels from H. The transducer induction from a sample set consists in building a prefix tree transducer and generalizing it by merging some states. For the wrapper induction however, we modify the procedure which will build a prefix tree transducer and then infer the wrapper extraction rules from it.

For a sample set $S = \{(x, y)\}$, we define the *prefix tree transducer* $PTT(S)$ as $(\Sigma, H, Q, q_0, F, \delta)$, where $X = \{x\}$, $Q = Pr(X)$, $F = \{X\}$, $\delta(u, a) = (ua, h)$, whenever $u, ua \in Q, a \in \Sigma, T[ua] = h$.

Example 2. Let the label set H include labels Author and Title and the annotated sample set S_1 be the following: { <hr>,
<hr>C(Author)<p>C(Title)<hr>C(Author)<p>
,
<hr>C(Author)<p>
C(Author)<p>
,
<hr>C(Author)<p>C(Title)<hr>}.
The prefix tree transducer for S_1 is given in Figure 4.

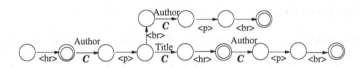

Fig. 4. Prefix tree transducer $PTT(S_1)$.

Unlike the prefix trees for finite-state automata which are always deterministic [1], prefix tree transducers can be deterministic, like transducer $PTT(S_1)$ above, or non-deterministic. Two wrapper induction algorithms introduced in the following sections are inspired by the OSTIA transducer inference method [15]. Our algorithms depend on whether the prefix tree transducer built for a sample set S is deterministic or not. First, we consider *deterministic prefix tree transducers* and develop a wrapper induction method based on the analysis of prefixes of labels in S and the construction of *minimal prefix sets*; analyzing such sets will be sufficient to detect unique labels for input tokens. Then, in Section 5 we consider the case the *nondeterministic prefix tree transducers* which raise the problem of *ambiguous* labeling; we will extend the first induction method with the combined analysis of prefixes and suffixes to disambiguate the token labeling.

4 Deterministic Prefix Tree Transducer

Let $h \in H$ label some occurrences of C in $s \in S$. We denote as $R(s, h)$ the set of all reverse prefixes for labeled tokens $C(h)$ in s, $R(s, h) = \{s_1^r | s = s_1 C(h) s_2\}$. The union of reverse prefixes for h in all $s \in S$ gives the set $R(h) = \{\cup_{s \in S} R(s, h)\}$.

In Example 2, the reverse prefix sets for labels `Title` and `Author` are the following:
$R(\text{Author})=\{$`<hr>`$,$`<hr>`$\mathcal{C}($`Title`$)$`<b>`$\mathcal{C}($`Author`$)$`<hr>`$,$`<br><p>`$\mathcal{C}($`Author`$)$`<hr>`$\}$
and $R(\text{Title})=\{$`<p>`$\mathcal{C}($`Author`$)$`<hr>`$\}$.

The following preposition establishes an important relationship between the determinism of a prefix tree transducer and the emptiness of intersection of reverse prefix sets.

Preposition 1 *For a sample set S, the corresponding prefix tree transducer $PTT(S)$ is deterministic iff for any pair of different labels h and h' in S, $R(h) \cap R(h') = \emptyset$.*

The preposition provides a general mechanism for the deterministic information extraction in wrappers induced from samples. Assume the proposition holds for a given set S, reverse prefix sets are built for all labels in S and we want to extract information from a new sample $x \in \Sigma^*$. Then, for any occurrence of $\mathcal{C}$ in x, it is sufficient to build its reverse prefix, comparing it to all sets $R(h)$ will uniquely identify the label for $\mathcal{C}$.

Preposition 1 uses the full reverse prefixes for labels in S. However, full reverse prefixes is of little practical use as they can require long learning and huge sample sets. Below we propose *minimal prefix sets* as an alternative to full prefix sets. This alternative representation, on one side, preserves the relationship established by Preposition 1 and, on other side, is compact and efficient in use.

4.1 Minimal Prefix Index

For a labeled sample $s = (x, y)$, k leading labeled tokens of s is called k-*prefix* and denoted by $s[k] = (x[k], y[k])$; if $len(s) < k$, $s[k] = s$. Given the prefix set $R(h)$ for label h is S, the set $R_k(h) = \{s[k] | s \in R(h)\}$ is called the k-*prefix* set of h in S, $k = 0, 1, 2, \dots$ For two distinct labels h and h', the *minimal prefix index* is given by $k(h, h') = min\{k | R_k(h) \cap R_k(h') = \emptyset\}$.

Example 3. For the sample set S_1 in Example 2, we obtain $k(\text{Author}, \text{Title}) = 1$. Indeed, since $R_1(\text{Author})=\{$`<hr>`$,$`<br>`$\}$ and $R_1(\text{Title})=\{$`<p>`$\}$, we obtain that $R_1(\text{Author}) \cap R_1(\text{Title})=\emptyset$.

For the entire set S, we calculate the *minimal prefix index* as the maximum among $k(h, h')$ for all label pairs in H: $k_S = max\{k(h, h') | h \neq h'\}$. The value k_S establishes the upper bound on the length of the reverse prefixes to deterministically label any $\mathcal{C}$ occurrence in S.

Minimal prefix set. The way we obtain the minimal prefix index k_S shows how to replace the full prefix sets $R(h)$ for all labels in S with minimal prefix sets, denoted $MR(h)$. The definition for minimal prefix sets is given below; in addition to the feature established in Preposition 1, called separability, such sets should satisfy two additional conditions, namely completeness and minimality.

Definition 1. *The minimal (reverse) prefix set MR for label h in a sample set S is such a set of reverse prefixes for which three following features hold:*

Separability: $\forall h' \neq h$ *in* S: $MR(h) \cap R(h') = \emptyset$.

Completeness: *for any reverse prefix s in $R(h)$, there exists a prefix $p \in MR(h)$ such that p is a prefix of s.*

Minimality: *$\forall p \in MR(h)$, replacement of p with any proper prefix of p results in loosing the separability feature.*

For any h, $MR(h)$ is obtained from $R(h)$ by replacing any element of $R(h)$, first with its k_S-prefix which satisfies the separability and completeness requirement above. Then, we can try to reduce the prefix further, till the minimality is reached. There exists an incremental procedure which constructs the minimal prefix sets for all labels in a sample set in polynomial time [2]. For the sample set S_1, we obtain the minimal prefix index k_S equals 1, and $MR(\text{Author})= \{\text{<hr>},\text{
}\}$ and $MR(\text{Title}) =\{\text{<p>}\}$.

5   Nondeterministic Prefix Tree Transducer

In the previous section, we have studied the case when the prefix tree transducer built from sample set S is deterministic. However, as we mentioned, $PTT(S)$ can be non-deterministic. In such a case, Preposition 1 does not hold and analysis of token prefixes is insufficient to disambiguate the token labeling. In this section, we extend the prefix-based analysis to suffixes as well and propose a wrapper induction method that copes with non-determinism in sample sets.

Assume that two annotated samples $s^1, s^2 \in S$ start with the prefixes $u\mathcal{C}(h)$ and $u\mathcal{C}(h')$, respectively, where h and h' are different labels of H. Any tree transducer built from set S will have a non-deterministic choice when trying to label the token $\mathcal{C}$, since samples s^1 and s^2 exemplify the different labeling of $\mathcal{C}$, with h and h', respectively.

Though S can be nondeterministic, we still assume that S is *consistent*, that is, there are no two different samples $s^1 = (x^1, y^1)$ and $s^2 = (x^2, y^2)$ in S, such that $x^1 = x^2$ but $y^1 \neq y^2$.

We will say that two distinct occurrences $\mathcal{C}(h)$ and $\mathcal{C}(h')$, $h, h' \in H$ conflict in sample set S, if $R(h) \cap R(h') \neq \emptyset$. As an example, consider the transducer T_2 in Figure 5. It has a nondeterministic choice at state q_1, where token $cal\mathcal{C}$ can be labeled as either as Author or Title. Consider an example of annotated sample set corresponding to this transducer.

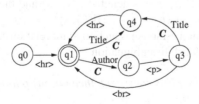

Fig. 5. Nondeterministic transducer T_2.

Example 4. Let the label set H include labels Author and Title and the annotated sample set S_2 be { <hr>, <hr>$\mathcal{C}$(Author)<p>$\mathcal{C}$(Title)<hr>$\mathcal{C}$(Author)<p>
,

`<hr>`$\mathcal{C}$`(Author)<p><br>`$\mathcal{C}$`(Author)<p><br>`,
`<hr>`$\mathcal{C}$`(Title)<hr>`$\mathcal{C}$`(Author)<p>`$\mathcal{C}$`(Title)<br>` }.

For the sample set S_2, we obtain the following inverse prefix sets for `Author` and `Title`:

$R(\mathcal{C}, \text{Author}) = \{$`<hr>`, `<hr>`$\mathcal{C}$`(Title)<p>`$\mathcal{C}$`(Author)<hr>`,
`<br><p>`$\mathcal{C}$`(Author)<hr>`, `<hr>`$\mathcal{C}$`(Title)<hr>`$\}$, and
$R(\mathcal{C}, \text{Title}) = \{$`<hr>`,`<p>`$\mathcal{C}$`(Author)<hr>`,`<p>`$\mathcal{C}$`(Author)<hr>`$\mathcal{C}$`(Title)<hr>`$\}$.

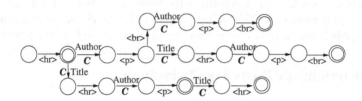

Fig. 6. Prefix tree transducer for S_2.

These two reverse prefix sets conflict as having the common item `<hr>`. The solution to the prefix conflicts is in extending the analysis, beyond prefixes, to suffixes of input tokens. Indeed, for a labeled token $\mathcal{C}(h)$ in two conflicting samples s^1 and s^2, the prefix comparison is insufficient, and the conflict resolution might require to lookahead and to compare suffixes of $u\mathcal{C}$ in s^1 and s^2. Such technique corresponds to postponing the conflict resolution in sub-sequential transducers [15]. If the sample set is consistent, observing both prefixes and suffixes can provide sufficient information to disambiguate labeling in conflict cases. Beyond the case of nondeterminism in sample sets, the analysis of suffixes can be equally helpful when the minimal prefix indexes and sets obtained by the previous method are too large. In such cases, considering *windows* which combine prefixes and suffixes can considerably reduce the number of context tokens needed for the label disambiguation.

Similar to prefix sets, we consider the set of all suffixes for $\mathcal{C}(h)$ in S. Let $\mathcal{C}(h)$ appear in $s \in S$, $s = s_1 \mathcal{C}(h) x'(y')$. The *window* for the given labeled token $\mathcal{C}(h)$ is defined as a pair (s_1^r, x'); it contains the (labeled) reverse prefix and (not labeled) suffix of $\mathcal{C}(h)$. The set of all windows of $\mathcal{C}(h)$ in s is denoted $W(h, s)$ and the set of all windows of $\mathcal{C}(h)$ in S is denoted $W(h)$: $W(h) = \{\cup_{s \in S} W(h, s)\}$.

The following preposition establishes an important relationship between the consistency of a sample set and label disambiguation.

Preposition 2 *If a sample set S is consistent, then for any pair of labels h and h' in S, we have $W(h) \cap W(h') = \emptyset$.*

Proof. (Sketch) From contradiction, let assume that a given sample set S is consistent but a pair of labels h and h' in S, $W(h) \cap W(h') \neq \emptyset$. Then there exists a window $w = (s, x)$ shared by both sets $W(h)$ and $W(h')$. Therefore S should have two samples s^1 and s^2 such that $s^1 = s\mathcal{C}(h)x(y)$ and $s^2 = s\mathcal{C}(h')x(y')$, and whatever y and y' are, S is not consistent.

5.1 Minimal Window Index

Preposition 2 gives a general method for the deterministic labeling when sample sets contain ambiguous translations. Similarly to the prefix case, now we introduce minimal window indexes and sets as compact alternative to the entire window sets. We will determine minimal window sets for all labels by observing the k-prefixes and l-suffixes, we can uniquely identify the labeling for any $\mathcal{C}$ occurrence in S.

Given the window set $W(h)$ for $\mathcal{C}(h)$, the set $W_{k,l}(h) = \{(s[k], u[l]|(s, u) \in W(h)\}$ is called the kl-window set of $\mathcal{C}(h)$ in S, $k, l = 0, 1, 2, ...$ For two distinct labels h and h', the minimal window index is given by $kl(h, h') = \{(k, l)|\ W_{k,l}(h) \cap W_{k,l}(h') = \emptyset\}$. and moreover the sum $k + l$ is minimal among all similar pairs.

For a given sample set S, we calculate the minimal window index as the maximal window index $kl_S = (k', l')$ for all pairs of labels in H, where

$$k' = max\{k|(k, l) = kl(h, h'), h \neq h'\},$$
$$l' = max\{l|(k, l) = kl(h, h'), h \neq h'\}.$$

The value kl_S establishes the upper bound on the lengths of k-prefix and l-suffix that guarantee the uniquely labeling of any occurrence of $\mathcal{C}$ in S.

Minimal preⁿx set. The minimal window set MW for all h in S are defined in the way similar to the minimal prefix sets. Unfortunately, unlike the minimal prefix sets, there may exist many different minimal window sets for the same set S and finding a globally minimal one is an computationally expensive task. However, there exists a greedy algorithm that build the (locally) minimal window sets for all labels in S.

For the sample set S_2 above, we obtain the (globally) minimal window sets for Author and Title as follows: MW(Author)=$\{(\emptyset, \texttt{<hr>}), ((\emptyset, \texttt{
}\}$ and MW(Title)=$\{(\emptyset, \texttt{<p>})\}$. Finally, kl(Author)=kl(Title)) = (0,1).

6   Related Work

The wrapper induction problem has been intensively studied over last years [4,6,9,11, 13,14]. In [11], Kushmerick first identified some simple classes of HTML wrappers which can be efficiently inferred from labeled samples. These classes assume a tabular structure of the response page. The wrapper inference is therefore reduced to the efficient detection of tag sequences preceding each label in such a tabular form. In [13], a wider set of HTML wrappers is considered. Beyond the tabular forms, the method also induces wrapper grammars in cases when some missing labels are they change the appearance order on the response page. Other wrapper classes has been proposed to treat multiple-valued labels, label permutations [9], nested labels in well-formed HTML pages [14] and disjunctions [4,9,13]. Some methods [9] are based on transducer-based extractors; however, because the simplifying assumptions about the page structure, none of these methods has however reached the 100% success rate.

7   Experiments and Analysis

For experiments, we have selected 16 information providers among about 100 ones generated for Xerox's AskOnce meta-searcher (http://www.mkms.xerox.com/askonce).

Selected providers cover two large domains, general-purpose search engines (8 sites) and bibliographic data providers (8 sites). They represent a wide range of complexity in response pages, including such different features as varying occurrences and permutations of labels, interleaving response items with advertisements, highlighting query keywords, label nesting, etc.

The complexity of a site is measured by the number of labels, by the size of minimal prefix/window sets (elements of either set are called extraction rules) and by minimal prefix/windows indexes. Complex sites have numerous labels and large MR and MW sets, and consequently, they require more samples for the accurate learning.

The wrappers based on both minimal prefix and minimal window sets have been successfully generated for all sites; in other words, sample sets for all sites are consistent and deterministic. In general, for the selected set, the window-based method outperforms the prefix-based method on 11% in the learning speed, reduces the total number of rules on 6% and number of tokens needed for disambiguation in 1.6 times. Table 1 reports the experiment results for all sites. Abbreviations used in the table are the following:

H - total number of labels in H, including λ and Stop,
Sz - total size of minimal prefix/window sets, $\sum_h |MR(h)|$ or $\sum_h |MW(h)|$,
RL-m(a), RL-a - maximal and average size of $MR(h)$ or $MW(h)$,
k_S, kl_S - minimal prefix/window indexes,
PL-a, WL-a - average length of prefixes/windows in $MR(h)$ or $MW(h)$, PL-a $\le k_S$,
     WL-a $\le kl_S$;
L-a - average number of samples needed to reach 99%-accuracy.

The label set H for all wrappers have been extended with a special label Stop which is learned like any other label; it results in halting the information extraction process. Using Stop allows wrappers to skip the mute tails of HTML pages and thus to make the minimal prefix/window sets smaller.

For each site, $|S| = 15$ labeled samples have been prepared for the evaluation of wrapper induction process. Accuracy of learning is measured by the percentage of correctly extracted and labeled tokens from a page. For each site, 5 tests have been performed, each test consists in learning the minimal prefix/window sets from i=1,2,3,... randomly chosen samples and testing the remaining (15-i) samples against the learned set. The average number (over 5 experiments) of samples needed to learn 99%-accurate prefix/window sets is reported in the table. Here we summarize some important results.

1. The second group of providers appears to be more complex than the first one. Deja.com and Go.com are the simplest among selected providers, their results have a regular table-like form. The prefix/window sets for both sites contain one rule per each valuable label and the remaining rules, 15 and 16 respectively, cope with label λ used to ignore HTML fragments before and within the answer list.
2. Many sites have a large gap between RL-m (referring always to label λ) and RL-a values. This gap is particularly important for advertisement-based sites like Altavista and Excite, while it remains minimal for no-advertisement sites (Google.com, DBLP, ACM[4] and Medline).

---

[4] http://www.informatik.uni-trier.de/ley/db, http://www.acm.org/dl/Search.html.

3. Cora is an example of search engines that visualize **query keywords** in answers by using a particular font. This splits a unique user label, such as Abstract, in multiple fragments; it results in an important number of rules for Abstract label, in both prefix-based and window-based induction methods.
4. Yahoo.com answers combine category entries and sites. These two sublists have common and different labels. This makes the learning of Yahoo wrapper much longer as compared to any other provider in the first group.
5. Medline differs from other sites by the large number of user labels (21). Although other parameters have values close to average ones, such a large number of labels and their combinations results in the biggest size of the sample set and the longest learning process.
6. The most difficult case takes place with CSBiblio and IEEE [5] sites where several labels like references to PDF/PS/HTML copies of a publication often share the same context (see Figure 1); this results in a very large prefix and window indexes (65 and 44 for CSBiblio, 45 and 23 for IEEE). Consequently, large prefixes/windows require a longer learning. Possible solutions for cases like CSBiblio and IEEE are either the normalization of conflicting labels by merging them in one joint label [3] or the extension of purely grammatical inference methods with some non-grammatical components (such as recognizers for explicit strings like 'PDF','HTML', etc.) [2,9, 11].

Table 1. Results of wrapper induction for 16 information providers.

Site	H	Prefixes						Windows					
		Sz	RL-a	RL-m	PL-a	k_S	L-a	Sz	RL-a	RL-m	WL-a	kl_S	L-a
Altavista.com	7	37	5.3	26	1.5	4	2.1	37	5.3	26	1.5	4	2.1
Google.com	9	29	3.2	11	2.4	4	2.3	27	3.0	11	2.3	3	2.1
Excite.com	7	27	3.9	19	1.4	3	2.0	27	3.9	19	1.3	3	2.0
Yahoo.com	6	30	5.0	14	3.8	20	4.4	29	4.8	14	1.3	4	3.8
Metacrawler.com	9	37	4.1	21	2.2	6	2.6	34	2.8	18	2.0	5	2.2
Go.com	6	21	3.5	16	1.8	8	1.2	19	3.2	14	1.5	4	1.1
Deja.com	6	20	3.3	15	1.6	4	1.1	17	2.8	12	1.4	3	1.1
CNN.com	7	36	5.1	22	1.5	4	2.2	35	5.1	21	1.5	4	2.2
DBLP	8	13	1.6	3	1.8	3	1.6	13	1.6	3	1.8	3	1.6
ResearchIndex	5	28	5.6	17	2.2	7	2.5	24	4.9	15	1.9	4	2.2
CSBiblio	10	32	3.2	17	4.6	65	8.7	32	3.2	17	3.8	44	8.2
ACM Search	9	18	2.0	9	2.1	4	1.6	18	2.0	9	2.1	4	1.6
IEEE DL	7	23	3.3	16	3.8	45	6.5	21	3.0	15	2.7	23	5.0
Elsevier	12	28	2.3	12	2.7	9	1.5	26	2.1	11	2.1	4	1.5
Medline	21	43	2.0	6	2.2	5	9.2	38	1.8	6	2.0	5	8.5
Cora	12	34	2.8	15	2.7	6	3.3	32	2.6	15	2.5	6	3.0
Average	8.8	28.5	3.5	14.9	2.4	12.3	3.3	26.8	3.2	14.1	2.0	7.7	3.0

---

[5] http://www.computer.org/search.htm

8 Conclusion

We have proposed two powerful wrapper classes for mediator and agent Web systems. The wrapper generation based on the transducer induction has been tested with a number of real Web information providers. Experiments have shown a large expressive power of new wrapper classes. Experiments with such sites as IEEE and CSBiblio have been particularly helpful, as they help to establish the limits of prefix-based and window-based methods, and pure grammar-based methods in general. They show that if the perfect information extraction and labeling is required from wrappers, pure grammatical methods should be extended with non-grammatical components.

References

1. Dana Angluin. Inference of Reversible Languages. *Journal of the ACM*, 29(3):741–765, July 1982.
2. Denis Bredelet and Bruno Roustant. Jwrap: Wrapper induction by grammar learning. Master's thesis, ENSIMAG, Grenoble, France, 2000.
3. B. Chidlovskii. Wrapper Generation by k-Reversible Grammar Induction. In *Proc. ECAI'00 Workshop on Machine Learning Inform. Extraction*, 2000.
4. B. Chidlovskii, J. Ragetli, and M. de Rijke. Wrapper Generation via Grammar Induction. In *11th European Conf. Machine Learning, Barcelona, Spain*, 2000.
5. D. Florescu, A. Levy, and A. Mendelzon. Database Techniques for the World-Wide Web: A Survey. *SIGMOD Record*, 27(3):59–74, 1998.
6. D. Freitag. Information extraction from HTML: Application of a general machine learning approach. In *Proc. AAAI/IAAI*, pages 517–523, 1998.
7. J. Hopcroft and J. Ullman. *Introduction to Automata Theory, Languages and Computation*. Addison-Wesley, N. Reading, MA, 1980.
8. C.-N. Hsu and C.-C. Chang. Finite-state transducers for semi-structured text mining. In *Proceedings of IJCAI-99 Workshop on Text Mining: Founda tions, Techniques and Applications*, 1999.
9. C.-N. Hsu and M.-T. Dung. Generating finite-state transducers for semistructured data extraction from the web. *Information Systems*, 23(8), 1998.
10. N. Kushmerick. Wrapper induction; efficiency and expressiveness. In *AAAI'98 Workshop on AI and Information Integration*, 19 98.
11. N. Kushmerick. Wrapper Induction: Efficiency and Expresiveness. *Artial Intelligence*, 118:15–68, 2000.
12. N. Kushmerick, D.S. Weld, and R. Doorenbos. Wrapper induction for information extraction. In *International Joint Conference on Artial Intelligence (IJCAI)*, 1997.
13. I. Muslea, S. Minton, and C. Knoblock. Stalker: Learning extraction rules for semistructured, web-based information sources. In *AAAI Workshop on AI and Information Integration*, 1998.
14. I. Muslea, S. Minton, and C. Knoblock. A hierarchical approach to wrapper induction. In *Proc. the Third Intern. Conf. on Autonomous Agents Conference, Seattle, WA*, pages 190–197, 1999.
15. J. Oncina, P. Garcia, and E. Vidal. Learning subsequential transducers for pattern recognition interpretation. *IEEE Trans. on Pattern Analysis*, 15:448–458, 1993.

Learning While Exploring: Bridging the Gaps in the Eligibility Traces

Fredrik A. Dahl and Ole Martin Halck

Norwegian Defence Research Establishment (FFI)
P.O. Box 25, NO-2027 Kjeller, Norway
{Fredrik-A.Dahl, Ole-Martin.Halck}@ffi.no

Abstract. The reinforcement learning algorithm TD(λ) applied to Markov decision processes is known to need added exploration in many cases. With the usual implementations of exploration in TD-learning, the feedback signals are either distorted or discarded, so that the exploration hurts the algorithm's learning. The present article gives a modification of the TD-learning algorithm that allows exploration without cost to the accuracy or speed of learning. The idea is that when the learning agent performs an action it perceives as inferior, it is compensated for its loss, that is, it is given an additional reward equal to its estimated cost of making the exploring move. This modification is compatible with existing exploration strategies, and is seen to work well when applied to a simple grid-world problem, even when always exploring completely at random.

1   Introduction

Reinforcement learning is a machine learning paradigm where agents learn "by themselves" from experience in a real or synthetic environment. Temporal difference learning (TD-learning) is a reinforcement learning algorithm that works by estimating the long-term utility of model states. It was originally designed for predicting the expected infinite-horizon return from Markov chains [1]. TD-learning tunes some evaluation function that assigns values to process states. It has been shown that TD-learning using lookup-tables for evaluating states converges toward the solution for states that are visited infinitely many times.

TD-learning can also be applied to Markov decision processes (MDPs), which are Markov chains where an agent has partial control over the process. This approach, due to Tesauro [2], transforms TD-learning from "a model-free algorithm for learning to predict, into a model-based algorithm for learning to control" [3]. An agent may use a state evaluation function as a *policy* for controlling the MDP by always choosing states with the highest possible evaluation (together with some strategy for breaking ties). If the evaluation function is correct, the derived policy is optimal. However, in a learning phase, there is a trade-off between exploiting the knowledge of the agent by following the derived policy, and exploring other options that may turn out to be better. One can easily see that an agent that never explores may fail to discover the best available policy. On the other hand, an agent that explores too often pays a price when the evaluation function is close to the optimal one. In addition –

L. De Raedt and P. Flach (Eds.): ECML 2001, LNAI 2167, pp. 73-84, 2001.
© Springer-Verlag Berlin Heidelberg 2001

and this is the problem this paper addresses – the TD-learning signals resulting from exploration will be distorted, and are therefore usually discarded.

The present article gives an algorithm that allows exploration without the downside of either discarding or distorting the learning signals. Our algorithm is based on the idea that the evaluation function can generate estimates of the cost of not following the greedy policy. We treat these estimates as rewards that the agent receives as compensation for making what it evaluates to be inferior actions.

The article is laid out as follows: Section 2 gives formal definitions of MDPs and TD-learning, with our preferred notation. In Section 3 we define our algorithm. Section 4 gives some experimental results in a simple grid world, Section 5 discusses some additional aspects of the algorithm, and Section 6 concludes the article.

2   Temporal Difference Learning and Markov Decision Processes

In this section we give some background on finite Markov decision processes and the temporal difference learning algorithm TD(λ) as applied to such processes. Over the years, a large body of literature on this and related subjects has appeared; we refer the reader to [4], [5], [6] and the references therein for more information on this field and reinforcement learning in general; most of this section is adapted from the former two works. A theoretical treatment of methods using value functions can be found in [7].

2.1   Markov Decision Processes

Informally, a (finite) *Markov decision process* (MDP) is a Markov process where in each state, an agent chooses an action, which influences the next step of the process and the reward the agent receives. We formalise an MDP as consisting of the following elements:

- A set S of *states*, with a subset $\Sigma \subseteq S$ of *terminal* states.
- A set A of *actions*, along with a function $A: S \rightarrow 2^A$ mapping each state to the set of admissible actions that can be taken when the process is in that state.
- A *transition* probability function $p_T(s'|s,a)$, giving the probability that a process in state s will move to state s' given action a.
- A *reward* probability function $p_R(r|s,a,s')$, giving the probability of receiving reward r upon moving from state s to state s' through action a.
- A discounting factor $\gamma \in (0,1]$.

An *episode* of an MDP proceeds as follows:

1. A starting state s_0 is given; $t \leftarrow 0$.
2. If $s_t \in \Sigma$, then $T \leftarrow t$ and end.
3. Choose an action $a_{t+1} \in A(s_t)$ according to some policy.
4. A new state s_{t+1} is drawn according to $p_T(\cdot | s_t, a_{t+1})$.

5. Receive a reward r_{t+1} drawn according to $p_R(\cdot \mid s_t, a_{t+1}, s_{t+1})$.

6. $t \leftarrow t+1$; go to step 2.

In practice, the reward r_{t+1} is often deterministic, depending for instance on (s_t, a_{t+1}) or on s_{t+1} alone.

The agent's total *return* from the episode is defined as the discounted sum of rewards $\sum_{t=0}^{T-1} \gamma^t r_{t+1}$ if the episode terminates, and $\sum_{t=0}^{\infty} \gamma^t r_{t+1}$ otherwise. In the latter case, $\gamma < 1$ is required to ensure that the return is finite.

For Markov (non-decision) processes, every state s has an associated *value* $V(s)$, giving the expected return from the process when starting at s. If, in an MDP, an agent employs a fixed policy π, that is, if in a given state each action has a fixed probability of being chosen by the agent, the MDP reduces to such a Markov process. In this case, we denote the value function of this process as V^π.

The *optimal value function* $V^* : S \to \mathbf{R}$ maps each state to the greatest expected return that can be achieved from that state, and is consequently defined by

$$\forall s \in S : V^*(s) = \max_\pi V^\pi(s). \tag{1}$$

By following a policy π^* achieving this maximum (there is always a deterministic policy of this kind), an agent maximises its expected return from the process. The optimal value function can in principle be found by using dynamic programming to solve the Bellman equations

$$V^*(s_t) = \max_{a_{t+1} \in A(s_t)} E[r_{t+1} + \gamma V^*(s_{t+1})], \tag{2}$$

where the expectation is taken with respect to p_T and p_R.[1] In practice, though, this set of equations is often too large to solve explicitly even if the MDP is known exactly, and this is where machine learning, and temporal difference learning in particular, comes in useful.

2.2 Temporal Difference Learning in MDPs

Sutton's original exposition of the TD(λ) algorithm mainly concentrates on the problem of predicting the outcome of Markov processes [1]. There, the algorithm is used for estimating the value function of the process. Clearly, the algorithm can then also be used for estimating the value function V^π of an MDP given a fixed policy π. On the other hand, if we have estimated such a value function, we may use this estimate to change the policy so that the expected return increases.

These two processes may be combined in a way that hopefully yields a good estimate of the optimal value function V^* and the optimal policy π^*. Exactly how value estimation and policy optimisation are interleaved may vary – for example, value estimates may be updated after each action, after each episode or after a batch

---

[1] For clarity we abuse the notation slightly, by suppressing the dependency of the new state on the old state and the action, and also the dependency of the reward on the action and the two states.

of episodes. For simplicity and ease of implementation, we consider a version of TD(λ) where the value estimates are updated after each episode, starting from the end of the episode. Similar formulations can be found in [3] and (less explicitly) in [2]. Using this formulation, we do not need explicit representations of the so-called eligibility traces (defined in e.g. [4]), since these are implicitly calculated along the way. Furthermore, we assume that the current estimate $\hat{V}$ of the value function is represented as a lookup-table. For a given $\lambda \in [0,1]$ and small, positive *step size* α, the training procedure we will refer to as *naive* TD(λ) then goes as follows:

1.   Initialise $\hat{V}(s)$ to 0 for each terminal s and (e.g.) randomly for all other $s \in S$.
2.   Run an episode of the MDP (as above).
3. $\delta \leftarrow 0$.
4.   For t from $T-1$ down to 0 do:

   4a. $\delta \leftarrow r_{t+1} + \gamma \hat{V}(s_{t+1}) - \hat{V}(s_t) + \gamma \lambda \delta$.

   4b. $\hat{V}(s_t) \leftarrow \hat{V}(s_t) + \alpha \delta$.

5.   If termination criterion is met, then end, else go to step 2.

2.3   Exploitation and Exploration in Learning

So far, we have not said explicitly *how* the agent is to choose its actions (step 3 in the MDP procedure). The seemingly obvious choice is to use a *greedy* policy, that is, to pick the action that it sees as best according to its current value estimates. Using this policy, the agent *exploits* its current beliefs in order to maximise its return. If we assume that the agent has full knowledge of the model (an assumption that will be kept in the following), the agent then chooses the action

$$a_{t+1} = \arg\max_{a \in A(s_t)} \hat{Q}(s_t, a) \equiv \arg\max_{a \in A(s_t)} E[r_{t+1} + \gamma \hat{V}(s_{t+1}) \mid a_{t+1} = a]. \tag{3}$$

The problem with this strategy is that the agent may have inaccurate value estimates, hindering it from discovering actions that may be more valuable than the one it believes to be the best. Therefore, it is necessary occasionally to *explore* the state space in order to find out whether there are better ways to act. The *exploitation–exploration dilemma* (see e.g. [8]) deals with the fact that exploring in order to discover new knowledge will usually also reduce the return given to the agent. A number of different strategies for handling the exploration–exploitation trade-off have been devised [8].

There is another fundamental problem with exploring, however, no matter which action selection policy is used. If the TD(λ) algorithm is used in the naive form above, the feedback signals will be negatively influenced by the exploring actions. Thus, even if the agent were to possess the optimal value function at some time, the feedback from the exploring actions will be biased and push the evaluations away from the correct ones. In fact, the only value function receiving unbiased learning signals in this process is the one that is optimal *under the given exploration policy*. (A parallel to this observation was made by John [9], who noted that the optimal value function and policy are no longer optimal under forced exploration.)

The usual way of dealing with this problem in TD-learning for control is *not* carrying the feedback across the exploring action – see for instance the tic-tac-toe example in the introduction to [4]. In our formulation of TD(λ) above, this means that step 4a is changed to:

4a'. If a_{t+1} was exploring, then $\delta \leftarrow 0$, else $\delta \leftarrow r_{t+1} + \gamma V(s_t) - V(s_t) + \lambda\delta$.

In the context of Q-learning, this approach corresponds to what [4] refers to as *Watkins's Q(λ)* [10]. We shall refer to this version as *trace-breaking* TD(λ), since it is equivalent to setting the eligibility traces to zero when an exploratory action is performed.

In this algorithm, having the optimal value function will lead to unbiased learning signals; thus, this function is stable if the process is deterministic. On the other hand, the algorithm has the disadvantage that it breaks the chain of feedback from later states to earlier ones when exploration occurs. This loss of information means that a greater number of episodes are needed for learning, especially if the agent explores frequently.

3   The Loss-Compensating Algorithm

The motivation of our algorithm is the observation that by breaking the signal chain at an exploring action, valuable information is lost. We want to remedy this loss by devising a way of carrying the learning signals across the exploring step, without at the same time distorting the learning signal as in the naive algorithm. The idea is to exploit the knowledge already present in the evaluation function in order to achieve this goal. Of course, this kind of bootstrapping – using the present value estimates for the purpose of finding better ones – is the principle behind all TD-learning; here it is taken one step further.

Our algorithm works in the following way: Whenever the agent makes an exploratory action, it gives itself a reward equal to its own evaluation of how inferior the action is. If the agent has a correct evaluation of every state, this will produce a TD-learning signal that is unbiased, because it then evaluates the downside of the "unwanted" exploration correctly. (If the process is deterministic, this means that the evaluations will remain correct.) Referring to the procedures given in Section 2, we can implement this algorithm by changing two steps. First, step 3 of the MDP is replaced by:

3'.   Act by performing the following steps:

    3'a. Find the greedy action: $\hat{a}_{t+1} \leftarrow \arg\max_a \hat{Q}(s_t, a)$.

    3'b. Choose an action a_{t+1} according to some policy.

    3'c. Calculate the perceived loss: $l_{t+1} \leftarrow \hat{Q}(s_t, \hat{a}_{t+1}) - \hat{Q}(s_t, a_{t+1})$.

Second, step 4a in the TD(λ) algorithm is changed to:

4a''. $\delta \leftarrow r_{t+1} + l_{t+1} + \gamma \hat{V}(s_{t+1}) - \hat{V}(s_t) + \gamma\lambda\delta$.

Preliminary experiments with this algorithm revealed one flaw: for certain parameter values – notably for high values of λ – the value estimates diverged by increasing exponentially. This is bad news, and can be explained informally as follows in the special case of $\lambda = 1$: The compensating rewards l are always non-negative, so for a given evaluation function, the expected value of the feedback may be higher than the actual expected return, but not lower. The feedback signals therefore have a positive bias, unless the evaluation function is correct. If the greedy use of the evaluation function recommends an inferior action at a given state, the compensating reward for exploring the actually correct action is the source of the bias. For a given state visited by the process, the bias in the feedback signal is equal to the expected sum of these future false rewards. Therefore, the feedback bias tends to be proportional to the average error of the evaluation function. This means that the feedback error tends to be proportional to the current error, which is a standard recipe for exponential explosion.

A simple fix for this instability – apart from tuning down λ – is implemented by truncating the evaluations at a maximum value M. After each training step, we set $\hat{V}(s_t) \leftarrow \min(M, \hat{V}(s_t))$. With this modification, there is of course no risk of exponential explosions beyond the limit M. In most cases, a good upper bound on the state values is available, either from prior knowledge of the problem, or from the actual payoffs achieved by the agent during training. Still, it may seem naive to hope that this simple trick will make an unstable algorithm convergent. However, the experiments that we present in the next section indicate that it actually works, at least in our grid-world example.

We are now able to write our full *loss-compensating* TD(λ) algorithm as follows: Given an MDP, λ, α, M, and an action selection policy:

1. Initialise $\hat{V}(s)$ to 0 for each terminal s and (e.g.) randomly for all other $s \in S$.
2. Run an episode of the MDP:
    M1. Initialise starting state s_0, $t \leftarrow 0$.
    M2. If $s_t \in \Sigma$, then $T \leftarrow t$ and go to step 3.
    M3. Act by performing the following steps:
        M3a. Find the greedy action: $\hat{a}_{t+1} \leftarrow \arg\max_a \hat{Q}(s_t, a)$.
        M3b. Choose an action a_{t+1} according to the action selection policy.
        M3c. $l_{t+1} \leftarrow \hat{Q}(s_t, \hat{a}_{t+1}) - \hat{Q}(s_t, a_{t+1})$.
    M4. A new state s_{t+1} is drawn according to $p_T(\cdot \mid s_t, a_{t+1})$.
    M5. Receive a reward r_{t+1} drawn according to $p_R(\cdot \mid s_t, a_{t+1}, s_{t+1})$.
    M6. $t \leftarrow t+1$; go to step M2.
3. Learn from the episode:
    L1. $\delta \leftarrow 0$.
    L2. For t from $T-1$ down to 0 do:
        L2a. $\delta \leftarrow r_{t+1} + l_{t+1} + \gamma \hat{V}(s_{t+1}) - \hat{V}(s_t) + \gamma \lambda \delta$.
        L2b. $\hat{V}(s_t) \leftarrow \min(M, \hat{V}(s_t) + \alpha \delta)$.
4. If termination criterion is met, then end, else go to step 2.

4   Experiments

The state space of our experimental MDP problem is the grid world of a fully connected rectangular 5×5 grid, with terminal states $\{(5,5),(2,4),(3,4),(4,4),(5,4)\}$. The node $(5,5)$ is the goal, and reaching this goal gives a reward of 1. The other four terminal nodes are "traps", which give a reward of -10. We set the discount factor γ to 0.9. On each time step, the agent can move along an arc in the network or stay put, and the starting point of the process is the lower left-hand corner $(1,1)$. Figure 1 shows the grid world. Clearly, the optimal policy is to move four times upwards and then four times to the right, which takes the process to the goal node in eight turns, for a return of γ^8.

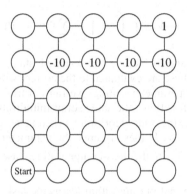

Fig. 1. The grid world

With the given formulation, the process may take a very long time to terminate, giving problems for our episode-based algorithm. To overcome this problem, we use the common technique of transforming the discount factor into a "survival rate" of the process: Instead of discounting future rewards directly, we apply a stopping probability of $1-\gamma$ at each time step. If this random draw stops the process, we let the process jump to an additional terminal node $(0,0)$ with payoff 0. In the MDP formalism above, this means that the transition probabilities from a state given an action are γ for entering the next node and $1-\gamma$ for going to $(0,0)$. (An exception occurs when the agent moves to a trap node, in which case the process never moves to $(0,0)$). For any given policy, this stochastic formulation gives the same expected payoff as the one using infinite horizons and discounted payoffs. Future payoffs are discounted indirectly, because they are less likely to occur. Note that this trick is applicable to any MDP with discounted rewards.

We apply "blind" exploration, so that for each decision there is a fixed probability $p_{explore}$ of the agent making a random action, with equal probability assigned to each possible action. We have tested a wide range of parameter settings for α, $p_{explore}$ and λ, and compared our loss-compensating algorithm to the trace-breaking algorithm.

We use two different error measures, designed to measure how quickly the algorithms learn to approximate the true value function $V*$ by their estimates $\hat{V}$. The error measures are defined as the root-mean-square difference between the true values and the estimates, taken along the optimal path and over all states, respectively. Denoting the shortest distance from a state s to the goal node by $d(s)$, we write the mathematical definitions of these error measures as

$$e^P_{rms} = \left(\frac{1}{8}\sum_{s \in P}\left(V*(s) - \hat{V}(s)\right)^2\right)^{1/2} = \left(\frac{1}{8}\sum_{s \in P}\left(\gamma^{d(s)} - \hat{V}(s)\right)^2\right)^{1/2} \tag{4}$$

– where $P = \{(1,1),(1,2),(1,3),(1,4),(1,5),(2,5),(3,5),(4,5)\}$ is the subset of S belonging to the optimal path – and

$$e^S_{rms} = \left(\frac{1}{20}\sum_{s \in S}\left(V*(s) - \hat{V}(s)\right)^2\right)^{1/2} = \left(\frac{1}{20}\sum_{s \in S}\left(\gamma^{d(s)} - \hat{V}(s)\right)^2\right)^{1/2}. \tag{5}$$

Note that it is not necessary to include the terminal states in the sums, since the algorithms guarantee that these are evaluated to the correct value of 0.

For each algorithm and parameter setting, we ran ten trials with different random initialisations of the value functions; the same set of initialisations was used for every algorithm and parameter setting. Our algorithm worked better in all cases, and Figures 2 and 3 give a typical example. In these figures, the parameters settings are $\alpha = 0.05$, $\lambda = 0.75$, and $p_{explore} = 0.5$. In the loss-compensating case, a maximum learning signal of $M = 1$ was used.

From the figures we see that our algorithm learns the task significantly faster than the benchmark algorithm does, although the long-term average performance is similar. This is compatible with the fact that our algorithm makes more use of the data available.

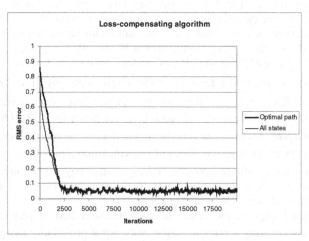

Fig. 2. RMS error as a function of iterations using the loss-compensating algorithm. Parameter settings: $\alpha = 0.05$, $\lambda = 0.75$, $p_{explore} = 0.5$, $M = 1$

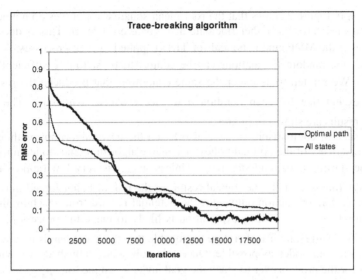

Fig. 3. RMS error as a function of iterations using the trace-breaking algorithm. Parameter settings: $\alpha = 0.05$, $\lambda = 0.75$, $p_{explore} = 0.5$

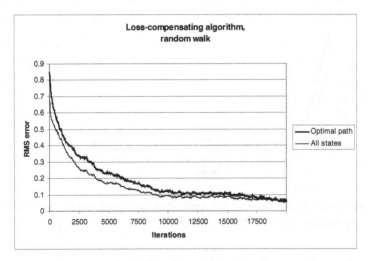

Fig. 4. RMS error of the loss-compensating algorithm learning from a random walk. Parameter settings: $\alpha = 0.05$, $\lambda = 0.75$, $p_{explore} = 1$, $M = 1$

Figure 4 shows the error curves of our algorithm with parameters $\alpha = 0.05$, $\lambda = 0.75$, and $p_{explore} = 1$. We see that the algorithm works even with a random walk exploration of the state space, so the agent learns the optimal value function simply by observing a completely random policy in action. The trace-breaking algorithm would not learn anything with $p_{explore} = 1$, as all feedback signals would be discarded.

The graph in Figure 2 shows that the root-mean-square error curves do not actually converge toward zero, but rather fluctuate at a given error level. This is due to the randomness of the MDP, and is typical for TD(λ) applied to such processes. As usual with TD(λ), the random fluctuations can be controlled by setting a sufficiently low step size α. We ran ten trials under the same conditions that produced the results in Figure 2, except that for each iteration n we set $\alpha = 0.1 \times (1 + n/500)^{-1}$. The rather successful results are shown in Figure 5.

For the sake of comparison we have also tested the naive algorithm, without ever observing discovery of the optimal policy. The naive algorithm tends to learn to move towards the starting node, and stay there. Unless $p_{explore}$ is very low (approximately 0.05 or less), this is actually the logical result, as the risk of being forced into a trap state by an exploratory action outweighs the potential reward from reaching the goal node. Even when $p_{explore}$ is low, exploration is likely to make the process hit a trap node once in a while, and it is therefore reasonable that the agent learns to stay as far away from the trap nodes as possible. Once this policy is established, it is virtually impossible for the process ever to reach the goal node, given the low $p_{explore}$.

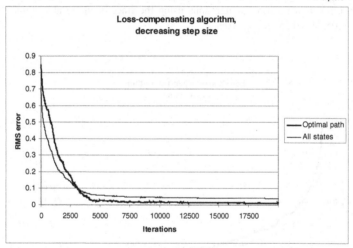

Fig. 5. RMS error of the loss-compensating algorithm using decreasing step size α. Other parameter settings: $\lambda = 0.75$, $p_{explore} = 0.5$, $M = 1$

5   Discussion

In the experiments, we used a very simple exploration policy, with a constant probability for exploring at each step, and uniform probabilities for choosing the exploring actions. However, our algorithm does not impose any constraint on how exploration is to be done. Consequently, it can be used regardless of what kind of exploration policy one might choose to employ.

Our trick of using the evaluation function for extracting rewards that compensate for exploration can be used beyond the context that we consider in the present article. It is not restricted to the episodic formulation of the algorithm, since its only additional requirement is the calculation of the loss l in step M3 above. It also generalises easily to model-based TD-learning where the agent must estimate the model – i.e. the transition and reward probabilities – in addition to the value function, and to $Q(\lambda)$. In fact, the idea of compensating the agent for the loss incurred by performing an inferior action has a parallel in simple one-step Q-learning [10] – that is, in $Q(0)$ – where the value estimate of a state–action pair is pushed towards the estimate associated with the *optimal* action in the subsequent state. Seen in this light, the relation between loss-compensating TD(0) and naive TD(0) is similar to that between $Q(0)$ and Sarsa(0).

This property of $Q(0)$ does not seem to have been extended in a consistent way to positive λ, although the algorithm that in [4] is called *Peng's $Q(\lambda)$* does make some use of the idea [11]. In Peng's $Q(\lambda)$, the feedback signal is a sum of components, each of which comes from the actual experience of the agent for a number of steps along the process, except for the signal from the last step, which is maximised over possible actions. Unlike our method as applied to $Q(\lambda)$, however, this algorithm does not produce unbiased learning signals if the optimal value function has been reached.

Our experiments indicate that our modification to the TD(λ) algorithm for learning control may significantly accelerate learning. However, the theoretical properties of the new algorithm are an important subject for future research.

6   Conclusion

We have presented a simple and intuitive modification of TD(λ) learning, based on the idea that the evaluation function can generate estimates of the cost of not following the greedy policy. We treat these estimates as rewards that the agent receives as compensations for making what it evaluates to be inferior actions. We have observed that the compensating rewards are all positive, so that the learning signal will be biased. This may result in exponential explosion of the value estimates, but simply truncating the value estimates at a given level appears to fix this problem, at least in our grid world application. In our experiments, the algorithm outperformed the version of the TD(λ) algorithm that works by truncating feedback signals over exploratory actions. The algorithm is compatible with arbitrary exploration policies. Furthermore, we observe that our trick is also applicable to $Q(\lambda)$, although this has not yet been tested.

References

1. Sutton, R.S.: Learning to predict by the methods of temporal differences. *Machine Learning* 3 (1988) 9–44.
2. Tesauro, G.J.: Practical issues in temporal difference learning. *Machine Learning* 8 (1992) 257–277.

3. Boyan, J.A., Moore, A.W.: Learning evaluation functions for large acyclic domains. In: Saitta, L. (ed.): *Proceedings of the Thirteenth International Conference on Machine Learning,* Morgan Kaufmann (1996) 63–70.
4. Sutton, R.S., Barto, A.G.: *Reinforcement Learning: an Introduction.* MIT Press (1998). URL: http://www-anw.cs.umass.edu/~rich/book/the-book.html
5. Kaelbling, L.P., Littman, M.L., Moore, A.W.: Reinforcement learning: a survey. *Journal of Artificial Intelligence Research* 4 (1996) 237–285.
6. Bertsekas, D.P., Tsitsiklis, J.N.: *Neuro-Dynamic Programming.* Athena Scientific (1996).
7. Szepesvari, C., Littman, M.L.: A unified analysis of value-function-based reinforcement-learning algorithms. *Neural Computation* 11 (1999) 2017–2060.
8. Thrun, S.B.: The role of exploration in learning control. In: White, D.A., Sofge, D.A. (eds.): *Handbook of Intelligent Control: Neural, Fuzzy and Adaptive Approaches,* Van Nostrand Reinhold, New York (1992).
9. John, G.H.: When the best move isn't optimal: Q-learning with exploration. In: *Proceedings, 10th National Conference on Artificial Intelligence,* AAAI Press (1994) 1464.
10. Watkins, C.J.C.H.: *Learning from Delayed Rewards.* PhD thesis, University of Cambridge, UK (1989).
11. Peng, J.: *Efficient Dynamic Programming-Based Learning for Control.* PhD thesis, Northeastern University, Boston (1993).

A Reinforcement Learning Algorithm Applied to Simplified Two-Player Texas Hold'em Poker

Fredrik A. Dahl

Norwegian Defence Research Establishment (FFI)
P.O. Box 25, NO-2027 Kjeller, Norway
Fredrik-A.Dahl@ffi.no

Abstract. We point out that value-based reinforcement learning, such as TD-
and Q-learning, is not applicable to games of imperfect information. We give a
reinforcement learning algorithm for two-player poker based on gradient search
in the agents' parameter spaces. The two competing agents experiment with
different strategies, and simultaneously shift their probability distributions
towards more successful actions. The algorithm is a special case of the lagging
anchor algorithm, to appear in the journal *Machine Learning*. We test the
algorithm on a simplified, yet non-trivial, version of two-player Hold'em poker,
with good results.

1   Introduction

A central concept in modern artificial intelligence is that of intelligent agents, that
interact in a synthetic environment. The game-theoretic structure of extensive form
games is a natural mathematical framework for studying such agents. The sub-field of
two-player zero-sum games, which contains games with two players that have no
common interest, has the added benefit of a strong solution concept (minimax) and a
corresponding well-defined performance measure.

In this article we apply a gradient-search-based reinforcement learning algorithm
for a simplified Texas Hold'em poker game. The algorithm is a simplified form of the
lagging anchor algorithm, to appear in the journal *Machine Learning* [1]. The
contribution of the present paper is the presentation of an application to a more
complex problem than those of the journal paper.

The structure of the paper is as follows: In Section 2 we explain a few key concepts
of game theory, and give a brief survey of reinforcement learning in games. Section 3
covers earlier work on Poker games. In Section 4 we describe our simplified Hold'em
Poker game, and Section 5 gives our agent design. Section 6 describes the lagging
anchor algorithm in general terms, together with a precise implementation of the
simplified form used in the present article. In Section 7 we give the performance
measures that we use, and Section 8 describes the experiments. Section 9 concludes
the article. For a more thorough treatment of the topics in Sections 2, 3, 6 and 7, we
refer to the journal article.

L. De Raedt and P. Flach (Eds.): ECML 2001, LNAI 2167, pp. 85-96, 2001.
© Springer-Verlag Berlin Heidelberg 2001

2   Reinforcement Learning in Games

Game theory [2] is a complex mathematical structure, and it is beyond the scope of this article to give more than an introduction to some of its key terms. We restrict our attention to two-player zero-sum games, which means that there are two players with opposite goals, and therefore no common interest. Under mild conditions, a two-player zero-sum game has a *minimax solution*. It consists of a pair of playing strategies for both sides that is in equilibrium, in the sense that neither side can benefit from changing his strategy as long as the opponent does not. The minimax solution gives the game a numeric *value*, which is the expected payoff (for the first player), given minimax play.

An important distinction is that between games of *perfect* and *imperfect* *information*. In perfect information games like chess and backgammon, both players know the state of the game at all times, and there are no simultaneous moves. In a perfect information game, each game state can be regarded as the starting state of a new game, and therefore has a value. If an agent knows the value of all game states in a perfect information game, it can easily implement a perfect strategy, in the minimax sense, by choosing a game state with the highest possible value (or lowest, if the value is defined relative to the opponent) at each decision point.

With imperfect information games such as two-player Poker or Matching Pennies (see below), the picture is more confusing, because minimax play may require random actions by the players. In Matching Pennies, both players simultaneously choose either "Heads" or "Tails". The first player wins if they make the same choice, and the second player wins otherwise. The minimax solution of this game is for both players to choose randomly with probability 0.5 (flip a coin). Under these strategies they have equal chances, and neither side can improve his chance by changing his strategy unilaterally. Obviously, there exists no deterministic minimax solution for this game. In Matching Pennies, the information imperfection is due to the fact that choices are made simultaneously, while in Poker games, it is a consequence of the private cards held by each player. Poker games typically also feature randomized (or *mixed*) minimax solutions. The randomization is best seen as a way of keeping the opponent from knowing the true state of the game. In a perfect information game, this has little point, as the opponent knows the game state at all times. Note that the concept of game state values, which is the key to solving perfect information games, does not apply to imperfect information games, because the players do not know from which game states they are choosing.

A game represents a closed world, formalized with rules that define the set of allowed actions for the players. Games are therefore suitable for algorithms that explore a problem "by themselves", commonly referred to as reinforcement learning. This term is actually borrowed from the psychological literature, where it implies that actions that turn out to be successful are applied more often in the future. In the machine-learning context, the term is often used more broadly, covering all algorithms that experiment with strategies and modify their strategies based on feedback from the environment.

The reinforcement learning algorithms that have been studied the most are TD-learning [3] and Q-learning [4]. These algorithms were originally designed for Markov decision processes (MDPs), which may be viewed as 1-player games. TD- and Q-learning work by estimating the utility of different states (and actions) of the process, which is the reason why they are referred to as value-based. Convergence results for value-based reinforcement learning algorithms are given in [5]. In an MDP, an accurate value function is all that it takes to implement an optimal policy, as the agent simply chooses a state with maximum value at each decision point.

The approach of deriving a policy from a state evaluator generalizes to two-player zero-sum games with perfect information, such as backgammon [6]. However, as we have seen in our brief game-theoretic survey, the value-based approach does not work with imperfect information, because the players may not know which game states they are choosing between. Also we have seen that optimal play in games of imperfect information may require random actions by the players, which is not compatible with the "greedy" policy of always choosing the game state with maximum value. It should be noted that the value-based approach can be extended to a subset of imperfect information games named *Markov games* by the use of matrix-game solution algorithms [7,8]. However, non-trivial Poker games are not Markov.

Summing up, established reinforcement learning algorithms like TD- and Q-learning work by estimating values (i.e. expected outcomes under optimal strategies) for process or game states. In (non-Markov) games of imperfect information, this paradigm does not apply.

3 Related Work on Poker

An important breakthrough in the area of solution algorithms for two-player games (not necessarily zero-sum) is that of sequential representation of strategies [9]. Prior to this work, the standard solution algorithm for two-player zero-sum games was based on enumerating all deterministic strategies for both players, assembling a corresponding game matrix, and solving the matrix game with linear programming [10]. The sequential strategy representation algorithm is an exponential order more efficient than the matrix game approach, and it has been applied to simple poker games [11]. However, even this algorithm quickly becomes intractable for non-trivial poker games.

A more practical view of computer poker is taken in the Hold'em-playing program "Loki" [12]. It uses parametric models of the habits of its opponents. Loki updates its opponent models "real time", based on the actions taken by its opponents. It estimates the utilities of different actions by approximate Bayesian analysis based on simulations with the current state of the opponent models. Apparently this approach has been quite successful, especially against weak and intermediate level humans. Note, however, that the objective of Loki is rather different from ours: We attempt to approximate game-theoretic optimal (minimax) behavior, while Loki attempts to exploit weaknesses in human play.

4 Simplified Two-Player Hold'em Poker

We now give the rules of our simplified two-player Hold'em poker game. Firstly, the full deck of 52 cards is shuffled. Then two private cards are dealt to each player (hereafter named *Blue* and *Red*). Blue then makes a forced blind bet of one unit, whereafter Red has the options of *folding*, *calling* and *raising* (by one unit). The betting process continues until one player folds or calls, except that Blue has the right to bet if Red calls the blind bet (the blind is "live"). Also there is a limit of four raises, so the maximum pot size is 10.

As usual in poker, a player loses the pot to the opponent if he folds. If the betting stops with a call, five open cards, called the *table*, are dealt. These are common to the players, so that both have seven cards from which they can choose their best five-card poker hand. The player with the better hand wins the pot. An example game may proceed as shown in Table 1.

Table 1. An example game of simplified Hold'em poker

	Blue	Red
Cards	♠A ♦K	♣5 ♣4
Betting	Blind bet	Raise
	Raise	Call
Table	♣A ♣K ♣2 ♠7 ♦7	
Best hand	♣A ♠A ♣K ♦K ♠7	♣A ♣K ♣5 ♣4 ♣2

In the example game, Red wins three units from Blue, because his flush beats Blue's two pair.

The decision tree of our game is given in Figure 1. Arrows pointing to the left represent folding, downward-pointing ones represent calling, while those pointing to the right represent raising. This is not the complete game tree, however, because the branching due to the random card deal is not represented. The nodes containing a "B" or an "R" represent decision nodes for Blue and Red, respectively. The leaf nodes contain Blue's payoff, where "+/–" indicates that the cards decide the winner.

Although our game is far simpler than full-scale Hold'em, it is complex enough to be a real challenge. We have not attempted to implement the sequential strategy algorithm, but we can indicate the amount of effort this would take. Essentially, that algorithm requires one variable for each available action for every information state, to represent a player's strategy. From Figure 1 this implies 13 variables for each different hand for Blue, and 14 for each hand Red can have. By utilizing the fact that suits are irrelevant (except whether or not the two cards are of the same suit), the number of different hands is reduced to 169. This implies that the strategy space of both sides has more than 2000 degrees of freedom. The algorithm requires the assembly (and processing) of a matrix with Blue degrees of freedom as columns and Red ones as rows (or vice versa), which implies a total of $169 \cdot 13 \cdot 169 \cdot 14 = 5,198,102$ matrix entries. The calculation of these entries also requires the calculation of the win probabilities of the various opposing hands ($169 \cdot 169 = 28,561$ combinations). One would probably have to estimate these probabilities by sampling, because the set of possible card combinations for the table is very large. All in all, it may be possible to solve our game using a present-day computer, but it will require massive use of computer time.

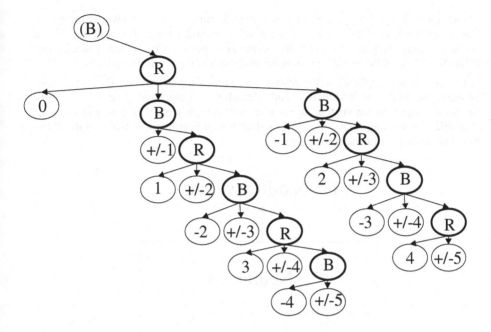

Fig. 1. The decision tree of simplified Hold'em poker. Arrows to the left signify *fold*, vertical arrows *call*, and arrows to the right *raise*

5 Agent Design

Our agents are designed to *act on the basis of available information*. This means that an agent bases its decision on its own two cards and the current decision node (in Figure 1). In game-theoretic terms this means that the agents act on *information sets* and represent behavioural strategies. From game theory, we know that strong play may require random actions by an agent, which means that it must have the capability to assign probabilities to the available actions in the given decision node. We use separate agents for playing Blue and Red.

The general agent design that we use with the lagging anchor algorithm is as follows: Let S represent the set of information states that the agent may encounter, and let $A(s)$ represent the (finite) set of available actions at state $s \in S$. For each $s \in S$ and $a \in A(s)$, the agent has a probability $P(s,a)$ of applying action a at information state s. Furthermore, we assume that the agent's behaviour is parameterised by $v \in V : P_v(s,a)$. We assume that V is a closed convex subset of $\mathbf{R}^n$ for some n. Summing up, our general agent design allows probability distributions over the set of legal actions for different information states, and these probability distributions may depend on a set of internal parameters of the agent (v). The goal of the learning algorithm is to find parameter values $v^* \in V$ so that the agent acts similarly to a minimax strategy.

Our agent design may give associations to Q-learning, which also works for agents that assign numeric values to combinations of states and actions. The main difference is one of interpretation; while Q-values estimate expected (discounted) rewards, our *P*-function dictates the agent's probability distribution over available actions.

For our present application, we design our agents using neural nets (NNs) that take as input the available information and a candidate action, and give a probability weight as output. When such an agent responds to a game state, it first evaluates all available actions, and then chooses a random action according to the outputs of the NN. The design is illustrated in Figure 2.

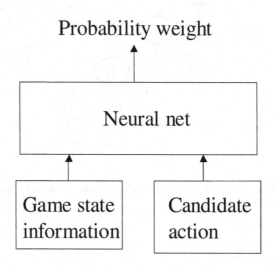

Fig. 2. Neural net agent design

For our NNs we have chosen a simple multi-layer perceptron design with one layer of hidden units and sigmoid activation functions. For updating we use standard back-propagation of errors [13]. The NN has the following input units (all binary): 13 units for representing the card denominators, one unit for signaling identical suit of the cards, one for signaling a pair, eight nodes for signaling the size of the pot, and finally three nodes signaling the candidate action (*fold*, *call* and *raise*). The single output node of the net represents the probability weight that the agent assigns to the action. The number of hidden nodes was set to 20. With this design, the internal parameters (*v*'s) are the NN weights, which will be tuned by the learning algorithm.

We denote Blue's NN function by $B_v(s,a)$, and Red's by $R_w(s,a)$. For Blue, the corresponding probability function is $P_v(s,a) = \dfrac{B_v(s,a)}{\sum\limits_{\bar{a} \in A(s)} B_v(\ ,\ )}$, and likewise for Red.

6   Learning Algorithm

The idea of our algorithm is to let Blue and Red optimize their parameters through simultaneous gradient ascent. Let $E(v, w)$ be Blue's expected payoff when Blue's playing strategy is given by v and Red's by w. By the zero-sum assumption, Red's expected payoff is $-E(v, w)$. If we set the step size to α, the following (idealized) update rule results:

$$v^{k+1} \leftarrow v^k + \alpha \nabla_v E(v^k, w^k)$$
$$w^{k+1} \leftarrow w^k - \alpha \nabla_w E(v^k, w^k)$$

$$(1)$$

In general, the basic gradient search algorithm (1) does not converge. In the context of matrix games (where E is bi-linear), Selten has shown that update rule (1) cannot converge towards mixed strategy solutions [14]. In [1] we show that in the case of matrix games with fully mixed randomised solutions, the paths of (v^k, w^k) converge towards circular motion around minimax solution points, when the step size falls towards zero. This fact is utilized in the lagging anchor algorithm: An anchor $\bar{v}^k$ maintains a weighted average of earlier parameter states for Blue. This "lagging anchor" pulls the present strategy state towards itself. Similarly, a lagging anchor $\bar{w}^k$ pulls Red's strategy towards a weighted average of previously used strategies, turning the oscillation of update rule (1) into spirals that, at least in some cases, converge towards a minimax solution. The (idealized) lagging anchor update rule looks like this:

$$v^{k+1} \leftarrow v^k + \alpha \nabla_v E(v^k, w^k) + \alpha \eta (\bar{v}^k - v^k)$$
$$w^{k+1} \leftarrow w^k - \alpha \nabla_w E(v^k, w^k) + \alpha \eta (\bar{w}^k - w^k)$$
$$\bar{v}^{k+1} \leftarrow \bar{v}^k + \alpha \eta (v^k - \bar{v}^k)$$
$$\bar{w}^{k+1} \leftarrow \bar{w}^k + \alpha \eta (w^k - \bar{w}^k)$$

where η is the anchor attraction factor.

In the present article, we use an approximate variant of learning rule (1), i.e. without anchors. The learning rule includes the calculation of the gradients of the expected payoff, with respect to the agents' internal parameters. We estimate these gradients through analysis of sample games. First the Blue and Red agents play a sample game to its conclusion. Then both Blue and Red perform the following "what-if" analysis: At each decision node (as in Figure 1) visited, an additional game is completed (by Blue and Red) for each decision not made in the original game. The outcomes of these hypothetical games provide estimates of how successful alternative decisions would have been. The agents then modify their NNs in order to reinforce those actions that would have been the most successful. We accomplish this through the use of training patterns of input and desired output: (gamestate+action , feedback). If a given (hypothetical) action turned out more successful than the others, for the given game state, the agent should apply it *more often*. This means that the training pattern feedback should be given by the NN's current evaluation of the state-action pair offset by the action's relative success compared to the other actions. Because of this relative nature of the feedback signals, there is a risk that the NN outputs may drift toward zero or one, which hurts the back-propagation learning. We prefer that the NN outputs approximate probability distributions, and therefore adjust the feedback signals in the NN training patterns accordingly.

In pseudo-code, the algorithm is given below, where we apply the convention of displaying vector quantities in **boldface**. Keywords are displayed in **boldface courier**. Blue's and Red's NN functions are denoted by $B(\cdot,\cdot)$ and $R(\cdot,\cdot)$, respectively.

repeat *Iteration* **times** {

    ⟨play a game g between Blue and Red⟩

    for ⟨each decision node $n \in g$⟩ **do** {

        $\mathbf{A} \leftarrow$ ⟨legal actions at n⟩

        $\mathbf{E} \leftarrow$ ⟨outcomes of games resulting from actions $\mathbf{A}$ at n⟩

        if ⟨Blue on turn in n⟩   { $\mathbf{P} \leftarrow B(s, \mathbf{A})$ }

        else   { $\mathbf{P} \leftarrow R(s, \mathbf{A})$ }

        $p_{sum} \leftarrow \mathbf{1}^T \mathbf{P}$

        $e \leftarrow \mathbf{P}^T \mathbf{E} / p_{sum}$

        $\mathbf{E} \leftarrow \mathbf{E} - \mathbf{1}e$

        $\mathbf{F} \leftarrow \mathbf{P} + \mathbf{E} - \mathbf{1}(p_{sum} - 1)$

        if ⟨Blue on turn in n⟩   { ⟨train B with patterns $\{(s, \mathbf{A}), \mathbf{F}\}$⟩ }

        else   { ⟨train R with patterns $\{(s, \mathbf{A}), \mathbf{F}\}$⟩ }

    }

}

Operations involving vectors are interpreted component-wise, so the notation implies several for-loops. As an example, the statement ⟨train B with patterns $\{(s, \mathbf{A}), \mathbf{F}\}$⟩ is implemented as:

for $(i = 1 \ldots length(\mathbf{A}))$ **do** { ⟨train B with pattern $((s, A_i), F_i)$⟩ }.

The vector $\mathbf{E}$ consists of outcomes (for the player on turn) of sample games that explore the different actions $\mathbf{A}$ in node n. In these games, the players' hands and the table cards are held fixed. Note that when we assemble $\mathbf{E}$, we take the outcome of the actual game as the estimated outcome from taking the action chosen in that game. The number e estimates the expected payoff for the player on turn, given his current probability distribution over the actions $\mathbf{A}$. The statement $\mathbf{E} \leftarrow \mathbf{E} - \mathbf{1}e$ normalizes $\mathbf{E}$ by deducting e from each component. $\mathbf{F}$ is the calculated vector of feedback, and the term $-\mathbf{1}(p_{sum} - 1)$ is included in order to push the NN function (B or R) towards valid probability distributions.

7   Evaluation Criteria

Defining evaluation criteria for two-player zero-sum games is less straightforward than one might believe, because agents tend to beat each other in circle. Ideally, we would like to apply the performance measure of *equity against globally optimizing opponent* (*Geq*) as described in [15]. The *Geq* measure is defined as the expected payoff when the agent plays against its most effective opponent (the *best response strategy* in game-theoretic terms). The *Geq* measure conforms with game theory in the sense that an agent applies a minimax strategy if, and only if, its *Geq* is equal to the game's value (which is the maximum *Geq* achievable).

Although we develop our Blue and Red players as separate agents that compete against each other, it is convenient for the purpose of evaluation to merge them into one agent that can play both sides. For agents of this form, a single game is implemented as a pair of games, so that both agents get to play both sides. For the sake of variance reduction, we hold the cards fixed in both games, so that both agents get to play the same deal from both sides. We take the average of the two outcomes as the merged game's outcome. The redefinition of the game as a pair of games has the advantage that the value is known to be zero, by symmetry.

We use a set of three reference players, named *Balanced-player*, *Aggressive-player* and *Random-player*. Balanced-player is our best estimate of a minimax-playing agent. Our first implementation of this agent turned out to have significant weaknesses, and the final one was developed through experimenting with (in parts even imitating) our NN agents. Aggressive-player is a modification of Balanced-player that folds only a few hands and raises often. Random-player makes completely random actions, with uniform probabilities over actions. It is included mostly for reference, as it is unlikely that it can ever be the most effective opponent.

8 Experimental Results

The step size for the NN back-propagation update started at 0.5 at the beginning of the training session, and was tuned down to 0.1 after 50,000 training games. The NNs were initialized with random weights. Figure 3 shows the estimated performance against the three reference opponents as a function of the number of training games.

We observe that the agent initially scores approximately 0 against Random-player, which is reasonable. We also see that Aggressive-player is the most effective opponent by a large margin at this point. The reason for this is that a randomly playing agent will sometimes fold after a sequence of raises, which is extremely costly. Against Balanced-player, the agent does not get the chance to make this error so often. Recall that our agent learns by adapting to its opponent (its own other half in the evaluation procedure). It therefore first learns strategies that are effective against a random opponent, which means that it begins to resemble Aggressive-player. This explains why it quickly scores so well against Random-player. Once the agent has learned not to fold so often, it starts to appreciate the value of good cards, and stops raising with weak hands. From then on, its strategy moves towards that of Balanced-player. The figure shows that when the agent becomes sufficiently skilled, it starts beating Aggressive-player, and Balanced-player takes over as the most effective opponent. The fluctuations in the diagrammed performance graphs are mainly due to randomness in the procedure of sampling the performances. Note that the random noise in the sampling of the performance against Balanced-player falls towards zero. This is because their strategies become similar, which makes the variance reduction trick of playing the same cards both ways more effective.

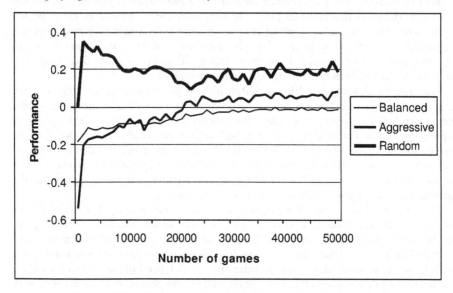

Fig. 3. Performance against reference opponents

The procedure of defining a set of opponents, and taking the result against the most effective of these, is a practical approach to estimating the *Geq* of an agent. According to this test, our NN based player appears to approach minimax play. Unfortunately, our small set of opponents is not sufficient to convince us. However, we are able to estimate the *Geq* quite accurately, through optimization. In this calculation we analyze one opponent hand at the time, and experimentally determine the most effective opponent strategy. For each of the 169 different hands, we have completed 10,000 test games for each deterministic playing strategy (derived from the decision tree of Figure 1). These calculations are rather time consuming, so we have not been able to produce learning curves with respect to this measure, but only analyzed the NN agent resulting from the complete training session. The learning curves of Figure 3 have actually been truncated, in order to highlight the interesting phenomena close to the start of the session. After 200,000 training games, our agent broke exactly even (to three decimal places) against Balanced-player. The massive optimization calculation gave a *Geq* estimate of –0.005 for this NN agent, which gives strong evidence that it is in fact close to minimax play.

Our fully trained agent has discovered a rather non-trivial fact that we hold to be true (or close to true) also for full-scale Hold'em: As Red it never calls the blind bet, but either folds or raises. Calling the blind bet is often a bad idea, because it leaves the opponent with the option of raising without putting on any pressure. If Red believes that he can make a profit by playing a hand (folding gives payoff 0), he should probably raise the stakes. Some humans like to call the blind bet with strong hands, with the intention of re-raising if Blue is tempted to raise. We do not think this is a sound strategy, because Red would also have to call with some weak or intermediate hands in order not to reveal his hand when he calls. We believe that the downside of playing these hands outweighs the benefit of sometimes getting to re-raise with the strong hands.

An open question that remains is why the algorithm works so well without the anchors. We know from formal analysis that the gradient ascent algorithm fails for matrix games with mixed strategy solutions, and the non-linearity of our Poker game is not likely to do any good. In our opinion, the reason is that there exist minimax strategies that are only marginally random. Every Poker player knows the importance of being unpredictable, so it may sound odd that good play requires little randomization. The explanation is that the random card deal does the randomization for the player. Although the player's betting is a deterministic function of his private cards, the randomness of the cards is sufficient to keep the opponent uncertain about the true state of the game. There probably exist borderline hands (e.g. hands on the border between an initial pass and raise for Red) that would be treated randomly by an exact minimax solution, but given the large number of possible hands, these are not very important.

9 Conclusion

We have implemented a reinforcement learning algorithm for neural net-based agents playing a simplified, yet non-trivial version of Hold'em poker. The experiments have been successful, as the agents appear to approximate minimax play. The algorithm is a special case of one that is to appear in the journal *Machine Learning*.

References

1. Dahl, F.A.: The lagging anchor algorithm. Reinforcement learning in two-player zero-sum games with imperfect information. *Machine Learning* (to appear).
2. Owen, G.: *Game Theory. 3rd ed.* Academic Press, San Diego (1995).
3. Sutton, R.S.: Learning to predict by the methods of temporal differences. *Machine Learning* 3 (1988) 9–44.
4. Watkins, C.J.C.H.: *Learning from Delayed Rewards.* PhD thesis, University of Cambridge, UK (1989).
5. Szepesvari, C., Littman, M.L.: A unified analysis of value-function-based reinforcement-learning algorithms. *Neural Computation* 11 (1999) 2017–2060.
6. Tesauro, G.J.: Practical issues in temporal difference learning. *Machine Learning* 8 (1992) 257–277.
7. Littman, M.L.: Markov games as a framework for multi-agent reinforcement learning. In: *Proceedings of the 11th International Conference on Machine Learning*, Morgan Kaufmann, New Brunswick (1994) 157–163.
8. Dahl F.A., Halck O.M.: Minimax TD-learning with neural nets in a Markov game. In: Lopez de Mantaras, R., Plaza, E. (eds.): *ECML 2000. Proceedings of the 11th European Conference on Machine Learning.* Lecture Notes in Computer Science Vol. 1810, Springer-Verlag, Berlin–Heidelberg–New York (2000) 117–128.

9. Koller, D., Megiddo, N., von Stengel, B.: Efficient computation of equilibria for extensive two-person games. *Games and Economic Behavior* 14 (1996) 247–259.
10. Luce, R.D., Raiffa, H.: *Games and Decisions*. Wiley, New York (1957).
11. Koller, D., Pfeffer, A.: Representations and solutions for game-theoretic problems. *Artificial Intelligence* 94 (1997) 167–215.
12. Schaeffer, J., Billings, D., Peña, L., Szafron, D.: Learning to play strong poker. In: Fürnkranz, J., Kubat, M. (eds.): *Proceedings of the ICML-99 Workshop on Machine Learning in Game Playing*, Jozef Stefan Institute, Ljubljana (1999).
13. Hassoun, M.H.: *Fundamentals of Artificial Neural Networks*. MIT Press, Cambridge, Massachusetts (1995).
14. Selten R. (1991). Anticipatory learning in two-person games, in: Selten, R. (ed.): *Game equilibrium models, vol. I: Evolution and game dynamics*, Springer-Verlag, Berlin.
15. Halck, O.M., Dahl, F.A.: On classification of games and evaluation of players – with some sweeping generalizations about the literature. In: Fürnkranz, J., Kubat, M. (eds.): *Proceedings of the ICML-99 Workshop on Machine Learning in Game Playing*, Jozef Stefan Institute, Ljubljana (1999).

Speeding Up Relational Reinforcement Learning through the Use of an Incremental First Order Decision Tree Learner

Kurt Driessens, Jan Ramon, and Hendrik Blockeel

Department of Computer Science K.U.Leuven
Celestijnenlaan 200A, B-3001 Leuven, Belgium
{kurt.driessens,jan.ramon,hendrik.blockeel}@cs.kuleuven.ac.be

Abstract. Relational reinforcement learning (RRL) is a learning technique that combines standard reinforcement learning with inductive logic programming to enable the learning system to exploit structural knowledge about the application domain.

This paper discusses an improvement of the original RRL. We introduce a fully incremental first order decision tree learning algorithm TG and integrate this algorithm in the RRL system to form RRL-TG.

We demonstrate the performance gain on similar experiments to those that were used to demonstrate the behaviour of the original RRL system.

1 Introduction

Relational reinforcement learning is a learning technique that combines reinforcement learning with relational learning or inductive logic programming. Due to the use of a more expressive representation language to represent states, actions and Q-functions, relational reinforcement learning can be potentially applied to a wider range of learning tasks than conventional reinforcement learning. In particular, relational reinforcement learning allows the use of structural representations, the abstraction from specific goals and the exploitation of results from previous learning phases when addressing new (more complex) situations.

The RRL concept was introduced by Džeroski, De Raedt and Driessens in [5]. The next sections focus on a few details and the shortcomings of the original implementation and the improvements we suggest. They mainly consist of a fully incremental first order decision tree algorithm that is based on the G-tree algorithm of Chapman and Kaelbling [4].

We start with a discussion of the implementation of the original RRL system. We then introduce the TG-algorithm and discuss its integration into RRL to form RRL-TG. Then an overview of some preliminary experiments is given to compare the performance of the original RRL system to RRL-TG and we discuss some of the characteristics of RRL-TG.

L. De Raedt and P. Flach (Eds.): ECML 2001, LNAI 2167, pp. 97–108, 2001.
© Springer-Verlag Berlin Heidelberg 2001

Initialise $\hat{Q}_0$ to assign 0 to all (s, a) pairs
Initialise Examples to the empty set.
e := 0
while true
    generate an episode that consists of states s_0 to s_i and actions a_0 to a_{i-1}
        (where a_j is the action taken in state s_j) through the use of a standard
        Q-learning algorithm, using the current hypothesis for $\hat{Q}_e$
    for j=i-1 to 0 **do**
        generate example $x = (s_j, a_j, \hat{q}_j)$,
            where $\hat{q}_j := r_j + \gamma max_{a'} \hat{Q}_e(s_{j+1}, a)$
        if an example $(s_j, a_j, \hat{q}_{old})$ exists in Examples, replace it with x,
            else add x to Examples
    update $\hat{Q}_e$ using TILDE to produce $\hat{Q}_{e+1}$ using Examples
    for j=i-1 to 0 **do**
        for all actions a_k possible in state s_j **do**
            if state action pair (s_j, a_k) is optimal according to $\hat{Q}_{e+1}$
            then generate example (s_j, a_k, c) where $c = 1$
            else generate example (s_j, a_k, c) where $c = 0$
    update $\hat{P}_e$ using TILDE to produce $\hat{P}_{e+1}$ using these examples (s_j, a_k, c)
    e := e + 1

Fig. 1. The RRL algorithm.

2   Relational Reinforcement Learning

The RRL-algorithm consists of two learning tasks. In a first step, the classical Q-learning algorithm is extended by using a relational regression algorithm to represent the Q-function with a logical regression tree, called the Q-tree. In a second step, this Q-tree is used to generate a P-function. This P-function describes the optimality of a given action in a given state, i.e., given a state-action pair, the P-function describes whether this pair is a part of an optimal policy. The P-function is represented by a logical decision tree, called the P-tree. More information on logical decision trees (classification and regression) can be found in [1,2].

2.1   The Original RRL Implementation

Figure 1 presents the original RRL algorithm. The logical regression tree that represents the Q-function in RRL is built starting from a knowledge base which holds correct examples of state, action and Q-function value triplets. To generate the examples for tree induction, RRL starts with running a normal episode just like a standard reinforcement learning algorithm [10,9,6] and stores the states, actions and q-values encountered in a temporary table. At the end of each episode, this table is added to a knowledge base which is then used for the tree induction phase. In the next episode, the q-values predicted by the generated tree are used to calculate the q-values for the new examples, but the Q-tree is generated again from scratch.

The examples used to generate the P-tree are derived from the obtained Q-tree. For each state the RRL system encounters during an episode, it investigates all possible actions and classifies those actions as optimal or not according to the q-values predicted by the learned Q-tree. Each of these classifications together with the according states and actions are used as input for the P-tree building algorithm.

Note that old examples are kept in the knowledge base at all times and never deleted. To avoid having too much old (and noisy) examples in the knowledge base, if a state–action pair is encountered more than once, the old example in the knowledge base is replaced with a new one which holds the updated q-value.

2.2   Problems with the Original RRL

We identify four problems with the original RRL implementation that diminish its performance. First, it needs to keep track of an ever increasing amount of examples: for each different state-action pair ever encountered a Q-value is kept. Second, when a state-action pair is encountered for the second time, the new Q-value needs to replace the old value, which means that in the knowledge base the old example needs to be looked up and replaced. Third, trees are built from scratch after each episode. This step, as well as the example replacement procedure, takes increasingly more time as the set of examples grows. A final point is that leaves of a tree are supposed to identify clusters of equivalent state-action pairs, "equivalent" in the sense that they all have the same Q-value. When updating the Q-value for one state-action pair in a leaf, the Q-value of all pairs in the leaf should automatically be updated; but this is not what is done in the original implementation; an existing (state,action,Q) example gets an updated Q-value at the moment when exactly the same state-action pair is encountered, instead of a state-action pair in the same leaf.

2.3   Possible Improvements

To solve these problems, a fully incremental induction algorithm is needed. Such an algorithm would relieve the need for the regeneration of the tree when new data becomes available. However, not just any incremental algorithm can be used. Q-values generated with reinforcement learning are usually wrong at the beginning and the algorithm needs to handle this appropriately.

Also an algorithm that doesn't require old examples to be kept for later reference, eliminates the use of old information to generalise from and thus eliminates the need for replacement of examples in the knowledge base. In a fully incremental system, the problem of storing different q-values for similar but distinct state-action pairs should also be solved.

In the following section we introduce such an incremental algorithm.

3   The TG Algorithm

3.1   The G-Algorithm

We use a learning algorithm that is an extension of the G-algorithm [4]. This is a decision tree learning algorithm that updates its theory incrementally as examples are added. An important feature is that examples can be discarded after they are processed. This avoids using a huge amount of memory to store examples.

On a high level (cf. Figure 2), the G-algorithm (as well as the new TG-algorithm) stores the current decision tree, and for each leaf node statistics for all tests that could be used to split that leaf further. Each time an example is inserted, it is sorted down the decision tree according to the tests in the internal nodes, and in the leaf the statistics of the tests are updated.

```
create an empty leaf
while data available do
    split data down to leafs
    update statistics in leaf
    if split needed then
        grow two empty leafs
endwhile
```

Fig. 2. The TG-algorithm.

The examples are generated by a simulator of the environment, according to some reinforcement learning strategy. They are tuples (*State, Action, QValue*).

3.2   Extending to First Order Logic

We extend the G algorithm in that we use a relational representation language for describing the examples and for the tests that can be used in the decision tree. This has several advantages. First, it allows us to model examples that can't be stored in a propositional way. Second, it allows us to model the feature space. Even when it would be possible in theory to enumerate all features, as in the case of the blocks world with a limited number of blocks, a problem is only tractable when a smaller number of features is used. The relational language can be seen as a way to construct useful features. E.g. when there are no blocks on some block A, it is not useful to provide a feature to see which blocks are on A. Also, the use of a relational language allows us to structure the feature space as e.g. on(State,block_a,block_b) and on(State,block_c,block_d) are treated in exactly the same way.

The construction of new tests happens by a refinement operator. A more detailed description of this part of the system can be found in [1].

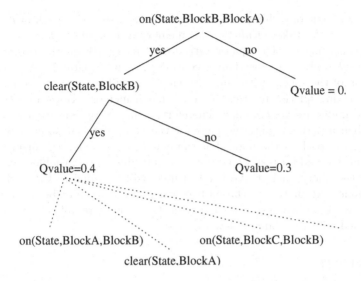

Fig. 3. A logical decision tree

Figure 3 gives an example of a logical decision tree. The test in some node should be read as the existentially quantified conjunction of all literals in the nodes in the path from the root of the tree to that node.

The statistics for each leaf consist of the number of examples on which each possible test succeeds, the sum of their Q values and the sum of squared Q values. Moreover, the Q value to predict in that leaf is stored. This value is obtained from the statistics of the test used to split its parent when the leaf was created. Later, this value is updated as new examples are sorted in the leaf. These statistics are sufficient to compute whether some test is significant, i.e. the variance of the Q-values of the examples would be reduced by splitting the node using that particular test. A node is split after some minimal number of examples are collected and some test becomes significant with a high confidence.

In contrast to the propositional system, keeping track of the candidate-tests (the refinements of a query) is a non-trivial task. In the propositional case the set of candidate queries consists of the set of all features minus the features that are already tested higher in the tree. In the first order case, the set of candidate queries consists of all possible ways to extend a query. The longer a query is and the more variables it contains, the larger is the number of possible ways to bind the variables and the larger is the set of candidate tests.

Since a large number of such candidate tests exist, we need to store them as efficiently as possible. To this aim we use the query packs mechanism introduced in [3]. A query pack is a set of similar queries structured into a tree; common parts of the queries are represented only once in such a structure. For instance, a set of conjunctions $\{(p(X), q(X)), (p(X), r(X))\}$ is represented as a term $p(X), (q(X); r(X))$. This can yield a significant gain in practice. (E.g., assuming a constant branching factor of b in the tree, storing a pack of n queries of length l ($n = b^l$) takes $O(nb/(b-1))$ memory instead of $O(nl)$.)

Also, executing a set of queries structured in a pack on the examples requires considerably less time than executing them all separately. An empirical comparison of the speeds with and without packs will be given in section 1.

Even storing queries in packs requires much memory. However, the packs in the leaf nodes are very similar. Therefore, a further optimisation is to reuse them. When a node is split, the pack for the new right leaf node is the same as the original pack of the node. For the new left sub-node, we currently only reuse them if we add a test which does not introduce new variables because in that case the query pack in the left leaf node will be equal to the pack in the original node (except for the chosen test which of course can't be taken again). In further work, we will also reuse query packs in the more difficult case when a test is added which introduces new variables.

3.3   RRL-TG

To integrate the TG-algorithm into RRL we removed the calls to the TILDE algorithm and use TG to adapt the Q-tree and P-tree when new experience (in the form of (*State, Action, QValue*) triplets) is available. Thereby, we solved the problems mentioned in Section 2.2.

- The trees are no longer generated from scratch after each episode.
- Because TG only stores statistics about the examples in the tree and only references these examples once (when they are inserted into the tree) the need for remembering and therefore searching and replacing examples is relieved.
- Since TG begins each new leaf with completely empty statistics, examples have a limited life span and old (possibly noisy) q-value examples will be deleted even if the exact same state-action pair is not encountered twice.

Since the bias used by this incremental algorithm is the same as with TILDE, the same theories can be learned by TG. Both algorithms search the same hypothesis space and although TG can be misled in the beginning due to its incremental nature, in the limit the quality of approximations of the q-values will be the same.

4   Experiments

In this section we compare the performance of the new RRL-TG with the original RRL system. Further comparison with other systems is difficult because there are no other implementations of RRL so far. Also, the number of first order regression techniques is limited and a full comparison of first order regression is outside the scope of this paper.

In a first step, we reran the experiments described in [5]. The original RRL was tested on the blocks world [8] with three different goals: unstacking all blocks, stacking all blocks and stacking two specific blocks. Blocks can be on the floor or can be stacked on each other. Each state can be described by a set (list) of facts, e.g., $s_1 = \{clear(a), on(a, b), on(b, c), on(c, floor)\}$. The available actions are then $move(x, y)$ where $x \neq y$ and x is a block and y is a block or the floor. The unstacking goal is reached when all blocks are on the floor, the stacking goal when only one block is on the floor. The goal of stacking two specific blocks (e.g. a and b) is reached when the fact $on(a, b)$ is part of the state description, note however that RRL learns to stack any two specific blocks by generalising from $on(a, b)$ or $on(c, d)$ to $on(X, Y)$ where X and Y can be substituted for any two blocks. In the first type of experiments, a Q-function was learned for state-spaces with 3, 4 and 5 blocks. In the second type, a more general strategy for each goal was learned by using policy learning on state-spaces with a varying number of blocks.

Afterwards, we discuss some experiments to study the convergence behaviour of the TG-algorithm and the sensitivity of the algorithm to some of its parameters.

4.1   Fixed State Spaces

For the experiments with a fixed number of blocks, the results are shown in Figure 4. The generated policies were tested on 10 000 randomly generated examples. A reward of 1 was given if the goal-state was reached in the minimal number of steps. The graphs show the average reward per episode. This gives an

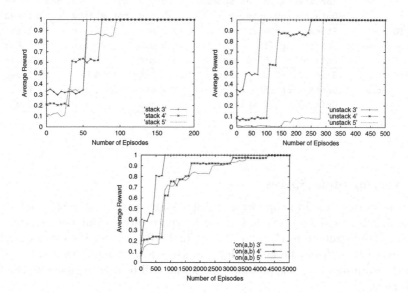

Fig. 4. The learning curves for fixed numbers of blocks

indication of how well the Q-function generates the optimal policy. Compared to the original system, the number of episodes needed for the algorithm to converge to the correct policy is much larger. This can be explained by two characteristics of the new system. Where the original system would automatically correct its mistakes when generating the next tree by starting from scratch, the new system has to compensate for the mistakes it makes near the root of the tree — due to faulty Q-values generated at the beginning — by adding extra branches to the tree. To compensate for this fact a parameter has been added to the TG-algorithm which specifies the number of examples that need to be filed in a leaf, before the leaf can be split. These two factors — the overhead for correcting mistakes and the delay put on splitting leaves — cause the new RRL system to converge slower when looking at the number of episodes.

However, when comparing timing results the new system clearly outperforms the old one, even with the added number of necessary episodes. Table 1 compares the execution times of RRL-TG with the timings of the RRL system given in [5]. For the original RRL system, running experiments in state spaces with more than 5 blocks quickly became impossible. Learning in a state-space with 8 blocks, RRL-TG took 6.6 minutes to learn for 1000 episodes, enough to allow it to converge for the stacking goal.

Table 1. Execution time of the RRL algorithm on Sun Ultra 5/270 machines.

		3 blocks	4 blocks	5 blocks
Original RRL	Stacking (30 episodes)	6.15 min	62.4 min	306 min
	Unstacking (30 episodes)	8.75 min	not stated	not stated
	On(a,b) (30 episodes)	20 min	not stated	not stated
RRL-TG without packs	Stacking (200 episodes)	19.2 sec	26.5 sec	39.3 sec
	Unstacking (500 episodes)	1.10 min	1.92 min	2.75 min
	On(a,b) (5000 episodes)	25.0 min	57 min	102 min
RRL-TG with packs	Stacking (200 episodes)	8.12 sec	11.4 sec	16.1 sec
	Unstacking (500 episodes)	20.2 sec	35.2 sec	53.7 sec
	On(a,b) (5000 episodes)	5.77 min	7.37 min	11.5 min

4.2   Varying State Spaces

In [5] the strategy used to cope with multiple state-spaces was to start learning on the smallest and then expand the state-space after a number of learning episodes. This strategy worked for the original RRL system because examples were never erased from the knowledge base, so when changing to a new state-space the examples from the previous one would still be used to generate the Q- and P-trees.

However, if we apply the same strategy to RRL-TG, the TG-algorithm first generates a tree for the small state-space and after changing to a larger state-space, it expands the tree to fit the new state space, completely forgetting what it has learned by adding new branches to the tree, thereby making the tests in the original tree insignificant. It would never generalise over the different state-spaces. Instead, we offer a different state-space to RRL-TG every episode. This way, the examples the TG-algorithm uses to split leaves will come from different state-spaces and allow RRL-TG to generalise over them. In the experiments on the blocks world, we varied the number of blocks between 3 and 5 while learning. To make sure that the examples are spread throughout several state-spaces we set the minimal number of examples needed to split a leaf to 2400, quite a bit higher than for fixed state-spaces. As a result, RRL-TG requires a higher number of episodes to converge.

At episode 15000, P-learning was started. Note that since P-learning depends on the presence of good Q-values, in the incremental tree learning setting it is unwise to start building P-trees from the beginning, because the Q-values at that time are misleading, causing suboptimal splits to be inserted into the P-tree in the beginning. Due to the incremental nature of the learning process, these suboptimal splits are not removed afterwards, which in the end leads to a more complex tree that is learned more slowly. By letting P-learning start only after a reasonable number of episodes, this effect is reduced, although not necessarily entirely removed (as Q-learning continues in parallel with P-learning).

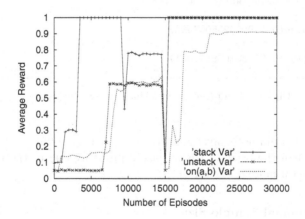

Fig. 5. The learning curves for varying numbers of blocks. P-learning is started at episode 15 000.

Figure 5 shows the learning curves for the three different goals. The generated policies were tested on 10 000 randomly generated examples with the number of blocks varying between 3 and 10. The first part of the curves indicate how well the policy generated by the Q-tree performs. From episode 15000 onwards, when P-learning is started, the test results are based on the P-tree instead of the Q-tree; on the graphs this is visible as a sudden drop of performance back to almost zero, followed by a new learning curve (since P-learning starts from scratch). It can be seen that P-learning converges fast to a better performance level than Q-learning attained. After P-learning starts, the Q-tree still gets updated, but no longer tested. We can see that although the Q-tree is not able to generalise over unseen state-spaces, the P-tree — which is derived from the Q-tree — usually can.

The jump to an accuracy of 1 in the Q-learning phase for stacking the blocks is purely accidental, and disappears when the Q-tree starts to model the encountered state-spaces more accurately. The generated Q-tree at that point in time is shown in Figure 6. Although this tree does not represent the correct Q-function in any way, it does — by accident — lead to the correct policy for stacking any number of blocks. Later on in the experiment, the Q-tree will be much larger and represent the Q-function much closer, but it does not represent an overall optimal policy anymore.

```
state(S),action_move(X,Y),numberofblocks(S,N)
  height(S,Y,H),diff(N,H,D),D<2 ?
    yes:
      qvalue(1.0)
    no:
      height(S,B,C),height(S,Y,D), D < C ?
        yes:
          qvalue(0.149220955007456)
        no:
          qvalue(0.507386078412001)
```

Fig. 6. The Q-tree for Stacking after 4000 episodes

The algorithm did not converge for the $On(A, B)$ goal but we did get better performance than the original RRL. This is probably due to the fact that we were able to learn more episodes.

4.3   The Minimal Sample Size

We decided to further explore the behaviour of the RRL-TG algorithm with respect to the delay parameter which specifies the minimal sample size for TG to split a leaf. To test the effect of the minimal sample size, we started RRL-TG for a total of 10 000 episodes and started P-learning after 5000 episodes. We then varied the minimal sample size from 50 to 2000 examples. We ran these tests with the unstacking goal.

Figure 7 shows the learning curves for the different settings, Table 2 shows the sizes of the resulting trees after 10 000 episodes (with P-learning starting at episode 5000. The algorithm does not converge for a sample size of 50 examples. Even after P-learning optimality is not reached. The algorithm makes too many

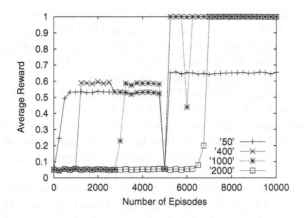

Fig. 7. The learning curves for varying minimal sample sizes

mistakes by relying on too small a set of examples when choosing a test. With an increasing sample size comes a slower convergence to the optimal policy. For a sample size of 1000 examples, the dip in the learning curve during P-learning is caused by a change in the Q-function (which is still being learned during the second phase). When looking at the sizes of the generated trees, it is obvious that the generated policies benefit from a larger minimal sample size, at the cost of slower convergence. Although experiments with a smaller minimal sample size have to correct for their early mistakes by building larger trees, they often still succeed in generating an optimal policy.

Table 2. The generated tree sizes for varying minimal sample sizes

	50	400	1000	2000
Q-tree	31	26	16	9
P-tree	9	10	8	8

5   Concluding Remarks

This paper described how we upgraded the G-tree algorithm of Chapman and Kaelbling [4] to the new TG-algorithm and by doing so greatly improved the speed of the RRL system presented in [5].

We studied the convergence behaviour of RRL-TG with respect to the minimal sample size TG needs to split a leaf. Larger sample sizes mean slower convergence but smaller function representations.

We are planning to apply the RRL algorithm to the Tetris game to study the behaviour of RRL in more complex domains than the blocks world.

Future work will certainly include investigating other representation possibilities for the Q-function. Work towards first order neural networks and Bayesian networks [7] seems to provide promising alternatives.

Further work on improving the TG algorithm will include the use of multiple trees to represent the Q- and P-functions and further attempts to decrease the amount of used memory. Also, some work should be done to automatically find the moment to start P-learning and the optimal minimal sample size. Both will influence the size of the generated policy and the convergence speed of TG-RRL.

Acknowledgements. The authors would like to thank Sašo Džeroski, Luc De Raedt and Maurice Bruynooghe for their suggestions concerning this work. Jan Ramon is supported by the Flemish Institute for the Promotion of Science and Technological Research in Industry (IWT). Hendrik Blockeel is a post-doctoral fellow of the Fund for Scientific Research of Flanders (FWO-Vlaanderen).

References

1. H. Blockeel and L. De Raedt. Top-down induction of first order logical decision trees. *Artificial Intelligence*, 101(1-2):285–297, June 1998.
2. H. Blockeel, L. De Raedt, and J. Ramon. Top-down induction of clustering trees. In *Proceedings of the 15th International Conference on Machine Learning*, pages 55–63, 1998. http://www.cs.kuleuven.ac.be/~ml/PS/ML98-56.ps.
3. H. Blockeel, B. Demoen, L. Dehaspe, G. Janssens, J. Ramon, and H. Vandecasteele. Executing query packs in ILP. In J. Cussens and A. Frisch, editors, *Proceedings of the 10th International Conference in Inductive Logic Programming*, volume 1866 of *Lecture Notes in Artificial Intelligence*, pages 60–77, London, UK, July 2000. Springer.
4. David Chapman and Leslie P. Kaelbling. Input generalization in delayed reinforcement learning: An algorithm and performance comparisions. In *Proceedings of the International Joint Conference on Artificial Intelligence*, 1991.
5. S. Džeroski, L. De Raedt, and K. Driessens. Relational reinforcement learning. *Machine Learning*, 43:7–52, 2001.
6. L. Kaelbling, M. Littman, and A. Moore. Reinforcement learning: A survey. *Journal of Artificial Intelligence Research*, 4:237–285, 1996.
7. K. Kersting and L. De Raedt. Bayesian logic programs. In *Proceedings of the tenth international conference on inductive logic programming, work in progress track*, 2000.
8. P. Langley. *Elements of Machine Learning*. Morgan Kaufmann, 1996.
9. T. Mitchell. *Machine Learning*. McGraw-Hill, 1997.
10. R. Sutton and A. Barto. *Reinforcement Learning: an introduction*. The MIT Press, Cambridge, MA, 1998.

Analysis of the Performance of AdaBoost.M2 for the Simulated Digit-Recognition-Example

Günther Eibl and Karl Peter Pfeiffer

Institute of Biostatistics, Innsbruck, Austria
guenther.eibl@uibk.ac.at

Abstract. In simulation studies boosting algorithms seem to be susceptible to noise. This article applies Ada.Boost.M2 used with decision stumps to the digit recognition example, a simulated data set with attribute noise. Although the final model is both simple and complex enough, boosting fails to reach the Bayes error. A detailed analysis shows some characteristics of the boosting trials which influence the lack of fit.

1 Introduction

Boosting algorithms were originally designed to turn weak classifiers into strong ones. The performance of such boosted classifiers turned out to be so good that they became an own discipline in the field of pattern recognition. However boosting algorithms seem to have disadvantages at noisy data sets ([1,4,6,7,10]). The aim of this paper is to apply a boosting algorithm to a simulated data set with attribute noise, analyze its behaviour and find some characteristics that affect the performance of boosting. The digit example is a well known artificial example, so it is possible to compare the result with the true structure of the problem. The chosen boosting classifier is AdaBoost.M2 with decision stumps as base classifiers.

2 AdaBoost.M2 with Decision Stumps for the Digit Dataset

2.1 The Digit Dataset

The artificial digit example is a simulation of a faulty digit display ([2]). The representation of a digit on a display consists of 7 lights, which can be lighted or not (Fig.1). Each representation x of a digit is an element of the set $\{0,1\}^7$, where $x_j = 1$ means, that light number j is lighted and $x_j = 0$ means, that light number j is not lighted. The proper representation of digits $0, \ldots, 9$ is given in figure 1. For example the proper representation of digit 1 is $x = (0, 0, 1, 0, 0, 1, 0)$. One can also say, that $x = (0, 0, 1, 0, 0, 1, 0)$ is the *prototype* of group 1.

The display is simulated to be faulty in displaying digits. All seven lights are independently properly lighted with probability 0.9 and faultily lighted with probability 0.1. So the probability, that a digit is properly represented is 0.9^7,

L. De Raedt and P. Flach (Eds.): ECML 2001, LNAI 2167, pp. 109–120, 2001.
© Springer-Verlag Berlin Heidelberg 2001

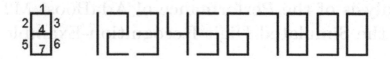

Fig. 1. Representation of a digit and prototypes of the digits

which is about 0.48. Now we define the *similarity* of a digit x to a group g as the number of identical lights of x and the prototype of group g. The Bayes classifier assigns an unknown digit x to the most similar group. If this most similar group is not uniquely defined, the group gets chosen by chance among the most similar groups. The error rate of the Bayes classifier is 0.26. The most important characteristics of the data set are given in Table 1

Table 1. Properties of the digit example

♯ groups	♯ input variables	♯ training set	Bayes error	SNR
10	7	1000	0.26	0.9

2.2   Decision Stumps

Since we use decision stumps as base classifiers we introduce some notation here. A decision stump h is a classification tree with 2 leaves. For the digit example this means that the decision stump chooses a variable j and divides the learning set $\{(x_1, g_1), \ldots, (x_N, g_N); x_i \in X, g_i \in G\}$ into the two leaves $l_0 := \{(x_i, g_i); x_{ij} = 0\}$ and $l_1 := \{(x_i, g_i); x_{ij} = 1\}$. Now we call N_k the number of elements of leave l_k and $N_k(g)$ the number of elements of group g in leave l_k. Then the decision stump estimates the probability that a new, unknown digit x belongs to group g as the corresponding group proportion $\pi_0(g) := N_0(g) \backslash N_0$ if $x_j = 0$ and $\pi_1(g) := N_1(g) \backslash N_1$ if $x_j = 1$.
The result is a map

$$h : \{0, 1\}^7 \times \{0, 1\}^{10} \to [0, 1], \quad h(x, g) := \pi_0(g)[[x_j = 0]] + \pi_1(g)[[x_j = 1]], \quad (1)$$

where $[[\cdot]]$ is a function of boolean values with $[[\text{true}]] = 1$ and $[[\text{false}]] = 0$.

2.3   AdaBoost.M2

Boosting algorithms are often designed for classification of two groups. There are several extensions for problems with more than two classes ([3,5,8,10]). With X

designating the input space and G designating the set of groups the straightforward multiclass extension, AdaBoost.M1, combines base classifiers of the form $h : X \to G$ by majority vote like in the twoclass case. A big drawback of this approach is that the error rate of each base classifier should be less than 50% which can be difficult to reach especially for the multiclass case. For the digit example the error rate of a single decision stump which assigns a case to the group with highest probability is about 80%. So the use of the straightforward multiclass extension with decision stumps has a poor performance.

A more sophisticated multiclass extension is AdaBoost.M2 (Fig.2) published by Freund and Schapire ([5]). AdaBoost.M2 changes the goal of the weak classifiers to predict a set of plausible groups and evaluates the weak classifiers using the pseudo-loss ϵ_t (step 3) which penalizes the weak classifiers for failing to include the correct group in the predicted plausible group set and for each incorrect label in the predicted plausible group set. The exact form of the pseudo-loss is under control of the algorithm so that the weak classifier can focus also on the groups which are hardest to distinguish from the correct group by changing the matrix q. The following theorem guarantees the decrease of the training error as long as the pseudo-loss is less than $1/2$ which is much more easier to achieve than training error less than 50%:

Theorem 1. *Let* $\epsilon_t \leq \frac{1}{2} - \gamma$ *for* $\gamma \in (0,1)$. *Then the training error of AdaBoost.M2 is upper bounded by*

$$(|G| - 1) \, 2^T \prod_{t=1}^{T} \sqrt{\epsilon_t(1 - \epsilon_t)} \leq \exp(-2\gamma^2 T).$$

In every boosting round t the algorithm takes a bootstrap sample, where each case (x_i, g_i) is weighted with $D_t(i)$, from the learning set. This bootstrap sample is used for the construction of the weak classifier (step 2). Then the pseudo-loss of this classifier is calculated (step 3). The pseudo-loss is used for three purposes: First it is used for updating the sampling weights $D(i)$ and the matrix q for the next boosting round (steps 4,5 and 1). The algorithm focuses more on cases that were difficult to classify properly at the previous boosting round. Second, according to the theorem above, the algorithm stops if the pseudo-loss reaches $1/2$ (step 3). The third time the pseudo-loss is used for the weighted majority-vote of the T base classifiers (step 4 and output).

3   Application of AdaBoost.M2 with Decision Stumps on the Digit-Example

To study the algorithm systematically we applied it to 50 independently generated data sets of size 1000. Other algorithms were also applied to these 50 data sets using the number of boosting rounds of the original algorithm. Since the example is artificial the expected error could be calculated directly, so there was no need for a test set. All figures come from trial 31, for which both minimal and final training error are near the corresponding mean errors over all datasets. In figure 3 and table 2 scores are multiplied with 100 for sake of readability.

Algorithm AdaBoost.M2

Input: learning set $\{(x_1, g_1), \ldots, (x_N, g_N); x_i \in X, g_i \in G\}$, $G = \{1, \ldots, |G|\}$
   weak classifier of the form $h : X \times G \to [0, 1]$
   T: maximum number of boosting rounds

Initialization: $D_1(i) = 1/N$, weight vector $w_{i,g}^1 = D_1(i)/(|G| - 1)$

For $t = 1, \ldots, T$:

1. Set $W_i^t = \sum\limits_{g = g_i} w_{i,g}^t$

   for $g \neq g_i :$ $q_{i,g}^t = \dfrac{w_{i,g}^t}{W_i^t}$

   and

   $$D_t(i) = W_i^t / \sum_{i=1}^{N} W_i^t$$

2. Call the weak classifier h_t with data sampled from the learning set with distribution D_t

3. Calculate the pseudo-loss ϵ_t of h_t:

   $$\epsilon_t = \tfrac{1}{2} \sum_{i=1}^{N} D_t(i) \left(1 - h_t(x_i, g_i) + \tfrac{1}{|G|-1} \sum_{g = g_i} q_{i,g}^t h_t(x_i, g) \right)$$

   if $\epsilon_t \geq \tfrac{1}{2}$: $T := t - 1$, **goto** output step

4. Set $\alpha_t = \tfrac{1}{2} \ln(\tfrac{1 - \epsilon_t}{\epsilon_t})$

5. For $i = 1 \ldots, N$ and $g \in G \backslash \{g_i\}$ set the new weight vectors to be
   $$w_{i,g}^{t+1} = w_{i,g}^t e^{- \alpha_t (1 - h_t(x_i, g_i) + h_t(x_i, g))}$$

Output: final classifier $h_f(x)$: Normalize $(\alpha_t)_{t=1,\ldots,T}$ and set

$$h_f(x) = \arg\max_{g \ G} \sum_{t=1}^{T} \alpha_t h_t(x, g)$$

Fig. 2. AdaBoost.M2

3.1   The Final Model

As we have seen in the previous section the final classifier has the following form:

$$h_f(x) \quad = \quad \arg\max_{g \in G} \sum_{t=1}^{T} \alpha_t h_t(x, g) \ . \tag{2}$$

We can interpret the sum in (2) as a score for group g. Digit x is classified as the digit g with the highest score for instance x. For decision stumps each base hypothesis h_t depends only on one variable j which we will call $j(t)$. Inserting the definition of the decision stumps (1) in (2) we get after some rearrangements of terms

$$h_f(x) \quad = \quad \arg\max_{g \in G} \sum_{t=1}^{T} \alpha_t \left(\pi_0^t(g)[[x_{j(t)} = 0]] + \pi_1^t(g)[[x_{j(t)} = 1]] \right)$$

$$= \quad \arg\max_{g \in G} \sum_{t=1}^{T} \alpha_t \left(\pi_0^t(g) + (\pi_1^t(g) - \pi_0^t(g))x_{j(t)} \right)$$

$$= \arg\max_{g \in G} \left(\sum_{t=1}^{T} \alpha_t \pi_0^t(g) + \sum_{t=1}^{T} \sum_{j=1}^{7} \alpha_t [[j = j(t)]](\pi_1^t(g) - \pi_0^t(g))x_j \right) .$$

Setting

$$a_0(g) := \sum_{t=1}^{T} \alpha_t \pi_0^t(g)$$

and

$$a_j(g) := \sum_{t=1}^{T} \alpha_t [[j = j(t)]](\pi_1^t(g) - \pi_0^t(g))$$

we finally get

$$h_f(x) = \arg\max_{g \in G} \text{score}(g)(x) \tag{3}$$

$$\text{score}(g)(x) = a_0(g) + \sum_{j=1}^{7} a_j(g)x_j . \tag{4}$$

The resulting classifier can be shown graphically (Fig.3).

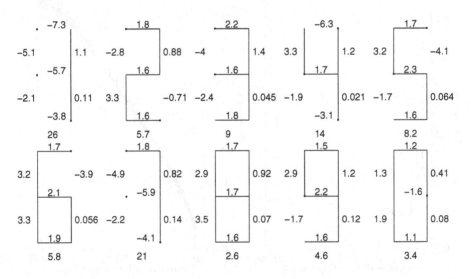

Fig. 3. Graphical representation of the resulting classifier

The figure consists of the prototypes of the 10 groups. To calculate for case x the score for group g look at the corresponding prototype. The number below is $a_0(g)$. Then for each of the 7 lights look at the number beside and above respectively and add it if light j of x is lighted ($x_j = 1$), otherwise add nothing.

As a result the final classifier can be represented by voting of the 10 scores score(1),...,score(10) where each score is a linear function of the 7 values x_j. The final classifier h_f is determined by fixing the 80 constants $a_j(g)$, $j = 0, \ldots, 7$, $g = 0, \ldots, 10$. This is a hint that we can get a quite complex classifier even from such simple base classifiers as decision stumps. Using classification trees with more leaves leads to interactions of higher orders with the disadvantage of loosing an easy interpretation like above.

3.2   Performance of the Algorithm

The boosting routine quickly diminishes the training error, showing some jumps of about 5 percent. The training error rate reaches a minimum and then slightly increases to a final training error (Fig.4). The jumps of the curve come from the fact, that at certain rounds t a prototype of a digit, which contains about 5% of all data, is assigned correctly and incorrectly respectively. Figure 4 shows that the pseudo loss increases with t, so the weights of the base classifiers in the combination step decrease. Therefore the changes of the final classifier get smaller which leads to the smoothness of the error curve at higher boosting rounds.

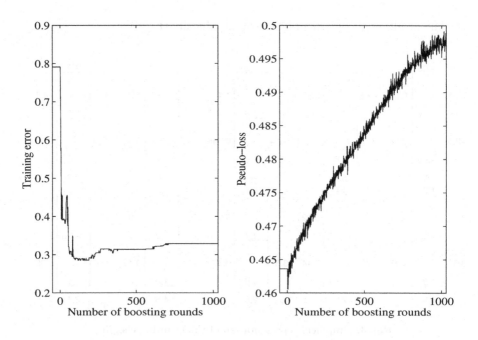

Fig. 4. Error (left) and pseudo loss (right) dependent on boosting round

This error curve is a typical one as can be seen by comparison with Table 3. The mean expected error of 34.3% is good in comparison with the error of the best single decision stump of 80%, but a comparison of the minimum test error with the Bayes error of 26% shows that there is much room for improvement.

Despite the additive structure of the problem and the simplicity of the final model the algorithm didn't manage to fit it well.

To be sure that the final model is complex enough we built an additive model whose scores are just the number of lights identical to the lights of the prototype of the corresponding group (Fig.5) which is just the Bayes classifier. Therefore we solved 10 systems of 128 linear equations. The ranks of all 10 corresponding matrices were full, so the representation of the desired score as an additive model is unique.

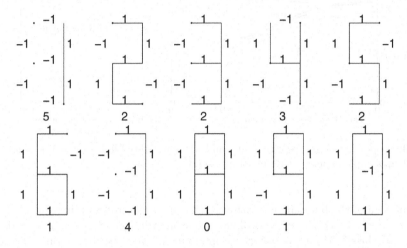

Fig. 5. Optimal additive model

An analysis of the results shows, that many digits are assigned wrongly to groups 1 and 7, because the scores for these two groups can get higher than the scores for the other eight groups (Table 2). An analysis of the algorithm shows that these two groups were chosen with higher probability the longer the boosting algorithm calculated (see Table 2 and Fig.6).

Table 2. Analysis of algorithm: $p_f(g)$: mean relative frequency of cases in the training set assigned to group g; score for group g: mean score(g) for cases in the training set of group g; Δp: mean difference between the group proportions at the last and the first boosting round in percent

group g	1	2	3	4	5	6	7	8	9	0
$p_f(g)$	**14.3**	8.9	6.5	10.0	10.1	12.0	**15.2**	9.1	6.1	7.8
score for group g	**23.0**	15.2	13.0	16.7	14.7	16.1	**19.6**	13.9	12.3	14.5
Δp	**9.9**	-3.8	-2.6	0.5	-2.9	-2.6	**10.7**	-2.6	-3.3	-3.4

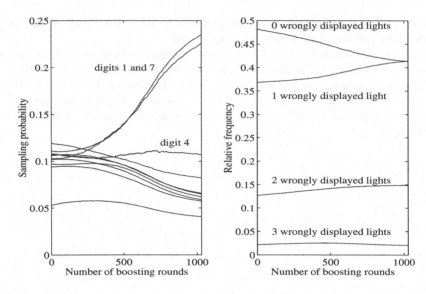

Fig. 6. Proportion of groups $\delta_t(g)$ (left) and wrongly lighted lights (right) in weighted bootstrap sample dependent on boosting round

The idea of the boosting algorithm is, that it concentrates on hard-to-classify training data. Since there is no obvious reason, why digits 1 and 7 should be harder to classify than the others we made an ad-hoc regularization of the algorithm by holding the group proportions constant. Therefore we inserted an additional normalization between step 1 and step 2 of AdaBoost.M2, we name it

$$\text{step } 1.5: \quad D_t(i) = D_t(i)\pi(g)/\delta_t(g), \quad \text{with } \delta_t(g) := \sum_{i;g_i=g} D_t(i) \ . \quad (5)$$

A natural choice for the constant group proportion $\pi(g)$ is the group prior estimated directly from the data

$$\pi(g) = \hat{\pi}(g) := \frac{N(g)}{N} \ .$$

We denote the algorithm using $\hat{\pi}(g)$ as AdaBoost$\hat{\pi}$. Since we know the real group proportion $\pi(g) = 0.1$ from theory we also used this choice and denote the corresponding algorithm as AdaBoostπ. Table 3 shows that AdaBoost$\hat{\pi}$ worked worse than the original algorithm, but AdaBoostπ brought a substantial improvement, so the exact knowledge about the true group proportions appears to be a crucial point for the modification. For a comparison we also applied bagging with confidence-rated votes to the data sets and got much worse classifiers (Table 3).

It's also interesting to see how the different error rates are made up of minimal training error, *overfit* and *generalization error*, where the overfit is defined as the difference between the final and minimal reached training error and the generalization error is the difference between the expected and training error of the classifier (Table 3). The two modified algorithms turned out to be more robust to overfitting, and as expected AdaBoostπ generalizes best. The greatest differences between the algorithms were seen in the minimal training error, where the 4 algorithms had the following ranking: AdaBoostπ, original AdaBoost.M2, AdaBoost$\hat{\pi}$, bagging. AdaBoost$\hat{\pi}$ comes closer to original AdaBoost.M2 because of its lower overfit, but this ranking also holds for the expected error of the final classifier.

Table 3. Comparison of algorithms

		AdaBoost.M2	AdaBoost$\hat{\pi}$	AdaBoostπ	Bagging
Final	MW	34,31	36,65	27,79	48,69
expected	STD	5,45	5,80	0,76	9,08
error	MIN	26,74	27,0	26,58	30,55
	MAX	48,69	53,77	30,20	74,80
Minimal	MW	28,67	32,54	26,06	40,06
training	STD	3,15	4,82	1,47	7,41
error	MIN	23,30	25,00	22,60	24,5
	MAX	37,20	47,20	29,70	61,5
Final	MW	32,60	34,26	27,33	45,32
training	STD	4,74	5,36	1,66	8,36
error	MIN	25,40	25,90	23,20	27,20
	MAX	45,40	48,80	30,80	71,10
Overfit	MW	3,93	1,72	1,27	5,26
	STD	2,98	2,03	0,79	5,51
	MIN	0,20	0,00	0,10	0,00
	MAX	12,4	7,30	3,50	31,00
Generalization	MW	1,71	2,39	0,47	3,37
error	STD	1,61	1,54	1,54	1,52
	MIN	-2,66	-1,18	-2,93	-1,21
	MAX	4,92	5,86	3,44	6,14

As we have seen above AdaBoost.M2 has some overfit which leads to the question how to choose the final boosting round T. We compared the original final classifier to the one which is the result of stopping at the minimal training error and the one which stops at the maximal sum of margins ([9], Table 4). Stopping at the minimal training error is clearly superior and leads to an improvement in expected error of $3.99 \pm 3.82\%$. The maximal margin approach was supposed to have less generalization error, but the generalization error was the same for all three stopping criteria.

Another interesting question is how noisy digits behave during the algorithm. To investigate this we saved at each boosting round the sampling weights of right

Table 4. Description of errors at the last round, the round with minimal training error (minerror) and the round with maximal margin (maxmargin)

method	T	training error(T)	expected error(T)
last round	1215±282	32.60±4.74	34.31±5.45
minerror	447±226	28.67±3.15	30.04±3.81
maxmargin	330±88	30.99±4.29	32.53±5.06

represented digits and digits with 1, 2 and 3 wrongly lighted lights respectively. As expected the proportion of digits with one and two wrongly lighted lights increased during boosting (Fig.6). Looking at the correlation of the proportion of lights with one and two false lights at the last step and the final test error we get -0.3516 and 0.391. Our interpretation is that most digits with one wrong light can get classified well whereas most digits with two wrong lights can't get classified well and can therefore be considered as noise.

4   Validation of Results with Two Other Databases

To validate the results of the previous section we applied our modifications to two additional datasets: the iris and the waveform dataset. We chose the iris dataset as a hard dataset, where boosting didn't work well in previous studies, the waveform dataset was chosen as an example, where boosting improved the base classifier with some space for improvement remaining by comparison with the Bayes classifier ([4,6]). We estimated the error by 10-fold crossvalidation for the iris dataset and by the use of a test set for the waveform dataset with 1000 cases in the learning and 4000 cases in the test set.

For both datasets AdaBoost.M2 again concentrated on some groups more than on others (Table 5).

Table 5. Analysis of algorithm: Difference Δp between the group proportions at the last and the first boosting round in percent

	group 1	group 2	group 3
Δp for iris	-23.7	12.4	11.3
Δp for waveform	7.3	1.0	-8.3

With a similar calculation as in 3.1 the final classifier can be interpreted as an additive model

$$\text{score}(g)(x) = \sum_j f(x_j, g)$$

with step functions $f(x_j, g)$. An additive model seems to be well suited for both datasets, because the algorithm showed a good performance for both datasets and is more than competitive to AdaBoost.M1 using classification trees (Table 6).

Table 6. Performance of AdaBoost.M2

	iris	waveform
Final error	4,0	16,4
Minimal training error	2,0	13,3
Final training error	2,3	13,6
Overfit	0,3	0,3
Generalization error	1,7	2,8

In the previous chapter we examined two modified boosting algorithms that held the group proportions constant. For the digit dataset AdaBoostπ was clearly superior to AdaBoost.M2. A look on the results for the iris and waveform datasets show that both modifications seem to worsen the algorithm for both datasets, but there is one thing that makes the comparison difficult. In ([1]) the problem of rounding errors at extreme differences between weights of cases was addressed, so for every boosting round we saved the ratio r between the maximal and the minimal weight for all boosting rounds. For the modified algorithms r was extremely high (about 10^{12}) for two of the iris trials which lead to much greater error for these two trials, r was also higher for the waveform trial (1695 and 5767 for AdaBoostπ and AdaBoost$\hat{\pi}$ compared to 135 for AdaBoost.M2) but had similar values for the digit dataset (28, 27, 38). We didn't expect this behaviour of the algorithm, in contrast we even saw the modification as a regularization step. As a result the validation confirmed that the weight distribution should be at least watched during boosting and that further research in this direction is needed.

5 Conclusion and Future Work

The final classifier of AdaBoost.M2 using decision stumps as base classifiers can be shown and interpreted very well as an additive model without interactions for the digit example. The performance of the algorithm for the digit example suffers from attribute noise leading to error rates far from the Bayes error, although the final model is complex enough to handle the problem. The additional error (8.29%) comes from the lack of fit for the training data (2.65%), overfitting (3.93%) and generalization (1.71%). During boosting the algorithm concentrates on the two groups 1 and 7. Holding group proportions constant on the can improve the algorithm considerably, but exact knowledge of the group proportions is crucial for the success of this method, which reduces the minimal training error and also errors resulting from overfitting and generalization.

In experiments with the iris and the waveform datasets the algorithm also concentrates on certain groups. The resulting classifiers are at least as good as classifiers resulting from AdaBoost.M1 with classification trees as base classifiers. As an additional advantage the resulting model is additive and therefore easier to interpret. Experiments to validate the good performance of the modified algorithm AdaBoostπ show no clear results but addressed the need to at least check the weight distribution during boosting. Additional work must be done in this area.

Future work will explore methods to take noise into account on one hand by changes within the algorithm and on the other hand by an additional analysis of the output of the algorithm. It will then be necessary to generalize the results to other algorithms, base classifiers and data sets.

References

1. E. Bauer, R. Kohavi, 1999. An empirical comparison of voting classification algorithms: bagging, boosting and variants. Machine Learning 36, 105-139.
2. L.Breiman, J.Friedman, R.Olshen, C.Stone, 1984. Classification and regression trees. Belmont, CA: Wadsworth.
3. T.G.Dietterrich, G.Bakiri, 1995. Solving multiclass learning problems via error-correcting output codes. Journal of Artificial Intelligence Research 2, 263-286.
4. T.G.Dietterrich, 2000. An experimental comparison of three methods for constructing ensembles of decision trees: bagging, boosting and randomization. Machine Learning 40,139-157.
5. Y.Freund, R.E.Schapire, 1997. A decision-theoretic generalization of online-learning and an application to boosting. Journal of Computer and System Sciences 55 (1), 119-139.
6. J.R.Quinlan, 1996. Bagging, boosting, and C4.5. Proceedings of the Thirteenth National Conference on Artificial Intelligence, 725-730.
7. G.Rätsch, T.Onoda, K.-R.Müller, 2000. Soft margins for AdaBoost. Machine Learning 42(3), 287-320.
8. R.E.Schapire, 1997. Using output codes to boost multiclass learning problems. Machine Learning: Proceedings of the Fourteenth International Conference, 313-321.
9. R.E.Schapire, Y.Freund, P.Bartlett, S.L.Wee, 1998. Boosting the margin: a new explanation for the effectiveness of voting methods. Annals of Statistics 26 (5), 1651-1686.
10. R.E. Schapire, Y.Singer, 1999. Improved boosting algorithms using confidence-rated predictions. Machine Learning 37, 297-336.

Iterative Double Clustering for Unsupervised and Semi-supervised Learning

Ran El-Yaniv and Oren Souroujon

Computer Science Department, Technion - Israel Institute of Technology
{rani, orenso}@cs.technion.ac.il

Abstract. This paper studies the Iterative Double Clustering (IDC) meta-clustering algorithm, a new extension of the recent Double Clustering (DC) method of Slonim and Tishby that exhibited impressive performance on text categorization tasks [1]. Using synthetically generated data we empirically demonstrate that whenever the DC procedure is successful in recovering some of the structure hidden in the data, the extended IDC procedure can incrementally compute a dramatically better classification, with minor additional computational resources. We demonstrate that the IDC algorithm is especially advantageous when the data exhibits high attribute noise. Our simulation results also show the effectiveness of IDC in text categorization problems. Surprisingly, this unsupervised procedure can be competitive with a (supervised) SVM trained with a small training set. Finally, we propose a natural extension of IDC for (semi-supervised) transductive learning where we are given both labeled and unlabeled examples, and present preliminary empirical results showing the plausibility of the extended method in a semi-supervised setting.

1 Introduction

Data clustering is a fundamental and challenging routine in information processing and pattern recognition. Informally, when we cluster a set of elements we attempt to partition it into subsets such that points in the same subset are more "similar" to each other than to points in other subsets. Typical clustering algorithms depend on a choice of a similarity measure between data points [2], and a "correct" clustering result can be dependent on an appropriate choice of a similarity measure. However, the choice of a "correct" measure is an ill-defined task without a particular application at hand. For instance, consider a hypothetical data set containing articles by each of two authors, so that half of the articles authored by each author discusses one topic, and the other half discusses another topic. There are two possible dichotomies of the data which could yield two different bi-partitions: one according to topic, and another, according to writing style. When asked to cluster this set into two sub-clusters, one cannot successfully achieve the task without knowing the goal: Are we interested in clusters that reflect writing style or semantics? Therefore, without a suitable target at hand and a principled method for choosing a similarity measure suitable for the target, it can be meaningless to interpret clustering results.

L. De Raedt and P. Flach (Eds.): ECML 2001, LNAI 2167, pp. 121–132, 2001.
© Springer-Verlag Berlin Heidelberg 2001

The *information bottleneck (IB)* method of Tishby, Pereira and Bialek [3] is a new framework that can sometimes provide an elegant solution to this problematic aspect of data clustering. Let the data be a set of observed values of some random variable S. The main idea of the IB method is to use some "target information" that can guide the clustering process towards the desired goal. Let this target information be the observed values of the random variable T. The goal is to extract the essence of S which can still predict T. Thus, we aim to compute a compressed representation $\tilde{S}$ of S (e.g., a clustering of S) so as to preserve $I(\tilde{S}, T)$, the mutual information between $\tilde{S}$ and T, as much as possible. Tishby et al. [3] also present an algorithm for computing the desired clustering $\tilde{S}$, which is a "soft" assignment of data points into cluster centroids.

In [4], Slonim and Tishby developed a simplified "hard" variant of this IB clustering, where there is a hard assignment of points to their clusters. Employing this hard IB clustering, the same authors introduced an effective two-stage clustering procedure called *Double Clustering (DC)* [1]. Roughly, the idea is as follows. Let X represent the data where each data point is a vector over real valued features. The goal is to cluster X based on the joint empirical distribution of data points and their features. Informally, during the first stage, a clustering of the features F is performed using the above (S, T)-IB procedure with S representing the features and T representing the data points. This results in a compressed representation $\tilde{F}$ of the features F that preserves information about the points. During the second stage, the data X is compressed with respect to the feature clusters $\tilde{F}$ (i.e. with $S = X$ and $T = \tilde{F}$), thus generating a clustering $\tilde{X}$ of the data X. An experimental study of DC on text categorization tasks [1] showed a consistent advantage of IB clustering over other clustering methods. A striking finding in [1] is that DC sometimes even attained results close to those of supervised learning.[1]

In this paper we present a powerful extension of the DC procedure which we term *Iterative Double Clustering (IDC)*. As its name suggests, IDC performs iterations of DC so that the input data variable of the next iteration is the clustered data of the previous DC iteration (and the first iteration is a standard DC). Whenever the first DC iteration succeeds in extracting a meaningful structure of the data, a number of the next consecutive iterations can continually improve the clustering quality. Intuitively, this continual improvement achieved by IDC is due to generation of progressively less noisy target variables that serve better the IB clustering of the features (see details in Section 3). Using synthetically generated data, we study some properties of the IDC method. Not only that IDC can dramatically outperform DC whenever the data is noisy, our experiments indicate that IDC attains impressive categorization results on text categorization tasks. In particular, we show that our unsupervised IDC procedure can outperform an SVM trained over a small sized training set.

These findings and the studies of Baker and McCallum [5] and of Slonim and Tishby [4,6] on *supervised* applications of the information bottleneck for

---

[1] Specifically, the DC method obtained in some cases accuracy close to that obtained by a naive Bayes classifier trained over a small sized sample [1].

word clustering provided us with the motivation for extending the IDC method into a semi-supervised setting, and we propose a natural extension of IDC for transductive and semi-supervised learning. Our preliminary empirical results indicate that our transductive IDC can yield effective text categorization.

2   Problem Setup and Preliminaries

We consider a data set X of *elements*, each of which is a d-dimensional vector over a set F of *features*. In this paper we focus on the case where feature values are non-negative real numbers. For every element $x = (f_1, \ldots, f_d) \in X$ we consider the empirical conditional distribution $\{p(f_i|x)\}$ of features given x, where $p(f_i|x) = f_i / \sum_{i=1}^{d} f_i$. For instance, X can be a set of documents, each of which is represented as a vector of word-features where f_i is the frequency of the ith word (in some fixed word enumeration). Thus, we represent each element as a distribution over its features, and are interested in a partition of the data based on these feature conditional distributions. Given a predetermined number of clusters, a straightforward approach to cluster the data using the above "distributional representation" would be to choose some (dis)similarity measure for distributions (e.g. based on some L_p norm or some statistical measure such as the KL-divergence) and employ some "plug-in" clustering algorithm based on this measure (e.g. agglomerative algorithms). Perhaps due to feature noise, this simplistic approach can result in mediocre results (see e.g. [1]).

2.1   The Information Bottleneck Method

Let S and T be two random variables. The *information bottleneck (IB)* method [3] aims to extract a compressed representation $\tilde{S}$ of S with minimum compromise of information content with respect to the variable T. Let $I(S,T) = \sum_{s \in S, t \in T} p(s,t) \log \frac{p(s,t)}{p(s)p(t)}$, the *mutual information* between S and T [7]. The IB method attempts to compute $p(\tilde{s}|s)$, a "soft" assignment of a data point s to clusters $\tilde{s}$, so as to minimize $I(S, \tilde{S}) - \beta I(\tilde{S}, T)$, given the Markov condition $T \to S \to \tilde{S}$ (i.e., T and $\tilde{S}$ are conditionally independent given S). Here, β is a Lagrange multiplier that controls a constraint on $I(\tilde{S}, T)$. As shown in [3], this minimization yields a system of coupled equations for the clustering mapping $p(\tilde{s}|s)$ in terms of the cluster representations $p(t|\tilde{s})$ and the cluster weights $p(\tilde{s})$. The paper [3] also presents an algorithm similar to deterministic annealing [8] for recovering a solution for the coupled equations.

Slonim and Tishby [4] proposed a simplified IB approach for the computation of "hard" cluster assignments. Specifically, for any cardinality $m = |\tilde{S}|$ (i.e. m is the desired number of clusters), the coupled equations in [3] induce, in the limit $\beta \to \infty$, the following coupled equations.

$$p(\tilde{s}|s) = \begin{cases} 1, & \text{if } s \in \tilde{s} \\ 0, & \text{otherwise} \end{cases} \qquad \forall s \in S$$

$$p(t|\tilde{s}) = \frac{1}{p(\tilde{s})} \sum_{s \in \tilde{s}} p(s,t) \qquad \forall t \in T$$

$$p(\tilde{s}) = \sum_{s \in \tilde{s}} p(s)$$

Using the above equations and the identity $I(S,T) = \sum_{s \in S, t \in T} p(s)$ $p(t|s) \log \frac{p(t|s)}{p(t)}$, a greedy agglomerative clustering algorithm was proposed in [4]. This algorithm initializes with a trivial clustering, where each data point s is a single cluster. Then, at each step, the algorithm merges the two clusters that minimize the loss of mutual information $I(\tilde{S},T)$. As shown in [4], the reduction in $I(\tilde{S},T)$ due to a merge of two clusters $\tilde{s}_i$ and $\tilde{s}_j$ is

$$(p(\tilde{s}_i) + p(\tilde{s}_j))D_{JS}[p(t|\tilde{s}_i), p(t|\tilde{s}_j)], \tag{1}$$

where, for any two distributions $p(x)$ and $q(x)$, with priors λ_p and λ_q, $\lambda_p + \lambda_q = 1$, $D_{JS}[p(x), q(x)]$ is the *Jensen-Shannon divergence* (see [9,10]),

$$D_{JS}[p(x), q(x)] = \lambda_p D_{KL}(p||\frac{p+q}{2}) + \lambda_q D_{KL}(q||\frac{p+q}{2}).$$

Here, $\frac{p+q}{2}$ denotes the distribution $(p(x) + q(x))/2$ and $D_{KL}(\cdot||\cdot)$ is the Kullbak-Leibler divergence [7]. The Jensen-Shannon divergence is non-negative, symmetric and bounded but does not satisfy the triangle inequality (and therefore is not a metric). Note that the priors used in the Jensen-Shannon divergence (1) for $p(t|\tilde{s}_i)$ and $p(t|\tilde{s}_j)$ are proportional to $p(\tilde{s}_i)$ and $p(\tilde{s}_j)$, respectively. For a detailed description of the (soft and hard) IB method the reader is referred to [3,4].

As all agglomerative clustering algorithms, the agglomerative IB clustering algorithm derived using the dissimilarity measure of Equation (1) is only *locally* optimal, since at each step it greedily merges the two most similar clusters. Another disadvantage of this algorithm is its time complexity, which can be accomplished in $O(n^2)$ for a data set of n elements (see [1] for details).

The IB method can be viewed as a meta-clustering procedure that, given observations of the variables S and T (via empirical co-occurrence samples of $p(s,t)$), attempts to cluster s-elements represented as distributions over t-elements. Clearly, one can attempt to approximate IB clustering using any vectorial clustering algorithm that can be applied within the simplex containing the distributional representations of the s-elements.

2.2 Double Clustering (DC)

Employed with the IB clustering method we now return to our problem setup (see Section 2) and describe the double clustering (DC) method of [1]. Notice that in the IB clustering method the roles of the random variables S and T can be switched. In our problem setup, this means that we can cluster elements as distributions over features, but can also cluster features as distributions over elements. For instance, we can cluster documents as distributions over words but also cluster words as distributions over documents.

DC is a two-stage procedure where during the first stage we cluster features represented as distributions over elements, thus generating *feature clusters*. During the second stage we cluster elements represented as distributions over the feature *clusters* (a more formal description follows). For instance, considering the document clustering domain, in the first stage we cluster words as distributions over documents to obtain word clusters. Then in the second stage we cluster documents as distributions over word clusters, to obtain document clusters.

Intuitively, the first stage in DC generates more coarse *pseudo* features (i.e. feature centroids), which can reduce noise and sparseness that might be exhibited in the original feature values. Then, in the second stage, elements are clustered as distributions over the "distilled" pseudo features, and therefore can generate more accurate element clusters. As reported in [1], this DC two-stage procedure outperforms various other clustering approaches as well as DC variants applied with other dissimilarity measures (such as the variational distance) different from the optimal JS-divergence of Equation (1). It is most striking that in some cases, the accuracy achieved by DC was close to that achieved by a supervised Naive Bayes classifier.

Input:
X (input data)
$N_{\tilde{X}}$ (number of element clusters)
$N_{\tilde{F}}$ (number of feature clusters to use)
k (number of iterations)
Initialize: $S \leftarrow F, T \leftarrow X,$
loop {k times}
    $N \leftarrow N_{\tilde{F}}$
    $\tilde{F} \leftarrow IB_N(T|S)$
    $N \leftarrow N_{\tilde{X}}, S \leftarrow X, T \leftarrow \tilde{F}$
    $\tilde{X} \leftarrow IB_N(T|S)$
    $S \leftarrow F, T \leftarrow \tilde{X}$
end loop
Output $\tilde{X}$

Fig. 1. Pseudo-code for IDC

3   Iterative Double Clustering (IDC)

Our Iterative Double Clustering (IDC) is a novel extension of the DC algorithm, which performs multiple iterations of the original DC. It works by feeding the element clusters output of each DC iteration as input to the first stage of the following DC iteration. As we shall later see, IDC consistently improves (in a sense to be defined) over DC whenever the data is noisy.

Denote by $IB_N(T|S)$ the clustering result, into N clusters, of the information bottleneck hard clustering procedure when the data is S and the target variable is T (see Section 2.1). For instance, if T represents documents and S represents words, the application of $IB_N(\text{documents}|\text{words})$ will cluster the words, represented as distributions over the documents, into N clusters. Using the notation of our problem setup, with X denoting the data, and F denoting the features, suppose we are interested in clustering X into $N_{\tilde{X}}$ clusters. In Figure 1 we provide a pseudo-code of the IDC meta-clustering algorithm. Note that the DC procedure is simply an application of IDC with $k = 1$.

The code of Figure 1 requires to specify k, the number of IDC iterations to run. It also requires as input both $N_{\tilde{X}}$, the number of element clusters (e.g. the desired number of of document clusters), and $N_{\tilde{F}}$, the number of feature clusters to use during each iteration. The question of how to choose these parameters requires study and some of the results we present in this paper provide partial answers. In general, a correct choice of $N_{\tilde{X}}$ is a model selection problem and is beyond the scope of this paper. In the experiments reported in the paper we always assumed that we know the correct $N_{\tilde{X}}$. A correct choice of $N_{\tilde{F}}$ is also related to model selection, but we cannot avoid it. Fortunately, as we discuss later, the algorithm is not too sensitive to an overestimate of $N_{\tilde{F}}$. We also studied the behavior of IDC as a function of the parameter k (number of iterations). Perhaps the first question to ask is whether or not IDC *converges* to a steady state (e.g. where two consecutive iterations generate identical partitions). Unfortunately, a theoretical understanding of this convergence issue is left open in this paper. Nevertheless, in all our experiments IDC converged. Our empirical experience with IDC is that convergence takes between a few iterations and a few dozens of iterations. We discovered that in most cases IDC achieved its best performance after 8-10 iterations. Unless otherwise is specified, in the experiments reported below we used a fixed $k = 15$.

The first DC iteration is the most computationally intensive. After this iteration the co-occurrence (joint) distribution maintained by IDC reduces in size from $|X||F|$ to $|\tilde{X}||F|$ where $|X|$ is the sample size, and $|\tilde{X}|$ is the number of clusters (which corresponds to the number of classes) and typically $|\tilde{X}| \ll |X|$.

As noted earlier, the "hard" implementation of IB-clustering (and of DC) originally presented by [1] uses an agglomerative procedure as the basic clustering algorithm (see Section 2.1). The "soft" implementation of IB [3] applies a deterministic annealing clustering [8] as its underlying clustering procedure. As already discussed, the IB method can be viewed as a meta-clustering algorithm. Therefore, we can employ many vectorial clustering algorithms in the underlying IB procedure used by DC and IDC. We implemented IDC using several clustering algorithms including agglomerative clustering and deterministic annealing. Since both

Input:
  a sample $x_1, \ldots, x_n$,
  a distance measure $d(\cdot, \cdot)$,
  the desired number of clusters k
Initialize:
  $c := 0$ (current number of clusters)
  for each point x_i in the sample **do**
    if $c > 0$ **then**
      Let c_j be the d-closest centroid to x_i
      Assign c_j to be the center of gravity
      of the cluster C_j together with x_i
    end if
    if $c = k$ **then**
      merge the two d-closest clusters
    end if
    create a new cluster containing x_i
  end for

Fig. 2. Pseudo-code for Add-C

these algorithms are computationally intensive, we also implemented IDC using a fast algorithm called *Add-C* proposed by Guedalia et al. [11]. Add-C is an online greedy clustering algorithm with linear running time.

A pseudo-code of Add-C appears in Figure 2. In the code we left the choice of the distance measure open. In order to better approximate the original hard information bottleneck procedure we applied Add-C with the Jensen-Shannon divergence of Equation (1). For the exact details of this algorithm, the reader is referred to [11]. Our experience with information bottleneck clustering with both Add-C and the agglomerative algorithm indicates that the IDC implementation with Add-C yields inferior results to those produced by IDC with the agglomerative clustering routine. Specifically, when we apply the first iteration of IDC (= DC) using the agglomerative routine we usually get better results than a first iteration of IDC applied with the Add-C routine. Nevertheless, we gain a significant runtime speed-up since Add-C maintains a linear time complexity in the number of points. Moreover, as we later discuss, several iterations of IDC applied with Add-C are always superior to one iteration (DC) applied with agglomerative clustering (or Add-C). Due to its computational intensity we have not experimented much with a (multi-round) IDC applied with the agglomerative routine.

Following [1] we chose to evaluate the performance of IDC with respect to a *labeled* data set. Specifically, we count the number of classification errors made by IDC as obtained from labeled data.

In order to better understand the properties of IDC, we first examined it within a controlled setup of synthetically generated data points whose feature values were generated by d-dimensional Gaussian distributions (for d features) of the form $N(\mu, \Sigma)$, where $\Sigma = \sigma^2 I$, with σ constant. In order to simulate different sources, we assigned different μ values (from a given constant range) to each combination of source and feature. Specifically, for data simulating m classes and $|F|$ features, $|F| \times m$ different distributions were selected.

Not surprisingly, when the range for selecting μ values was large in proportion to σ (i.e. the sources were far apart), both DC and IDC performed well and gave results close to the Bayes error. Our next step was to introduce feature noise and see how IDC reacts. We used the following two noise models.

Constant feature noise: Distorts each of the features by adding random values sampled from $N(0, \sigma^2)$, where σ is a constant "noise amplitude". Resulting negative values are rounded to zero.

Proportional feature noise: Distorts each entry with value v by adding a random sample from $N(0, (\alpha \cdot v)^2)$, where α is the "noise amplitude". Resulting negative values are again rounded to zero.

In figure 3(a), we plot the average accuracy of 10 runs of IDC. The solid line plots (average) accuracies achieved in the last (15th) round of IDC vs. proportional feature noise amplitude (α). The dashed line plots first rounds of IDC (equivalent to DC) vs. σ. Each error bar specifies one standard deviation. As can be seen, at low level noise amplitudes IDC attains perfect accuracy. When the noise amplitude increases, both IDC and DC deteriorate but the multiple rounds of IDC can better resist the extra noise. A similar effect is observed when applying constant feature noise.

After observing the large accuracy gain between DC and IDC at a specific interval of noise amplitude within the proportional feature noise setup, we set the noise amplitude to a value in that interval and examined the behavior of the IDC run in more detail. Figure 3(b) shows a trace of the accuracy obtained at each of the 20 iterations of an IDC run over noisy data. This learning curve shows a quick improvement in accuracy during the first few rounds, and then reaches a plateau.

4   Empirical Results for Text Categorization

Following [1] we used the *20 Newsgroups (NG20)* [12] data set to evaluate IDC on real, labeled data. NG20 consists of 20,000 newsgroup articles from 20 different newsgroups, each group containing 1,000 documents. In this section we describe experiments with various subsets of NG20. We chose subsets with various degrees of difficulty. In the first set of experiments we used the following four newsgroups (denoted as NG4), two of which deal with sports subjects: 'rec.sport.baseball', 'rec.sport.hockey', 'alt.atheism' and 'sci.med'. In these experiments we tested some basic properties of IDC. In all the experiments reported in this section we performed the following preprocessing: We lowered the case of all letters, filtered out low frequency words which appeared only 3 times in the entire set and filtered out numerical and non-alphabetical characters. We also stripped off newsgroup headers which contain the class labels.

In Figure 3(c) we display accuracy vs. number of feature clusters ($N_{\tilde{F}}$). The accuracy deteriorates when $N_{\tilde{F}}$ is too small and we see a slight negative trend when it increases. A possible interpretation is that when the number of clusters is too small, there are not enough clusters to represent the inherent structure (in our case, word clusters with contextually similar meanings) of the data. It may also suggest that when the number of clusters is too large, either not enough features are grouped together to form 'semantic' units, or not enough noise is filtered by the clustering procedure. We performed an additional experiment which tested the performance using very large numbers of feature clusters. Indeed, these results indicate that after a plateau in the range of 10-20 there is a minor negative trend in the accuracy level. Thus, with respect to this data set, the IDC algorithm is not too sensitive to an overestimation of the number $N_{\tilde{F}}$ of feature clusters.

Other experiments over the NG4 data set confirmed the results of [1] that the JS-divergence dissimilarity measure of Equation (1) outperforms other measures, such as the variational distance (L_1 norm), the KL-divergence, the square-Euclidean distance and the 'cosine' distance. Details of all these experiments will be presented in the full version of the paper.

In the next set of experiments we tested IDC's performance on the same newsgroup subsets used in [1]. Table 1(a) compares the accuracy achieved by DC to the the last (15th) round of IDC with respect to all data sets described

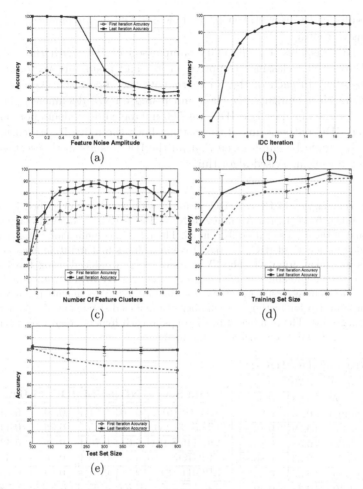

Fig. 3. (a) Average accuracy over 10 trials for different amplitudes of proportional feature noise. Data set: A synthetically generated sample of 200 500-dimensional elements in 4 classes (max $\mu = 50$, $\sigma = 50$). (b) A trace of a single IDC run. The x-axis is the number of IDC iterations and the y-axis is accuracy achieved in each iteration. Data set: Synthetically generated sample of 500, 400-dimensional elements in 5 classes (max $\mu = 50$, $\sigma = 45$); Noise: Proportional feature noise with $\alpha = 1.0$; (c) Average accuracy (10 trials) for different numbers of feature clusters. Data set: NG4. (d) Average accuracy of (10 trials of) transductive categorization of 5 newsgroups. Sample size: 80 documents per class, X-axis is training set size. Upper curve shows trans. IDC-15 and lower curve is trans. IDC-1. (e) Average accuracy of (10 trials of) transductive categorization of 5 newsgroups. Sample size: constant training set size of 50 documents from each class. The x-axis counts the number of unlabeled samples to be categorized. Upper curve is trans. IDC-15 and lower curve is trans. IDC-1. Each error bar (in all graphs) specifies one std.

in [1]. Results of DC were taken from [1] where DC is implemented using the agglomerative routine.

Table 1(b) displays a preliminary comparison of IDC with the results of a Naive Bayes (NB) classifier (reported in [6]) and a support vector machine (SVM) classifier. In each of the 5 experiments the supervised classifiers were trained using 25 documents per class and tested on 475 documents per class. The input for the unsupervised IDC was 500 unlabeled documents per class. As can be seen, IDC outperforms in this setting both the naive Bayes learner and the SVM. It should be emphasized that all the IDC results in this section were achieved by an unsupervised algorithm.

Table 1. (a) Accuracy of DC vs. IDC on most of the data sets described in [1]. DC results are taken from [1]; (b) Accuracy of Naive Bayes (NB) and SVM classifiers vs. IDC on some of the data sets described in [6]. The IDC-15 column shows final accuracy achieved at iteration 15 of IDC; the IDC-1 column shows first iteration accuracy. The NB results are taken from [6]. The SVM results were produced using the LibSVM package [13] with its default parameters. In all cases the SVM was trained and tested using the same training/test set sizes as described in [6] (25 documents per newsgroup for training and 475 for testing; the number of unlabeled documents fed to IDC was 500 per newsgroup). The number of newsgroups in each hyper-category is specified in parenthesis (e.g. COMP contains 5 newsgroups).

Newsgroup	DC	IDC-15
$Binary1$	0.70	0.85
$Binary2$	0.68	0.83
$Binary3$	0.75	0.80
$Multi5_1$	0.59	0.86
$Multi5_2$	0.58	0.88
$Multi5_3$	0.53	0.86
$Multi10_1$	0.35	0.56
$Multi10_2$	0.35	0.49
$Multi10_3$	0.35	0.55
Average	**0.54**	**0.74**

Data Set	NB	SVM	IDC-15	IDC-1
COMP (5)	0.50	0.51	0.50	0.34
SCIENCE (4)	0.73	0.68	0.79	0.44
POLITICS (3)	0.67	0.76	0.78	0.42
RELIGION (3)	0.55	0.78	0.60	0.38
SPORT (2)	0.75	0.78	0.89	0.76
Average	**0.64**	**0.70**	**0.71**	**0.47**

(a)   (b)

5   Learning from Labeled and Unlabeled Examples

The impressive performance of IDC in unsupervised classification of data raises the question of whether the IDC procedure can serve for (semi) supervised learning or transductive learning. In this section, we present a natural extension of

IDC for transductive and semi-supervised learning that can utilize *both* labeled and unlabeled data. In transductive learning, the testing is done on the unlabeled examples in the training data, while in semi-supervised learning it is done on previously unseen data.

For motivating the transductive IDC, consider a data set X that has emerged from a statistical mixture which includes several sources (classes). Let C be a random variable indicating the class of a random point. During the first iteration of a standard IDC we cluster the features F so as to preserve $I(F, X)$. Typically, X contains predictive information about the classes C. In cases where $I(X, C)$ is sufficiently large, we expect that the feature clusters $\tilde{F}$ will preserve some information about C as well. Having available some *labeled* data points, we may attempt to generate feature clusters $\tilde{F}$ which preserve more information about class labels.

This leads to the following straightforward idea. During the first IB-stage of the IDC first iteration, we cluster the features F as distributions over *class labels* (given by the labeled data). This phase results in feature clusters $\tilde{F}$. Then we continue as usual; that is, in the second IB-phase of the first IDC iteration we cluster X, represented as distributions over $\tilde{F}$. Subsequent IDC iterations use all the unlabeled data.

In Figure 3(d) we show the accuracy obtained by DC and IDC in categorizing 5 newsgroups as a function of the training (labeled) set size. For instance, we see that when the algorithm has 10 documents available from each class it can categorize the entire unlabeled set, containing 90 unlabeled documents in each of the classes, with accuracy of about 80%. The benchmark accuracy of IDC with no labeled examples obtained about 73%.

In Figure 3(e) we see the accuracy obtained by DC and transductive IDC trained with a constant set of 50 labeled documents, on different unlabeled (test) sample sizes. The graph shows that the accuracy of DC significantly degrades, while IDC manages to sustain an almost constant high accuracy.

6   Concluding Remarks

Our contribution is threefold. First, we present a natural extension of the successful double clustering algorithm of [1]. Empirical evidence indicates that our new iterative DC algorithm has distinct advantages over DC, especially in noisy settings. Second, we applied the *unsupervised* IDC on text categorization problems which are typically dealt with by supervised learning algorithms. Our results indicate that it is possible to achieve performance competitive to supervised classifiers that were trained over small samples. Finally, we present a natural extension of IDC that allows for transductive learning. Our preliminary empirical evaluation of this scheme over text categorization is very promising.

A number of interesting questions are left for future research. First, it would be of interest to gain better theoretical understanding of several issues: the generalization properties of DC and IDC, the convergence of IDC to a steady state and precise conditions on attribute noise settings within which IDC is advantageous. Second, it would be important to test the empirical performance of IDC with respect to different problem domains. Finally, we believe it would be of great interest to better understand and characterize the performance of transductive IDC in settings having both labeled and unlabeled data.

Acknowledgements. We thank Naftali Tishby and Noam Slonim for helpful discussions and for providing us with the detailed descriptions of the NG20 data sets used in [1]. We also thank Ron Meir for useful comments and discussions. This research was supported by the Israeli Ministry of Science. R. El-Yaniv is a Marcella S. Geltman Memorial academic lecturer.

References

1. Noam Slonim and Naftali Tishby. Document clustering using word clusters via the information bottleneck method. In *ACM SIGIR 2000*, 2000.
2. A.K. Jain and R.C. Dubes. *Algorithms for Clustering Data*. Prentice-Hall, New Jersey, 1988.
3. F.C. Pereira N. Tishby and W. Bialek. Information bottleneck method. In *37-th Allerton Conference on Communication and Computation*, 1999.
4. N. Slonim and N. Tishby. Agglomerative information bottleneck. In *NIPS99*, 1999.
5. L. D. Baker and A. K. McCallum. Distributional clustering of words for text classification. In *Proceedings of SIGIR'98*, 1998.
6. N. Slonim and N. Tishby. The power of word clustering for text classification. To appear in the European Colloquium on IR Research, ECIR, 2001.
7. T.M. Cover and J.A. Thomas. *Elements of Information Theory*. John Wiley & Sons, Inc., 1991.
8. K. Rose. Deterministic annealing for clustering, compression, classification, regression and related optimization problems. *Proceedings of the IEEE*, 86(11):2210–2238, 1998.
9. J. Lin. Divergence measures based on the shannon entropy. *IEEE Transactions on Information Theory*, 37(1):145–151, 1991.
10. R. El-Yaniv, S. Fine, and N. Tishby. Agnostic classification of markovian sequences. In *NIPS97*, 1997.
11. I.D. Guedalia, M. London, and M. Werman. A method for on-line clustering of non-stationary data. *Neural Computation*, 11:521–540, 1999.
12. 20 newsgroup data set. http://www.ai.mit.edu/jrennie/20_newsgroups/.
13. Libsvm. http://www.csie.ntu.edu.tw/cjlin/libsvm.

On the Practice of Branching Program Boosting

Tapio Elomaa and Matti Kääriäinen

Department of Computer Science, P.O. Box 26
FIN-00014 University of Helsinki, Finland
{elomaa,matti.kaariainen}@cs.helsinki.fi

Abstract. Branching programs are a generalization of decision trees. From the viewpoint of boosting theory the former appear to be exponentially more efficient. However, earlier experience demonstrates that such results do not necessarily translate to practical success. In this paper we develop a practical version of Mansour and McAllester's [13] algorithm for branching program boosting. We test the algorithm empirically with real-world and synthetic data. Branching programs attain the same prediction accuracy level as C4.5. Contrary to the implications of the boosting analysis, they are not significantly smaller than the corresponding decision trees. This further corroborates the earlier observations on the way in which boosting analyses bear practical significance.

1 Introduction

The *weak learning model* or *boosting* theory [16,6] has been able to offer an analytical explanation for the practical success of top-down induction of decision trees (subsequently DTs for short) [9,12]. Earlier attempts to explain the success of DT learning in theoretical models have not been successful. Even though the weak learning framework may better suit analyzing and designing practical learning algorithms than the PAC model and its variants, one must exercise care in drawing conclusions about the practical implications of boosting analyses [4]. In this paper we provide further evidence to support meticulous consideration.

A *branching program* (BP) is an abstract model of computation that takes the form of a directed acyclic graph (DAG). BPs have been well-studied in theoretical computer science. In this paper we view them as classifiers. In empirical machine learning a similar representation formalism — *decision graphs* — has been studied to some extent [14,10,11]. BPs are a strict generalization of DTs. Thus, their learning in computational learning frameworks is hard [5,1].

Mansour and McAllester [13] devised a boosting algorithm for BPs. The main advantage obtained by using BPs rather than DTs is that their training error is guaranteed to decline exponentially in the square root of the size of the program. When DT learning algorithms are viewed as boosting algorithms, the training error declination is only polynomial in the size of the tree [9,12]. The learning algorithm for BPs is basically very similar to the algorithms used in top-down induction of DTs [3,15]. It greedily searches for good splits of the nodes in the last level of the evolving program. The central difference between a BP and a

L. De Raedt and P. Flach (Eds.): ECML 2001, LNAI 2167, pp. 133–144, 2001.
© Springer-Verlag Berlin Heidelberg 2001

DT is that in the former branches may grow together, while in the latter two separate branches never unite.

In this paper we experiment with a practical learning algorithm based on the results of Mansour and McAllester [13]. We clarify the algorithm and test it with data sets from the UCI Repository [2] and some synthetic data. In the experiments BPs attain the same overall prediction accuracy level as unpruned DTs. Domain specific differences, though, are observed; in particular, on some synthetic domains the differences are clear. BPs appear to be slightly smaller than unpruned DTs, but there is no clear difference.

In Section 2 we recapitulate weak learning and boosting, introducing at the same time the framework used subsequently. We also review Kearns and Mansour's [9] analysis of DT learning as a boosting algorithm. Section 3 presents the boosting algorithm for BPs and the motivation behind its details. We also briefly touch the related work of learning decision graphs. In Section 4 empirical experiments with the BP algorithm are reported. The results are contrasted with those obtained by C4.5. Lessons learned from the experimentation are reflected upon in Section 5. Finally, we present the concluding remarks of this paper.

2   Weak Learning, Boosting, and Decision Tree Induction

Let f be a boolean target function over an input space X. A set $\mathcal{H}$ of base classifiers or predicates on X fulfills the β-weak learning hypothesis (with respect to f), where $\beta \in (0, 1/2]$, if it contains, for any distribution D on X, a classifier $h \in \mathcal{H}$ such that

$$\mathbf{Pr}_D\{ h(x) \neq f(x) \} \leq \frac{1}{2} - \beta.$$

In other words, the weak learning hypothesis guarantees the existence of a predicate with a predictive *advantage* of at least β on f over random guessing.

Boosting algorithms exploit the weak learning hypothesis by combining many different predicates from $\mathcal{H}$ on different filtered distributions of the original sample. Thus, they amplify the small predictive advantages over random guessing iteratively to obtain a combined function, whose training error is less than any desired error threshold [16,6]. A natural type of boosting algorithm is a *voting* algorithm, which uses some number of iterations to assemble a collection of weak classifiers — e.g., decision stumps — and at the end uses weighted voting to determine the classification of future instances. For example, AdaBoost [8] is such an algorithm.

By interpreting the node predicates as weak classifiers, one can apply the boosting framework also to DT learning. In top-down induction of DTs predicates are assigned to the leaves of the evolving tree. Usually the predicates test the value of a single attribute. They filter subsets of the original sample forward in the tree. A *splitting criterion* is used to rank candidate predicates. It favors predicates that reduce the impurity of the class distribution in the subsets that result from splitting the data. Since the filtered distributions gradually lose impurity, they usually become easier as we go down in the tree. The final predictor is combined from the node predicates. Thus, viewing node predicate selection as a form of weak learning enables to explain the learning behavior of such successful DT learners as CART [3] and C4.5 [15].

Under the weak learning hypothesis, choosing a suitable predicate class and using an appropriate splitting criterion, the training error of the DT is driven down polynomially in its size [9]. This bound, which is close to optimal for any DT learning algorithm, is exponentially worse than that of AdaBoost [8]. However, empirically the error reduction with respect to the classifier size in AdaBoost is not essentially any better than that in C4.5 [4,7].

Let T be a binary DT constructed on the basis of sample S. We denote the set of leaves of T by $L(T)$. Throughout this paper we assume that leaves are labeled by the majority class of the examples reaching them. For a node $v \in T$ let $S_v \subseteq S$ be the set of examples reaching it. By $S_v^1 \subseteq S_v$ we denote the set of positive training examples reaching node v. The fraction of the sample reaching node v is denoted by $\hat{p}_v = |S_v|/|S|$ and the proportion of positive examples from those that reach v is denoted by $\hat{q}_v = |S_v^1|/|S_v|$.

A splitting criterion is a mapping $F : [0,1] \to [0,1]$. It assigns an impurity value to an observed class frequency distribution. Pure distributions, where $\hat{q} \in \{0,1\}$, have no impurity; i.e., for them $F(\hat{q}) = 0$. The most mixed distribution is the one in which $\hat{q} = 1/2$ and it has the maximal impurity, $F(1/2) = 1$. In addition to these properties, Kearns and Mansour [9] required a *permissible* splitting criterion F to be symmetric about $1/2$, $F(x) = F(1-x)$ for any $x \in [0,1]$, and to be concave. Commonly-used impurity functions fulfilling these properties include the binary entropy of C4.5 [15] and the Gini function of the CART algorithm [3]. Also the criterion that is used in the BP learning algorithm, $G(\hat{q}) = 2\sqrt{\hat{q}(1-\hat{q})}$ [9], is permissible.

Let the *index* of the tree T be

$$F(T) = \sum_{\ell \in L(T)} \hat{p}_\ell F(\hat{q}_\ell).$$

For any $h \in \mathcal{H}$ let T_h be the DT consisting of a single internal node labeled with h and two leaves corresponding to its values 0 and 1. Let $F(T_h, S)$ denote the index of T_h as measured with respect to S. Then, the change in the index, when node v is split using predicate h, is $\Delta(S_v, h) = F(\hat{q}_v) - F(T_h, S_v)$. Selecting a split to replace a node entails choosing the attribute that gives the most decrease to the value of the splitting criterion. Evaluation of attributes, on its part, entails determining the best binary partition for the domain of the attribute.

The *empirical error* of decision tree T is the weighted sum of the error of its leaves

$$\hat{\epsilon}(T) = \sum_{\ell \in L(T)} \hat{p}_\ell \min\{\hat{q}_\ell, 1 - \hat{q}_\ell\}.$$

It is bounded by the index $F(T)$, because $F(\hat{q}_\ell) \geq \min\{\hat{q}_\ell, 1 - \hat{q}_\ell\}$ by the properties required from a permissible splitting criterion.

Kearns and Mansour [9] showed that when the splitting criterion $G(\hat{q}) = 2\sqrt{\hat{q}(1-\hat{q})}$ is used in connection with DT learning, then assuming the β-weak

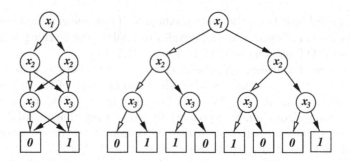

Fig. 1. Minimal BP and DT for computing the exclusive-or of three bits, $x_1 \oplus x_2 \oplus x_3$. Arcs with a black arrow head correspond to value 1 and those with a white head correspond to value 0.

learning hypothesis for $\mathcal{H}$, for any sample S_v from X there exists an $h \in \mathcal{H}$ such that $\Delta(S_v, h) \geq (\beta^2/16)G(\hat{q}_v)$. Based on this result Mansour and McAllester [12] defined that $\mathcal{H}$ and F satisfy the γ-*weak index reduction hypothesis* if for any sample S_v from X there exists an $h \in \mathcal{H}$ such that $\Delta(S_v, h) \geq \gamma F(\hat{q}_v)$.

By approximating — according to the weak learning hypothesis — the reduction of the index obtained by growing the size of the tree, one can bound the empirical error of the tree as a polynomial of its size:

$$\hat{\epsilon}(T) \leq F(T) \leq |T|^{-\gamma}.$$

The best known bound for γ with respect to β is obtained by using the splitting criterion G.

3   Branching Program Boosting

The polynomial reduction of a DT's error is inefficient from the analytical point of view [4]. Mansour and McAllester [13] showed that using the more compact DAG representation of BPs one can exploit the γ-weak index reduction hypothesis more efficiently than when DTs are used.

We are concerned with *leveled* BPs in the following. Let P_d be such a BP of depth d. The nodes of P_d form a two-dimensional lattice. There are $d+1$ levels $L_0, L_1, \ldots, L_d$ and each L_j has its individual width. All the arcs from the nodes of L_j go to the nodes of L_{j+1}. The first level consists of the root of the program and the nodes at level d are leaves. Leaves may already appear at earlier levels.

Internal nodes of a BP contain a predicate. Leaves are labeled by one of the two classes. Each instance x has a unique path from the root of the program to one of its leaves: At an internal node containing the predicate h decide for x whether $h(x) = 0$ or $h(x) = 1$ and follow the corresponding arc to the next level. Finally, after at most d internal nodes a leaf is reached. The label of the leaf determines the class prediction for x. Fig. 1 gives an example of a BP and a DT recognizing the same function.

3.1   The BP Learning Algorithm

Let us start by sketching the main points of the learning algorithm. We fill in the missing details and describe the analytical background subsequently.

The analysis of Mansour and McAllester [13] is based on a constant γ over all levels. No such constant is available in practice. In the following algorithm, instead, each level j has its own γ_j. Together with the current index, its value determines the width w_j of a grid of *potential nodes*. From those the ones that get connected to nodes of the previous level, will make up L_j. Potential nodes help to merge leaves of P_j whose class distribution is close enough to each other. We discuss the intuition behind potential nodes in more detail in the next subsection.

Algorithm LearnBP(S)

Initialize: Let L_0 consist of the root node of the BP. Associate the whole sample S with the root. Let P_0 be this single node program.

Main Loop: For j in $\{0, \ldots, d-1\}$ define L_{j+1} as follows.

1. Let *leaves$_j$* consist of the pure nodes of L_j and set $L'_j = L_j \setminus leaves_j$. If L'_j is empty, then terminate.
2. **Predicate Selection:** For each $v \in L'_j$ choose the predicate h_v that most reduces the value of the splitting criterion F. In other words, for each $v \in L'_j$ check all attributes and determine their optimal binary splits with respect to S_v using F. Choose the best attribute and its optimal binary split to v. Technically, we choose v as the predicate h that maximizes $\Delta(S_v, h) = F(\hat{q}_v) - F(T_h, S_v)$.
3. **Program Expansion:** Let P'_{j+1} be the BP obtained from P_j by splitting the leaves in L'_j. Determine the average reduction of index, $\gamma_{j+1} > 0$, obtained by P'_{j+1}. That is,
$$\gamma_{j+1} = \frac{F(P_j) - F(P'_{j+1})}{F(P_j)}. \tag{1}$$
4. **Potential Node Grid Choosing:** Using γ_{j+1} and $F(P_j)$ determine the width w_{j+1} (the number of subintervals) of a one-dimensional grid of potential nodes each corresponding to an interval in $[0, 1]$. Determine the widths of the intervals.
5. **Leaf Merging:** Associate each leaf v of P'_{j+1} with the potential node that corresponds to the subinterval of $[0, 1]$ that contains the proportion, $\hat{q}_v$, of positive examples within v.
6. Those potential nodes that have at least one incoming arc make up L_{j+1}. Other potential nodes are discarded. The resulting program is P_{j+1}.

The parts that are not fully elaborated in the above algorithm are steps 3–6. They also comprise the theoretically most demanding points in this algorithm. The next subsection will review the analytical motivation behind these steps.

3.2   Analytical Background

A key difficulty in learning BPs is to have a sufficiently finely spaced grid so that when subsets from two or more nodes get merged, the loss in index reduction is not too large. On the other hand, in order to restrict the growth of the hypothesis size, one must limit the number of potential nodes in the grid. Next, we go through those parts of the analysis of Mansour and McAllester [13] that motivate the choice of the grid of potential nodes used in LearnBP.

Consider, first, growing a leveled BP, where the nodes never get merged. This leveled DT growing yields the same polynomial error declination with respect to the tree size as other DT learning algorithms. Hence, to improve the error reduction with respect to the classifier size, nodes must be merged in the BP.

In the following we consider what happens to the index of a program, when P_j is expanded to P_{j+1} using the two-phase process, where all nodes $v \in L'_j$ are first split in two to produce P'_{j+1}. By Eq. 1, the index of the expanded program is $(1 - \gamma_{j+1})F(P_j)$. After expansion the grid of potential nodes is chosen. It helps to merge together leaves of P'_{j+1} to produce the final nodes of P_{j+1}.

The potential nodes $n_1, \ldots, n_{w_{j+1}}$ correspond to a division of $[0, 1]$ into consecutive intervals $I_i = [u_{i-1}, u_i)$, where $0 = u_0 < u_1 < \cdots < u_{w_{j+1}} = 1$. Let N_i denote those leaves v of P'_{j+1} for which $\hat{q}_v \in I_i$. The nodes belonging to N_i are merged together to potential node n_i. If $N_i = \emptyset$, the node n_i is discarded.

Let us see how the index of the BP changes due to merging of nodes. Before any such operations

$$F(P'_{j+1}) = \sum_{v \in L(P'_{j+1})} \hat{p}_v F(\hat{q}_v) = \sum_{i=1}^{w_{j+1}} \hat{p}_i F_i,$$

where $\hat{p}_i = \sum_{v \in N_i} \hat{p}_v$ and $F_i = \sum_{v \in N_i} (\hat{p}_v / \hat{p}_i) F(\hat{q}_v)$. After the merging, node n_i receives all the examples that arrived in P'_{j+1} to the leaves belonging to N_i. Hence, $\hat{p}_i$ is the proportion of examples received by n_i out of all examples. Let $\hat{q}_i$ denote, as usual, the fraction of positive examples out of those reaching n_i. Then, the index after the mergings is

$$F(P_{j+1}) = \sum_{i=1}^{w_{j+1}} \hat{p}_i F(\hat{q}_i).$$

The change in the index of the BP can, thus, be expressed as

$$F(P_{j+1}) - F(P'_{j+1}) = \sum_{i=1}^{w_{j+1}} \hat{p}_i (F(\hat{q}_i) - F_i).$$

Now, $\inf_{x \in I_i} F(x) \leq F_i \leq F(\hat{q}_i) \leq \sup_{x \in I_i} F(x)$, because $\hat{q}_i \in I_i$ and F is concave (see Fig. 2). Thus, the index increases, but the increase is small provided that F maps the points of each interval I_i close to each other.

In order not to lose the whole index reduction obtained by P'_{j+1}, the increase of index due to mergings has to be small with respect to γ_{j+1} and $F(P_j)$. This can be obtained by setting $u_m = 1/2$, where $m = w_{j+1}/2$, and $u_{m \pm k} = F_\pm^{-1}(1/(1 + \gamma_{j+1}/3)^k)$, for $0 < k < m$. Above, F_- is F restricted to $[0, 1/2]$ and F_+ to $[1/2, 1]$. Now, $\sup_{x \in I_i} F(x) = (1 + \gamma_{j+1}/3) \inf_{x \in I_i} F(x)$, whenever $1 < i < w_{j+1}$.

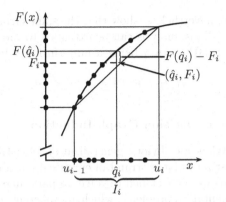

Fig. 2. Leaves with a fraction of positive examples in the interval $I_i = [u_{i-1}, u_i)$ make up N_i and are gathered to the potential node n_i. Combined these leaves have index $\hat{p}_i F_i$ and proportion $\hat{q}_i$ of positive examples within them. The point $(\hat{q}_i, F_i)$ is a convex combination of points $(\hat{q}_v, F(\hat{q}_v))$, $v \in N_i$ and, thus, falls within the region bounded by $F(x)$ in between end points u_{i-1} and u_i and the line connecting these end points. The index value assigned to n_i, $\hat{p}_i F(\hat{q}_i)$, is higher than $\hat{p}_i F_i$.

To keep the width of the grid under control n_1 and $n_{w_{j+1}}$ are handled as special cases. By setting

$$w_{j+1} = 2 + 2 \left\lceil \frac{\ln(6/(\gamma_{j+1}F(P_j)))}{\ln(1 + \gamma_{j+1}/3)} \right\rceil,$$

it holds that $1/(1 + \gamma_{j+1}/3)^{w_{j+1}/2} \leq (\gamma_{j+1}/6)F(P_j)$. Hence, the first and the last potential node represent (a subset of) those leaves $v \in L(P'_{j+1})$ for which $F(\hat{q}_v) \leq (\gamma_{j+1}/6)F(P_j)$. When the grid is chosen as presented above, then

$$F(P_{j+1}) - F(P'_{j+1}) \leq \frac{\gamma_{j+1}}{3} \sum_{i=2}^{w_{j+1}-1} \hat{p}_i \inf_{x \in I_i} F(x) + (\hat{p}_1 + \hat{p}_{w_{j+1}})\frac{\gamma_{j+1}}{6}F(P_j)$$

$$\leq \left(\frac{\gamma_{j+1}}{3} + \frac{\gamma_{j+1}}{6} \right) F(P_j).$$

On the other hand, by Eq. 1, $F(P'_{j+1}) = (1 - \gamma_{j+1})F(P_j)$. Thus, $F(P_{j+1}) \leq (1 - \gamma_{j+1}/2)F(P_j)$. In other words, at least half of the index reduction obtained by P'_{j+1} is retained also after merging nodes together.

It remains to show that $|P_j|$ grows slowly enough. Let us first assume that γ_j equals a fixed $\gamma > 0$ and that $F(P_{j+1}) = (1 - \gamma/2)F(P_j)$ for each j. This is the least index reduction conforming to the above analysis. Now, the index of P_j is at most $(1 - \gamma/2)^j$. The increase in width, $w_{j+1} - w_j$, depends only on γ, not on j. Therefore, $|P_j|$ grows only quadratically in j. Together these observations imply that in this case the error reduction of a BP is exponential in the square root of its size. When it is also allowed that $F(P_{j+1}) < (1 - \gamma/2)F(P_j)$ —the analysis becomes more complicated, because $w_{j+1} - w_j$ may now vary. Mansour and McAllester [13], nevertheless, show that the same error declination holds in general for a fixed γ. This analysis can be extended to show that for a program P produced by LearnBP, with γ being a uniform lower bound for γ_j, it holds that

$$\hat{\epsilon}(P) \leq F(P) \leq e^{-\Omega(\gamma\sqrt{|P|})}.$$

3.3   Related Work: Decision Graph Induction

Even though a DAG is an obvious generalization of a tree, learning decision graphs (DGs) is just an isolated strand in empirical machine learning. The DG induction algorithms were developed to solve, in particular, the subtree replication and data fragmentation problems, which are inherent to top-down induction of DTs. DGs resemble BPs, but are not exactly alike.

Oliver's [14] iterative hill-climbing algorithm uses a Minimum Message Length (MML) criterion to determine whether to split a leaf or to join a pair of leaves in the evolving DG. In experiments the algorithm attained the same accuracy level as MML-based DT learners and C4.5. DGs were observed to give particularly good results in learning disjunctive concepts.

Kohavi [10], originally, proposed constructing DGs in a bottom-up manner. Despite some empirical success, the algorithm was not able to cope with numerical attributes and lacked methods for dealing with irrelevant attributes. Subsequently Kohavi and Li [11] presented a method that post-processes a DT top-down into a DG. Special requirements were put to the initial DT; it was required to be *oblivious*, that is, test the same variable at each node in the same level of the tree. This approach was proposed as an alternative to the bottom-up pruning of DTs. The reported experiments exhibit classification accuracies comparable to those of C4.5, but with smaller classifier sizes.

Despite these few approaches, learning DAG-formed classifiers has not yet been thoroughly studied. Neither has sufficient analysis been presented for them.

4   Empirical Evaluation

We now test LearnBP in practice. As splitting criterion we use Kearns and Mansour's [9] function G. The analysis above only covers two class problems. Also, the algorithm LearnBP can only handle predicates. Therefore, we restrict our attention to domains with two classes. For nominal variables with more than two values, we search their optimal binary grouping with respect to G and use it. Numerical value ranges are binarized.

The classifier sizes are compared to see whether the BPs with zero empirical error are smaller than the corresponding DTs like they should be by the analysis (assuming the index reduction hypothesis). In order to evaluate the practical applicability of BPs, we compare the prediction accuracies of BPs and DTs.

It suffices to test LearnBP against C4.5, because the relation of C4.5 and AdaBoost is known [4,7]. In order to make the comparison fair to BPs, we contrast them against unpruned DTs built by C4.5. Moreover, we force C4.5 to drive the empirical error to zero, if possible, like LearnBP does.[1] In order to make the comparison fair to DTs, we avoid repetitive counting of leaves, and measure classifier sizes by the number of internal nodes.

As test domains we use well-known binary data sets from the UCI Repository [2] and some synthetic domains. From the UCI Repository also relatively large domains were included. (Adult has approx. 32,500 and Connect some 67,500 examples; the latter was changed into a binary problem by uniting classes draw and lost). Some data sets were manipulated to rid the effects of missing attribute values. The synthetic data sets used are the majority function on 10 and 50 bits (denoted by MAJ10 and MAJ50, respectively), the multiplexor function with 3 address bits (MPLX3) [15], and the exclusive-or function on 6 and 8 bits (XOR6 and XOR8). For all synthetic data sets two different-sized random samples were generated. Our test strategy is 10-fold cross-validation repeated 10 times.

Table 1 gives the average prediction accuracies and sizes for BPs and DTs. It also records whether the observed differences are statistically significant as measured by the two-tailed Student's t-test at significance level 0.01 (99%).

4.1   Results on the UCI Data

On "real-world" data sets the accuracies of the learning algorithms are close to each other. In seven out of the total fifteen UCI domains statistically significant differences in the prediction accuracies are observed. On five of these cases the differences are in favor of LearnBP and on two cases of the unpruned DTs of C4.5. On some domains BPs may benefit from the fact that due to subset mergings the split decisions are often based on a larger population of training examples than the corresponding decisions in DTs. The obtained accuracy levels are lower than when using pruning, but not dramatically.

In hypothesis sizes the fact that pruning is disabled is, of course, observed. Some of the classifier average sizes are very large. On ten domains BPs are smaller than unpruned DTs and in the remaining five UCI domains unpruned DTs are smaller than the corresponding BPs. The algorithm that produces smaller hypotheses tends to have the better prediction accuracy. There are only three exceptions to this rule.

4.2   Results on Synthetic Data

On synthetic data, BPs are systematically more accurate on the majority problems. In addition to those there is only one further significant difference (in favor of C4.5). The results on the majority domains can be explained by the utility of merging leaves in the evolving program. Consider two leaves that are merged. Their fractions of positive examples have to be close to each other. Thus, even though different bits were tested en route to the leaves, the subsets associated

---

[1] It is not possible to set the parameters of Release 8 of C4.5 to produce perfect unpruned trees. Therefore, in this comparison we use Release 5 [15].

Table 1. Average classification accuracies and classifier sizes (with standard deviations) for LearnBP and C4.5 on the test domains. Statistically significant differences between the two learning algorithms are indicated by a double asterisk.

DATA SET		LEARNBP	C4.5	BP SIZE	DT SIZE
ADULT		81.6 ±0.2	81.3 ±0.1	3,959.6 ±50.0	4,870.1 ±13.5
BREAST W		94.6 ±0.6	93.9 ±0.6	26.0 ±0.5	29.6 ±1.1
CHESS		99.5 ±0.1	99.7 ±0.1	46.1 ±0.9	44.3 ±0.3
CONNECT		82.5 ±0.1	84.3 ±0.1	11,012.0 ±30.7	9,058.0 ±9.8
DIABETES		70.3 ±1.5	69.4 ±1.0	119.9 ±2.1	131.8 ±1.7
EUTHYROID		91.0 ±0.5	90.1 ±0.5	135.6 ±0.7	161.4 ±2.3
GERMAN		69.4 ±0.7	67.6 ±0.6	157.7 ±2.0	167.1 ±1.6
GLASS2		79.9 ±1.6	80.8 ±1.7	18.4 ±0.3	14.8 ±0.6
HEART H		72.7 ±2.3	72.8 ±1.2	43.9 ±0.9	52.6 ±0.8
HEPATITIS		75.7 ±2.0	78.0 ±1.9	13.6 ±0.3	15.0 ±0.5
IONOSPHERE		88.4 ±1.1	89.8 ±1.3	18.0 ±0.3	15.4 ±0.8
LIVER		65.4 ±1.8	63.4 ±1.5	70.7 ±1.7	77.6 ±1.4
SONAR		77.6 ±1.6	74.5 ±1.5	15.5 ±0.3	16.5 ±0.5
TIC-TAC-TOE		93.7 ±0.9	86.8 ±1.0	81.6 ±2.9	107.5 ±2.1
VOTING		86.6 ±0.7	86.2 ±0.6	41.0 ±1.2	35.7 ±0.3
MAJ10	200	82.3 ±2.5	78.7 ±2.5	40.2 ±1.2	42.8 ±0.8
	400	87.0 ±1.9	84.8 ±1.5	67.2 ±1.9	74.6 ±1.4
MAJ50	1000	66.2 ±1.1	61.4 ±1.2	159.7 ±1.7	191.1 ±2.2
	2000	70.2 ±1.3	63.8 ±0.9	296.3 ±2.1	368.3 ±2.6
MPLX3	400	82.8 ±1.8	84.4 ±1.3	101.2 ±3.6	96.5 ±2.6
	800	95.2 ±1.0	94.6 ±0.7	109.2 ±5.4	113.8 ±5.0
XOR6	300	98.1 ±0.8	98.4 ±0.7	71.5 ±2.1	59.7 ±0.1
	600	99.0 ±0.8	100.0 ±0.1	75.6 ±2.8	63.0 ±0.1
XOR8	500	81.2 ±2.2	81.6 ±0.8	257.7 ±5.5	207.6 ±0.5
	1000	96.6 ±0.6	96.7 ±0.7	321.5 ±4.8	245.6 ±0.9

with the leaves are likely to consist of examples with similar numbers of positive and negative bits. On the other hand, sometimes mergings are disadvantageous.

Over the ten synthetic domains the race for the smaller hypothesis is tied. This time there is no exception to the rule that the algorithm that produces the smaller hypothesis also has the better prediction accuracy.

In summary, the overall performance of BPs and unpruned DTs is very similar in both measured parameters. Nevertheless, BPs seem to perform slightly better than DTs.

5   Discussion

The empirical observations in the comparison between AdaBoost and C4.5 were explained with their different *advantage sequences* [4], i.e., how the weak learning parameter β changes from round to round. This depends on the algorithm and the data. The parameter characterizes the difficulty of the classification problems posed to the weak learners. While C4.5 produces increasingly refined partitions of the sample, thus obtaining increasing advantage, AdaBoost concentrates on the examples that are falsely classified by earlier weak classifier, thus producing harder and harder filtered distributions and losing advantage.

Advantage sequences cannot directly be used in analyzing LearnBP, since it chooses many weak classifiers at a time. However, there is reason to believe that the γ-sequences of BPs are worse than those of DTs, because merging may make the task of separating the two classes more difficult. The advantage in LearnBP grows as the original sample is refined, but subset mergings lead to slow growth. Consider, e.g., the exclusive-or on eight bits. Assume that LearnBP has grown P_8'. Let u and v be two leaves that will be merged in P_8. If seven different bits have been tested on the paths from the root to u and v, splitting the leaves by testing the remaining bit produces pure leaves and, thus, gives a large reduction in index. On the other hand, when u and v are merged, the examples reaching them get mixed and it is impossible to separate the positive and negative examples by testing a single bit. We obtain a smaller value for γ_9, and also a larger BP since all information lost has to be gathered anew.

We may note that the width of the grid of potential nodes explodes with respect to the width of the corresponding program level. While the program levels typically are up to 30 nodes wide, the width of the grid of potential nodes may be close to 30,000 intervals. In the analysis of Mansour and McAllester [13] potential nodes determine the size of a program, which is much larger than the actual program size. Quite often the programs produced by LearnBP are actually DTs or almost such, i.e., they have very few node mergings. Sometimes the BP consists of several consecutive trees; i.e., there are nodes that gather all the remaining examples and the program construction starts anew.

We have compared BPs with unpruned DTs to better relate their sizes. However, DTs can be easily pruned to enhance classifier compactness. In this respect our empirical setting was not fair; with pruning C4.5 would easily beat LearnBP in classifier size. On the other hand, we wanted to obtain an understanding of the basic properties of a new interesting learning approach and test how the boosting analysis is reflected to practice.

LearnBP can be seen to work in the same explicit merging approach as some DG learning algorithms do, where all leaves of the evolving program are first expanded and then merged heuristically. Using the grid of potential nodes is an analytically motivated heuristic. Other heuristics could be used as well.

6   Conclusion

Constructing DAG-formed classifiers rather than tree-formed ones is a natural idea. However, since the former are harder to interpret and prune, they have not become more popular. Moreover, no evident advantage for using BPs has been known. The new analysis [13] gives a promise of a concrete advantage that could bear fruit in practice. However, our empirical evaluation indicates that this theoretical advantage does not directly materialize in experiments. The results, though, are comparable to those obtained using unpruned DTs. Altogether, learning BPs (or DGs) is an interesting new idea which might deserve more empirical attention.

References

1. Bergadano, F., Bshouty, N.H., Tamon, C., Varricchio, S.: On learning branching programs and small depth circuits. In: Ben-David, S. (ed.): Computational Learning Theory: Proc. Third European Conference. Lecture Notes in Artificial Intelligence, Vol. 1208, Springer-Verlag, Berlin Heidelberg New York (1997) 150–161
2. Blake, C.L., Merz, C.J.: UCI repository of machine learning databases. Department of Information and Computer Science, University of California, Irvine (1998). http://www.ics.uci.edu/~mlearn/MLRepository.html
3. Breiman, L., Friedman, J.H., Olshen, R.A., Stone, C.J.: Classification and regression trees. Wadsworth, Pacific Grove, CA (1984)
4. Dietterich, T., Kearns, M., Mansour, Y.: Applying the weak learning framework to understand and improve C4.5. In: Saitta, L. (ed.): Proc. Thirteenth Internationl Conference on Machine Learning, Morgan Kaufmann, San Francisco (1996) 96–104
5. Ergün, F., Kumar, R.S., Rubinfeld, R.: On learning bounded-width branching programs. In: Proc. Eighth Annual Conference on Computational Learning Theory, ACM Press, New York (1995) 361–368
6. Freund, Y.: Boosting a weak learning algorithm by majority. Inf. Comput. **121** (1995) 256–285
7. Freund, Y., Schapire, R.E.: Experiments with a new boosting algorithm. In: Saitta, L. (ed.): Proc. Thirteenth International Conference on Machine Learning. Morgan Kaufmann, San Francisco (1996) 148–156
8. Freund, Y., Schapire, R.E.: A decision-theoretic generalization of on-line learning and an application to boosting. J. Comput. Syst. Sci. **55** (1997) 119–139
9. Kearns, M., Mansour, Y.: On the boosting ability of top-down decision tree learning algorithms. J. Comput. Syst. Sci. **58** (1999) 109–128
10. Kohavi, R.: Bottom-up induction of oblivious read-once decision graphs. In: Bergadano, F., De Raedt, L. (eds.): Machine Learning: Proc. Seventh European Conference. Lecture Notes in Artificial Intelligence, Vol. 784, Springer-Verlag, Berlin Heidelberg New York (1994) 154–169
11. Kohavi, R., Li, C.-H.: Oblivious decision trees, graphs, and top-down pruning. In: Proc. Fourteenth International Joint Conference on Artificial Intelligence. Morgan Kaufmann, San Francisco, CA (1995) 1071–1079
12. Mansour, Y., McAllester, D.: Boosting with multi-way branching in decision trees. In: Solla, S.A., Leen, T.K., Müller, K.-R. (eds.): Advances in Neural Information Processing 12. MIT Press, Cambridge, MA (2000) 300–306
13. Mansour, Y., McAllester, D.: Boosting using branching programs. In: Cesa-Bianchi, N., Goldman, S. (eds): Proc. Thirteenth Annual Conference on Computational Learning Theory. Morgan Kaufmann, San Francisco, CA (2000) 220–224
14. Oliver, J.J.: Decision graphs — an extension of decision trees. In: Proc. Fourth International Workshop on Artificial Intelligence and Statistics. Society for Artificial Intelligence and Statistics (1993) 343–350
15. Quinlan, J.R.: C4.5: Programs for machine learning. Morgan Kaufmann, San Mateo, CA (1993)
16. Schapire, R.E.: The strength of weak learnability. Mach. Learn. **5** (1990) 197–227

A Simple Approach to Ordinal Classification

Eibe Frank and Mark Hall

Department of Computer Science
University of Waikato
Hamilton, New Zealand
{eibe, mhall}@cs.waikato.ac.nz

Abstract. Machine learning methods for classification problems commonly assume that the class values are unordered. However, in many practical applications the class values do exhibit a natural order—for example, when learning how to grade. The standard approach to ordinal classification converts the class value into a numeric quantity and applies a regression learner to the transformed data, translating the output back into a discrete class value in a post-processing step. A disadvantage of this method is that it can only be applied in conjunction with a regression scheme.

In this paper we present a simple method that enables standard classification algorithms to make use of ordering information in class attributes. By applying it in conjunction with a decision tree learner we show that it outperforms the naive approach, which treats the class values as an unordered set. Compared to special-purpose algorithms for ordinal classification our method has the advantage that it can be applied without any modification to the underlying learning scheme.

1 Introduction

Classification algorithms map a set of attribute values to a categorical target value, represented by a class attribute. Practical applications of machine learning frequently involve situations exhibiting an order among the different categories represented by the class attribute. However, standard classification algorithms cannot make use of this ordering information: they treat the class attribute as a nominal quantity—a set of unordered values.

Statisticians differentiate between four basic quantities that can be represented in an attribute, often referred to as levels of measurement [9]. There are four types of measurements: nominal, ordinal, interval, and ratio quantities. The difference between nominal and ordinal quantities is that the latter exhibit an order among the different values that they can assume. An ordinal attribute could, for example, represent a coarse classification of the outside temperature represented by the values *Hot*, *Mild*, and *Cool*. It is clear that there is an order among those values and that we can write $Hot > Mild > Cool$.

Interval quantities are similar to ordinal quantities in that they exhibit an order. They differ because their values are measured in fixed and equal units. This implies that the difference between two values can be determined by subtracting

L. De Raedt and P. Flach (Eds.): ECML 2001, LNAI 2167, pp. 145–156, 2001.
© Springer-Verlag Berlin Heidelberg 2001

them. This does not make sense if the quantity is ordinal. Temperature measured in degrees Fahrenheit is an interval quantity. Ratio quantities additionally exhibit a zero point. This means that it is possible to multiply their values.

Standard classification algorithms for nominal classes can be applied to ordinal prediction problems by discarding the ordering information in the class attribute. However, some information is lost when this is done, information that can potentially improve the predictive performance of a classifier.

This paper presents a simple method that enables standard classification algorithms to exploit the ordering information in ordinal prediction problems. Empirical results—obtained using the decision tree learner C4.5 [7]—show that it indeed improves classification accuracy on unseen data. A key feature of our method is that it does not require any modification of the underlying learning algorithm—it is applicable as long as the classifier produces class probability estimates.

The method is explicitly designed for ordinal problems—in other words, for classification tasks with ordered categories. Standard regression techniques for numeric prediction problems can be applied when the target value represents an interval or ratio quantity. However, their application to truly ordinal problems is necessarily *ad hoc*.

This paper is structured as follows. In Section 2 we present our approach to ordinal classification. Section 3 contains experimental results on a collection of benchmark datasets, demonstrating that the predictive accuracy of decision trees can be improved by applying this method to exploit ordering information in the class. Section 4 discusses related work on custom-made learning algorithms for ordinal problems and approaches that use regression techniques for ordinal classification. Section 5 summarizes the contributions made in this paper.

2   Transforming the Ordinal Classification Problem

Figure 1 shows in diagrammatic form how our method allows a standard classification learner to be applied to an ordinal prediction task. The data is from a fictional temperature prediction problem and has an ordinal class attribute with three values (*Cool, Mild* and *Hot*). The upper part depicts the training process and the lower part the testing process.

A simple trick allows the underlying learning algorithms to take advantage of ordered class values. First, the data is transformed from a k-class ordinal problem to $k-1$ binary class problems. Figure 2 shows the process of converting an ordinal attribute A^* with ordered values $V_1, V_2, ..., V_k$ into $k - 1$ binary attributes, one for each of the original attribute's first $k - 1$ values. The ith binary attribute represents the test $A^* > V_i$.

Training starts by deriving new datasets from the original dataset, one for each of the $k - 1$ new binary class attributes. In Figure 1 there are two derived datasets, the first has a class attribute that represents $Target > Cool$ and the second has a class attribute that represents $Target > Mild$. Each derived dataset contains the same number of attributes as the original, with the same attribute values for each instance—apart from the class attribute. In the next

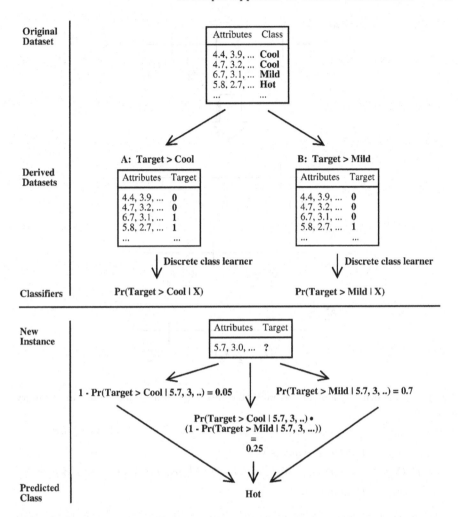

Fig. 1. How standard classification algorithms are applied to ordinal prediction

step the classification algorithm is applied to generate a model for each of the new datasets.

To predict the class value of an unseen instance we need to estimate the probabilities of the k original ordinal classes using our $k - 1$ models. Estimation of the probability for the first and last ordinal class value depends on a single classifier. The probability of the first ordinal value ($Cool$) is given by $1 - Pr(Target > Cool)$. Similarly, the last ordinal value (Hot) is computed from $Pr(Target > Mild)$. For class values in the middle of the range—in this case there is only one ($Mild$)—the probability depends on a pair of classifiers. In this example it is given by $Pr(Target > Cool) \times (1 - Pr(Target > Mild))$. In general, for class values V_i,

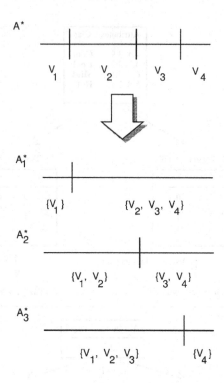

Fig. 2. Transformation of an ordinal attribute with four values into three binary attributes

$$Pr(V_1) = 1 - Pr(Target > V_1)$$
$$Pr(V_i) = Pr(Target > V_{i-1}) \times (1 - Pr(Target > V_i)) \ , 1 < i < k$$
$$Pr(V_k) = Pr(Targe > V_{k-1})$$

At prediction time, an instance of unknown class is processed by each of the $k - 1$ classifiers and the probability of each of the k ordinal class values is calculated using the above method. The class with maximum probability is assigned to the instance.

3   Experimental Results

To test the hypothesis that the above method improves the generalization performance of a standard classification algorithm on ordinal prediction problems, we performed experiments on artificial and real-world datasets in conjunction with the C4.5 decision tree learner [7]. We used a collection of benchmark datasets representing numeric prediction problems and converted the numeric target values into ordinal quantities using equal-frequency binning. This unsupervised discretization method divides the range of observed values into a given number of intervals so that the number of instances in each interval is approximately

Table 1. Datasets and their characteristics

Dataset	Instances	Attributes	Numeric	Nominal
Abalone	4177	9	7	2
Ailerons	13750	41	40	1
Delta Ailerons	7129	6	5	1
Elevators	16599	19	18	1
Delta Elevators	9517	7	6	1
2D Planes	40768	11	10	1
Pole Telecomm	15000	49	48	1
Friedman Artificial	40768	11	10	1
MV Artificial	40768	11	7	4
Kinematics of Robot Arm	8192	9	8	1
Computer Activity (1)	8192	13	12	1
Computer Activity (2)	8192	22	21	1
Census (1)	22784	9	8	1
Census (2)	22784	17	16	1
Auto MPG	398	8	4	4
Auto Price	159	16	15	1
Boston Housing	506	14	12	2
Diabetes	43	3	2	1
Pyrimidines	74	28	27	1
Triazines	186	61	60	1
Machine CPU	209	7	6	1
Servo	167	5	0	5
Wisconsin Breast Cancer	194	33	32	1
Pumadyn Domain (1)	8192	9	8	1
Pumadyn Domain (2)	8192	33	32	1
Bank Domain (1)	8192	9	8	1
Bank Domain (2)	8192	33	32	1
California Housing	20640	9	8	1
Stocks Domain	950	10	9	1

constant. The resulting class values are ordered, representing variable-size intervals of the original numeric quantity. This method was chosen because of the lack of benchmark datasets involving ordinal class values.

The datasets were taken from a publicly available collection of regression problems [8]. The properties of these 29 datasets are shown in Table 1. For each dataset we created three different versions by discretizing the target value into three, five, and ten intervals respectively. This was done to evaluate the influence of different numbers of classes on the schemes' relative performance.

All accuracy estimates were obtained by averaging the results from 10 separate runs of stratified 10-fold cross-validation. In other words, each scheme was applied 100 times to generate an estimate for a particular dataset. Throughout, we speak of two results for a dataset as being "significantly different" if the difference is statistically significant at the 1% level according to a paired two-sided t-test, each pair of data points consisting of the estimates obtained in one ten-fold cross-validation run for the two learning schemes being compared. A significant difference in this sense means that, with high probability, a complete cross-validation [4] on the dataset would result in a difference in accuracy.[1]

Table 2 shows the accuracy estimates for the decision tree learner C4.5[2] in the five-class situation, applied (a) without any modification of the input and output (C4.5), (b) in conjunction with the ordinal classification method presented in Section 2 (C45-ORD), and (c) using the standard one-per-class method (see, e.g., [9]) for applying a two-class learner to a multi-class problem (C4.5-1PC). We have included C4.5-1PC in the comparison to ascertain whether overall differences in performance are due to the fact that we transform the multi-class problem into several two-class problems. Standard deviations are also shown (based on the 10 accuracy estimates obtained from the 10 cross-validation runs).

Results for C4.5 and C4.5-1PC are marked with ○ if they show significant improvement over the corresponding results for C4.5-ORD, and with ● if they show significant degradation. Table 3 shows how the different methods compare with each other. Each entry indicates the number of datasets for which the method associated with its column is (significantly) more accurate than the method associated with its row.

The results show that the ordinal classification method frequently improves performance compared to plain C4.5. On 17 datasets, C4.5-ORD is significantly more accurate than C4.5, and significantly worse on only one. The results also show that the performance difference is not due to the fact that each learning problem has been converted into several two-class problems: C45-ORD is significantly more accurate than C4.5-1PC on 16 datasets, and significantly worse on only five.

A sign test confirms the hypothesis that the ordinal classification procedure from Section 2 improves performance. Note that the results for the two different versions of the computer activity, census domain, pumadyn domain, and bank domain datasets are highly correlated. Consequently we ignore the smaller version of each of these four datasets when we perform the sign test (i.e. we only consider version number 2 in each case). If this is done, C4.5-ORD wins against plain C4.5 on 19 datasets and looses on only four (not taking the significance of the individual differences into account). According to a two-sided sign test this ratio is significant at the 0.005%-level. The win/loss-ratio between C4.5-ORD and C4.5-1PC is 18/6 and significant at the 0.05%-level.

An interesting question is whether the difference in accuracy depends on the number of class values in the problem. A reasonable hypothesis is that the performance difference increases as the number of classes increases. To investigate this we also ran the three schemes on the same datasets with different discretizations of the target value.

Tables 4 and 5 summarize the results for the three-bin discretization. They show that there is relatively little to be gained by exploiting the ordering information in the class. Compared to C4.5, C4.5-ORD is significantly more accurate on 15 datasets, and significantly worse on none. However, C4.5-ORD does not

---

[1] A complete cross-validation is performed by averaging across all possible cross-validation runs that can be performed for a particular dataset.

[2] We used the implementation of C4.5 that is part of the WEKA machine learning workbench.

Table 2. Experimental results for target value discretized into five bins: percentage of correct classifications, and standard deviation

Dataset	C4.5-ORD	C4.5	C4.5-1PC
Abalone	47.86±0.45	46.34±0.73 •	49.55±0.65 ∘
Ailerons	59.24±0.30	56.97±0.35 •	55.58±0.34 •
Delta Ailerons	55.76±0.34	55.54±0.50	56.77±0.15 ∘
Elevators	50.32±0.24	47.76±0.29 •	50.72±0.33 ∘
Delta Elevators	49.78±0.31	47.63±0.42 •	50.34±0.29 ∘
2D Planes	75.37±0.10	75.37±0.06	75.29±0.07
Pole Telecomm	95.05±0.12	95.05±0.10	94.94±0.07
Friedman Artificial	66.50±0.19	64.83±0.18 •	64.01±0.13 •
MV Artificial	99.19±0.04	99.20±0.04	99.19±0.02
Kinematics of Robot Arm	47.28±0.34	43.69±0.41 •	42.58±0.70 •
Computer Activity (1)	65.96±0.38	63.75±0.32 •	65.03±0.32 •
Computer Activity (2)	68.69±0.47	66.80±0.47 •	66.76±0.44 •
Census Domain (1)	53.32±0.22	50.20±0.36 •	51.46±0.34 •
Census Domain (2)	51.49±0.26	48.96±0.33 •	50.97±0.21 •
Auto MPG	59.74±0.98	59.58±1.86	59.46±1.25
Auto Price	66.80±2.20	62.39±2.71 •	63.50±1.43 •
Boston Housing	60.97±1.41	59.34±1.49 •	59.70±1.65
Diabetes	29.00±3.14	26.55±5.21	33.80±2.63 ∘
Pyrimidines	43.27±2.85	42.27±3.51	42.68±2.78
Triazines	40.03±2.51	38.90±3.07	37.14±2.40 •
Machine CPU	58.10±1.32	56.78±2.78	56.62±2.43
Servo	52.45±1.60	55.16±2.09 ∘	49.82±1.65 •
Wisconsin Breast Cancer	21.36±2.04	22.92±3.48	21.71±1.40
Pumadyn Domain (1)	49.83±0.30	46.04±0.43 •	48.28±0.34 •
Pumadyn Domain (2)	65.75±0.35	62.67±0.42 •	63.51±0.37 •
Bank Domain (1)	74.04±0.24	73.14±0.31 •	73.27±0.36 •
Bank Domain (2)	38.68±0.52	37.37±0.59 •	36.01±0.22 •
California Housing	64.83±0.24	63.30±0.18 •	64.36±0.18 •
Stocks Domain	86.85±0.67	87.05±0.88	85.19±0.53 •

∘, • statistically significant improvement or degradation

Table 3. Pair-wise comparison for target value discretized into five bins: number indicates how often method in column (significantly) outperforms method in row

	C4.5-ORD	C4.5	C4.5-1PC
C4.5-ORD	–	**4 (1)**	**6 (5)**
C4.5	**23 (17)**	–	15 (11)
C4.5-1PC	**22 (16)**	14 (7)	–

Table 4. Experimental results for target value discretized into three bins: percentage of correct classifications, and standard deviation

Dataset	C4.5-ORD	C4.5	C4.5-1PC
Abalone	66.07±0.26	63.90±0.24 •	65.91±0.34
Ailerons	75.37±0.31	74.78±0.37 •	73.79±0.34 •
Delta Ailerons	80.54±0.26	80.34±0.17	80.9 ±0.17 ∘
Elevators	64.43±0.17	62.22±0.25 •	63.63±0.36 •
Delta Elevators	70.83±0.22	69.89±0.26 •	70.73±0.27
2D Planes	86.61±0.04	86.61±0.05	86.52±0.09 •
Pole Telecomm	95.90±0.12	95.64±0.10 •	95.58±0.1 •
Friedman Artificial	80.78±0.09	80.23±0.14 •	80.3 ±0.18 •
MV Artificial	99.51±0.02	99.53±0.02	99.55±0.03 ∘
Kinematics of Robot Arm	64.37±0.37	63.76±0.24 •	64.88±0.38 ∘
Computer Activity (1)	79.04±0.39	78.44±0.43 •	78.38±0.31 •
Computer Activity (2)	81.02±0.42	80.76±0.31	80.21±0.4 •
Census Domain (1)	70.53±0.17	69.58±0.27 •	70.95±0.18 ∘
Census Domain (2)	69.53±0.21	68.19±0.28 •	69.61±0.23
Auto MPG	78.81±1.26	78.12±1.14	79.16±1.32
Auto Price	86.25±1.38	85.36±1.60	85.87±1.27
Boston Housing	75.52±1.07	74.83±1.72	74.79±1.18
Diabetes	54.45±2.61	51.00±3.91	54.45±2.61
Pyrimidines	56.89±3.98	50.11±2.95 •	55.12±3.31
Triazines	54.47±3.28	54.18±3.20	54.11±2.84
Machine CPU	73.88±2.39	71.85±2.44	74.26±2.77
Servo	77.24±1.16	75.56±1.26 •	79.22±1.27 ∘
Wisconsin Breast Cancer	35.98±2.33	37.40±3.23	35.71±2.11
Pumadyn Domain (1)	66.71±0.37	66.02±0.28 •	67.37±0.32 ∘
Pumadyn Domain (2)	78.83±0.15	77.65±0.41 •	77.64±0.3 •
Bank Domain (1)	85.89±0.28	86.02±0.28	85.61±0.11 •
Bank Domain (2)	57.15±0.45	55.84±0.38 •	53.94±0.26 •
California Housing	78.94±0.11	79.02±0.17	79.42±0.16 ∘
Stocks Domain	91.74±0.53	91.24±0.53	91.77±0.45

∘, • statistically significant improvement or degradation

Table 5. Pair-wise comparison for target value discretized into three bins: number indicates how often method in column (significantly) outperforms method in row

	C4.5-ORD	C4.5	C4.5-1PC
C4.5-ORD	–	**4 (0)**	**11 (7)**
C4.5	**24 (15)**	–	18 (11)
C4.5-1PC	**17 (10)**	11 (4)	–

perform markedly better than C4.5-1PC: it is significantly more accurate on 10 datasets, and significantly worse on seven. It is interesting to see that the one-per-class encoding outperforms plain C4.5 on these three-class datasets.

If the significance of the individual differences is not taken into account and ignoring the smaller version of each pair of datasets from the same domain, C4.5-ORD wins against C4.5 on 20 datasets, and looses on four. This difference is statistically significant according to a two-sided sign test: the corresponding p-value is 0.0008. However, compared to C4.5-1PC, the win/loss-ratio for C4.5-ORD is 15/10, with a corresponding p-value of 0.21. Thus there is only very weak evidence that the ordinal classification method improves on the standard one-per-class encoding.

For the ten-bin case we expect a more significant difference, in particular when compared to the one-per-class method. This is confirmed in the experimental results summarized in Tables 6 and 7. The difference in performance between C4.5-ORD and C4.5 remains high but increases only slightly when moving from five to ten bins. C4.5-ORD outperforms C4.5 on all but seven of the datasets. It is significantly more accurate on 22 datasets, and significantly less accurate on only two. Compared to C4.5-1PC, C4.5-ORD is significantly more accurate on 25 datasets, and significantly worse on two. This is a marked improvement over the five-bin case and suggests that ordering information becomes more useful as the number of classes increases.

Not considering the significance of individual differences and ignoring the smaller version of each pair of datasets from the same domain, C4.5-ORD wins against C4.5 on 19 datasets, and looses on six. According to a two-sided sign test this ratio is significant at the 0.01%-level. Thus there is strong evidence that C4.5-ORD outperforms C4.5 on a collection of datasets of this type. Compared to C4.5-1PC, the win/loss-ratio for C4.5-ORD is 21/4, with a corresponding p-value of 0.0005. Consequently there is very strong evidence that the ordinal classification method improves on the standard one-per-class encoding.

4   Related Work

The ordinal classification method discussed in this paper is applicable in conjunction with any base learner that can output class probability estimates. Kramer *et al.* [5] investigate the use of a learning algorithm for regression tasks—more specifically, a regression tree learner—to solve ordinal classification problems. In this case each class needs to be mapped to a numeric value. Kramer *et al.* [5] compare several different methods for doing this. However, if the class attribute represents a truly ordinal quantity—which, by definition, cannot be represented as a number in a meaningful way—there is no principled way of devising an appropriate mapping and this procedure is necessarily *ad hoc*.

Herbrich *et al.* [3] propose a strategy for ordinal classification that is based on a loss function between pairs of true ranks and predicted ranks. They present a corresponding algorithm similar to a support vector machine, and mention that their approach can be extended to other types of linear classifiers.

Potharst and Bioch [6] present a decision tree learning algorithm for *monotone* learning problems. In a monotone learning problem both the input at-

Table 6. Experimental results for target value discretized into ten bins: percentage of correct classifications, and standard deviation

Dataset	C4.5-ORD	C4.5	C4.5-1PC
Abalone	29.48±0.36	26.68±0.61 ●	27.43±0.58 ●
Ailerone	39.36±0.33	36.64±0.37 ●	35.76±0.32 ●
Delta Ailerons	43.06±0.37	41.31±0.61 ●	43.30±0.30
Elevators	31.41±0.34	28.58±0.35 ●	29.77±0.38 ●
Delta Elevators	39.86±0.33	36.9 ±0.44 ●	41.44±0.23 ○
2D Planes	54.95±0.14	53.00±0.14 ●	51.25±0.32 ●
Pole Telecomm	91.18±0.08	90.85±0.14 ●	89.34±0.15 ●
Friedman Artificial	44.55±0.17	41.06±0.10 ●	32.79±0.38 ●
MV Artificial	98.11±0.03	98.17±0.05	97.36±0.06 ●
Kinematics of Robot Arm	25.83±0.36	24.39±0.28 ●	20.37±0.38 ●
Computer Activity (1)	45.61±0.38	42.20±0.46 ●	42.12±0.34 ●
Computer Activity (2)	48.77±0.55	45.58±0.65 ●	45.60±0.48 ●
Census (1)	32.58±0.18	30.5 ±0.23 ●	29.00±0.21 ●
Census (2)	31.51±0.27	29.33±0.22 ●	28.95±0.19 ●
Auto MPG	36.55±1.18	39.63±1.70 ○	24.65±1.09 ●
Auto Price	48.40±2.01	36.82±2.40 ●	34.37±3.01 ●
Boston Housing	42.66±1.00	38.61±1.25 ●	35.93±1.65 ●
Diabetes	14.55±3.12	23.00±3.12 ○	19.80±2.06 ○
Pyrimidines	19.39±2.95	23.89±2.69	15.93±1.83 ●
Triazines	20.51±1.21	16.50±1.94 ●	12.22±1.74 ●
Machine CPU	36.35±2.47	36.23±1.48	30.59±1.93 ●
Servo	34.57±0.98	34.60±1.47	13.18±0.03 ●
Wisconsin Breast Cancer	10.73±1.91	11.24±3.15	11.33±1.24
Pumadyn Domain (1)	26.49±0.38	23.69±0.61 ●	16.6 ±0.43 ●
Pumadyn Domain (2)	45.76±0.44	41.87±0.42 ●	41.21±0.54 ●
Bank Domain (1)	52.76±0.37	49.57±0.44 ●	43.58±0.82 ●
Bank Domain (2)	25.51±0.42	24.20±0.33 ●	24.06±0.39 ●
California Housing	44.77±0.28	42.67±0.32 ●	39.47±0.27 ●
Stocks Domain	74.83±1.33	72.69±0.76 ●	72.09±0.70 ●

○, ● statistically significant improvement or degradation

Table 7. Pair-wise comparison for target value discretized into ten bins: number indicates how often method in column (significantly) outperforms method in row

	C4.5-ORD	C4.5	C4.5-1PC
C4.5-ORD	–	**6 (2)**	**4 (2)**
C4.5	**23 (22)**	–	6 (3)
C4.5-1PC	**25 (25)**	22 (17)	–

tributes and the class attribute are assumed to be ordered. This is different from the setting considered in this paper because we do not assume that the input is ordered.

Although machine learning algorithms for ordinal classification are rare, there are many statistical approaches to this problem. However, they all rely on specific distributional assumptions for modeling the class variable and also assume a stochastic ordering of the input space [3].

The technique of generating binary "dummy" attributes to replace an ordered attribute can also be applied to the attributes making up the input space. Frank and Witten [2] show that this often improves performance compared to treating ordered attributes as nominal quantities. In cases where both the input and the output are ordered, this technique can be applied in addition to the method discussed in this paper to obtain further performance improvements.

The method presented in this paper is also related to the use of error-correcting output codes for (unordered) multi-class problems [1]. Instead of using error-correcting bit vectors to represent each class, we use bit vectors that reflect the ordering of the class values. As opposed to choosing the bit vector with the closest Hamming distance when making a prediction, our method selects the vector which corresponds to the largest estimated class probability (computed according to the procedure discussed in Section 2).

5   Conclusions

This paper presents a simple method that enables standard classification algorithms to make use of ordering information in ordinal class attributes. The method converts the original ordinal class problem into a series of binary class problems that encode the ordering of the original classes. Empirical results based on C4.5 show that this procedure is significantly more accurate than plain C4.5, and C4.5 used in conjunction with the standard one-per-class method. They also show that the performance gap increases with the number of classes. Our findings demonstrate that the improvement in performance is a result of exploiting ordering information and not simply as a side effect of transforming the problem into a series of binary-class problems.

References

1. T. G. Dieterich and G. Bakiri. Solving multiclass learning problems via error-correcting output codes. *Journal of Artificial Intelligence Research*, 2:263–286, 1995.
2. E. Frank and I. H. Witten. Making better use of global discretization. In *Proceedings of the Sixteenth International Conference on Machine Learning*, Bled, Slovenia, 1999. Morgan Kaufmann.
3. R. Herbrich, T. Graepel, and K. Obermayer. Regression models for ordinal data: A machine learning approach. Technical report, TU Berlin, 1999.
4. R. Kohavi. *Wrappers for Performance Enhancement and Oblivious Decision Graphs*. PhD thesis, Stanford University, Department of Computer Science, 1995.
5. S. Kramer, G. Widmer, B. Pfahringer, and M. DeGroeve. Prediction of ordinal classes using regression trees. *Fundamenta Informaticae*, 2001.

6. R. Potharst and J.C. Bioch. Decision trees for ordinal classification. *Intelligent Data Analysis*, 4(2):97–112, 2000.
7. R. Quinlan. *C4.5: Programs for Machine Learning*. Morgan Kaufmann, San Francisco, 1993.
8. L. Torgo. Regression Data Sets. University of Porto, Faculty of Economics, Porto, Portugal, 2001. [`http://www.ncc.up.pt/~ltorgo/Regression/DataSets.html`].
9. I. H. Witten and E. Frank. *Data Mining: Practical Machine Learning Tools and Techniques with Java Implementations*. Morgan Kaufmann, San Francisco, 2000.

Fitness Distance Correlation of Neural Network Error Surfaces: A Scalable, Continuous Optimization Problem

Marcus Gallagher

School of Computer Science and Electrical Engineering
University of Queensland, QLD 4072, Australia
marcusg@csee.uq.edu.au

Abstract. This paper investigates neural network training as a potential source of problems for benchmarking continuous, heuristic optimization algorithms. Through the use of a student-teacher learning paradigm, the error surfaces of several neural networks are examined using so-called fitness distance correlation, which has previously been applied to discrete, combinatorial optimization problems. The results suggest that the neural network training tasks offer a number of desirable properties for algorithm benchmarking, including the ability to scale-up to provide challenging problems in high-dimensional spaces.

1 Introduction

Heuristic optimization algorithms such as Evolutionary Algorithms (EAs) are expected to be capable of solving high-dimensional, complex problems, requiring only the ability to be able to evaluate the objective function at any feasible point in the search space. These kinds of optimization problems arise frequently many areas, and are often a fundamental part of methods used for data-driven tasks such as supervised and unsupervised learning. In recent years, heuristic optimization algorithms have been the focus of a very large amount of research, as well as being successfully applied to many challenging real-world problems.

Researchers face several difficulties when trying to evaluate the effectiveness of a given algorithm at solving problems. In particular, a set of benchmark optimization problems which can be usefully scaled to high-dimensions is an important requirement. Unfortunately, commonly used test functions have a number of short-comings in meeting this need. This paper investigates a particular form of a well-known task: training a feedforward neural network, as a possible source of test optimization problems. The evaluation of continuous heuristic optimization algorithms is discussed further in the following section. Section 3 considers the exploration of continuous optimization problems using correlation statistics and scatterplots. The student-teacher neural network training problem is then described in Section 4, and experimental results for a set of such problems is presented in Section 5. Section 6 concludes and summarizes these results. Note that here we are concerned mainly with solving continuous multivariate optimization problems, using algorithms which work directly with a continuous representation of solution vectors.

L. De Raedt and P. Flach (Eds.): ECML 2001, LNAI 2167, pp. 157–166, 2001.
© Springer-Verlag Berlin Heidelberg 2001

2   Heuristic Algorithms and Continuous Optimization

The standard multidimensional optimization problem involves a parameter vector $\mathbf{w} = (w_1, \ldots, w_n)$, with the quality of a candidate solution being measurable by an objective function $f(\mathbf{w})$. The goal of optimization can then be simply to find a solution vector $\mathbf{w}^*$, which yields the best possible objective function value, subject to given resources (e.g, computation time). In some fields (e.g, evolutionary computation), optimization is normally defined as maximization of $f()$ (a fitness function) while in others (e.g, neural networks) the problem is equivalently framed as minimization of a cost (e.g, error) function. To describe and visualize an optimization algorithm (which performs an iterative, guided search in the space of possible solutions), the ideas of hill-climbing on a fitness landscape [5] and searching for the minimum of an error surface [10] have become well-known.

The focus of this paper is on continuous optimization problems (i.e, $\mathbf{w} \in I\!R^n$). Although heuristic algorithms have been successfully applied to many real-world optimization problems, interest in quantifying what kind of problems are easy or hard for algorithms such as EA's to solve has increased. This interest is partly due to the No Free Lunch (NFL) theorems, which indicate that there is no algorithm that outperforms all other algorithms in any general sense [12].

Researchers seek to understand and evaluate heuristic algorithms by empirical testing on sets of benchmark problems. Many of the test functions that have been used are analytical functions of continuous variables. Such functions can be easily visualized in one or two dimensions, and the locations of local and globally optimal points are often known precisely. Unfortunately, commonly used functions have a number of shortcomings [11]. Desirable properties for test functions include [4,7,11]:

P1. difficult to solve using simple methods such as hill-climbing
P2. nonlinear, nonseparable and nonsymmetric
P3. scalable in terms of problem dimensionality
P4. scalable in terms of time to evaluate the cost function
P5. tunable by a small number of user parameters
P6. can be generated at random and are difficult to reverse engineer
P7. exhibit an array of landscape-like features.

Despite the large amount of research in developing new algorithms, very few attempts have been made to identify problems that possess many of these properties. Whitley et al. [11] and Michalewicz et al. [7] propose methods for generating analytical test functions for unconstrained and constrained optimization respectively.

3   Correlation Measures of Landscapes

A number of researchers (see, e.g. [9] and the references therein) have considered examining the correlation between fitness and distances between points on discrete fitness landscapes. These studies include the cost versus average distance of an optimum point to all other points within a sample of local optima [2,8] and cost versus distance of local optima from the best optima found [6]. These studies on artificial and combinatorial optimization landscapes have indicated that a "Massif Central" [6] or "big valley" [2] structure seems to exist in many landscapes. That is, perhaps not surprisingly, cost in general seems to increase with distance from the best minimum, providing an intuitive picture of the landscape as a big bowl-like structure with smaller ridges, valleys and other structure imposed on it. These approaches require collecting a sample of local optimum points, which is infeasible in the continuous case.

One correlation measure which can be adapted to continuous error surfaces is the Fitness Distance Correlation (FDC) of Jones [5]. FDC is intended to provide a measure of the global structure of the surface in question, by examining how the value of the cost (fitness) function varies with the distance between a given point and a global optimum. A sample of random points on the surface P is chosen, and the standard sample correlation coefficient is calculated:

$$r = \frac{Cov(D, E)}{\sigma_D \sigma_E} \tag{1}$$

$$= \frac{n \sum^n DE - (\sum^n D)(\sum^n E)}{\sqrt{[n \sum^n D^2 - (\sum^n D)^2][n \sum^n E^2 - (\sum^n E)^2]}} \tag{2}$$

where D is a set of distances for a sample of points from the global optimum, E is the corresponding set of fitness function values for the sample and $Cov(D, E)$ is the covariance of D and E. σ_X is the standard deviation of X. The value of r is in the range $[-1, +1]$, with a value of $+1$ suggesting perfect, positive linear correlation between the objective function and the distance from the global optimum, and a value of -1 suggesting perfect negative correlation between these quantities.

FDC was proposed as an indicator of the difficulty of a search space for a Genetic Algorithm (GA) to solve [5]. The results support this measure, indicating that problems with a low FDC coefficient are hard for a GA to solve, whereas those with a high FDC coefficient value are GA-easy. While it has been shown that this correlation coefficient is not always successful at predicting the "GA-difficulty" of a problem [1,9], Jones suggests that FDC scatterplots provide a useful visualization of this relationship, even when the FDC coefficient does not summarize the relationship well [5].

4   The Neural Network Training Task

The Multi-layer Perceptron (MLP) [10] is the standard feedforward neural network model used in supervised learning problems. The model consists of a layer of N_i inputs, connected to one or more layers of "hidden" units, which are themselves connected to a final layer of N_o output units. Input signals propagate through the units in the network, via weighted connections, to the outputs.

The network mapping for a single hidden layer is given by

$$\mathbf{y} = \Psi(\mathbf{x}, \mathbf{u}, \mathbf{v}) \tag{3}$$

$$y_i = g_o(\sum_j u_{ij} h_j) \tag{4}$$

$$h_j = g_h(\sum_k v_{jk} x_k) \tag{5}$$

where $\mathbf{x}$ is an input vector, $\mathbf{u}$ and $\mathbf{v}$ are vectors of weights on the input connections to the hidden and output layers respectively, $\mathbf{y} = (y_1, \ldots, y_{N_o})$ is an output vector, g_h is a sigmoidal activation function and g_o is typically either an identity function or another sigmoid. The latter is employed if the outputs are to be constrained to an interval (e.g. $(-1, 1)$). A linear bias term is also normally included as an input and is connected directly to the hidden and output layers, by setting $x_0 = \pm 1 \ \forall \ \mathbf{x} = (x_0, x_1, \ldots, x_{N_i})$. This network architecture is known to be a universal approximator (with a sufficient number of hidden units) by appropriate choice of connection weight values $u_{ij}, v_{jk} \in I\!R$ [10].

MLP networks are typically trained to perform supervised learning tasks from a set of training data. As mentioned earlier, training is usually formulated as the minimization of an appropriate error function. The error surface of MLP networks has an interesting structure, which is dependent on a number of factors, such as the number of nodes in each layer, and the given training set. Although precise results concerning the structure of error surfaces are limited, they are typically considered to consist of a number of wide, flat plateaus, narrow ravines, symmetries due to the network topology and often a small number of unique non-global minima [3].

In this set of experiments, an artificial learning task is used, which is sometimes referred to as the *student-teacher* learning model (see [3]). In this problem, two networks are created. One network, the teacher, is initialized in some way, and then represents the "oracle" for the learning task. The training set is produced by generating random input vectors and passing these inputs to the teacher network, producing the desired output vectors. The other network, the student, is then trained using this data.

The main advantage, from an optimization viewpoint, of using this student-teacher model of learning is that it guarantees the presence of a known globally minimum point (ie, a parameter vector identical to the teacher weight configuration), where the value of the error function is zero. Symmetries in neural network error surfaces mean that there are $2^{N_h} N_h!$ functionally equivalent weight vectors to the teacher network, which are also global minima. Knowledge of the global minimum is required for calculating the FDC, which is normally not available on neural network training tasks derived from simple test problems like XOR, or from real world supervised learning datasets [10].

The error surface of an student-teacher MLP training task can be seen as having many of the properties listed in Section 2. Error surfaces are not easy to optimize over using simple methods like gradient descent [10] (P1). They are clearly nonlinear and nonseparable (part of (P2)), and scalable in problem dimensionality (P3) (furthermore, their properties can be changed by varying user-parameters such as the number of training patterns and units in the network (P5)). The time to evaluate the cost function scales linearly with these user-parameters (P4), and networks can be generated randomly as desired (part of (P6)). This paper explores the possible features of these error surfaces (P7), in relation to varying three network parameters (P5), through a series of experiments and FDC-scatterplots[1].

In the following experiments, the student-teacher model is used to generate FDC results for MLP's. Throughout, mean-squared error is used as the error function and Euclidean distance is the distance measure. Teacher networks are generated by choosing their weights from a Normal distribution (with mean zero, standard deviation 5), in an attempt to generate networks with realistic weights (i.e. some large weights leading to some units saturating their outputs [3]). The "student" networks' weights are chosen from a Normal distribution (with mean $\mu_{teacher}$, standard deviation 1) distribution, and the weight vector is then scaled to a length chosen uniformly between 0 and 100. 5000 points are used to calculate the FDC coefficients, while for clarity only 2000 are used for the fitness-distance scatterplots. The number of input units, number of hidden units and the number of training patterns are varied in the experiments. All networks have a single output unit. The hidden and output units use the *tanh* activation function (i.e g_h and g_o). Each unique training instance is run 10 times with different random initializations of teacher networks.

5   FDC Results for Error Surfaces

The FDC coefficient results are shown in Table 1. Each table entry reports the mean and standard deviation of the 10 different experiments for each training instance. Firstly, all coefficient values are positive, confirming intuition that moving away from a global minimum cannot lead to a *decrease* in error. At worst ($r \approx 0$), there is basically no correlation between the error value and the distance to the global minimum - the current location of a search or the trajectory up to some point in the search yields no information regarding the location of the global minimum. A general trend in this table is from relatively low r values for small numbers of inputs, hidden units and training patterns, to high values as these variables are increased. Standard deviations can be reasonably high for small values of the variables, and remain high even for large training sets when the network size is small.

From these r values alone, the indication is that for networks with more inputs and hidden units, distance from the global minimum and the current error value are related - implying that algorithms that are able to utilize this property will perform well in this situation. To allow a more detailed insight into the nature of these error surfaces however, the scatterplots of the experiments must be examined.

---

[1] The FDC acronym is used in this paper, although error (minimization) rather than fitness (maximization) is being considered.

Table 1. Fitness-Distance correlation values for student-teacher experiments.

No. Patterns	No. Inputs (y)/No. Hidden (x)				
		1	5	10	100
1	1	0.185 (0.069)	0.214 (0.074)	0.228 (0.101)	0.269 (0.097)
	5	0.245 (0.067)	0.189 (0.104)	0.273 (0.066)	0.248 (0.100)
	10	0.207 (0.088)	0.260 (0.064)	0.249 (0.094)	0.198 (0.130)
	100	0.322 (0.083)	0.283 (0.049)	0.183 (0.123)	0.113 (0.096)
5	1	0.176 (0.073)	0.285 (0.083)	0.378 (0.049)	0.423 (0.073)
	5	0.266 (0.078)	0.401 (0.075)	0.409 (0.400)	0.466 (0.043)
	10	0.304 (0.082)	0.466 (0.053)	0.493 (0.051)	0.480 (0.087)
	100	0.403 (0.091)	0.476 (0.089)	0.494 (0.137)	0.309 (0.148)
10	1	0.213 (0.069)	0.318 (0.073)	0.314 (0.059)	0.459 (0.059)
	5	0.305 (0.058)	0.469 (0.073)	0.494 (0.075)	0.588 (0.107)
	10	0.317 (0.076)	0.529 (0.054)	0.573 (0.086)	0.594 (0.067)
	100	0.454 (0.128)	0.548 (0.103)	0.612 (0.063)	0.523 (0.089)
100	1	0.194 (0.073)	0.320 (0.120)	0.401 (0.056)	0.529 (0.051)
	5	0.378 (0.121)	0.534 (0.072)	0.689 (0.064)	0.827 (0.037)
	10	0.383 (0.140)	0.670 (0.085)	0.744 (0.060)	0.880 (0.020)
	100	0.418 (0.108)	0.787 (0.117)	0.883 (0.056)	0.864 (0.026)
1000	1	0.180 (0.069)	0.280 (0.104)	0.382 (0.065)	0.488 (0.063)
	5	0.335 (0.152)	0.585 (0.059)	0.694 (0.052)	0.845 (0.024)
	10	0.377 (0.110)	0.631 (0.122)	0.798 (0.055)	0.926 (0.017)
	100	0.506 (0.161)	0.854 (0.050)	0.926 (0.044)	0.970 (0.005)

Figures 1-4 show a representative sample of the kinds of scatterplots which were observed from the experiments. The general nature of all of the experiments can be summarized by this sample.

Figure 1(a) shows an FDC scatterplot for a 10-5-1(#1) network (i.e. a 10 input, 5 hidden unit, 1 output MLP) with a single training pattern). Clearly, two error values dominate the sample, over the range of distances examined - one which is very close to the global minimum and one which is also the highest (worst) error value found ($E \approx 2$). This result indicates that this error surface is largely dominated by two plateaus, and the small number of points at intermediate error values suggests that the transition between these two levels is relatively sharp. Note also that the high plateau is not seen until a distance of roughly $||\mathbf{w}|| \simeq 20$ from the global minimum. In this case, the area surrounding the global minimum is quite flat, which will cause problems for algorithms seeking to converge to the exact global minimum. In practice however, this may be less of a concern - any point with an error so close to zero would probably be sufficient to halt training.

In Figure 1(b) the number of training patterns has increased to 5 for a 10-5-1(#5) network. The observable effect is the appearance of a number of intermediate levels between the $E \approx 0$ and the $E \approx 2$ levels. In addition, the levels appear incrementally as the distance increases. This observation accounts for the higher correlation coefficient ($r = 0.5235$) compared to Figure 1(a). The levels are equidistant, separated by $E \approx 0.4$ in error. This result implies that the

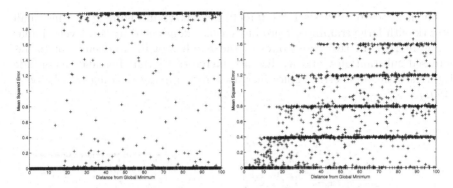

Fig. 1. (a)FDC scatterplot; 10-5-1(#1) network; $r = 0.3846$. (b)FDC scatterplot; 10-5-1(#5) network; $r = 0.5235$.

number of levels are directly related to the number of training patterns in this experiment. Lastly, the number of intermediate points between the levels has increased. The overall impression is that the global minimum is now situated in a "smaller bowl", in that walking a shorter distance from the global minimum leads to much worse error values. The number of points at a level close to the global minimum also drops off with increasing distance, again suggesting a unique global minimum and surrounding neighbourhood.

Increasing the number of training patterns further leads to an extension of these trends. Figure 2(a) shows the scatterplot for a 10-5-1(#10) network. A greater number of levels dominate the plot, though the levels themselves are becoming less defined as the number of points between them increases and as they become closer together. The rate at which higher error values appear moving away from the global minimum has also increased, indicating a reduced region around the global minimum with small error values (and producing a lower correlation value $r = 0.4330$. At a large distance, points with $E \approx 0$ are becoming increasingly rare.

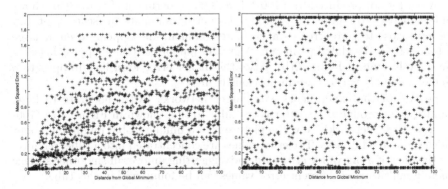

Fig. 2. (a)FDC scatterplot; 10-5-1(#10) network; $r = 0.4330$. (b)FDC scatterplot; 1-1-1(#1000) network; $r = 0.1501$.

The next scatterplot is a 1-1-1(#1000) net, shown in Figure 2(b). This small network with large training set produces a plot dominated by two levels similar to Figure 1(a). In this case however, the number of intermediate points has increased substantially, and as distance increases the number and magnitude of points with worse error values increases more rapidly (leading to a low $r = 0.1501$).

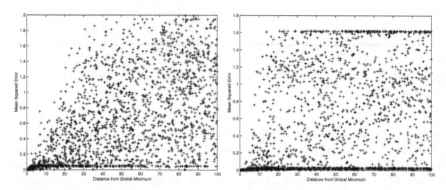

Fig. 3. (a)FDC scatterplot; 1-100-1(#1000) network; $r = 0.5040$. (b)FDC scatterplot; 100-1-1(#1000) network; $r = 0.3064$.

In Figure 3(a) (1-100-1(#1000) net), the levels which have dominated the above examples are all but gone. A significant number of points exist at one level at a value slightly above the global minimum, but only for smaller distances. A wide range of different error values is spread over the majority of the distance values. Note however that the intuition of a bowl surrounding the global minimum is supported with the smooth increase in worse error values moving away from the global minimum. The value of r has increased significantly from Figure 2(b) to Figure 3(a), due mainly to the disappearance of the high plateau of points and the diminishing lower plateau for high values of distance from the global minimum.

A scatterplot produced by a 100-1-1(# 1000) experiment (Figure 3(b)) shows some similarity to Figure 2(b). Two levels of error dominate the scatterplot, but the level close to zero error is much more common, and appears even at large distances from the global minimum. A greater number of points appear between these levels than in Figure 2(b). Also, the higher error level has dropped to a smaller value ($E \approx 1.6$) than in previous figures.

Several of the experiments with larger networks (with moderate to large training sets) produced a scatterplot similar to that shown in Figure 4(a) (100-100-1(# 1000) network). Now the picture is of a unique global minimum, about which error steadily rises. The error values are concentrated into a tube, reinforcing the idea of a big-valley structure and suggesting an overall smoother surface where a multitude of different error values can be found within this tube.

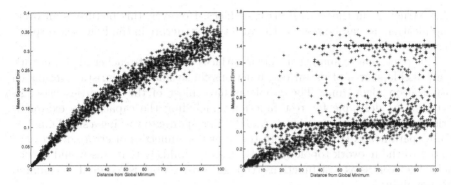

Fig. 4. (a)FDC scatterplot; 100-100-1(#1000) network; $r = 0.9706$. (b)FDC scatter-plot; 100-1-1(#1000) network; $r = 0.5748$.

6   Discussion

These results show that a number of different phenomena can be observed in the structure of MLP error surfaces. A small number of training patterns induces a number of distinct levels onto the error surface. For small values of inputs and hidden units, the number of levels was observed to have an upper bound of $(k+1)$, where k is the number of training patterns. As the number of training patterns increases, the effect becomes more like a smoothing of the error surface - as levels blur together and intersect in various different ways. Restricted numbers of hidden units and inputs (e.g. Figures 2(b) and 3(b)) seem to be factors in producing levels in the scatterplots. As all three variables (inputs, hidden units, number of training patterns) become large, the error surface becomes globally smoother, with a near-continuous range of error values at various distances from the global minimum.

The above experiments attempt to describe the fundamentally different features of scatterplots observed. Nevertheless, several experiments produced plots whose behaviour can be described as some kind of combination of such features. An example is shown in Figure 4(b), for a 100-1-1(# 100) experiment. The "tube"-like structure seen in Figure 4(a) is evident for lower values of distance and error, but a two-leveled structure becomes increasingly prominent as distance increases (cf. Figure 3(b)). Three of the ten 100-1-1(# 100) experiments produced scatterplots similar to Figure 4(b), while the other seven closely resembled Figure 3(b). A more detailed study would be required to explain the interaction of these effects with varying numbers of inputs, hidden units and numbers of training patterns.

Overall, the FDC experiments indicate that the error surface has a complex structure. Furthermore, the structure of the error surface is sensitive to factors that are commonly varied when MLP's are used - the number of inputs, number of hidden units and the number of training patterns. This observation suggests that the performance of an optimization algorithm can be expected to vary widely across different values for these variables, and across different training tasks. The positive values in Table 1 support the idea of a global big valley structure in these MLP error surfaces. However, this picture is an over-simplification, as can be seen by the variety of structure in the FDC scatterplots above.

This paper has examined the error surfaces of student-teacher MLP network as a possible source of useful test functions for evaluating heuristic continuous optimization algorithms. The problems have most of the properties listed in Section 2 as desirable for test functions, including the capacity to exhibit a variety of different structural features (P7) in response to varying a small number of user parameters (P5). Although the known symmetries of error surfaces are related to the network topology [3,11], it seems unlikely that this would reduce their effectiveness as test functions (though further work is required to examine this possibility).

Heuristic global optimization algorithms typically do not require any knowledge about a problem other the ability to evaluate the objective function. Hence, it is straightforward to apply several of these algorithms to the student-teacher MLP training problem and compare their performance empirically, in relation to FDC scatterplots and the parameters of this problem domain. A large-scale application of the test problems to several optimization algorithms is an obvious, fundamental extension of the feasibility study presented in this paper.

References

[1] ALTENBERG, L. Fitness distance correlation analysis: An instructive counterexample. In *Seventh International Conference on Genetic Algorithms (ICGA97)* (San Francisco, CA, 1997), T. Baeck, Ed., Morgan Kauffman, pp. 57–64.

[2] BOESE, K. D. *Models for Iterative Global Optimization*. PhD thesis, University of California, Los Angeles, 1996.

[3] GALLAGHER, M. *Multi-layer perceptron error surfaces: visualization, structure and modelling*. PhD thesis, Dept. Computer Science and Electrical Engineering, University of Queensland, 2000.

[4] HOLLAND, J. H. Building blocks, cohort genetic algorithms, and hyperplane-defined functions. *Evolutionary Computation 8*, 4 (2000), 373–391.

[5] JONES, T. *Evolutionary Algorithms, Fitness Landscapes and Search*. PhD thesis, University of New Mexico, 1995.

[6] KAUFFMAN, S. *The Origins of Order*. Oxford University Press, Oxford, 1993, ch. 2, pp. 33–67.

[7] MICHALEWICZ, Z., DEB, K., SCHMIDT, M., AND STIDSEN, T. Test-case generator for nonlinear continuous parameter optimization techniques. *IEEE Transactions on Evolutionary Computation 4*, 3 (2000), 197–215.

[8] MÜHLENBEIN, H., GORGES-SCHLEUTER, M., AND KRÄMER, O. Evolution algorithms in combinatorial optimization. *Parallel Computing 7* (1988), 65–85.

[9] NAUDTS, B., AND KALLEL, L. A comparison of predictive measures of problem difficulty in evolutionary algorithms. *IEEE Transactions on Evolutionary Computation 4*, 1 (2000), 1–15.

[10] REED, R. D., AND II, R. J. M. *Neural Smithing: supervised learning in feedforward artificial neural networks*. The MIT Press, Cambridge, MA, 1999.

[11] WHITLEY, D., MATHIAS, K., RANA, S., AND DZUBERA, J. Evaluating evolutionary algorithms. *Artificial Intelligence 85*, 1-2 (1996), 245–276.

[12] WOLPERT, D. H., AND MACREADY, W. G. No free lunch theorems for search. Tech. Rep. SFI-TR-95-02-010, Santa Fe Institute, February 1995.

Extraction of Recurrent Patterns from Stratified Ordered Trees

Jean-Gabriel Ganascia

Laboratoire d'Informatique de Paris 6 - CNRS
8, rue du Capitaine Scott, 75015 Paris, FRANCE
Jean-Gabriel.Ganascia@lip6.fr

Abstract. This paper proposes a new algorithm for pattern extraction from Stratified Ordered Trees (SOT). It first describes the SOT data structure that renders possible a representation of structured sequential data. Then it shows how it is possible to extract clusters of similar recurrent patterns from any SOT. The similarity on which our clustering algorithm is based is a generalized edit distance, also described in the paper. The algorithms presented have been tested on text mining: the aim was to detect recurrent syntactical motives in texts drawn from classical literature. Hopefully, this algorithm can be applied to many different fields where data are naturally sequential (e.g. financial data, molecular biology, traces of computation, etc.)

1   Introduction

Much work has been done in fields as molecular biology [8], music [7] or text analysis to compare sequences of characters. In the past, an important amount of good results have been obtained on the exact matching problems between strings, areas or binary trees [4], [5]. Other approaches have dealt with approximate pattern matching. Some of them used dynamic programming techniques based on the notion of edit distance [9]; however, those techniques mainly consider flat sequential data, such as strings, without any structure. Some authors have attempted to replace flat sequential data by binary or n-ary ordered or non-ordered trees, but the inherent complexity of pattern extraction algorithms makes them intractable in general cases. It has been proved that some efficient procedures exist [11] under strict conditions, but the imposed restrictions preclude their use for practical machine learning problems. This paper shows that, by restricting the structured input to SOT, i.e. to Stratified Ordered Trees, it is possible to build a new efficient pattern extraction algorithm. This algorithm uses as input a huge SOT containing 100,000 or more nodes, and generates

L. De Raedt and P. Flach (Eds.): ECML 2001, LNAI 2167, pp. 167–178, 2001.
© Springer-Verlag Berlin Heidelberg 2001

clusters of small similar SOTs that appear to have multiple occurrences in the input SOT. The technique can be used in many different applications, the one presented here being text mining, i.e. the detection of approximate syntactical patterns with multiple occurrences in natural language texts. Of course, there are numerous other applications to machine learning in all domains where data are essentially sequential, as is the case with financial data, molecular biological data, etc.

The main body of the paper consists of four main parts. The first section briefly introduces the notion of SOT; the second recalls the classical definition of edit distance and shows how it has been generalized to be able to deal with SOTs. The third section presents the generation algorithm that builds the similarity graph and the clustering procedure which induces patterns with multiple approximate occurrences. The fourth and final section provides some information about the use of the algorithm on text mining and considers its efficiency in practical terms.

2   Stratified Ordered Trees

2.1   Ordered Trees

According to a classical definition, an ordered tree is a tree where left to right order between siblings is significant. All sequential data can obviously be represented with a depth-1 ordered tree. By adding levels to ordered trees, it is possible to organize data in a way that represents implicit background knowledge. For instance, a text, i.e. a sequence of characters, is a list of sentences, each of which is composed of words and punctuation marks. Therefore, it can be represented using a depth-3 tree that makes this structure explicit.

2.2   Sorts and Stratification

Ordered trees increase representation power and it is possible to detect similar sub-trees, with respect to this data organization. It is also possible to extract general patterns that have multiple approximate occurrences. For instance, any specific recurrent sequence of syntactical groups extracted from a parsing tree may be detected without considering the corresponding words or their categories.

Nevertheless, due to the high number of potential pairs of sub-trees recurrent pattern detection is intractable. To make it manageable, nodes are categorized into sorts in such a way that two successfully matched nodes must be of the same sort. In other words, a match between two trees is valid if and only if the corresponding nodes in the matching are of the same sort.

In addition, we suppose that there exists a total order on the set of sorts and that, with respect to this order, the sort of the son(s) is identical to, or immediately follows that of the father. This constraint defines the so-called stratification and the resulting structure is a SOT — Stratified Ordered Tree —. More formally, by defining an ordered set, $\mathscr{S}$ (set of sorts), and a function $sort(x)$ which associates a sort to each labeled node belonging to $\mathscr{L}$, we can specify a SOT as an ordered tree where each node sort is either equal to its father sort or to its immediate successor, except for the root which has no father. In case of syntactical trees resulting from natural language text parsing, it means that the ordered set of sorts $\mathscr{S}$ may contain five categories {Text, Sentence, Syntagma, Category, Word} such that Text < Sentence < Syntagma < Category < Word. Let us note that Syntagmas may correspond to syntactical groups or propositions, depending on the syntactical parser, and that they can be recursive. For instance, the son of a proposition may be a proposition.

3   Edit Distance and Similarity Measure

3.1   Edit model

Edit distances have been widely used to detect approximate string pattern matching [9] and a general overview of these techniques can be found in [1]. Let us just recall here some of the basic principles.

Definition: An *edition* is an operator that replaces one character or one sub-string of a string, or more generally one node of a tree, by another one. For instance, a substitution is an edition if it transforms a character of a string into another one in the same position. An insertion (respectively deletion) which inserts (respectively deletes) a character in a string is also an edition.

Remark: in the following, we note $\mathscr{A}$ any set of editions, i.e. any set of transformations from a string or a tree, and $\mathscr{A}_s$ the standard set of editions composed of the three basic operations, *substitution*, *deletion* and *insertion*.

Definition: An *edit distance* between two strings or two trees is based on the minimum number of editions that transform one string or one tree into another. For instance, here is an edit transformation based on the standard set of editions $\mathscr{A}$ from the string "WHICH" to the string "THAT":

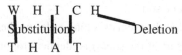

Fig. 1. A set of editions that derives THAT from WHICH

It follows from this definition that the edit distance from "WHICH" to "THAT", i.e. $\text{edit}_{\mathscr{A}}$(WHICH, THAT), is lower than the cost of this transformation (Cf. fig. 1) which is equal to the sum of all the corresponding edition costs, i.e. cost(substitution(W, T)) + cost(substitution(I, A)) + cost(substitution(C, T) + cost(deletion(H)).

3.2   Edit distance between strings

Let us now consider that strings x and y are given as two tables of length n and m, i.e. as x[1..n] and y[1..m]. Then it is possible to build a matrix (n+1)×(m+1) called $\text{EDIT}_{\mathscr{A}}$ where $\text{EDIT}_{\mathscr{A}}$(i, j) is filled with the value of $\text{edit}_{\mathscr{A}}$(x[1..i], y[1..j]) for i∈[1..n] and j∈[1..m], while EDIT(0, j) corresponds to the cost of the insertion of y(j) i.e. *insertion(y(j)),* and EDIT(i, 0) to the cost of the deletion of x(i), i.e. *deletion(x[i]).* A simple formula summarizes the way the matrix elements are computed:

$$\text{edit}_{\mathscr{A}}(x[1..i], y[1..j]) = \min \begin{cases} \text{edit}_{\mathscr{A}}(x[1..i-1], y[1..j]) + \textit{deletion}(x(i)) \\ \text{edit}_{\mathscr{A}}(x[1..i-1], y[1..j-1]) + \textit{substitution}(x(i), y(j)) \\ \text{edit}_{\mathscr{A}}(x[1..i], y[1..j-1]) + \textit{insertion}(y(j)) \end{cases} \tag{1}$$

where *deletion*(x(i)), *insertion*(y(j)) and *substitution*(x(i), y(j)) correspond to the cost of respectively the deletion of x(i), the insertion of y(j) and the substitution of x(i) by y(j).

This recursive definition is appropriate for computation since the distance between two chains of size n is obtained from the distance between chains with a size less than n. Since the edit distance increases with the size of the chains, the closest pairs will be computed first. So, given a threshold beyond which pairs of chains are not considered as similar, it will be easy to discard pairs of chains when some of their sub-chains have already been discarded.

3.3   Extension of the edit model to SOTs

The edit model can easily be extended to SOTs (Stratified Ordered Trees). It is just to remark that the *left-hand exploration* (i.e. the pre-order) of a SOT unambiguously represents it as a list of node occurrences. Due to the stratification of SOTs, the node sorts refer directly to their level in trees. This representation is unambiguous since if the subsequent node sort is greater than the current node sort, it is its son ; if it is equal it is its brother ; if it is lower, it is one of its ancestors.

Therefore the comparison of sequences of nodes resulting from the left-hand exploration of two trees is equivalent to the comparison of those trees. Taking this remark into account, the edit distance between two SOTs is equivalent to the edit distance between the sequences of nodes resulting from the left-hand exploration of those SOTs. In a more formal way, by denoting $lhe(T)$ the left-hand exploration of SOT T, the edit distance edit(T, T') between two SOTs T and T' can be expressed by $\text{edit}_{se}(lhe(T), lhe(T'))$.

1. The Whole Processing Chain

To summarize, the whole processing chain that transforms a natural language text into a set of frequent patterns is given below (fig. 2)

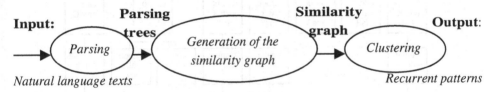

Fig. 2. The whole processing chain

The main input of the system consists of a natural language text that is a sequence of sentences, each being affirmative, interrogative or exclamatory. A natural language analysis performs the first step, through parsing or categorization. It associates labels to words (noun, verb, etc.) and to groups of words (noun group, verb group, etc.). Since the paper is not focused on this natural language analysis, the parser and the categorization process used are not described in detail. We shall just focus on the generality of the approach that has as input any natural language parsing tree with different grammar and different sets of labels. The important point is that the analysis transforms texts into trees or forests, i.e. into sequences of trees, which means that general graphs are excluded. Most of the time, trees are layered, i.e. depending on the level of the trees, labels belong to distinct classes. For instance, one level corresponds to non-recursive syntagmas, i.e. noun groups or verb groups; the second to word categories, i.e. articles or nouns; the third to attributes like gender or number; the following one to lemma, i.e. canonical forms of verbs or nouns, and the last to words as they appear in sentences. Note that our approach is not restricted to syntactical decomposition in non-recursive groups. The only limitation is that the result of the analysis has to be structured in a Stratified Ordered Tree (SOT)

2. The Similarity Graph

Using the edit distance, a labeled graph called the *similarity graph* is built making the distances between patterns explicit when they do not go beyond a fixed threshold.

4.1.1   Patterns

This similarity graph is of crucial importance; it constitutes the main input of the clustering module and includes all the *patterns* that generalize sub-trees of the input SOT. This implicit generalization is a key-point in the overall algorithm, since it generates all general patterns including non-balanced ordered trees. In the case of natural language parsing trees, generated patterns may look like the following:

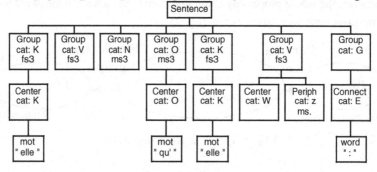

Fig. 3. A non-balanced pattern covering *"Elle exécuta ce qu'elle avait projeté :"*

Note that in Vergne [10] parsing formalism *Group* is a kind of syntagmas that refers to a syntactical group while *Center, Periph* and *Connect* are syntactical categories corresponding to the central or peripheral role of the word in the syntactical group and to a connector (here an external connector, i.e. a punctuation mark).

4.1.2   Computing the Similarity Graph

To compute the similarity graph, all pairs of patterns T_1 and T_2 have to be produced and then the value of the edit distance from T_1 to T_2 has to be checked. The upper bound of the computational complexity of this algorithm is $|S(T)|^2$, $S(T)$ being the set of all sub-trees of T. However, it may be considerably reduced using properties of the edit distance on which the similarity graph relies.

Given any total order $<_e$ on patterns, the symmetry of the edit distance reduces the test to ordered pairs of patterns $\{T_1, T_2\}$ where $T_1 <_e T_2$.

A second important property of the edit distance comes from the restriction to the standard set of editions, i.e. to the three basic operations *insertion*, *deletion* and *substitution*. Let us now suppose that $T_1 \leq_e T_2$, and that edit$(T_1, T_2) \geq \theta$. It is then easy to prove that edit$(T_1, T_3) \geq \theta$ for any T_3 such that $T_2 \leq_e T_3$.

4.2   Pattern extraction

The last step is the pattern extraction. Since the similarity graph records all similarities between patterns, it is natural to extract clusters of similar patterns from this graph. However, the way in which we can build such clusters may differ.

The classical approach is to detect highly connected sub-graphs of the similarity graph [4], [5]. However, for many reasons, this approach appears to be inappropriate to solve our problem. A more satisfactory approach is adopted here. Called the "center star" algorithm, it has been introduced by Gusfield [2] to detect homology on molecular biology data. Then Rolland and Ganascia [7] developed and applied it to extract patterns in music. As this approach has already been published, we shall not describe it here in detail. Let us just define a *star centered* on N as a graph of which all vertices contain node N. In other words, a star centered on N is composed of all nodes P such that the pair $\{N, P\}$ is a vertex.

To each node N of the similarity graph is associated its centered star that is ranked taking into account two criteria: the number of nodes belonging to it and their similarity to the center. The following formula provides a way to evaluate the centered star associated to each node of the similarity graph and to classify it:

$$\text{star\_value}(N) = \sum_{\{N'/\{N,N'\}\in \text{Similarity \_graph}\}} \text{similarity}(N,N') \qquad (2)$$

Once the similarity graph has been built, this function is easy to compute. However, the evaluation of each arc of the similarity graph, i.e. its similarity, has to be derived from the edit distance that needs to be converted. Given a distance (here the edit distance), many different similarity measures can be introduced such that they obey the classical definition.

Because the edit distance heavily depends on the length of patterns, we have introduced this length in the similarity formula. It means that the error ratio, i.e. the number of tolerated deletions, insertions and substitutions, depends on the size of the patterns considered. Among the possible formulae the following has been proved to be efficient and useful in practice, even if some others have been tested without substantially modifying the results.

$$s_\alpha(i,j) = \frac{1}{1 + \alpha \times (\text{edit}(i,j)/\min(\text{length}(i), \text{length}(j)))^4} \tag{3}$$

Remark: α is a positive number acting as a parameter. Its current value is fixed to 0.01 in all our experiments. However, it was experimentally modified from 0.05 to 0.001 without notably changing the obtained results.

Using any similarity measure, the "center star" algorithm first computes all the star evaluations for all nodes of the similarity graph, then the best star is selected and the nodes belonging to it are discarded from the similarity graph before the process iterates.

5   Evaluation

The generated patterns are mathematically specified as recurrent sub-trees, i.e. as sub-trees with multiple occurrences. Edit distance renders possible to extend this definition to approximate occurrences; clustering makes it possible to specify the minimum number of occurrences belonging to patterns. As a consequence, the global evaluation of the overall algorithm does not relate to the nature of the results which are perfectly specified, but to the practical complexity and to the usefulness of the system. This is the reason why it was evaluated on some practical application.

5.1   Application to syntactical pattern extraction

Among many applications of our algorithm, we focus here on the extraction of syntactical patterns resulting from syntactical analysis of natural language texts. The goal of this application is to detect some recurrent syntactical patterns in natural language texts, i.e. patterns with multiple approximate occurrences. There are three reasons for doing this research. The first is to characterize the personal style of authors as we claim that the style of writing is embedded within their choice of syntactical structure and lexicon. The second reason is educational. Our aim is to help school children, students or young writers to evaluate the richness and the diversity of their own writing style, to identify classical mistakes and propose corrections. The third reason is an academic one. The science of language, linguistics, could take advantage of such a study in order to distinguish different registers of language and to characterize them.

The system was tested on more than 75 18th and 19th centuries short stories and novels written by Madame de Lafayette, Guy de Maupassant, Alphonse Allais, Marcel Schwob, Alphonse Daudet, Eugène Mouton, Hégésippe Moreau and George Sand, among others. The texts were first parsed using the Vergnes-98 analyzer [10] and then the resulting sequence of syntactical trees was transformed into one SOT.

5.2 Efficiency

We studied the empirical complexity by relating execution time in seconds to input size in thousands of words, by reporting it on a log-log scale, and by applying a linear regression algorithm. It clearly appears (see figure 4) that the regression coefficient (i.e. the slope of the line) is equal to 2, which empirically shows that the temporal complexity is quadratic.

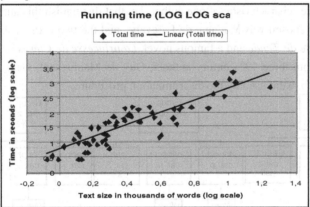

Fig. 4. Empirical Evaluation on 75 Short Stories and Novels (with the same parameters)

This first empirical result is highly satisfactory since the theoretical complexity of our algorithm is at least quadratic with the size of the input text. It comes from the way our algorithm computes the similarity graph, by exploring all the pairs of patterns. Because of the tree structure of texts, the number of sub-trees is linear with the number of sentences, so the global complexity cannot be any lower. To avoid misunderstanding, it should be said that in the case of exact repetition [4] the procedure is clearly more efficient, but not in the case of approximate matching, as it is the case. On the other hand, the center star algorithm that is a greedy algorithm, appears to be linear with the size of the similarity graph, i.e. quadratic with the number of nodes it contains. Here again, the complexity should not be any lower.

The system has been implemented in C++ and tests are run on a Macintosh G3, with a 300 MHz processor. Extracting patterns from short stories takes a few seconds while, in the case of full novels, it may take one hour or more. This means in practice that it is possible to apply our algorithm to extract patterns that are characteristic of full books, but not to deal with the lifetime work of an author. However, as we shall see in the next subsection, it can already be of great help.

5.3   Examples of extracted patterns

The pattern extraction program is completed by a discrimination procedure. Given two texts, this procedure detects the recurrent patterns covering multiple occurrences of some syntactical structure in the first text without detecting any occurrence of this structure in the second. This discrimination procedure has been employed to detect syntactical structures characteristic of one author, i.e. that distinguish this author from others. The author chosen was Madame de Lafayette, and the two texts, a short story entitled *La comtesse de Tende* and a famous novel, *La princesse de Clèves*. More than 25 short stories from three 19th century authors, Guy de Maupassant, Georges Sand and Marcel Schwob, were used by the discrimination procedure.

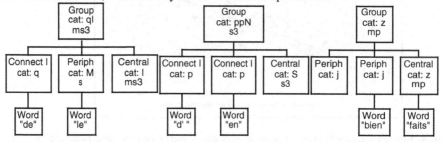

Fig. 5. Three Patterns present in the Lafayette texts without any occurrences in other texts

Among others, the first pattern (cf. fig. 5) covers the following French expression: "*de le supplier*", "*de l'éviter*", "*de l'aimer*", and others like "*de la tromper*", "*à le servir*", "*pour l'obliger*" etc. The second covers "*d'en avoir*", "*d'en attendre*", "*d'en garantir*", "*d'en faire*" etc. but also, "*sans en avoir*" and others which appear to have a very similar structure. While the third covers the following three fragments "*admirablement bien faits*", "*parfaitement bien faits*", "*très bien fait*".

There are many others specific syntactical patterns characteristic of Madame de Lafayette. Among those, here is a syntactical structure which is frequently repeated:

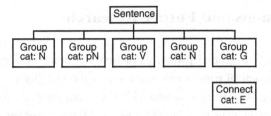

Fig. 6. A syntactical structure characteristic of Madame de Lafayette writings

It closely covers all those fragments (and others in Madame de Lafayette's work) whereas it is virtually absent from the other authors: *"Le prince de Navarre prit la parole :"*, *"La reine de Navarre avait ses favorites"*, , *"Monsieur de Nemours prit la reine dauphine"*, *"Madame de Clèvcs ne répondit rien"*, *"Le comte de Tende aimait déjà le chevalier de Navarre ;"*, *"La passion de la reine surmonta enfin toutes ses irrésolutions."*, etc.

There exists also many fragments less closely covered by this pattern. For instance: *"Madame de Chartes avait une opinion opposée"*, *"Le comte de Tende sentit son procédé dans toute sa dureté ;"*, *"La comtesse reçut ce billet avec joie"*, *"L'humeur ambitieuse de la reine lui faisait trouver une grande douceur à régner"*, etc.

There are also some very surprising results. For instance, in most of those phrases (more than 80%), the word *"comte"* which means count in French and refers to a member of the aristocracy, is matched against other words like *"prince"*, *"madame"* (i.e. madam), *"monsieur"* (i.e. sir), *"reine"* (i.e. queen) and *"comtesse"* (i.e. countess). Since no semantics has been given, this example shows how the syntax may convey semantics. As the reader might well imagine, there are many other hypotheses that may be investigated using this procedure.

All those results were presented to experts of French literature. They recognize some of the pattern as characteristic of the 18th century style of writing, while others seemed to be more specific to Madame de Lafayette. We are now currently integrating our program to a reading environment.

Note that there exists already many Computer-Assisted Research on Literature (CARL) known as stylometric analysis [3], [6]. However, those studies are based on the words, on their repetition, on their size, on their number or on their categories, not on the syntactical structure.

6   Conclusions and Future Research

We have developed a general pattern extraction algorithm working on a SOT. An application to syntactical pattern extraction shows the viability of this algorithm on real life problems. We are now programming a visual interface that displays these results. This program may be applied to many different problems where data are sequential, for instance financial analysis or molecular biology.

Among all the possible applications, one is now under development; it is to analyze traces of computation. Our algorithm is particularly well adapted because traces are easily expressed using a SOT. The two main goals of such an investigation of computing traces are to study the use of new information technology and to detect frequent patterns of commands which are the seeds of new macro operators. In other words, the algorithm can be used to build intelligent learning agents.

References

1. Crochemore M, Rytter W *Text Algorithms*, "Approximate matching", (1994): 237-251.
2. Gusfield D. *Efficient methods for multiple sequence Alignment with Guaranteed Error Bounds*, Bull. Math. Biol., 55 (1993); 141-154.
3. Holmes D Autorship Attribution, *Computers and the Humanities*, 28 (1994): 87-106.
4. Karp R M., Miller R E., Rosenberg A L. *Rapid Identification of Repeated Patterns in Strings, Trees and Arrays*, in Proc. 4th. ACM Symp. Theory of Computing, (1972): 125-136.
5. Landraud A M., Avril J-F, Chrétienne P *An algorithm for Finding a Common Structure Shared by a Family of Strings*, IEEE transactions on Pattern Analysis and Machine Intelligence, 11 (8), (1989): 890-895.
6. Lowe D, Matthews R *Shakespeare Vs. Fletcher: A Stylometric Analysis by Radial Basis Function*, Computer and the Humanities, 29 (1995): 449-461.
7. Rolland, P-Y, Ganascia J-G, *Musical Pattern Extraction and Similarity Assessment*. In Miranda, E. (ed.). Readings in Music and Artificial Intelligence. Contemporary Music Studies - Vol 20. Harwood Academic Publishers. (1999).
8. Sagot, Viari A. A Double Combinatorial Approach to Discovering Patterns in Biological Sequences, *Combinatorial Pattern Matching*, Springer Verlag, LNCS 1075 (1996): 168-208
9. Sankoff D., Kruskal J.B. *Time Warps, String Edits and Macromolecules: The Theory and Practice of Sequence Comparison*, Addison-Wesley, Reading, Mass. (1983)
10. Vergne J., *Analyseur linéaire avec dictionnaire partiel, décembre 1999*, convention d'utilisation de l'analyseur de Jacques Vergne. (1999)
11. Zhang K. *Fast algorithms for the constrained editing distance between ordered labeled trees and related problems*, report N°361, Department of computer science, University of Western Ontario, London, Ontario, Canada. (1993)

Understanding Probabilistic Classifiers

Ashutosh Garg and Dan Roth

Department of Computer Science and the Beckman Institute
University of Illinois, Urbana, IL. 61801, USA
{ashutosh,danr}@uiuc.edu

Abstract. Probabilistic classifiers are developed by assuming generative models which are product distributions over the original attribute space (as in naive Bayes) or more involved spaces (as in general Bayesian networks). While this paradigm has been shown experimentally successful on real world applications, despite vastly simplified probabilistic assumptions, the question of why these approaches work is still open.

This paper resolves this question. We show that *almost all* joint distributions with a given set of marginals (i.e., all distributions that could have given rise to the classifier learned) or, equivalently, almost all data sets that yield this set of marginals, are very close (in terms of distributional distance) to the product distribution on the marginals; the number of these distributions goes down exponentially with their distance from the product distribution. Consequently, as we show, for almost all joint distributions with this set of marginals, the penalty incurred in using the marginal distribution rather than the true one is small. In addition to resolving the puzzle surrounding the success of probabilistic classifiers our results contribute to understanding the tradeoffs in developing probabilistic classifiers and will help in developing better classifiers.

1 Introduction

Probabilistic classifiers and, in particular, the archetypical naive Bayes classifier, are among the most popular classifiers used in the machine learning community and increasingly in many applications. These classifiers are derived from generative probability models which provide a principled way to the study of statistical classification in complex domains such as natural language and visual processing.

The study of probabilistic classification is the study of approximating a joint distribution with a product distribution. Bayes rule is used to estimate the conditional probability of a class label y, and then assumptions are made on the model, to decompose this probability into a product of conditional probabilities.

$$Pr(y|x) = Pr(y|x^1, x^2, \ldots x^n) = \Pi_{i=1}^n Pr(x^i|x^1, \ldots x^{i-1}, y)\frac{Pr(y)}{Pr(x)} = \Pi_{j=1}^{n'} Pr(y^j|y)\frac{Pr(y)}{Pr(x)},$$

where $x = (x^1, \ldots, x^n)$ is the observation and the $y^j = g_j(x^1, \ldots x^{i-1}, x^i)$, for some function g_j, are independent given the class label y.

While the use of Bayes rule is harmless, the final decomposition step introduces independence assumptions which may not hold in the data. The functions g_j encode the probabilistic assumptions and allow the representation of any Bayesian network, e.g., a Markov model. The most common model used in classification, however, is the *naive*

L. De Raedt and P. Flach (Eds.): ECML 2001, LNAI 2167, pp. 179–191, 2001.
© Springer-Verlag Berlin Heidelberg 2001

Bayes model in which $\forall j, g_j(x^1, \ldots x^{i-1}, x^i) \equiv x^i$. That is, the original attributes are assumed to be independent given the class label.

Although the naive Bayes algorithm makes some unrealistic probabilistic assumptions it has been found to work remarkably well in practice [4,3]. Roth [10] develops a partial answer to this unexpected behavior using techniques from learning theory. It is shown that naive Bayes and other probabilistic classifiers are all "Linear Statistical Query" classifiers; thus, PAC type guarantees [12] can be given on the performance of the classifier on future, previously unseen data, as a function of its performance on the training data, independently of the probabilistic assumptions made when deriving the classifier. However, the key question that underlies the success of probabilistic classifiers is still open. That is, why is it even possible to get good performance on the training data, i.e., to "fit the data"[1] with a classifier that relies heavily on extremely simplified probabilistic assumptions on the data?

This paper resolves this question and develops arguments that could explain the success of probabilistic classifiers and, in particular, that of naive Bayes. We start by quantifying the optimal Bayes error as a function of the entropy of the data. We develop upper and lower bounds on this term, and discuss where do most of the distributions lie relative to these bounds. While this gives some idea as to what can be expected in the best case, we would like to quantify what happens in realistic situations, when the probability distribution is not known. Quantifying the penalty incurred due to the independence assumptions allows us to show its direct relation to the distributional distance between the true (joint) and the product distribution over the marginals used to derive the classifier. This is used to derive the main result of the paper which, we believe, explains the practical success of product distribution based classifiers. Informally, we show that *almost all* joint distributions with a given set of marginals (that is, all distributions that could have given rise to the classifier learned)[2] are very close to the product distribution on the marginals - the number of these distributions goes down exponentially with their distance from the product distribution. Consequently, the error incurred when predicting using the product distribution is small for *almost all* joint distributions with the same marginals.

There is no claim in this paper that distributions governing "practical" problems are sampled according to a uniform distribution over these marginal distributions. Clearly, there are many distributions for which the product distribution based algorithm will not perform well (e.g., see [10]) and in some situations, these could be the interesting distributions. The counting arguments developed here suggest, though, that "bad" distributions are relatively rare.

Finally, we show how these insights may allow one to quantify the potential gain achieved by the use of complex probabilistic models thus explaining phenomena observed previously by experimenters.

It is important to note that this paper ignores small sample effects. We do not attend to learnability issues but rather assume that good estimates of the statistics required by the classifier can be obtained; the paper concentrates on analyzing the properties of the resulting classifiers.

---

[1] We assume here a fixed feature space; clearly, by blowing up the feature space it is always possible to fit the data.

[2] Or, equivalently, as we show, almost all data sets with this set of marginals.

2   Preliminaries

We consider the standard binary classification problem in a probabilistic setting. In this model one assumes that data elements (x, y) are sampled according to some arbitrary distribution P on $\mathcal{X} \times \{0, 1\}$. $\mathcal{X}$ (e.g., $\mathcal{X} = \Re^M$) is the instance space and $y \in \{0, 1\}$ is the label. The goal of the learner is to determine, given a new example $x \in \mathcal{X}$, its most likely corresponding label $y(x)$, which is chosen as follows:

$$y(x) = \arg \max_{i \{0,1\}} P(y = i | x) = \arg \max_{i \{0,1\}} P(x | y = i) \frac{P(y = i)}{P(x)}.$$

We define the following distributions over $\mathcal{X}$: $P_0 \doteq P(x | y = 0)$ and $P_1 \doteq P(x | y = 1)$. With this notation, the Bayesian classifier predicts $y = 0$ iff $P_0(x) > P_1(x)$.

Throughout the paper we will use capital letters (X, Y, Z) to denote random variables and lower case (x, y, z) to denote particular instantiation of them. $P(x)$ refers to the probability of random variable X taking on value x. $P^n(\cdot)$ refers to the joint probability of observing a sequence of n i.i.d samples distributed according to P.

Deﬁnition 1. *Let $X = (X^1, X^2, ..., X^M) \in \mathcal{X}$ be a random vector and P a probability distribution over $\mathcal{X}$. The* marginal distribution *of the ith component of X (P^i) and the* product distribution(P_m) *induced by P over $\mathcal{X}$ are deﬁned, resp. as $P^i = \sum_{X \setminus X^i} P(X);$ $P_m = \prod_i P^i$. P_m is identical to P under the assumption that the components X^i of X are independent of each other. We sometimes call P_m the* marginal distribution *of P.*

Deﬁnition 2 (Entropy; Kullback-Leibler Distance). *For probability distributions P, Q over $\mathcal{X}$ the entropy of P and the Kullback-Leibler distance between P and Q and the conditional entropy of a random variable x given y, are deﬁned, resp. by*

$$H(P) = -\sum_{x \in \mathcal{X}} P(x) \log P(x) \; ; \; D(P||Q) = \sum_{x \in \mathcal{X}} P(x) \log \frac{P(x)}{Q(x)} \; ; \; H(x|y) = -\sum_{x \in \mathcal{X}} \sum_{y \in \{0,1\}} P(x, y) \log P(x|y)$$

3   Bayes Optimal Error and Entropy

Given a sample $\{(x, y)\}_1^n$ sampled according to P we are interested in studying the optimal Bayes error achievable on it. Assuming, for simplicity, that the two classes are equally likely ($P(y = 1) = P(y = 0) = \frac{1}{2}$), the optimal Bayes error is given by $\frac{1}{2} P_0(\{x | P_1(x) > P_0(x)\}) + P_1(\{x | P_0(x) > P_1(x)\})$.

Lemma 1. *[2] The Bayes optimal error under the uniform class prob. assumption is:*

$$\epsilon = \frac{1}{2} - \frac{1}{4} \sum_x |P_0(x) - P_1(x)|. \tag{1}$$

Note that $P_0(x)$ and $P_1(x)$ are independent quantities and can be changed without influencing each other. [2] also gives the relation between the Bayes optimal error and the entropy of the class label conditioned upon the data, $P(y|x)$.

$$-\log(1 - \epsilon) \le H(P(y|x)) \le -\epsilon \log \epsilon - (1 - \epsilon) \log(1 - \epsilon), \tag{2}$$

where the left hand side inequality is same as the Fano's inequality [1] and the right side follows by the direct application of the Jensen's inequality. However, $P(y|x)$ is typically not always available and thus the use of this bound depends on learning a probabilistic classifier. Now we derive a relation between the lowest achievable Bayes error and the conditional entropy of the input data given the class label thus allowing for an assessment of the optimal performance of the Bayes classifier just by looking at the given data. Naturally, the relation obtained between error and entropy is much loser, compared to the one given in Eqn 2, as has been documented in previous attempts to develop bounds of this sort[5]. We assume a domain of size M, $x \in \{0, 1, \ldots, M - 1\}$ and $y \in \{0, 1\}$. Let $H_b(p)$ denotes the binary entropy $H_b(p) = -(1 - p) \log(1 - p) - p \log p$. Then we have:

Theorem 1. *Assuming equal class probabilities and an optimal Bayes error of ϵ, the conditional entropy $H(x|y)$ of input data conditioned upon class label is bounded by*

$$\frac{1}{2} H_b(2\epsilon) \leq H(x|y) \leq H_b(\epsilon) + \log \frac{M}{2}. \tag{3}$$

We prove the theorem using the following sequence of lemmas (For proofs, please see [8]). For simplicity, our analysis assumes that M is an even number. The general case follows similarly.

Lemma 2. *Consider two probability distributions P, Q de□ned over $x \in \{0, 1, \ldots, M - 1\}$. Let $p_i = P(x = i)$ and $q_i = Q(x = i)$. Assume that the two distributions are constrained such that $\sum_i |p_i - q_i| = \alpha$. Then the sum of the entropy $(H(P) + H(Q))$ of two distributions is maximized when for some $0 \leq K \leq M$,*

$$\forall i : 0 \leq i \leq K \ p_i = c_1, \ q_i = d_1 \quad \forall i : K < i \leq M \ p_i = c_2, \ q_i = d_2$$

Where c_1, c_2, d_1, d_2 are some constants (which are functions of α, K, M).

Lemma 3. *The entropy $H(P) + H(Q)$ from Lemma 2 achieves maxima at K=M/2.*

When M is odd, due to the concavity and symmetry of the entropy function, maximum entropy is achieved when K is either $\frac{M+1}{2}$ or $\frac{M-1}{2}$.

The next lemma is used later to develop the lower bound on the conditional entropy.

Lemma 4. *Let P, Q be probability distributions such that $\sum_i |p_i - q_i| = \alpha$. The sum $H(P) + H(Q)$ of their entropies is minimized when for some K and some $j, 0 \leq j \leq K$, $p_j = \frac{\alpha}{2}$ and $\forall i : 0 \leq i \leq K, i \neq j, p_i = 0$ and $\forall i : 0 \leq i \leq K, q_i = 0$. And for some $j : K < j \leq M, p_j = 1 - \frac{\alpha}{2}, q_j = 1$ and $\forall i \neq j : K < i \leq M, p_i, q_i = 0$. That is,*

$$P = \{p_1 = 0, .., p_j = \frac{\alpha}{2}, 0, p_K = 0, ..., p_i = 1 - \frac{\alpha}{2}, ..0\} \quad Q = \{0, .., 0, 0, 0, ..., p_i = 1, 0, ..., 0\}$$

Now we are in a position to prove Theorem 1. Lemma 2 and 3 are used to prove the upper bound and Lemma 4 is used to prove the lower bound on the entropy.

Proof: (**Theorem 1**) We assume $P(y=0) = P(y=1) = \frac{1}{2}$ and a Bayes optimal error of ϵ. For upper bound we would like to obtain P_0 and P_1 that achieve the maximum conditional entropy, given by $H(x|y) = \frac{1}{2}H(P_0(x)) + \frac{1}{2}H(P_1(x))$. Since we are constraining the Bayes optimal error to be ϵ, we can write it as $\sum_x |P_0(x) - P_1(x)| = 4 - 2\epsilon = \alpha$. Since the distributions that maximize the conditional entropy will also maximize the sum of the entropies of the two distributions (P_0, P_1 because of equal class probability assumption), we can use the results given in Lemma 2,3 to obtain such distributions. Treating $P_1(x)$ as P and $P_0(x)$ as Q, we obtain the distributions that maximize the conditional entropy:

$$P_0 = \{\frac{1+\frac{\alpha}{2}}{M}, \frac{1+\frac{\alpha}{2}}{M}, ..., \frac{1-\frac{\alpha}{2}}{M}, \frac{1-\frac{\alpha}{2}}{M}\} \quad P_1 = \{\frac{1-\frac{\alpha}{2}}{M}, \frac{1-\frac{\alpha}{2}}{M}, ..., \frac{1+\frac{\alpha}{2}}{M}, \frac{1+\frac{\alpha}{2}}{M}\}$$
(4)

The conditional entropy for this distribution is $H(x|y) = H_b(\epsilon) + \log \frac{M}{2}$.

To prove the lower bound on the conditional entropy given Bayes optimal error of ϵ we use the distributions given by Lemma 4:

$$P_0 = \{0, 0, ..., 1 - \frac{\alpha}{2}, ..., 0, \frac{\alpha}{2}, 0, ..., 0\} \quad P_1 = \{0, 0, ..., 1, ..., 0, 0, 0, ..., 0\} \quad (5)$$

The entropy for this distribution is given by $H(x|y) = \frac{1}{2}H_b(2\epsilon)$. $\blacksquare$

The results of the theorem are depicted in Figure 1 for $M = 4$. The bounds imply that the points outside the shaded area cannot be realized. It is interesting to see that the bound is tight in the sense that there are distributions on the boundary of the curves. This also addresses the common misconception that "low entropy implies low error and high entropy implies high error". Our analysis shows that while the latter is correct, the former may not be. We observe that when the entropy is zero, the error can either be 0 (no error, perfect classifier, point (A) on graph) or 50% error (point (B) on graph). Although somewhat counterintuitive, consider:

Example 1. Let $P_0(x = 1) = 1$ and $P_0(x = i) = 0, \forall i \neq 1$ and $\forall x, P_1(x) = P_0(x)$. Then $H(x|y) = 0$ since $H(P_0(x)) = H(P_1(x)) = 0$ and the probability of error is 0.5.

The other critical points on this curve are also realizable. Point "D", which corresponds to the maximum entropy is achieved only when $P_0(x) = \frac{1}{M}, \forall x$ and $P_1(x) = \frac{1}{M}$. Again the error is 0.5. Point (C) corresponds to the maximum entropy with 0 achievable error. It is given by $H(P(y|x)) = \log \frac{M}{2}$. Finally, point (E) corresponds to the minimum entropy for which there exists a distribution for any value of optimal error. This corresponds to $entropy = 0.5$. Continuity arguments imply that all the shaded area is realizable. At a first glance it appears that the points (A) and (C) are very far apart, as (A) corresponds to 0 entropy where as (C) corresponds to entropy of $\log \frac{M}{2}$. One might think that most of the joint probability distributions are going to be between (A) and (C) - a range for which the bounds are vacuous. It turns out, however, that most of the distributions actually lie beyond the $\log \frac{M}{2}$ entropy point.

Theorem 2. *Consider a probability distribution over $x \in \{0, 1, ..., M-1\}$ given by $P = [p_0, ..., p_{M-1}]$ and assume that $H(p) \leq \log \frac{M}{2}$. Then, $\forall \delta : 0 < \delta < \frac{1}{M}$, the distribution Q defined by $q_i = \frac{1}{M} + \delta(p_i - \frac{1}{M})$, $\forall i$ satisfies $H(Q) > \log \frac{M}{2}$.*

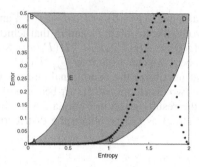

Fig. 1. The relation between the error and the conditional entropy of the data. The shaded region represents the feasible region (the distributions with the corresponding error and entropy are realizable). The dotted curve gives the empirical distribution of the joint distributions over a given set of input features.

Proof: To show that $H(Q) > \log \frac{M}{2}$ consider $H(Q) - \log \frac{M}{2} = -\sum_{i=1}^{M} q_i \log \left(q_i \frac{M}{2} \right)$. Now if $0 < \delta < 1$ then it is straightforward to see that $\forall i, q_i > 0$, and if $0 < \delta < \frac{1}{M}$ then $\forall i$, $\frac{M}{2} q_i < 1$, implying that $H(Q) > \log \frac{M}{2}$. Since $H(P) \leq \log \frac{M}{2}$, $P \neq Q$. Hence, for each δ we have defined a 1-1 mapping of distributions with entropy below $\log \frac{M}{2}$ to those with entropy above it. ∎

Consequently, the number of distributions with entropy above $\log \frac{M}{2}$ is at least as much as the number of those with entropy below it. This is illustrated using the dotted curve in Figure 1 for the case $M = 4$. For the simulations we fixed the resolution and did not distinguish between two probability distributions for which the probability assignments for all data points is within some small range. We then generated all the conditional probability distributions and their (normalized) histogram. This is plotted as the dotted curve superimposed on the bounds in Figure 1. It is evident that most of the distributions lie in the high entropy region, where the relation between the entropy and error in Thm. 1 carries useful information.

4   Classiﬁcation Error

While previously we bounded the Bayes optimal error assuming the correct joint probability is known, in this section we start investigating the more interesting case – the mismatched probability distribution. We assume that the learner has estimated a probability distribution that is different from the true joint distribution. The performance measure used in our study is the *probability of error*. We can look at the probability of misclassification from the perspective of hypothesis testing. That is, this is the probability of misclassifying a sample as coming from hypothesis $H_0 \sim P_0(X^1, ..., X^M)$ when it actually came from $H_1 \sim P_1(X^1, ..., X^M)$, and vice versa. Although slightly different from the standard classification problem, the hypothesis testing framework provides two advantages. It provides tools for the analysis of the mismatched probability distributions and at the same time, allows one to analyze the asymptotic probability of error. Since it is assumed that the distributions P_0, P_1 have already been estimated from data, this perspective (i.e., looking at many samples $X^1, ..., X^M$) allows us to obtain better bounds for the performance of these estimates. Under this framework, the probability of error can be grouped into two categories α, β. Where α (Type I error) is the probability of misclassification when the true hypothesis is $H_0 \sim P_0$ and β (Type II error) is the misclassification error when the true hypothesis is $H_1 \sim P_1$. Formally, if $A = \{x : \frac{P_0(x)}{P_1(x)} > \tau\}$ is the acceptance region for hypothesis H_0 then $\alpha = P_0(A^c)$; $\beta = P_1(A)$. Now, A_n, α_n, β_n denote the corresponding terms when the decision is made for n random vectors.

Stein's lemma [1] gives asymptotic bounds on the performance of a classifier which is using Likelihood ratio test for deciding between the two hypotheses. It shows that under the condition that $\alpha_n < \epsilon$, and for $0 < \epsilon < \frac{1}{2}$, defining $\beta_n^\epsilon = \min_{\alpha_n < \epsilon} \beta_n$ gives

$$\lim_{\epsilon \to 0} \lim_{n \to \infty} \frac{1}{n} \log \beta_n^\epsilon = -D(P_0 || P_1) \tag{6}$$

In practice, however, rather than the true joint distribution over the samples, the induced product distribution (derived using conditional independence assumptions) is used. The standard Stein's lemma doesn't hold in this case and we prove a modified version of it for this case.

Theorem 3. *(Modified Stein's Lemma) Let $X_1, ..., X_n$ be i.i.d $\sim Q$. Consider the hypothesis test between two hypothesis $Q \sim P_0$, and $Q \sim P_1$. Let A_n be the acceptance region for hypothesis $H_0 = Q \sim P_0$. The probabilities of error can then be written as $\alpha_n = P_0^n(A_n^c)$; $\beta_n = P_1^n(A_n)$. Assume P_0' is used instead of P_0 for the likelihood ratio test. Then if A_n is chosen such that $\alpha_n < \epsilon$, then the type II error (β) is given by*

$$\lim_{\epsilon \to 0} \lim_{n \to \infty} \frac{1}{n} \log \beta_n^\epsilon = -D_{P_0}(P_0' || P_1) = -E_{P_0}(\log \frac{P_0'}{P_1}). \tag{7}$$

For the proof, please refer to [8]. By writing $D_{P_0}(P_0' || P_1)$ in a more recognizable form, the asymptotic bound on the error can be written as

$$\frac{1}{n} \log(error) \leq -D_{P_0}(P_0' || P_1) = -D(P_0 || P_1) + D(P_0 || P_0') \tag{8}$$

The first term on the right hand side of Eqn 8 is the same as the one in the original Stein's Lemma. Since Stein's lemma gave the minimum error achievable by any algorithm, we can't do better than this quantity which can be viewed as a "baseline" term. Improving the approximation affects the second term - the distance between the true distribution and the approximation - which acts as the actual penalty.

Although the bound is derived under the assumption that only the distribution corresponding to one hypothesis is approximated, a similar bound can be derived for the more general case (when the distributions corresponding to both hypothesis are unknown) under the condition that $P_1(x) \leq K P_1'(x)$ for some finite K. In this case, the bound will be given by $\log D_{P_0}(P_0' || P_1')$. The condition is fairly general and always holds for product distributions. However, the bound given by Eqn 7 highlights some basic properties of the distributions and will be analyzed in the rest of the paper. The general case follows similar arguments. Eqn 8 shows that the additional penalty term is related to $D(P_0 || P_0')$,

---

[2] For the purpose of the analysis of the performance, we study performance using error on the sample.

with P_0 being the true distribution and P_0' the approximation. In the special case when both P_1 and P_0' are product form distributions, we have

$$D_{P_0}(P_0'||P_1) = \sum_x P_0(x) \log \frac{P_0'(x)}{P_1(x)} = \sum_{x^1, x^2, ..., x^n} P_0(x^1, x^2, ..., x^n) \sum_i \log \frac{P_0(x^i)}{P_1(x^i)}$$

$$= \sum_i P_0(x^i) \log \frac{P_0'(x^i)}{P_1(x^i)} = D(P_0'||P_1) = D(P_0||P_1) - D(P_0||P_0') \quad (9)$$

Corollary 1. *If both P_0' and P_1 are product distributions then $\frac{1}{n} \log(error) \leq -D(P_0'||P_1)$, i.e. the bound is independent of the joint distribution and depends just on the marginals.*

5   Density of Distributions

Let P_m be the product distribution induced by P. As mentioned before, given data sampled according to P, probabilistic algorithms estimate P_m and use it for classifying future data. In this section we explain why making classifications using an induced product distribution rather than the true joint distribution works well in practice.

Given the bound in Eq. 8, classifying data from P using P_m incurs penalty $D(P||P_m)$ (in addition to the baseline term there, which reflects the error *any* classifier must make). This section shows that given P_m, for almost all distributions P that induce P_m, the error term $D(P||P_m)$ is small; equivalently, as we show, for almost all data sets sampled according to distributions that induce P_m the error term is small.

For analysis, discrete domain $\{0, 1\}^m$ is assumed (although it can be extended to the case of continuous random variables). The analysis is based on the *method of types* [1] which allows one to study the number of sequences of length n that can be observed when sampling according to distribution P. We first provide some preliminaries.

Definition 3. *Let $x = \{x_1, ... x_n\}$ be a sequence of n symbols from an alphabet $\mathcal{H}$. The type P_x (or empirical probability distribution) of a sequence $x_1, ..., x_n$ is the relative proportion of occurrences of each symbol of $\mathcal{H}$, i.e. $P_x = \frac{N(a|x)}{n}$ for all $a \in \mathcal{H}$, where $N(a|x)$ is the number of times symbol a occurs in the sequence $x \in \mathcal{H}^n$.*

Definition 4. *Let $\mathcal{P}_n$ denotes the set of types with denominator n (i.e. set of empirical probability distributions derived from sequences of length n.) For $P \in \mathcal{P}_n$, the set of sequences of length n and type P is called the type class of P, denoted $T(P)$.*

Example 2. Let $\mathcal{H} = \{1, 2, 3\}$, $x = 11321$. The type P_x is $P_x(1) = 3/5, P_x(2) = 1/5, P_x(1) = 1/5$. The type class of P_x is the set of all sequences of length 5 with three 1's, one 2 and one 3. There are 20 such sequences, that is $|T(P_x)| = 20$.

Notice the similarity to the case studied in this paper (with $\mathcal{H} = \{0, 1\}^M$). All data sets in $T(P_x)$ induce the same product distribution P_x *conditional entropy* of a random variable x given y

Theorem 4. *[1] For any probability distribution $P \in \mathcal{P}_n$, $\frac{1}{(n+1)^{|\mathcal{H}|}} 2^{nH(P)} \leq |T(P)| \leq 2^{nH(P)}$. That is, within a polynomial approximation $|T(P)| = 2^{nH(P)}$. (Here $|\mathcal{H}|$ is the alphabet size.)*

We note that it is possible to write an exact term for $|T(P)|$ as a multinomial; $|T(P)| = \frac{n!}{\prod_{a \in \mathcal{H}} (nP(a))!}$ where $(nP(a))$ is the expected number of time one observes symbol a in a sequence of length n. However, we will use the powerful relation to entropy and thus to prediction error. The following lemma uses the concept of sample entropy defined as $-\frac{1}{n} \log P^n(x_1, x_2, ..., x_n) = -\sum_{a \in \mathcal{H}} \frac{N(a)}{n} \log P(x = a)$. Here $N(a)$ refers to the number of time $x = a$ is observed in the sample (i.i.d) of length n. We know that as $n \to \infty$, $\frac{N(a)}{n} \to P(a)$ and hence known as sample entropy

Theorem 5. *[1] Let A_δ^n (typical set) denote the set of all the sequences with sample entropy as*
$$H(P) - \delta \leq -\frac{1}{n} \log P^n(x_1, x_2, ..., x_n) \leq H(P) + \delta \text{ Then } |A_\delta^n| \leq 2^{n(H(P) + \delta)}$$

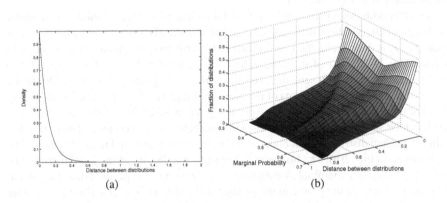

(a)   (b)

Fig. 2. (a) Density of sequences of length n. Y-axis gives the number of sequences ($K2^{-n\epsilon}$) as a function of the distance of the true joint distribution from the product distribution ($D(P_0 \| P_{m0}) = \epsilon$) in the X-axis. (b) shows the decay in the number of the distributions as a function of the entropy of the marginal distribution and the distance of the joint distribution and its induced product distribution. Plots are based on a two attributes case. P_m varies from [0.3 0.3] to [0.7 0.7] (i.e., the attributes have the same marginal distribution.)

This theorem gives a bound on the number of sequences with a given entropy. We now present the main result of this section:

Theorem 6. *Let P_m be a product distribution and let $\mathcal{P}$ be the collection of all probability distributions P that induce P_m, and such that $D(P \| P_m) = \epsilon$. Then, the number of sequences with joint probability P, for $P \in \mathcal{P}$, is equal to (within a polynomial approximation) $K \, 2^{-n\epsilon}$, for some constant K that is independent of P.*

Proof: **(Sketch)** Consider a probability distribution P such that $D(P||P_m) = \epsilon$. We know that

$$D(P||P_m) = \sum_x P(x) \log P(x) - \sum_x P(x) \log P_m(x) = H(P_m) - H(P), \qquad (10)$$

where the second equality follows from the argument given in Eqn 9. That is, the entropy of distributions for which $D(P||P_m) = \epsilon$ is $H(P) = H(P_m) - \epsilon$ and it decays as the distance between P, P_m increases. We know from the law of large numbers that the sample entropy converges to the true entropy, as the number of sample increases. Thus the number of sequences with entropy P is given by (using Theorem 5)

$$2^{n(H(P)+\delta)} = 2^{n(H(P_m)-\epsilon+\delta)} = K2^{-n\epsilon}, \qquad (11)$$

where δ (a small number) goes to zero as n increases. ∎

The theorem shows that a randomly picked sequence of n elements $x \in \{0,1\}^M$ (a "data set") with a given marginal distribution over the individual features is likely to have true joint distribution that is very close to the marginal distribution. Equivalently, the probability of a data set which is ϵ away from the product distribution decays exponentially with ϵ (Figure 2(a)).

Together with the penalty results in Sec. 4 it is clear why we represent this in terms of the distance between the distributions. If, as probabilistic classifier do, classification with respect to P is done using the induced product distribution P_m, then the error incurred is related to $D(P||P_m)$ (disregarding the baseline term in Eq. 8). Therefore, Thm 6 implies that for most data sets, the classification error is going to be small. While the results above are phrased in terms of the number of data sets that are sampled according to distributions in a certain distance from the given product distribution, an equivalent result can be shown for the number of joint distributions in a certain distance from the induced product distribution. In both cases the decay is exponential in the distance. This is illustrated in Fig. 2(b). The histogram shows that the density of the joint distributions which have the same marginal distribution, as a function of the product distribution and the distance between the joint and the product distribution $(D(P||P_m)^3)$. e.g., consider two random variables $x^1, x^2 \in \{0,1\}$. Lets fix $P(x^1 = 1) = 0.8$ and $P(x^2 = 1) = 0.2$ (i.e. fixing the marginal distribution). This means that $P(x^1 = 1, x^2 = 1)$ can take only finite number of values (if we limit the resolution of the probabilities to say 0.001.) Thus it shows that the "bad" cases (when the distribution is far from marginal) are rare when considering the space of all possible distributions with a given marginal distribution (or all data sets sampled according to distributions with a given marginal). Note that, this is a upper bound analysis . Sometimes this bound is tight, as shown in Sec. 4 for the case in which P_1 is in product form. Nevertheless, there could be cases in which the bound is loose. However, the bound goes in the right direction, and in the majority of the cases the upper bound is small.

To show what happens in practice, some simulations are presented in Fig. 3. We considered a case of 2 and 3 features as input and the case of a binary classifier. In each case, 1000 sequences of fixed length were randomly sampled according to different joint distributions, all having the same induced product distribution. Plots of the number of

---

[3] Notice that this distance is always finite since P_m is 0 iff P is zero.

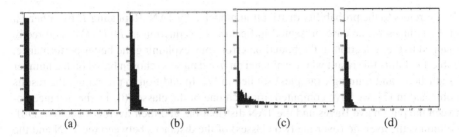

| (a) | (b) | (c) | (d) |

Fig. 3. The plots (a),(b) gives the density of the joint distribution as a function of the distance from the product distribution. Plots (c),(d) gives the ratio of the errors after approximation (product distribution assumption) over the bayes optimal error (modeling complete joint distribution.)

Table 1. This table compares the performance of naive Bayes classifier with the Tree augmented Bayes classifier (TAN). The results presented here are the ones published.The Avr. Diff. column is the average (over the two classes) of the distances between the TAN and the naive product distributions. It is evident that it explains the success (e.g., rows 3, 5) and failure (row 2) of TAN over the naive distribution.

Dataset	$D(P_0\|P_{m0})$	$D(P_1\|P_{m1})$	$D(P_0\|P_1)$	$D(P_1\|P_0)$	Avg. Diff	NB Res	TAN Res
Pima	0.0957	0.0226	0.9432	0.8105	0.8177	75.51±1.63	75.13±1.36
Breast	0.1719	0.4458	6.78	9.70	7.9311	97.36±0.50	*95.75±1.25*
Mofn-3-7-10	0.3091	0.3711	0.1096	0.1137	-0.2284	86.43±1.07	**91.70±0.86**
Diabetes	0.0228	0.0953	0.7975	0.9421	0.8108	74.48±0.89	75.13±0.98
Flare	0.5512	0.7032	0.8056	0.8664	0.2088	79.46±1.11	**82.74±1.60**

sequences, with a joint distribution at a certain distance from the product distribution are given in Fig. 3 (a&c)(for 2&3 features resp.). As expected, the histogram looks very similar to the Fig. 2. Also shown (Fig. 3(b&d) for 2&3 features resp.) are the resulting classification errors as a function of the distance between the joint and the product distribution. The figures give the ratio of the errors made during classification when one uses the product distribution vs. the use of the true joint distribution. As expected the error ratio ($exp(-D(P\|P_m))$) has an exponential decay.

6   Complex Probabilistic Models and Small Sample Effects

In the practice of machine learning [9,11] the use of probabilistic classification algorithms is preceded by the generation of new features from the original attributes in the space which can be seen as using complex probabilistic classifiers. We analyze the particular case of tree augmented Bayesian (TAN) classifier introduced in [7], which is a sophisticated form of the naive Bayesian classifier modeling higher (second) order probabilistic dependencies between the attributes. They [7] conducted a number of experiments and reported improved results on some of the datasets. It is easy to see that by modeling the TAN distribution, one is essentially decreasing the distance between the true (joint) and the approximated distribution. i.e. $D(P\|P_m) \geq D(P\|P_{TAN})$ where

P_{TAN} refers to the probability distribution modeled by TAN. Replacing P by either P_0 or P_1 reduces to the case presented in Section 4. Reduction in $D(P||P_m)$ is directly mapped to the reduction in the bound on error, thus explaining the better performance. Table 1 exhibits this result when evaluated on five data sets (chosen based on the number of attributes and training examples) studied in [7]. In addition to presenting the results published in [7], we have computed, for each one of the classes (0, 1), the distance between the pure naive Bayes and the TAN distribution, and their average. The Avr. Diff. column is the average (over the two classes) of the distances between the TAN and the product distributions. Clearly our results predict well the success (rows 3, 5) and failure (row 2) of TAN over the naive Bayesian distribution.

As mentioned before, in this paper we have ignored small sample effects, and assumed that good estimates of the statistics required by the classifier can be obtained. In general, when the amount of data available is small, the naive Bayes classifier may actually do better than the more complex probability models because of the insufficient amount of data that is available. In fact, this has been empirically observed and discussed by a number of researchers [6,7].

7 Conclusions

In the last few years we have seen a surge in learning work that is based on probabilistic classifiers. While this paradigm has been shown experimentally successful on many real world applications, it clearly makes vastly simplified probabilistic assumptions. This papers uses an information theoretic framework to resolve the fundamental question of: why do these approaches work. On the way to resolving this puzzle we develop methods for analyzing probabilistic classifiers and contribute to understanding the tradeoffs in developing probabilistic classifiers and thus to the development of better classifiers.

Acknowledgments. Research supported by NSF grants ITR-IIS-0085836, ITR-IIS-0085980 and IIS-9984168.

References

1. T. M. Cover and J. A. Thomas. *Elements of Information Theory.* Wiley and Sons, 1991.
2. L. Devroye, L. Gyorfi, and G. Lugosi. *A Probabilistic Theory of Pattern Recognition.* Applications of Mathematics. Springer Verlag, 1996.
3. P. Domingos and Pazzani. M. Beyond independence: Conditions for the optimality of simple bayesian classifier. *Machine Learning,* 29:103–130, 1997.
4. C. Elkan. Boosting and naive bayesian learning. Technical Report CS97-557, Department of Computer Science, University of California, San Diego, 1997.
5. M Feder and N. Merhav. Relation between entropy and error probability. *IEEE Trans. on Information Theory,* 40:259–266, 1994.
6. J. H. Friedman. On bias, variance, 0/1-loss and curse-of-dimensionality. *Data Mining and Knowledge Discovery,* 55, 1997.
7. N. Friedman, D. Geiger, and M. Goldszmidt. Bayesian network classifiers. *Machine Learning,* 29:131–163, 1997.

8. A. Garg and D. Roth. Understanding probabilistic classifiers. Technical Report UIUCDCS-R-2001-2206, UIUC Computer Science Department, March 2001.

9. A. R. Golding. A Bayesian hybrid method for context-sensitive spelling correction. In *Proceedings of the 3rd workshop on very large corpora, ACL-95*, 1995.

10. D. Roth. Learning in natural language. In *Proc. of the International Joint Conference of Artincial Intelligence*, pages 898–904, 1999.

11. H. Schneiderman and T. Kanade. A statistical method for 3D object detection applied to faces and cars. In *The IEEE Conference on Computer Vision and Pattern Recognition*, volume 1, pages 746–751, 2000.

12. L. G. Valiant. A theory of the learnable. *Communications of the ACM*, 27(11):1134–1142, November 1984.

Efficiently Determining the Starting Sample Size for Progressive Sampling

Baohua Gu[1], Bing Liu[2], Feifang Hu[3], and Huan Liu[4]

[1] Dept. of Computer Science, National Univ. of Singapore
gubh@comp.nus.edu.sg
[2] Dept. of Computer Science, National Univ. of Singapore
liub@comp.nus.edu.sg
[3] Dept. of Stat. & Applied Prob. National Univ. of Singapore
stahuff@nus.edu.sg
[4] Dept. of Computer Sci. and Eng., Arizona State Univ
hliu@asu.edu

Abstract. Given a large data set and a classification learning algorithm, Progressive Sampling (PS) uses increasingly larger random samples to learn until model accuracy no longer improves. It is shown that the technique is remarkably efficient compared to using the entire data. However, how to set the starting sample size for PS is still an open problem. We show that an improper starting sample size can still make PS expensive in computation due to running the learning algorithm on a large number of instances (of a sequence of random samples before achieving convergence) and excessive database scans to fetch the sample data. Using a suitable starting sample size can further improve the efficiency of PS. In this paper, we present a statistical approach which is able to efficiently find such a size. We call it the *Statistical Optimal Sample Size* (*SOSS*), in the sense that a sample of this size sufficiently resembles the entire data. We introduce an information-based measure of this resemblance (Sample Quality) to define the SOSS and show that it can be efficiently obtained in one scan of the data. We prove that learning on a sample of SOSS will produce model accuracy that asymptotically approaches the highest achievable accuracy on the entire data. Empirical results on a number of large data sets from the UCIKDD repository show that SOSS is a suitable starting size for Progressive Sampling.

1. Introduction

Classification is an important learning task. It is often solved by the decision tree approach [19]. Most decision tree algorithms require the data to reside in main memory. This presents a major problem if the data set is too large to fit in the memory. Even if a large data set is able to fit into memory, running a tree-building algorithm on the whole data can be very expensive. A natural way to overcome this problem is to do sampling [2]. One of the recent works towards improving tree-building efficiency (both in terms of time and memory space required) by sampling is Boat by Gehrke et al [6]. [6] builds an initial decision tree using a small sample and then refines it via bootstrap to produce exactly the same tree as that would be

L. De Raedt and P. Flach (Eds.): ECML 2001, LNAI 2167, pp. 192-202, 2001.
© Springer-Verlag Berlin Heidelberg 2001

produced using the entire data. Boat is able to achieve excellent efficiency in tree construction. However, due to the large size of the data, the produced tree can be very complex and large, which makes it hard for human understanding. It has been observed that the tree size often linearly increases with the size of training data, and additional complexity in the tree results in no significant increase in model accuracy [15]. Another recent work on improving the efficiency of tree building for large data sets is Progressive Sampling (PS for short) proposed by Provost et al [17]. By means of a learning curve (see an example learning curve in Figure 1, and related concepts in [4][17]) which depicts the relationship between sample size and model accuracy, PS searches for the optimal model accuracy (the highest achievable on the entire data) by feeding a learning algorithm with progressively larger samples. Assuming a well-behaved learning curve, it will stop at a sample size equal to or slightly larger than the *Optimal Sample Size* (*OSS* for short) corresponding to the optimal model accuracy[1]. [17] shows that PS is more efficient than using the entire data. Besides, it can in fact produce a less complex tree or simpler model (if the real *OSS* is far less than the total data size). Therefore, PS is able to achieve two goals by means of sampling: first, to avoid loading the whole data set into memory; second, to produce good as well as simple model from the data. In this paper, we restrict our attention to PS and aim to improve it further by finding a good starting sample size for it, which is still an open problem.

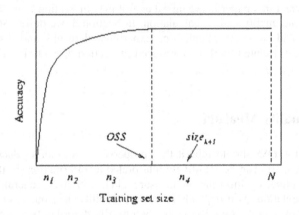

Fig. 1. Learning Curve and Progressive Samples

Obviously, the efficiency of PS gets to the highest when the starting sample size is equal to the *OSS*; and the smaller the difference between the two, the higher the efficiency. The following analysis shows how much benefit can be gained from a proper starting sample size. Suppose we use the simple geometric sampling schedule suggested by [17]. We denote the sample size sequence by $\{n_0, a \times n_0, a^2 \times n_0, a^3 \times n_0, ...\}$, where $n_0 > 0$ is the starting sample size, $a > 1$ is the increment ratio. If the convergence

---

[1] Upon each sample size, PS uses a special procedure to evaluate if the learning accuracy has converged [17]. The evaluation is independent of the previous samples.

is detected at the $(k+1)$-th sample (its size being $size_{k+1} = a^k \times n_0 \approx OSS$), then the total size of the previous k samples will be $size_{1..k} = n_0 \times (1 + a + a^2 + ... + a^{k-1}) = n_0 \times (a^k - 1)/(a-1) = (size_{k+1} - n_0)/(a-1)$. When $a=2$, this is almost the same as the $size_{k+1}$. Given a learning algorithm whose runtime complexity is typically $O(n^c)$ ($c>1$), in terms of the instance number n used in learning, the computation spent on these pre-convergence samples could be very expensive. Obviously, this extra cost could be significantly reduced if n_0 is set near to the OSS. Moreover, as $k = log_a (size_{k+1}/n_0) \approx log_a (OSS/n_0)$, if n_0 is much less than OSS, then k, the number of samples needed before convergence, will be large. Note that generating a random sample from a single-table database typically requires scanning the entire table once [18]. Thus a large k will result in considerably high disk I/O cost. Therefore setting a good starting sample size can further improve the efficiency of PS by cutting the two kinds of costs.

In this paper, we find such a size via a statistical approach. The intuition is that a sample with the OSS should sufficiently resemble its mother data (the entire data set). We implement this intuition via three steps. First, we define an information-based measure of the resemblance (we call *Sample Quality*). Based on this measure, we then define a *Statistical Optimal Sample Size* (*SOSS* for short). We prove that learning on a sample of the SOSS will produce a model accuracy that is sufficiently close to that of the *OSS*. We show that the *SOSS* can be efficiently determined in one scan of the mother data. Our experiments on a number of UCIKDD [1] data sets show that our approach is effective.

The remainder of this paper is organized as follows. In Section 2, we introduce the measure of sample quality and its calculation. In Section 3, we define *SOSS*, prove a useful theorem and show its calculation. Experimental results and discussions are given in Section 4. Related work is introduced in Section 5. Section 6 concludes the paper.

2. Sample Quality Measure

A sample with the *OSS* should inherit the "property" of its mother data as much as possible. This property can be intuitively interpreted as information. In this work, we make use of Kullback's information measure [11], which is generally called the divergence or deviation, as it depends on two probability distributions and describes the divergence between the two. Below we first briefly describe its related definitions and conclusions, and then introduce our measure of sample quality.

2.1 Underlying Information Theory

Suppose x is a specific value (i.e., an observation) of a generic variable X, and H_i is the hypothesis that X is from a statistical population with generalized probability densities (under a probability measure λ) $f_i(x)$, $i = 1, 2$, then the information divergence is defined by

$$J(1,2) = \int (f_1(x) - f_2(x)) \log(f_1(x) / f_2(x)) d\lambda(x) \tag{1}$$

According to [11], $J(1,2)$ is a measure of the divergence between hypotheses H_1 and H_2, and is a measure of the difficulty of discriminating between them. Specifically, for two multinomial populations with c values (c categories), if p_{ij} is the probability of occurrence of the j-th value in population i ($i=1, 2,$ and $j=1, 2,..., c$), then the information divergence is

$$J(1,2) = \sum_{j=1}^{c} (p_{1j} - p_{2j}) \log(p_{1j} / p_{2j})$$ (2)

The information divergence has a good limiting property described in Theorem 1 below (see [11] for its proof), based on which we will prove an important theorem about $SOSS$ in Section 3.

Theorem 1 Given a probability density function $f(x)$ and a series of probability density functions $f_n(x)$, where $n \to \infty$, denote the information divergence from $f_n(x)$ to $f(x)$ as $J(f_n(x), f(x))$, we have, if $J(f_n(x), f(x)) \to 0$, then $f_n(x)/f(x) \to 1$ [λ], uniformly. Here [λ] means that the limitation and the fraction hold in a probability measure λ. #

2.2 Definition and Calculation

We borrow the concept of information divergence between two populations and define our sample quality measure below. The idea is to measure the dissimilarity of a sample from its mother data by calculating the information divergence between them.

Definition 1 Given a large data set D (with r attributes) and its sample S, denote the information divergence between them on attribute k as $J_k(S, D)$, ($k=1, 2, ..., r$), then the sample quality of S is

$$Q(S)=exp(-J)$$ (3)

where the averaged information divergence J is

$$J = \frac{1}{r}\sum_{k=1}^{r} J_k(S, D)$$ (4)

In calculating $J_k(S, D)$, we treat a categorical (nominal) attribute as a multinomial population. For a continuous (numerical) attribute, we build its histogram (e.g., using a simple discretization), and then treat it also as a multinomial population by taking each bin as a categorical value and the bin size as its frequency. According to [14], the information divergence $J > 0$, therefore $0 < Q \le 1$, where $Q = 1$ means that no information divergence exists between S and D. The larger the information divergence J, the smaller the sample quality Q; and vice versa. For numerical attributes, if we have prior knowledge about their distributions, further improvement on the calculation of J can be achieved by directly applying them to formula (1) to get the information divergence.

The calculation of Q is straightforward. In one scan of the data, both the occurrences of categorical values and the frequencies of numerical values that fall in the bins can be incrementally gathered. At the end of the scan, Q can be worked out by using formula (2) for each attribute and then using formula (4) for the averaged J. Therefore the time complexity of calculating sample quality is $O(N)$ (N is the total number of instances or records of the mother data), while the space complexity is $O(r*v)$ (v is the largest number of distinct values or bins of each attribute). Note that a random sample can be obtained also in one scan. Thus we can calculate a sample's quality while generating it.

3. Statistical Optimal Sample Size

From the definition of sample quality, we can observe that the larger the sample size, the higher the sample quality. This is because as sample size increases, a sample will have more in common with its mother data, therefore the information divergence between the two will decrease. We can imagine that when a sample is sufficiently large, its sample quality should be sufficiently close to the mother data thus should sufficiently "resemble" the mother data in distribution. Below we define the *SOSS* and introduce its calculation.

3.1 Definition

We define the Statistical Optimal Sample Size (*SOSS*) as follows:
Definition 2 Given a large data set D, its *SOSS* is the size at which its sample quality Q is sufficiently close to 1. That is, $|1-Q| < \delta$ where $\delta > 0$ is given by user. #

Clearly, the *SOSS* only depends on the data set D, while the *OSS* depends on both the data set and the learning algorithm. Therefore, the *SOSS* is not necessarily the *OSS*. However, by the following theorem, we can see that their corresponding model accuracies can be very close.

Given a learning algorithm L and a sufficiently large data set D with probability density function $f(x)$, we take L as an operator mapping $f(x)$ to a real number (namely the model accuracy), i.e., $L : f(x) \rightarrow Acc^*$, where Acc^* is the maximum accuracy obtained on D. Assume that a random sample of the size *OSS* has the probability density function $f_{oss}(x)$, and a random sample of the size *SOSS* has $f_{soss}(x)$. Let the model accuracies on the two samples be Acc_{oss} and Acc_{soss} respectively. We have the following theorem.

Theorem 2 If a random sample S of D has a probability density function $f_s(x)$ and L satisfies: $f_s(x) / f(x) \rightarrow 1[\lambda] \Rightarrow |L(f_s(x)) - L(f(x))| \rightarrow 0$, then $Acc_{oss} \rightarrow Acc_{soss}$.
Proof (Sketch): Suppose we have a series of n random samples of D with incrementally larger sample sizes. Denote the size of the i-th sample as S_i, and the corresponding sample quality of the sample with $Q(S_i)$, $i=1, 2, ..., n$. According to the definition of *SOSS*, when $S_i \rightarrow SOSS$, $Q(S_i) \rightarrow 1$, i.e., the information divergence of S_i from D is $J(S_i, D) \rightarrow 0$. Applying Theorem 1, we have, $f_{si}(x) / f(x) \rightarrow 1[\lambda]$. From the condition, we have $|L(f_{si}(x)) - L(f(x))| \rightarrow 0$. In an asymptotic sense, $L(f_{si}(x)) \rightarrow L(f_{soss}(x)) \rightarrow Acc_{soss}$, and $L(f(x)) \rightarrow Acc^* \rightarrow Acc_{oss}$, that is, $Acc_{soss} \rightarrow Acc_{oss}$. #

The premise of the theorem means that if two data sets are quite similar in their probability distributions, then the learning algorithm should produce quite close model accuracy on them. This is reasonable for a typical learning algorithm. Based on this theorem, we can search for the *SOSS* by measuring sample quality instead of directly searching for the *OSS* by running an expensive learning algorithm. We can also expect that the two are close in terms of model accuracy.

3.2 Calculation

To calculate the *SOSS* of *D*, we can set *m* sample sizes S_i spanning the range of [1, *N*] and compute the corresponding qualities Q_i (*i*=1,2,...,*m*). We then draw a sample quality curve (the relationship between sample size and sample quality) using these (S_i, Q_i) points. The *SOSS* is estimated using the curve. To be efficient, we can calculate all samples' qualities at the same time in one sequential scan of *D* by using the idea of Binomial Sampling [16]. That is, upon reading in each instance or data record, a random number *x* uniformly distributed on [0.0, 1.0) is generated. If $x < S_i / N$, then corresponding statistics (by counting a categorical value or binning a numerical value) are gathered for the *i*-th sample. This is repeated for all samples before reading the next instance. We describe the procedure using the pseudo algorithm below.

Pseudo Algorithm *SOSS*
input: a large data set *D* of size *N*, *m* sample sizes {S_i | *i* = 1, 2, ..., *m*};
output: *m* pairs of (S_i, Q_i);
begin
1. for each instance *k* in *D* (*k* ∈ [1, *N*])
  {
      update corresponding statistics for *D*;
      for each sample *i* ∈ [1, *m*]
      {
        r ← *UniformRandomNumber*(0.0,1.0);
        if $r < S_i / N$, then update corresponding statistics for sample *i*;
      }
  }
2. for each sample *i* ∈ [1, *m*]
  {
      calculate its Q_i and output (S_i, Q_i);
  }
end

It is easy to see that its runtime complexity and the memory needed are *m* times that of computing sample quality for a single sample. With these (S_i, Q_i) points in hand, we draw the quality curve and decide the *SOSS* in the following way: starting from the first point, we do a linear regression on every *l* consecutive points (we set *l*=5 in our experiment), if the 95% confidence interval of the slope of the regressed line includes zero, then the size of the middle point is the SOSS.

4. Experimental Results and Discussions

We evaluate our measure on four large UCIKDD data sets: *adult*, *led*, *census*, and *covtype*. The number of instances in training data/testing data are, 36k/12.8k for *adult*, 100k/50k for *led*, 199.5k/99.8k for *census*, and 400k/181k for *covtype*. The classification algorithm we use is C5.0, the latest improvement of C4.5 [19]. We first draw the learning curve for each data set by running C5.0 on a number of sample sizes from 1% to 100% of all training data. All accuracies are tested against the corresponding testing data. Then we draw the quality curve for each data set by calculating multiple sample qualities in one scan. We set the bin number to be 20 for discretizing numerical attributes[2]. We use 50 sample sizes equally covering [1, N].

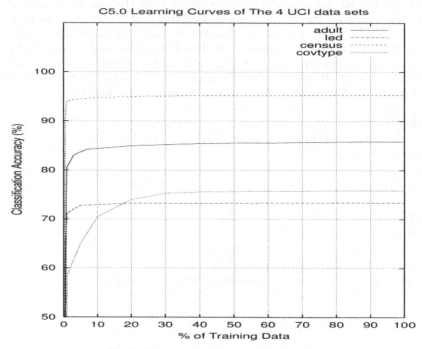

Fig. 2. C5.0 Learning Curves of the four data sets

The learning curves and quality curves (averaged on 10 runs for the four data sets) are shown in Figure 2 and Figure 3 respectively. We decide the *OSS* as the size corresponding to 99.5%×*Acc**, where *Acc** is the model accuracy on all instances. The *SOSS* is determined by the method in Section 3. The resulting *OSS* and *SOSS* with their corresponding tree sizes (S_{tree}) and tested accuracies (*Acc*) are listed in Table 1.

We can see that for *led* and *census*, the *SOSS* is equal to or very close to the *OSS*[3]. If starting from this size, PS will reach the optimal model accuracy at once. For *adult* and *covtype* data sets, the SOSS is about half of the OSS, which means only one more iteration is needed for PS (if the size increment ratio *a*=2) starting with the *SOSS*. In

---

[2] In our experiments, we also test other bin numbers. We find that a too small bin number (e.g., 5, or 10) is not good in representing distributions, while a too large bin number (e.g., 50 or 100) increases the needs of memory but improves little in representing distributions.

[3] It happens that the *SOSS* is slightly larger than the *OSS* for census. This may be due to the way we decide the *OSS*. Intuitively, the *SOSS* could not be far larger than the *OSS*, unless the learning algorithm produces very different learning accuracy on two similar distributions.

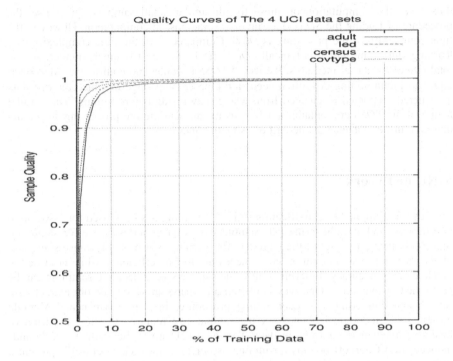

Fig. 3. Quality Curves of the four data sets

Table 1. Results of the 4 data sets

dataset	N (×1k)	S_{tree}	Acc^* (%)	OSS (×1k)	S_{tree}	Acc (%)	$SOSS$ (×1k)	S_{tree}	Acc (%)	$t_{PS+SOSS}$ (t_{PS}/t_N)(sec)
adult	36	344	86.2	14	170	85.8	8	127	85.6	18 (20/22)
Led	100	3896	73.3	10	480	72.9	10	480	72.9	14 (38/41)
census	199.5	848	95.3	30	91	94.8	35	108	94.9	94 (152/176)
covtype	400	10970	75.8	140	4402	75.4	70	2417	73.0	668(766/1330)

all data sets, the resulting tree sizes with both the *SOSS* and the *OSS* are significantly smaller than those with the full size, while their accuracy are very close. We also empirically compare the execution time used for PS starting with the found *SOSS* ($t_{PS+SOSS}$) (including the time for finding the *SOSS*) to that without the *SOSS* (t_{PS}) [4]. The execution time of directly learning on the entire data (t_N) is also given. They are all in the last column of Table 1. We can see that the *SOSS* indeed speeds up PS in all the data sets. All these results support our expectation that the *SOSS* can be used as a good starting sample size for PS.

As we have shown, the benefit of using the *SOSS* to start a PS actually lies in that it directly starts learning from a sample that sufficiently resembles the mother data, and

---

[4] We use the geometric size scheme for PS as suggested in [17]. The sample size starts from 1% of the total data and doubles in the next iteration ($a=2$) and so on. All experiments run on SUN Sparc 450.

thus saves the computation on those too dissimilar small samples. Of course, the procedure of finding the *SOSS* does involve some cost in computation. However, the time complexity of the procedure is $O(N)$. Compared with the time complexity of a learning algorithm, which is typically $O(N^c)$ $(c>1)$, this cost is much smaller. As the total size of a data set increases, the use of *SOSS* becomes more attractive. Moreover, a practical data mining task often needs a pre-processing stage in which the raw data are filtered, extracted or cleaned from where they reside before mining. The parallel nature of the *SOSS* computation enables us to run it in the pre-processing stage, and thus can further enhance the benefit of using the *SOSS*.

5. Related Work

Besides being applied to classification [6][17], sampling has been used for association rule mining [21] and clustering [7]. Sample size is an important issue for sampling. Since only using a subset of the total data for learning will probably cause some loss of accuracy, a proper amount of data is necessary to gain efficiency while not lose too much learning accuracy. In terms of how the sample size is decided, sampling can be performed in two ways. One way is to find a proper sample size before extracting a sample and delivering it to data mining procedure. In [10], Kivinen and Mannila present some theoretical bounds for the sample size required to show the truth or falsity of a set of regularities in data. Toivonen [21] gives the sample size bounds induced from Chernoff bounds for mining association rules. Guha et al [7] present a sufficient sample size for clustering also using Chernoff bounds, which aims to produce a sample so that the probability of missing clusters is low. However, Chernoff bounds are found to be too conservative in practice [3][21].

The other way is not to fix the sample size *a priori*, but directly start learning from a small sample and continue trying larger samples until some stopping criterion is satisfied. Progressive Sampling works in this way. It directly uses the convergence of learning curve as the stopping criterion. Musick et al [14] use the expected loss in information gain, which is associated with choosing an attribute in decision tree construction, as the stopping criterion. Domingo et al [3] and Scheffer and Wrobel [20] propose some *utility functions*, which measure the "goodness" of rules or hypotheses on a given data set, as the stopping criterion. John and Langley [9] define a *"Probably Close Enough"* (PCE) criterion, which also makes use of the convergence of learning curve like Progressive Sampling [17].

The proposed *SOSS* can be viewed as the first way. It balances the need of efficiency and accuracy by directly measuring the similarity of a sample to the entire data. It also has a desirable property: the *SOSS* only depends on the data set and is independent of the learning algorithm. Although we present it for classification in Progressive Sampling, this property makes it applicable to other DM techniques.

The work that we find most similar to ours is that given in [5], where Ganti et al introduce a measure to quantify the difference between two data sets in terms of the models built by a given data mining algorithm. Our measure is different as it is based on statistical information divergence of the data sets. Although [5] also addresses the issue of building models using random samples and shows that bigger samples produce better models, it does not study how to determine a proper sample size.

Learning curve and similarity measure are essential to our work. They have long been addressed by machine learning researchers. Haussler et al [8] theoretically characterize the asymptotic behavior of learning curves (they call *sample complexity*) for Bayesian learning. Frey and Fisher [4] empirically study the behavior of learning curves for decision tree algorithm. Latorrette [12] measures the explanatory similarity between exemplars and applies it to nearest neighbor classification. Lin [13] proposes a general information-based definition of similarity and suggests its uses in different domains. Our similarity measure is different from [13] in that we do not measure the similarity of two instances, instead we measure the similarity between a sample and its mother data. Our measure is similar to that of [13] in that both have roots in information theory and require a probabilistic distribution. However, [13] does not associate similarity with a sufficient sample size, while we do.

6. Concluding Remark

[17] shows that Progressive Sampling is more efficient than learning on the entire data, and eliminates the need to load the entire data into memory. In this paper, we showed that a proper starting sample size could further improve its efficiency. With the intuition that a sample "must" sufficiently resemble its mother data in order to produce a good model, we proposed a technique to find a suitable starting sample size by measuring the similarity of a sample and its mother data. An information-based sample quality or similarity measure was introduced. Based on this measure, we defined the *SOSS*, and proved that asymptotically, the *SOSS* will achieve a model accuracy very close to that of the *OSS*. This claim was supported by our experimental results on UCIKDD data sets. Furthermore, the *SOSS* can also be efficiently determined in one scan of the mother data and is independent of learning algorithms. All these clearly suggest that the proposed *SOSS* can be used to start a Progressive Sampling. It can save many runs on unnecessary small samples, which are too dissimilar to the entire data.

References

[1] S. D. Bay. The UCI KDD Archive [http://kdd.ics.uci.edu], 1999.

[2] M. S. Chen, J. W. Han, and P. S. Yu. Data Mining: An Overview from a Database Perspective. IEEE Transactions on Knowledge and Data Engineering, 1996.

[3] C. Domingo, R. Gavalda and O. Watanabe. Adaptive Sampling Methods for Scaling Up Knowledge Discovery Algorithms. Book Chapter in "Instance Selection and Construction for Data Mining", Edited by H. Liu and H. Motoda. Kluwer Academic Publishers, 2001.

[4] L. J. Frey, and D. H. Fisher. Modeling Decision Tree Performance With the Power Law. The 7th Workshop on AI and Stat (Uncertainty'1999).

[5] V. Ganti, J. Gehrke, R. Ramakrishnan, and W. Y. Loh. A Framework for measuring Changes in Data Characteristics. In Proceedings of PODS'1999.

[6] J. Gehrke, V. Ganti, R. Ramakrishnan, and W. Y. Loh. Boat—Optimistic Decision Tree Construction. In Proceedings of ACM SIGMOD'1999.

[7] S. Guha, R. Rastogi, and K. Shim. CURE: An Efficient Clustering Algorithm for Large Databases. In Proceedings of SIGMOD'1998.

[8] D. Haussler, M. Kearns, and R. Schapire. Bounds on the Sample Complexity of Bayesian Learning Using Information Theory and the VC Dimension. In Proceedings of the Fourth Annual Workshop on Computational Learning Theory (COLT'1991).

[9] G. H. John and P. Langley. Static Versus Dynamic Sampling for Data Mining. In Proceedings of KDD'1996.

[10] J. Kivinen and H. Mannila. The Power of Sampling in Knowledge Discovery. In Proceedings of ACM SIGMOD/PODS'1994.

[11] S. Kullback. Information Theory and Statistics. John Wiley & Sons, Inc, New York, 1959.

[12] M. Latourrette. Toward an Explanatory Similarity Measure for Nearest Neighbor Classification. In Proceedings of ECML'2000.

[13] D. Lin. An Information-theoretic Definition of Similarity. In Proceedings of ICML'1998.

[14] R. Musick, J. Catlett, and S. Russell. Decision Theoretic Subsampling for Induction on Large Databases. In proceedings of ICML'1993.

[15] T. Oates and D. Jensen. The Effects Of Training Set Size on Decision Tree Complexity. In Proceedings of ICML'1997.

[16] F. Olken. Random Sampling from Databases. PhD thesis, Department of Computer Science, University of California Berkeley, 1993.

[17] F. Provost, D. Jensen, and T. Oates. Efficient Progressive Sampling. In Proceedings of KDD'1999.

[18] F. Provost and V. Kolluri. A Survey of Methods for Scaling Up Inductive Algorithms. Data Mining and Knowledge Discovery, 3(2), 131-169, 1999.

[19] J. R. Quinlan. C4.5: Programs for Machine Learning. Morgan Kaufmann, 1993.

[20] T. Scheffer and S. Wrobel. A Sequential Sampling Algorithm for a General Class of Utility Criteria. In Proceedings of KDD'2000.

[21] H. Toivonen. Sampling Large Databases for Association Rules. In Proceedings of VLDB'1996.

Using Subclasses to Improve Classification Learning

Achim Hoffmann, Rex Kwok, and Paul Compton

School of Computer Science and Engineering,
The University of New South Wales,
UNSW SYDNEY NSW 2052,
Australia
{achim,rkwok,compton}@cse.unsw.edu.au

Abstract. We propose to use systematic simulation studies as opposed to the use of real-world benchmark datasets to better understand the behaviour, strengths and weaknesses of machine learning algorithms. Simulated data sets allow much better control and understanding of the nature of the learning problem than empirical benchmark data sets.

To demonstrate the value of our proposed research methodology, we describe in this paper the results of our studies concerning the problem of learning multiple classes. We derived the following hypothesis: *"Learning classification functions using decision tree learners can be helped by providing additional subclass labels."* To illustrate, for learning a two class problem "car is OK/car needs service" it can be helpful to provide a finer-grained classification in the training data such as "car OK", "faulty brakes", "faulty engine", "faulty lights", etc.

This hypothesis was corroborated using a number of 'real-world' multi-class data sets from the UCI ML repository. Our empirical studies demonstrate the usefulness of the proposed research methodology using artificial data sets as an important methodological complement to using real-world datasets.

1 Introduction

The careful evaluation of the effectiveness of a particular approach in AI is important but often difficult to conduct in practice. Empirical studies have been conducted in a large number of subfields of AI, including theorem proving, constraint satisfaction, vision, machine learning and neural networks. Usually benchmark datasets are used for the comparison of approaches and evaluation studies. Benchmark datasets, such as the UCI machine learning (ML) repository, are often obtained from real data.

This paper demonstrates the use of simulated domains in investigating the strengths and weaknesses of machine learning techniques. A model of a domain is developed that provides a (probabilistic) source of examples and a target classification function which is the target of the learning process. The major insight that has arisen from the work reported in this paper is that the simulated domain approach enables one to investigate how the domain structure affects the performance of machine learning techniques much more readily than using 'real-world' data where the target function is unknown.

In fact, using simulated domains, we found an intriguing behaviour of decision tree learners (C4.5) when dealing with a large number of different classes: With an increasing

L. De Raedt and P. Flach (Eds.): ECML 2001, LNAI 2167, pp. 203–213, 2001.
© Springer-Verlag Berlin Heidelberg 2001

number of classes that need to be distinguished, the accuracy of C4.5 *increased* for target concepts of comparable complexity.

This observation lead us to hypothesise a new approach to achieving increased accuracy on classification problems with two or only few classes as follows:

If the provided examples can be divided into 'meaningful' subclasses then using the subclass label to train a learner may result in improved accuracy for classifying according to the initial set of two or only a few classes. The critical question here is, what exactly constitutes meaningful subclasses. Ultimately, the success of using subclass labels depends on the distribution of the data of each subclass in the instance space. If it is distributed as in our simulation studies, it will be successful. If it is distributed differently, we don't know how useful it is. In practice, given our current understanding, we have to deal with the question of meaningful subclasses on a rather intuitive basis. Intuitively, meaningful subclasses of a class should be ontologically justifiable. I.e. each subclass should occupy a separate area in the instance space, such that the learner can represent a suitable separating function of low complexity (i.e. few additional nodes in a decision tree). On the other hand, the domain must be sufficiently complex to represent a challenge for the learner when no subclass labels are provided.

The paper is organised as follows: In section 2 we discuss our methodology and rationale for using artificial data sets as a general useful strategy for exploring issues in machine learning that complements the widespread use of 'real' data sets (often from UCI) for experimental studies. The following section presents the details of our simulated domain approach. In section 4 we present our empirical corroboration of our hypothesis using 'real-world data' from the UCI repository. Section 5 contains a discussion of our approach and our new hypothesis.

2   Simulation Studies

In this paper we advocate simulation studies as a complement to both empirical studies using 'real-world' data sets as well as to rigorous mathematical analyses of learning tasks and techniques.

Empirical studies using 'real-world' data sets, taken from the UCI ML repository or 'fresh' data sets from an available application domain, may reveal certain aspects of the domain the data comes from. This is an important objective in itself, although characteristics of domains may be more effectively studied by not compounding the analysis of the data with the study of learning algorithms whose characteristics are insufficiently understood.

Similarly, the study of the learning techniques using 'real-world' data sets is compounded by the poorly understood nature of the domains the data sets come from. Some simple characteristics of 'real-world' data sets have been drawn up, e.g. in the STAT-LOG project [6] where domains were characterised by the number and types of attributes (whether numerical or non-numerical etc.). It is clear that such a coarse characterisation is only the beginning of understanding peculiarities of domains.

In theoretical/mathematical studies of learning algorithms and learning tasks, it is usually very difficult both, to characterise a given learning algorithm in detail as well as to characterise a learning task. As a consequence, the results achieved so far in computational learning theory are rather coarse results, where many practitioners tend to question whether these studies have any relevance whatsoever for the practice of machine learning.

Artificial data sets or the simulation of a domain have been used on many occasions in Machine Learning research mainly to provide evidence for the validity of a particular statement; in many cases for showing the superiority of one learning technique over another one. See e.g. [1,7,4]. In [2] a data generator was used which is available from the UCI ML repository.

On other occasions, artificially generated benchmark data sets have been used to gauge the abilities of learning techniques. E.g. the two spiral problem in neural networks [3] is an example of that, where the purpose of such benchmarks is rather questionable, as it is not clear at all that solving such artificial problems is a worthwhile endeavour.

In this paper, we advocate the use of simulated domains and to run implemented learning algorithms on them. By properly setting up the simulation environment for domains and running systematic experiments, results can be achieved in a much easier way than in the traditional mathematical analysis of computational learning theory. The simulation results can have the same rigour as mathematical proofs. The results are in principle reproducible without the recourse to empirical data. I.e. the used data is generated using a data source that can be described in a mathematically rigorous way. Similarly, the learning algorithm can also be described in a mathematically precise way, as the actual program code would warrant. However, to study how a given learning algorithm would perform on a precisely characterised domain (the domain would be described as a probabilistic source of data) is virtually impossible by traditional mathematical approaches as the analysis of the execution of perhaps many million computing steps of a program on perhaps ten thousand or more data points is practically infeasible.

On the other hand, simulation studies can very easily study the behaviour of algorithms on large data sets at least in individual instances (running an algorithm on a particular data set). Mathematical theorems have usually a generality which covers a whole range of learning tasks or training data sets. Similar generality on the basis of simulation experiments can only be achieved by drawing conclusions from experimental results very carefully. However, in many cases it is not really necessary to establish 'absolute' validity of a conclusion drawn from simulation experiments. This is the case, for example, where one moves in uncharted territory and one first wants to obtain a coarse impression of the phenomena around which, if they appear sufficiently important, in turn can be studied in more detail. Such initial studies would just serve the purpose of hypotheses generation. Once interesting hypotheses have been found, further studies can be designed and conducted to establish the validity of a hypothesis.

Gaining such a coarse survey and the generation of interesting hypotheses is comparably simple using simulated domains and requires only very limited resources. Yet it is much more revealing and effective than empirical studies involving 'real-world' data sets.

The missing link to the practice of machine learning, is the relationship between the characteristics of the simulated domains and the characteristics of the real domains. While this remains a critically important relationship to explore, it appears still that progress can and should be achieved via simulation studies: The simulation studies have the potential to allow us further insight into why a given learning algorithm performs well or poorly upon a particular characteristic of the simulated domain. On the basis of such findings, one can build a conceptual framework of important characteristics or features one need to look for in assessing 'real-world' domains.

Studying 'real-world' domains has at least two objectives that can be distinguished: To develop better learning techniques and to ascertain the suitability of already existing learning techniques.

The choice of a learning technique for a given domain can then be guided either by characteristics of the individual domain, perhaps gauged by preliminary data analysis, or by characteristics that are commonly found among *similar* domains. Of course, in turn it is not clear what it might mean that two domains are similar.

In any case, in order to find useful characteristics of real-world domains, and in order to become clearer about what constitutes similar domains, simulation studies have the potential to lay the conceptual foundation by clarifying the aspects in a domain upon which the success of one or more learning techniques depend. Those aspects which do not significantly influence the performance of a learning technique can safely be ignored when it comes to characterising and assessing real-world domains.

3   Learning Multiple Classes by Decision Trees

Learning multiple classes is an important learning task as recent research [8,5] on extending learning techniques to deal with multiple classes shows. C4.5 or decision tree learners generally are naturally suited to the task. In our simulation studies, we wanted to explore the ability of C4.5 to handle large numbers of classes in more detail.

3.1   Simulations

The target concepts we generate are binary decision trees. At each node an attribute is randomly chosen and a random threshold (a floating point value between 0 and 100) is generated. Leaf nodes are randomly assigned a class. Parameters are used to control the depth of the tree, the number of classes and the number of available attributes. Given a decision tree, examples are generated simply by picking uniformly distributed random points in the instance space and seeing how the tree classifies the point.

The study presented here looks at how the number of classes affects the error rate produced by C4.5. Typical results can be seen in Figure 1. The only variable that is varied is the class number. As the number of classes increases, the error rate initially decreases and then plateaus out. In this case, the error rate with only 2 classes is more than double the error rate when there are 40 classes. This result is surprising for three reasons. Firstly, the complexity of the target concepts are similar, since the number of cuts and divisions to the instance space is determined by the depth of the target concept. Increasing the class number only increases the number of labels with which the divisions can be named. Secondly, guessing becomes harder. With fewer classes, a guess is more likely to produce the correct answer than when there are more classes. Finally, when there are fewer classes, the target concept often receives some pruning. For instance,

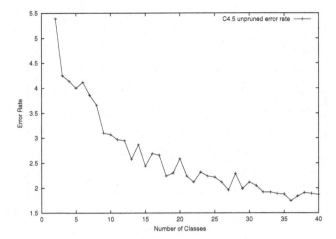

Fig. 1. Varying the number of classes in the simulated domain. Each point is the average over 20 trials.

consider a target concept with two classes. When two adjacent leaf nodes are attributed the same class (there is a 50% chance of this happening), the last attribute test is rendered redundant.

The graph in Figure 1 is quite general. Changes to the depth of the target concept or the number of available attributes has only a slight effect. The main variable affecting the trend is the average number of examples presented to C4.5 for each leaf node in the target concept. As this number increases, the curve shifts downwards.

The reason for the trend may be due to the anecdotally known weakness of C4.5 to handle target concepts where a class is scattered across the instance space. With only two classes, half of the leaf nodes in the target concept will be assigned to one class. With more classes, the probability that the class is represented by a few convex regions in the instance space becomes greater. One hypothesis to account for the degradation in performance is that C4.5 is oversimplifying the target concept by joining close regions with the same class. The 'small' intervening region where the class alternates would then be misclassified.

If this is true, then it might be expected that smaller trees are produced when there are fewer classes. In fact, the opposite is the case. With fewer classes, larger trees are produced. The plot of tree size corresponding to the target concepts in Figure 1 can be seen in Figure 2. Further research will be required to determine the exact cause for these results.

4   Results with UCI Datasets

The simulation results in the previous section clearly show that C4.5 performs better when there are more class labels. This is in spite of the fact that the complexity of the target concept remains the same. This hypothesis can be corroborated by using datasets from the UCI repository. Since we cannot increase the number of classes for a single

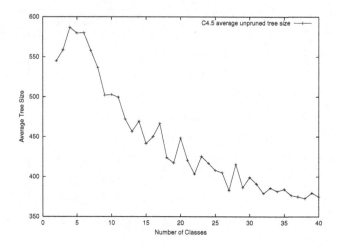

Fig. 2. Varying class number and the resulting C4.5 tree sizes. The tree size decreases with an increasing number of classes.

dataset (except arbitrarily), we study the contrapositive to our hypothesis. By grouping or conflating classes in a dataset, we would expect the performance of C4.5 to degrade.

In conflating several classes for a dataset, the learning task becomes simpler. To compensate for this, *confusion errors* between equivalent classes need to be eliminated. For example, suppose that a dataset X contains two classes, A and B. Also, suppose that X is altered to Y by setting A and B to the same class. To compare the performance of C4.5 on X and Y, it is necessary to eliminate the errors where A type examples are misclassified as B (and *vice versa*) from the result of C4.5 on X.

A summary of the UCI results can be seen in Figure 3. For each dataset, trials were carried out by grouping classes in a certain manner. Each grouping was then given equal weight in determining the average. To generate some variation in the amount of training data, both 2-fold and 10-fold cross-validation trials were carried out. With the 10-fold cross-validation trials, only two datasets seem to confirm our hypothesis to any degree. However, the 2-fold cross-validation trials gave a far better confirmation of our hypothesis. This agrees with our simulation results which show that the trend towards improved performance with increasing class numbers is more accentuated with fewer training examples.

The exact groupings and the performance of C4.5 for each particular grouping can be seen in the following figures. For each data set we show the average error rates of the pruned trees of 50 2-fold cross validation results and the average error rates from 50 10-fold cross validations. The first line for each dataset shows the performance of C4.5 without altering the data. The last column lists the classes present in the dataset.

The average improvements using subclasses as listed in figure 3 cannot be taken too seriously, as averaging results from a collection of sometimes more or less arbitrarily chosen class groupings is not a mathematically meaningful operation. However, it should provide a first glance.

The car evaluation dataset (see Figure 4) best corroborates our hypothesis. An example in the dataset describes the price and technical features of a car and is assigned

Dataset	Average Improvement in % (2-fold trials)	Average Improvement in % (10-fold trials)
car evaluation	37.9	19.95
dermatology	7.4	1.3
glass identification	9.6	0.3
nursery	1.9	0.7
handwritten digits	4.1	0.8
image segmentation	11.4	11.9

Fig. 3. Summary of UCI trials.

Error in % (2fold cv)		Error in % (10-fold cv)		Groupings
normal	subclasses	normal	subclasses	
17.46	17.46	8.06	8.06	{unacc(u)}, {acc(a)}, {good(g)}, {vgood(v)}
8.06	8.565	5.03	4.60	{a, g, v}, {u}
18.90	17.03	8.53	6.50	{u, v}, {a}, {g}
26.34	11.18	4.91	3.65	{u, a}, {v}, {g}

Fig. 4. The **car evaluation** data set (6 atts, 4 classes): The groupings were done on the basis of forming larger groups of similar cars according to their rated quality (in the class label).

one of four classes. The distribution of the examples is heavily weighted towards two classes. There is also an intuitive ordering to the classes, ranging from unacceptable to very good. In all but one trial, grouping classes results in a significantly higher error rate than the adjusted error rate.

Error in % (2fold cv)		Error in % (10-fold cv)		Groupings
normal	subclasses	normal	subclasses	
7.09	7.09	6.21	6.21	{psoriasis(p)}, {seboreic dermatitis(sd)}, {lichen planus(lp)}, {pityriasis rosea(pr)}, {cronic dermatitis(cd)}, {pityriasis rubra pilaris(prp)}
7.08	7.08	7.07	6.21	{pr, prp}, {p}, {sd}, {lp}, {cd}
6.37	7.08	5.80	6.21	{pr, prp}, {sd, cd}, {p}, {lp}
8.74	6.57	5.29	5.30	{p, lp}, {sd}, {cd}, {pr}, {prp}
7.25	6.81	5.57	5.67	{sd, lp}, {p}, {cd}, {pr}, {prp}

Fig. 5. The **dermatology** data set (34 atts, 6 classes): As we have no knowledge of the various conditions being classified here, the groupings have to be considered random groupings, which are presumably not meaningful.

The dermatology, glass identification, and nursery datasets (Figure 5,6,7) all show only a slight tendency for C4.5 to perform worse when classes are grouped together.

However, there are two significant results in the 2-fold cross-validation trials. In one dermatology trial and one glass identification trial the adjusted error rate was exceeded by some 30%. It can be argued that the class groupings used for these particular trials are counter-intuitive. Consultation with domain experts would be required to determine whether this is the case.

Some of the dermatology results may point to an interesting finding. The groupings in the first two dermatology trials resulted in virtually no change in the adjusted error. This means that C4.5 is not confused between the classes in those groupings. However, when the dataset is changed to reflect these groupings, two contrasting results are obtained. In one trial, an absolute increase in error (in the order of 10%) is observed. In the other, a decrease is error (in the order of 6%) is observed.

Error in % (2fold cv)		Error in % (10-fold cv)		Groupings
normal	subclasses	normal	subclasses	
36.98	36.98	32.73	32.73	{building_windows_float_processed(bwf)}, {building_windows_non_float_proc'd(bwnf)}, {vehicle_windows(vw)}, {containers(c)}, {tableware(t)},{headlamps(h)}
21.72	20.78	19.21	19.62	{bwf, bwnf}, {vw}, {c}, {t}, {h}
38.86	36.74	32.64	32.55	{t, vw}, {bwf}, {bwnf}, {c}, {h}
34.81	34.44	31.70	31.60	{vw, c, t, h}, {bwf}, {bwnf}
42.92	33.84	30.78	29.96	{bwf, h}, {bwnf, t}, {c}, {vw}

Fig. 6. The **glass identification** data set (10 atts, 6 classes): As we have no knowledge of the various kinds of glass being classified here, the groupings have to be considered random groupings, which are presumably not meaningful.

Error in % (2fold cv)		Error in % (10-fold cv)		Groupings
normal	subclasses	normal	subclasses	
6.80	6.80	3.51	3.51	{not_recom(nr)}, {recommend(r)}, {very_recom(vr)}, {priority(p)}, {spec_prior(sp)}
6.94	6.80	3.54	3.51	{nr, sp}, {r}, {vr}, {p}
6.47	6.78	3.48	3.50	{nr, r, vr}, {p}, {sp}
5.34	4.94	2.35	2.31	{nr, r}, {vr, p}, {sp}

Fig. 7. The **nursery** data set (8 atts, 5 classes): The groupings were done on the basis of forming larger groups according to their ratings (in the class label).

Handwritten digits (Figure 8) only present a moderate trend. This is perhaps a little surprising because the dataset shares some important characteristics of the target concepts used in the simulation studies. It contains a reasonable number (10) of classes and errors result from a number of digits being confused with other digits. However, there

Error in % (2fold cv)		Error in % (10-fold cv)		Groupings
normal	subclasses	normal	subclasses	
11.51	11.51	9.52	9.52	{0}, {1}, {2}, {3}, {4}, {5}, {6}, {7}, {8}, {9}
8.48	7.25	7.11	5.96	{0, 1, 2, 3, 4}, {5, 6, 7, 8, 9}
5.54	5.51	4.53	4.62	{0, 2, 4, 6, 8}, {1, 3, 5, 7, 9}
7.57	7.12	5.80	5.97	{0, 1, 2, 3, 4, 7}, {5, 6, 8, 9}
5.72	6.10	4.58	5.13	{0, 1, 4, 6, 8, 9}, {2, 3, 5, 7}
9.36	9.11	7.62	7.51	{3, 7, 9}, {2, 8}, {5, 6}, {0}, {1}, {4}, {8}

Fig. 8. The **handwritten digits** data set (64 atts, 10 classes): We listed various grouping of the 10 digits. The numbers 5, 6, 8, 9, appear to have a rather similar shape for the human eye. This group is reflected in the first and second grouping where we have the groups {0, 1, 2, 3, 4} vs. {5, 6 ,7 8, 9} on the one hand and the same grouping with the 7 shifted to the lower digits on the other hand. In the first case grouping resulted in a significant improvement over the normal training. When the 7 was shifted to the lower digits, the absolute error rate dropped further. However, C4.5 managed to perform significantly better than with the first grouping, resulting in no improvement over the normal training procedure. The result suggests that the instance space may be less fractured for the classes {0, 1, 2, 3, 4, 7} vs. {5, 6, 8, 9}, resulting in a better performance of C4.5 and a lower relative advantage using subclass labels.

are two stand out results. In one, the digits are divided into two groups, those between 0 and 4 and those between 5 and 9. For this trial, the error rate is approximated 18% greater than the adjusted rate. In another trial where the digits are separated according to whether they are prime or not, the error rate is 6–11% lower than the adjusted value.

Error in % (2fold cv)		Error in % (10-fold cv)		Groupings
normal	subclasses	normal	subclasses	
6.21	6.21	3.38	3.38	{grass(g)}, {foliage(f)}, {window(w)}, {sky(s)}, {cement(c)}, {path(p)}
6.60	5.56	3.97	3.30	{g, f}, {w, s}, {c, p}
3.75	3.60	2.09	2.02	{g, f, s}, {w, c, p}

Fig. 9. The **image segmentation** data set (19 atts, 7 classes): The first grouping was done on the basis of similarity to the human eye. The second grouping is about natural and artificial surfaces, which appears to be a more arbitrary grouping. The results show a marked improvement for the intuitive grouping while the improvement for the second grouping is rather marginal.

In Figure 9 the results from image data are shown. For image domains intuitive similarities to the human eye are rather easy to determine. However, what appears similar to the human eye is not necessarily a good grouping for the learner, depending on the extracted features of the image used as the image representation to the learner.

Besides these observations of the behaviour of the error rates, we made another noteworthy observation concerning the tree sizes: The sizes of the learned trees using subclasses was about the same size as the trees trained without subclasses. No clear trend had been observed, although occasionally marked differences occurred. The results with the UCI data sets did not show the same clear trend we observed on our simulated domains. In the simulated domains we had a clear trend towards smaller trees when more classes had to be covered by a single tree. We do not yet understand why the same trends were not reproduced for the learning trials using the UCI data.

This suggests that our simulated domains are not accurately reflecting the domain structure of the UCI data. At the same time we are vindicated with our approach of using simulation studies to enhance the understanding of learning processes, as the results with the UCI data were rather mixed.

The mixed results are due to significant differences in the various domains of the UCI data, which are poorly understood at this stage. To enhance our understanding, further studies on simulated domains in comparison to 'real-world' data sets are necessary in order to understand which domain features are responsible for what effects. This is not limited to studying the effect of subclasses but includes also many other important aspects of learning, such as overfitting, noise handling, model selection, or the effectiveness of committee classifiers.

5   Discussion and Conclusion

While using artificial data sets is not new in machine learning research, it has not been widely used as a tool to obtain a better understanding of the domain characteristics that determine the relative success or lack of success of a given technique. We believe that a host of important insights into characteristics of ML techniques and domains can be obtained using the presented methodology more extensively. The purpose of such simulations is insight into the nature of learning algorithms and reasons why they behave as they do. Using artificial domains it is much easier to understand the characteristics of learning algorithms as the domains are well-controlled and can easily be modified to validate emerging hypotheses.

We demonstrated our point by presenting results showing an intriguing behaviour of C4.5 to improve its classification error when more classes have to be distinguished. We explained the behaviour, that is at first sight counterintuitive, with the fact that more classes may make it easier for C4.5 to find an appropriate split point for an attribute. This is due to the fact that with few classes a single split on an attribute is likely to split also those training examples apart which belong to the same class (but lie in different pockets in the instance space). In contrast to that when C4.5 deals with many classes, it is more likely that C4.5 will find a split on an attribute which does not split apart the examples belonging to the same class. In this sense, the subclasses can be viewed as additional information provided to the learner for guiding the learning process.

In other words, it is easier for C4.5 to learn target functions that assign to each class one or a few convex areas in the object space, as opposed to rather complex shaped areas for only a few classes.

Guessing the correct class becomes drastically more difficult with an increased number of classes. In this light, it is still surprising that the additional information provided to C4.5 using subclasses more than outweighs the increased difficulty of 'guessing'.

Our observation led us to the hypothesis that it may be advantageous for learning tasks for only few classes, to provide additional subclass labels to C4.5, as C4.5 may use the additional information to find the proper splits. Obviously, this is only going to work, where the subclass labels are assigned in a meaningful way (ideally selecting a single convex sub-area of the object space). Under what circumstances subclass labels would be meaningful in the above sense is not easy to decide at this stage.

However, our empirical studies with the UCI data suggest that using subclass labels can indeed be used as a general heuristic which may well lead to better results for many practical data sets. Further studies are needed to better understand the observed effects. Our results so far show that the effect of using subclasses can significantly differ from application to application.

Another intriguing avenue for further research seems to be the exploration of how other learners react to additional subclass labels. In particular, for some learners, such as Naive Bayes, which let the 'different classes compete' against each other to make a decision on a classification, additional subclasses may have significantly more pronounced effects than for decision tree learners. For decision tree learners the recognition phase is not at all affected by the finer grained classifications, as each subclass is uniquely mapped to one of the grouped classes.

The fact that the empirical UCI data sets produced mixed results confirms our methodological approach to a deeper understanding of learning by using artificial data sets. Using the real-world data sets leads often to mixed results and it is very difficult to understand the reason of the varying results without further studies that involve different types of domain models in a controlled way.

References

1. T. Dieterich. Approximate statistical tests for comparing supervised classification learning algorithms. *Neural Computation*, 7(10):1895–1924, 1998.
2. J. H. Gennari, P. Langley, and D. Fisher. Model of incremental concept formation. *Artificial Intelligence*, 40:11–61, 1989.
3. K. Lang and M. Witbrock. Learning to tell 2-spirals apart. In *Connectionist Models Summer School*, 1988.
4. D. D. Margineantu and T. G. Dietterich. Bootstrap methods for the cost-sensitive evaluation of classifiers. In *Proceedings of the 17th International Conference on Machine Learning*, pages 582–590. Kaufmann, 2000.
5. C. Mesterharm. A multi-class linear learning algorithm related to Winnow. In *Neural Information Processing Systems (NIPS-12)*, pages 519–525. MIT Press, 2000.
6. D. Michie and D. Spiegelhalter. *Machine Learning, Neural and Statistical Classification*. Ellis Horwood, 1994.
7. T. Scheffer. Predicting the generalization performance of cross validatory model selection criteria. In *Proceedings of the 17th International Conference on Machine Learning*. Kaufmann, 2000.
8. J. Weston and C. Watkins. Multi-class support vector machines. Technical Report CSD–TR–98–04, Royal Holloway, University of London, 1998.

Learning What People (Don't) Want

Thomas Hofmann

Department of Computer Science Brown University
th@cs.brown.edu

Abstract. Recommender systems make use of a database of user ratings to generate personalized recommendations and help people to find relevant products, items, or documents. In this paper, we present a probabilistic, model-based framework for user ratings based on a novel collaborative filtering technique that performs an automatic decomposition of user preferences. Our approach has several benefits, including highly accurate predictions, task-optimized model learning, mining of interest groups and patterns, as well as a highly efficient and scalable computation of predictions and recommendation lists.

1 Introduction

Kowing what one really wants is far from obvious. In order to figure out which book to read, which movie to watch, or which Web site to visit, we often rely on advise given to us by other people. Yet, in many situations one would like to automate the process of recommending items by anticipating user preferences. For example, in an electronic commerce setting customer may want to automatically receive accurate recommendations. Similarly, in the case of news groups or Web communities one would like to have some form of automated support, since these user groups are often far too large to allow its members to directly share experiences or to interchange recommendation. And even if one is lucky enough to get a persons advise on a subject, the question of whos advise to trust on which issue always remains a crucial question.

Recommender systems have been proposed and utilized in this context to leverage existing user data (ratings, profiles, logs) and to help people share their evaluations. Prominent Internet sites like amazon.com or CDnow use such systems for personalized product recommendation and to complement the traditional content-oriented search functionality. The predominant technique that powers recommender systems is *collaborative filtering* [2] and the most popular methods are variations around the memory-based approach proposed in the GroupLens [10,8] project. The underlying principle is extremely simple - for a given (so-called *active*) user, find people with similar interests and use their ratings and judgements to recommend new items.

In this paper, we propose a radically different approach to collaborative filtering which uses a sparse matrix decomposition technique called Probabilistic Latent Semantic Analysis [5] to automatically discover preference patterns in user profile data. In order to motivate our approach, we will first briefly discuss the dominant paradigm for collaborative filtering in Section 2 and point out what we think are its conceptional flaws. Section 3 presents our approach whereas Section 4 deals with an experimental evaluation and discussion.

L. De Raedt and P. Flach (Eds.): ECML 2001, LNAI 2167, pp. 214–225, 2001.
© Springer-Verlag Berlin Heidelberg 2001

2   Memory-Based Approaches

The by far most popular class of algorithms for collaborative filtering relies on the following principle. Given an active user a and a database of user profiles, recommendations are determined by, (i) computing the similarity between the active user and all the users in the database, (ii) for each item, forming a weighted and properly normalized vote over all (or some) users in the database, where the weights reflect the similarity computed in (i).

More specifically, the Pearson correlation has been proposed in many landmark papers [8,11], which computes the similarity between user profiles as

$$w(a, u) = \sum_{y \in V_a \cap V_u} \frac{(v_{a,y} - \bar{v}_a)(v_{u,y} - \bar{v}_u)}{\sqrt{\sigma_a \sigma_u}}. \tag{1}$$

Here $v_{u,y}$ denotes the (known) vote of user u on item y, while $\bar{v}_u$ and σ_u refer to the mean and standard deviation of votes of user u, respectively. Based on these weights a predictive vote for the active user is computed as follows,

$$p_{a,y} = \frac{\sum_{u:y \in V_u} w(a, u) v_{u,y}}{\sum_{u:y \in V_u} |w(a, u)|}. \tag{2}$$

Variations of this basic methodology include the use of different correlation measures like the Spearman correlation [4], the thresholding of weights, and the inhomogeneous weighting of items. These methods are often called *memory-based* methods or neighbor-based methods, since predicted votes are computed directly from the database of user profiles.

What is the fundamental assumption underlying this class of algorithms? Most importantly in our opinion, it is the idea of a *constant similarity* measure between user profiles. Here "constant" refers to the fact that $w(a, u)$ does not depend on the actual item y under consideration.[1] This is a very strong assumption, since it presupposes that in making a prediction for an active user, the "degree of trust" in the rating of some other user does not depend on the specific item. Similar assumptions are made be many model-based and hybrid approaches, e.g., the clustering approach of [12] and the personality diagnostics approach in [9]. The dependency network approach proposed in [3] on the other hand, builds a predictive model for each item and hence does not suffer from this limitation.

Potential problems that come with the above assumption can best be illustrated with an example: imagine we would like to recommend music to an active user A who likes opera. In the database, we find a very "post-modern character", B, who also adores opera but at the same time likes Salsa rhythms. Should one recommend Salsa to the purist opera fan? Or should one effectively eliminate B from the neighbor set of A, although B's opera recommendations could be highly relevant? Similarly, in the opposite situation, imagine that "typically" opera and Salsa are negatively correlated and most people who like one genre

---

[1] Only the overall normalization in Eq. (2) is different for every item, although one can hardly consider this to be an "item-specific" weighting.

dislike the other one. This would imply that recommending items of one or the other type to B, but never both, dependent on the exact similarity weights and proportions.

Intuitively, what is missing in standard memory-based approaches is the possibility to model that fact that one person is a reliable recommender for another person with respect to a *subset of items*, but not necessarily for all possible items. This deficit is expected to become more relevant with increasing diversity of the item set and users'interest patterns. In general, we strongly believe that the simple notion of similarity between one person and another person fails to capture the multi-dimensional nature of human preferences.

We see the solution to this problem in a method that couples recommendation with a decomposition of preferences, where each preference pattern models an interest or trait shared among a community of people. There is a reciprocal characterization of user communities by sets of items and vice versa, along with the typical ratings that describe the nature of the relation, be it positive, neutral, or negative.

3   Decomposing Preferences

We propose a probabilistic model-based approach to collaborative filtering which overcomes the major limitations of memory-based methods and offers a number of additional advantages:

- User profiles are explicitly decomposed into statistically significant *interest patterns*, each pattern typically dealing with a subset of the items. This allows to selectively share recommendations among users by introducing a dependency on the specific item or type of item, thereby increasing accuracy.
- The preference decomposition also perform *data mining* by revealing hidden patterns that drive user ratings. This can be used for identifying user communities as well as for data visualization.
- The probabilistic preference model can be used to tailor recommender systems to the task at hand. Often items come with specific costs or utilities and one can optimize the recommendations to maximize the expected utility.
- Once the model is trained, the database is no longer required to make recommendations. A model-based approach thus avoids the need to have a potentially huge database available to make recommendations. This has advantages in terms of memory requirements as well as system speed.

3.1   Latent Class Models for User Ratings

There are two variants of probabilistic models that we investigate in this paper. They correspond to different settings of the recommendation problem: (I) predicting a user rating for an unknown item, i.e., estimating $P(v|u,y)$ or $p_{u,y} \equiv \sum_v v\, P(v|u,y)$ and (II) predicting a rating in conjunction with a selection, i.e., estimating $P(v,y|u)$. Which setting is more appropriate depends on the actual application and objective. For example, in an electronic commerce setting, $P(y|u)$ may model the fact whether a user is likely to purchase a product, which may be an important part of the system, irrespective of the actual user satisfaction expressed by the rating v.

Formally, let us introduce a latent variable $z_{u,y}$ for each (actual and potential) observation triplet $(u, y, v_{u,y})$, thus defining the complete data of an elementary rating event by $(u, y, v_{u,y}, z_{u,y})$. Intuitively, each quadruple is supposed to model the fact that a person u votes on item y with rating $v_{u,y}$, "because of" $z_{u,y}$. Each latent variable is intended to offer a hypothetical explanation for a rating. For example, a high rating of a person on a piece of music, say Fidelio", might be explained by the fact that the person is interest in the particular genre (opera). However, an alternative explanation could be that a person likes works by a specific composer (Beethoven) and the genre might be completely irrelevant. & a third person might like Fidelio"because of its political message and its praise of freedom and love. Of course, it is not clear *a priori* which possible explanations should be considered. And even for a finite candidate set of causes the question remains to what cause is in effect in each individual case. Each item may be liked or disliked for different reasons and persons may have more than a single interest, different aspects of their taste being relevant for different ratings. In summary, we are looking for a method that would automatically find potential causes, determine which subset of the causes are likely to be relevant for a specific item as well as for a specific person, and in each individual case assign a probability to the fact that a cause will be áctive"for a given rating.

Assume for now that the number of potential causes is fixed beforehand, i.e., each variable $z_{u,y}$ may take one out of a finite number of say K values. Then the joint probability of an observation triplet will be given by summing over all possible states of the latent variable,

$$P(u, y, v) = \sum_z P(u, y, v, z) = \sum_z P(v, y|z, u)P(z|u)P(u).$$ (3)

We make the crucial independence assumption that conditioned on the true cause z, the vote as well as the selection of the item are independent of the user, implying that $P(v, y|z, u) = P(v, y|z)$. The resulting model can be written as

$$P(v, y|u) = \sum_z P(v, y|z)P(z|u)$$ (4)

where we have neglected the user probability $P(u)$. In the first case, where one conditions on both, the user as well as the item, one will get similarly

$$P(v|u, y) = \sum_z P(v|y, z)P(z|u)$$ (5)

These parameters have a very intuitive meaning: $P(z|u)$ represents to what extend a user ṕarticipates"in a common interest pattern, or more precisely, which fraction of a users ratings are explained by hidden cause z. $P(v, y|z)$ models which items and item/vote combinations are more likely or less likely to occur in the interest group described by z. Similarly, $P(v|y, z)$ models the probability that a user as a member of interest group z will vote with v on item y.

One can also investigate models in which the role of users and items are reversed, in particular in the symmetric setting of estimating $P(v|u, y)$. Notice that in the typical case where the number of users exceeds the number of items, the dimensionality of the resulting model will be quite different.

The presented approach is closely related to sparse matrix decomposition techniques and the paper effectively extends a model called *Probabilistic Latent Semantic Analysis* which has been used mainly in the context of information retrieval [6]. More details about the conceptional foundations can be found in [5]. A simplified model and preliminary experiments for collaborative filtering have been presented in [7], which mainly dealt with a conceptual framework for latent class models for collaborative filtering.

3.2   Expectation Maximization Algorithm

The Expectation Maximization (EM) algorithm is a standard method for maximum likelihood estimation in latent variable models. The EM algorithm performs two steps in alternation, an E-step, where the expected value for the unobserved variables are computed given the current parameters and a M-step, where these values are used to update the parameters. More details can be found in [5]. In our case the E-step computes the probability that a cause z is associated with an observation triplet $(u, y, v_{u,y})$. By Bayes'rule one obtains

$$P(z|u, y, v_{u,y}) = \frac{P(z|u)\rho(v_{u,y}, z, y)}{\sum_{z'} P(z|u)\rho(v_{u,y}, z, y)}, \tag{6}$$

where $\rho(v_{u,y}, z, y) = P(v_{u,y}|z, y)$ in case (I) and $\rho(v_{u,y}, z, y) = P(v_{u,y}, y|z)$ in case (II). Notice that the occurrence of a vote on y matters in the computation of the posterior probabilities for z according to (II), but not in case (I).

In the M-step one updates the parameters, i.e., re-estimates the conditional probabilities that define the model. The user participation probabilities are given by

$$P(z|u) = \frac{\sum_{(y,v_{u,y})} P(z|u, y, v_{u,y})}{\sum_{z'} \sum_{(y,v_{u,y})} P(z'|u, y, v_{u,y})} = \frac{\sum_{(y,v_{u,y})} P(z|u, y, v_{u,y})}{|\{(u, y, v_{u,y})\}|}. \tag{7}$$

The update equations for $P(v|y, z)$ and $P(v, y|z)$, respectively, depend on the parametric form that one chooses for those distributions. We assume that the rating scale is quantized, e.g., a rating v might be an integral number between 0 and 5 (as it is the case for the EachMovie data set). In the quantized case one can work directly with multinomial/binomial probability distributions, leading to

$$P(v|y, z) = \frac{\sum_u P(z|u, y, v)}{\sum_{v'} \sum_u P(z|u, y, v')}. \tag{8}$$

Other choices are possible, for example a normal distribution with mean $\mu_{y,z}$ and variance $\sigma^2_{y,z}$ for each combination of items and hidden causes. In this case, the mean would simply be re-estimated in the M-step according to

$$\mu_{y,z} = \frac{\sum_v \sum_u v \, P(z|u, y, v)}{\sum_v \sum_u P(z|u, y, v)}. \tag{9}$$

The Gaussian model has shown slightly worse performance in the experiments, we have therefore focused on the multinomial/binomial model in the experiments.

4 Experimental Evaluation

4.1 Evaluation Criteria

A thorough empirical analysis of collaborative filtering algorithms has been presented in [1] and we have adapted most of the proposed evaluation criteria. The effectiveness of collaborative filtering techniques can be measured in various ways dependent on how the recommender system is used and how results are presented to the user.

In the case that individual items are presented to the user, we use two evaluation metrics. The first score is the absolute deviation of the predicted and actual vote,

$$E_1(u, y) = |p_{u,y} - v_{u,y}|. \tag{10}$$

Moreover, for quantized votes, we also evaluate the score

$$E_0(u, y) = \begin{cases} 0, \text{ if } p_{u,y} = v_{u,y} \\ 1, \text{ else.} \end{cases} \tag{11}$$

which only measures whether or not the vote was correctly predicted.

For ranked lists of items we have to assign score to permutations of items. We denote a permutation by τ and the rank of an item y with respect to τ by $\tau(y)$, e.g., the top ranked item y will have $\tau(y) = 1$, the second item $\tau(y) = 2$, and so forth. Items with known votes are not included in the ranking. We then use the following rank score for τ,

$$R(u, \tau) = \sum_y 2^{-\frac{\tau(y)-1}{\alpha-1}} \max(v_{u,y} - \bar{v}, 0), \tag{12}$$

with $\bar{v}$ denoting the overall mean vote. The rationale behind this score is that when presented with a ranked list of items, users will sift through the list starting at the top, until they find a relevant item or simply give up. The probability that a user will ever take notice of an item at rank r is modeled as an exponential distribution with a half-life constant α (set to 4 in our experiments). The total score for a population of users is then measured by (cf. [1])

$$R = 100 \frac{\sum_u R(u, \tau_u)}{\sum_u \max_{\tau'} R(u, \tau')}. \tag{13}$$

4.2   Evaluation Protocols

In the evaluation experiments the observed user ratings are partitioned into a training set and a test set. For each user the training data is used to compute votes on unrated items as well as a ranked list of recommendations. For the split into training and test data, we have used a leave-one-out protocol, where we randomly leave out one of the ratings for each user who has at least two observed ratings. This has been called the *All but 1* protocol in [1].

Notice that the above ranking measure takes a very simple form in this case: If the hold-out rating is below the average, simply skip this user. Otherwise, compute the rank of the hold out positive"item and evaluate the expression corresponding to this item. The maximum achievable score would be to have the test item always be in first place.

4.3   Data Set

Unfortunately, there are very few data sets available to the academic community to test recommender systems. This seems largely because of the potential commercial value of user data and because of privacy issues. The data set we have used in our experiments is the EachMovie data. There are 1623 items in this data set and more than 60,000 user profiles with a total of over 2.8 million ratings. The rating scale is discrete taking values from 0 to 5.[2]

4.4   Results

We have compared our statistical approach with the memory based approach using the Pearson correlation as a similarity measure. The results on predicting ratings for given items are summarize in Table 1. As one can see, the model-based approach achieves great performance gains in terms of absolute error as well as in terms of prediction accuracy. According to both scores, the model-based approach performs significantly better. The improvement grows with the number of states chosen for the latent class variables, but more or less levels out at around $K = 100$. Notice that we have used early stopping on validation data to avoid overfitting (cf. [5] for more details on complexity control issues).

Although we have not implemented other collaborative filtering techniques like Bayesian clustering or Bayesian networks, the comparison in [1] have demonstrated that memory-based methods achieve excellent results on this benchmark. The results reported in the latter paper on memory-based methods are also in good agreement with the outcome of our experiments. This makes the results in Table 1 even more remarkable. It can also be seen that models with reversed role of users and items show a weaker performance.

The results for generating ranked recommendation lists, the more typical setting for recommender systems are shown in Table 2. Notice that in this case the model denoted by case (II) has been used, which not only predicts the outcome of the rating, but also whether or not a person is familiar with a particular

---

[2] The original ratings have been multiplied by a factor of 5.

Table 1. Results for predicting individual test ratings on the Each Movie data set. K denotes the number of latent states used to perform the decomposition.

Method	Absolute Deviation	Relative Improvement	Prediction Accuracy	Relative Improvement
Baseline	1.091	0.00	33.4	0.00
Memory-based	0.951	12.8%	35.3	6.3%
Model-based				
K=5	0.972	10.9%	39.3	17.6%
K=10	0.951	12.8%	39.8	19.1%
K=20	0.947	13.2%	39.9	19.5%
K=50	0.937	14.1%	40.1	20.0%
K=100	0.927	15.0%	40.6	21.6%
K=150	0.926	15.1%	40.7	21.9%
K=200	0.924	15.3%	40.8	22.2%
K=400	0.916	16.0%	41.4	24.0%
Model-based (Role of items and users reversed)				
K=20	0.983	9.9%	37.7	12.8%
K=50	0.975	10.6%	38.4	14.9%
K=100	0.973	10.8%	38.5	15.2%

item and/or has rated an item. The achieved performance gains are even more substantial than for predicting ratings of single items. The relative performance gain over the baseline method of ranking items by overall popularity is more than 70%

4.5 Performance Issues

The advantages of the model-based approach in terms of memory and computation time are also considerable. As far as the memory requirement is concerned, one only needs to store the parameters $P(v, y|z)$ or $P(v, |y, z)$, respectively. The user-specific parameters $P(z|u)$ can be reconstructed as needed. In fact, it is simple to show that the problem of finding $P(z|u)$ reduces to an independent convex cross-entropy minimization problem for each user u. Since the number of users is typically much larger than the number of items, this can make a crucial difference. On the other hand, memory-based approaches suffer greatly from the fact that the data can not be compressed into a model, but has to be kept in main memory at recommendation time.

Similarly there are great savings in terms of computation time. In memory-based approaches, user correlations have typically to be performed on-line which is a very time consuming process. In comparison, the model-based approach only requires to perform of the order of K operations to compute the probability for a single rating or rating/item pair. Since the probabilities $P(z|u)$ are typically very sparse, the actual savings will often be even larger for a slight sacrifice in accuracy. In our experiments, the model-based approach was typically more

Table 2. Rank score results for ordered recommendation lists on the Each Movie data set. K denotes the number of latent states used to perform the decomposition.

Method	Rank Score	Relative Improvement
Baseline	26.95	0.00
Memory-based	36.71	36.2%
Model-based		
K=20	44.64	65.6%
K=50	45.91	70.3%
K=100	45.98	70.6%

than 10-20 times faster compared to the memory-based approach. In practice, memory-based methods often have to subsample the user profile base to allow real-time recommendations for large databases. This is not necessary for our model-based approach.

The main disadvantage of the model-based approach is the computational burden of the model training stage. For the EachMovie data, a typical training run took between 5 and 60 minutes on a Pentium III w/800 MHz (dependent on the dimensionality of the model). Yet, training can be performed off-line where computational resources are typically abundant or at least much less critical.

4.6   Mining User Preferences

Finally, we would like to illustrate that the decomposition of user ratings may lead to the discovery of interesting patterns and regularities that describe user interests as well as dislikes. To that extend we have visualized the items for each latent variable state by sorting them according to the popularity within an interest group as measured by $P(y|z)$ (irrespective of the actual vote). The average vote $\sum_v vP(v|y,z)$ is displayed in rectangular brackets as well. Figure 1 and 2 display the interest groups extracted by the model with $K = 40$, ordered according to the average "positiveness"of each group, computed as $\sum_{y,v} vP(v|y,z)P(y|z)$.

4.7   Conclusion

We have presented a powerful method for collaborative filtering and mining of user data. The method achieves a very good recommendation and prediction accuracy compared to previously proposed methods, in addition it is highly scalable, and extremely flexible. Conceptionally, the decomposition of user preferences is a radically novel idea that clearly distinguishes this approach from traditional memory-based approaches. The use as a data mining tool is another unique benefit of our method.

Acknowledgements. The EachMovie dataset was generously provided by Digital Equipment Corporation. This work was supported in part by the Air Force and the Defense Advanced Research Projects Agency under Grant No. F30602-00-2-0599 and by the National Science Foundation, under Grant No. IIS-0085836.

Fig. 1. EachMovie interest groups number 1-20 out of 40.

224   T. Hofmann

The screenshot shows a Microsoft Internet Explorer window titled:
`\\Plato\Repository\Academic\CollFilter\EachMovie\Visual.html - Microsoft Internet...`

Menu bar: File Edit View Favorites Tools Help

Interest Group 21, *3.5*	Interest Group 22, *3.4*	Interest Group 23, *3.1*	Interest Group 24, *3.1*	Interest Group 25, *3*
Smoke [*3.7*] [0.024]	Money Train [*3.2*] [0.017]	Jumanji [*3.5*] [0.026]	Jurassic Park [*3.2*] [0.08]	Jerry Maguire [*3.5*] [0.021]
Mighty Aphrodite [*3.3*] [0.018]	Terminal Velocity [*3.2*] [0.016]	Oliver and Company... [*3.1*] [0.023]	Forrest Gump [*3.5*] [0.079]	The People vs. Lar... [*3.5*] [0.016]
Fargo [*4.1*] [0.018]	The Shadow [*3.3*] [0.015]	Muppet Treasure Is... [*3.1*] [0.022]	The Fugitive [*3.6*] [0.066]	Mars Attacks! [*2.6*] [0.015]
Four Weddings and ... [*3.3*] [0.018]	Hard Target [*3.4*] [0.015]	Powder [*3.5*] [0.021]	Terminator 2: Judg... [*3.6*] [0.056]	The Lost World: Ju... [*2.8*] [0.015]

Interest Group 26, *2.8*	Interest Group 27, *2.7*	Interest Group 28, *2.7*	Interest Group 29, *2.6*	Interest Group 30, *2.2*
Dances With Wolves [*3.4*] [0.11]	Naked Gun 33 1/3: ... [*2.4*] [0.02]	I.Q. [*2.8*] [0.022]	Mrs. Doubtfire [*3*] [0.049]	Mulholland Falls [*2.1*] [0.018]
Batman (1989) [*2.4*] [0.11]	The Hudsucker Prox... [*3.3*] [0.019]	French Kiss [*2.9*] [0.019]	Pretty Woman [*2.9*] [0.047]	The Arrival (Shock... [*2.5*] [0.017]
Pulp Fiction [*3.4*] [0.1]	Hot Shots! Part De... [*2.3*] [0.019]	Nine Months [*2.5*] [0.019]	Ghost [*3*] [0.042]	Primal Fear [*2.9*] [0.017]
Apollo 13 [*3.6*] [0.094]	So I Married an Ax... [*2.6*] [0.016]	Junior [*2.4*] [0.018]	The Mask [*2.5*] [0.042]	City Hall [*2.4*] [0.016]

Interest Group 31, *2.2*	Interest Group 32, *2*	Interest Group 33, *1.8*	Interest Group 34, *1.8*	Interest Group 35, *1.7*
E.T.: The Extrater... [*2.6*] [0.01]	Lord of Illusions [*1.6*] [0.011]	Sleepless in Seatt... [*1.8*] [0.017]	Toy Story [*2.4*] [0.05]	Striptease [*0.025*] [0.033]
The Sound of Music... [*2.3*] [0.0086]	Tales From the Hoo... [*1.6*] [0.0087]	The Firm [*1.8*] [0.015]	Mission: Impossibl... [*1.8*] [0.049]	Independence Day (... [*0.87*] [0.029]
Top Gun (1986) [*2.3*] [0.0086]	Mallrats [*2.4*] [0.0083]	Pretty Woman [*1.5*] [0.015]	Independence Day (... [*2.1*] [0.048]	The Cable Guy [*0.16*] [0.028]
Mary Poppins (1964... [*2.3*] [0.0083]	Wes Craven's New N... [*2*] [0.0082]	Dave [*2*] [0.015]	Twister [*1.8*] [0.043]	Barb Wire [*4.9e-005*] [0.025]

Interest Group 36, *1.1*	Interest Group 37, *0.68*	Interest Group 38, *0.39*	Interest Group 39, *0.16*	Interest Group 40, *0.16*
Super Mario Bros. [*0.11*] [0.017]	Mighty Morphin Pow... [*0.017*] [0.033]	Dumb and Dumber [*0.0025*] [0.038]	Kazaam [*0.028*] [0.014]	Tales From the Hoo... [*0.022*] [0.0075]
The Beverly Hillbi... [*0.34*] [0.016]	The Brady Bunch Mo... [*0.28*] [0.024]	Ace Ventura: Pet D... [*0.016*] [0.034]	Children of the Co... [*0.021*] [0.014]	Vampire in Brookly... [*1.3e-005*] [0.007]
Richie Rich [*0.22*] [0.015]	Mortal Kombat [*0.21*] [0.018]	Ace Ventura: When ... [*0.00067*] [0.033]	A Very Brady Seque... [*0.083*] [0.012]	The Baby-Sitters C... [*0.0063*] [0.007]
The Next Karate Ki... [*0.21*] [0.014]	The Bridges of Mad... [*0.015*] [0.018]	Waterworld [*0.034*] [0.028]	Halloween: The Cur... [*0.035*] [0.012]	Candyman: Farewell... [*0.0039*] [0.0065]

Status bar: `http://us.imdb.com/M/title-exact?Arrival, The (1996)`   Local intranet

Fig. 2. EachMovie interest groups number 21-40 out of 40.

References

1. J. S. Breese, D. Heckerman, and C. Kardie. Empirical analysis of predictive algorithms for collaborative filtering. In *Proceedings of the 14th Conference on Uncertainty in Artificial Intelligence*, pages 43–52, 1998.
2. D. Goldberg, D. Nichols, B. Oki, and D. Terry. Using collaborative filtering to weave an information tapestry. *Communications of the ACM*, 35(2):61–70, 1992.
3. D. Heckerman, D. M. Chickering, C. Meek, R. Rounthwait, and C. Kadie. Dependency networks for density estimation, collaborative filtering, and data visualization. In *Proceedings of the 16th Conference on Uncertainty in Artificial Intelligence*, 2000.
4. J. Herlocker, Konstanm J., Al Borchers, and J. Riedl. An algorithmic framework for collaborative filtering. In *Proceedings of SIGIR'99*, 1999.
5. T. Hofmann. Probabilistic latent semantic analysis. In *Proceedings of the 15th Conference on Uncertainty in Artificial Intelligence*, pages 289–296, 1999.
6. T. Hofmann. Probabilistic latent semantic indexing. In *Proceedings of the 22nd ACM-SIGIR International Conference on Research and Development in Information Retrieval, Berkeley, California*, pages 50–57, 1999.
7. T. Hofmann and J. Puzicha. Latent class models for collaborative filtering. In *Proceedings of the International Joint Conference on Artificial Intelligence*, 1999.
8. J. Konstan, B. Miller, D. Maltz, J. Herlocker, L. Gordon, and J. Riedl. Grouplens: Applying collaborative filtering to Usenet news. *Communications of the ACM*, 40(3):77–87, 1997.
9. D. M. Pennock, E. Horvitz, S. Lawrence, and C. L. Giles. Collaborative filtering by personality diagnosis: A hybrid memory- and model-based approach. In *Proceedings of the 16th Conference on Uncertainty in Artificial Intelligence*, pages 473–480, 2000.
10. P. Resnik, I. Neophytos, M. Suchak, P. Bergstrom, and J. Rield. Grouplens: An open architecture for collaborative filtering of netnews. In *Proceedings of ACM CSCW'94 Conference on Computer-Supported Cooperative Work*, pages 175–186, 1994.
11. U. Shardanand and P. Maes. Social information filtering: Algorithms for automatic 'word of mouth'. In *ACM CHI'95 Conference on Human Factors in Computing Systems*, pages 210–217, 1995.
12. L.H. Ungar and D.P. Foster. Clustering methods for collaborative filtering. In *Workshop on Recommendation Systems at the Fifteenth National Conference on Artificial Intelligence*, 1998.

Towards a Universal Theory of Artificial Intelligence Based on Algorithmic Probability and Sequential Decisions

Marcus Hutter

IDSIA, Galleria 2, CH-6928 Manno-Lugano, Switzerland,
marcus@idsia.ch,
http://www.idsia.ch/~marcus

Abstract. Decision theory formally solves the problem of rational agents in uncertain worlds if the true environmental probability distribution is known. Solomonoff's theory of universal induction formally solves the problem of sequence prediction for unknown distributions. We unify both theories and give strong arguments that the resulting universal AIξ model behaves optimally in any computable environment. The major drawback of the AIξ model is that it is uncomputable. To overcome this problem, we construct a modified algorithm AIξ^{tl}, which is still superior to any other time t and length l bounded agent. The computation time of AIξ^{tl} is of the order $t \cdot 2^l$.

1 Introduction

The most general framework for Artificial Intelligence is the picture of an *agent* interacting with an environment [RN95]. If the goal is not pre-specified, the agent has to learn by occasional reinforcement feedback [SB98]. If the agent shall be universal, no assumption about the environment may be made, besides that there *exists* some exploitable structure at all. We may ask for the most intelligent way an agent could behave, or, about the optimal way of learning in terms of real world interaction cycles. *Decision theory* formally[1] solves this problem only if the true environmental probability distribution is known (e.g. Blackjack) [Bel57,BT96,SB98]. On the other hand, there is a universal theory for a subset of machine learning, namely, passively predicting unseen data after exposure to training examples. [Sol64,Sol78] formally solved this *induction* problem if the true distribution is unknown, but only if the agent cannot influence the environment (e.g. weather forecasts) [LV97]. Here, we combine both ideas to obtain a universal machine learner for the general case where the learner can actively influence its world. We claim that the resulting *parameterless model AIξ behaves optimally in any computable environment* (e.g. prisoner or auction problems,

---

[1] With a formal solution we mean a rigorous mathematical definition, uniquely specifying the solution. For problems considered here this always implies the existence of an algorithm which asymptotically converges to the correct solution.

L. De Raedt and P. Flach (Eds.): ECML 2001, LNAI 2167, pp. 226–238, 2001.
© Springer-Verlag Berlin Heidelberg 2001

poker, car driving). To get an *effective solution*, a modification $AI\xi^{tl}$, superior to any other time t and length l bounded agent, is constructed. The computation time of $AI\xi^{tl}$ per interaction cycle is of the order $t \cdot 2^l$. The computation time is still not practical, but $AI\xi^{tl}$ represents the first learning algorithm with generalization capability at all which makes no specific assumptions (Markov property, known transition matrix, observablility, similarity relations, ...) on the structure of the environment. The $AI\xi$ and $AI\xi^{tl}$ models lead to many new insights into learning agents. The main goal of this work is to derive and discuss both models, and to clarify the meanings of *universal, optimal, superior, etc.* It summarizes a long report and is necessarily succinct. Details can be found in the technical report [Hut00].

2   Rational Agents & Sequential Decisions

Agents in probabilistic environments: A very general framework for intelligent systems is that of rational agents [RN95]. In cycle k, an agent performs *action* $y_k \in Y$ (output word) which results in a *perception* $x_k \in X$ (input word), followed by cycle $k+1$ and so on. If agent and environment are deterministic and computable, the entanglement of both can be modeled by two Turing machines with two common tapes (and some private tapes) containing the action stream $y_1 y_2 y_3...$ and the perception stream $x_1 x_2 x_3...$ (The meaning of $x_k \equiv x'_k r_k$ is explained in the next paragraph):

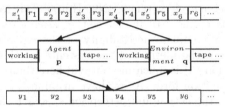

The program p is called the *policy* of the agent interacting with environment q. We write $p(x_{<k}) = y_{1:k}$ to denote the output $y_{1:k} \equiv y_1...y_k$ of the agent p on input $x_{<k} \equiv x_1...x_{k-1}$ and similarly $q(y_{1:k}) = x_{1:k}$ for the environment q. We call Turing machines p and q behaving in this way *chronological*. In the more general case of a *probabilistic environment*, given the history $yx_{<k}y_k \equiv yx_1...yx_{k-1}y_k \equiv y_1 x_1...y_{k-1}x_{k-1}y_k$, the probability that the environment leads to perception x_k in cycle k is (by definition) $\mu(yx_{<k}y\underline{x}_k)$. The underlined argument $\underline{x}_k$ in μ is a random variable and the other non-underlined arguments $yx_{<k}y_k$ represent conditions. We call probability distributions like μ *chronological*. Details on the notation can be found in [Hut00].

The $AI\mu$ Model: The goal of the agent is to maximize future *rewards*, which are provided by the environment through the inputs x_k. The inputs $x_k \equiv x'_k r_k$ are divided into a regular part x'_k and some (possibly empty or delayed) reward r_k. The μ-expected reward sum of future cycles k to m (called the value) with outputs $y_{k:m} \equiv y^p_{k:m}$ generated by the agent's policy p can be written compactly as

$$V^p_\mu(\dot{y}\dot{x}_{<k}) := \sum_{x_k...x_m} (r_k + ... + r_m)\mu(\dot{y}\dot{x}_{<k}y\underline{x}_{k:m}), \qquad (1)$$

where m is the *lifespan* of the agent, and the dots above $\ddot{y}\ddot{x}_{<k}$ indicate the actual action and perception history. The value with outputs y_i generated by the *ideal agent* which maximizes the expected future rewards is

$$V_\mu^*(\ddot{y}\ddot{x}_{<k}) := \max_{y_k}\sum_{x_k} ... \max_{y_m}\sum_{x_m}(r_k + ... + r_m)\mu(\ddot{y}\ddot{x}_{<k}y\underline{x}_{k:m}), \qquad (2)$$

i.e. the best expected reward is obtained by averaging over the x_i and maximizing over the y_i. This has to be done in chronological order to correctly incorporate the dependency of x_i and y_i on the history. The output $\dot{y}_k$, which achieves the maximal value defines *the AIμ model*:

$$\dot{y}_k := \arg\max_{y_k}\sum_{x_k} ... \max_{y_m}\sum_{x_m}(r_k + ... + r_m)\mu(\ddot{y}\ddot{x}_{<k}y\underline{x}_{k:m}). \qquad (3)$$

The AIμ model is optimal in the sense that no other policy leads to higher μ-expected reward. A detailed derivation and other recursive and functional versions can be found in [Hut00].

Sequential decision theory: Eq. (3) is essentially an Expectimax algorithm/ sequence. One can relate (3) to the Bellman equations [Bel57] of sequential decision theory by identifying complete histories $y\underline{x}_{<k}$ with states, $\mu(y\underline{x}_{<k}y\underline{x}_k)$ with the state transition matrix, $V_\mu^*(y\underline{x}_{<k})$ with the value of history/state $y\underline{x}_{<k}$, and y_k with the action in cycle k [BT96,RN95,Hut00]. Due to the use of complete histories as state space, the AIμ model neither assumes stationarity, nor the Markov property, nor complete accessibility of the environment. Every state occurs at most once in the lifetime of the system. For this and other reasons the explicit formulation (3) is much more useful here than to enforce a pseudo-recursive Bellman equation form. As we have in mind a universal system with complex interactions, the action and perception spaces Y and X are huge (e.g. video images), and every action or perception itself occurs usually only once in the lifespan m of the agent. As there is no (obvious) universal similarity relation on the state space, an effective reduction of its size is impossible, but there is no principle problem in determining $\dot{y}_k$ as long as μ is known and computable and X, Y and m are finite.

Reinforcement learning: Things dramatically change if μ is unknown. Reinforcement learning algorithms [KM96,SB98,BT96] are commonly used in this case to learn the unknown μ. They succeed if the state space is either small or has effectively been made small by generalization or function approximation techniques. In any case, the solutions are either *ad hoc*, work in restricted domains only, have serious problems with state space exploration versus exploitation, or have non-optimal learning rate. There is no universal and optimal solution to this problem so far. In Section 4 we present a new model and argue that it formally solves all these problems in an optimal way. The true probability distribution μ will not be learned directly, but will be replaced by a universal prior ξ, which is shown to converge to μ in a sense.

3   Algorithmic Complexity and Universal Induction

The problem of the unknown environment: We have argued that currently there is no universal and optimal solution to solving reinforcement learning problems. On the other hand, [Sol64] defined a universal scheme of inductive inference, based on Epicurus' principle of multiple explanations, Ockhams razor, and Bayes' rule for conditional probabilities. For an excellent introduction one should consult the book of [LV97]. In the following we outline the theory and the basic results.

Kolmogorov complexity and universal probability: Let us choose some universal prefix Turing machine U with unidirectional binary input and output tapes and a bidirectional working tape. We can then define the (conditional) prefix Kolmogorov complexity [Cha75,Gác74,Kol65,Lev74] as the length l of the shortest program p, for which U outputs the binary string $x = x_{1:n}$ with $x_i \in \{0,1\}$:

$$K(x) := \min_p\{l(p) : U(p) = x\},$$

and given y

$$K(x|y) := \min_p\{l(p) : U(p,y) = x\}.$$

The *universal semimeasure* $\hat{\xi}(\underline{x})$ is defined as the probability that the output of U starts with x when provided with fair coin flips on the input tape [Sol64, Sol78]. It is easy to see that this is equivalent to the formal definition

$$\hat{\xi}(\underline{x}) := \sum_{p \,:\, \exists \omega : U(p) = x\omega} 2^{-l(p)} \qquad (4)$$

where the sum is over minimal programs p for which U outputs a string starting with x. U might be non-terminating. As the short programs dominate the sum, $\hat{\xi}$ is closely related to $K(x)$ as $\hat{\xi}(\underline{x}) = 2^{-K(x)+O(K(l(x)))}$. $\hat{\xi}$ has the important universality property [Sol64] that it dominates every computable probability distribution $\hat{\rho}$ up to a multiplicative factor depending only on $\hat{\rho}$ but not on x:

$$\hat{\xi}(\underline{x}) \geq 2^{-K(\hat{\rho})-O(1)} \cdot \hat{\rho}(\underline{x}). \qquad (5)$$

The Kolmogorov complexity of a function like $\hat{\rho}$ is defined as the length of the shortest self-delimiting coding of a Turing machine computing this function. $\hat{\xi}$ itself is *not* a probability distribution[2]. We have $\hat{\xi}(\underline{x}0) + \hat{\xi}(\underline{x}1) < \hat{\xi}(\underline{x})$ because there are programs p which output just x, neither followed by 0 nor 1. They just stop after printing x or continue forever without any further output. We will call a function $0 \leq \hat{\rho} \leq 1$ with the property $\sum_{x_n} \hat{\rho}(\underline{x}_{1:n}) \leq \hat{\rho}(\underline{x}_{<n})$ a *semimeasure*. $\hat{\xi}$ is a semimeasure and (5) actually holds for all enumerable semimeasures $\hat{\rho}$.

Universal sequence prediction: (Binary) sequence prediction algorithms try to predict the continuation x_n of a given sequence $x_1...x_{n-1}$. In the following we

---

[2] It is possible to normalize $\hat{\xi}$ to a probability distribution as has been done in [Sol78, Hut99] by giving up the enumerability of $\hat{\xi}$. Bounds (6) and (8) hold for both definitions.

will assume that the sequences are drawn from a probability distribution and that the true probability of a string starting with $x_1...x_n$ is $\hat{\mu}(\underline{x}_{1:n})$. The probability of x_n given $x_{<n}$ hence is $\hat{\mu}(x_{<n}\underline{x}_n)$. Usually $\hat{\mu}$ is unknown and the system can only have some belief $\hat{\rho}$ about the true distribution $\hat{\mu}$. Now the universal probability $\hat{\xi}$ comes into play: [Sol78] has proved that the mean squared difference between $\hat{\xi}$ and $\hat{\mu}$ is finite for computable $\hat{\mu}$:

$$\sum_{k=1}^{\infty} \sum_{x_{1:k}} \hat{\mu}(\underline{x}_{<k})(\hat{\xi}(x_{<k}\underline{x}_k) - \hat{\mu}(x_{<k}\underline{x}_k))^2 \; < \; \ln 2 \cdot K(\hat{\mu}) + O(1). \qquad (6)$$

A simplified proof can be found in [Hut99]. So the difference between $\hat{\xi}(x_{<n}\underline{x}_n)$ and $\hat{\mu}(x_{<n}\underline{x}_n)$ rapidly tends to zero $n \to \infty$ with $\hat{\mu}$ probability 1 for *any* computable probability distribution $\hat{\mu}$. The reason for the astonishing property of a single (universal) function to converge to *any* computable probability distribution lies in the fact that the sets of $\hat{\mu}$-random sequences differ for different $\hat{\mu}$. Past data $x_{<n}$ are exploited to get a (with $n \to \infty$) improving estimate $\hat{\xi}(x_{<n}\underline{x}_n)$ of $\hat{\mu}(x_{<n}\underline{x}_n)$. The learning rule is deeply hidden in the Bayesian mechanism. The universality property (5) is the central ingredient for proving (6).

Error bounds: If we measure prediction quality as the number of correct predictions, the best possible system predicts the x_n with the highest probability. Let SPρ be a probabilistic sequence predictor, predicting x_n with probability $\hat{\rho}(x_{<n}\underline{x}_n)$. If $\hat{\rho}$ is only a semimeasure the SPρ system might refuse any output in some cycles n. Further, we define a deterministic sequence predictor SPΘ_ρ predicting the x_n with highest $\hat{\rho}$ probability. $\Theta_\rho(x_{<n}\underline{x}_n) := 1$ for one x_n with $\hat{\rho}(x_{<n}\underline{x}_n) \geq \hat{\rho}(x_{<n}\underline{x}_n') \; \forall x_n'$ and $\Theta_\rho(x_{<n}\underline{x}_n) := 0$ otherwise. SPΘ_μ is the best prediction scheme when $\hat{\mu}$ is known. If $\hat{\rho}(x_{<n}\underline{x}_n)$ converges quickly to $\hat{\mu}(x_{<n}\underline{x}_n)$ the number of additional prediction errors introduced by using Θ_ρ instead of Θ_μ for prediction should be small in some sense. Let us define the total number of expected erroneous predictions the SPρ system makes for the first n bits:

$$E_{n\rho} := \sum_{k=1}^{n} \sum_{x_{1:k}} \hat{\mu}(\underline{x}_{1:k})(1 - \hat{\rho}(x_{<k}\underline{x}_k)). \qquad (7)$$

The SPΘ_μ system is best in the sense that $E_{n\Theta_\mu} \leq E_{n\rho}$ for any $\hat{\rho}$. In [Hut99] it has been shown that SPΘ_ξ is not much worse

$$E_{n\Theta_\xi} - E_{n\rho} \; \leq \; H + \sqrt{4E_{n\rho}H + H^2} \; = \; O(\sqrt{E_{n\rho}}) \qquad (8)$$

$$\text{with} \quad H \; < \; \ln 2 \cdot K(\hat{\mu}) + O(1)$$

and the tightest bound for $\hat{\rho} = \Theta_\mu$. For finite $E_{\infty\Theta_\mu}$, $E_{\infty\Theta_\xi}$ is finite too. For infinite $E_{\infty\Theta_\mu}$, $E_{n\Theta_\xi}/E_{n\Theta_\mu} \overset{n\to\infty}{\longrightarrow} 1$ with rapid convergence. One can hardly imagine any better prediction algorithm as SPΘ_ξ without extra knowledge about the environment. The values of the $O(1)$ terms in the bounds (6) and (8) depend on the chosen universal Turing machine [LV97]. For real-sized problems (but not for toy problems), $K(\hat{\mu}) \gg O(1)$. Therefore the bounds, and hence the prediction quality, is only marginally effected by different Turing machine choices. In

[Hut01], (6) and (8) have been generalized from binary to arbitrary alphabet and to general loss functions. Apart from computational aspects, which are of course very important, the problem of sequence prediction could be viewed as essentially solved.

4   The Universal AIξ Model

Definition of the AIξ Model: We have developed enough formalism to suggest our universal AIξ model. All we have to do is to suitably generalize the universal semimeasure $\hat{\xi}$ from the last section and to replace the true but unknown probability $\hat{\mu}$ in the AIμ model by this generalized ξ. In what sense this AIξ model is universal and optimal will be discussed thereafter.

We define the generalized universal probability ξ as the $2^{-l(q)}$ weighted sum over all chronological programs (environments) q which output $x_{1:k}$, similar to (4) but with $y_{1:k}$ provided on the input tape:

$$\xi(\underline{y}\underline{x}_{1:k}) := \sum_{q:q(y_{1:k})=x_{1:k}} 2^{-l(q)}. \tag{9}$$

Replacing μ by ξ in (3) the *AIξ system* outputs

$$\dot{y}_k := \arg\max_{y_k} \sum_{x_k} \dots \max_{y_m} \sum_{x_m} (r_k + \dots + r_m)\xi(\dot{y}\dot{x}_{<k}\underline{y}\underline{x}_{k:m}). \tag{10}$$

in cycle k given the history $\dot{y}\dot{x}_{<k}$.

(Non)parameters of AIξ: The AIξ model and its behaviour is completely defined by (9) and (10). It (slightly) depends on the choice of the universal Turing machine, because $K()$ and $l()$ are defined only up to terms of order 1 [LV97]. The AIξ model also depends on the choice of X and Y, but we do not expect any bias when the spaces are chosen sufficiently large and simple, e.g. all strings of length 2^{16}. Choosing $I\!N$ as word space would be ideal, but whether the maxima (or suprema) exist in this case, has to be shown beforehand. The only non-trivial dependence is on the horizon m. Ideally we would like to chose $m = \infty$, but there are several subtleties to be discussed later, which prevent at least a naive limit $m \to \infty$. So apart from m and unimportant details, the AIξ system is uniquely defined by (10) and (9) without adjustable parameters. It does not depend on any assumption about the environment apart from being generated by some computable (but unknown) probability distribution, as we will see.

Universality of ξ: It can be shown that ξ defined in (9) is universal and converges to μ analogously to the SP case (5) and (6). The proofs are generalizations from the SP case. The actions y are pure spectators and cause no difficulties in the generalization. This will change when we analyze error/value bounds analogously to (8). The major difference when incorporating y is that in (4), $U(p) = x\omega$ produces strings starting with x, whereas in (9) we can demand q to output exactly n words $x_{1:n}$ as q knows n from the number of input words $y_1...y_n$. ξ dominates all *chronological enumerable semimeasures* [Hut00]

$$\xi(\underline{y}\underline{x}_{1:n}) \geq 2^{-K(\hat{\rho})-O(1)}\hat{\rho}(\underline{y}\underline{x}_{1:n}). \tag{11}$$

ξ is a universal element in the sense of (11) in the set of all enumerable chronological semimeasures. This can be proved even for infinite (countable) alphabet [Hut00].

Convergence of ξ to μ: From (11) one can show

$$\sum_{k=1}^{n} \sum_{x_{1:k}} \mu(y\!x_{<k})\Big(\mu(y\!x_{<k}y\!x_k) - \xi(y\!x_{<k}y\!x_k)\Big)^2 < \ln 2 \cdot K(\mu) + O(1) \qquad (12)$$

for computable chronological measures μ. The main complication in generalizing (6) to (12) is the generalization to non-binary alphabet [Hut01]. The y are, again, pure spectators. (12) shows that the μ-expected squared difference of μ and ξ is finite for computable μ. This, in turn, shows that $\xi(y\!x_{<k}y\!x_k)$ converges to $\mu(y\!x_{<k}y\!x_k)$ for $k \to \infty$ with μ probability 1. If we take a finite product of ξ-s and use Bayes' rule, we see that also $\xi(y\!x_{<k}y\!x_{k:k+r})$ converges to $\mu(y\!x_{<k}y\!x_{k:k+r})$. More generally, in the case of a bounded horizon $h_k \equiv m_k - k + 1 \leq h_{max} < \infty$, it follows that

$$\xi(y\!x_{<k}y\!x_{k:m_k}) \overset{k\to\infty}{\longrightarrow} \mu(y\!x_{<k}y\!x_{k:m_k}) \qquad (13)$$

with μ-probability 1. Eq. (13) does not guarantee $\dot{y}_k^\xi \to \dot{y}_k^\mu$, since $\dot{y}_k^{\mu/\xi}$ are discontinuous functions of μ/ξ due to the discontinuous arg max operation in (3/10). This gap is already present in the SPΘ_ρ models, but nevertheless good error bounds could be proved. This gives confidence that the outputs $\dot{y}_k^\xi$ of the AIξ model (10) could converge to the outputs $\dot{y}_k^\mu$ of the AIμ model (3), at least for a bounded horizon h_k. The problems with a fixed horizon $m_k = m$ and especially $m \to \infty$ will be discussed later.

Universally optimal AI systems: We want to call an AI model *universal*, if it is μ-independent (unbiased, model-free) and is able to solve any solvable problem and learn any learnable task. Further, we call a universal model, *universally optimal*, if there is no program, which can solve or learn significantly faster (in terms of interaction cycles). As the AIξ model is parameterless, ξ converges to μ in the sense of (12,13), the AIμ model is itself optimal, and we expect no other model to converge faster to AIμ by analogy to SP (8),

we expect AIξ to be universally optimal.

This is our main claim. Further support is given in [Hut00] by a detailed analysis of the behaviour of AIξ for various problem classes, including prediction, optimization, games, and supervised learning. The difficulties in obtaining a precise formulation and a general proof, as well as suggestions to overcome them, are analyzed in detail. A first (weak) bound for the passive case is proven.

The choice of the horizon: The only significant arbitrariness in the AIξ model lies in the choice of the lifespan m or the $h_k \equiv m_k - k + 1$ if we allow a cycle dependent m. We will not discuss *ad hoc* choices of h_k for specific problems. We are interested in universal choices. The book of [Ber95] thoroughly discusses the mathematical problems regarding infinite horizon systems.

   In many cases the time we are willing to run a system depends on the quality of its actions. Hence, the lifetime, if finite at all, is not known in advance. Exponential discounting $r_k \rightsquigarrow r_k \cdot \gamma^k$ solves the mathematical problem of $m \to \infty$ but is no real solution, since an effective horizon $h \sim \ln \frac{1}{\gamma}$ has been introduced. The scale invariant discounting $r_k \leadsto r_k \cdot k^{-\alpha}$ has a dynamic horizon $h \sim k$. This choice has some appeal, as it seems that humans of age k years usually do not plan their lives for more than the next $\sim k$ years. From a practical point of view this model might serve all needs, but from a theoretical point we feel uncomfortable with such a limitation in the horizon from the very beginning. A possible way of taking the limit $m \to \infty$ without discounting and its problems can be found in [Hut00].

Another objection against too large choices of m_k is that $\xi(y\!x_{<k}y\underline{x}_{k:m_k})$ has been proved to be a good approximation of $\mu(y\!x_{<k}y\underline{x}_{k:m_k})$ only for $k \gg h_k$, which is never satisfied for $m_k = m \to \infty$. On the other hand it may turn out that the rewards $r_{k'}$ for $k' \gg k$, where ξ may no longer be trusted as a good approximation of μ, are in a sense randomly disturbed with decreasing influence on the choice of $\dot{y}_k$. This claim is supported by the forgetfulness property of ξ (see next paragraph) and can be proved when restricting to factorizable environments [Hut00].

We are not sure whether the choice of m_k is of marginal importance, as long as m_k is chosen sufficiently large and of low complexity, $m_k = 2^{2^{16}}$ for instance, or whether the choice of m_k will turn out to be a central topic for the AIξ model or for the planning aspect of any universal AI system in general. Most if not all problems in agent design of *balancing exploration and exploitation* vanish by a sufficiently large choice of the (effective) horizon and a sufficiently general prior. We suppose that the limit $m_k \to \infty$ for the AIξ model results in correct behaviour for weakly separable (defined in the next paragraph) μ, and that even the naive limit $m \to \infty$ may exist.

Value bounds and separability concepts: The values V_ρ^* associated with the AIρ systems correspond roughly to the negative error measure $-E_{n\rho}$ of the SPρ systems. In the SP case we were interested in small bounds for the error excess $E_{n\Theta_\xi} - E_{n\rho}$. Unfortunately, simple value bounds for AIξ or any other AI system in terms of V^* analogously to the error bound (8) cannot hold [Hut00]. We even have difficulties in specifying what we can expect to hold for AIξ or any AI system which claims to be universally optimal. In SP, the only important property of μ for proving error bounds was its complexity $K(\mu)$. In the AI case, there are no useful bounds in terms of $K(\mu)$ only. We either have to study restricted problem classes or consider bounds depending on other properties of μ, rather than on its complexity only. In [Hut00] the difficulties are exhibited by two examples. Several concepts, which might be useful for proving value bounds are introduced and discussed. They include forgetful, relevant, asymptotically learnable, farsighted, uniform, (generalized) Markovian, factorizable and (pseudo) passive μ. They are approximately sorted in the order of decreasing generality and are called *separability concepts*. A first weak bound for passive μ has been proven.

5   Time Bounds and Effectiveness

Non-effectiveness of AIξ: ξ is not a computable but only an enumerable semimeasure. Hence, the output $\dot{y}_k$ of the AIξ model is only asymptotically computable. AIξ yields an algorithm that produces a sequence of trial outputs eventually converging to the correct output $\dot{y}_k$, but one can never be sure whether one has already reached it. Besides this, convergence is extremely slow, so this type of asymptotic computability is of no direct practical use. Furthermore, the replacement of ξ by time-limited versions [LV97], which is suitable for sequence prediction, has been shown to fail for the AIξ model [Hut00]. This leads to the issues addressed next.

Time bounds and effectiveness: Let $\tilde{p}$ be a policy which calculates an acceptable output within a reasonable time $\tilde{t}$ per cycle. This sort of computability assumption, namely, that a general purpose computer of sufficient power and appropriate program is able to behave in an intelligent way, is the very basis of AI research. Here it is not necessary to discuss what exactly is meant by 'reasonable time/intelligence' and 'sufficient power'. What we are interested in is whether there is a computable version of the AIξ system which is superior or equal to any policy p with computation time per cycle of at most $\tilde{t}$.

What one can realistically hope to construct is an AI$\xi^{\tilde{t}\tilde{l}}$ system of computation time $c \cdot \tilde{t}$ per cycle for some constant c. The idea is to run all programs p of length $\leq \tilde{l} := l(\tilde{p})$ and time $\leq \tilde{t}$ per cycle and pick the best output in the sense of maximizing the *universal value* V_ξ^*. The total computation time is $c \cdot \tilde{t}$ with $c \approx 2^{\tilde{l}}$. Unfortunately V_ξ^* cannot be used directly since this measure is itself only semi-computable and the approximation quality by using computable versions of ξ given a time of order $c \cdot \tilde{t}$ is crude [LV97,Hut00]. On the other hand, we *have* to use a measure which converges to V_ξ^* for $\tilde{t}, \tilde{l} \to \infty$, since we want the AI$\xi^{\tilde{t}\tilde{l}}$ model to converge to the AIξ model in that case.

Valid approximations: A solution satisfying the above conditions is suggested in [Hut00]. The main idea is to consider *extended chronological incremental policies p*, which in addition to the regular output y_k^p *rate* their own output with w_k^p. The AI$\xi^{\tilde{t}\tilde{l}}$ model selects the output $\dot{y}_k = y_k^p$ of the policy p with highest rating w_k^p. p might suggest any output y_k^p but it is not allowed to rate itself with an arbitrarily high w_k^p if one wants w_k^p to be a reliable criterion for selecting the best p. One must demand that no policy p is allowed to claim that it is better than it actually is. In [Hut00] a logical predicate VA(p), called *valid approximation*, is defined, which is true if, and only if, p *always* satisfies $w_k^p \leq V_\xi^p(y\!x_{<k})$, i.e. never overrates itself. $V_\xi^p(y\!x_{<k})$ is the ξ expected future reward under policy p. Valid policies p can then be (partially) ordered w.r.t. their rating w_k^p.

The universal time bounded AI$\xi^{\tilde{t}\tilde{l}}$ system: In the following, we describe the algorithm p^* underlying the AI$\xi^{\tilde{t}\tilde{l}}$ system. It is essentially based on the selection of the best algorithms p_k^* out of the time $\tilde{t}$ and length $\tilde{l}$ bounded policies p, for which there exists a proof P of VA(p) with length $\leq l_P$.

1. Create all binary strings of length l_P and interpret each as a coding of a mathematical proof in the same formal logic system in which VA($\cdot$) has been formulated. Take those strings which are proofs of VA(p) for some p and keep the corresponding programs p.
2. Eliminate all p of length $> \tilde{l}$.

3. Modify all p in the following way: all output $w_k^p y_k^p$ is temporarily written on an auxiliary tape. If p stops in $\tilde{t}$ steps the internal òutput'is copied to the output tape. If p does not stop after $\tilde{t}$ steps a stop is forced and $w_k^p := -\infty$ and some arbitrary y_k^p is written on the output tape. Let $\mathcal{P}$ be the set of all those modified programs.

4. Start first cycle: $k := 1$.

5. Run every $p \in \mathcal{P}$ on extended input $\ddot{y}\ddot{x}_{<k}$, where all outputs are redirected to some auxiliary tape: $p(\ddot{y}\ddot{x}_{<k}) = w_1^p y_1^p ... w_k^p y_k^p$. This step is performed incrementally by adding $\ddot{y}\ddot{x}_{k-1}$ for $k > 1$ to the input tape and continuing the computation of the previous cycle.

6. Select the program p with highest rating w_k^p: $p_k^* := \arg \max_p w_k^p$.

7. Write $\dot{y}_k := y_k^{p_k^*}$ to the output tape.

8. Receive input $\dot{x}_k$ from the environment.

9. Begin next cycle: $k := k+1$, goto step 5.

Properties of the p^* algorithm: Let p be any extended chronological (incremental) policy of length $l(p) \leq \tilde{l}$ and computation time per cycle $t(p) \leq \tilde{t}$, for which there exists a proof of VA(p) of length $\leq l_P$. The algorithm p^*, depending on $\tilde{l}$, $\tilde{t}$ and l_P but not on p, has always higher rating than any such p. The setup time of p^* is $t_{setup}(p^*) = O(l_P^2 \cdot 2^{l_P})$ and the computation time per cycle is $t_{cycle}(p^*) = O(2^{\tilde{l}} \cdot \tilde{t})$. Furthermore, for $l_P, \tilde{t}, \tilde{l} \to \infty$, policy p^* converges to the behavior of the AIξ model.

Roughly speaking, this means that if there exists a computable solution to some AI problem at all, then the explicitly constructed algorithm p^* is such a solution. This claim is quite general, but there are some limitations and open questions, regarding the setup time, regarding the necessity that the policies must rate their own output, regarding true but not (efficiently) provable VA(p), and regarding ïnconsistent"policies [Hut00].

6 Outlook & Discussion

This section contains some discussion and remarks on otherwise unmentioned topics.

Value bounds: Rigorous proofs of value bounds for the AIξ theory are the major theoretical challenge –general ones as well as tighter bounds for special environments μ. Of special importance are suitable (and acceptable) conditions to μ, under which $\dot{y}_k$ and finite value bounds exist for infinite Y, X and m.

Scaling AIξ down: [Hut00] shows for several examples how to integrate problem classes into the AIξ model. Conversely, one can downscale the AIξ model by using more restricted forms of ξ. This could be done in a similar way as the theory of universal induction has been downscaled with many insights to the Minimum Description Length principle [Ris89] or to the domain of finite automata [FMG92]. The AIξ model might similarly serve as a super model, from which specialized models could be derived.

Applications: [Hut00] shows how a number of AI problem classes, including *sequence prediction, strategic games, function minimization* and *supervised learning* fit into the general AIξ model. All problems are claimed to be formally solved by the AIξ model. The solution is, however, only formal, because the AIξ model is uncomputable or, at best, approximable. First, each problem class is formulated in its natural way (when μ^{problem} is known) and then a formulation within the AIμ model is constructed and their equivalence is proven. Then, the consequences of replacing μ by ξ are considered. The main goal is to understand how the problems are solved by AIξ.

Implementation and approximation: The AI$\xi^{\tilde{t}\tilde{l}}$ model suffers from the same large factor $2^{\tilde{l}}$ in computation time as Levin search for inversion problems [Lev73]. Nevertheless, Levin search has been implemented and successfully applied to a variety of problems [Sch97,SZW97]. Hence, a direct implementation of the AI$\xi^{\tilde{t}\tilde{l}}$ model may also be successful, at least in toy environments, e.g. prisoner problems. The AI$\xi^{\tilde{t}\tilde{l}}$ algorithm should be regarded only as the first step toward a *computable universal AI model*. Elimination of the factor $2^{\tilde{l}}$ without giving up universality will probably be a very difficult task. One could try to select programs p and prove VA(p) in a more clever way than by mere enumeration. All kinds of ideas like, heuristic search, genetic algorithms, advanced theorem provers, and many more could be incorporated. But now we have a problem.

Computability: We seem to have transferred the AI problem just to a different level. This shift has some advantages (and also some disadvantages) but presents, in no way, a solution. Nevertheless, we want to stress that we have reduced the AI problem to (mere) computational questions. Even the most general other systems the author is aware of, depend on some (more than complexity) assumptions about the environment, or it is far from clear whether they are, indeed, universally optimal. Although computational questions are themselves highly complicated, this reduction is a non-trivial result. A formal theory of something, even if not computable, is often a great step toward solving a problem and has also merits of its own (see previous paragraphs).

Elegance: Many researchers in AI believe that intelligence is something complicated and cannot be condensed into a few formulas. They believe it is more a combining of enough *methods* and much explicit *knowledge* in the right way. From a theoretical point of view, we disagree as the AIξ model is simple and seems to serve all needs. From a practical point of view we agree to the following extent. To reduce the computational burden one should provide special purpose algorithms (*methods*) from the very beginning, probably many of them related to reduce the complexity of the input and output spaces X and Y by appropriate pre/post-processing methods.

Extra knowledge: There is no need to incorporate extra *knowledge* from the very beginning. It can be presented in the first few cycles in *any* format. As long as the algorithm that interprets the data is of size $O(1)$, the AIξ system will ünderstand"the data after a few cycles (see [Hut00]). If the environment μ is complicated but extra knowledge z makes $K(\mu|z)$ small, one can show that the bound (12) reduces to $\ln 2 \cdot K(\mu|z)$ when $x_1 \equiv z$, i.e. when z is presented in the first cycle. Special purpose algorithms could also be presented in x_1, but it would be cheating to say that no special purpose algorithms have been implemented in AIξ. The boundary between implementation and training is blurred in the AIξ model.

Training: We have not said much about the training process itself, as it is not specific to the AIξ model and has been discussed in literature in various forms and disciplines. A serious discussion would be out of place. To repeat a truism, it is, of course, important to present enough knowledge x'_k and evaluate the system output y_k with r_k in a reasonable way. To maximize the information content in the reward, one should start with simple tasks and give positive reward to approximately the better half of the outputs y_k, for instance.

The big questions: [Hut00] contains a discussion of the big"questions concerning the mere existence of any computable, fast, and elegant universal theory of intelligence, related to Penroses non-computable environments, and Chaitins number of wisdom' Ω.

References

[Bel57]   R. Bellman. *Dynamic Programming.* Princeton University Press, New Jersey, 1957.

[Ber95]   D. P. Bertsekas. *Dynamic Programming and Optimal Control, Vol. (II).* Athena Scientific, Belmont, Massachusetts, 1995.

[BT96]   D. P. Bertsekas and J. N. Tsitsiklis. *Neuro-Dynamic Programming.* Athena Scientific, Belmont, MA, 1996.

[Cha75]   G. J. Chaitin. A theory of program size formally identical to information theory. *Journal of the ACM,* 22(3):329–340, 1975.

[FMG92]   M. Feder, N. Merhav, and M. Gutman. Universal prediction of individual sequences. *IEEE Transactions on Information Theory,* 38:1258–1270, 1992.

[Gác74]   P. Gács. On the symmetry of algorithmic information. *Russian Academy of Sciences Doklady. Mathematics (formerly Soviet Mathematics–Doklady),* 15:1477–1480, 1974.

[Hut99]   M. Hutter. New error bounds for Solomonoff prediction. *Journal of Computer and System Science, in press,* 1999.
ftp://ftp.idsia.ch/pub/techrep/IDSIA-11-00.ps.gz.

[Hut00]   M. Hutter. A theory of universal artificial intelligence based on algorithmic complexity. Technical report, 62 pages, 2000.
http://arxiv.org/abs/cs.AI/0004001.

[Hut01]   M. Hutter. General loss bounds for universal sequence prediction. Technical Report, Manno(Lugano), CH, 2001.
ftp.idsia.ch/pub/techrep/IDSIA-03-01.ps.gz.

[KLM96]   L. P. Kaelbling, M. L. Littman, and A. W. Moore. Reinforcement learning: a survey. *Journal of AI research,* 4:237–285, 1996.

[Kol65]   A. N. Kolmogorov. Three approaches to the quantitative definition of information. *Problems of Information and Transmission,* 1(1):1–7, 1965.

[Lev73]   L. A. Levin. Universal sequential search problems. *Problems of Information Transmission,* 9:265–266, 1973.

[Lev74]   L. A. Levin. Laws of information conservation (non-growth) and aspects of the foundation of probability theory. *Problems of Information Transmission,* 10:206–210, 1974.

[LV97]   M. Li and P. M. B. Vitányi. *An introduction to Kolmogorov complexity and its applications.* Springer, 2nd edition, 1997.

[Ris89]   J. J. Rissanen. *Stochastic Complexity in Statistical Inquiry.* World Scientific Publ. Co., 1989.

[RN95]   S. J. Russell and P. Norvig. *Artificial Intelligence. A Modern Approach.* Prentice-Hall, Englewood Cliffs, 1995.

[SB98]   R. Sutton and A. Barto. *Reinforcement learning: An introduction.* Cambridge, MA, MIT Press, 1998.

[Sch97]   J. Schmidhuber. Discovering neural nets with low Kolmogorov complexity and high generalization capability. *Neural Networks*, 10(5):857–873, 1997.

[Sol64]   R. J. Solomonoff. A formal theory of inductive inference: Part 1 and 2. *Inform. Control*, 7:1–22, 224–254, 1964.

[Sol78]   R. J. Solomonoff. Complexity-based induction systems: comparisons and convergence theorems. *IEEE Trans. Inform. Theory*, IT-24:422–432, 1978.

[SZW97]   J. Schmidhuber, J. Zhao, and M. Wiering. Shifting inductive bias with success-story algorithm, adaptive Levin search, and incremental self-improvement. *Machine Learning*, 28:105–130, 1997.

Convergence and Error Bounds for Universal Prediction of Nonbinary Sequences

Marcus Hutter

IDSIA, Galleria 2, CH-6928 Manno-Lugano, Switzerland,
marcus@idsia.ch[*]
http://www.idsia.ch/~marcus

Abstract. Solomonoff's uncomputable universal prediction scheme ξ allows to predict the next symbol x_k of a sequence $x_1...x_{k-1}$ for any Turing computable, but otherwise unknown, probabilistic environment μ. This scheme will be generalized to arbitrary environmental classes, which, among others, allows the construction of computable universal prediction schemes ξ. Convergence of ξ to μ in a conditional mean squared sense and with μ probability 1 is proven. It is shown that the average number of prediction errors made by the universal ξ scheme rapidly converges to those made by the best possible informed μ scheme. The schemes, theorems and proofs are given for general finite alphabet, which results in additional complications as compared to the binary case. Several extensions of the presented theory and results are outlined. They include general loss functions and bounds, games of chance, infinite alphabet, partial and delayed prediction, classification, and more active systems.

1 Introduction

The Bayesian framework is ideally suited for studying induction problems. The probability of observing x_k at time k, given past observations $x_1...x_{k-1}$, can be computed with Bayes' rule if the generating probability distribution μ, from which sequences $x_1x_2x_3...$ are drawn, is known. The problem, however, is that in many cases one does not even have a reasonable estimate of the true generating distribution. What is the true probability of weather sequences or stock charts? In order to overcome this problem we define a universal distribution ξ as a weighted sum of distributions $\mu_i \in M$, where M is any finite or countable set of distributions including μ. This is a generalization of Solomonoff induction, in which M is the set of all enumerable semi-measures [Sol64,Sol78]. We show that using the universal ξ as a prior is nearly as good as using the unknown generating distribution μ. In a sense, this solves the problem, that the generating distribution μ is not known, in a universal way. All results are obtained for general finite alphabet. Convergence of ξ to μ in a conditional mean squared sense and with μ probability 1 is proven. The number of errors E_{Θ_ξ} made by the universal prediction scheme Θ_ξ based on ξ minus the number of errors E_{Θ_μ} of

---

[*] This work was supported by SNF grant 2000-61847.00 to Jürgen Schmidhuber.

L. De Raedt and P. Flach (Eds.): ECML 2001, LNAI 2167, pp. 239–250, 2001.
© Springer-Verlag Berlin Heidelberg 2001

the optimal informed prediction scheme Θ_μ based on μ is proven to be bounded by $O(\sqrt{E\Theta_\mu})$.

Extensions to arbitrary loss functions, games of chance, infinite alphabet, partial and delayed prediction, classification, and more active systems are discussed (Section 5). The main new results are a generalization of the universal probability ξ [Sol64] to arbitrary probability classes and weights (Section 2), a generalization of the convergence [Sol78] $\xi \to \mu$ (Section 3) and the error bounds [Hut99] to arbitrary alphabet (Section 4). The non-binary setting causes substantial additional complications. Non-binary prediction cannot be (easily) reduced to the binary case. One may have in mind a binary coding of the symbols x_k in the sequence $x_1x_2\ldots$. But this makes it necessary to predict a block of bits x_k, before receiving the true block of bits x_k, which differs from the bit-by-bit prediction considered in [Sol78,LV97,Hut99].

For an excellent introduction to Kolmogorov complexity and Solomonoff induction one should consult the book of Li and Vitányi [LV97] or the article [LV92] for a short course. Historical surveys of inductive reasoning and inference can be found in [AS83,Sol97].

2 Setup

2.1 Strings and Probability Distributions

We denote strings over a finite alphabet $\mathcal{A}$ by $x_1x_2\ldots x_n$ with $x_k \in \mathcal{A}$. We further use the abbreviations $x_{n:m} := x_n x_{n+1}\ldots x_{m-1}x_m$ and $x_{<n} := x_1\ldots x_{n-1}$. We use Greek letters for probability distributions and underline their arguments to indicate that they are probability arguments. Let $\rho(\underline{x_1\ldots x_n})$ be the probability that an (infinite) sequence starts with $x_1\ldots x_n$:

$$\sum_{x_{1:n} \in \mathcal{A}^n} \rho(\underline{x}_{1:n}) = 1, \quad \sum_{x_n \in \mathcal{A}} \rho(\underline{x}_{1:n}) = \rho(\underline{x}_{<n}), \quad \rho(\epsilon) = 1. \tag{1}$$

We also need conditional probabilities derived from Bayes' rule. We prefer a notation which preserves the order of the words, in contrast to the standard notation $\rho(\cdot|\cdot)$ which flips it. We extend the definition of ρ to the conditional case with the following convention for its arguments: An underlined argument $\underline{x}_k$ is a probability variable and other non-underlined arguments x_k represent conditions. With this convention, Bayes' rule has the following look:

$$\rho(x_{<n}\underline{x}_n) = \rho(\underline{x}_{1:n})/\rho(\underline{x}_{<n}) \quad , \quad \rho(\underline{x_1\ldots x_n}) = \rho(\underline{x}_1)\cdot\rho(x_1\underline{x}_2)\cdot\ldots\cdot\rho(x_1\ldots x_{n-1}\underline{x}_n). \tag{2}$$

The first equation states that the probability that a string $x_1\ldots x_{n-1}$ is followed by x_n is equal to the probability that a string starts with $x_1\ldots x_n$ divided by the probability that a string starts with $x_1\ldots x_{n-1}$. The second equation is the first, applied n times.

2.2   Universal Prior Probability Distribution

Most inductive inference problem can be brought into the following form: Given a string $x_{<k}$, take a guess at its continuation x_k. We will assume that the strings which have to be continued are drawn from a probability[1] distribution μ. The maximal prior information a prediction algorithm can possess is the exact knowledge of μ, but in many cases the generating distribution is not known. Instead, the prediction is based on a guess ρ of μ. We expect that a predictor based on ρ performs well, if ρ is close to μ or converges, in a sense, to μ. Let $M := \{\mu_1, \mu_2, ...\}$ be a finite or countable set of candidate probability distributions on strings. We define a weighted average on M

$$\xi(\underline{x}_{1:n}) := \sum_{\mu_i \in M} w_{\mu_i} \cdot \mu_i(\underline{x}_{1:n}), \quad \sum_{\mu_i \in M} w_{\mu_i} = 1, \quad w_{\mu_i} > 0. \tag{3}$$

It is easy to see that ξ is a probability distribution as the weights w_{μ_i} are positive and normalized to 1 and the $\mu_i \in M$ are probabilities. For finite M a possible choice for the w is to give all μ_i equal weight ($w_{\mu_i} = \frac{1}{|M|}$). We call ξ universal relative to M, as it multiplicatively dominates all distributions in M

$$\xi(\underline{x}_{1:n}) \geq w_{\mu_i} \cdot \mu_i(\underline{x}_{1:n}) \quad \text{for all} \quad \mu_i \in M. \tag{4}$$

In the following, we assume that M is known and contains[2] the true generating distribution, i.e. $\mu \in M$. We will see that this is not a serious constraint as we can always chose M to be sufficiently large. In the next section we show the important property of ξ converging to the generating distribution μ in a sense and, hence, might being a useful substitute for the true generating, but in general, unknown distribution μ.

2.3   Probability Classes

We get a rather wide class M if we include *all* computable probability distributions in M. In this case, the assumption $\mu \in M$ is very weak, as it only assumes that the strings are drawn from *any computable* distribution; and all valid physical theories (and, hence, all environments) *are* computable (in a probabilistic sense).

We will see that it is favorable to assign high weights w_{μ_i} to the μ_i. Simplicity should be favored over complexity, according to Occams razor. In our context this means that a high weight should be assigned to simple μ_i. The prefix Kolmogorov complexity $K(\mu_i)$ is a universal complexity measure [Kol65,

---

[1] This includes deterministic environments, in which case the probability distribution μ is 1 for some sequence $x_{1:}$ and 0 for all others. We call probability distributions of this kind *deterministic*.

[2] Actually all theorems remain valid for μ being a finite linear combination of $\mu_i \in L \subseteq M$ and $w_\mu := \min_{\mu_i \in L} w_{\mu_i}$ [Hut01].

Ł70,LV97]. It is defined as the length of the shortest self-delimiting program (on a universal Turing machine) computing $\mu_i(x_{1:n})$ given $x_{1:n}$. If we define

$$w_{\mu_i} := \frac{1}{\Omega}2^{-K(\mu_i)} \quad , \quad \Omega := \sum_{\mu_i \in M} 2^{-K(\mu_i)}$$

then, distributions which can be calculated by short programs, have high weights. Besides ensuring correct normalization, Ω (sometimes called the number of wisdom) has interesting properties in itself [Cal98,Cha91]. If we enlarge M to include all enumerable semi-measures, we attain Solomonoff's universal probability, apart from normalization, which has to be treated differently in this case [Sol64,Sol78]. Recently, M has been further enlarged to include all cumulatively enumerable semi-measures [Sch00]. In all cases, ξ is not finitely computable, but can still be approximated to arbitrary but not pre-specifiable precision. If we consider *all* approximable (i.e. asymptotically computable) distributions, then the universal distribution ξ, although still well defined, is not even approximable [Sch00]. An interesting and quickly approximable distribution is the Speed prior S defined in [Sch00]. It is related to Levin complexity and Levin search [Lev73, Lev84], but it is unclear for now which distributions are dominated by S. If one considers only finite-state automata instead of general Turing machines, one can attain a quickly computable, universal finite-state prediction scheme related to that of Feder et al. [FMG92], which itself is related to the famous Lempel-Ziv data compression algorithm. If one has extra knowledge on the source generating the sequence, one might further reduce M and increase w. A detailed analysis of these and other specific classes M will be given elsewhere. Note that $\xi \in M$ in the enumerable and cumulatively enumerable case, but $\xi \notin M$ in the computable, approximable and finite-state case. If ξ is itself in M, it is called a universal element of M [LV97]. As we do not need this property here, M may be *any* finite or countable set of distributions. In the following we consider generic M and w.

3   Convergence

3.1   Upper Bound for the Relative Entropy

Let us define the relative entropy (also called Kullback Leibler divergence [Kl59]) between μ and ξ:

$$h_k(x_{<k}) := \sum_{x_k \in \mathcal{A}} \mu(x_{<k}\underline{x}_k) \ln \frac{\mu(x_{<k}\underline{x}_k)}{\xi(x_{<k}\underline{x}_k)}. \tag{5}$$

H_n is then defined as the sum-expectation, for which the following upper bound can be shown

$$H_n := \sum_{k=1}^{n} \sum_{x_{<k} \in \mathcal{A}^{k-1}} \mu(\underline{x}_{<k}) \cdot h_k(x_{<k}) = \sum_{k=1}^{n} \sum_{x_{1:k} \in \mathcal{A}^k} \mu(\underline{x}_{1:k}) \ln \frac{\mu(x_{<k}\underline{x}_k)}{\xi(x_{<k}\underline{x}_k)} = \tag{6}$$

$$= \sum_{x_{1:n}} \mu(x_{1:n}) \ln \prod_{k=1}^{n} \frac{\mu(x_{<k}x_k)}{\xi(x_{<k}x_k)} = \sum_{x_{1:n}} \mu(x_{1:n}) \ln \frac{\mu(x_{1:n})}{\xi(x_{1:n})} \leq \ln \frac{1}{w_\mu} =: d_\mu$$

In the first line we have inserted (5) and used Bayes' rule $\mu(x_{<k}) \cdot \mu(x_{<k}x_k) = \mu(x_{1:k})$. Due to (1), we can further replace $\sum_{x_{1:k}} \mu(x_{1:k})$ by $\sum_{x_{1:n}} \mu(x_{1:n})$ as the argument of the logarithm is independent of $x_{k+1:n}$. The k sum can now be exchanged with the $x_{1:n}$ sum and transforms to a product inside the logarithm. In the last equality we have used the second form of Bayes' rule (2) for μ and ξ. Using universality (4) of ξ, i.e. $\ln \mu(x_{1:n})/\xi(x_{1:n}) \leq \ln \frac{1}{w_\mu}$ for $\mu \in M$ yields the final inequality in (6). The proof given here is simplified version of those given in [Sol78] and [LV97].

3.2 Lower Bound for the Relative Entropy

We need the following inequality to lower bound H_n

$$\sum_{i=1}^{N} (y_i - z_i)^2 \leq \sum_{i=1}^{N} y_i \ln \frac{y_i}{z_i} \quad \text{for} \quad y_i \geq 0, \quad z_i \geq 0, \quad \sum_{i=1}^{N} y_i = 1 = \sum_{i=1}^{N} z_i. \quad (7)$$

The proof of the case $N = 2$

$$2(y-z)^2 \leq y \ln \frac{y}{z} + (1-y) \ln \frac{1-y}{1-z}, \quad 0 < y < 1, \quad 0 < z < 1 \quad (8)$$

will not be repeated here, as it is elementary and well known [LV97]. The proof of (7) is one point where the generalization from binary to arbitrary alphabet is not trivial[3] We will reduce the general case $N > 2$ to the case $N = 2$. We do this by a partition $\{1, ..., N\} = G^+ \cup G^-$, $G^+ \cap G^- = \{\}$, and define $y^{\pm} := \sum_{i \in G^{\pm}} y_i$

and $z^{\pm} := \sum_{i \in G^{\pm}} z_i$. It is well known that the relative entropy is positive, i.e.

$$\sum_{i \in G^{\pm}} p_i \ln \frac{p_i}{q_i} \geq 0 \quad \text{for} \quad p_i \geq 0, \quad q_i \geq 0, \quad \sum_{i \in G^{\pm}} p_i = 1 = \sum_{i \in G^{\pm}} q_i. \quad (9)$$

Note that there are 4 probability distributions (p_i and q_i for $i \in G^+$ and $i \in G^-$). For $i \in G^{\pm}$, $p_i := y_i/y^{\pm}$ and $q_i := z_i/z^{\pm}$ satisfy the conditions on p and q. Inserting this into (9) and rearranging the terms we get $\sum_{i \in G^{\pm}} y_i \ln \frac{y_i}{z_i} \geq y^{\pm} \ln \frac{y^{\pm}}{z^{\pm}}$. If we sum this over $\pm$ and define $y \equiv y^+ = 1 - y^-$ and $z \equiv z^+ = 1 - z^-$ we get

$$\sum_{i=1}^{N} y_i \ln \frac{y_i}{z_i} \geq \sum_{\pm} y^{\pm} \ln \frac{y^{\pm}}{z^{\pm}} = y \ln \frac{y}{z} + (1-y) \ln \frac{1-y}{1-z}. \quad (10)$$

---

[3] We will not explicate every subtlety and only sketch the proofs. Subtleties regarding $y, z = 0/1$ have been checked but will be passed over. $0 \ln \frac{0}{z_i} := 0$ even for $z_i = 0$. Positive means ≥ 0.

For the special choice $G^\pm := \{i : y_i \gtrless z_i\}$, we can upper bound the quadratic term by

$$\sum_{i \in G^\pm} (y_i - z_i)^2 \leq \left(\sum_{i \in G^\pm} |y_i - z_i| \right)^2 = \left(\sum_{i \in G^\pm} y_i - z_i \right)^2 = (y^\pm - z^\pm)^2.$$

The first equality is true, since all $y_i - z_i$ are positive/negative for $i \in G^\pm$ due to the special choice of $G^\pm$. Summation over $\pm$ gives

$$\sum_{i=1}^{N} (y_i - z_i)^2 \leq \sum_{\pm} (y^\pm - z^\pm)^2 = 2(y - z)^2 \tag{11}$$

Chaining the inequalities (11), (8) and (10) proves (7). If we identify

$$\mathcal{A} = \{1, ..., N\}, \quad N = |\mathcal{A}|, \quad i = x_k, \quad y_i = \mu(x_{<k}\underline{x}_k), \quad z_i = \xi(x_{<k}\underline{x}_k) \tag{12}$$

multiply both sides of (7) with $\mu(\underline{x}_{<k})$ and take the sum over $x_{<k}$ and k we get

$$\sum_{k=1}^{n} \sum_{x_{1:k}} \mu(\underline{x}_{<k}) \Big(\mu(x_{<k}\underline{x}_k) - \xi(x_{<k}\underline{x}_k) \Big)^2 \leq \sum_{k=1}^{n} \sum_{x_{1:k}} \mu(\underline{x}_{1:k}) \ln \frac{\mu(x_{<k}\underline{x}_k)}{\xi(x_{<k}\underline{x}_k)}. \tag{13}$$

3.3 Convergence of ξ to μ

The upper (6) and lower (13) bounds on H_n allow us to prove the convergence of ξ to μ in a conditional mean squared sense and with μ probability 1.

Theorem 1 (Convergence). *Let there be sequences $x_1 x_2 ...$ over a finite alphabet $\mathcal{A}$ drawn with probability $\mu(\underline{x}_{1:n})$ for the first n symbols. The universal conditional probability $\xi(x_{<k}\underline{x}_k)$ of the next symbol x_k given $x_{<k}$ is related to the generating conditional probability $\mu(x_{<k}\underline{x}_k)$ in the following way:*

$$i)\; \sum_{k=1}^{n} \sum_{x_{1:k}} \mu(\underline{x}_{<k}) \Big(\mu(x_{<k}\underline{x}_k) - \xi(x_{<k}\underline{x}_k) \Big)^2 \leq H_n \leq d_\mu = \ln \frac{1}{w_\mu} < \infty$$

$$ii)\; \xi(x_{<k}\underline{x}_k) \to \mu(x_{<k}\underline{x}_k) \quad \text{for } k \to \infty \text{ with } \mu \text{ probability 1}$$

where H_n is the relative entropy (6), and w_μ is the weight (3) of μ in ξ.

(*i*) follows from (6) and (13). For $n \to \infty$ the l.h.s. of (*i*) is an infinite k-sum over positive arguments, which is bounded by the finite constant d_μ on the r.h.s. Hence the arguments must converge to zero for $k \to \infty$. Since the arguments are μ expectations of the squared difference of ξ and μ, this means that $\xi(x_{<k}\underline{x}_k)$ converges to $\mu(x_{<k}\underline{x}_k)$ with μ probability 1 or, more stringent, in a mean square sense. This proves (*ii*). The reason for the astonishing property of a single (universal) function ξ to converge to *any* $\mu_i \in M$ lies in the fact that the sets of μ-random sequences differ for different μ. Since the conditional probabilities are the basis of all prediction algorithms considered in this work, we expect a good prediction performance if we use ξ as a guess of μ. Performance measures are defined in the following sections.

4   Error Bounds

We now consider the following measure for the quality of a prediction: making a wrong prediction counts as one error, making a correct prediction counts as no error.

4.1   Total Expected Numbers of Errors

Let Θ_μ be the optimal prediction scheme when the strings are drawn from the probability distribution μ, i.e. the probability of x_k given $x_{<k}$ is $\mu(x_{<k}\underline{x}_k)$, and μ is known. Θ_μ predicts (by definition) $x_k^{\Theta_\mu}$ when observing $x_{<k}$. The prediction is erroneous if the true k^{th} symbol is not $x_k^{\Theta_\mu}$. The probability of this event is $1 - \mu(x_{<k}\underline{x}_k^{\Theta_\mu})$. It is minimized if $x_k^{\Theta_\mu}$ maximizes $\mu(x_{<k}\underline{x}_k^{\Theta_\mu})$. More generally, let Θ_ρ be a prediction scheme predicting $x_k^{\Theta_\rho} := \text{maxarg}_{x_k} \rho(x_{<k}\underline{x}_k)$ for some distribution ρ. Every deterministic predictor can be interpreted as maximizing some distribution. The μ probability of making a wrong prediction for the kth symbol and the total μ-expected number of errors in the first n predictions of predictor Θ_ρ are

$$e_{k\Theta_\rho}(x_{<k}) := 1 - \mu(x_{<k}\underline{x}_k^{\Theta_\rho}) \quad , \quad E_{n\Theta_\rho} := \sum_{k=1}^{n} \sum_{x_1...x_{k-1}} \mu(\underline{x}_{<k}) e_{k\Theta_\rho}(x_{<k}). \tag{14}$$

If μ is known, Θ_μ is obviously the best prediction scheme in the sense of making the least number of expected errors

$$E_{n\Theta_\mu} \leq E_{n\Theta_\rho} \quad \text{for any} \quad \Theta_\rho, \tag{15}$$

since $e_{k\Theta_\mu}(x_{<k}) = 1 - \mu(x_{<k}\underline{x}_k^{\Theta_\mu}) = \min_{x_k}(1 - \mu(x_{<k}\underline{x}_k)) \leq 1 - \mu(x_{<k}\underline{x}_k^{\Theta_\rho}) = e_{k\Theta_\rho}(x_{<k})$ for any ρ.

4.2   Error Bound

Of special interest is the universal predictor Θ_ξ. As ξ converges to μ the prediction of Θ_ξ might converge to the prediction of the optimal Θ_μ. Hence, Θ_ξ may not make many more errors than Θ_μ and, hence, any other predictor Θ_ρ. Note that $x_k^{\Theta_\rho}$ is a discontinuous function of ρ and $x_k^{\Theta_\xi} \to x_k^{\Theta_\mu}$ can not be proved from $\xi \to \mu$. Indeed, this problem occurs in related prediction schemes, where the predictor has to be regularized so that it is continuous [FMG92]. Fortunately this is not necessary here. We prove the following error bound.

Theorem 2 (Error bound). *Let there be sequences $x_1 x_2...$ over a finite alphabet $\mathcal{A}$ drawn with probability $\mu(\underline{x}_{1:n})$ for the first n symbols. The Θ_ρ-system predicts by definition $x_n^{\Theta_\rho} \in \mathcal{A}$ from $x_{<n}$, where $x_n^{\Theta_\rho}$ maximizes $\rho(x_{<n}\underline{x}_n)$. Θ_ξ is the universal prediction scheme based on the universal prior ξ. Θ_μ is the optimal*

informed prediction scheme. The total μ-expected number of prediction errors $E_{n\Theta_\xi}$ and $E_{n\Theta_\mu}$ of Θ_ξ and Θ_μ as defined in (14) are bounded in the following way

$$0 \le E_{n\Theta_\xi} - E_{n\Theta_\mu} \le H_n + \sqrt{4E_{n\Theta_\mu}H_n + H_n^2} \le 2H_n + 2\sqrt{E_{n\Theta_\mu}H_n}$$

where $H_n \le \ln\frac{1}{w_\mu}$ is the relative entropy (6), and w_μ is the weight (3) of μ in ξ.

First, we observe that the number of errors $E_{\infty\Theta_\xi}$ of the universal Θ_ξ predictor is finite if the number of errors $E_{\infty\Theta_\mu}$ of the informed Θ_μ predictor is finite. This is especially the case for deterministic μ, as $E_{n\Theta_\mu} \equiv 0$ in this case[4], i.e. Θ_ξ makes only a finite number of errors on deterministic environments. More precisely, $E_{\infty\Theta_\xi} \le 2H_\infty \le 2\ln\frac{1}{w_\mu}$. A combinatoric argument shows that there are M and $\mu \in M$ with $E_{\infty\Theta_\xi} \ge \log_2 |M|$. This shows that the upper bound $E_{\infty\Theta_\xi} \le 2\ln|M|$ for uniform w must be rather tight. For more complicated probabilistic environments, where even the ideal informed system makes an infinite number of errors, the theorem ensures that the error excess $E_{n\Theta_\xi} - E_{n\Theta_\mu}$ is only of order $\sqrt{E_{n\Theta_\mu}}$. The excess is quantified in terms of the information content H_n of μ (relative to ξ), or the weight w_μ of μ in ξ. This ensures that the error densities E_n/n of both systems converge to each other. Actually, the theorem ensures more, namely that the quotient converges to 1, and also gives the speed of convergence $E_{n\Theta_\xi}/E_{n\Theta_\mu} = 1 + O(E_{n\Theta_\mu}^{-1/2}) \longrightarrow 1$ for $E_{n\Theta_\mu} \to \infty$.

4.3   Proof of Theorem 2

The first inequality in Theorem 2 has already been proved (15). The last inequality is a simple triangle inequality. For the second inequality, let us start more modestly and try to find constants A and B that satisfy the linear inequality

$$E_{n\Theta_\xi} \le (A+1)E_{n\Theta_\mu} + (B+1)H_n. \tag{16}$$

If we could show

$$e_{k\Theta_\xi}(x_{<k}) \le (A+1)e_{k\Theta_\mu}(x_{<k}) + (B+1)h_k(x_{<k}) \tag{17}$$

for all $k \le n$ and all $x_{<k}$, (16) would follow immediately by summation and the definition of E_n and H_n. With the abbreviations (12) and the abbreviations $m = x_k^{\Theta_\mu}$ and $s = x_k^{\Theta_\xi}$ the various error functions can then be expressed by $e_{k\Theta_\xi} = 1-y_s$, $e_{k\Theta_\mu} = 1-y_m$ and $h_k = \sum_i y_i \ln\frac{y_i}{z_i}$. Inserting this into (17) we get

$$1-y_s \le (A+1)(1-y_m) + (B+1)\sum_{i=1}^N y_i \ln\frac{y_i}{z_i}. \tag{18}$$

---

[4] Remember that we named a probability distribution *deterministic* if it is 1 for exactly one sequence and 0 for all others.

By definition of $x_k^{\Theta_\mu}$ and $x_k^{\Theta_\varepsilon}$ we have $y_m \geq y_i$ and $z_s \geq z_i$ for all i. We prove a sequence of inequalities which show that

$$(B+1) \sum_{i=1}^{N} y_i \ln \frac{y_i}{z_i} + (A+1)(1-y_m) - (1-y_s) \geq \; \ldots \tag{19}$$

is positive for suitable $A \geq 0$ and $B \geq 0$, which proves (18). For $m = s$ (19) is obviously positive since the relative entropy is positive ($h_k \geq 0$). So we will assume $m \neq s$ in the following. We replace the relative entropy by the sum over squares (7) and further keep only contributions from $i=m$ and $i=s$.

$$\ldots \; \geq \; (B+1)[(y_m - z_m)^2 + (y_s - z_s)^2] + (A+1)(1-y_m) - (1-y_s) \; \geq \; \ldots$$

By definition of y, z, m and s we have the constraints $y_m + y_s \leq 1$, $z_m + z_s \leq 1$, $y_m \geq y_s \geq 0$ and $z_s \geq z_m \geq 0$. From the latter two it is easy to see that the square terms (as a function of z_m and z_s) are minimized by $z_m = z_s = \frac{1}{2}(y_m + y_s)$. Furthermore, we define $x := y_m - y_s$ and eliminate y_s.

$$\ldots \; \geq \; (B+1)\tfrac{1}{2}x^2 + A(1-y_m) - x \; \geq \; \ldots \tag{20}$$

The constraint on $y_m + y_s \leq 1$ translates into $y_m \leq \frac{x+1}{2}$, hence (20) is minimized by $y_m = \frac{x+1}{2}$.

$$\ldots \; \geq \; \tfrac{1}{2}[(B+1)x^2 - (A+2)x + A] \; \geq \; \ldots \tag{21}$$

(21) is quadratic in x and minimized by $x^* = \frac{A+2}{2(B+1)}$. Inserting x^* gives

$$\ldots \; \geq \; \frac{4AB - A^2 - 4}{8(B+1)} \geq 0 \quad \text{for} \quad B \geq \tfrac{1}{4}A + \tfrac{1}{A}, \quad A > 0, \quad (\Rightarrow B \geq 1). \tag{22}$$

Inequality (16) therefore holds for any $A > 0$, provided we insert $B = \frac{1}{4}A + \frac{1}{A}$. Thus we might minimize the r.h.s. of (16) w.r.t. A leading to the upper bound

$$E_{n\Theta_\varepsilon} \leq E_{n\Theta_\mu} + H_n + \sqrt{4E_{n\mu}H_n + H_n^2} \quad \text{for} \quad A^2 = \frac{H_n}{E_{n\Theta_\mu} + \frac{1}{4}H_n}$$

which completes the proof of Theorem 2 $\square$.

5   Generalizations

In the following we discuss several directions in which the findings of this work may be extended.

5.1   General Loss Function

A prediction is very often the basis for some decision. The decision results in an action, which itself leads to some reward or loss. To stay in the framework of (passive) prediction we have to assume that the action itself does not influence the environment. Let $l^k_{x_k y_k}(x_{<k}) \in [l_{min}, l_{min} + l_\Delta]$ be the received loss when taking action $y_k \in \mathcal{Y}$ and $x_k \in \mathcal{A}$ is the kth symbol of the sequence. For instance, if we make a sequence of weather forecasts $\mathcal{A} = \{$sunny, rainy$\}$ and base our decision, whether to take an umbrella or wear sunglasses $\mathcal{Y} = \{$umbrella, sunglasses$\}$ on it, the action of taking the umbrella or wearing sunglasses does not influence the future weather (ignoring the butterfly effect). The error assignment of section 4 falls into this class. The action was just a prediction ($\mathcal{Y} = \mathcal{A}$) and a unit loss was assigned to an erroneous prediction ($l_{x_k y_k} = 1$ for $x_k \neq y_k$) and no loss to a correct prediction ($l_{x_k x_k} = 0$). In general, a Λ_ρ action/prediction scheme $y_k^{\Lambda_\rho} :=$ minarg$_{y_k} \sum_{x_k} \rho(x_{<k} \underline{x}_k) l_{x_k y_k}$ can be defined that minimizes the ρ-expected loss. Λ_ξ is the universal scheme based on the universal prior ξ. Λ_μ is the optimal informed scheme. In [Hut01] it is proven that the total μ-expected losses $L_{n\Lambda_\xi}$ and $L_{n\Lambda_\mu}$ of Λ_ξ and Λ_μ are bounded in the following way: $0 \leq L_{n\Lambda_\xi} - L_{n\Lambda_\mu} \leq l_\Delta H_n + \sqrt{4(L_{n\Lambda_\mu} - n l_{min}) l_\Delta H_n + l_\Delta^2 H_n^2}$. The loss bound has a similar form as the error bound of Theorem 2, but the proof is much more evolved.

5.2 Games of Chance

The general loss bound stated in the previous subsection can be used to estimate the time needed to reach the winning threshold in a game of chance (defined as a sequence of bets, observations and rewards). In step k we bet, depending on the history $x_{<k}$, a certain amount of money s_k, take some action y_k, observe outcome x_k, and receive reward r_k. Our profit, which we want to maximize, is $p_k = r_k - s_k \in [p_{max} - p_\Delta, p_{max}]$. The loss, which we want to minimize, can be identified with the negative profit, $l_{x_k y_k} = -p_k$. The Λ_ρ-system acts as to maximize the ρ-expected profit. Let $\bar{p}_{n\Lambda_\rho}$ be the average expected profit of the first n rounds. One can show that the average profit of the Λ_ξ system converges to the best possible average profit $\bar{p}_{n\Lambda_\mu}$ achieved by the Λ_μ scheme ($\bar{p}_{n\Lambda_\xi} - \bar{p}_{n\Lambda_\mu} = O(n^{-1/2}) \to 0$ for $n \to \infty$). If there is a profitable scheme at all, then asymptotically the universal Λ_ξ scheme will also become profitable with the same average profit. In [Hut01] it is further shown that $(\frac{2p_\Delta}{\bar{p}_{n\Lambda_\mu}})^2 \cdot d_\mu$ is an upper bound for the number of bets n needed to reach the winning zone. The bound is proportional to the relative entropy of μ and ξ.

5.3 Infinite Alphabet

In many cases the basic prediction unit is not a letter, but a number (for inducing number sequences), or a word (for completing sentences), or a real number or vector (for physical measurements). The prediction may either be generalized to a block by block prediction of symbols or, more suitably, the finite alphabet $\mathcal{A}$ could be generalized to countable (numbers, words) or continuous (real or vector) alphabet. The theorems should generalize to countably infinite alphabets by appropriately taking the limit $|\mathcal{A}| \to \infty$ and to continuous alphabets by a denseness or separability argument.

5.4 Partial Prediction, Delayed Prediction, Classification

The Λ_ρ schemes may also be used for partial prediction where, for instance, only every m^{th} symbol is predicted. This can be arranged by setting the loss l^k to zero when no prediction is made, e.g. if k is not a multiple of m. Classification could be interpreted as partial sequence prediction, where $x_{(k-1)m+1:km-1}$ is classified as x_{km}. There are better ways for classification by treating $x_{(k-1)m+1:km-1}$ as pure conditions in ξ, as has been done in [Hut00] in a more general context. Another possibility is to generalize the prediction schemes and theorems to delayed sequence prediction, where the true symbol x_k is given only in cycle $k+d$. A delayed feedback is common in many practical problems.

5.5 More Active Systems

Prediction means guessing the future, but not influencing it. A tiny step in the direction to more active systems, described in subsection 5.1, was to allow the Λ system to act and to receive a loss $l_{x_k y_k}$ depending on the action y_k and the outcome x_k. The probability μ is still independent of the action, and the loss function l^k has to be known in advance. This ensures that the greedy strategy is optimal. The loss function may be generalized to depend not only on the history $x_{<k}$, but also on the historic actions $y_{<k}$ with μ still independent of the action. It would be interesting to know whether the scheme Λ and/or the loss bounds generalize to this case. The full model of an acting agent influencing the environment has been developed in [Hut00], but loss bounds have yet to be proven.

5.6 Miscellaneous

Another direction is to investigate the learning aspect of universal prediction. Many prediction schemes explicitly learn and exploit a model of the environment. Learning and exploitation are melted together in the framework of universal Bayesian prediction. A separation of these two aspects in the spirit of hypothesis learning with MDL [VL00] could lead to new insights. Finally, the system should be tested on specific induction problems for specific M with computable ξ.

6 Summary

Solomonoff's universal probability measure has been generalized to arbitrary probability classes and weights. A wise choice of M widens the applicability by reducing the computational burden for ξ. Convergence of ξ to μ and error bounds have been proven for arbitrary finite alphabet. They show that the universal prediction scheme Λ_ξ is an excellent substitute for the best possible (but generally unknown) informed scheme Λ_μ. Extensions and applications, including general loss functions and bounds, games of chance, infinite alphabet, partial and delayed prediction, classification, and more active systems, have been discussed.

References

[AS83]   D. Angluin and C. H. Smith. Inductive inference: Theory and methods. *ACM Computing Surveys*, 15(3):237–269, 1983.

[Cal98]   C. S. Calude et al. Recursively enumerable reals and Chaitin Ω numbers. In *15th Annual Symposium on Theoretical Aspects of Computer Science*, volume 1373 of *lncs*, pages 596–606, Paris France, 1998. Springer.

[Cha91]   G. J. Chaitin. Algorithmic information and evolution. *in O.T. Solbrig and G. Nicolis, Perspectives on Biological Complexity, IUBS Press*, pages 51–60, 1991.

[FMG92]   M. Feder, N. Merhav, and M. Gutman. Universal prediction of individual sequences. *IEEE Transactions on Information Theory*, 38:1258–1270, 1992.

[Hut99]   M. Hutter. New error bounds for Solomonoff prediction. *Journal of Computer and System Science, in press*, 1999. ftp://ftp.idsia.ch/pub/techrep/IDSIA-11-00.ps.gz.

[Hut00]   M. Hutter. A theory of universal artificial intelligence based on algorithmic complexity. Technical report, 62 pages, 2000. http://arxiv.org/abs/cs.AI/0004001.

[Hut01]   M. Hutter. Optimality of universal Bayesian prediction for general loss and alphabet. Technical Report IDSIA-09-01, Istituto Dalle Molle di Studi sull'Intelligenza Artificiale, Manno(Lugano), Switzerland, 2001.

[Kol65]   A. N. Kolmogorov. Three approaches to the quantitative definition of information. *Problems of Information and Transmission*, 1(1):1–7, 1965.

[Kul59]   S. Kullback. *Information Theory and Statistics*. Wiley, 1959.

[Lev73]   L. A. Levin. Universal sequential search problems. *Problems of Information Transmission*, 9:265–266, 1973.

[Lev84]   L. A. Levin. Randomness conservation inequalities: Information and independence in mathematical theories. *Information and Control*, 61:15–37, 1984.

[LV92]   M. Li and P. M. B. Vitányi. Inductive reasoning and Kolmogorov complexity. *Journal of Computer and System Sciences*, 44:343–384, 1992.

[LV97]   M. Li and P. M. B. Vitányi. *An introduction to Kolmogorov complexity and its applications*. Springer, 2nd edition, 1997.

[Sch00]   J. Schmidhuber. Algorithmic theories of everything. Report IDSIA-20-00, quant-ph/0011122, IDSIA, Manno (Lugano), Switzerland, 2000.

[Sol64]   R. J. Solomonoff. A formal theory of inductive inference: Part 1 and 2. *Inform. Control*, 7:1–22, 224–254, 1964.

[Sol78]   R. J. Solomonoff. Complexity-based induction systems: comparisons and convergence theorems. *IEEE Trans. Inform. Theory*, IT-24:422–432, 1978.

[Sol97]   R. J. Solomonoff. The discovery of algorithmic probability. *Journal of Computer and System Sciences*, 55(1):73–88, 1997.

[VL00]   P. M. B. Vitányi and M. Li. Minimum description length induction, Bayesianism, and Kolmogorov complexity. *IEEE Transactions on Information Theory*, 46(2):446–464, 2000.

[ZL70]   A. K. Zvonkin and L. A. Levin. The complexity of finite objects and the development of the concepts of information and randomness by means of the theory of algorithms. *RMS: Russian Mathematical Surveys*, 25(6):83–124, 1970.

Consensus Decision Trees: Using Consensus Hierarchical Clustering for Data Relabelling and Reduction

Branko Kavšek [1], Nada Lavrač [1], and Anuška Ferligoj [2]

[1] Institute Jožef Stefan, Jamova 39, 1000 Ljubljana, Slovenia
branko.kavsek@ijs.si, nada.lavrac@ijs.si
[2] University of Ljubljana, 1000 Ljubljana, Slovenia
anuska.ferligoj@uni-lj.si

Abstract. In data analysis, induction of decision trees serves two main goals: first, induced decision trees can be used for classification/prediction of new instances, and second, they represent an easy-to-interpret model of the problem domain that can be used for explanation. The accuracy of the induced classifier is usually estimated using N-fold cross validation, whereas for explanation purposes a decision tree induced from all the available data is used. Decision tree learning is relatively non-robust: a small change in the training set may significantly change the structure of the induced decision tree. This paper presents a decision tree construction method in which the domain model is constructed by consensus clustering of N decision trees induced in N-fold cross-validation. Experimental results show that consensus decision trees are simpler than C4.5 decision trees, indicating that they may be a more stable approximation of the intended domain model than decision tree, constructed from the entire set of training instances.

1 Introduction

Decision tree induction (Breiman et al. 1984, Quinlan, 1986) has been recognized as one of the standard data analysis methods. In particular, variants of Quinlans C4.5 (Quinlan, 1993) can be found in virtually all commercial and academic data mining packages.

In data analysis, induction of decision trees serves two main goals: first, induced decision trees can be used for the classification (or prediction) of new instances, and second, they represent an easy-to-interpret model of the problem domain that can be used for explanation. In the standard decision tree learning methodology (e.g., as implemented in the WEKA system (Witten & Frank, 1999)) the accuracy of the induced classifier is estimated using N-fold cross-validation, whereas for explanation purposes a decision tree induced from all the available data is used. Its explanation capability is evaluated qualitatively by the domain expert, whereas quantitative measures estimate only the simplicity of decision trees, measured by the number of leaves and nodes.

L. De Raedt and P. Flach (Eds.): ECML 2001, LNAI 2167, pp. 251–262, 2001.
© Springer-Verlag Berlin Heidelberg 2001

The main advantages of decision tree learning are computational efficiency, reasonable accuracy and simplicity of explanations. It is well known, however, that decision tree learning is a rather non-robust method: a small change in the training set may significantly change the structure of the induced decision tree, which may result in experts' distrust in induced domain models. Improved robustness and improved accuracy results can be achieved e.g., by bagging/boosting (Breiman, 1996) at a cost of increased model complexity and decreased explanatory potential.

This paper addresses the model selection problem of the standard decision tree learning methodology in which the induced domain model is the decision tree induced from all the available data. The accuracy of the induced classifier is estimated using N-fold cross-validation, which is a bias-free (Stone, 1974) but not variance-free (Kang, 1992, Khavi, 1995) estimate of the true accuracy, i.e., the accuracy of a classifier that is learned by the same algorithm on the complete data set. For model selection purposes, a 63,2% bootstrap (Efron 1979) may be preferable to learning from a complete set of training instances (Scheffer & Herbrich, 1997). The bootstrap approach is based on re-sampling of a number of training sets of size n from an original data set of size n by randomly drawing samples with replacement, leading to 63,2% distinct samples in the training set, on the average.

Despite the statistical advantages of this method for choosing the optimal model, this method is still non-robust in the case of decision tree learning. To improve robustness, this paper presents a decision tree construction method in which the domain model in the form of a decision tree is constructed by consensus clustering of N decision trees induced in N-fold cross-validation. Experimental results show that consensus decision trees are simpler than C4.5 decision trees, indicating that they may be a more stable approximation of the intended domain model than decision trees constructed from the entire set of training instances.

The paper is organized as follows. Section 2 presents the basic methodology of decision tree induction and hierarchical clustering, Section 3 outlines the novel approach of consensus decision tree construction, and Section 4 provides the experimental evaluation of the proposed approach. We conclude by a summary and plans for further work.

2   Background Methodology

2.1   Decision Trees

Induction of decision trees is one of the most popular machine learning methods for learning of attribute-value descriptions (Breiman et al., 1984, Quinlan, 1986). The basic decision tree learning algorithm builds a tree in a top-down greedy fashion by recursively selecting the best'attribute on the basis of an information measure, and splitting the data set accordingly. Various modifications of the basic algorithm can be found in the literature, the most popular being Quinlans C4.5 (Quinlan, 1993). In our work we used the WEK (Witten and Frank, 1999) implementation of C4.5.

2.2   Hierarchical Clustering

Clustering methods in general aim at building clusters (groups) of objects so that similar objects fall into the same cluster (internal cohesivity) while dissimilar objects fall into separate clusters (external isolation). A particular class of clustering methods, studied and widely used in statistical data analysis (e.g., Sokal and Sneath, 1963; Gordon, 1981; Hartigan, 1975) are *hierarchical clustering* methods.

The purpose of hierarchical clustering is to fuse objects (instances) into successively larger clusters, using some measure of (dis)similarity. A typical result of this type of clustering is a hierarchical tree or dendrogram.

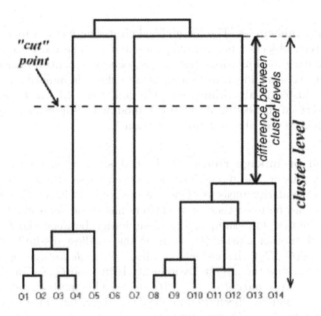

Fig. 1. A sample dendrogram obtained as a result of hierarchical clustering.

As shown in Figure 1, a dendrogram is a binary tree where single objects form the leaves of the tree and each node of the tree represents a cluster of similar objects. The further the node is from the tree root, the more similar the items are under the node. The height of the branches (vertical lines) in a dendrogram are directly proportional to the dissimilarity between clusters. Thus, for each node in the dendrogram (where a new cluster is formed) we can read off the dissimilarity at which the respective objects were joined together into a new single cluster. This dissimilarity is called the *cluster level* and is used to determine the most appropriate number of clusters that reflects the real structure in the data.

The dendrogram illustrates the actual procedure of hierarchical clustering. It starts by forming N clusters, each consisting of one single object (training instance). Then, step by step, the threshold regarding the decision when to declare two objects to be members of the same cluster is lowered. As a result, larger clusters of increasingly dissimilar objects are aggregated. Finally, in the last step, all objects are joined to form a single cluster. The cluster levels are computed and where the difference between successive cluster levels is maximal (Figure 1) the dendrogram is ċut,̦ producing the partition where each cluster is the most internally cohesive and there is the highest external isolation between clusters. Note that the number of clusters is determined dynamically through the procedure of dendrogram ċutting.̦

There is one last question that remains to be answered in order to understand the hierarchical clustering: ħow should we measure the (dis)similarity between objects and between clusters of objects?These questions are addressed in the following two paragraphs, respectively.

Dissimilarity measures. The hierarchical clustering method uses the dissimilarities between objects when forming the clusters. The most straightforward way of computing dissimilarities between objects in a multi-dimensional space is to compute the Euclidean distances; many other dissimilarity measures are also used in clustering algorithms (e.g., Gordon, 1981: 13-32). In our CDT algorithm, described in Section 3, we use a modified disagreement dissimilarity measure which we describe in detail in Section 1.

Aggregation or linkage rules. At the first step, when each object represents its own cluster, the dissimilarities between these objects are defined by the chosen dissimilarity measure. Once several objects have been aggregated, the dissimilarities between these new clusters has to be determined. There are various possibilities: for example, the dissimilarity between the fused cluster $(C_i \cup C_j)$ and another cluster (C_k) can be the smallest dissimilarity between $d(C_i, C_k)$ and $d(C_j, C_k)$; this method is called the *single linkage* method. Alternatively, one may use the largest dissimilarity between $d(C_i, C_k)$ and $d(C_j, C_k)$, i.e., $d(C_i \cup C_j, C_k) = max(d(C_i, C_k), d(C_j, C_k))$. This method, called the *complete linkage* method, has been used in our CDT algorithm. There are numerous other linkage rules (e.g., Gordon, 1981).

An example of hierarchical clustering. To better illustrate the hierarchical clustering method, a simple example is presented in Figure 2. Having five points (x,y,z,w,v) in a two-dimensional space (Figure 2a), we want to assign these points to clusters. Taking the Euclidian distance between points as the dissimilarity measure, we compute the dissimilarity matrix (Figure 2b). What follows is one step of the hierarchical clustering algorithm: find the smallest dissimilarity value in the matrix (Figure 2b - encircled value), fuse the appropriate elements together (Figure 2b - points x and y), delete from the matrix the row and column containing this (smallest) value and recompute the dissimilarity matrix according to the complete linkage aggregation rule. Figure 2c is what we get after applying one step of this algorithm. Repeating the step until the dissimilarity matrix śhrinks'to a single value (Figures 2c,d,e; the last step is not shown), we obtain a dendrogram (Figure 2f). The cluster levels 1, 1, 1.41

and 5.66 correspond to the encircled values in Figures 2b,c,d,e; the differences between successive cluster levels are thus: 0, 0.41 and 4.25. The dendrogram in Figure 2f is cut where this difference is maximal (4.25), yielding two clusters of points: (x,y,z) and (w,v).

Consensus clustering. Consensus hierarchical clustering deals with the following problem: given a set of concept hierarchies (represented by dendrograms), find a *consensus concept hierarchy* by merging the given concept hierarchies in such a way that similar instances (those that belong to the same concept/cluster) will remain similar also in the merged concept hierarchy. In the last thirty years many consensus clustering methods have been proposed (e.g., Regnier, 1965; Adams, 1972; McMorris and Neuman, 1983; Day, 1983). In 1986, a special issue of the Journal of Classification was devoted to consensus classifications. Excellent reviews of this topic are also available (Faith, 1988; Leclerc, 1988).

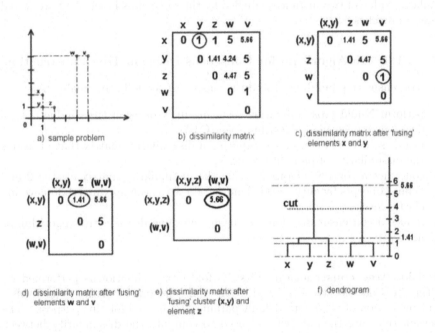

Fig. 2. A short example problem solved using hierarchical clustering with complete linkage aggregation rule.

3   Consensus Decision Tree Construction

3.1   Motivation

As pointed out by Langley (Langley, 1996), decision tree induction can be seen as a special case of induction of concept hierarchies. A concept is associated with each node of the decision tree, and as such a tree represents a kind of taxonomy, a hierarchy of many concepts. In this case, a concept is identified by the set of instances in a node of the decision tree. Hierarchical clustering also results in a taxonomy of concepts, equally identified by the set of instances in a 'node' of a dendrogram representing the concept hierarchy. Concept hierarchies can be induced in a supervised or unsupervised manner: decision tree induction algorithms perform supervised learning, whereas induction by hierarchical clustering is unsupervised.

Our idea of building consensus decision trees is inspired by the idea of consensus hierarchical clustering. A consensus decision tree should be constructed in such a way that instances that are similar in the original decision trees should remain being similar also in the consensus decision tree. To this end, it is crucial to define an appropriate measure of similarity between instances. This measure may only consider the distances between instances or may also profit from the fact that instances are labelled by class labels and appropriately increase the similarity value of two instances labelled by the same class label. We have tested both approaches.

3.2   CDT: An Algorithm for Consensus Decision Tree Construction

The consensus tree building procedure consists of the following main steps:

1. perform N-fold cross-validation resulting in N decision trees induced by a decision tree learning algorithm (e.g., C4.5),
2. use these decision trees for computing a dissimilarity matrix that measures the dissimilarity of pairs of instances,
3. construct a concept hierarchy using the dissimilarity matrix of step 2 and define concepts by cutting'the dendrogram w.r.t. the maximal difference in cluster levels,
4. induce a consensus decision tree using the same decision tree algorithm as in step 1.

Decision tree construction. First, N-fold cross-validation is performed resulting in N decision trees induced by the C4.5 learning algorithm (the WEK implementation of C4.5 with default parameters[1] is used for this purpose). The decision trees are then stored and used to compute the dissimilarity between pairs of instances.

Dissimilarity between instances. The dissimilarities between pairs of instances are computed from the N stored decision trees in the following way:

- first we measure the similarity s between instances i and j by counting (for all N decision trees) how many times the two instances belong to the same leaf (i.e., are described by the same path of attribute-value tests leading

---

[1] The default parameters were: *binary splits = NO, confidence factor for pruning = 0.25, minimum number of objects in a leaf = 2.*

from the root to the leaf of the decision tree). Therefore $s(i, j)$ is defined as follows:

$$s(i,j) = \sum_{l=1}^{N} T_l(i,j)$$

where

$$T_l(i,j) = \begin{cases} 1, \text{ if } i \text{ and } j \text{ belong to the same leaf (are described by} \\ \quad \text{ the same attribute values) in the } l\text{--th decision tree} \\ \\ 0, \text{ otherwise} \end{cases}$$

- then we compute the dissimilarity measure $d(i, j)$ by simply subtracting the similarity $s(i, j)$ from the number of trees N, i.e., $d(i, j) = N - s(i, j)$, which gives the same results as its normalized variant:

$$d(i,j) = 1 - \frac{s(i,j)}{N}$$

By calculating the dissimilarities for all pairs of instances, we obtain the dissimilarity matrix, which is the input for the hierarchical clustering algorithm.

Concept hierarchy construction. A concept hierarchy is constructed using the following hierarchical clustering algorithm:

Each instance is a cluster: $C_i = \{i\}$;
REPEAT
      find the nearest'pair of clusters C_p and C_q:
         $d(C_p, C_q) = \min_{u,v} d(C_u, C_v)$;
      fuse clusters C_p and C_q in a new cluster $C_r = C_p \cup C_q$;
      replace clusters C_p and C_q by the cluster C_r;
      determine the dissimilarities between C_r and the other clusters
         using the complete linkage method;
UNTIL one cluster is left

This algorithm produces a dendrogram as its output. The concepts (clusters) can then be identified by cutting'this dendrogram according to the maximal difference in cluster levels (as described in Section 2.2). If needed, we increase the height of the cutpoint to ensure that the number of clusters remains greater or equal to the number of classes of the given classification problem. Consequently, we sometimes force the algorithm to cut the dendrogram producing more clusters than the optimal number of clusters according to the maximal difference between successive cluster levels.

Induction of consensus decision trees. Within each cluster of instances, we select the majority class. We have tested the following versions of the algorithm:

Learning by data relabelling. In this algorithm, not reported in this paper, we re-classify the instances belonging to non-majority classes by assigning them to the majority class. We then use the C4.5 learning algorithm to induce a consensus decision tree from the set of all instances, some being relabelled.

Learning by data reduction. In the algorithm reported in this paper, we remove from the cluster all instances not belonging to the majority class. We then use the C4.5 learning algorithm to induce the consensus decision tree from the remaining subset of instances.

In all runs of the C4.5 algorithm the same (default) parameter setting is used (as in the first step of this algorithm). Notice that in the case of a tie (two or more classes being the majority class), a random choice between these class assignments is made. The results of learning by data reduction slightly (non-significantly) outperform the results of learning by data relabelling. Due to the lack of space, only the results of learning by data reduction are reported in Table 2.

4   Experimental Evaluation

4.1   Experimental Design

In standard 10-fold cross-validation, the original data set is partitioned into 10 folds with (approximately) the same number of examples. Training sets are built from 9 folds, leaving one fold as a test set. Let G denote the entire data set, T_i an individual test set (consisting of one fold), and G_i the corresponding training set ($G_i \leftarrow G \setminus T_i$, composed of nine folds). In this way, 10 training sets G_1– G_{10}, and 10 corresponding test sets T_1–T_{10} are constructed. Every example occurs exactly once in a test set, and 9 times in training sets.

In the first experiment we used C4.5 (WEK implementation, default parameter setting[2]) to induce decision trees on training sets G_1–G_{10}. We measured the average accuracy $Acc(C4.5(G))$ (and standard deviation) and the information score[3] $Info(C4.5(G))$ of ten hypotheses $C4.5(G_i)$ constructed by C4.5 on training sets G_i, $i \in [1, 10]$, where $Acc(C4.5(G)) = \frac{1}{10} \sum_1^{10} Acc(C4.5(G_i))$, and $Info(C4.5(G)) = \frac{1}{10} \sum_1^{10} Info(C4.5(G_i))$. The average size of decision trees $Leaves/Nodes(C4.5(G))$ was measured by the number of leaves and the number of all decision tree nodes (number of leaves + number of internal nodes), averaged over 10 folds.

The above result presents the baseline for comparing the quality of our consensus tree building algorithm CDT, measured by the average accuracy $Acc(CDT(G))$, $Leaves/Nodes(CDT(G))$, and information score $Info(CDT(G))$ over ten consensus decision trees $CDT(G_i)$.

---

[2] See footnote 1 in Section 3.2.

[3] Whereas accuracy computes the relative frequency of correctly classified instances, the information score takes into the account also the improvement of accuracy compared to the prior probability of classes, see (Kononenko and Bratko, 1991).

As described in Section 3.2, a consensus decision tree is constructed from ten C4.5 decision trees. Building of consensus decision trees was performed in a nested 10-fold cross-validation loop: for each G_i, $i \in [1, 10]$, training sets G_{ij}, $j \in [1, 10]$ were used to construct decision trees $C4.5(G_{ij})$ by the C4.5 algorithm. Training sets G_{ij} were obtained by splitting each G_i into ten test sets T_{ij} (consisting of one sub-fold), and ten training sets $G_{ij} \leftarrow G_i \setminus T_{ij}$ (composed of nine sub-folds).

Ten decision trees $C4.5(G_{ij})$ were merged into a single consensus decision tree $CDT(G_i)$. Let $Acc(CDT(G_i))$ denote its accuracy tested on T_i. Accordingly, $Acc(CDT(G)) = \frac{1}{10}\sum_1^{10} Acc(CDT(G_i))$, and information contents $Info(CDT(G)) = \frac{1}{10}\sum_1^{10} Info(CDT(G_i))$. $Leaves/Nodes(CDT(G))$ is also the average of $Leaves/Nodes(CDT(G_i))$.

In order to compare accuracy, tree size and information score of consensus trees and C4.5 trees, we calculate their *relative improvements* as follows: $Rel(Acc(G)) = \frac{Acc(CDT(G))}{Acc(C4.5(G))} - 1$, $Rel(Leaves/Nodes(G)) = 1 - \frac{Leaves/Nodes(CDT(G))}{Leaves/Nodes(C4.5(G))}$, $Rel(Info(G)) = \frac{Info(CDT(G))}{Info(C4.5(G))} - 1$.

Table 1. Characteristics of data sets.

Data set	#Attr.	#Class.	#Inst.	Class distribution (%)
Anneal	38	5	898	1:11:**76**:8:4
Audiology	69	24	226	1:1:**25**:9:1:1:8:21:1:2:1:2:1:1:3:1:1:1:9:2:1:2:4:1
Australian	14	2	690	**56**:44
Autos	25	6	205	1:11:**33**:26:16:13
Balance	4	3	625	**46**:8:**46**
Breast	9	2	286	**70**:30
Breast-w	9	2	699	**66**:34
Car	6	4	1728	**70**:22:4:4
Colic	22	2	368	**63**:37
Credit-a	15	2	690	44:**56**
Credit-g	20	2	1000	**70**:30
Diabetes	8	2	768	**65**:35
Glass	9	6	214	33:**36**:8:6:4:14
Heart-c	13	2	303	**54**:46
Heart-stat	13	2	270	**56**:44
Hepatitis	19	2	155	21:**79**
Ionosphere	34	2	351	36:**64**
Iris	4	3	150	**33:33:33**
Labor	16	2	57	35:**65**
Lymph	18	4	148	1:**55**:41:3
Prim. tumor	17	21	339	**25**:5:3:4:11:1:4:2:1:8:4:2:7:1:1:3:8:2:1:1:7
Segment	19	7	2310	**14:14:14:14:14:14:14**
Sonar	60	2	208	47:**53**
Tic-tac-toe	9	2	958	**65**:35
Vehicle	18	4	846	25:**26:26**:24
Vote	16	2	435	**61**:39
Wine	13	3	178	33:**40**:27
Zoo	17	7	101	**41**:20:5:13:4:8:10

4.2   Results of Experiments

Experiments were performed on 28 UCI data sets whose characteristics are outlined in Table 1 (boldface denoting the majority class). Results of experiments are shown in Table 2 (boldface meaning that CDT performed equally well or better than C4.5).

Table 2. Results of the experiments.

Data set	C4.5 Acc(Sd)	leaves /nodes	info.	CDT Acc(Sd)	leaves /nodes	info.	Relative improvement Acc	leaves /nodes	info.
Anneal	97,14 (0,0893)	39/77	2,7130	**99,13 (0,0497)**	52/103	**2,7811**	0,0205	-0,333/-0,338	0,0251
Audiol.	77,88 (0,1193)	32/54	2,6579	**80,09 (0,1288)**	**29/49**	2,5316	0,0284	0,094/0,093	-0,0475
Austral.	85,51 (0,3455)	31/45	0,6183	84,64 (0,3919)	**17/24**	**0,6813**	-0,0102	0,452/0,467	0,1019
Autos	82,44 (0,2022)	49/69	1,8198	80,49 (0,2361)	39/57	1,7598	-0,0237	0,204/0,174	-0,0330
Balance	77,76 (0,3567)	58/115	0,6778	69,12 (0,4537)	**8/15**	0,5598	-0,1111	0,862/0,870	-0,1741
Breast	75,17 (0,4423)	4/6	0,1005	72,73 (0,5222)	13/17	**0,2630**	-0,0326	-2,250/-1,833	**1,6169**
Brst-w	95,28 (0,2116)	16/31	0,8020	94,85 (0,2269)	**9/17**	**0,8189**	-0,0045	0,438/0,452	0,0211
Car	92,48 (0,1628)	131/182	1,0218	68,66 (0,3946)	**29/41**	0,2687	-0,2576	0,779/0,775	-0,7370
Colic	85,87 (0,3518)	4/6	0,4993	83,42 (0,4071)	11/17	**0,6023**	-0,0285	-1,750/-1,833	**0,2063**
Crdt-a	85,94 (0,3402)	30/42	0,6221	85,07 (0,3864)	**18/25**	**0,6901**	-0,0101	0,400/0,405	0,1093
Crdt-g	69,70 (0,4922)	103/140	0,1193	69,50 (0,5523)	**82/114**	**0,1949**	-0,0029	0,204/0,186	0,6337
Diab.	74,09 (0,4356)	22/43	0,2993	73,96 (0,5103)	**21/41**	**0,3766**	-0,0018	0,045/0,047	0,2583
Glass	67,29 (0,2837)	30/59	1,3307	**68,69 (0,2991)**	23/45	**1,3524**	0,0208	0,233/0,237	0,0163
Heart-c	79,21 (0,2619)	30/51	0,5354	**79,21 (0,2884)**	**18/29**	**0,5917**	0,0000	0,400/0,431	0,1052
Heart-s	77,78 (0,4322)	18/35	0,4847	75,93 (0,4907)	21/41	**0,5054**	-0,0238	-0,167/-0,171	**0,0427**
Hepat.	79,35 (0,4200)	11/21	0,1445	77,42 (0,4752)	**8/15**	**0,1510**	-0,0244	0,273/0,286	0,0450
Ionos.	90,88 (0,2887)	18/35	0,7416	89,74 (0,3203)	**16/31**	0,7247	-0,0125	0,111/0,114	-0,0228
Iris	95,33 (0,1707)	5/9	1,4663	94,67 (0,1886)	**3/5**	**1,4692**	-0,0070	0,400/0,444	0,0020
Labor	78,95 (0,4285)	3/5	0,3496	**80,70 (0,4393)**	3/5	**0,5257**	0,0222	0,000/0,000	0,5037
Lymph	77,03 (0,3274)	21/34	0,6074	**77,70 (0,3339)**	**18/28**	**0,6712**	0,0088	0,143/0,176	0,1050
Prim.t.	40,71 (0,1961)	47/88	1,2050	**41,30 (0,2310)**	29/54	**1,2396**	0,0145	0,383/0,386	0,0287
Segment	97,14 (0,0893)	39/77	2,7130	96,02 (0,1067)	52/103	2,6867	-0,0116	-0,333/-0,338	-0,0097
Sonar	74,04 (0,4986)	18/35	0,4662	**75,81 (0,4952)**	15/29	**0,5050**	0,0239	0,167/0,171	0,0832
T-tac-t	84,76 (0,3485)	95/142	0,5613	78,91 (0,4592)	**71/106**	0,4793	-0,0690	0,253/0,254	-0,1461
Vehicle	73,40 (0,3272)	98/195	1,3607	70,92 (0,3813)	**56/111**	1,2996	-0,0338	0,429/0,431	-0,0449
Vote	96,78 (0,1650)	6/11	0,8580	96,55 (0,1857)	6/11	**0,8908**	-0,0024	0,000/0,000	0,0382
Wine	94,94 (0,1776)	5/9	1,4476	93,26 (0,2120)	7/13	1,4192	-0,0178	-0,400/-0,444	-0,0196
Zoo	92,08 (0,1359)	9/17	2,1435	**92,08 (0,1504)**	9/17	2,1014	0,0000	0,000/0,000	-0,0196
Average	82,10 (0,2900)	34,71/ 58,32	1,01	80,38 (0,3300)	24,39/ 41,54	1,01	-0,0195	0,037/ 0,051	0,0960

Results of experiments show that there is no significant difference in average accuracy between the consensus decision trees and the decision trees induced by C4.5 ($t = 1.8664$, $df = 27$, $p = 0.0729$, using two-tailed t-test for dependent samples, where t, df and p stand for t-statistics, degrees of freedom and significance level, respectively), using a 95%significance level (the bound used throughout this paper). Notice, however, that the CDT algorithm improves the information score (compared to C4.5) in 18 domains (9.6%improvement on the average).

Our hypothesis that the structure of CDT is simpler than the structure of the induced C4.5 decision trees was confirmed: indeed, the average number of leaves of CDT is significantly smaller than the average number of leaves of the C4.5 decision trees ($t = 2.3787$, $df = 27$, $p = 0.0247$, using two-tailed t-test for dependent samples). Moreover, the average tree size (measured by the number of all decision tree nodes) of CDT is also significantly smaller than that of C4.5 ($t = 2.4413$, $df = 27$, $p = 0.0215$, using two-tailed t-test for dependent samples).

The relative improvement in tree size also shows that in 19 domains the CDT algorithm learned smaller decision trees than C4.5 yielding, on the average, 3.7% smaller trees according to the number of leaves (5.1% according to the number of all nodes).

5   Summary and Conclusions

Results show that consensus decision trees are, on the average, as accurate as C4.5 decision trees, but simpler (smaller w.r.t. the number of leaves and nodes). Moreover, consensus decision trees improve the information score compared to C4.5 decision trees[4].

We also tested alternative ways of constructing consensus decision trees. First, the similarity measure that only considers the distances between instances was replaced by a measure that takes into the account that instances are labelled by class labels; the similarity value of two instances labelled by the same class label was appropriately increased. Opposed to our expectations, this way of measuring similarities between instances has not proved to be better than the one described in this paper.

Second, instead of labelling instances by class labels, instances may be labelled by cluster labels, considering clusters generated by consensus clustering as classes for learning by C4.5. This approach has turned out to be inferior compared to the approaches described in the paper.

In further work we are planning to measure the similarities between instances not just by counting how many times two instances belong to the same leaf (have the same attribute-value representation), but also by putting different weights on the segments of this path (higher weights assigned to segments closer to the root).

Moreover, our plan is to test the hypothesis that consensus decision trees are more robust with respect to adding of new instances, i.e., that the structure of the consensus decision tree would change less than the structure of C4.5 decision trees. To this end we need to propose new measures of tree structure variability, and measure the robustness accordingly. The current results indicate that a step in the direction of improving the robustness has been achieved, assuming that simpler tree structures are more robust.

There is however a performance drawback that we should take into account when using the CDT method for building decision trees. Since the CDT algorithm builds 11 decision trees (10 in the cross-validation process and the final one) and does also the hierarchical clustering, it is much slower than the traditional decision tree building algorithm.

Acknowledgements. Thanks to Saso Džeroski, Ljupčo Todorovski and Marko Grobelnik for useful comments on the draft of this paper. Thanks also to Bernard

---

[4] There are two data sets in which a C4.5 decision tree outperforms CDT in accuracy, simplicity and information score; on the other hand, in five domains CDT is better in all the three characteristics.

žnko for his help when using WEK. The work reported in this paper was supported by the Slovenian Ministry of Education, Science and Sport, and the IST-1999-11495 project Data Mining and Decision Support for Business Competitiveness: A European Virtual Enterprise.

References

1. Adams, E.N. (1972). Consensus techniques and the comparison of taxonomic trees. *Systematic Zoology*, 21, 390–397.
2. Breiman, L., Friedman, J., Olshen, R., and Stone, C. (1984). *Classification and Regression Trees*. Wadsworth International Group, Belmont, CA.
3. Breiman, L. (1996). Bagging predictors. *Machine Learning*, 24:123–140,1996.
4. Day, W.H.E. (1983). The role of complexity in comparing classifications. *Mathematical Biosciences*, 66, 97–114.
5. Efron, B. (1979). Bootstrap methods: Another look at the jackknife. *Annals of Statistic*, 7(1): 1–26.
6. Faith, D.P. (1988). Consensus applications in the biological sciences. In: Bock, H.H. (Ed.) *Classification and Related Methods of Data Analysis*, Amsterdam: North-Holland, 325–332.
7. Fisher, D.H. (1989). Noise-tolerant conceptual clustering. *Proceedings of the Eleventh International Joint Conference on Artificial Intelligence* 825–830. San Francisco: Morgan Kaufmann.
8. Gordon, A.D. (1981). *Classification*. London: Chapman and Hall.
9. Hartigan, J.A. (1975). *Cluster Algorithms*. New York: Wiley.
10. Kohavi, R. (1995). Wrappers for performance enhancement and oblivious decision graphs. Doctoral dissertation, Stanford University.
11. Kononenko, I. and Bratko, I. (1991). Information based evaluation criterion for classifier's performance. *Machine Learning*, 6, (1), 67–80.
12. Langley, P. (1996). *Elements of Machine Learning*. Morgan Kaufmann.
13. Leclerc, B. (1988). Consensus applications in the social sciences. In: Bock, H.H. (Ed.) *Classification and Related Methods of Data Analysis*, Amsterdam: North-Holland, 333–340.
14. McMorris, F.R. and Neuman, D. (1983). Consensus functions defined on trees. *Mathematical Social Sciences*, 4, 131–136.
15. Quinlan, J.R. (1986). Induction of decision trees. *Machine Learning*, 1(1): 81–106.
16. Quinlan, J.R. (1993). *C4.5: Programs for Machine Learning*. California: Morgan Kaufmann.
17. Regnier, S. (1965). Sur quelques aspects mathematiques des problems de classification automatique. *I.I.C. Bulletin*, 4, 175–191.
18. Scheffer, T. and Herbrich, R. (1997). Unbiased assessment of learning algorithms. In *Proceedings of the International Joint Conference on Artificial Intelligence*, 798–803.
19. Sokal, R.R. and Sneath, P.H.A. (1963). *Principles of Numerical Taxonomy*. San Francisco: Freeman.
20. Stone, M. (1974). Cross-validatory choice and assessment of statistical predictions. *Journal of the Royal Statistical Society*, B 36, 111–147.
21. Witten, I.H. and Frank, E. (1999). *Data Mining: Practical Machine Learning Tools and Techniques with Java Implementations*. Morgan Kaufmann, San Francisco.
22. Zhang, J. (1992). On the distributional properties of model selection criteria. *Journal of the American Statistical Association*, 87(419) 732–737.

Learning of Variability for
Invariant Statistical Pattern Recognition

Daniel Keysers, Wolfgang Macherey, Jörg Dahmen, and Hermann Ney

Lehrstuhl für Informatik VI, Computer Science Department
RWTH Aachen - University of Technology, D-52056 Aachen, Germany
{keysers,w.macherey,dahmen,ney}@informatik.rwth-aachen.de
http://www-i6.informatik.rwth-aachen.de

Abstract. In many applications, modelling techniques are necessary which take into account the inherent variability of given data. In this paper, we present an approach to model class specific pattern variation based on tangent distance within a statistical framework for classification. The model is an effective means to explicitly incorporate invariance with respect to transformations that do not change class-membership like e.g. small affine transformations in the case of image objects. If no prior knowledge about the type of variability is available, it is desirable to learn the model parameters from the data. The probabilistic interpretation presented here allows us to view learning of the variational derivatives in terms of a maximum likelihood estimation problem. We present experimental results from two different real-world pattern recognition tasks, namely image object recognition and automatic speech recognition. On the US Postal Service handwritten digit recognition task, learning of variability achieves results well comparable to those obtained using specific domain knowledge. On the SieTill corpus for continuously spoken telephone line recorded German digit strings the method shows a significant improvement in comparison with a common mixture density approach using a comparable amount of parameters. The probabilistic model is well-suited to be used in the field of statistical pattern recognition and can be extended to other domains like cluster analysis.

1   Introduction

In many applications, it is important to carefully consider the inherent variability of data. In the field of pattern recognition it is desired to construct classification algorithms which tolerate variation of the input patterns that leaves the class-membership unchanged. For example, image objects are usually subject to affine transformations of the image grid like rotation, scaling and translation. Conventional distance measures like the Euclidean distance or the Mahalanobis distance [3] do not take into account such transformations or do so only if the training data contains a large number of transformed patterns, respectively. One method to incorporate *invariance* with respect to such transformations into a classifier is to use invariant distance measures like the *tangent distance*, which has been successfully applied in image object recognition during the last years [9,14,15].

L. De Raedt and P. Flach (Eds.): ECML 2001, LNAI 2167, pp. 263–275, 2001.
© Springer-Verlag Berlin Heidelberg 2001

Tangent distance (TD) is usually applied by explicitly modelling the derivative of transformations which are known a priori. This is especially effective in cases where the training set is small. But not in all domains such specific knowledge is available. For example, the transformation effects on the feature vectors of a speech signal that are used in automatic speech recognition are generally difficult to obtain or unknown.

In this paper we present a method to automatically *learn* the derivative of the variability present in the data within a statistical framework, thus leading to an increased robustness of the clasifier. To show the practical value of the approach we present results from experiments in two real-world application areas, namely optical character recognition (OCR) and automatic speech recognition (ASR).

To classify an observation $x \in \mathbb{R}^D$, we use the Bayesian decision rule

$$x \longmapsto r(x) = \operatorname*{argmax}_k \{p(k) \cdot p(x|k)\}. \tag{1}$$

Here, $p(k)$ is the *a priori* probability of class k, $p(x|k)$ is the *class conditional* probability for the observation x given class k and $r(x)$ is the decision of the classifier. This decision rule is known to be optimal with respect to the expected number of classification errors if the required distributions are known [3]. However, as neither $p(k)$ nor $p(x|k)$ are known in practical situations, it is necessary to choose models for the respective distributions and estimate their parameters using the training data. The class conditional probabilities are modelled using *Gaussian mixture densities* (GMD) or *kernel densities* (K) in the experiments. The latter can be regarded as an extreme case of the mixture density model, where each training sample is interpreted as the center of a Gaussian distribution. A Gaussian mixture is defined as a linear combination of Gaussian component densities, which can approximate any density function with arbitrary precision, even if only component densities with diagonal covariance matrices are used. This restriction is often imposed in order to reduce the number of parameters that must be estimated. The necessary parameters for the GMD can be estimated using the Expectation-Maximization (EM) algorithm [3].

2   Invariance and Tangent Distance

There exists a variety of ways to achieve invariance or transformation tolerance of a classifier, including normalization, extraction of invariant features and invariant distance measures [19]. Distance measures are used for classification as dissimilarity measures, i.e. the distances should ideally be small for members of the same class and large for members of different classes. An invariant distance measure ideally takes into account transformations of the patterns, yielding small values for patterns which mostly differ by a transformation that does not change class-membership. In the following, we will give a brief overview of one invariant distance measure called *tangent distance*, which was introduced in [15,16].

Let $x \in \mathbb{R}^D$ be a pattern and $t(x, \alpha)$ denote a transformation of x that depends on a parameter L-tuple $\alpha \in \mathbb{R}^L$, where we assume that t does not

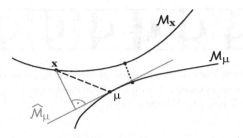

Fig. 1. Illustration of the Euclidean distance between an observation x and a reference μ (dashed line) in comparison to the distance between the corresponding manifolds (dotted line). The tangent approximation of the manifold of the reference and the corresponding (one-sided) tangent distance is depicted by the light gray lines.

affect class membership (for small α). The set of all transformed patterns now comprises a manifold $\mathcal{M}_x = \{t(x, \alpha) \; : \; \alpha \in \mathbb{R}^L\} \subset \mathbb{R}^D$ in pattern space. The distance between two patterns can then be defined as the minimum distance between the manifold $\mathcal{M}_x$ of the pattern x and the manifold $\mathcal{M}_\mu$ of a class specific prototype pattern μ, which is truly invariant with respect to the regarded transformations (cf. Fig. 1):

$$d(x, \mu) = \min_{\alpha, \beta \in \mathbb{R}^L} \left\{ ||t(x, \alpha) - t(\mu, \beta)||^2 \right\} \tag{2}$$

However, the resulting distance calculation between manifolds is a hard non-linear optimization problem in general. Moreover, the manifolds usually cannot be handled analytically. To overcome these problems, the manifolds can be approximated by a *tangent subspace* $\widehat{\mathcal{M}}$. The *tangent vectors* x_l that span the subspace are the partial *derivatives* of the transformation t with respect to the parameters α_l ($l = 1, \ldots, L$), i.e. $x_l = \partial t(x, \alpha) / \partial \alpha_l$. Thus, the transformation $t(x, \alpha)$ can be approximated using a Taylor expansion around $\alpha = 0$:

$$t(x, \alpha) = x + \sum_{l=1}^{L} \alpha_l x_l + \sum_{l=1}^{L} \mathcal{O}(\alpha_l^2) \tag{3}$$

The set of points consisting of all linear combinations of the pattern x with the tangent vectors x_l forms the tangent subspace $\widehat{\mathcal{M}}_x$, which is a first-order approximation of $\mathcal{M}_x$:

$$\widehat{\mathcal{M}}_x = \left\{ x + \sum_{l=1}^{L} \alpha_l x_l \; : \; \alpha \in \mathbb{R}^L \right\} \subset \mathbb{R}^D \tag{4}$$

Using the linear approximation $\widehat{\mathcal{M}}_x$ has the advantage that distance calculations are equivalent to the solution of linear least square problems or equivalently projections into subspaces, which are computationally inexpensive operations. The approximation is valid for small values of α, which nevertheless is sufficient in many applications, as Fig. 2 shows for examples of OCR data. These examples illustrate the advantage of TD over other distance measures, as the depicted

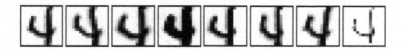

Fig. 2. Example of first-order approximation of affine transformations and line thickness. (Left to right: original image, diagonal deformation, scale, line thickness increase, shift left, axis deformation, line thickness decrease)

patterns all lie in the same subspace. The TD between the original image and any of the transformations is therefore zero, while the Euclidean distance is significantly greater than zero. Using the squared Euclidean norm, the TD is defined as:

$$d_{2S}(x,\mu) = \min_{\alpha,\beta \in \mathbb{R}^L} \left\{ \left\| (x + \sum_{l=1}^{L} \alpha_l x_l) - (\mu + \sum_{l=1}^{L} \beta_l \mu_l) \right\|^2 \right\} \tag{5}$$

Eq. (5) is also known as *two-sided* tangent distance (2S) [3]. In order to reduce the effort for determining $d_{2S}(x,\mu)$ it may be convenient to restrict the calculation of the tangent subspaces to the prototype (or the reference) vectors. The resulting distance measure is called *one-sided* tangent distance (1S):

$$d_{1S}(x,\mu) = \min_{\alpha \in \mathbb{R}^L} \left\{ \left\| x - (\mu + \sum_{l=1}^{L} \alpha_l \mu_l) \right\|^2 \right\} \tag{6}$$

The presented considerations are based on the Euclidean distance, but equally apply when using the Mahalanobis distance [3] in a statistical framework. They show that a suitable first-order model of variability is a subspace model based on the derivatives of transformations that respect class-membership, where the variation is modelled by the tangent vectors or subspace components, respectively. In the following we will concentrate on properties of the model and the estimation of subspace components if the transformations are not known.

3   Learning of Variability

We first discuss a probabilistic framework for TD and then show, how learning of the tangent vectors can be considered as the solution of a maximum likelihood estimation problem. This estimation is especially useful for cases where no prior knowledge about the transformations present in the data is available.

3.1   Tangent Distance in a Probabilistic Framework

To embed the TD into a statistical framework we will focus on the one-sided TD, assuming that the references are subject to variations. A more detailed presentation including the remaining cases of variation of the observations and the two-sided TD can be found in [8].

We restrict our considerations here to the case where the observations x are normally distributed with expectation μ and covariance matrix Σ. The extension to Gaussian mixtures or kernel densities is straightforward using maximum approximation or the EM algorithm. In order to simplify the notation, class indices are omitted. Using the first-order approximation of the manifold $\mathcal{M}_\mu$ for a mean vector μ, we obtain the probability density function (pdf) for the observations:

$$p(x \,|\, \mu, \alpha, \Sigma) = \mathcal{N}(x \,|\, \mu + \sum_{l=1}^{L} \alpha_l \mu_l, \Sigma) \qquad (7)$$

The integral of the joint distribution $p(x, \alpha \,|\, \mu, \Sigma)$ over the unknown transformation parameters α then leads to the following distribution:

$$\begin{aligned} p(x \,|\, \mu, \Sigma) &= \int p(x, \alpha \,|\, \mu, \Sigma) \, d\alpha \\ &= \int p(\alpha \,|\, \mu, \Sigma) \cdot p(x \,|\, \mu, \alpha, \Sigma) \, d\alpha \\ &= \int p(\alpha) \cdot p(x \,|\, \mu, \alpha, \Sigma) \, d\alpha \end{aligned} \qquad (8)$$

Without loss of generality, the tangent vectors of the pdf in Eq. (7) can be assumed orthonormal with respect to Σ, as only the spanned subspace determines the modelled variation. Hence, it is always possible to achieve the condition

$$\mu_l^T \Sigma^{-1} \mu_m = \delta_{l,m} \qquad (9)$$

using e.g. a singular value decomposition, where $\delta_{l,m}$ denotes the Konecker delta. Note that we assume that α is independent of μ and Σ, i.e. $p(\alpha \,|\, \mu, \Sigma) \equiv p(\alpha)$. Furthermore, $\alpha \in \mathbb{R}^L$ is assumed to be normally distributed with mean 0 and a covariance matrix $\gamma^2 I$, i.e. $p(\alpha) = \mathcal{N}(\alpha \,|\, 0, \gamma^2 I)$, where I denotes the identity matrix and γ is a hyperparameter describing the standard deviation of the transformation parameters. These assumptions reduce the complexity of the calculations but do not affect the general result. The evaluation of the integral in Eq. (8) leads to the following expression:

$$p(x|\mu, \Sigma) = \mathcal{N}(x|\mu, \Sigma') = \det(2\pi \Sigma')^{-\frac{1}{2}} \exp\left(-\frac{1}{2}\left[(x - \mu)^T \Sigma'^{-1}(x - \mu)\right]\right) \quad (10)$$

$$\Sigma' = \Sigma + \gamma^2 \sum_{l=1}^{L} \mu_l \mu_l^T, \qquad \Sigma'^{-1} = \Sigma^{-1} - \frac{1}{1 + \frac{1}{\gamma^2}} \Sigma^{-1} \sum_{l=1}^{L} \mu_l \mu_l^T \Sigma^{-1} \quad (11)$$

Note that the exponent in Eq. (10) leads to the conventional Mahalanobis distance for $\gamma \to 0$ and to TD for $\gamma \to \infty$. Thus, the incorporation of tangent vectors adds a corrective term to the Mahalanobis distance that only affects the covariance matrix which can be interpreted as structuring Σ [8]. For the limiting case $\Sigma = I$, a similar result was derived in [6]. The probabilistic interpretation of TD can also be used for a more reliable estimation of the parameters of the distribution [2,8]. Note that $\det(\Sigma') = (1 + \gamma^2)^L \det(\Sigma)$ [5, pp. 38ff.] which is independent of the tangent vectors and can therefore be neglected in the following maximum likelihood estimation.

3.2 Estimation of Subspace Components

In order to circumvent the restriction that the applicable transformations must be known a priori, the tangent vectors can be learned from the training data. This estimation can be formulated within a maximum likelihood approach.

Let the training data be given by $x_{n,k}, n = 1, \ldots, N_k$ training patterns of $k = 1, \ldots, K$ classes. Assuming that the number L of tangent vectors is known (note that L can be determined automatically [1]) we consider the log-likelihood as a function of the unknown tangent vectors $\{\mu_{kl}\}$ (for each class k):

$$
\begin{aligned}
F(\{\mu_{kl}\}) &:= \sum_{k=1}^{K} \sum_{n=1}^{N_k} \log \mathcal{N}(x_{n,k} | \mu_k, \Sigma_k') \\
&= \frac{1}{1 + \frac{1}{\gamma^2}} \sum_{k=1}^{K} \sum_{n=1}^{N_k} \sum_{l=1}^{L} ((x_{n,k} - \mu_k)^T \Sigma^{-1} \mu_{kl})^2 + \text{const} \\
&= \frac{1}{1 + \frac{1}{\gamma^2}} \sum_{k=1}^{K} \sum_{l=1}^{L} \mu_{kl}^T \Sigma^{-1} S_k \Sigma^{-1} \mu_{kl} + \text{const}
\end{aligned}
\tag{12}
$$

with $S_k = \sum_{n=1}^{N_k} (x_{n,k} - \mu_k)(x_{n,k} - \mu_k)^T$ as the class specific scatter matrix. Σ and S_k can be regarded as covariance matrices of two competing models. Taking the constraints of orthonormality of the tangent vectors with respect to Σ^{-1} into account, we obtain the following result [5, pp. 400ff.]: The class specific tangent vectors μ_{kl} maximizing Eq. (12) have to be chosen such that the vectors $\Sigma^{-1/2}\mu_{kl}$ are those eigenvectors of the matrix $\Sigma^{-1/2} S_k (\Sigma^{-1/2})^T$ with the largest corresponding eigenvalues.

As the above considerations show, two different models have to be determined for the covariance matrices Σ and S_k. While S_k is defined as a class specific scatter matrix, a globally pooled covariance matrix is a suitable choice for Σ in many cases. Using these models, the effect of incorporating the tangent distance into the Mahalanobis distance is equivalent to performing a global whitening transformation of the feature space and then using the L class specific eigenvectors with the largest eigenvalues as tangent vectors for each class. This reduces the effect of those directions of class specific variability that contribute the most variance to Σ. While the maximum likelihood estimate leads to results similar to conventional principal component analysis (PCA), the estimated components are used in a completely different manner here. In conventional PCA, the principal components are chosen to minimize the reconstruction error. In contrast to that, these components span the subspace with minor importance in the distance calculation in the approach presented here. This can be interpreted as reducing the effect of specific variability, motivated by the fact that it does not change class membership of the patterns. The tangent distance has the property that it also works very well in combination with global feature transformations as for instance a linear discriminant analysis (LDA), since Σ can be assumed as a global covariance matrix of an LDA-transformed feature space.

4 Experimental Results

To show the applicability of the proposed learning approach, we present results obtained on two real-world classification tasks. The performance of a classifier is measured by the obtained *error rate* (ER), i.e. the ratio of misclassifications to the total number of classifications. For speech recognition a suitable measure is the *word error rate* (WER), which is defined as the ratio of the number of incorrectly recognized words to the total number of words to be recognized. The difference to the correct sentence is measured using the Levenshtein or edit distance, defined as the minimal number of insertions (ins), deletions (del) or replacements of words necessary to transform the correct sentence to the recognized sentence. The *sentence error rate* (SER) is defined as the fraction of incorrectly recognized sentences.

4.1 Image Object Recognition

Results for the domain of image object recognition were obtained on the well known US Postal Service handwritten digit recognition task (USPS). It contains normalized greyscale images of size 16×16 pixels, divided into a training set of 7,291 images and a test set of 2,007 images. Reported recognition error rates for this database are summarized in Table 1. In our preliminary experiments, we used kernel densities to model the distributions in Bayes' decision rule and we applied *appearance based* classification, i.e. no feature extraction was applied. The use of tangent distance based on derivatives (6 affine derivatives plus line thickness) and virtual training and testing data (by shifting the images 1 pixel into 8 directions, keeping training and test set separated) improved the error

Table 1. Summary of results for the USPS corpus (error rates, [%]).

: training set extended with 2,400 machine-printed digits

method		ER[%]
human performance	[SIMARD et al. 1993] [15]	2.5
relevance vector machine	[TIPPING et al. 2000] [17]	5.1
neural net (LeNet1)	[LeCun et al. 1990] [14]	4.2
invariant support vectors	[SCHÖLKOPF et al. 1998] [13]	3.0
neural net + boosting	[DRUCKER et al. 1993] [14]	2.6
tangent distance	[SIMARD et al. 1993] [15]	2.5
nearest neighbor classifier	[9]	5.6
mixture densities	[2] baseline	7.2
	+ LDA + virtual data	3.4
kernel densities	[9] tangent distance, derivative, one-sided (μ)	3.7
	one-sided (x)	3.3
	two-sided	3.0
	+ virtual data	2.4
	+ classifier combination	**2.2**
kernel densities	tangent distance, learned, one-sided (μ), $L = 12$	3.7

Table 2. Results for learning of tangent vectors (ER [%], USPS, KD)

#references/class	$L = 0$	$L = 7$	$L = 12$	$L = 20$	derivative tangent vectors ($L = 7$)
1	18.6	6.4	5.5	5.5	11.8
≈700	5.5	3.8	3.9	3.7	3.7

rate to 2.4%This shows the effectivity of the tangent distance approach in combination with prior knowledge. Finally, using classifier combination, where different test results were combined using the sum rule, we obtained an error rate of 2.2%[9].

For our experiments on learning of variability, we used two different settings. First, we used a single Gaussian density, i.e. one reference per class, and varied the number of estimated tangents. As shown in Table 2, the error rate can be reduced from 18.6%to 5.5%with the estimation of tangent vectors from class specific covariance matrices as proposed above. Using only $L = 7$ tangent vectors, the result of 6.4%compares favorably to the use of the derivative, here with 11.8%error rate. This is probably due to the fact that the means of the single densities are the average of a large number of images and therefore very blurred, which is a disadvantage for the derivative tangent vectors. Here, the estimated tangent vectors outperform those based on the derivative.

Interestingly, when using all 7,291 training patterns in a kernel density based classifier, the result obtained without tangent model is the same as for a single density model with 12 estimated tangents. In this case, the single densities with estimated tangent subspace obtain the same result using about 50 times fewer parameters. In the second setting with about 700 references per class (KD), the error rate can be reduced to 3.7%for 20 estimated tangents. Fig. 3(a) shows the evolution of the error rate for different number of tangent vectors. Here, the tangent vectors were estimated using a local, class specific covariance matrix obtained from the set of local nearest neighbors for each training pattern. Therefore, the method is only applied to the one-sided tangent distance with tangents on the side of the reference. The obtained error rate is the same as for the derivative tangents, although somewhat higher for the same number of tangents. This shows that the presented method can be effectively used to learn the class specific variability on this dataset. Note that using the tangents on the side of the observations resp. on both sides, the obtained error rate is significantly lower (cf. Table 1).

Fig. 3(b) shows the error rate with respect to the subspace standard deviation γ for derivative tangents and estimated tangents using $L = 7$ each. It can be seen that, on this data, no significant improvement can be obtained by restricting the value of γ, while there may be improvements for other pattern recognition tasks.

So far we have not discussed the computational complexity of the tangent method. Due to the structure of the resulting model, the computational cost of the distance calculation is increased approximately by a factor of $(L + 1)$, in comparison with the baseline model that corresponds to the Euclidean distance.

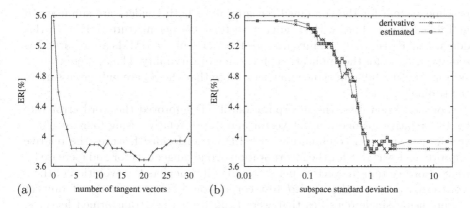

(a)   number of tangent vectors   (b)   subspace standard deviation

Fig. 3. (a) ER w.r.t. number of estimated tangents (USPS, KD). (b) ER w.r.t. subspace standard deviation γ for $L = 7$ derivative and estimated tangent vectors (USPS, KD).

4.2   Automatic Speech Recognition

Experiments for the domain of speech recognition were performed on the *SieTill* corpus [4] for telephone line recorded German continuous digit strings. The corpus consists of approximately 43k spoken digits in 13k sentences for both training and test set. In Table 3 some information on corpus statistics is summarized.

The recognition system is based on whole-word Hidden Markov Models (HMMs) using continuous emission densities. The baseline system is characterized as follows:

- vocabulary of 11 German digits including the pronunciation variant '*zwo*',
- gender-dependent whole-word HMMs, with every two subsequent states being identical,
- for each gender 214 distinct states plus one for silence,
- Gaussian mixture emission distributions,
- one globally pooled diagonal covariance matrix Σ,
- 12 cepstral features plus first derivatives and the second derivative of the first feature component.

The baseline recognizer applies maximum likelihood training using the Viterbi approximation in combination with an optional LDA. A detailed description of the baseline system can be found in [18]. The word error rates obtained with the

Table 3. Corpus statistics for the SieTill corpus.

corpus	female		male	
	sent.	digits	sent.	digits
test	6176	20205	6938	22881
train	6113	20115	6835	22463

baseline system for the combined recognition of both genders are summarized in Table 4 (in the lines with 0 tangent vectors (tv) per mixture (mix)). In this domain, all densities of the mixtures for the states of the HMMs are regarded as separate *classes* for the application of learning of variability. The S_k were trained as state specific full covariance matrices. Note that the S_k are only necessary in the training phase.

For single densities, the incorporation of TD improved the word error rate by 18.1%relative for one tangent vector and 21.6%relative using four tangent vectors per state. In combination with LDA transformed features the relative improvement was 13.8%for the incorporation of one tangent vector and increased to 28.6%for five tangent vectors per state. Fig. 4(a) depicts the evolution of the word error rates on the *SieTill* test corpus for different numbers of tangent vectors using single densities that were trained on LDA transformed features. For this setting the optimal choice for gender dependent trained references was five tangent vectors per state.

Using mixture densities, the performance gain in word error rate decreased but was still significant. Thus the relative improvement between the baseline result and tangent distance was 6.7%(16 densities plus one tangent vector per mixture) for untransformed features and 13.6%for LDA transformed features (16 dns/mix, 1 tv/mix). The same applies for the optimal number of tangent vectors which was found at one tangent vector per mixture. Consequently, a larger number of densities is able to partially compensate for the error that is made in the case that the covariance matrix is estimated using the conventional method. The best result was obtained using 128 densities per mixture in combination with LDA transformed features and the incorporation of one tangent vector per state. Using this setting, the word error rate decreased from 1.85% to 1.67%which is a relative improvement of 5%Fig. 4(b) depicts the evolution of word error rates for conventional training in comparison with TD using equal

Table 4. Word error rates (WER) and sentence error rates (SER) on the SieTill corpus obtained with the tangent distance. In column 'tv/mix' the number of used tangent vectors per mixture is given. A value of 0 means that the conventional Mahalanobis distance is used. 'dns/mix' gives the average number of densities per mixture.

without LDA					with LDA				
dns/mix	tv/mix	error rates [%]			dns/mix	tv/mix	error rates [%]		
		del - ins	WER	SER			del - ins	WER	SER
1	0	1.17-0.83	4.59	11.34	1	0	0.71-0.63	3.78	9.74
	1	1.17-0.52	3.76	9.22		1	0.97-0.49	3.26	8.46
	4	0.69-1.07	3.60	9.10		**5**	**0.48-0.88**	**2.70**	**7.18**
16	0	0.59-0.83	2.67	6.92	16	0	0.44-0.68	2.28	5.92
	1	0.54-0.58	2.49	6.56		1	0.58-0.40	1.97	5.06
	4	0.46-0.80	2.60	6.76		4	0.38-0.55	1.97	5.35
128	0	0.52-0.54	2.24	5.87	128	0	0.45-0.39	1.85	4.94
	1	0.50-0.48	2.12	5.75		**1**	**0.42-0.34**	**1.67**	**4.50**
	4	0.55-0.49	2.13	5.71		4	0.39-0.41	1.76	4.81

numbers of parameters. Even though the incorporation of tangent vectors into the Mahalanobis distance increases the number of parameters, the overall gain in performance justifies the higher expense.

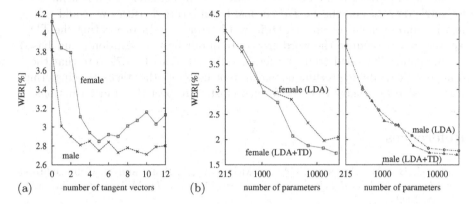

Fig. 4. (a) Word error rates as a function of the number of tangent vectors on the SieTill test corpus for single densities using ML training on LDA transformed features. (b) Comparison of WER for mixture densities on the SieTill test corpus using equal overall model parameter numbers.

5   Discussion and Conclusion

In this paper we presented an approach for modelling and learning variability for statistical pattern recognition, embedding tangent distance into a probabilistic framework. In contrast to principal component analysis based methods like [12] the model disregards the specific variability of the patterns when determining the distance or the log-likelihood, respectively, which leads to an incorporation of transformation tolerance and therefore improves the classification performance. This is due to the basic difference between the *distance in feature space* and the *distance from feature space*, which seems to be more appropriate for classification [11]. The presented model in its local version is adaptive to specific local variability and therefore similar to [7]. Note that the presented model assigns to the subspace components a weight γ that was found to be usually larger than the corresponding eigenvalue, which is a main difference to subspace approximations to the full covariance matrix based on eigenvalue decomposition like e.g. [10]. The overrepresentation of estimated variational subspace components may lead to an increased transformation tolerance. The new model proved to be very effective for pattern recognition, including the combination with globally operating feature transformations as the linear discriminant analysis. Thus, theoretical findings are supported by the experimental results. Comparative experiments were performed on the USPS corpus for image object recognition and on the *SieTill* corpus for continuous German digit strings for automatic speech recognition. On the USPS corpus, single density and kernel density error rates could be significantly improved, and the obtained results were well comparable to the use of tangents based on prior knowledge. Using the one-sided TD, a relative improvement in word error rate of approximately 20%was achieved for single densities on the *SieTill* corpus. For mixture densities we could gain a relative improvement of up to 13.6%in word error rate. Incorporating the TD we were able to reduce the word error rate of our best recognition result based on maximum likelihood trained references from 1.85%to 1 .67%Note that the probabilistic modelling technique may also be used for other tasks like clustering, where first results show that the formed clusters respect the transformations.

References

1. C. M. Bishop. Bayesian PCA. In M. Kearns, S. Solla, and D. Cohn, editors, *Advances in Neural Information Processing Systems 11*. MIT Press, pages 332–388, 1999.
2. J. Dahmen, D. Keysers, H. Ney, and M. O. Güld. Statistical Image Object Recognition using Mixture Densities. *Journal of Mathematical Imaging and Vision*, 14(3):285–296, May 2001.
3. R. O. Duda, P. E. Hart, and D. G. Stork. *Pattern Classification*. John Wiley & Sons, Inc., New York, 2nd edition, 2000.
4. T. Eisele, R. Haeb-Umbach, and D. Langmann. A comparative study of linear feature transformation techniques for automatic speech recognition. In *Proc. of Int. Conf. on Spoken Language Processing*, volume I, Philadelphia, PA, pages 252–255, Oct. 1996.
5. K. Fukunaga. *Introduction to Statistical Pattern Recognition*. Computer Science and Scientific Computing Academic Press Inc., San Diego, CA, 2nd edition, 1990.
6. T. Hastie and P. Simard. Metrics and Models for Handwritten Character Recognition. *Statistical Science*, 13(1):54–65, January 1998.
7. T. Hastie and R. Tibshirani. Discriminative Adaptive Nearest Neighbor Classification. *IEEE Transactions on Pattern Analysis and Machine Intelligence*, 18(6):607–616, June 1996.
8. D. Keysers, J. Dahmen, and H. Ney. A Probabilistic View on Tangent Distance. In *22. DAGM Symposium Mustererkennung 2000*, Springer, Kiel, Germany, pages 107–114, September 2000.
9. D. Keysers, J. Dahmen, T. Theiner, and H. Ney. Experiments with an Extended Tangent Distance. In *Proceedings 15th International Conference on Pattern Recognition*, volume 2, Barcelona, Spain, pages 38–42, September 2000.
10. P. Meinicke and H. Ritter. Local PCA Learning with Resolution-Dependent Mixtures of Gaussians. In *Proc. of ICANN'99, 9th Intl. Conf. on Artificial Neural Networks, Edinburgh, UK*, pages 497–502, September 1999.
11. B. Moghaddam and A. Pentland. Probabilistic Visual Learning for Object Representation. *IEEE Transactions on Pattern Analysis and Machine Intelligence*, 19(7):696–710, July 1997.
12. T. R. Payne and P. Edwards. Dimensionality Reduction through Sub-space Mapping for Nearest Neighbor Algorithms. In *Proceedings ECML 2000, 11th European Conference on Machine Learning*, volume 1810 of *Lecture Notes in Artificial Intelligence*, Springer, Barcelona, Spain, pages 331–343, May 2000.

13. B. Schölkopf, P. Simard, A. Smola, and V. Vapnik. Prior Knowledge in Support Vector Kernels. In M. I. Jordan, M. J. Kearns, and S. A. Solla, editors, *Advances in Neural Inf. Proc. Systems*, volume 10. MIT Press, pages 640–646, 1998.
14. P. Simard, Y. Le Cun, J. Denker, and B. Victorri. Transformation Invariance in Pattern Recognition — Tangent Distance and Tangent Propagation. In G. Orr and K.-R. Müller, editors, *Neural networks: tricks of the trade*, volume 1524 of *Lecture Notes in Computer Science*, Springer, Heidelberg, pages 239–274, 1998.
15. P. Simard, Y. Le Cun, and J. Denker. Efficient Pattern Recognition Using a New Transformation Distance. In S. Hanson, J. Cowan, and C. Giles, editors, *Advances in Neural Inf. Proc. Systems*, volume 5, Morgan Kaufmann, San Mateo CA, pages 50–58, 1993.
16. P. Simard, Y. Le Cun, J. Denker, and B. Victorri. An Efficient Algorithm for Learning Invariances in Adaptive Classifiers. In *Proceedings 11th International Conference on Pattern Recognition*, The Hague, The Netherlands, pages 651–655, August 1992.
17. M. E. Tipping. The Relevance Vector Machine. In S. Solla, T. Leen, and K. Müller, editors, *Advances in Neural Information Processing Systems 12*. MIT Press, pages 332–388, 2000.
18. L. Welling, H. Ney, A. Eiden, and C. Forbrig. Connected Digit Recognition using Statistical Template Matching. In *1995 Europ. Conf. on Speech Communication and Technology*, volume 2, Madrid, Spain, pages 1483–1486, Sept. 1995.
19. J. Wood. Invariant Pattern Recognition: A Review. *Pattern Recognition*, 29(1):1–17, January 1996.

The Evaluation of Predictive Learners: Some Theoretical and Empirical Results

Kevin B. Korb, Lucas R. Hope, and Michelle J. Hughes

School of Computer Science and Software Engineering
Monash University, VIC 3800, Australia,
{korb,lhope,mjh}@csse.monash.edu.au,

Abstract. With the growth of interest in data mining, there has been increasing interest in applying machine learning algorithms to real-world problems. This raises the question of how to evaluate the performance of machine learning algorithms. The standard procedure performs random sampling of predictive accuracy until a statistically significant difference arises between competing algorithms. That procedure fails to take into account the *calibration* of predictions. An alternative procedure uses an information reward measure (from I.J. Good) which is sensitive both to domain knowledge (predictive accuracy) and calibration. We analyze this measure, relating it to Kullback-Leibler distance. We also apply it to five well-known machine learning algorithms across a variety of problems, demonstrating some variations in their assessments using accuracy vs. information reward. We also look experimentally at information reward as a function of calibration and accuracy.

Keywords: Evaluation, information reward, predictive accuracy, scoring rules, machine learning, Kullback-Leibler distance.

1 Introduction

With the growing accessibility of computational power and accumulation of data in large databases, machine learning is rapidly becoming a central concern for both academia and industry, as the growing interest in applying machine learning to data mining demonstrates. A difficult and important meta-question has yet to be answered satisfactorily: how do we decide whether one machine learning algorithm is superior to another?The standard practice has been to take some collection of samples in the domain of interest, select some random subset as training cases to which the machine learning algorithm is applied and run the representation thus learned on the test cases remaining, using the resultant estimate of predictive accuracy as the index of success for the algorithm. This is not a bad practice, particularly once the standards of statistical inference were attended to and, especially, sample sizes were increased, allowing for the calculation of a sensible estimate of the standard deviation in predictive accuracy.

Nevertheless, there are a number of likely objections to this use of predictive accuracy for assessment. Orthodox statistical practices, and in particular the

L. De Raedt and P. Flach (Eds.): ECML 2001, LNAI 2167, pp. 276–287, 2001.
© Springer-Verlag Berlin Heidelberg 2001

significance testing which this practice relies upon, are beset with foundational difficulties. For example, it is easy to find circumstances in which the finding of a significant result leading to the rejection of the null hypothesis, per Jerzy Neyman results in an   *increased* posterior probability that the null hypothesis is true. Or, again, one can derive 95% classical confidence interval estimates (equivalent to significance tests under a transformation) which have a probability of *zero* of capturing the population parameter of interest [Leslie, 1998]. These sorts of objections are commonly advanced by Bayesians and, if taken seriously, should lead to reform in the selection and use of statistical inference techniques.

But there is an even more telling, even compelling, objection to the standard practice of assessment by predictive accuracy. Predictive accuracy entirely disregards the confidence of the prediction. In binomial classification, for example, a prediction of a mushroom's edibility with a probability of 0.51 counts exactly the same as a prediction of edibility with a probability of 1.0. Now, if *we* were confronted with the first prediction, we might rationally hesitate to consume such a mushroom. The predictive accuracy measurement does not hesitate. According to standard evaluation practice in machine learning and data mining every prediction is as good as every other. Any business, or animal, which behaved this way would have a very short life span.

The typical Bayesian approach to prediction is to calculate the expected value of a classification, which explicitly incorporates the probability given to a class. Indeed, Bayesianism typically goes further than to hesitate concerning a predicted class, it even hesitates about the model used to classify; that is, the ideal Bayesian approach is to compute a posterior distribution over the entire model space, and then to combine the individual predictions of the models, weighting them according to their posteriors. This mixed prediction will typically provide better predictions than those of any of the individual models, including that one with the highest posterior probability. This is the hard-core Bayesian method, as advocated, for example, by Richard Jeffrey [Jeffrey, 1983]. But there are many situations where this ideal method is unavailable. It is in many (or most) inductive environments computationally intractable, requiring joint probability distributions over all variables in the model space, extending to any hypotheses in other domains that may be found to be relevant. More typical of actual scientific practice is that we come to believe a particular scientific theory, which is then applied *individually* to make predictions or to guide interventions in related domains. So, in machine learning, a possible compromise approach to evaluating machine learners would be to take the posterior probabilities of individual hypotheses put forward by the machine learners as guidance as to which algorithm is the best. Of course, if one of the machine algorithms under consideration is Bayesian, then this Bayesian assessment will always favor it. So, it would be useful to have some evaluation metric for the predictive success of learning algorithms which does not simply assume Bayesianism, as Bayesian principles are in part what is at stake in the methodology of machine learning.

A good starting point for such an alternative is the concept of Kllback-Leibler distance. This measures the distance"between two probability distributions $p(\cdot)$ and $q(\cdot)$, according to the formula [Cover and Thomas, 1991]:

$$KL(p,q) = \sum_{x \in X} p(x) \log \frac{p(x)}{q(x)} = E_p \log \frac{p(x)}{q(x)} \qquad (1)$$

This measure records the distance from p to q, from the point of view"of p. When p and q are *identical*, the K distance is zero; as they diverge, the K distance may tend towards infinity. This is the right measure when there is a preferred point of view"–when the true probability distribution is known, and if that is p in equation (1), then K distance reports how close a learned distribution q is to the generating distribution. This provides a performance measure for machine learning algorithms that increases monotonically as the learned distribution diverges from the truth. Also, being based strictly upon the output distribution of a machine learning algorithm, it is invariant to the internal properties of the algorithm itself, including the complexity of the representations used, as is appropriate since such a performance measure is not attempting to assess the probability of those representations directly. The drawback to K distance is simply that when assessing algorithms in the real world, the true model is necessarily unknown. We would like a performance measure with similar properties, but which does not depend on prior knowledge of the truth.

2   Knowledge and Meta-knowledge

There are two fundamental ingredients to predictive success: knowledge of the system whose behavior is being predicted and knowledge of the limits of that knowledge. With the former comes a greater ability to predict target states; with the latter comes an improved ability to assess the probability that those predictions are in error. These two are not in a trade-off relationship: they can be jointly maximized. Given fixed domain knowledge, it is a theorem that to maximize betting reward, one must calibrate the oddsover- or under-estimating them guarantees (in the long run) suboptimal performance ([Cover and Thomas, 1991], chapter 6).[1] And, as [Ramsey, 1931] argued effectively, betting is a pertinent metaphor for every kind of decision making under uncertainty, including the prediction tasks to which machine learners might be put.

Orthodox machine learning assessment of accuracy for classification tasks simply sums up all the test cases classified correctly and divides by the total number of cases. Clearly, using such a metric, it does not pay to withhold classification, for that guarantees a failure to classify correctly, which is all that is being rewarded here. In general, it does not pay to express any doubts whatsoever about one's classifications: given that a probability of a target class is greater than 0.5 (in the binomial case) one should always act as if the probability is 1.

---

[1] In philosophy this is recognized in David Lewis's "Principal Principle", which asserts that one's subjective probability for an event, conditioned upon the knowledge of a physical probability of that event, should equal the latter [Lewis, 1980].

As noted above, such behavior applied to ordinary tasks of an agent trying to get around in the world would lead to rapid extinction. This metric ignores the costs of misclassification and the rewards of correct classification, as some AI researchers have begun pointing out (e.g., [Turney, 1995,Provost et al., 1998]; also see the earlier [Pearl, 1978]). A more appropriate metric, therefore, would be a sample estimate of the expected value of the classification, that is, something like:

$$\frac{\text{reward} \times s + \text{penalty} \times (n - s)}{n} \tag{2}$$

where n is the number of test items, s the number of correct predictions and reward and penalty the rewards for correct and incorrect predictions respectively. Such a metric (or more complex relatives) we think to be correct, whenever applicable. Unfortunately, they are often not applicable. In general, in science one cannot well anticipate the uses to which scientific inferences will be put, and so one cannot know the values associated with correct or incorrect conclusions. This holds also for evaluating machine learning and data mining techniques: the number and range of applications is entirely open ended, and so too therefore are the rewards and penalties. We need a metric which somehow produces results consistent with "normal"values for penalties and rewards.

3   The Information Reward

We suggest a proper such metric for assessing machine learning algorithms is simply how well those algorithms would perform in guiding the betting behavior of agents located in the domain or world of interest. In other words, if the learning algorithm can consistently beat its competitors when betting on domain events, then it is superior to its competitors (within that domain). This is an ability which the orthodox measure of predictive accuracy fails to assess.[2]

Lacking an exact characterization of costs and rewards available for incorrect and correct classifications, we use the information-theoretic reward [Good, 1952,Dowe et al., 1996]: reward $= \sum_i [1 + \log_2 P(X_i)]$ where i indexes the test cases, X_i is the actual class of the ith test case and $P(X_i)$ is the probability of that event asserted by the learner.[3] This function demonstrably has the two properties we require of our metric. First, given perfect calibration, the reward is monotonic to domain knowledge, with the limit of 1 bit"for each classification known with certainty and 0 bits for complete ignorance in the binomial classification task (i.e., $P(X_i) = 0.5$). This reward is one minus the length of a message conveying the actual event in a language efficient for agents with

---

[2] [Kononenko and Bratko, 1991] also criticize the use of predictive accuracy as a comparative scoring function, and provide an information based scoring function which explicitly takes prior probabilities of classes into account. Their work will be dealt with in a more comprehensive paper.

[3] For multinomial classification we used the above equation for successful classifications; for misclassifications we treated all the non-selected classes as a contrast class (i.e., grouping them into one class) — i.e., $1 + \log_2(1 - P(X_i))$.

the learners beliefs (i.e., a language that minimizes entropy for them). [4] Second, given fixed domain knowledge, it is maximized by perfect calibration. Taking the binomial case for simplicity, let c be the physical probability (chance) that some test case is in the target class and p the probability estimated by the machine learner. Then the expected reward function is:

$$[1 + \log_2 p]c + [1 + \log_2(1 - p)](1 - c)$$

To find the maximum we take the derivative with respect to p and set it to zero:

$$
\begin{aligned}
0 &= \frac{d}{dp}\left([1 + \log_2 p]c + [1 + \log_2(1 - p)](1 - c)\right) \\
&= \frac{c}{p} + \frac{1 - c}{1 - p}\frac{d}{dp}(1 - p) \\
&= \frac{c}{p} - \frac{1 - c}{1 - p} \\
c &= p
\end{aligned}
$$

which last equation reports that perfect calibration maximizes reward.

4   A Calibration Measure

The information reward measures domain knowledge and meta-knowledge (calibration) jointly. It would be useful to be able to tease these apart: if we can measure calibration directly, then by comparison with the information reward we can measure domain knowledge indirectly; also, we can use calibration measures to improve performance by recalibrating our prediction probabilities. Calibration has been measured by cognitive psychologists investigating how human cognition deviates from the ideal [Lichtenstein et al., 1977]. The basic idea is to measure how much the probability estimate of the agent deviates from the frequency of truth of events estimated at each particular level. Thus, if the agent gets right 70% of events that the agent accords a probability of 0.9, then the agent is overconfident at least, of events which are given that probability (such overconfidence, by the way, is typical of non-expert humans[Lichtenstein et al., 1977]). A measure of miscalibration suggested by this is:

$$\text{miscalibration} = \sqrt{\sum_{i \in I}\sum_{j \in J}\frac{(\frac{\sum_k f_{ik}}{n_i} - p_{ij})^2}{n_i - 1}} \tag{3}$$

where I partitions the range of probabilistic predictions from 0 to 1, so we are summing over the partition cells; J and K index the predictions within each

---

[4] Note that such a message is infinite if it is attempting to communicate an event that has been deemed to be impossible, that is, to have probability zero.

partition cell.[5] What we sum is the average of the squared deviations of the prediction probabilities (p_{ij}) from the average frequency of truth within each cell (so f_{ij} is 1 or 0 depending upon whether that particular prediction was correct or not).[6]

5   Results

For this study we tested five well-known machine learning algorithms, using the same datasets employed by [Holte, 1993]:

- **C4.5** [Quinlan, 1993]: This learns pruned classification trees; the leaves have associated probability distributions over classes.
- **MML classification trees** [Wallace and Patrick, 1993]: This uses MML (Minimum Message Length [Wallace and Boulton, 1968]) to learn classification trees, with probabilities.
- **MML classification graphs** [Oliver, 1993]: This uses MML to learn classification graphs, with branches that may split or join (making disjunctive concepts easier to learn); leaves have associated classification probabilities.
- **Holte's decision stumps** [Holte, 1993]: Robert Holte demonstrated that classification trees with only a single internal node (i.e., with classification based only on a single attribute) can achieve predictive accuracies comparable over many data sets to those of C4.5, which usually learns far more complex representations.
- **Naive Bayes:** Instead of splitting on a single attribute these simple models split on class membership, with the leaves representing the different available attributes. The models are "naive" because they assume that the attributes, given knowledge of class membership, are independent of each other. Observed attribute values are filled in and a simple Bayesian net propagation provides a posterior probability of class membership. We implemented the algorithm as described in [Mitchell, 1997].[7]

Each algorithm was applied to each dataset, with two-thirds of the data randomly allocated as training data and one-third for testing. Each such test was repeated 25 times to obtain the 95% confidence intervals shown in Tables 1, 2 and 3.

In assessing the information reward for each algorithm we require a probability associated with each predicted class. In the case of the MML algorithms, predicting probabilities is an integral aspect of their operation. For C4.5, leaf nodes have probabilities associated with classes internally (called "class weights"); we

---

[5] In our experimental work below we divided the range of probabilities into cells so that each cell was guaranteed to contain at least 10 sample points and as few as possible above that number.

[6] This measure does not distinguish between over- and under-confidence, but can easily be adjusted to do so.

[7] Our results for Naive Bayes (Table 1) are comparable with other experimental reports (e.g., [Domingos and Pazzani 1996]).

modified the source code to externalize those probabilities. For Naive Bayes and decision stumps, we used the frequency associated with the predicted class amongst training set items classified to the appropriate node. Since the information reward can penalize wrong predictions without limit –for example, probabilities of 0 and 1 correspond to offering infinite odds, and so when wrong are penalized infinitely –we applied a cutoff to extreme probability estimates supported by MML theory [Dowe, 2000], enforcing the range:

$$\left[\frac{(1/2)}{(n+1)}, \frac{(n+1/2)}{(n+1)} \right]$$

where n is the sample size.

Table 1. Predictive accuracy results ($\pm$ 1.96 standard deviations). Boldface indicates statistically significant differences for high results (relative to non-boldface results).

Data set	C4.5	MML Tree	MML Graph	Naive Bayes	DStump
BC	0.700 ± 0.079	0.685 ± 0.085	0.698 ± 0.064	0.706 ± 0.062	0.682 ± 0.055
CH	$\mathbf{0.992 \pm 0.007}$	$\mathbf{0.989 \pm 0.009}$	$\mathbf{0.984 \pm 0.014}$	0.704 ± 0.062	0.676 ± 0.020
GL	0.663 ± 0.112	0.623 ± 0.142	0.607 ± 0.137	0.626 ± 0.098	0.558 ± 0.134
G2	0.772 ± 0.120	0.742 ± 0.094	0.737 ± 0.129	0.780 ± 0.139	0.711 ± 0.110
HD	0.759 ± 0.086	0.615 ± 0.083	0.628 ± 0.060	0.808 ± 0.084	0.732 ± 0.059
HE	0.802 ± 0.135	0.796 ± 0.072	0.782 ± 0.060	0.809 ± 0.097	0.812 ± 0.091
HO	0.858 ± 0.052	0.857 ± 0.064	0.853 ± 0.063	0.807 ± 0.070	0.817 ± 0.063
HY	$\mathbf{0.992 \pm 0.006}$	$\mathbf{0.993 \pm 0.004}$	$\mathbf{0.992 \pm 0.005}$	0.951 ± 0.007	0.972 ± 0.006
IR	0.935 ± 0.065	0.942 ± 0.049	0.943 ± 0.065	0.896 ± 0.089	0.875 ± 0.075
LA	0.773 ± 0.226	0.629 ± 0.170	0.663 ± 0.193	0.848 ± 0.150	0.796 ± 0.120
LY	0.781 ± 0.089	0.718 ± 0.137	0.691 ± 0.109	0.782 ± 0.119	0.733 ± 0.113
MU	$\mathbf{1.000 \pm 0.000}$	$\mathbf{1.000 \pm 0.000}$	$\mathbf{1.000 \pm 0.000}$	0.910 ± 0.010	0.986 ± 0.004
SE	$\mathbf{0.978 \pm 0.007}$	$\mathbf{0.978 \pm 0.008}$	$\mathbf{0.977 \pm 0.009}$	0.909 ± 0.014	0.902 ± 0.015
SO	0.975 ± 0.087	0.988 ± 0.050	0.975 ± 0.128	0.960 ± 0.212	0.777 ± 0.166
VO	$\mathbf{0.961 \pm 0.030}$	$\mathbf{0.954 \pm 0.025}$	$\mathbf{0.953 \pm 0.036}$	0.889 ± 0.037	$\mathbf{0.956 \pm 0.022}$
V1	0.890 ± 0.049	0.881 ± 0.040	0.871 ± 0.044	0.869 ± 0.052	0.874 ± 0.053

In general, information reward follows predictive accuracy fairly closely. Since information reward is a partial function of accuracy, this is unsurprising. But we would expect information reward to diverge significantly from the assessment of predictive accuracy when the calibration differs substantially between learners. And, in these results we see exactly that in a number of cases. For example, C4.5 performs well in predictive accuracy on the glass data (GL; Table 1); however, its information reward for GL is clearly the worst (despite high variance; Table 2), which is explained by its high miscalibration rating.

The pattern of correlations between the three variables is striking: predictive accuracy is fairly strongly negatively correlated with miscalibration (Table 6); predictive accuracy is even more strongly positively correlated with information reward (Table 4); and miscalibration is negatively correlated with information reward (Table 5). This pattern is consistent with our interpretation above of information reward.

Table 2. Average information reward ($\pm$ 1.96 standard deviations). Boldface indicates statistically significant differences for high results (relative to non-boldface results).

Data set	C4.5	MML Tree	MML Graph	Naive Bayes	DStump
BC	0.016 ± 0.269	0.131 ± 0.173	0.157 ± 0.098	0.136 ± 0.194	0.095 ± 0.167
CH	$\mathbf{0.945 \pm 0.051}$	$\mathbf{0.930 \pm 0.044}$	$\mathbf{0.946 \pm 0.035}$	0.200 ± 0.036	0.097 ± 0.025
GL	-0.809 ± 0.859	0.034 ± 0.181	0.018 ± 0.174	0.147 ± 0.086	-0.058 ± 0.214
G2	-0.206 ± 0.827	0.096 ± 0.343	0.128 ± 0.261	0.321 ± 0.194	-0.095 ± 0.401
HD	-0.215 ± 0.457	0.059 ± 0.088	0.062 ± 0.077	0.409 ± 0.171	0.122 ± 0.127
HE	0.180 ± 0.452	0.307 ± 0.152	0.283 ± 0.184	0.297 ± 0.412	0.244 ± 0.341
HO	0.374 ± 0.209	0.403 ± 0.160	0.403 ± 0.134	0.325 ± 0.178	0.329 ± 0.151
HY	$\mathbf{0.933 \pm 0.060}$	$\mathbf{0.948 \pm 0.027}$	$\mathbf{0.942 \pm 0.031}$	0.526 ± 0.084	$\mathbf{0.890 \pm 0.060}$
IR	0.604 ± 0.443	0.678 ± 0.213	0.659 ± 0.352	0.378 ± 0.090	0.593 ± 0.165
LA	0.086 ± 0.543	0.020 ± 0.201	0.042 ± 0.157	0.591 ± 0.395	0.185 ± 0.569
LY	-0.047 ± 0.485	0.132 ± 0.188	0.092 ± 0.144	0.331 ± 0.229	0.230 ± 0.208
MU	$\mathbf{1.000 \pm 0.000}$	$\mathbf{1.000 \pm 0.000}$	0.999 ± 0.011	0.636 ± 0.038	0.908 ± 0.018
SE	$\mathbf{0.849 \pm 0.051}$	$\mathbf{0.874 \pm 0.037}$	$\mathbf{0.868 \pm 0.031}$	0.025 ± 0.174	$\mathbf{0.586 \pm 0.237}$
SO	0.828 ± 0.518	0.903 ± 0.299	0.865 ± 0.448	0.721 ± 0.315	0.496 ± 0.339
VO	0.809 ± 0.106	0.784 ± 0.097	0.766 ± 0.159	0.587 ± 0.136	0.764 ± 0.116
V1	0.528 ± 0.226	0.536 ± 0.134	0.530 ± 0.117	0.518 ± 0.173	0.459 ± 0.167

Table 3. Miscalibration results ($\pm$ 1.96 standard deviations). Boldface indicates statistically significant differences for high results (relative to non-boldface results)

Data set	C4.5	MML Tree	MML Graph	Naive Bayes	DStump
BC	0.562 ± 0.277	0.516 ± 0.274	0.475 ± 0.232	0.571 ± 0.276	$\mathbf{1.176 \pm 0.239}$
CH	0.309 ± 0.215	0.383 ± 0.159	0.411 ± 0.299	2.155 ± 0.236	$\mathbf{4.925 \pm 0.099}$
GL	0.855 ± 0.281	0.472 ± 0.279	0.505 ± 0.302	0.437 ± 0.245	0.678 ± 0.284
G2	0.461 ± 0.299	0.363 ± 0.266	0.359 ± 0.311	0.312 ± 0.170	0.451 ± 0.248
HD	0.717 ± 0.326	0.549 ± 0.244	0.512 ± 0.206	0.412 ± 0.204	0.501 ± 0.176
HE	0.412 ± 0.258	0.290 ± 0.161	0.299 ± 0.156	0.471 ± 0.348	0.355 ± 0.204
HO	0.446 ± 0.149	0.432 ± 0.165	0.428 ± 0.207	0.462 ± 0.211	0.497 ± 0.133
HY	0.326 ± 0.244	0.301 ± 0.134	0.317 ± 0.119	$\mathbf{1.732 \pm 0.266}$	0.789 ± 0.271
IR	0.204 ± 0.184	0.192 ± 0.114	0.187 ± 0.140	$\mathbf{0.572 \pm 0.190}$	$\mathbf{0.531 \pm 0.302}$
LA	0.157 ± 0.159	0.093 ± 0.183	0.124 ± 0.166	0.155 ± 0.059	0.157 ± 0.111
LY	0.489 ± 0.219	0.392 ± 0.232	0.368 ± 0.183	0.329 ± 0.185	0.354 ± 0.167
MU	0.000 ± 0.000	0.002 ± 0.002	0.013 ± 0.116	$\mathbf{2.386 \pm 0.312}$	1.070 ± 0.223
SE	0.551 ± 0.165	0.528 ± 0.147	0.515 ± 0.190	$\mathbf{1.835 \pm 0.252}$	$\mathbf{1.881 \pm 0.514}$
SO	0.026 ± 0.089	0.016 ± 0.043	0.026 ± 0.103	0.181 ± 0.102	0.213 ± 0.089
VO	0.262 ± 0.177	0.284 ± 0.201	0.321 ± 0.165	0.507 ± 0.229	0.268 ± 0.118
V1	0.408 ± 0.227	0.448 ± 0.200	0.427 ± 0.185	0.515 ± 0.277	0.459 ± 0.199

The results of testing information reward are unlikely to revolutionize data mining practice. However, they can tell an importantly different story from that of accuracy measures alone. For example, both Naive Bayes and decision stumps have received much publicity in recent years as techniques which are effective on many problems while being supremely simple. The results here show that they are both much more poorly calibrated than the more sophisticated methods they might replace and so that they are worse performers than many had thought.

Table 4. Correlations between information reward and predictive accuracy. (NaN (not a number) occurs because one of the datasets for correlation consists entirely of 1's.)

Data set	C4.5	MML Tree	MML Graph	Naive Bayes	DStump
BC	0.410	0.810	0.689	0.865	0.434
CH	0.902	0.834	0.703	0.960	0.930
GL	0.711	0.388	0.558	0.499	0.308
G2	0.823	0.594	0.868	0.960	0.477
HD	0.659	0.868	0.554	0.910	0.893
HE	0.879	0.605	0.689	0.901	0.648
HO	0.855	0.928	0.905	0.878	0.899
HY	0.939	0.867	0.872	0.988	0.638
IR	0.955	0.879	0.916	0.518	0.957
LA	0.725	0.928	0.833	0.880	0.538
LY	0.658	0.789	0.730	0.817	0.715
MU	NaN	NaN	1.000	0.881	0.998
SE	0.756	0.916	0.822	0.990	0.226
SO	1.000	1.000	0.948	0.937	0.803
VO	0.791	0.772	0.766	0.746	0.905
V1	0.814	0.603	0.708	0.895	0.787

Table 5. Correlations between information reward and miscalibration.

Data set	C4.5	MML Tree	MML Graph	Naive Bayes	DStump
BC	−0.602	−0.664	−0.087	−0.762	0.231
CH	−0.800	−0.417	−0.701	0.405	−0.893
GL	−0.892	−0.788	−0.736	0.398	−0.492
G2	−0.932	−0.712	−0.734	−0.253	−0.610
HD	−0.827	−0.479	−0.152	−0.546	−0.261
HE	−0.725	−0.191	−0.266	−0.833	−0.646
HO	−0.487	−0.565	−0.520	−0.462	−0.384
HY	−0.855	−0.648	−0.394	−0.559	0.201
IR	−0.929	−0.634	−0.761	0.052	−0.988
LA	−0.750	−0.667	−0.198	−0.774	−0.468
LY	−0.746	−0.239	−0.285	−0.046	−0.244
MU	NaN	−0.639	−0.999	−0.755	−0.914
SE	−0.591	−0.631	−0.575	−0.781	0.638
SO	−1.000	−0.998	−0.957	−0.851	−0.702
VO	−0.631	−0.110	−0.447	−0.696	−0.347
V1	−0.616	−0.297	−0.567	−0.680	−0.635

Table 6. Correlations between predictive accuracy and miscalibration.

Data set	C4.5	MML Tree	MML Graph	Naive Bayes	DStump
BC	0.606	−0.631	−0.326	−0.878	−0.330
CH	−0.940	−0.455	−0.752	0.491	−0.838
GL	−0.829	−0.588	−0.551	0.293	−0.035
G2	−0.838	−0.545	−0.562	−0.344	−0.692
HD	−0.834	−0.519	−0.344	−0.447	−0.269
HE	−0.710	0.412	0.016	−0.946	−0.647
HO	−0.235	−0.497	−0.499	−0.287	−0.228
HY	−0.805	−0.488	−0.495	−0.622	0.086
IR	−0.882	−0.400	−0.703	0.834	−0.955
LA	−0.797	−0.351	0.345	−0.817	−0.518
LY	−0.461	−0.127	−0.211	0.107	−0.102
MU	NaN	NaN	−1.000	−0.682	−0.911
SE	−0.642	−0.598	−0.741	−0.811	−0.005
SO	−1.000	−0.998	−0.999	−0.644	−0.815
VO	−0.807	0.419	−0.581	−0.656	−0.397
V1	−0.789	−0.350	−0.534	−0.866	−0.738

Table 7. Properties of the datasets employed.

Dataset	Training set size	Test set size	Attributes	Classes
BC	190	96	9	2
CH	2130	1066	36	2
GL	142	72	9	6
G2	108	55	9	2
HD	202	101	13	2
HE	103	52	19	2
HO	245	123	22	2
HY	2108	1055	25	2
IR	100	50	4	3
LA	38	19	16	2
LY	98	50	18	4
MU	5416	2708	22	2
SE	2108	1055	25	2
SO	31	16	35	4
VO	290	145	16	2
V1	290	145	15	2

6   Conclusion

Information reward provides an effective, general-purpose performance measure for machine learning algorithms. It combines measures of domain understanding and calibration, and it provides means for these two to be analyzed separately and together. In future work we will compare information reward with ROC and lift curves, which provide another popular evaluation method. We will also look at using feedback on calibration (over- and under-confidence) to improve performance in incremental learning tasks.

Acknowledgement. We acknowledge the Monash Data Mining Centre for assisting with the experimental work reported here. Thanks to Richard McConachy for useful comments.

References

[Brier, 1950] Brier, G.W. (1950). Verification of forecasts expressed in terms of probability. *Monthly Weather Review, 78*, 1-3.

[Cover and Thomas, 1991] Cover, T.M. and Thomas, J.A. (1991). *Elements of information theory.* New York: Wiley.

[Domingos and Pazzani 1996] Domingos, P. and Pazzani, M. (1996). Beyond independence: Conditions for the optimality of the simple bayesian classifier. In *Proceedings of the Thirteenth International Conference on Machine Learning*, (pp. 105–112), Bari, Italy. Morgan Kaufmann.

[Dowe et al., 1996] Dowe, D.L., Farr, G.E., Hurst, A.J. and Lentin, K.L. (1996). Information-theoretic football tipping. *Technical Report 96/297*, Dept. of Computer Science, Monash University.

[Dowe, 2000] Dowe, D.L. (2000). *Learning and prediction notes.* School of Computer Science and Software Engineering, Monash University.

[Good, 1952] Good, I.J. (1952). Rational decisions. *Jrn. of the Royal Statistical Society, B, 14*, 107-114. Reprinted in *Good thinking: The foundations of probability and its applications*, Minnesota, 1983.

[Griffen and Tversky, 1992] Griffen, D., and Tversky, A. (1992). The weighing of evidence and the determinants of confidence. *Cognitive Psychology, 24*, 411-435.

[Holte, 1993] Holte, R. C., (1993). Very simple classification rules perform well on most commonly used datasets. *Machine Learning, 11*, 63-91.

[Jeffrey, 1983] Jeffrey, R. (1983). *The logic of decision*, 2nd ed. New York: McGraw-Hill.

[Kononenko and Bratko, 1991] Kononenko, I., and Bratko, I. (1991). Information-based evaluation criterion for classifier's performance. *Machine Learning, 6*, 67-80.

[Leslie, 1998] Leslie, C. (1998). *Lack of confidence.* MA Thesis, Department of History and Philosophy of Science, University of Melbourne.

[Lewis, 1980] Lewis, D. (1980). A subjectivist's guide to objective chance. In Jeffrey (Ed.) *Studies in inductive logic and probability, vol II* (pp. 263-293). Univ of California.

[Lichtenstein et al., 1977] Lichtenstein, S., Fischhoff, B., and Phillips, L.D. (1977). Calibration of probabilities: The state of the art. In H. Jungermann and G. de Zeeuw (Eds.), *Decision making and change in human affairs* (pp. 275-324). Dordrecht: Reidel.

[Matheson and Winkler, 1976] Matheson, J.E., and Winkler, R. L. (1976). Scoring rules for continuous probability distributions. *Management Science, 22.*

[McClelland and Bolger, 1994] McClelland, A. G. R., and Bolger, F. (1994). The calibration of subjective probabilities: Theories and models, 1980-1994. In G. Wright and P. Ayton (Eds.)*Subjective probability,* Wiley.

[Mitchell, 1997] Mitchell, T. (1997]). *Machine learning.* McGraw-Hill.

[Morgan and Henrion, 1990] Morgan, M. G., and Henrion, M. (1990). *Uncertainty: A guide to dealing with uncertainty in quantitative risk and policy analysis.* Cambridge University.

[Murphy and Winkler, 1984] Murphy, A. H., and Winkler, R. L. (1984). The probability of precipitation forecasts. *Journal of the American Statistical Association, 79,* 391-400.

[Oliver, 1993] Oliver, J. (1993). Decision graphs - an extension of decision trees. *Fourth Int. Conf. Artificial Intelligence and Statistics,* pp. 343-350

[Pearl, 1978] Pearl, J. (1978). An economic basis for certain methods of evaluating probabilistic forecasts. *International Journal of Man-Machine Studies, 10,* 175-183.

[Provost et al., 1998] Provost, F., Fawcett, T. and Kohavi, R. (1998). The case against accuracy estimation for comparing induction algorithms. *International Conference on Machine Learning, 1998,* Morgan Kaufmann.

[Quinlan, 1993] Quinlan, J. R. (1993). *C4.5: programs for machine learning.* Morgan Kaufmann.

[Ramsey, 1931] Ramsey, F.P. (1931). *The foundations of mathematics and other logical essays,* edited by R.B. Braithwaite. New York: Humanities Press.

[Savage, 1971] Savage, L.J. (1971). Elicitation of personal probabilities and expectations. *Journal of the American Statistical Association, 66.*

[Turney, 1995] Turney, P. (1995). Cost-sensitive classification: Empirical evaluation of a hybrid genetic decision tree induction algorithm. *Journal of Artificial Intelligence Research,* 369-409.

[Wallace and Boulton, 1968] Wallace, C.S., and Boulton, D.M. (1968). An information measure for classification. *The Computer Journal, 11,* 185-194.

[Wallace and Patrick, 1993] Wallace, C.S., and Patrick, J. D. (1993). Coding decision trees. *Machine Learning, 11,* 7-22.

An Evolutionary Algorithm for Cost-Sensitive Decision Rule Learning

Wojciech Kȩdlo and Marek Kȩtowski

Institute of Computer Science, Technical University of Białystok
Wiejska 45a, 15-351 Białystok, Poland
e-mail: {wkwedlo, mkret}@ii.pb.bialystok.pl
http://aragorn.pb.bialystok.pl/~{wkwedlo, mkret}

Abstract. Most of classification learning methods aim at the reduction of the number of errors. However, in many real-life applications it is misclassification cost, which should be minimized. In the paper we propose a new method for cost-sensitive learning of decision rules from datasets. Our approach consists in modifying the existing system EDRL-MD (Evolutionary Decision Rule Learner with Multivariate Discretization). EDRL-MD learns decision rules using an evolutionary algorithm (EA). We propose a new fitness function, which allows the algorithm to minimize misclassification cost rather than the number of classification errors. The remaining components of EA i.e., the representation of solutions and the genetic search operators are not changed. The performance of our method is compared to that of C5.0 learning system. The results show, that the modified EDRL-MD is able to effectively process datasets with non-equal error costs.

1 Introduction

Classification is one of the most important tasks in machine learning and data mining. There exist many effective methods for building classifiers [16], but in most cases the goal is to minimize the number of prediction errors. However, in many practical applications the assumption that all errors are equally important is invalid. For example, in medical domain misclassifying an ill patient as a healthy one is usually much more harmful than treating a healthy patient as an ill one and sending him for additional examinations. In database marketing the cost of mailing to a non-respondent is very small, but the cost of not mailing to someone who would respond is the entire profit lost [6].

In the paper a new approach based on the existing system EDRL-MD [12] (EDRL-MD, for Evolutionary Decision Rule Learner with Multivariate Discretization) is proposed. The system learns decision rules using an *evolutionary algorithm* [15] (EA). EAs are stochastic techniques, which have been inspired by the process of biological evolution. Their advantage over greedy search methods is the ability to avoid local optima.

The main novelty of EDRL-MD lies in dealing with continuous-valued attributes. Most of decision rule systems employ univariate discretization methods, which search for threshold values for only one attribute at the same time. In

L. De Raedt and P. Flach (Eds.): ECML 2001, LNAI 2167, pp. 288–299, 2001.
© Springer-Verlag Berlin Heidelberg 2001

contrast to them, EDRL-MD learns rules simultaneously searching for threshold values for all continuous-valued attributes. This approach is called [12] *multi-variate discretization*.

The goal of the original EDRL-MD is to minimize the number of classification errors. In order to enable our system to minimize misclassification cost we modified the *fitness function*, which is optimized by the evolutionary search process.

Several EA-based systems, which learn decision rules in either propositional (e.g., GABIL [5], GIL [10], EDRL [13]) or first order form (e.g., REGAL [9]) were proposed. According to our knowledge, they are unable to process continuous-valued features directly and they cannot minimize misclassification costs.

The remainder of the paper is organized as follows. The next section briefly discusses the related research on cost-sensitive learning. Section 3 contains a short presentation of EDRL-MD. Section 4 describes the modifications of the fitness function, which enable the learning system to minimize misclassification cost. In Section 5 an experimental evaluation on several real-life datasets and a short discussion of the results are presented. The last section contains our conclusions and the directions of the future work.

2   Related Work on Cost-Sensitive Learning

The process of inductive learning may involve different costs [21] e.g., costs of tests (features), costs of cases, costs of errors. In the literature the latter kind of costs is the most commonly discussed one.

Several attempts to incorporate misclassification costs into decision tree or decision rule learning were made so far. The first approach was introduced by Breiman et al. [3] in CART decision tree learning system. Their method consists in modification of the class prior probabilities used in the splitting criterion. The cost-based measure is also used for tree pruning.

In a simpler approach (e.g., [2], [11]) error costs are taken into consideration during the pruning phase, but not during the induction phase. In such case the pruning procedure has a limited capability to change the structure of the classifier obtained by the error-based learning. Consequently, ignoring the misclassification cost at the first phase is the main drawback of this approach.

Pazzani et al. [17] introduced three cost-sensitive algorithms for decision list induction. Their method was applied to a real telephone network troubleshooting problem.

Ting [19] proposed a modified version of C4.5 using instance-weighting for induction of cost-sensitive decision trees. This approach requires the conversion of the cost matrix into the cost vector, which may result in poor performance in multi-class problems.

In [6] Domingos presented a method for making an arbitrary classifier cost-sensitive by wrapping a cost-minimizing procedure around it. However his approach may be computationally inefficient because it requires many runs of the basic learning algorithm.

As for applications of EAs to cost-sensitive learning, Turney [20] described a system called ICET, which learns decision trees taking into account both feature costs and misclassification costs. In his approach a genetic algorithm is used to evolve a population of biases for the induction algorithm (a modified C4.5).

3   Learning Decision Rules with EDRL-MD

In this section we briefly present the main topics (i.e., representation of solutions and genetic search operators) of the learning system EDRL-MD. More detailed description can be found in [12].

We assume that a learning set $E = \{e_1, e_2, \ldots, e_M\}$ consists of M examples. Each example $e \in E$ is described by N attributes (features) $A_1, A_2, \ldots, A_N$ and labeled by a class $c(e) \in C$. The domain of a nominal (discrete-valued) attribute A_i is a finite set $V(A_i)$, while the domain of a continuous-valued attribute A_j is an interval $V(A_j) = [l_j, u_j]$. For each class $c_k \in C$ by $E^+(c_k) = \{e \in E : c(e) = c_k\}$ we denote the set of *positive examples* and by $E^-(c_k) = E - E^+(c_k)$ the set of *negative examples*. A *decision rule* R takes the form IF $t_1 \wedge t_2 \wedge \ldots \wedge t_r$ THEN c_k, where $c_k \in C$ and the left-hand side (LHS) is a conjunction of $r(r \leq N)$ conditions $t_1, t_2, \ldots, t_r$; each of them concerns one attribute. The right-hand side (RHS) of the rule determines class membership of an example. A *ruleset RS* is a disjunctive set of decision rules with the same RHS. By $c_{RS} \in C$ we denote the class on the right-hand side of the ruleset *RS*.

In our approach the EA is called once for each class $c_k \in C$ to find the ruleset separating the set of positive examples $E^+(c_k)$ from the set of negative examples $E^-(c_k)$. The search criterion, in terminology of EAs called the *fitness function* prefers rulesets consisting of few conditions, which cover many positive examples and very few negative ones. Detailed description of the fitness functions used for error reduction and misclassification cost reduction is presented in Section 4.

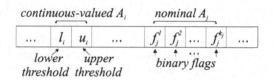

Fig. 1. The string encoding the LHS of a decision rule ($k_j = |V(A_j)|$). The chromosome representing the ruleset is the concatenation of strings. The number of strings in a chromosome can be adjusted by some search operators.

3.1   Representation

The EA processes a population of candidate solutions to a search problem called *chromosomes*. In our case a single chromosome encodes a ruleset *RS*. Since the number of rules in the optimal ruleset for a given class is not known, we use variable-length chromosomes and provide the search operators, which change the number of rules. The chromosome representing the ruleset is a concatenation of *strings*. Each fixed-length string represents the LHS of one decision rule. Because the EA is called to find a ruleset for the given class c_{RS} there is no need for encoding the RHS.

The string is composed (Fig. 1) of N *substrings*. Each substring encodes a condition related to one attribute. The LHS is the conjunction of these conditions. In case of a continuous-valued attribute A_i the substring encodes the lower l_i and the upper u_i threshold of the condition $l_i < A_i \leq u_i$. It is possible that $l_i = -\infty$ or $u_i = +\infty$.

Both l_i and u_i are selected from the finite set of all *boundary thresholds*. A boundary threshold for the attribute A_i is defined (Fig. 2) as a midpoint between such a successive pair of examples in the sequence sorted by the increasing value of A_i, that one of the examples is positive and the other is negative. Evaluating only the boundary thresholds is sufficient [7] for finding the maximum of two fitness functions (1) and (4) discussed in the paper.

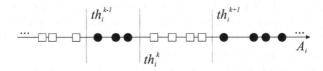

Fig. 2. An example illustrating the notion of boundary threshold. The boundary thresholds $th_i^1, \ldots, th_i^k, \ldots, th_i^{NT_i}$ for the continuous-valued attribute A_i are placed between groups of negative ($\bullet$) and positive ($\square$) examples.

For a nominal attribute A_j the substring consists of binary flags. Each of the flags corresponds to one value of the attribute.

Note that it is possible that a condition related to an attribute is not present on the LHS. For a continuous-valued attribute A_i it can be achieved by setting both $l_i = -\infty$ and $u_i = +\infty$. For a nominal A_j it is necessary to set all the flags $f_j^1, f_j^2, \ldots, f_j^{|V(A_j)|}$.

Figure 3 shows an example chromosome for a dataset with two numerical attributes: *Salary* and *Amount*, and one nominal attribute *Purpose*. It is assumed that the EA is searching for the optimal ruleset for the class *Accept*.

3.2   Genetic Operators

Our system employs six search operators. Four of them: *changing condition*, *positive example insertion*, *negative example removal*, *rule drop* are applied to a single ruleset RS (represented by a chromosome). The other two: *crossover* and *rule copy* require two arguments RS_1 and RS_2.

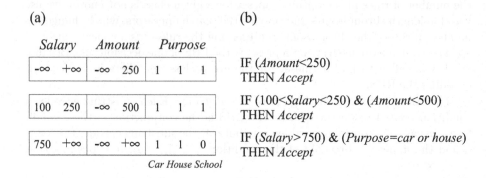

(a)

Salary		Amount		Purpose		
-∞	+∞	-∞	250	1	1	1

Salary		Amount		Purpose		
100	250	-∞	500	1	1	1

Salary		Amount		Purpose		
750	+∞	-∞	+∞	1	1	0

Car House School

(b)

IF (*Amount*<250)
THEN *Accept*

IF (100<*Salary*<250) & (*Amount*<500)
THEN *Accept*

IF (*Salary*>750) & (*Purpose*=car or house)
THEN *Accept*

Fig. 3. Representation of rulesets: (a) an example chromosome consisting of three strings, (b) the corresponding ruleset.

A similar approach was proposed by Janikow. His GIL system [10] conducts the search for rulesets using 14 operators. However, GIL is not able to handle continuous-valued attributes directly, since it represents a condition as a sequence of binary flags corresponding to the values of an attribute (we use the same representation for nominal attributes).

The changing condition is a mutation-like operator, which alters a single condition related to an attribute A_i. If A_i is nominal, a flag randomly chosen from $f_i^1, f_i^2, \ldots, f_i^{|V(A_i)|}$ is flipped. For a continuous-valued attribute a threshold (l_i or u_i) is replaced by a random boundary threshold.

The positive example insertion operator modifies a single decision rule R in the ruleset RS to allow it to cover a new random positive example $e^+ \in E^+(c_{RS})$, currently uncovered by R. All conditions in the rule, which conflict with e^+ have to be altered. In case of a condition related to a nominal attribute A_i the flag, which corresponds to $A_i(e^+)$, is set. If A_i is a continuous-valued attribute and the condition $l_i < A_i \le u_i$ is not satisfied because $u_i < A_i(e^+)$ the threshold u_i is replaced by $\hat{u}_i$, where $\hat{u}_i$ is the smallest boundary threshold such that $\hat{u}_i \ge A_i(e^+)$. The case when $A_i(e^+) \le l_i$ is handled in a similar way.

The negative example removal operator alters a single rule R from the ruleset RS. It selects at random a negative example e^- from the set of all the negative examples covered by R. Then it alters a random condition in R in such a way, that the modified rule does not cover e^-. If the chosen condition concerns a nominal attribute A_i the flag which corresponds to $A_i(e^-)$ is cleared. If A_i is a continuous-valued attribute then the condition $l_i < A_i \le u_i$ is narrowed down either to $\hat{l}_i < A_i \le u_i$ or to $l_i < A_i \le \hat{u}_i$, where $\hat{l}_i$ is the smallest boundary threshold such that $A_i(e^-) \le \hat{l}_i$ and $\hat{u}_i$ is the largest boundary threshold such that $\hat{u}_i < A_i(e^-)$.

Rule drop and rule copy operators were used previously by Janikow. They are the only ones capable of changing the number of rules in a ruleset. The single argument rule drop removes a random rule from a ruleset RS. The two argument rule copy adds to one of its arguments RS_1, a copy of a rule selected at random from RS_2, provided that the number of rules in RS_1 is lower than max_R. max_R is an user-supplied parameter, which limits the maximal number of rules in the ruleset.

The crossover operator selects at random two rules R_1 and R_2 from the respective arguments RS_1 and RS_2. Then it applies an uniform crossover [15] to the strings representing R_1 and R_2.

4   Adaptation to Cost-Sensitive Learning

To convert EDRL-MD for cost-sensitive learning we modified the fitness function used to guide the search process. We start this section with the presentation of the fitness function used when the goal of learning is the reduction of the number of errors [12]. Then we describe the changes which allow the EA to minimize the expected misclassification cost rather than the error rate. We also present the cost-sensitive methods for resolving conflicts between rules and for choosing a default class.

We define E_{RS} as the set of examples covered by ruleset RS. The class on the right-hand side of RS is denoted by c_{RS}. Then $E_{RS}^+ = E_{RS} \cap E^+(c_{RS})$ is the set of positive examples correctly classified by RS and $E_{RS}^- = E_{RS} \cap E^-(c_{RS})$ denotes the set of negative examples covered by the ruleset. The total number of positive and negative cases in the learning set are denoted by $POS = |E^+(c_{RS})|$ and $NEG = |E^-(c_{RS})| = M - POS$ respectively. The ruleset RS correctly classifies $pos = |E_{RS}^+|$ positive examples and $NEG - neg$ negative ones, where $neg = |E_{RS}^-|$.

4.1   The Fitness for Error Reduction

In the case of the error-based classification (i.e., with equal misclassification costs) EDRL-MD employs the fitness function f_{error} given by:

$$f_{error}(RS) = \frac{Pr(RS)}{Compl(RS)}, \tag{1}$$

where $Pr(RS)$ is the probability of classifying correctly an example from the learning set by the ruleset RS and $Compl(RS)$ is the complexity of the ruleset. We are interested in maximizing the probability and minimizing the complexity (to obtain the compact ruleset and to avoid overfitting). $Pr(RS)$ and $Compl(RS)$ are given respectively by:

$$Pr(RS) = \frac{pos + NEG - neg}{POS + NEG}. \tag{2}$$

and

$$Compl(RS) = (L/N + 1)^\alpha, \tag{3}$$

where L is the total number of conditions in the ruleset, N is the number of attributes and α is an user supplied parameter (typically $\alpha \in [0.1 \ldots 0.001]$).

4.2   The Fitness for Misclassification Cost Reduction

Let $Cost(c_i, c_j)$ be the cost of misclassifying an object from the class c_j as belonging to class c_i. We assume the costs for correct decisions are equal zero i.e., $Cost(c_i, c_i) = 0$ for all c_i.

To adapt the fitness function (1) to the cost-sensitive classification we have to change only $Pr(RS)$, because the complexity term is independent of costs. We replace $Pr(RS)$ by the cost-sensitive $Pr_{cost}(RS)$. The new fitness f_{cost} is defined as follows:

$$f_{cost}(RS) = \frac{Pr_{cost}(RS)}{Compl(RS)}. \tag{4}$$

Classification errors made by the ruleset RS can be divided into two groups: the errors caused by covering a negative example and the errors caused by leaving a positive example not covered. The cost of the former group of errors is denoted by $NC(RS)$ (*Negative examples misclassification Cost*) defined as:

$$NC(RS) = \sum_{e \in E_{RS}^-} Cost(c_{RS}, c(e)). \tag{5}$$

The latter case, when positive examples are not covered by the ruleset is more complicated. Because the EA is called to find the ruleset for one class c_{RS} we cannot figure out to which class a positive example not covered by RS will be classified. This information is available after $|C|$ runs of the EA, when the complete classifier i.e., disjunction of $|C|$ rulesets is learned. Since we do not know the exact cost of a single misclassified (not covered) positive example, we use an approximate measure called $AvgPC(c_{RS})$ (*Average Positive example misclassification Cost*):

$$AvgPC(c_{RS}) = \sum_{c_i \neq c_{RS}} \frac{|E^+(c_i)|}{|E^-(c_{RS})|} * Cost(c_i, c_{RS}). \tag{6}$$

The cost of all misclassified (not covered) positive examples $PC(RS)$ (*Positive examples misclassification Cost*) is given by:

$$PC(RS) = (POS - pos) * AvgPC(c_{RS}). \tag{7}$$

Finally, we define the cost-sensitive replacement for $Pr(RS)$ as:

$$Pr_{cost}(RS) = \frac{MaxNC(c_{RS}) + MaxPC(c_{RS}) - NC(RS) - PC(RS)}{MaxNC(c_{RS}) + MaxPC(c_{RS})}, \tag{8}$$

where $MaxNC(c_{RS})$ and $MaxPC(c_{RS})$ are maximal possible values for $NC(RS)$ and $PC(RS)$ respectively. We can observe $MaxNC(c_{RS})$ when the ruleset covers all the negative examples:

$$MaxNC(c_{RS}) = \sum_{c_i \neq c_{RS}} |E^+(c_i)| * Cost(c_{RS}, c_i), \tag{9}$$

and $MaxPC(c_{RS})$ when none of the positive examples is covered by the ruleset:

$$MaxPC(c_{RS}) = POS * AvgPC(c_{RS}). \tag{10}$$

Because $MaxNC(c_{RS})$ and $MaxPC(c_{RS})$ do not depend on the left-hand side of the ruleset RS, through the maximization of $Pr_{cost}(RS)$ we minimize the total misclassification cost $(NC(RS) + PC(RS))$.

$Pr_{cost}(RS)$ has the following properties: $0 \leq Pr_{cost}(RS) \leq 1$, $Pr_{cost}(RS) = 1$ iff the ruleset covers all positive examples $(pos = POS)$ and no negative ones $(neg = 0)$, $Pr_{cost}(RS) = 0$ iff the ruleset covers all the negative examples $(neg = NEG)$ and no positive ones $(pos = 0)$. The above properties hold also for $Pr(RS)$. Furthermore one can show, that if the costs of classification errors are equal then $Pr_{cost}(RS) = Pr(RS)$. It means that Pr is a special case of Pr_{cost} when the goal is to minimize the number of errors rather than the cost.

4.3   Conflict Resolution and Default Class

Contrary to decision trees, the prediction obtained by a set of decision rules can be ambiguous. Such a situation arises when either at least two rules predicting different classes cover an example or none of rules covers an example.

In the former case the classifier has to resolve a conflict between rules. The most common approach to conflict resolution is based on assessment of rule quality [4]. The rule with the highest quality among the conflicting rules is chosen as the winner'and the class on the RHS of this rule becomes the final decision of the classifier.

A similar approach was adopted in EDRL-MD. The conflicting rules are ranked according to *average conflict cost(ACC)*, which is given by:

$$ACC(R) = \frac{1}{|E_R^{CL}|} * \sum_{e \in E_R^{CL}} Cost(c_R, c(e)), \tag{11}$$

where c_R denotes the class on the RHS of the rule R. It is assumed that each example from the set $E_R^{CL} \subset E$ causes a conflict involving the rule R. The rule, which offers the lowest ACC is chosen as the winner.

If an example is not covered by any rule it is classified into a *default class*. To select the default we consider the training examples not covered by any rule. The class, which minimizes the total misclassification cost of these examples is chosen as the default.

5   Experimental Evaluation

In this section experimental results are presented. We have tested our method on ten datasets from UCI repository [1]. The description of the datasets is shown in Table 1. We compared EDRL-MD to C4.5 [18] and its newer, unpublished version C5.0[1]. Contrary to its predecessor C5.0 is capable of taking misclassification costs into consideration. In all the experiments EDRL-MD was using the fitness function (4).

---

[1] Both C4.5 and C5.0 generate rules by converting a decision tree.

Table 1. The datasets used in the experiments

Dataset	Size	No. of attributes (Numeric/Nominal)	No. of classes
german credit	1000	7/13	2
heart disease	270	7/6	2
cmc	1473	2/7	3
housing	506	12/1	3
breast wisconsin	683	9/0	2
page blocks	5473	10/0	5
pima	532	7/0	2
bupa	345	6/0	2
vehicle	846	18/0	4
crx	690	6/9	2

5.1   Experimental Methodology

Unfortunately, publicly available datasets with known misclassification costs are rare. In the UCI repository only two such datasets (*german credit* and *heart disease*) are provided. These datasets were previously the subject of the cost-sensitive classification experiments in the EU StatLog project [16]. In our experiments the expected misclassification cost and the error rate were estimated by running ten times complete ten-fold crossvalidation. The results are shown in the Table 2.

Table 2. Misclassification cost and error rate for datasets with known cost matrices. Averages and standard deviations are given. The best results for each dataset are shown in bold.

Dataset	Misclassification cost			Error rate		
	C4.5	C5.0	EDRL-MD	C4.5	C5.0	EDRL-MD
german credit	$.960 \pm .05$	$.656 \pm .02$	$\mathbf{.558 \pm .01}$	$.272 \pm .01$	$.333 \pm .01$	$.453 \pm .01$
heart disease	$.662 \pm .05$	$\mathbf{.476 \pm .04}$	$.499 \pm .04$	$.207 \pm .02$	$.243 \pm .02$	$.375 \pm .02$

For the remaining datasets, for which cost matrices are not available, we used a different experimental setup. The results presented in Table 3 are averaged over ten runs of ten-fold crossvalidation. In each run a cost matrix was generated randomly. The off-diagonal elements of the cost matrix were drawn from the uniform distribution over the range $[0, 10]$. The diagonal elements were always zero. For each single crossvalidation run the same random cost matrix was used for all three tested algorithms. For this experiment the standard deviations are not reported because they would incorporate the difference between cost matrices used in different crossvalidation runs.

Similar procedures for generating cost matrices were used in [19] and [14].

Table 3. Average misclassification cost and error rate for datasets with cost matrices generated randomly. The best results for each dataset are shown in bold.

Dataset	Misclassification cost			Error rate		
	C4.5	C5.0	EDRL-MD	C4.5	C5.0	EDRL-MD
cmc	1.98	1.67	**1.39**	.460	.523	.566
housing	1.08	1.00	**0.85**	.246	.322	.334
breast wisconsin	.202	.235	**.187**	.040	.085	.063
page blocks	.140	.135	**.134**	.031	.058	.052
pima	1.22	1.00	**.982**	.240	.268	.287
bupa	1.65	1.44	**1.37**	.321	.411	.418
vehicle	1.20	1.13	**1.09**	.270	.392	.411
crx	.758	**.623**	.624	.152	.186	.207

5.2 Discussion of the Results

The results confirm that an algorithm (in our case C4.5), which optimizes the error rate cannot be applied to datasets with non-equal misclassification costs. For all datasets, except *breast wisconsin* C4.5 obtained the highest misclassification cost. As for two cost-sensitive algorithms, EDRL-MD outperformed C5.0 for eight datasets although for four datasets the difference was marginal (less than 10% C5.0 achieved slightly better results only for two datasets.

C4.5 achieved lower error rates than its cost-sensitive competitors. One could expect such results since error rate and misclassification cost cannot be optimized at the same time.

It should be noted that EDRL-MD requires significantly more processing time than the other algorithms. Nevertheless the learning time required by our system is acceptable. For instance EDRL-MD needs 51 seconds of CPU time on a PC workstation (PIII 700 MHz) to learn decision rules for the largest of datasets (*page blocks*) whereas C5.0 needs about 1 s.

6 Conclusions and Future Work

In this paper we presented the method of incorporation of misclassification costs into the decision rule learning system EDRL-MD. Contrary to some approaches based on the cost-sensitive pruning our method takes the error costs into account during the inductive search. The results are promising, especially when compared with the results obtained by the cost-sensitive learning system C5.0.

Several directions of the future research exist. One of them is an extension of our cost model. For instance, it would be relatively easy to add costs of features (tests) to the fitness function. Moreover in some applications e.g., fraud detection [8] cost of an error depends on the amount of money involved in the given example. Our approach could be extended to cover such situations as well. In this case instead of using a single cost matrix for the whole dataset the algorithm should associate a cost vector with each single observation and employ a modified fitness function.

Since in many practical applications of classification one has to deal with increasingly large databases, the computational complexity of learning methods becomes important. As for evolutionary algorithms, it is the well known fact [9], that their efficiency can be significantly improved by implementation in a distributed environment (e.g., cluster of workstations). Currently we are developing such a solution for EDRL-MD.

Acknowledgments. The authors are grateful to Prof. Leon Bobrowski for his support and useful comments. This work was supported by the grant W/II/1/00 from Technical University of Białystok.

References

1. Blake, C., Keogh, E., Merz, C.J.: *UCI repository of machine learning databases*,[http://www.ics.uci.edu/~mlearn/MLRepository.html]. Irvine, CA: University of California, Dept. of Computer Science (1998).
2. Bradford, J.P., Kunz, C., Kohavi, R., Brunk, C., Brodley, C.E.: Pruning decision trees with misclassification costs. In *Proc. of the Tenth European Conf. on Machine Learning*. Springer Verlag (1998) 131-136.
3. Breiman, L., Friedman, R.A., Olshen, R., Stone, C.J.: *Classification and Regression Trees*. Wadsworth (1984).
4. Bruha, I., Quality of decision rules: Definitions and classification schemes for multiple rules. In: Nakhaeizadeh, G., Taylor, C.C., (eds.) *Machine Learning and Statistics. The Interface*. Wiley-Interscience (1997) 107-131.
5. De Jong, K., Spears, W.M., Gordon, D.F.: Using genetic algorithm for concept learning. *Machine Learning* 13 (1993) 168-182.
6. Domingos, P.: MetaCost: A general method for making classifiers cost-sensitive. In *Proc. of Int. Conf. on Knowledge Discovery and Data Mining, KDD'99*. ACM Press (1999) 155-164.
7. Fayyad, U.M., Irani, K.B.: Multi-interval discretization of continuous-valued attributes for classification learning. In *Proc. of IJCAI'93*. Morgan Kaufmann (1993) 1022-1027.
8. Fawcett, T., Provost, F.J., Adaptive fraud detection, *Data Mining and Knowledge Discovery* 1 (1997)
9. Giordana, A., Neri, F.: Search-intensive concept induction. *Evolutionary Computation* 3(4) (1995) 375-416.
10. Janikow, C.: A knowledge intensive genetic algorithm for supervised learning. *Machine Learning* 13 (1993) 192-228.
11. Knoll, U., Nakhaeizadeh, G., Tausend, B.: Cost-sensitive pruning of decision trees. In *Proc. of the 8th European Conf. on Machine Learning*. Springer LNCS 784 (1994) 383-386.
12. Kwedlo, W., Krętowski, M.: An evolutionary algorithm using multivariate discretization for decision rule induction. In *Principles of Data Mining and Knowledge Discovery. 3rd European Conference PKDD'99*. Springer LNCS 1704 (1999) 392-397.
13. Kwedlo, W., Krętowski, M.: Discovery of decision rules from databases: an evolutionary approach. In *Principles of Data Mining and Knowledge Discovery. 2nd European Symposium PKDD'98*. Springer LNCS 1510 (1998) 370-378.

14. Margineantu, D.D., Dietterich, T.G.: Bootstrap methods for the cost-sensitive evaluation of classifiers, In *Proc. 17th Int. Conf. on Machine Learning ICML'2000*, Morgan Kaufmann (2000) 583-590.
15. Michalewicz, Z.: *Genetic Algorithms + Data Structures = Evolution Programs*. 3rd edn. Springer (1996).
16. Michie, D., Spiegelhalter, D.J., Taylor, C.C.: *Machine Learning, Neural and Statistical Classification*. Ellis Horwood Ltd. (1994) [also available at http://www.amsta.leeds.ac.uk/~charles/statlog/index.html].
17. Pazzani, M., Merz, C., Murphy, P., Ali, K., Hume, T., Brunk, C.: Reducing misclassification costs. In *Proc. of Int. Conf. on Machine Learning, ICML'94*. Morgan Kaufmann (1994) 217-225.
18. Quinlan, J.R.: *C4.5: Programs for Machine Learning*. Morgan Kaufmann (1993).
19. Ting, K.M.: Inducing cost-sensitive trees via instance weighting. In *Principles of Data Mining and Knowledge Discovery*. 2nd *European Symposium PKDD'98*. Springer LNCS 1510 (1998) 139-147.
20. Turney, P.: Cost-sensitive classification: Empirical evaluation of a hybrid genetic decision tree induction algorithm. *Journal of Artificial Intelligence Research* 2 (1995) 369-409.
21. Turney, P.: Types of cost in inductive concept learning. In *Proc. of ICML'2000 Workshop on Cost-Sensitive Learning*. Stanford, CA (2000).

A Mixture Approach to Novelty Detection Using Training Data with Outliers

Martin Lauer

Institut für Logik, Komplexität und Deduktionssysteme
Universität Karlsruhe
D-76128 Karlsruhe, Germany
lauer@ira.uka.de

Abstract. This paper describes an approach to handle multivariate training data which contain outliers. The aim is to analyze the training patterns and to detect anomalous patterns. Therefore we explicitly model the existence of outliers in the training data using a widespread outlier distribution. Indicator variables assign each pattern to either the outlier distribution or the distribution of normal patterns. Thus we can estimate the data distribution using the EM-algorithm or Data Augmentation. We present the general approach as well as a concrete realization where we use Gaussian mixture models to describe the patterns' distribution. Experimental results show the applicability of this approach for practical studies.

1 Introduction

Novelty detection is concerned with the identification of anomalous patterns in data sets. These patterns are often faulty values generated by flaws in data ascertainment. Possible reasons are faulty measurement instruments or mistakes when feeding the computer with data, among others.

Furthermore outlying patterns may influence the analysis of data a lot. Standard approaches for regression analysis like the least sum of squares approach or for density estimation like the method of moments suffer a lot from their sensitivity to outliers. Even an outlier rate fewer than one per cent may corrupt the result of such a statistical analysis. Some examples illustrating this problem are given in [11]. Therefore it is necessary to detect outlying patterns and to eliminate them from the training data.

Several approaches have been proposed to tackle the task of novelty detection. Almost all approaches are based on the idea to learn a model of the data distribution and afterwards classify the patterns according to a density level. Two types of approaches can be distinguished: a) approaches working only with outlier-free training sets which are designed to find outliers in test data and b) approaches working on training data with a known number of outliers. The models which are used for data description are Gaussian mixture models (GMMs) [10,9], auto-associating neural networks [6,15], self organizing maps [16,8] and a class of sets based on support vector representation [12,2], among others.

L. De Raedt and P. Flach (Eds.): ECML 2001, LNAI 2167, pp. 300–311, 2001.
© Springer-Verlag Berlin Heidelberg 2001

In this paper we want to extend the approach based on GMMs for the use of training data which contain outliers themselves. Up to now GMMs were only used to estimate the density of a data distribution from outlier-free training data. Afterwards these estimates can be used to find anomalous patterns in other data sets which are taken from the same distribution but which contain supplementary outliers. Our approach is more robust against outliers so that it tolerates even a small amount of outliers in the training data. To calibrate the algorithm we need to have either classified validation patterns or a rough knowledge of the outlier proportion in the training data. But in contrast to the above mentioned approaches we do not need to know the exact number of outliers.

2   Key Idea

We start from the presumption that the training data contain a small amount of outliers. Thus we can model the pattern distribution as the composition of a) a big percentage of normal patterns[1] and b) a small proportion of corrupted patterns. If we denote the proportion of anomalous patterns with λ, the distribution of normal patterns with P_N and the distribution of outliers with P_O we can describe the distribution of the whole training set by:

$$P(x) = (1 - \lambda) \cdot P_N(x) + \lambda \cdot P_O(x) \tag{1}$$

λ can be interpreted as the prior probability for outlying patterns. The modeling described in (1) is called the "mixture alternative"in [1].

The learning task can now be split up into three steps:

1. estimate $P(x)$ from the given training set
2. decompose $P(x)$ into $P_N(x)$ and $P_O(x)$
3. decide whether x is an outlier given the probabilities $P_N(x)$, $P_O(x)$ and the prior probability λ

The second step is a delicate task since there are many possibilities to decompose $P(x)$ into two parts. Additionally we neither know which training patterns are outlying nor the exact number of anomalous patterns. If we assume an outlier percentage of $\leq 1\%$ and a number of training patterns ≤ 1000 the number of outliers is anyway too small to estimate the distribution $P_O(x)$ reliably. Therefore we cannot perform the second step directly.

Instead we assume that we know the outliers'distribution P_O and the outlier proportion λ or at least have a rough idea which we can use as an approximation for P_O and λ. We focus on the special problem of determining appropriate P_O and λ in sect. 5. Then we can derive the distribution of normal patterns from (1):

$$P_N(x) = \frac{1}{1 - \lambda} P(x) - \frac{\lambda}{1 - \lambda} \cdot P_O(x) \tag{2}$$

---

[1] We use the term "normal pattern" as complement to "outlier" or "anomalous pattern", not in the sense of a pattern derived from a Gaussian distribution.

The second step is now to estimate $P_N(x)$ from the training patterns. The rough knowledge of $P_O(x)$ and λ will help to restrain the outliers'influence on the estimation of $P_N(x)$. Thus we can work with training data which contain anomalous patterns.

If we would omit to consider the outlier distribution $P_O(x)$ and try to estimate $P_N(x)$ directly from the training patterns we would actually learn $P(x)$ which can be substantially different from $P_N(x)$. In particular $P(x)$ will be much more widespread than $P_N(x)$. If we assume the patterns to be distributed according to a parameterized model, e.g. a Gaussian distribution, the estimated parameters will be corrupted by the outliers, e. g. the variances of the Gaussian will be too large. Thus the explicit modeling of an outlier distribution P_O preserves the estimate from being corrupted by outliers.

The third step of classifying patterns according to $P_N(x)$, $P_O(x)$ and λ is an application of the Bayesian classification approach. λ is the prior probability for outliers, $P_O(x)$ and $P_N(x)$ are the distributions for anomalous and normal patterns, respectively. Thus a new pattern x is classified as outlier if the probability of belonging to the set of outliers is larger than the probability of being a normal pattern, i.e. equation (3) holds:

$$x \text{ is classified as outlier } \quad \text{if and only if} \quad \lambda \cdot P_O(x) > (1 - \lambda) \cdot P_N(x) \quad (3)$$

3   Implementation of the Outlier Detection Approach

So far we have described the general approach. Now we want to show how to estimate the probability distribution $P_N(x)$. In this paper we want to concentrate on the use of parameterized models. Thus the estimation of $P_N(x)$ becomes the determination of a distribution's parameters. Firstly we want to show how to use an arbitrary parameterized distribution for $P_N(x)$ and afterwards we will describe the case of Gaussian mixture models as a special choice.

Now we assume that the distribution P_N is parameterized by a parameter vector ϑ which we want to estimate from the given training patterns $x_1, \ldots, x_n$. Unfortunately we do not know which patterns are normal and which are anomalous. Therefore we introduce an indicator variable z_i for every training pattern x_i which is either one if x_i is anomalous or zero if the respective pattern is normal. If we knew the indicator variables z_i we could use a standard estimation procedure like maximum likelihood or another appropriate approach to estimate the parameter ϑ from the normal training patterns indicated by $z_i = 0$.

Since we do not know the z_i we have to estimate them in parallel with the parameter ϑ, i.e. we have to estimate the vector $(\vartheta, z_1, \ldots, z_n)$. Thereto we can use the EM-algorithm [4] or Data Augmentation [14].

Both algorithms split up the vector $(\vartheta, z_1, \ldots, z_n)$ into ϑ and $(z_1, \ldots, z_n)$. Alternately the EM-algorithm estimates the indicator variables'distribution by its expectation value given a current estimate of ϑ and the parameter ϑ given a current estimate of the indicator variables. A convergence theorem guarantees that the EM-algorithm converges into a local maximum of the likelihood function for a large number of iterations. It is therefore a maximum likelihood estimator.

In contrast the Data Augmentation algorithm is a Bayesian approach. It alternately samples parameters ϑ given current indicator variables $(z_1, \ldots, z_n)$ and the indicator variables given the current parameter ϑ. Although the current parameters are random it can be shown that they are anyhow samples from the distribution of parameters given the training data $P(\vartheta|x_1, \ldots, x_n)$. Taking the expectation value of this distribution yields an estimate for ϑ.

The approach based on indicator variables can be interpreted as the estimation of the parameters of a mixture distribution composed of two components, namely the distribution of normal patterns $P_N(x|\vartheta)$ and the outlier distribution $P_O(x)$ weighted by $1 - \lambda$ and λ, respectively. The indicator variables assign each pattern to one of the mixture components, either to the outlier component or to the component of normal patterns. The only difference from the standard applications of mixture distributions is the fact that the outlier component has no parameters to estimate.

4   Gaussian Mixture Models

In this section we want to describe a special choice for the distribution $P_N(x)$, namely Gaussian mixture models (GMMs). They are a very flexible class of probability distributions and thus they are well suited for the modeling of unknown data. Subsequently we will give a brief review of GMMs and explain the peculiarity of GMM fitting in our framework.

Given d-variate patterns the density of a GMM is defined as:

$$p(x) = \sum_{j=1}^{k} \frac{w_j}{\sqrt{(2\pi)^d \cdot det(\Sigma_j)}} \exp\left(-\frac{1}{2}(x - \mu_j)^T \Sigma_j^{-1}(x - \mu_j) \right) \qquad (4)$$

A GMM can be understood as the combination of k Gaussian distributions. Each component j is described by its mean vector μ_j, its covariance matrix Σ_j and its contribution to the mixture $w_j \geq 0$ which we name the mixing weight. w_j can be understood as the prior probability of a pattern belonging to the j-th component. Thereto the mixing weights have to fulfill the condition $\sum_{j=1}^{k} w_j = 1$. The complete parameter vector of a GMM contains the mixing weights, means and covariances of each component: $\vartheta = (w_1, \ldots, w_k, \mu_1, \ldots, \mu_k, \Sigma_1, \ldots, \Sigma_k)$. The number of components k controls the amount of distributions which can be approximated by a GMM. A survey of the topic of mixture models is given in [7].

Up to now the modeling is a two-level approach: on the top level the complete data distribution $P(x)$ is a mixture with two components, the distribution of normal patterns and the outlier distribution. On the second level the distribution of normal patterns is again modeled as a mixture, i.e. a GMM. These two mixtures can be unified such that the overall distribution $P(x)$ is a single mixture distribution with a) a single fix component modeling the outliers and b) several Gaussians which constitute the distribution of normal patterns. The mixing weight of the outlier component is λ and the mixing weights of the components of normal patterns sum to $1 - \lambda$.

The estimation of the parameters of the complete mixture can again be done using either the EM-algorithm or Data Augmentation. The necessary extension from the 2-component case described above and the case with k components is that the indicator variables can now take on values in the range of $1, \ldots, k$.

The EM-algorithm has two disadvantages: a) the dependency of the result from the initialization and b) the danger of overfitting. Both problems are not really serious if the parameters of all components are adapted and the number of components is chosen adequately. But the first difficulty becomes a snare when at least one component is not adapted to the data. This phenomenon is explained by the fact that the EM-algorithm locally maximizes the likelihood-function and that the existence of the outlier component bounds the log-likelihood below. Think of a training pattern x lying in an area of input space where the density of the outlier component is much greater than the density of the other components according to a current parameter vector ϑ_t. Then there are two aspects to consider: 1.) the influence of the pattern x onto the non-outlier components is very small and 2.) changing the parameter vector does not reduce the contribution of pattern x to the log-likelihood function since its contribution is bounded below by the logarithm of the the outlier components density at x. Thus the next parameter vector ϑ_{t+1} is computed without considering x. If x is an outlier this behavior is desired but if x is a normal pattern at the edge of the distribution this behavior leads to a GMM fitting that treats x by mistake as an outlier.

Due to the described problem we used Data Augmentation for all experiments. It has the advantage to search the parameter space globally. Therefore it does not get stuck in local optima and the result does not depend so much from the initial choice of parameters.

As priors for Data Augmentation we used non-informative priors which do not bias the resulting parameters. Additionally we used Data Augmentation to control the number of components k of the mixture distribution: we started with a large number of components and examined in every iteration whether there is a component j without assignments, i.e. all indicator variables z_i are $\neq j$. Then this component was deleted. A similar proceeding is described in [5].

5 Determining the Outlier Distribution

An essential of our approach is the use of an explicit outlier distribution P_O and an outlier rate λ. They cannot be estimated from the training data but have to be derived from a model of outlier generation.

If there is no explicit model of outlier generation we have to determine P_O and λ as plausible as possible. E. g. in an application working on measured data a typical outlier is generated by an erroneous shift of a decimal point when copying the measured value. Thus a plausible outlier distribution is normal with ten times the standard deviation of the normal data.

But, however, the determination of the outlier distribution and the outlier rate is delicate. A change in these parameters may influence the result a lot.

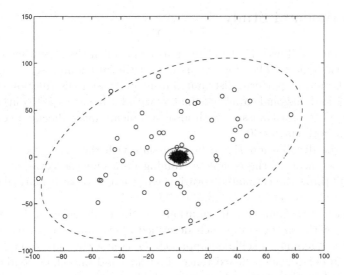

Fig. 1. Influence of λ onto the result of the outlier detection. The pattern set contains 1000 normal patterns indicated by "+" and 50 outliers indicated by "o". The dashed line shows the computed contour discriminating outliers from normal patterns for $\lambda = 0.01$ while the solid line shows the discriminating contour for $\lambda = 0.05$. The assumed outlier distribution P_O was set to be Gaussian with covariance equal to 100 times the estimated covariance of the pattern set. Further increasing λ would lead the algorithm to classify normal patterns by mistake as outliers.

In any case, the outlier distribution should be widespread since we expect the outliers to lie widespread in the data space.

A possibility to determine the outlier distribution and λ is to choose P_O to be an arbitrary widespread distribution, e.g. a Gaussian with very large variances or an improper distribution with constant density. Running our approach with different values for λ and fix P_O results in different outlier quota. Thus we can determine λ so that the resulting outlier rate resembles the expected proportion. Although this way of determining λ does not match the theoretical analysis exactly it can successfully be used in practice. Certainly, λ cannot be interpreted as the outlier rate anymore but rather as a parameter of the algorithm to adjust the sensitivity against anomalous patterns.

Furthermore, if a validation set with tagged outliers is available or if we know the outlier rate in a validation set we can use cross-validation to calibrate the unknown λ. Figure 1 shows the outcome of the presented algorithm for different values of λ on a 2-dimensional pattern set. Note that a modification of λ does not only influence the classification of patterns given a fix distribution of normal patterns but also influences the estimation of the distribution of normal patterns itself: a smaller λ increases the number of training patterns which contribute to the distribution of normal data.

6 Experimental Study

Firstly we want to illustrate the algorithms behavior in the case where P_N is a Gaussian distribution. Therefore we used an artificial training set composed of 300 bivariate normal patterns distributed from a Gaussian distribution with zero mean vector and diagonal covariance matrix with both entries 4. 15 outliers were added derived from a Gaussian with also zero mean and a diagonal covariance matrix with both entries 400.

We set the distribution P_O to be Gaussian with the mean vector equal to the estimated mean of the complete training data and the covariance matrix equal to 100 times the estimated covariance of the complete training data. The parameter λ varied between 0.01 and 0.999.

We trained two Gaussian distributions on the training data. The first one was trained with the new approach described above and the second one was fitted using a maximum likelihood approach. Of course the maximum likelihood approach did not consider the existence of outliers and thus the second estimate was corrupted by the outliers. In contrast the first estimate was very similar to the original distribution of normal data for all $\lambda \in [0.01, 0.9]$. Larger values of λ produced too many false outliers on a test set of normal patterns while very small values did not avoid the estimate to be corrupted by the outliers. The resulting estimates for the maximum likelihood estimate and the new approach are illustrated by their covariance ellipses in Fig. 2. Although the choice of λ was not critical in this example it is in general not easy to calibrate.

In a second experimental study we investigated the Biomed dataset [3] from the StatLib archive [13]. This benchmark has already been used in [2] to analyze the performance of a novelty detection algorithm.

The Biomed data are taken from a study of medical diagnosis. The aim is to detect the carriers of a rare disease. The patterns consist of four measurements on blood samples. 127 patterns of healthy patients and 67 of carriers are available. We used 27 patterns of healthy patients and 57 patterns of carriers as test set and the remaining patterns for training. The training sets were composed of

1. 100 patterns from healthy patients, no carriers
2. 100 patterns from healthy patients and 5 patterns from carriers
3. 100 patterns from healthy patients and 10 patterns from carriers

As model for P_N we used a GMM with a variable number of components. The training was performed by Data Augmentation. The outlier distribution was set to be Gaussian with the mean equal to the mean of the training patterns and the covariance equal to 100 times the covariance of the training patterns.

Figure 3 shows the error rates on the test sets for the model trained on the second training set with various λ between 0.001 and 0.999. Comparing this figure with Fig. 4 in [2] shows two important similarities:

− the rate of undetected outliers is less than 60% even if the parameters of the algorithms are chosen inappropriate (small λ)

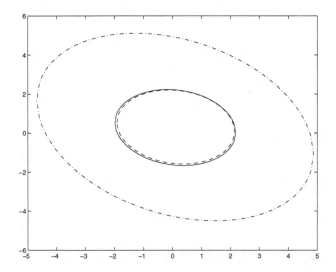

Fig. 2. Estimated covariance ellipses for the training patterns derived from a Gaussian distribution. The solid line shows the covariance ellipse of the true distribution while the dashed line shows the estimated distribution computed with the above presented new approach with $\lambda = 0.5$. The dash-dot line gives the maximum likelihood estimate.

- the point of intersection between the rate of misclassified normal patterns and undetected carriers is about 15% in both approaches

These circumstances suggest that both algorithms lead to a comparable result. But in contrast to the Linear Programming approach of [2] our algorithm was trained on data which contained 5% anomalous patterns while the Linear Programming approach was trained on outlier-free data. Figure 4 shows that even an increase in the rate of anomalous patterns in the training set does not worsen the results critically.

In a third experiment we want to show that our approach is also able to model more complex data distributions. Thereto we used an artificial bivariate data set. It consisted of 300 (1000) normal patterns which are distributed in the shape of a horseshoe. Additional 15 (50) outliers were randomly generated according to a uniform distribution in a square area of the two-dimensional plane.

The outlier distribution P_O was again set to be Gaussian with 100 times the covariance of the training patterns. As a model for normal patterns we used a GMM with variable number of components. The Fig. 5 and 6 show the 315 (1050) training patterns and the computed contour discriminating outliers from normal patterns. In both cases the algorithm recognized that the distribution of normal patterns is not convex and it classified the anomalous patterns in the inner of the horseshoe correctly as outliers.

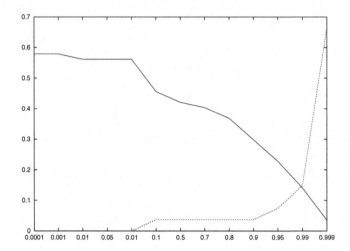

Fig. 3. Error rates (on the y-axis) for the Biomed data versus λ. The solid line shows the rate of undetected outliers, the dotted line shows the rate of misclassified normal patterns. Note that the labels on the x-axis are not equidistant.

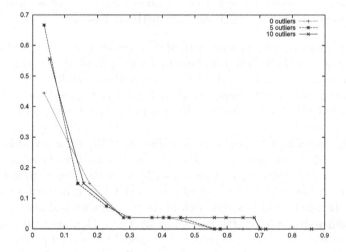

Fig. 4. Rate of misclassified outliers (x-axis) versus rate of misclassified normal patterns on a test set in the Biomed data domain. The three models are trained on an outlier-free training set (dotted line) of 100 patterns, a training set with additional 5 outliers (dashed line) and a training set with additional 10 outliers (solid line).

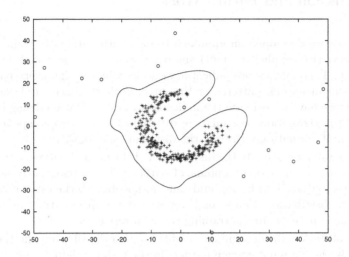

Fig. 5. Training patterns of the horseshoe data. Outliers are indicated by "o" and normal patterns by "+". The solid line gives the contour which was computed to discriminate outliers from normal patterns. λ was set to 0.05. The number of training patterns was 300 normal and 15 anomalous patterns.

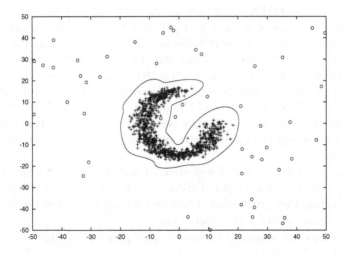

Fig. 6. Training patterns of the horseshoe data. Outliers are indicated by "o" and normal patterns by "+". The solid line gives the contour which was computed to discriminate outliers from normal patterns. λ was set to 0.2. The number of training patterns was 1000 normal and 50 anomalous patterns.

7   Discussion and Future Work

In this paper we developed an approach to deal with outliers in training data. The key idea is to explicitly model the occurrence of outliers with an outlier distribution. Therefore we use indicator variables which assign every pattern to either the set of normal patterns or the set of outliers. Since we do not know the outliers we have to estimate the indicator variables. This modeling is closely related to the estimation of a mixture distribution with two components: the distribution of normal patterns and the distribution of outliers.

This allows us to estimate the distribution of the normal patterns from training data that contain a small amount of outliers: the outlying patterns are assigned to the outlier distribution and thus do not disturb the estimation of the normal data distribution. In a second step we can use this distribution to detect the anomalous patterns in the training set or in test data.

A difficult task is the determination of the outlier distribution and the outlier rate. Mostly there are not enough outliers in the training data so that a reliable estimation is not possible. Thus these parameters have to be set explicitly. We propose the use of an arbitrary widespread distribution and to vary the outlier rate. Cross validation helps to find a suitable parameter. In our future work we hope to find a rule of thumb how to set these parameters depending on the dimensionality of the data and the spread of the training patterns.

Another problem sometimes occurs when the normal pattern distribution is modeled by a flexible class of distributions like GMMs. Then it may happen that a component of the GMM specializes on the outlying patterns or on a subset of the outliers. Especially if the GMM parameters are estimated with the EM-algorithm such a component overfits the outlying data. Therefore these outliers cannot be detected. If instead Data Augmentation with non-informative priors is used this problem is not so serious because Data Augmentation does not overfit the data but estimates a very broad component with a very small density which is often smaller than the density of the outlier distribution. Thus the outliers are found anyhow. In our future work we will focus on this phenomenon and examine in which way the outlier distribution influences the occurrence of such a component.

If we use a model for the distribution of normal patterns which is not so flexible like a single Gaussian distribution the above described problem does not occur since fitting the distribution of normal patterns to outliers would seriously worsen the description of normal patterns.

The experimental results presented in this paper show that our approach can successfully be applied in practical studies. It bounds the influence of the outliers on the estimation of the distribution of normal patterns and it is able to model even complex data distributions.

Acknowledgments. Thanks to Martin Riedmiller for helpful comments that improved this paper.

References

[1] Vic Barnett and Toby Lewis. *Outliers in Statistical Data*. John Wiley & Sons, 1978.

[2] Colin Campbell and Kristin P. Bennett. A linear programming approach to novelty detection. In *Advances in Neural Information Processing Systems 13 (to appear)*, 2001.

[3] L. H. Cox, M. M. Johnson, and K. Kafadar. Exposition of statistical graphics technology. In *ASA Proceedings of the Statistical Computation Section*, pages 55–56, 1982.

[4] A. P. Dempster, N. M. Laird, and D. B. Rubin. Maximum likelihood from incomplete data via the EM algorithm. *Journal of the Royal Statistical Society Series B*, 39:1–38, 1977.

[5] Jean Diebolt and Christian P. Robert. Estimation of finite mixtures through bayesian sampling. *Journal of the Royal Statistical Society Series B*, 56(2):363–375, 1994.

[6] Nathalie Japkowicz, Catherine Myers, and Mark Gluck. A novelty detection approach to classification. In *Proceedings of the 14th International Joint Conference on Artificial Intelligence*, pages 518–623, 1995.

[7] Geoffrey McLachlan and David Peel. *Finite Mixture Models*. John Wiley & Sons, 2000.

[8] Alberto Munõz and Jorge Muruzabál. Self-organizing maps for outlier detection. *Neurocomputing*, 18(1-3):33–60, 1998.

[9] Alexandre Nairac, Timothy A. Corbett-Clark, Ruth Ripley, Neil W. Townsend, and Lionel Tarassenko. Choosing an appropriate model for novelty detection. In *Proceedings of the Fifth International Conference on Artificial Neural Networks*, pages 117–122, 1997.

[10] Stephen Roberts and Lionel Tarassenko. A probabilistic ressource allocation network for novelty detection. *Neural Computation*, 6(2):270–284, 1994.

[11] Peter J. Rousseeuw and Annick M. Leroy. *Robust Regression and Outlier Detection*. John Wiley & Sons, 1987.

[12] Bernhard Schölkopf, Robert C. Williamson, Alex Smola, and John Shawe-Taylor. SV estimation of a distribution's support. In *Advances in Neural Information Processing Systems 12*, pages 582–588, 2000.

[13] Statlib–datasets archive. cf. http://lib.stat.cmu.edu/datasets.

[14] Martin A. Tanner and Wing Hung Wong. The calculation of posterior distributions by data augmentation. *Journal of the American Statistical Society*, 82(398):528–550, 1987.

[15] Geoffrey G. Towell. Local expert autoassociators for anomaly detection. In *Proceedings of the Seventeenth International Conference on Machine Learning*, pages 255–262, 2000.

[16] Alexander Ypma and Robert P. W. Duin. Novelty detection using self-organizing maps. In *Progress in Connectionist-Based Information Systems*, volume 2, pages 1322–1325, 1997.

Applying the Bayesian Evidence Framework to ν-Support Vector Regression

Martin H. Law and James T. Kok

Department of Computer Science
Hong Kong University of Science and Technology
Clear Water Bay
Hong Kong
{martin,jamesk}@cs.ust.hk

Abstract. Following previous successes on applying the Bayesian evidence framework to support vector classifiers and the ϵ-support vector regression algorithm, in this paper we extend the evidence framework also to the ν-support vector regression (ν-SVR) algorithm. We show that ν-SVR training implies a prior on the size of the ϵ-tube that is dependent on the number of training patterns. Besides, this prior has properties that are in line with the error-regulating behavior of ν. Under the evidence framework, standard ν-SVR training can then be regarded as performing level one inference, while levels two and three allow automatic adjustments of the regularization and kernel parameters respectively, without the need of a validation set. Furthermore, this Bayesian extension allows computation of the prediction intervals, taking uncertainties of both the weight parameter and the ϵ-tube width into account. Performance of this method is illustrated on both synthetic and real-world data sets.

1 Introduction

Recently, there is growing interest in using the support vector machines (SVMs) for various classification and regression problems. SVMs are motivated by results from statistical learning theory [8], and have shown superior performance over traditional techniques in many practical applications. The two commonly used SVM methods for regression problems are the ϵ-support vector regression (ϵ-SVR) algorithm [7] and the ν-support vector regression (ν-SVR) algorithm [5]. In particular, ν-SVR, which will be the focus in this paper, has the advantage of being able to automatically adjust the width of the ϵ-tube.

However, to obtain a high level of performance, some parameters in the ν-SVR algorithm still have to be tuned. These include 1) a kernel parameter that helps to define the feature space; and 2) two regularization parameters that determine the tradeoff between the value of ϵ, the training accuracy and model complexity. Data-resampling techniques such as cross-validation can be used, but they are usually very expensive in terms of computation and/or data.

In this paper, we address this issue by adopting the Bayesian approach. In general, the Bayesian approach is attractive in being logically consistent,

L. De Raedt and P. Flach (Eds.): ECML 2001, LNAI 2167, pp. 312–323, 2001.
© Springer-Verlag Berlin Heidelberg 2001

simple and flexible. Recently, various Bayesian techniques have been applied to SVMs for classification problems. Here, we follow [2,3] in applying the evidence framework [4] to ν-SVR. The evidence framework is divided into three levels of inference, and is computationally equivalent to the type II maximum likelihood method in Bayesian statistics. Its use in feedforward neural networks has allowed the automatic selection of regularization parameters and network architectures, without the need of a validation set [4].

The rest of this paper is organized as follows. Brief overviews of the ν-SVR and the evidence framework will be given in Sections 2 and 3 respectively. Application of the evidence framework to ν-SVR will be discussed in Section 4. Simulation results are presented in Section 5, and the last section gives some concluding remarks.

2 ν-Support Vector Regression

In this section, we first introduce ϵ-SVR and then present ν-SVR as an improvement. Interested readers may consult [7,8] for details.

Let the training data D be $\{(\mathbf{x}_i, y_i)\}_{i=1}^{N}$, with input $\mathbf{x}_i$ and output $y_i \in \Re$. In ϵ-SVR, $\mathbf{x}$ is first mapped to $\mathbf{z} = \phi(\mathbf{x})$ in feature space $\mathcal{F}$, then a linear function $f(\mathbf{x}, \mathbf{w}) = \mathbf{w}^T \mathbf{z} + b$ is constructed in $\mathcal{F}$ such that it deviates least from the training data according to the ϵ-insensitive loss function

$$|y - f(\mathbf{x})|_\epsilon = \begin{cases} 0 & \text{if } |y - f(\mathbf{x})| \le \epsilon, \\ |y - f(\mathbf{x})| - \epsilon & \text{otherwise,} \end{cases}$$

while at the same time is as flat"as possible (i.e., $\|\mathbf{w}\|$ is as small as possible). Mathematically, this means minimizing $\frac{1}{2}\|\mathbf{w}\|^2 + C \sum_{i=1}^{N}(\xi_i + \xi_i^*)$, subject to

$$y_i - f_i \le \epsilon + \xi_i^*, \quad f_i - y_i \le \epsilon + \xi_i, \quad \xi_i, \xi_i^* \ge 0, \tag{1}$$

for $1 \le i \le N$, where $f_i = f(\mathbf{x}_i, \mathbf{w})$ and C is a user-defined constant. Notice that after training, those nonzero ξ_iš and ξ_i^*š will be exactly equal to the difference between the corresponding y_i and f_i.

A drawback of ϵ-SVR is that ϵ can be difficult to tune. ν-SVR alleviates this problem by trading off ϵ against model complexity and training error using a parameter $\nu > 0$. Mathematically, the problem now becomes

$$\underset{\mathbf{w}, \epsilon, \xi_i, \xi_i^*}{\text{minimize}} \quad \frac{1}{2}\|\mathbf{w}\|^2 + C\left(\nu\epsilon + \frac{1}{N}\sum_{i=1}^{N}(\xi_i + \xi_i^*)\right), \tag{2}$$

subject to (1) and $\epsilon \ge 0$. Schlkopf $et\ al.$ [5] showed that asymptotically, with probability 1, ν equals both the fraction of data points that become support vectors and the fraction of data points lying outside the ϵ-tube[1]. This suggests that in situations where some prior knowledge on these fractions is available, ν may be easier to adjust than ϵ.

---

[1] Notice that data points lying outside the ϵ-tube are also the error patterns.

3   The Evidence Framework

A model $\mathcal{H}$, with a k-dimensional parameter vector $\mathbf{w}$, consists of its functional form f, the distribution $p(D|\mathbf{w}, \beta, \mathcal{H})$ that the model makes about the data, and a prior parameter distribution $p(\mathbf{w}|\alpha, \mathcal{H})$. Here, α and β are usually called the hyper-parameters. Moreover, $p(D|\mathbf{w}, \beta, \mathcal{H})$ and $p(\mathbf{w}|\alpha, \mathcal{H})$ are often written as:

$$p(D|\mathbf{w}, \beta, \mathcal{H}) \propto \exp(-\beta E_D(D|\mathbf{w}, \mathcal{H})), \tag{3}$$

$$p(\mathbf{w}|\alpha, \mathcal{H}) \propto \exp(-\alpha E_W(\mathbf{w}|\mathcal{H})). \tag{4}$$

3.1   Level 1 Inference

The evidence framework is divided into three levels of inference. For given values of α and β, the first level infers the posterior distribution of $\mathbf{w}$ by the Bayes rule: $p(\mathbf{w}|D, \alpha, \beta, \mathcal{H}) \propto p(D|\mathbf{w}, \beta, \mathcal{H})p(\mathbf{w}|\alpha, \mathcal{H})$. Substituting in (3) and (4), finding the *maximum a posteriori* (MAP) estimate $\mathbf{w}_{MP}$ of $\mathbf{w}$ is then the same as minimizing $M(\mathbf{w}) \equiv \alpha E_W + \beta E_D$.

3.2   Level 2 Inference

The second level of inference determines α and β by maximizing $p(\alpha, \beta|D, \mathcal{H})$. When $p(\alpha, \beta|\mathcal{H})$ is flat, the *evidence* $p(D|\alpha, \beta, \mathcal{H})$ can be used instead. By approximating $p(\mathbf{w}|D, \alpha, \beta, \mathcal{H})$ with a Gaussian at $\mathbf{w}_{MP}$, it can be shown that

$$\log p(D|\alpha, \beta, \mathcal{H}) = -\alpha E_W^{MP} - \beta E_D^{MP} - \frac{1}{2}\log\det\mathbf{A} + \frac{k}{2}\log\alpha + \frac{N}{2}\log\beta - \frac{N}{2}\log 2\pi,$$

where $\mathbf{A} = \frac{\partial^2 M}{\partial \mathbf{w}^2}$ is the hessian matrix, E_W^{MP} and E_D^{MP} are the values of E_W and E_D evaluated at $\mathbf{w}_{MP}$. Optimal values of α and β (denoted by α_{MP} and β_{MP} respectively) are then obtained by iterating the process of finding $\mathbf{w}_{MP}$ from the level 1 inference and estimating α, β by maximizing $p(D|\alpha, \beta, \mathcal{H})$ above.

3.3   Level 3 Inference

The third level of inference ranks different models by $p(\mathcal{H}|D)$. Assuming a flat $p(\mathcal{H})$ for all models, different models are then rated by $p(D|\mathcal{H})$. This can be computed by again taking a Gaussian approximation for $p(D|\alpha, \beta, \mathcal{H})$ at $(\alpha_{MP}, \beta_{MP})$.

4   Applying the Evidence Framework to ν-SVR

4.1   Probabilistic Model and Level 1 Inference

The ϵ-insensitive cost function corresponds to the following noise model [7]:

$$p(y_i|\mathbf{x}_i, \mathbf{w}, \epsilon, \beta, \mathcal{H}) = \frac{\beta}{2(1 + \epsilon\beta)} \exp(-\beta|y_i - f_i|_\epsilon). \tag{5}$$

Notice that [7] does not have the factor β, but is added here to play the important role of controlling the noise variance. For $\mathbf{w}$, we adopt the commonly-used weight decay prior

$$p(\mathbf{w}|\alpha, \mathcal{H}) = (\frac{\alpha}{2\pi})^{\frac{k}{2}} \exp(-\frac{\alpha}{2}\|\mathbf{w}\|^2). \tag{6}$$

Comparing (5), (6) with (3), (4), we see that $E_D(D|\mathbf{w}, \mathcal{H}) = \sum_{i=1}^{N} |y_i - f_i|_\epsilon$, and $E_W(\mathbf{w}|\mathcal{H}) = \frac{1}{2}\|\mathbf{w}\|^2$. For ϵ, we adopt the following prior

$$p(\epsilon|\beta, \nu, \mathcal{H}) = c(\beta, \nu)(1 + \epsilon\beta)^N \exp(-N\beta\nu\epsilon), \tag{7}$$

where $c(\beta, \nu) = (N\nu)^{N+1}\beta/(\exp(N\nu)\Gamma(N+1, N\nu))$ is the normalization factor. Here, $\Gamma(a, x) = \int_x^\infty t^{a-1} \exp(-t)\, dt$ is related to the incomplete gamma function. Justifications for this prior will be discussed in Section 4.2.

Assuming that the patterns are i.i.d., then by using the Bayes rule, finding the MAP estimates of $\mathbf{w}$ and ϵ is equivalent to

$$\underset{\mathbf{w}, \epsilon}{\text{maximize}} \quad \log p(\mathbf{w}|\alpha, \mathcal{H}) + \log p(\epsilon|\beta, \nu, \mathcal{H}) + \sum_{i=1}^{N} \log p(y_i|\mathbf{x}_i, \mathbf{w}, \epsilon, \beta, \mathcal{H}).$$

Plugging in (5), (6) and (7), this becomes

$$\underset{\mathbf{w}, \epsilon}{\text{minimize}} \quad \frac{\alpha}{2}\|\mathbf{w}\|^2 + N\beta\left(\nu\epsilon + \frac{1}{N}\sum_{i=1}^{N} |y_i - f_i|_\epsilon\right).$$

Setting $C = N\beta/\alpha$, we obtain the same optimization problem as in (2). Thus, ν-SVR training can be regarded as performing level 1 inference under this probabilistic model.

4.2   Properties of the Prior $p(\epsilon|\beta, \nu, \mathcal{H})$

Assuming that the model is unbiased and the true noise really follows (5), the probability that a particular $\mathbf{x}$ will have its corresponding y lying outside the ϵ-tube (and thus considered as an error) is equal to

$$1 - \int_{-\epsilon}^{\epsilon} \frac{\beta}{2(1 + \epsilon\beta)} \exp(-\beta \cdot 0)d\delta = \frac{1}{1 + \epsilon\beta}.$$

Now, at the peak of $p(\epsilon|\beta, \nu, \mathcal{H})$, $d\log p(\epsilon|\beta, \nu, \mathcal{H})/d\epsilon = 0$, which gives $\nu = 1/(1 + \epsilon\beta)$. Thus, the prior prefers the value of ϵ such that ν equals the fraction of errors. This is in line with the observation that ν equals the fraction of errors asymptotically with probability one [5]. Moreover, as ν increases, the prior distribution shifts towards zero (Figure 1a). If $\nu = 1$, then $p(\epsilon|\beta, \nu, \mathcal{H})$ has maximum at $\epsilon = 0$. When ν increases beyond 1, $p(\epsilon|\beta, \nu, \mathcal{H})$ becomes strictly decreasing with ϵ. These observations are also in line with [5] in that when $\nu > 1$, the value of ϵ obtained after training will be zero.

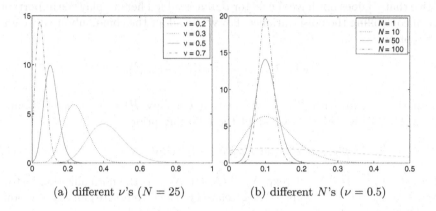

(a) different ν's ($N = 25$)   (b) different N's ($\nu = 0.5$)

Fig. 1. Variations of $p(\epsilon|\beta, \nu, \mathcal{H})$ with ν and N ($\beta = 10$).

Moreover, notice that ϵ appears as a product with β at the peak of $p(\epsilon|\beta, \nu, \mathcal{H})$. Hence, the preferred value of ϵ by the prior is inversely proportional to β. Or, in other words, this preferred ϵ has a linear dependency with the scale parameter $1/\beta$ of the noise model in (5). In fact, it can be shown that the mean value of ϵ under this prior distribution also exhibits the same trend. These are thus in line with the observation in [6] that there is a linear scaling between the optimal ϵ and the noise in the data.

Besides, unlike traditional Bayesian priors, this prior depends on the size of training data and becomes more concentrated around the peak with more training data (Figure 1b). Notice that while the effect of a traditional Bayesian prior diminishes with the arrival of more data, the logarithm of the prior in (7) scales linearly with N just like the log likelihood. Hence, our prior belief, which embodies the idea that ν governs the fraction of errors, will not be overwhelmed with the arrival of more data.

4.3   Level 2 Inference

The second level of inference determines the hyperparameters α, β and ν by maximizing $p(\alpha, \beta, \nu|D, \mathcal{H}) \propto p(D|\alpha, \beta, \nu, \mathcal{H})p(\alpha, \beta, \nu|\mathcal{H})$. When $p(\alpha, \beta, \nu|\mathcal{H})$ is a flat prior, the evidence for α, β and ν, $p(D|\alpha, \beta, \nu, \mathcal{H})$, can be used instead. Now, $\mathcal{E} \equiv \log p(D|\alpha, \beta, \nu, \mathcal{H})$ can be obtained by integrating out $\mathbf{w}$ and ϵ, as:

$$\mathcal{E} = \log \int P(D|\mathbf{w}, \epsilon, \beta, \mathcal{H})P(\mathbf{w}|\alpha, \mathcal{H})P(\epsilon|\beta, \nu, \mathcal{H}) \, d\mathbf{w} \, d\epsilon. \qquad (8)$$

As in [4], we approximate the joint posterior distribution of $\mathbf{w}$ and ϵ using a single Gaussian at their MAP values ($\mathbf{w}_{MP}$ and ϵ_{MP} respectively). This entails computation of the hessian matrix $\mathbf{A} = \frac{\partial^2}{\partial[\mathbf{w}\epsilon]^2}(\alpha E_W + \beta E_D + N\beta\nu\epsilon)$, and consequently derivatives of E_D. However, E_D is not differentiable due to the non-smooth nature of the underlying ϵ-insensitive loss function. Hence, similar to [3], we approximate this loss function by a smooth function

$$V(u) = \varsigma_\eta(u - \epsilon) + \varsigma_\eta(-u - \epsilon), \tag{9}$$

where $\varsigma_\eta(u) = \frac{1}{\eta} \log(1 + \exp(\eta u)), \eta > 0$.

Define $r(u) \equiv d^2\varsigma_\eta(u)/du^2 = \eta/((1 + e^{\eta u})(1 + e^{-\eta u})), r_i \equiv r(y_i - f_i - \epsilon) + r(f_i - y_i - \epsilon)$ and $s_i \equiv r(y_i - f_i - \epsilon) - r(f_i - y_i - \epsilon)$. To obtain $\mathcal{E}$, we can first solve the eigen system[2] for the $N \times N$ matrix $\tilde{\mathbf{K}}$ with entries $r_i K(\mathbf{x}_i, \mathbf{x}_j)$, where K is the kernel function. Denote the resultant n non-zero eigenvalues and the corresponding eigenvectors by ρ_j and $\mathbf{u}_j$ respectively. Then,

$$\mathcal{E} = -\alpha E_W^{MP} - \beta E_D^{MP} - N\beta\nu\epsilon_{MP} + \frac{n}{2}\log\alpha - \frac{1}{2}\sum_{j=1}^{n}\log(\alpha + \beta\rho_j)$$

$$+(N + 1)\log\beta - N\nu + (N + 1)\log(N\nu) - \log\Gamma(N + 1, N\nu) - \frac{1}{2}\log\psi$$

$$+ \log\left(1 + \mathrm{erf}(\sqrt{\frac{\psi}{2}}\epsilon_{MP})\right) - (N + 1)\log 2 + \frac{1}{2}\log(2\pi), \tag{10}$$

where

$$\psi = \beta\sum_{i=1}^{N}r_i - \frac{\beta^2}{\alpha}\left(\sum_{i=1,j=1}^{N}s_is_jK(\mathbf{x}_i, \mathbf{x}_j) - \sum_{j=1}^{n}\frac{\beta\rho_j}{\alpha + \beta\rho_j}(\sum_{l=1}^{N}u_{jl}\sum_{i=1}^{N}s_iK(\mathbf{x}_i, \mathbf{x}_l))^2\right), \tag{11}$$

and $\mathrm{erf}(x) = \frac{2}{\sqrt{\pi}}\int_0^x \exp(-t^2)\,dt$ is the error function.

Iteration formula for α, β and ν to maximize $\mathcal{E}$ can be devised. However, they will not be described here because of the lack of space.

4.4   Level 3 Inference

The third level of inference rates different models by their $p(D|\mathcal{H})$. This, again, is obtained by integrating out α, β and ν, as:

$$p(D|\mathcal{H}) = \int p(D|\alpha, \beta, \nu, \mathcal{H})p(\alpha|\mathcal{H})p(\beta|\mathcal{H})p(\nu|\mathcal{H})d\alpha\,d\beta\,d\nu.$$

As α and β are scale parameters, we take uniform priors over $\log\alpha$ and $\log\beta$, whereas for ν we take a uniform prior over $[0, 1]$. As in the level 2 inference, we also adopt the Gaussian approximation for $p(D|\alpha, \beta, \nu, \mathcal{H})$. It can be shown that $\log p(D|\mathcal{H})$ is given by:

---

[2] Solving this eigen system takes $O(N^3)$ time. However, notice that r_i is significant only when $|y_i - f_i| - \epsilon$ is small. Hence, we need only include into $\tilde{\mathbf{K}}$ those patterns that are lying close to the edges of the ϵ-tube.

$$\log p(D|\mathcal{H}) = \log p(D|\alpha_{MP}, \beta_{MP}, \nu_{MP}, \mathcal{H}) - \frac{1}{2}\log(\alpha_{MP}E_W^{MP}) - \frac{1}{2}\log \kappa$$

$$+ \log \mathrm{erf}\left(\sqrt{\frac{\kappa}{2\beta_{MP}(E_D^{MP} + N\nu_{MP}\epsilon_{MP})}}\right) + \text{constant}, \tag{12}$$

where $\kappa = \beta_{MP}(E_D^{MP} + N\nu_{MP}\epsilon_{MP})(\frac{N+1}{\nu_{MP}^2} - \Delta(\Delta + \frac{N(1-\nu_{MP})}{\nu_{MP}})) - (N\nu_{MP}\beta_{MP})^2,$

$$\Delta = N\exp(-\log\Gamma(N+1, N\nu) + N\log(N\nu) - N\nu). \tag{13}$$

4.5   Posterior Predictive Distribution and Error Bars

To compute the posterior predictive distribution $p(y|\mathbf{x}, D, \mathcal{H})$ at a particular $\mathbf{x}$, the Bayesian approach again requires integrating out the posterior uncertainty of $\mathbf{w}$ and ϵ from $p(y|\mathbf{x}, D, \mathbf{w}, \epsilon, \mathcal{H})$. As mentioned in Section 4.3, the joint posterior distribution of $\mathbf{w}$ and ϵ is approximated by a single Gaussian at their MAP values. This joint distribution can be decomposed into the product of $p(\mathbf{w}|D, \epsilon, \mathcal{H})$ and $p(\epsilon|D, \mathcal{H})$. It can be shown that $p(\mathbf{w}|D, \epsilon, \mathcal{H})$ is a Gaussian distribution with mean $\mathbf{w}_{MP} + \mathbf{A}_{11}^{-1}\mathbf{a}_{12}(\epsilon - \epsilon_{MP})$, and $p(\epsilon|D, \mathcal{H})$ is a normal distribution with peak at ϵ_{MP} and truncated at $\epsilon = 0$ (because $\epsilon \geq 0$). Here $\mathbf{A}_{11}$ and $\mathbf{a}_{12}$ are sub-matrices of the hessian matrix $\mathbf{A}$.

The mean of the posterior predictive distribution can be computed as:

$$\int yp(y|\mathbf{x}, D, \mathbf{w}, \epsilon, \mathcal{H})p(\mathbf{w}, \epsilon|D, \mathcal{H})d\mathbf{w}\,d\epsilon\,dy$$

$$= \int\left(\int yp(y|\mathbf{x}, D, \mathbf{w}, \epsilon, \mathcal{H})p(\mathbf{w}|D, \epsilon, \mathcal{H})d\mathbf{w}dy\right)p(\epsilon|D, \mathcal{H})d\epsilon$$

$$= \int\left(\mathbf{z}^T\left(\mathbf{w}_{MP} + \mathbf{A}_{11}^{-1}\mathbf{a}_{12}(\epsilon - \epsilon_{MP})\right) + b\right)p(\epsilon|D, \mathcal{H})d\epsilon$$

$$= f(\mathbf{x}, \mathbf{w}_{MP}) + \mathbf{z}^T\mathbf{A}_{11}^{-1}\mathbf{a}_{12}(E[\epsilon] - \epsilon_{MP}),$$

where $E[\epsilon] = \epsilon_{MP} + \int \epsilon p(\epsilon|D, \mathcal{H})d\epsilon = p(\epsilon = 0|D, \mathcal{H})/\psi$ (recall that ψ is given by (11)), while

$$\mathbf{z}^T\mathbf{A}_{11}^{-1}\mathbf{a}_{12} = \beta\sum_{i=1}^{n} s_i\left(\frac{1}{\alpha}K(\mathbf{x'x}_i) - \frac{1}{\alpha}\sum_{j=1}^{N}\frac{\beta\rho_j}{\alpha + \beta\rho_j}(\sum_{l=1}^{N}u_{jl}K(\mathbf{x}, \mathbf{x}_l))(\sum_{l=1}^{N}u_{jl}K(\mathbf{x}_i, \mathbf{x}_l))\right).$$

Similarly, the variance $\sigma_y^2(\mathbf{x})$ of the predictive distribution can be shown to be:

$$\int y^2 p(y|\mathbf{x}, D, \mathbf{w})p(\mathbf{w}, \epsilon|D, \mathcal{H})d\mathbf{w}\,d\epsilon\,dy - \left(\int yp(y|\mathbf{x}, D, \mathbf{w})p(\mathbf{w}, \epsilon|D, \mathcal{H})d\mathbf{w}\,d\epsilon\,dy\right)^2$$

$$= \mathbf{z}^T\mathbf{A}_{11}^{-1}\mathbf{z} + (\mathbf{z}^T\mathbf{A}_{11}^{-1}\mathbf{A}_{12})^2\mathrm{VAR}[\epsilon]$$

$$+ \frac{1}{3\beta^2}\left(\beta^2 E[\epsilon^2]^2 + 2\beta E[\epsilon] + 4 + \int_{-\psi\epsilon_{MP}}^{\cdot}\frac{2c(2\pi)^{-1/2}}{(-\frac{\beta}{\psi}t + \beta\epsilon_{MP} + 1)}\exp(-\frac{1}{2}t^2)dt,\right)$$

where $c = 1/\Phi(-\epsilon_{MP}\sqrt{\psi})$ with $\Phi(z)$ being the area under the Gaussian distribution $N(0, 1)$ from z to ∞, $\mathrm{VAR}[\epsilon^2] = \epsilon_{MP}(E[\epsilon] - \epsilon_{MP}) + \frac{1}{\psi}$, and the last integral can be computed by numerical integration.

5   Result

In this section, we report results on applying the evidence framework to ν-SVR, using the Gaussian kernel $K(\mathbf{x}_i, \mathbf{x}_j) = \exp(-\omega\|\mathbf{x}_i - \mathbf{x}_j\|^2)$. Three data sets are used in the experiments. Two of them are real-world data from the UCI machine learning repository [1].

The first one is the toy data $\mathrm{sinc}(x) = \sin(x)/x$, with x uniformly distributed over $[-12, 12]$. In one set of experiments, we add Gaussian noise $N(0, 0.05^2)$ to the outputs; while in another set, we add noise following the noise model in (5), with $\epsilon = 0.05$ and $\beta = 50$. The test set has 10,000 patterns. The experiment is repeated using 10 independent training sets, each of size 80.

The second one is the abalone data, and the task is to predict the ages of the abalones based on 8 input attributes. We used 256 patterns for training and the remaining 3921 patterns for testing. The experiment is repeated 25 times.

The third data set is the Boston housing data, and the task is to predict housing values in the Boston suburbs using 13 input attributes. We used 128 patterns for training and the remaining 378 patterns for testing. The experiment is repeated 10 times.

5.1   Choosing the Regularization and Kernel Parameters

Figure 2 illustrates the choice of $C = N\beta/\alpha$ for a particular ν by using level 2 inference. Figure 3 illustrates the choice of the kernel parameter ω by using level 3 inference. As can be seen from these figures, evidence from the level 2 and level 3 inference follows the testing error closely.

For comparison, 10-fold cross-validation has also been performed, and the average validation set errors are reported in Figures 2 and 3. As can be seen, cross-validation also yields a close match to the testing error. However, this procedure is very computationally demanding[3]. For example, in preparing the curve in Figure 2 for the sinc data, we experimented with 17 values of C and 11 values of ν. Each C, ν combination requires 10 SVMs to be trained (for 10-fold cross-validation), leading to a total of $17 \times 11 \times 10 = 1870$ SVMs for each independent training set. It becomes even worse in choosing the kernel parameter. In the cross-validation experiments, we experimented with 9 values of ω, giving a total of $1870 \times 9 = 16830$ SVMs to be trained.

On the contrary, our proposed method is iterative and, for a fixed ω, this usually takes 10 to 50 iterations to find a good enough C and ν. The computational demand in each iteration comes mainly from the SVM training and the eigen decomposition of $\tilde{\mathbf{K}}$. As $\tilde{\mathbf{K}}$ is dominated by points with large r_is (which lie close to the edges of the ϵ-tube and are thus usually small in number), we can discard those data points with small r_is and thus result in a much smaller eigen problem. Hence, in practice, most of the time is spent on the SVM training. In comparison with cross-validation, we required just around 10 to 50 SVMs in

---

[3] In fact, cross-validation is so computationally demanding that experiments on choosing the kernel parameters for the two real datasets have not been performed.

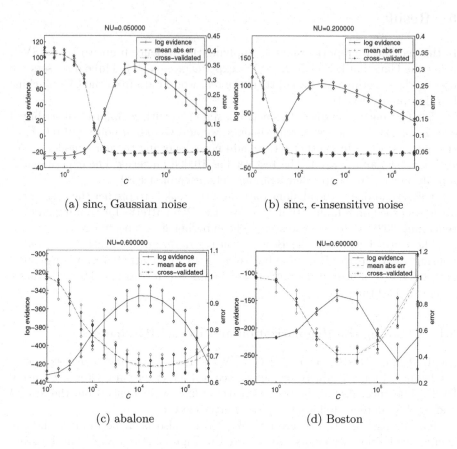

Fig. 2. Plots showing the logarithm of the evidence $p(D|\alpha, \beta, \nu, \mathcal{H})$, the testing errors and the average validation set errors at different values of C's. The error bars correspond to the ± 1 standard deviations based on the 10 repetitions.

preparing the Figure 2 curve for the sinc data, and on average $30 \times 9 = 270$ SVMs in preparing the one in Figure 3.

As on the question of how the choice of η affects the inference results, Figure 4 shows the level 2 and level 3 results for the sinc data set at different ηs. One can see that the evidence curves are all similar in shape as η varies. In particular, their peaks are all located at the same position.

5.2   Error Bars

Figure 5 shows the output predictions on a variation of the sinc problem, with the training patterns distributed unevenly in the input space. As expected, $\sigma_y^2(\mathbf{x})$ increases in regions where the data are sparse. For distant $\mathbf{x}$s, the uncertainty reduces to that of the prior uncertainty.

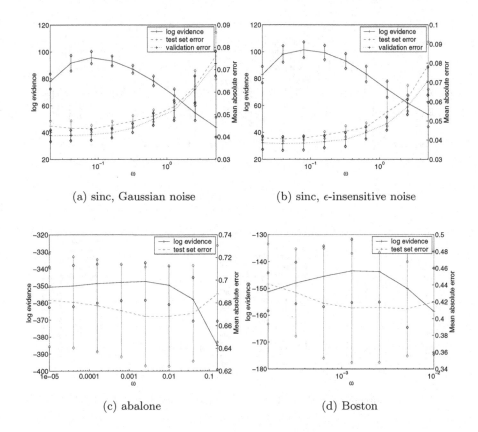

(a) sinc, Gaussian noise

(b) sinc, ϵ-insensitive noise

(c) abalone

(d) Boston

Fig. 3. Plots showing the logarithm of the evidence $p(D|\mathcal{H})$, the test set error (with C and ν selected by the proposed method), and the validation set error (with the best C and ν). The error bars correspond to the ± 1 standard deviations based on the 10 repetitions.

6   Conclusion

In this paper, we extend the application of the evidence framework to ν-SVR. This allows automatic adjustment of the regularization and kernel parameters to their near-optimal values, without the need to set data aside in a validation set. Moreover, posterior predictive distribution and error bars can also be computed, which can then be used as a measure of uncertainty associated with ν-SVR's output predictions.

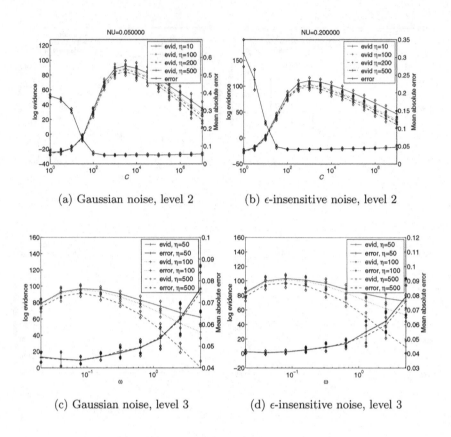

(a) Gaussian noise, level 2   (b) ϵ-insensitive noise, level 2

(c) Gaussian noise, level 3   (d) ϵ-insensitive noise, level 3

Fig. 4. Plots showing the effect of η on level 2 and level 3 inference with the sinc dataset.

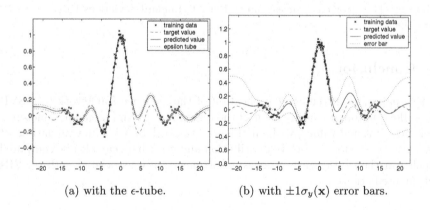

(a) with the ϵ-tube.   (b) with $\pm 1\sigma_y(\mathbf{x})$ error bars.

Fig. 5. Uncertainties in output predictions on the sinc dataset ($\nu = 0.56$).

References

1. C. Blake, E. Keogh, and C.J. Merz. UCI repository of machine learning databases, 1998. http://www.ics.uci.edu/~mlearn/MLRepository.html University of California, Irvine, Department of Information and Computer Sciences.
2. J.T. Kwok. Moderating the outputs of support vector machine classifiers. *IEEE Transactions on Neural Networks*, 10:1018–1031, 1999.
3. J.T. Kwok. The evidence framework applied to support vector machines. *IEEE Transactions on Neural Networks*, 11(5):1162–1173, 2000.
4. D.J.C. MacKay. Bayesian interpolation. *Neural Computation*, 4(3):415–447, May 1992.
5. B. Schölkopf and A.J. Smola. New support vector algorithms. NeuroCOLT2 Technical Report NC2-TR-1998-031, GMD FIRST, 1998.
6. A.J. Smola, N. Murata, B. Schölkopf, and K.-R. Müller. Asymptotically optimal choice of ϵ-loss for support vector machines. In *Proceedings of the International Conference on Artificial Neural Networks*, 1998.
7. A.J. Smola and B. Schölkopf. A tutorial on support vector regression. NeuroCOLT2 Technical Report NC2-TR-1998-030, Royal Holloway College, 1998.
8. V. Vapnik. *Statistical Learning Theory*. Wiley, 1998.

DQL: A New Updating Strategy for Reinforcement Learning Based on Q-Learning

Carlos E. Mariano[1] and Eduardo F. Morales[2]

[1] Instituto Mexicano de Tecnología del Agua, Paseo Cuahunáhuac 8532, Jiutepec, Morelos, 62550, MEXICO
cmariano@tlaloc.imta.mx
[2] ITESM-Campus Cuernavaca, Paseo de la Reforma 182-A, Col. Lomas de Cuernavaca, Temixco, Morelos, 62589, MEXICO
emorales@campus.mor.itesm.mx

Abstract. In reinforcement learning an autonomous agent learns an optimal policy while interacting with the environment. In particular, in one-step Q-learning, with each action an agent updates its Q values considering immediate rewards. In this paper a new strategy for updating Q values is proposed. The strategy, implemented in an algorithm called DQL, uses a set of agents all searching the same goal in the same space to obtain the same optimal policy. Each agent leaves traces over a copy of the environment (copies of Q-values), while searching for a goal. These copies are used by the agents to decide which actions to take. Once all the agents reach a goal, the original Q-values of the best solution found by all the agents are updated using Watkins' Q-learning formula. DQL has some similarities with Gambardella's Ant-Q algorithm [4], however it does not require the definition of a domain dependent heuristic and consequently the tuning of additional parameters. DQL also does not update the original Q-values with zero reward while the agents are searching, as Ant-Q does. It is shown how DQL's guided exploration of several agents with selected exploitation (updating only the best solution) produces faster convergence times than Q-learning and Ant-Q on several testbed problems under similar conditions.

1 Introduction

Reinforcement learning is an on-line technique that approximates dynamic programming. The external environment is modeled as a discrete-time, finite state, Markov decision process. Each action is associated with a reward. The task of reinforcement learning is to maximize the long-term discounted reward per action.

Reinforcement learning has been recently applied to multi agent settings. The main purpose is to coordinate agents to complete a task. In coordination problems, each agent is responsible for a portion of the problem, and most of the time, decisions of an agent affect other agents' performance or solution. Examples include the solution of network routing problems in [6] and coordination

L. De Raedt and P. Flach (Eds.): ECML 2001, LNAI 2167, pp. 324–335, 2001.
© Springer-Verlag Berlin Heidelberg 2001

games such as soccer [7]. Multi agent reinforcement learning have also been used in pursuit games, where a hunter'tries to capture a prey: In these problems, agents share sensations of the location of the prey, communicate its location to its partners and update their relative location in order reach the prey'[13]. Price and Boutilier [10] proposed a method called *implicit imitation*. In this approach apprentice agents learn from the experience of mentor agents about its own capabilities in unvisited parts of the space. Imitation is performed extracting a model from the experienced agent behavior. This approach was proved in the solution of mazes using model based reinforcement learning algorithms, speeding learning dramatically. Other interesting problems, solved using multi agent reinforcement learning, are those known as *n-player cooperative repeated games*. In these problems agents interact in a limited resource environment selecting actions that maximize reward. The chosen actions constitute a joint action. Each joint action is associated with a reward function; the decision problem is cooperative since there is a single reward function reflecting the utility assessment of all the agents. Agents must cooperate in order to select those actions representing the maximal individual and team benefit. Some approaches to establish cooperative behavior between agents for these kind of problems include [1,2,5].

In most of these approaches, single agent reinforcement learning methods are applied without much modification. In this paper, we propose an alternative strategy for updating value functions. The main motivation behind this research is to improve the convergence times of Q-learning with a distributed reinforcement learning setting, where a set of agents"have the same goal, and together cooperate"by leaving traces to find an optimal policy for the same problem. The hypothesis is that using more exploration with a set of agents and a controlled exploitation, by leaving traces between agents and reinforcing only the best solution proposed by the agents, produces faster convergence times.

DQ performance was compared against Q-learning [14] and Gambardella and Dorigo's Ant-Q algorithm [4], which is a distributed reinforcement learning algorithm used in the solution of the traveling salesman problem. The three algorithms were tested on several problems over the whole range of the α and γ parameters used in the Q-learning formula. It is shown that DQ has faster convergence times than one-step Q-learning and Ant-Q under similar conditions.

The paper is organized as follows. Section 2 gives a brief overview of Q-learning and Ant-Q Section 3 describes DQ. Section 4, presents the four test problems used to measure the algorithms'performance and discusses the main results. Finally, Section 5 concludes and gives future research directions.

2   Q-Learning

In this study, each reinforcement learning agent uses the one-step *Q-learning* algorithm [14]. Its learned decision policy is determined by the state-action pair value function, $Q(s, a)$, which estimates long-term discounted rewards for each state-action pair. Given a current state $s \in \mathcal{S}$ and available actions $a_i \in \mathcal{A}_s$, a Q-learning agent selects most of the time an action a with the highest estimated

$Q(s, a)$ and with a small probability $\varepsilon \approx 0$, selects an alternative action. The agent then executes the action, receives an immediate reward r, and moves to the next state s'.

In each step, the agent updates $Q(s, a)$ by recursively discounting future utilities and weighting them by a positive learning rate α:

$$Q(s, a) \leftarrow Q(s, a) + \alpha \left[r + \gamma \max_{a' \in \mathcal{A}'_s} Q(s', a') - Q(s, a) \right] \tag{1}$$

where $(0 \leq \gamma \leq 1)$ is a discount parameter.

As an agent explores the state space, its estimate Q improves gradually, and, eventually, each $\max_{a' \in \mathcal{A}'_s} Q(s', a')$ approaches: $E\left\{ \sum_{n=1}^{\infty} \gamma^{n-1} r_{t+n} \right\}$. Here r_t is the reward received at time t due the action chosen at time $t - 1$. Watkins and Dayan [15] have shown that this Q-learning algorithm converges to an optimal decision policy for a finite Markov decision process.

2.1 Ant-Q

An interesting distributed reinforcement algorithm, originally proposed by Gambardella and Dorigo [4], is Ant-Q. Ant-Q was used to solve traveling salesman problems and can be seen as an improvement over a previous system called ant systems [3]. The general idea of Ant-Q is to use a set of agents searching for the same best policy. Following an analogy with ant colonies, each agent updates its Q-values, as in Q-learning, but without considering any reward ($r = 0$ in Eq. 1), after executing each action. This updating represent traces that can be followed by other agents. Once all the agents reach a goal (an episode), state-action pair evaluation functions of the best solution are updated using a delayed reward ($r \neq 0$) as expressed in Eq. 1. This means that some Q-values will be updated several times on each episode, first without rewards by all the agents that followed the same state-action pair, and once more with rewards if the state-action pair is part of the best path. This repeated updating is not clearly justified and is difficult to prove if the convergence properties of Q-learning still hold.

Ant-Q introduced several additional mechanisms to the Q-learning framework. In particular, the selection policy is defined as a combination of a domain dependent heuristic function ($HE(s, a)$) and the best Q-values. This combination introduces two new parameters (δ and β) that estimate the relevance of $HE(s, a)$ with respect to $Q(s, a)$ values and that need to be tuned for each particular application domain. In general an ϵ-greedy strategy is used and HE is combined with Q values as follows: $argmax_a \{ AQ(s, a)^\delta \times HE(s, a)^\beta \}$.

3 DQL

DQL follows similar ideas of Ant-Q but without loosing the main properties of Q leaning nor introducing extra parameters or heuristics. The general ideas, and main differences with Ant-Q are that it does not use any domain dependent heuristic (and consequently no additional parameters) and it updates the Q values only once (for the best solution found by all the agents).

DQ allows more exploration, as several agents are searching at the same time, and promotes better exploitation, since the updates on the Q-values are performed only over the best solutions[1].

All the agents have access to a temporary copy of the state-action pair evaluation functions ($Q_C(s, a)$). Each time an agent has to select an action, it looks at this copy and decides, based on its information, which action to take. Once the agent performs the selected action, it updates the copy of the state-action value pair using Eq. 2, where $Q_C(s, a)$ represents a copy of the original $Q(s, a)$ pairs.

$$Q_C(s, a) \leftarrow Q_C(s, a) + \alpha \left[\gamma \max_{a' \in \mathcal{A}_s} Q_C(s', a') - Q_C(s, a) \right] \qquad (2)$$

This is similar to what Ant-Q does, however in this case the updates are performed over copies of the original Q-values and the original Q-values are consequently not affected at this stage. All the agents are moved one step at a time, updating and sharing their common Q_C values until reaching a stopping criterion. The agents use the copies of the Q-values to decide which actions to take following an $\epsilon-greedy$ policy. When all the agents have found a solution the Q-value copies are discarded and the state-action pairs considered in the best solution receive a reward which reinforce their values according to Eq. 1. This updates the original Q-values from which a new copy is created for the next cycle. The whole process is repeated until reaching a termination criterion (see Table 1).

Table 1. DQL algorithm.

Initialize $Q(s, a)$ arbitrarily
Repeat (for n episodes)
    Initialize s, copy $Q(s, a)$ to $Q_C(s, a)$
    Repeat (for each step of episode)
        Repeat (for m agents)
            Take action a, observe r, s
            $Q_C(s, a) \leftarrow Q_C(s, a) + \alpha \left[\gamma \max_{a'} Q_C(s, a) - Q_C(s, a) \right]$
            $s \leftarrow s$;
        Until s is terminal
    Evaluate the m proposed solutions
    Assign rewards to the best solution found and
        update the Q values:
    $Q(s, a) \leftarrow Q(s, a) + \alpha \left[r + \gamma \max_{a'} Q(s, a) - Q(s, a) \right]$

---

[1] In the tested problems, the best solution of one episode is the shortest path found by one agent in that episode.

All the agents act on the same environment and have access to the same Q and Q_C values. The copies of the Qvalues are used as guidances to the agents of what seems to be promising states. However, only the best solution found by all the agents receives an actual reward. There are two main differences with respect to Ant-Q

- Partial updates are performed over copies of the Qvalues avoiding multiple updates with and without rewards.
- There is no need to define a domain dependent heuristic or to tune extra parameters as in Ant-Q

The main motivation behind DQ is that it allows:

- More exploration as more agents are used during search
- More exploitation as only relevant (best) solutions are effectively rewarded

The hypothesis is that this alternative strategy for updating value functions achieves, in general, faster convergence times than one-step Qearning, regardless the values of α and γ. To test this hypothesis, we performed several experiments over four problems with different complexity and nature, comparing Qearning, Ant-Qand DQ performance. Although, the tests were performed of deterministic state transition domains, our framework can also be applied to stochastic state transition functions.

4   Experimental Results

All the experiments were performed on the same machine and the algorithms were similarly coded by the same author[2]. Although DQ and Ant-Quse multiple agents the algorithms are implemented sequentially.

Two maze problems were first considered as they are problems where Q learning normally shows good performance. For these problems the algorithms were tested over all possible α and γ values with 0.25 increments. $\varepsilon = 0.1$ was considered for the three algorithms in both maze problems. Each experiment was performed thirty times and we report the mean CPU time, mean number of episodes, and mean number of steps per episode[3]. Algorithm execution stops when the optimal policy (solid lines in Figure 1) is reached in five consecutive episodes.

As mentioned earlier, the Ant-Qalgorithm was designed for the solution of traveling salesman problems (TSPs). Two TSP instances previously solved with Ant-Qre also included in the tests. The same parameter values and stopping criteria used with Ant-Qwere used for DQ and Qearning. Tables of results include best solution found, standard deviation of solutions, the mean of all the solutions, and the mean CPU time to reach the stopping criterion. In this case, every algorithm was executed 15 times over 200 episodes.

---

[2] All algorithms are coded in C++.
[3] The mean number refers to the mean of all the solutions found at a particular episode.

4.1   Grid World with Wind

The first experiment was run on the windy grid world shown in Figure 1 left. The objective is to find the optimal path from S to G considering a wind force, which shifts upwards the resulting state when moving horizontally, the strength of which varies from column to column as shown at the bottom of Figure 1. For instance, moving horizontally (either left or right) from a square which has a wind force"of 1 (indicated at the bottom of Figure 1), causes the agent to move one square above its intended destination. However, moving vertically (either down or up) does not produce any effect[4]. Ant-Qand DQ were both run with 3 agents. Ant-Qwas tested with and without a heuristic. The results are shown in Figures 2 and 3 without heuristic for Ant-Q

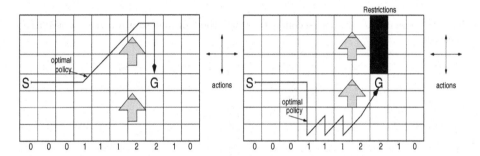

Fig. 1. Grid world in which horizontal movement is altered by a location-dependent upward "wind" (left) and windy world with restrictions (right).

Results from the three algorithms are plotted using three different line types, dashed for Ant-Qdash-dot for Qearning, and continuous for DQ There are four lines for each algorithm, one for each value of γ. The + symbol correspond to $\gamma = 0.25$, ○ to $\gamma = 0.5$, ◇ to $\gamma = 0.75$, and □ to $\gamma = 1.0$.

Figure 2 shows the mean CPU time required for each algorithm to reach the stopping criterion. For Ant-Qand DQ this time corresponds to the mean time required for all the solutions found at each episode. As can be seen from the results, both Ant-Qand DQ clearly outperformed Qearning for all the tested values of α and γ, significantly reducing the convergence times.

Figure 3 shows the mean number of episodes and the mean number of steps per episode required for the three algorithms to reach the stopping criterion. For these two metrics DQ performance was the best of the three algorithms, and Qeaning was able to outperform Ant-Qfor $\alpha \geq 0.5$.

The previously described results are for Ant-Qwithout using any heuristic. When Ant-Qwas tested using as heuristic the inverse of the Manhattan distance,

---

[4] An agent is not allowed to move outside the borders.

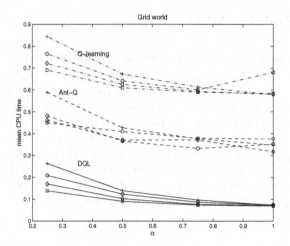

Fig. 2. Mean CPU time in seconds to reach the optimal solution five consecutive episodes.

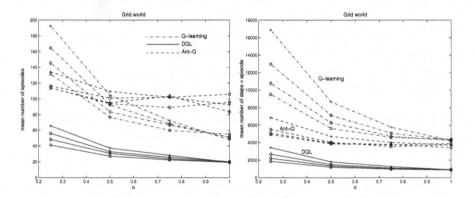

Fig. 3. Mean episodes (left) and steps per episode (right) required to reach the optimal solution.

it was not able to converge[5] with three different combinations of (δ, β): $(1, 1)$ Q values and heuristic function equally important, $(2, 1)$ Q values more important than the heuristic function, and $(1, 2)$ heuristic function more important than Q values. Although, the heuristic used may be reasonable for some maze problems, it is clear that in general, finding a suitable heuristic may be a very difficult task.

We also decided to test a variant of DQ called DQ-2, where each agent performs a complete episode before starting with the next agent. That is, performing m episodes in sequence without sharing information while performing the task. Figure 4 compares the mean CPU times of DQ (here as DQ-1)

---

[5] Reach the optimal policy five consecutive episodes before reaching 500,000 transitions.

against this "episodic"updating approach (DQ-2). As it can be appreciated in the figure, sharing information while performing a task reduces convergence times. Although not shown in the paper, due to restrictions in space, similar results were observed in the other problems.

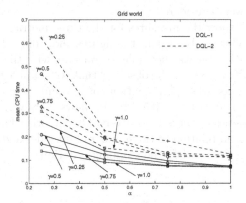

Fig. 4. Mean CPU times in seconds between DQL and an "episodic" variant (DQL-2)

We also measured the average number of total updates of Q-values ($Q_C + Q$) in DQ against the number of Q-updates of Q-learning (see Figure 5). As can be seen in the figure, although DQ updates a larger number of total Q values, it converges faster. We believe that the extra information shared by the agents during the process helps to reduce convergence times. Similar behavior was observed on the other problems.

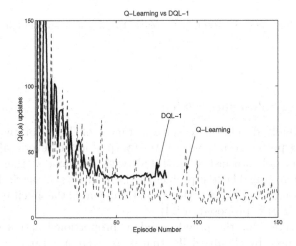

Fig. 5. Average number of total Q-value updates for DQL and Q-learning.

4.2   Grid World with Wind and Trap

This problem was designed to generate a more difficult maze. An obstacle block-
ing the optimal path is included to the windy grid world, forcing agents to search
for an alternative route. Figure 1 right shows the maze and the optimal policy
that agents must find. The same operation conditions and parameters used in
the previous maze were considered.

Figures 6 and 7 show the measures for the three metrics obtained with the
three algorithms under study. Again, the figures show only the performance of
Ant-Q without heuristic as it was not able to converge with the Manhattan distance heuristic. In Figure 6 it can be observed that Ant-Q is able to outperformed
DQ mean CPU time for some combinations of α and γ: ($\alpha = 0.25, \gamma \neq 0.25$),
$\alpha = 0.5, \gamma = 0.5$, and ($\alpha = 1, \gamma = 0.5, 1.0$). It shows, however, to be much more
dependent on the values of these parameters. On the other hand, DQ shows a
more stable behavior in relation to the number of episodes and steps per episode
required for the agents to satisfy the stopping criterion.

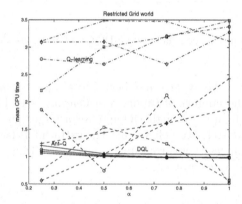

Fig. 6. Mean CPU time in seconds to reach the optimal solution five consecutive
episodes.

4.3   Traveling Salesman Problems

Ant-Q was originally developed to solve instances of TSP. For them, the authors of Ant-Q reported results where Ant-Q outperformed several alternative
algorithms. We took two instances of TSP with the same settings used in the
original Ant-Q paper [4]. The first problem is the 30 cities symmetric TSP known
as *Oliver30* proposed in [9], and the second problem is the 48 cities asymmetric
TSP known as *Ry48p* proposed in [11].

Ant-Q parameters for the pseudo random proportional action choice rule
were the same used by Gambardella, that is, $\beta = 2.0$, $\delta = 1.0$, $\alpha = 0.1$, $\gamma = 0.3$,
and $HE(i, j) = 1/d_{i,j}$, being i, j cities and $d_{i,j}$ the distance between them. For

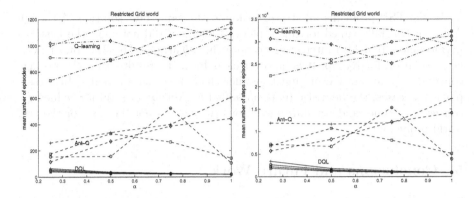

Fig. 7. Mean episodes (left) and steps per episode (right) required to reach the optimal solution.

DQ and Q-learning, the same values for the α and γ parameters were used. $Q(s,a)$ values were initialized to the inverse of the number of cities times the average length of edges, and an ε-greedy selection policy, with $\varepsilon = 0.1$ [6]. The algorithms considered 200 steps or transitions for *Oliver30* problem, and 600 for *ryp48*. The number of agents were the same in DQ and Ant-Q: 30 for *Oliver30* and 48 for *Ry48p*. For Q-learning a single agent was used.

The performance was evaluated repeating each trial 15 times. We report the average performances. The CPU time correspond to the average running times to reach the best result.

Table 2. Results for the two TSPs.

		Oliver30	*Ry48p*
Best		423.74	14422
DQL	Mean	424.61	14600
	Std. Dev.	3.25	100
	CPU	3.48	13.29
Q-learning	Mean	425.32	14520
	Std. Dev.	4.12	150
	CPU	25.92	97.32
Ant-Q HE	Mean	424.92	14750
	Std. Dev.	3.7	189
	CPU	6.39	32.39
Ant-Q no HE	Mean	435.43	15365
	Std. Dev.	12.7	210
	CPU	46.84	76.98

[6] This policy is equivalent to consider $q_0 = 0.9$ in the original Ant-Q algorithm

In the TSP problems all strategies found the same best solution. Although Ant-Q was specially "tuned" for this type of problems it did not show the best performance. It is also interesting to note that Q-learning show the lowest average solution for Ry48p. It is however clear from the results, that the average convergence times of DQ are much smaller than the other strategies. In these particular cases, the heuristic function added to Ant-Q was useful for reducing convergence times and standard deviations (which was not the case for the grid world problems).

5   Conclusions and Future Work

This paper introduces a new strategy for updating Q-values implemented in an algorithm called DQ. DQ uses a set of agents searching the same goal in the same space. Traces (copies of Q-values updated without rewards) are used to guide the exploration of agents. The original Q-values of only the best solution found by all the agents is updated using the one-step Q-learning formula. It was shown how DQ's guided exploration of several agents with selected exploitation (updating only the best solution) produces faster convergence times than Q-learning and Ant-Q on several testbed problems under similar conditions.

The heuristic and extra parameters needed by Ant-Q does not seem to be producing any benefits. Additionally, selecting a good heuristic can be a difficult task. DQ, on the other hand, does not require extra parameters and shows, in general, better convergence times.

DQ updating strategy is performed only on the best path among m solutions. In order to preserve the convergence properties of Q-learning, we need to show that all the Q-value state-action pairs have a non zero probability of being updated. This is part of our future work.

Before trying a parallel version, which seems a natural extension, we would like to perform more tests and compare the results against different strategies for updating Q-values, such as Monte Carlo. It will also be interesting to run DQ without updating the copies of the Q-values to assess its influence in the results (which is like running Q-learning several times without updating and then update the best results found so far).

Acknowledgments. Thanks to the anonymous reviewers for their helpful comments on the initial draft of this paper. The first author was supported by IMTA. This research was supported by CONACyT under grant 33000-A.

References

1. Boutilier, C.: Sequential Optimality and Coordination in Multi agent Systems, In *Proc. of IJCAI-99*, Stockholm, Sweden, 1999.
2. Claus, C., Boutilier, C.: The Dynamics of Reinforcement Learning in Cooperative Multiagents Systems, In *Proc. of AAAI-97 Multiagent Learning Workshop*, pg. 13-18, Providence, 1997.

3. Dorigo, M.: *Optimization, Learning, and Natural Algorithms*, PhD thesis, Politecnico da Milano, Italy, 1992.
4. Gambardella, L., M., Dorigo, M.: Ant-Q: A reinforcement Learning Approach to the Traveling Salesman Problem, In *Proceedings of the 12th International Conference on Machine Learning*, pp. 252-260, Morgan Kaufmann, 1995.
5. Hu, J., Wellman, M.: Multiagent Reinforcement Learning: Theoretical Framework and an Algorithm, In *Proc. 15th Int. Conf. on Machine Learning*, pp. 242-250, Morgan Kaufmann, 1998.
6. Littman, M., Boyan, J.: A Distributed Reinforcement Learning Scheme for Network Routing, In *Proc. Int. Workshop on Applications of Neural Networks to Telecommunications*, pp. 45-51, J. Alspector, et al., (eds.), Lawrence Erlbaum, Hillsdale, NJ, 1993.
7. Littman, M.: Markov Games as a Framework for Multiagent Reinforcement Learning, In *Proc. 11th Int. Conf. on Machine Learning*, pp. 157-163, New Brunswick, NJ, 1994, Morgan Kaufmann.
8. Mariano, C., Morales, E.: A New Distributed Reinforcement Learning Algorithm for the solution of Multiple Objective Optimization Problems, In O. Cairo et al., eds. *Lecture Notes in Artificial Intelligence*, 1793:212-223, April 2000.
9. Oliver, I., Smith, D., Holland, J.R.: A study of Permutation Crossover Operators on the Traveling Salesman Problem, In *Proc. 2nd Int. Conf. an Genetic Algorithms*, pp. 224-230, J.J. Grefenstette (ed.), Lawrence Erlbaum, Hillsdale, NJ, 1987.
10. Price, B., Boutilier, C.: Implicit Imitation in Multiagent Reinforcement Learning, In *Proc. 16th Int. Conf. on Machine Learning*, pp. , 1999.
11. Reinelt, G.: The Traveling Salesman: Computational Solutions for TSP Applications, Springer Verlag, Berlin, 1994.
12. Sutton, R., Barto, A.: *Reinforcement Learning an Introduction*, MIT Press, Cambridge, MA, 1998.
13. Tan, M.: Multiagent Reinforcement Learning: Independent vs. Cooperative Agents, In *Proc. 10th Int. Conf. on Machine Learning*, pp. 330-337, Amherst, MA, 1993.
14. Watkins, C.: *Learning from Delayed Rewards*. PhD thesis, Cambridge University, Cambridge, MA, 1978.
15. Watkins, C., Dayan, P.: Q-Learning, *Machine Learning*, 3:279-292, 1992.

A Language-Based Similarity Measure

Lionel Martin and Frédéric Moal

LIFO - Université d'Orléans,
rue Léonard de Vinci, BP 6759,
45067 Orleans cedex 2, FRANCE
{martin,moal}@lifo.univ-orleans.fr

Abstract. This paper presents an unified framework for the definition of similarity measures for various formalisms (attribute-value, first order logic...). The underlying idea is that the similarity between two objects does not depend only on the attribute values of the objects, but more especially on the set of the potentially relevant definitions of concepts for the problem considered.

In our framework, the user defines a language with a grammar to specify the similarity measure. Each term of the language represents a property of the objects. The similarity between two objects is the probability that these two objects both satisfy or both reject simultaneously the properties of the given language. When this probability is not computable, we use a stochastic generation procedure to approximate it.

This measure can be applied for both clustering and classification tasks. The empirical evaluation on common classification problems shows a very good accuracy.

1 Introduction

Distance or similarity measures play a central role in many machine learning problems. Usually, the definition of similarity between objects depends on the formalism used for the object description. Two main approaches have been proposed: weight-based similarity measure, relying on a weighted sum of similarity of different parts of objects (used in attribute-value languages) and description-based similarity measure based on the construction of object descriptions, used in both attribute-value languages and first order logic.

In the case of attribute-value languages, objects are vectors and the similarity between objects depends on the similarity of vectors components; two types of attributes are separately considered: nominal attributes (having value in an unordered finite -and generally small- set of symbolic values) and numerical ones. In most cases, two different values of a nominal attribute are not similar (similarity=0), otherwise they are similar (similarity=1): in this case, the similarity between two objects is the number of common attributes. In some cases, the frequency of values is used to define the similarity of nominal attributes [CS93, SW86]. Numerical attributes can be considered in various ways: the similarity can be defined from their Euclidean distance or their normalized distance [Aha89,GCM95] or values are discretized and then considered as nominal attributes. The final similarity between tuples is the sum of the similarity induced

L. De Raedt and P. Flach (Eds.): ECML 2001, LNAI 2167, pp. 336–347, 2001.
© Springer-Verlag Berlin Heidelberg 2001

by the nominal attributes and the similarity induced by the numerical attributes. This sum can be weighted with different techniques: weights are computed by statistical techniques [MT94], based on conditional probabilities [SW86], or are obtained by an optimization technique such as a genetic algorithm.

Another way to build a similarity function consists of producing a description of objects. When such descriptions are sets (of atoms), the similarity is based on description intersections [Bis92,EW96]; when descriptions are rules, the similarity between two objects is given by the number of rules satisfied by the two objects [Seb97,SS94]. RISE [Dom95] builds rules for attribute-value objects and proposes an extension of weight-based similarity in the case of generalized attribute-value vectors.

In any case, two objects are considered to be similar when they share some properties. However, it is important to notice that the main expectation from a similarity measure is the ordering induced, i.e. such measure is used to state that object e_1 is more similar to e_2 than e_3 is. Then e_1 can be considered to be more similar to e_2 than e_3 is, if e_1 shares more properties with e_2 than with e_3. This is achieved by several rule-based similarity measures [Dom95,SS94,Seb97,EW96] which consider a finite set of properties, made of rules learned to characterize some objects. The common point of these approaches is that the considered rules have a discriminating power: a rule is built to discriminate a set of examples from a set of counter-examples, and then the similarity is induced in a supervised manner. So this set of rules is strongly biased by the original set of objects and the induction technique used.

In this paper, we propose to base the similarity measure on a language, representing a possibly infinite set of properties or rules. This language is composed of terms that represent concept descriptions. Each term of the language is associated with an evaluation function, able to test whether an object satisfies the property or not. In the case of a finite language, the similarity between two objects is given by the number of properties both objects satisfy or reject simultaneously. In the case of infinite languages, we propose to approximate the similarity by randomly generating a finite subset of the language.

The next section formalizes our similarity definition for finite languages. We focus on the properties of this similarity and its limitations for infinite languages. The Section 3 presents a constraint tree grammar formalism used to specify a language and to generate a finite subset of this language. In Section 4, we present experimental results of this similarity: it has been implemented for a classification task based on a nearest neighbor algorithm and tested on some well-known attribute-value problems.

2   A Similarity Measure

We consider a set of objects $\mathcal{E} = \{e_1, \dots, e_m\}$ and a language $\mathcal{L}$, i.e. a (possibly infinite) set of terms $\{t_1, \dots, t_n, \dots\}$. In this paper, a term $t \in \mathcal{L}$ represents a property (for example *color=blue*); for each object $e \in \mathcal{E}$, either e satisfies t (noted $t(e) = 1$) or e does not satisfy t (noted $t(e) = 0$). We will consider further (Section 2.5) the case where, due to incomplete or imprecise data, we cannot state that $t(e) = 1$ or $t(e) = 0$.

Now, given two objects e_i and e_j in $\mathcal{E}$ and a property $t \in \mathcal{L}$, we say that e_i and e_j are equivalent w.r.t. t if $t(e_i) = t(e_j)$ (e_i and e_j can not be distinguished by t). When e_i and e_j are equivalent w.r.t. most terms (resp. a few terms) of $\mathcal{L}$, we propose to consider that the similarity between e_i and e_j be high (resp. low). We propose to formalize this similarity by using a probability measure.

2.1   Finite Languages

Let $\mathcal{L}$ be a language. A probability measure [DeG86] is defined over a space $(\Omega, \mathcal{B})$ where $\mathcal{B}$ is an α-algebra over the basic space Ω. We define the basic space $\Omega = \mathcal{L}$, i.e. terms $t \in \mathcal{L}$ are elementary events.

In the case of finite languages $\mathcal{L}$, the space $(\mathcal{L}, \mathcal{P}(\mathcal{L}))$, where $\mathcal{P}(\mathcal{L})$ is the powerset of $\mathcal{L}$, is probabilisable. The similarity between e_i and e_j can then be defined as the probability that e_i and e_j are equivalent w.r.t. a term t randomly chosen in $\mathcal{L}$. Let $\mathcal{L}_{e_i,e_j} = \{t \in \mathcal{L} | t(e_i) = t(e_j)\}$ be the set of terms of $\mathcal{L}$ for which e_i and e_j are equivalent; $\mathcal{L}_{e_i,e_j} \in \mathcal{P}(\mathcal{L})$ and we define the previous similarity as the probability of the event $\mathcal{L}_{e_i,e_j}$

Definition 1. *Let $\mathcal{L}$ be a finite language and P a probability measure over $(\mathcal{L}, \mathcal{P}(\mathcal{L}))$. Let e_i and e_j be two objects of $\mathcal{E}$ and $\mathcal{L}_{e_i,e_j} = \{t \in \mathcal{L} | t(e_i) = t(e_j)\} \in \mathcal{P}(\mathcal{L})$. The similarity with respect to $\mathcal{L}$ between e_i and e_j, noted $sim_{\mathcal{L}}(e_i, e_j)$, is defined by $sim_{\mathcal{L}}(e_i, e_j) = P(\mathcal{L}_{e_i,e_j})$.*

In the following, we will write $sim(e_i, e_j)$ for $sim_{\mathcal{L}}(e_i, e_j)$ when $\mathcal{L}$ is not ambiguous.

In the case of a uniform probability over $\mathcal{L}$, i.e. each term $t \in \mathcal{L}$ has the same probability: $P(t) = \frac{1}{|\mathcal{L}|}$, this definition is equivalent to

$$ sim(e_i, e_j) = \frac{1}{|\mathcal{L}|} \cdot \sum_{t \in \mathcal{L}} \delta_t(e_i, e_j) $$

where $\delta_t(e_i, e_j) = 1$ if $t(e_i) = t(e_j)$ and $\delta_t(e_i, e_j) = 0$ if $t(e_i) \neq t(e_j)$.

In this definition, the similarity between e_i and e_j is the rate of terms $t \in \mathcal{L}$ such that $t(e_1) = t(e_j)$. Previous works propose a similarity measure based on a sum of weights associated with learned rules [SS94], attributes [CS93,SW86] or occurrences [Bis92]. In the previous definition, the sum is not weighted and is computed for any term of the language.

2.2   Example

In this example, objects are glasses of colored water. Each object is described by a couple $< col, temp >$ where col (resp. $temp$) is the color (resp. temperature expressed in fahrenheit degrees) of the object.

$e_1 = < green, 14 >$	$e_3 = < orange, 221 >$
$e_2 = < red, 203 >$	$e_4 = < pink, 266 >$

Language $\mathcal{L}_1$. The first language considered here focuses on the temperature of the water; it contains 30 terms: $\mathcal{L}_1 = \{temp > 0, temp > 10, \ldots, temp > 290\}$ and we consider a uniform probability over $\mathcal{L}_1$. For each e_i and e_j, we can compute $sim(e_i, e_j)$: for example, $sim(e_1, e_2) = 11/30$, $sim(e_1, e_3) = 9/30$, $\ldots$ and we can see that the most similar objects w.r.t $\mathcal{L}_1$ are e_2 and e_3 which is intuitive if we focus on the temperature.

Language $\mathcal{L}_2$. The second language considered here focuses on the chemical state of the water (gaseous, liquid, solid): the language $\mathcal{L}_2$ is defined by two terms: $\{temp \leq 32, temp \leq 212\}$ and we consider a uniform probability over $\mathcal{L}_2$. With respect to this language, the most similar objects are e_3 and e_4 ($sim(e_3, e_4) = 1$). Moreover, $sim(e_2, e_4) = 1/2$ and $sim(e_1, e_4) = 0$, i.e the object e_4 (gaseous) is less far from the object e_2 (liquid) than the object e_1 (solid).

Let us notice that if we had added an attribute *state* to the object description, the language $\mathcal{L}'_2 = \{state = solid, state = liquid, state = gazeous\}$ would lead to a different result since then, $sim(e_3, e_4) = 1$ but $sim(e_2, e_4) = 1/3$.

Language $\mathcal{L}_3$. Let us consider now a language focusing on the color of objects. With respect to the language $\{col = green, col = pink, col = red, col = orange\}$, for any e_i, e_j with $e_i \neq e_j$, we have $sim(e_i, e_j) = 1/2$. In such cases, we would like to use a distance over the domain of color, indicating that red and pink are more similar than red and orange, $\ldots$. In this case, we propose to extend the previous language by adding $\{(color=red \ or \ color=pink), \ (color=red \ or \ color=orange), \ \ldots\}$. With this language, e_2 and e_4 share the property *(color=red or color=pink)* and then $sim(e_2, e_4) > sim(e_1, e_4)$. Finally we can consider a non-uniform probability over $\mathcal{L}_3$, given a greater weight to *(color=red or color=pink)* than to *(color=red or color=orange)*. Finally, we can consider the following language (the probability of each term is written in boxes) :

$\mathcal{L}_3 = \{col=green \boxed{20\%}, col=pink \boxed{20\%}, col=red \boxed{20\%}, col=orange \boxed{20\%},$ *(color=red or color=pink)* $\boxed{12\%}$, *(color=red or color=orange)* $\boxed{6\%}$, *(color=pink or color=orange)* $\boxed{2\%}$ $\}$. With such a language, the most similar objects are now e_2 and e_4 ($sim(e_2, e_4) = 20 + 0 + 0 + 20 + 12 + 0 + 0 = 52\%$)

Preliminary conclusion. In this example, the similarity between objects depends on the language considered. It shows that the similarity is not intrinsic to the objects, but depends on the point of view by which objects are considered, i.e. on properties (or concept definitions) that are relevant to the user. The language can then be viewed as a central bias on the similarity definition. We propose in Section 3 to use a grammar to express such a bias.

2.3 A Pseudo-Distance

For any $e_i, e_j \in \mathcal{E}$, $sim(e_i, e_j) \in [0, 1]$; a dissimilarity measure can be naturally defined as $dissim(e_i, e_j) = 1 - sim(e_i, e_j) = P(\overline{\mathcal{L}_{e_i, e_j}})$. It is easy to see that *dissim* is symmetric. To show that *dissim* satisfies the triangle inequality, i.e. for any e_1, e_2, e_3, $dissim(e_1, e_3) \leq dissim(e_1, e_2) + dissim(e_2, e_3)$, we have to prove that $P(\overline{\mathcal{L}_{e_1,e_3}}) \leq P(\overline{\mathcal{L}_{e_1,e_2}}) + P(\overline{\mathcal{L}_{e_2,e_3}})$. For any $t \in \mathcal{L}$, if $t(e_1) \neq t(e_3)$ then either $t(e_1) \neq t(e_2)$ or $t(e_2) \neq t(e_3)$ which prove the triangle inequality.

Since $dissim(e,e) = 0$ for any e, $dissim$ is a pseudo distance. However $dissim$ is not a distance since it may exist $e_i, e_j \in \mathcal{E}$ with $dissim(e_i, e_j) = 0$ but $e_i \neq e_j$. This case happens when the language does not allow to distinguish two objects ($\forall t \in \mathcal{L}, t(e_i) = t(e_j)$): in Example 2.2, objects $e_5 =< blue, 18 >$ and $e_1 =< green, 14 >$ are equivalent w.r.t. $\mathcal{L}_1$ ($dissim_{\mathcal{L}_1}(e_1, e_5) = 0$); for practical purpose, e_1 and e_2 are equivalent but they are not equal.

2.4   Usual Languages

For objects described by a set of attributes $A = \{Att_i\}$, with a domain D_i for Att_i with nominal values, a (finite) language can be defined by $\mathcal{L}_{A=v} = \{Att_i = v_{i_j} | v_{i_j} \in D_i\}$.

The dissimilarity associated with this language is a distance equivalent to the Hamming distance if each attribute is binary.

If we consider objects described by a set of numerical attributes $A = \{Att_i\}$, various languages can be considered:

$$\mathcal{L}_{A=n} = \{Att_i = v_{i_j}\}$$
$$\mathcal{L}_{A \leq x} = \{Att_i \leq v_{i_j}\}$$
$$\mathcal{L}_{A \geq x} = \{Att_i \geq v_{i_j}\}$$
$$\mathcal{L}_{x \leq A \leq y} = \{v_{i_k} \leq Att_i \leq v_{i_j}\}$$
$$\ldots$$

where v_{i_j} is chosen among the possible values of Att_i or is taken from a given range.

We can also consider languages such as $\{Exp \leq v\}$ where Exp is a numeric expression (linear or not) involving attributes, such as

$$\mathcal{L}_{Lin} = \{a_0^i + a_1^i Att_1 + \ldots + a_n^i Att_n \geq 0 | a_k^i \in I\!R\}$$

Finally, any combination of these languages can be considered, also extended with conjunctions and disjunctions.

For object described by atoms built with a predicate p, the language can be defined as the set of clauses (constrained or not) having the predicate p for head:

$$\mathcal{L}_{FOL}(p) = \{h \leftarrow l_1, \ldots l_n | h = p(X_1, \ldots, X_k)\}.$$

For example, consider objects called $a, b, c, \ldots$, where some objects are contained into others. This can be represented in a first order theory with predicates *contains*, *shape* and *nb_elements*: an example is shown in Fig. 1.

With this representation, we can define a similarity measure between atoms $object(a), object(b), \ldots$ with respect to the set of clauses:

$$object(X) \leftarrow shape(X, circle).$$
$$object(X) \leftarrow shape(X, square).$$
$$object(X) \leftarrow shape(X, triangle).$$
$$object(X) \leftarrow contains(X, Y), shape(Y, circle).$$
$$object(X) \leftarrow contains(X, Y), shape(Y, square).$$
$$object(X) \leftarrow contains(X, Y), shape(Y, triangle).$$

Two objects are similar if they are both covered or rejected by the same clauses. In the previous example, the similarity between $object(b)$ and $object(f)$ is maximum ($sim(object(b), object(f)) = 1$).

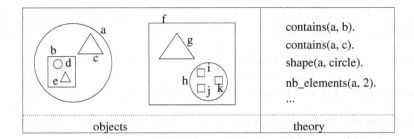

Fig. 1. Example in first order logic

We can also consider a language involving the number of objects (predicate *nb_elements*) by considering clauses such as

$object(X) \leftarrow nb\_elements(X, N), N \geq 2.$

In this framework, the similarity measure is different from [HWB01] and [Pla95] which is based on the structure of terms.

In the case of infinite languages, it can be more complicated or impossible to build a probability measure. Moreover, even for finite languages, it can be hard to compute exactly the similarity between two objects. For these reasons, we propose to define the similarity using a finite subset of the language, stochastically generated. In the next section, we propose a grammatical formalism to generate such sub-language.

2.5   Handling Missing and Constrained Values

The previous similarity definition can be extended to treat missing values: when a value is missing in e_i, it may be impossible to evaluate $t(e_i)$ for some $t \in \mathcal{L}$. Let $\mathcal{L}_{(e_i)}$ be the set of $t \in \mathcal{L}$ such that $t(e_i)$ can be evaluated. To express the similarity between e_i and e_j, the language is restricted to terms t such that both $t(e_i)$ and $t(e_j)$ can be evaluated:

$sim_{\mathcal{L}}(e_i, e_j) = sim_{\mathcal{L}_{e_i} \cap \mathcal{L}_{e_j}}(e_i, e_j)$

Moreover, attribute-value languages do not allow to handle approximate values. Consider an object for which an attribute is not precisely known, but is known to be ≤ 10. Such an attribute is then either considered unknown (value ? or is specified by a symbolic attribute, which require that each value for this attribute is symbolic.

The similarity proposed here may support an attribute-value specification, with constraints: an object is then a constrained vector $c\square < x_1, \ldots, x_n >$ where c express constraints on variables x_i. For example,

$e_6 : (temp \leq 10) \,\square\, < col, temp >$

is a constrained vector for which the color is unknown and temperature is not precisely known, but known to be $\leq 10°F$.

With this formalism, a term $t \in \mathcal{L}$ can be expressed using constraints (like all languages of example 2.2) and we note $\neg t$ the negation of t; in most cases (languages made with equalities, inequalities, disequalities, conjunction, disjunction), $\neg t$ is also a constraint. Let $e = c\square < x_1, \ldots, x_n >$ and t a term, to determine if e satisfies t ($t(e) = 1$) or not ($t(e) = 0$),we have to compute the inconsistency of a constraint:

- $t(e) = 0$ iff t, c is inconsistent,
- $t(e) = 1$ iff $\neg t, c$ is inconsistent,
- otherwise $t(e)$ is undetermined.

For example, let $t_1 = (temp \geq 15)$, $t_2 = (temp \leq 20)$ and $t_3 = (temp \geq 5)$: $t_1(e_6) = 0$, $t_2(e_6) = 1$ and $t_3(e_6)$ is undetermined,

Finally, as for missed values, $sim(e_i, e_j)$ can be defined by restricting the language to the set of terms t such that both $t(e_i)$ and $t(e_j)$ are defined. In example 2.2, object e_6 is highly similar to e_1 with respect to both $\mathcal{L}_1$ and $\mathcal{L}_2$.

3   Constraint Tree Grammars

We propose in this section a new formalism able to express a language specification: constraint tree grammars. Regular tree grammars are commonly used to specify language composed of structured terms. Such grammars [GS84] are defined by

- a set of constructors $\mathcal{F}$ (function symbols and their arity) such as $=$, $\geq$, or, red, $color$, ... We denote $T(\mathcal{F})$ the set of terms over $\mathcal{F}$ (for example $or(=(color, red), \geq (temp, 10)))$,
- a set of non-terminal symbols containing an axiom noted A,
- and a set of production rules.

The set of production rules specify how terms can be built. In order to handle context dependent informations, we propose to extend this formalism by adding constraints to the production rules. In most constraint languages [MS98], constraints are defined over a structure $\mathcal{D}$ composed of a set of function symbols, an interpretation domain D, a set of constraint predicate symbols and a set of evaluation functions: these functions define the evaluation of terms on D and the boolean values of constrained atoms.

The idea is to use constraints to declaratively define biases on the language. This formalism has been deeply studied in [Moa00]. The main advantage here is the compositionality: from different languages (specified by their grammar), we can build a new grammar representing the union or intersection of initial languages.

Moreover production rules can be used to stochastically generate terms of the language for building a finite subset of the (possibly infinite) language specified by the grammar. Finally, weights can be associated with each rules in order to specify different probabilities.

3.1   Formal Definition

Formally, a constraint tree grammar is defined as follows:

Definition 2. *A* **Constraint Tree Grammar** *is a tuple* $G = (A, N, \mathcal{F}, \mathcal{D}, R)$ *where:*
- *A is the axiom,*
- *N is a set of non-terminal symbols* $X(x_1, x_2, \ldots, x_n)$, *where* $(x_1, x_2, \ldots, x_n)$ *represents the set of attributes linked to the symbol X.* $\tilde{N}$ *represents the set of symbols of N, without their attributes specifications* $(A \in \tilde{N})$.
- $\mathcal{F}$ *is a set of terminal symbols, with their arities,*
- $\mathcal{D}$ *is constraint domain,*
- *R is a finite set of production rules* $X \to \alpha \square c$, *where* $X \in \tilde{N}$, $\alpha \in T(\mathcal{F} \cup \tilde{N})$, *and c is a set of constraints on the attributes of the non-terminals occurring in the rule. This set is interpreted as a conjunction of constraints.*

For instance, the language composed of disjunctions of terms in $\mathcal{L}_2 \cup \mathcal{L}_3$ (§2.2) with at most two disjunctions is specified by the grammar in Table 1.

We use the classical notation of attribute grammars: the value of the attribute a in the non-terminal N is denoted by $N.a$, and if there are more than one occurrence of the same non-terminal in a rule, these occurrences are numbered from left to right, starting from 0.

Table 1. A Constraint Tree Grammar.

$G_c = \{\ A,$
$\qquad \{A(d), B(d), T, Temp, Col\},$
$\qquad \{or/2, =/2, \leq/2, temp, col, red, pink, orange, blue, 32, 212\},$
$\qquad (\ \mathbb{N}, \{+, 0, 1\}, \{=\}),$
$\qquad \{$

A	$\to B \ \square\{A.d \leq 2, A.d = B.d\}$	
B_0	$\to or(B_1, B_2) \ \square\{B_0.d = 1 + B_1.d + B_2.d\}$	
B	$\to T \ \square\{B.d = 0\}$	
T	$\to \leq (temp, Temp)$	
T	$\to = (col, Col)$	
Col	$\to red \mid pink \mid blue \mid orange$	
$Temp$	$\to 32 \mid 212 \quad \}$	$\}$

In this grammar, $Temp \to 32 \mid 212$ is an abbreviation for the two rules $Temp \to 32$ and $Temp \to 212$ (we omit the constraint when it is *true*). The non-terminal symbol A has an attribute d indicating the number of disjunctions in a term. This number must be less or equal than 2 ($A.d \leq 2$).

3.2   Generated Language

We describe now the process of generating a term from a constraint tree grammar. The starting point for this process is made of the atom and an empty set of constraints $\emptyset$: $< A \square \emptyset >$.

Then, a derivation step for a constrained term $< t \square c >$ consists of choosing a non-terminal symbol X in t, choosing a derivation rule $X \to \alpha \square c'$, substituting X with α in t to get t' and adding the constraint c' to c (the symbols A.n occurring in the constraints are considered as variable in constraints; for this reason, these variables must be renamed in c').

In the previous example, the term $< A\square\emptyset >$ can be derived in $< B\square\{A.d < 2, A.d = B.d\} >$ using the first production rule. Then, this term can be derived either in $< or(B_1, B_2)\square\{A.d \geq 2, A.d = B.d, B.d = B_1.d + B_2.d\} >$ using the second production rule, or in $< T\square\{A.d \geq 2, A.d = B.d, B.d = 0\} >$ using the third one.

Definition 3. *Given a Constraint Tree Grammar $G = (A, N, \mathcal{F}, \mathcal{D}, R)$, the language generated from G (noted $L(G)$) is the set of ground terms (without nonterminal symbol) t such that there exists a constrained term $< t\square c >$ obtained by derivations from $< A\square\emptyset >$ and where the set of constraints c is satisfiable.*

Let us notice that when a term is generated, if the derivation leads to a terms $< t\square c >$ such that c is not satisfiable, the derivation can be stopped (or backtrack) since no term of the language can be built by derivation from $< t\square c >$.

For example, if we use the second rule from the term $< or(B_1, B_2)\square\{A.d \geq 2, A.d = B.d, B.d = 1 + B_1.d + B_2.d\} >$, we can derive the term $< or(or(B_3, B_4), B_2) \ \square\{A.d \geq 2, A.d = B.d, B.d = 1 + B_1.d + B_2.d, B_1.d = 1 + B_3.d + B_4.d\} >$. If the second rule is use again, we can obtain the term $< or(or(or(B_5, B_6), B_4), B_2) \ \square\{A.d \geq 2, A.d = B.d, B.d = 1 + B_1.d + B_2.d, B_1.d = 1 + B_3.d + B_4.d, B_3.d = 1 + B_5.d + B_6.d\} >$ for which the set of constraints is unsatisfiable (the number of disjunctions was limited to 2 and this terms has 3 disjunctions).

3.3 Generating Random Values

The formalism of constraint tree grammars can only be used when the number of terminal symbol is finite. Most numeric domains are infinite and then the language $\mathcal{L}_{A\leq x} = \{Att_i \leq v_{i_j}, v_{i_j} \in [a_i, b_i\}$ can not be specified with such grammar. In this case, we propose to add one (or more) non-terminal symbol(s) Rnd: this non-terminal symbol will be derived in a randomly generated value. In our experimentations (in attribute-value case), we have considered mainly two ways for generating a values for an attribute Att_i, depending on two domains:

$D_{discrete}$: the values are selected from the set of possible values (appearing in the object descriptions)

$D_{continuous}$: the values are chosen in a range $[Min_i, Max_i]$ where Min_i (resp. Max_i) may be, for example, the minimum (resp. maximum) value for attribute Att_i in the set of objects.

4   Application to Classification

To test our approach, we apply our measure to classification: we compute the similarity between objects to classify and objects for which the class is known. Then the class of the most similar object is assigned (in case of equi-similar objects, the most frequent class is affected).

This evaluation has to answer some questions: do we need a great subset of the language, does this method is efficient?The Figure 2 shows the accuracy of the method on the mushrooms dataset with various languages: $\mathcal{L}_1$ is $\mathcal{L}_{A=v}$ with values generated by a random selection in the domain, $\mathcal{L}_2$ is $\mathcal{L}_{A=v}$ with values generated by randomly selecting an object and returning the corresponding attributes. $\mathcal{L}_2$, which gives a great weight to frequent values, has better accuracy. $\mathcal{L}_{AND}$ is $\mathcal{L}_2$ with conjunction and $\mathcal{L}_{OR}$ is $\mathcal{L}_2$ with disjunction. $\mathcal{L}_{AND}$ contains more specific terms than $\mathcal{L}_{OR}$ and its accuracy is better, but the best is $\mathcal{L}_2$.

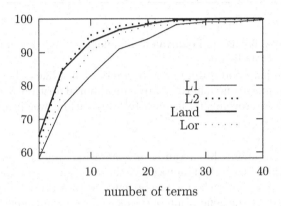

Fig. 2. Evolution of the accuracy with different languages

These tests consist of predicting the class of 5%(406 mushrooms) of the base using the 95%remaining (7719). Our classifier $\mathcal{L}^{class}$, written in C and running on an Ultra Sparc 5, takes 270 sec for this classification, generating 100 terms. Notice that the accuracy is 100%with 100 terms, even if $|\mathcal{L}_{A=v}| = 123$. Moreover, the 100%accuracy is obtained with an average of 32.5 terms using $\mathcal{L}_2$.

The following table shows the accuracy of $\mathcal{L}^{class}$ on the Glass problem with different languages: $\mathcal{L}^c_{A\leq x}$ (resp. $\mathcal{L}^d_{A\leq x}$) for continuous (resp. discrete) domains, in the same way $\mathcal{L}^c_{x\leq A\leq y}$ and $\mathcal{L}^d_{x\leq A\leq y}$ and we test $\mathcal{L}_{A=n}$ with discrete domains that can be considered because most values occur several times.

$\mathcal{L}^c_{A\ x}$	$\mathcal{L}^d_{A\ x}$	$\mathcal{L}^c_{x\ A\ y}$	$\mathcal{L}^d_{x\ A\ y}$	$\mathcal{L}_{A=n}$
75.04%	80.26%	75.5%	76.13%	49.39%

These results are obtained from 50 runs, with 10%of objects to classify, and with 1000 terms (one run = 1 second). Notice that 80%accuracy is one of the best results on the Glass problem. Moreover, we test with $\mathcal{L}^c_{A\leq x} \cup \mathcal{L}^c_{x\leq A\leq y}$ and get 77.39%accuracy. This example shows that results with an union of languages can be better than results with languages taken separately.

The Table 2 compares average accuracies on some domains of the UCI repository [BM98], for different well-known classifiers. These results are extract from [LM98].

The accuracy is measured by a 10-fold cross-validation. For $\mathcal{L}^{class}$, the accuracy is the average measure over 50 runs, with a random cross-validation (10%

Table 2. Comparison of accuracy on different domains.

DOMAINS	$\mathcal{L}^{class}$	SCOPE	RISE	PEBLS	C4.5	CN2	SE-LEARN
ECHOCARDIOGRAM	82.2	69.3	62.7	63.7	68.0	70.1	67.8
GLASS	80.2	74.3	72.0	69.7	63.3	62.1	71.4
HEPATITIS	78.0	78.7	76.9	82.4	81.6	81.2	-
IRIS	94.6	94.7	95.3	95.5	95.8	94.0	96.0
WINE	96.1	95.5	98.9	97.7	94.9	92.7	98.8
ZOOLOGY	96.0	94.0	96.0	95.5	88.6	90.0	95.0

testing set), 1000 terms, and equivalent languages ($\mathcal{L}_{A \leq x}$ for numeric attributes, and $\mathcal{L}_{A=v}$ for symbolic ones).

Our system has good results over several domains, like Echocardiogram, even with a basic language and a ñaive'hearest-neighbor algorithm. We are currently studying some improvements: using a KNN algorithm, weighting terms in the language, ...

Complexity: The algorithm requires a generation function and an evaluation function associated with the language. We have chosen to represent the language with a grammar where each rule is associated with a probability to be selected: the time needed for the generation of terms is insignificant. Let N be the number of known objects and let M be the number of objects to classify.

We propose to compute a matrix storing the distance between each object to classify and each known object: the size of this matrix is $M \times N$. Let T be the number of terms generated. For each term, we have to compute $M + N$ evaluations and $N.M$ comparisons to compute the similarity. Then the time complexity depends on $T.(a(M+N)+b(N.M))$ which is polynomial (a represents time for an evaluation, b represents time for a comparison). However, when $M.N$ is high this method requires a large amount of memory to store the distance matrix.

5   Conclusion and Further Works

We proposed in this paper a generic similarity measure based on a language specification, that allows to cope with various formalisms in a uniform way: attribute-values, first order logic, constraint FOL. The language allows to express relevant (or supposed relevant) properties of objects, and to easily introduce biases. The language is specified by a grammar that allows to generate terms.

For the moment, it has been implemented in the system $\mathcal{L}^{class}$ for attribute-value objects and for classification tasks.

The experiments show that the quality of classification task depend on the language used. For many practical domains, $\mathcal{L}^{class}$ gets comparable or better results than usual approaches with simple languages.

We now plan to test this similarity measure in a constraint first order logic framework and with unstrutured datas like texts.

References

[Aha89]   D. Aha. Incremental, instance based-learning of independent and graded concept descriptions. In *Sixth International Machine Learning Workshop (ML89)*, pages 387–391, 1989.

[Bis92]   G. Bisson. Learning in FOL with a similarity measure. In *11th National Conf. on Artificial Intelligence (AAAI), San Jose, CA.*, pages 82–87. AAAI Press, 1992.

[BM98]   C.L. Blake and C.J. Merz. UCI repository of machine learning databases, 1998.

[CS93]   S. Cost and S. Salzberg. A weighted nearest neighbor algorithm for learning with symbolic features. *Machine Learning ,10(1), 57–78*, 1993.

[DeG86]   Morris H. DeGroot. *Probability and Statistics*. Addison-Wesley Series in Statistics. Addison-Wesley, Reading, MA, USA, 2nd edition, 1986.

[Dom95]   P. Domingos. Rule induction and instance-based learning: A unified approach. In *Fourteenth International Joint Conference on Artificial Intelligence (IJCAI'95), Montreal, Canada*, pages 1226–1232. Morgan & Kaufmann, 1995.

[EW96]   W. Emde and D. Wettschereck. Relational instance-based learning. In Saitta L., editor, *13th Int. Conf. on Machine Learning (ICML'96), Bari, Italy*, pages 122–130. Morgan & Kaufmann, 1996.

[GCM95]   C. Giraud-Carrier and T. Martinez. An efficient metric for heterogeneous inductive learning applications in the attribute-value language. In *Proceedings of GWIC'94*, pages Vol. 1, 341–350. Kluwer Academic Publishers, 1995.

[GS84]   F. Gécseg and M. Steinby. *Tree Automata*. Akadémiai Kidoó, Budapest, 1984.

[HWB01]   Tamás Horváth, Stefan Wrobel, and Uta Bohnebeck. Relational instance-based learning with lists and terms. *Machine Learning*, 43(1/2):53–80, 2001.

[LM98]   N. Lachiche and P. Marquis. Scope classification: An instance-based learning algorithm with a rule-based characterization. *Lecture Notes in Computer Science*, 1398:268–??, 1998.

[Moa00]   F. Moal. *Langages de biais en Apprentissage Symbolique*. PhD thesis, LIFO, Université d'Orléans, France, December 2000.

[MS98]   Kim Marriott and Peter J. Stuckey. *Programming with Constraints: An Introduction*. The MIT Press, 1998.

[MT94]   T. Mohri and H. Tanaka. An optimal weighting criterion of case indexing for both numeric and symbolic attributes. In *Case-Based Reasoning Workshop*, pages 123–127. AAAI Press, 1994.

[Pla95]   Enric Plaza. Cases as terms: A feature term approach to the structured representation of cases. In *ICCBR*, pages 265–276, 1995.

[Seb97]   M. Sebag. Distance induction in first order logic. In *Proceedings of ILP'97*, pages 264–272. Springer-Verlag, 1997.

[SS94]   M. Sebag and M. Schoenauer. *Topics in Case-Based Reasonning*, volume 837 of *LNAI*, chapter A Rule-based Similarity Measure, pages 119–130. Springer-Verlag, 1994.

[SW86]   C. Stanfill and D. Waltz. Toward memory-based reasoning. *Communication of the ACM*, 29(12):1213-1228, 1986.

Backpropagation in Decision Trees for Regression

Victor Medina-Chico[1], Alberto Suárez[1], and James F. Lutsko[2]

[1] Escuela Técnica Superior de Informática
Universidad Autónoma de Madrid
Ciudad Universitaria de Cantoblanco
28049 Madrid, Spain
[2] Center for Nonlinear Phenomena and Complex Systems
Université Libre de Bruxelles
C.P. 231 Campus Plaine
B-1050 Brussels, Belgium

Abstract. A global optimization algorithm is designed to find the parameters of a CART regression tree extended with linear predictors at its leaves. In order to render the optimization mathematically feasible, the internal decisions of the CART tree are made continuous. This is accomplished by the replacement of the crisp decisions at the internal nodes of the tree with soft ones. The algorithm then adjusts the parameters of the tree in a manner similar to the backpropagation algorithm in multilayer perceptrons. With this procedure it is possible to generate regression trees optimized with a global cost function, which give a continuous representation of the unknown function, and whose architecture is automatically fixed by the data. The integration in one decision system of complementary features of symbolic and connectionist methods leads to improvements in prediction efficiency in both synthetic and real-world regression problems.

1 Introduction

The use of decision trees in regression problems has been limited by their reduced expressive capacity. For instance, CART regression trees [1] yield a rather coarse approximation of the unknown real-valued function in terms of patches of constant value. The origin of this piecewise representation is the divide-and-conquer strategy used in the generation of the decision tree: The original regression problem is decomposed into a series of simpler problems by a recursive partitioning procedure that divides the attribute space into disjoint regions. Each of these divisions is generated by a Boolean test on the attributes. The parameters of the splits are found by minimizing a cost function that measures the local prediction error. This implies that the tree is an approximation that presents finite-size jump discontinuities at the decision boundaries. Furthermore the greedy strategy used in the tree generation implies that the final predictor need not be globally optimal. There are also statistical implications in subdividing the initial space

L. De Raedt and P. Flach (Eds.): ECML 2001, LNAI 2167, pp. 348–359, 2001.
© Springer-Verlag Berlin Heidelberg 2001

into smaller regions. Every time a split is made, the problem generally becomes simpler to solve, but the number of examples available for the learning is also reduced. In more precise terms, dividing the data can have favorable consequences for the bias of the predictor, but it generally increases its variance. The decomposition of the prediction error in terms of bias and variance is a well-known decomposition in regression [11]. The bias term may be understood as the error that remains even if we had an infinite number of observations while the variance term is a measure of the fluctuations due to the finite number of observations.

It is thus desirable to design a method to construct decision trees that are optimized with a global cost function while retaining the advantages of a symbolic knowledge representation. In this work, a backpropagation algorithm is presented that adjusts the parameters of a decision tree whose architecture is selected by a standard tree generation algorithm [21]. This algorithm is similar to the backpropagation algorithm in multilayer perceptrons. It solves the credit assignment problem by propagating the errors from the leaves of the tree up to its root, following an inverse path to that used in prediction. The advantage of the resulting predictor is that its architecture is not fixed beforehand, but is generated automatically by the data itself. The regression tree obtained is subject to the limitations of the base tree generation algorithm in finding an architecture as close as possible to the optimal one, and of the numerical optimization procedure, which may get trapped in a local minimum of the cost function.

To implement this backpropagation algorithm on the architecture of the tree needs to be reinterpreted in terms of membership functions. A classical decision tree, such as CART [1] or C4.5 [18] is characterized by Boolean membership functions. A fuzzy decision tree incorporates continuous membership functions to allow the possibility of partial memberships in the nodes of the tree. This reformulation makes it possible to employ analytic tools to adjust the tree parameters to optimize a global cost function. The starting point for the generation of fuzzy regression trees is a CART tree [1] extended with linear models at each of the leaves of the tree [22], instead of the traditional constant models used in CART. These linear models at each of the leaves have the effect of extending the expressive capabilities of the traditional CART tree and of reducing its size. Once the crisp tree is constructed, the Boolean splits are replaced by continuous sigmoidal splits that can be continuously tuned. In a manner similar to backpropagation in neural networks, the learning process involves the propagation of the tree estimates from the leaves to the root node.

There are several advantages in this approach. The representation given by a fuzzy regression tree is continuous and the parameters can be adjusted to optimize a global error function. Instead of discarding data at every decision in the tree, all training data is assigned to every node, although with different degrees of membership. Since no single tree leaf is solely responsible for the prediction, some of the model interpretability is lost. Nonetheless, the final estimator can be thought of as a hierarchical mixture of experts [14]. The optimized model is not just a smoothed version of a piecewise linear representation, and can significantly differ form the original CART tree.

The organization of the paper is as follows: In Section 2, connections with other approaches such as M5 [12], ensemble methods (bagging, boosting, PC - perturb & combine) and HME (hierarchical mixtures of experts) are outlined. In Section 3, the generation of crisp trees is reinterpreted in terms of membership functions. This interpretation leads to the design of a global optimization algorithm and to the formulation of the backpropagation algorithm for regression. The results of the experiments are presented in Section 4. Finally, Section 5 summarizes the results and conclusions of this work.

2   Relation to Previous Work

A decision tree with linear models at the leaves, M5, was proposed in Ref. [12]. In the M5 system, a fully developed regression tree giving a piecewise constant representation of the objective function is pruned by replacing the subtree attached to an inner node by a linear model whenever the latter outperforms the subtree model. The linear models are artificially restricted to using only those variables involved in the splits in the eliminated subtree. The final tree gives a piecewise linear (i.e. discontinuous) representation. No attempt is made to select the tree parameters by optimizing a global cost function.

Much of the current research on regression trees strives to overcome the shortcomings and rigidity of piecewise representations. Divide-and-conquer algorithms approach a complex task by dividing it into more elementary tasks whose solutions can be combined to yield a solution to the original problem. This leads to simple and elegant algorithms. However, one should be concerned about the statistical consequences of dividing the input space, specially when the training data available are limited. Dividing the data generally leads to an increased variance because one has more hypotheses that fit the reduced number of data points.

For unstable algorithms such as CART [1], C4.5 [18] or ID3 [19], a possible solution is to to combine different realizations of the same predictor. These different realizations are obtained by perturbing the training set in various ways. Examples are bagging [2], boosting [8], arcing [4] and output smearing [5]. All of them need some amount of instability of the base learner to small changes in the training set. The reason for this is that the predictors need to be different to reduce the variance.

The performance of ensemble methods is often quite remarkable given their simplicity. In fact, these algorithms are more immune to overfitting than one would expect considering the large amount of parameters involved. In regression, the performance of ensemble methods can be studied in terms of a decomposition of the error in terms of bias and variance [3]. The combination of the base learners leads to a reduction in the variance. In classification, the explanation is not so clear since there is not a single decomposition in terms of bias and variance [4], [15] or [16]. Besides, boosting has been argued to be more than a variance-reducing device and an explanation in terms of the margin of classification has also been proposed [20].

The main disadvantage of voting methods is their complexity. Because the amount of parameters involved and because the final hypothesis is the average of the hypotheses of the different predictors, the interpretation of a voting method is not as straightforward as that of a single predictor. The computational costs are also larger both in terms of memory and prediction speed.

The present work proposes to take advantage of combinations of different models, as well, but from a radically different perspective. Whereas ensembles of learners generally give similar weights to all the individual predictor, we propose a weighted combination the predictions given by the different units that make up a single learner. The starting point for our algorithm is a CART regression tree, extended with linear models at the leaves. The unknown function is approximated by the Piecewise Linear Model (PLM) encoded by the regression tree. The weights for combining the linear models are computed by applying a succession of fuzzy splits that replace the Boolean splits in the internal nodes of the CART tree. The resulting predictor can be thought of as a hierarchical mixture of linear predictors [14] whose architecture is fixed by the training data itself. The parameters of both the fuzzy splits and of the linear models are adjusted by minimization of a global cost function.

3   Optimization of PLM Regression Trees

In order to design a procedure to optimize the parameters of the tree structure with respect to a global cost function, one has to take into account the fact that the decisions taken in its construction are formulated in terms of hard splits. The global cost function for the tree can be written in terms of Boolean membership functions of the training examples in the leaf nodes [21]. These functions are discontinuous step functions. Therefore, their parameters cannot be tuned by standard analytical optimization routines, which require smoothness of the function and its derivatives. The solution to this problem is to replace these functions by continuous ones. This means that the decisions become smooth and that a point may simultaneously belong to different leaves, thus bringing fuzzy character into the tree structure. Following Suárez and Lutsko [21] we review the construction of a crisp regression tree in terms of membership functions. This reformulation allows the possibility of considering real-valued (fuzzy) membership functions and renders the design of a global optimization algorithm feasible. The introduction of the fuzzy character is made once the tree architecture is fixed. This is a procedure analogous to that used in the construction of a neural network. It has the advantage that selection of the architecture is an automatic process guided by the data itself and not by heuristics. There are many different algorithms to generate decision trees [1,10,19] . In this paper the base classifier is CART, designed by Breiman et $al.$ [1].

The dataset from which the tree is induced consists of examples in the form of pairs $(\boldsymbol{x}_n, y_n); n = 1, \ldots, N$, where $\mathbf{x}_n = \{x_{n1}, x_{n2}, \ldots, x_{nD}\}$ is the vector of attributes (also known as predictor or independent variables) and y_n is the dependent variable to be predicted. We assume that both the dependent variable and the attributes are ordinal variables (regression). Nominal attributes can also be handled by the decision tree. However, the possibility of fuzzifying nominal splits is not considered.

Following the usual procedure, the dataset is partitioned into a training set, with N_{train} examples, which is used to learn the model, and a statistically independent test set, with N_{test} examples, which is used to evaluate the quality of the generated model. The training set is used to build a tree (T) composed of a collection of nodes ($t_i \in T; i = 0, 1, 2...$) arranged in a hierarchical manner. The CART method is a top-down algorithm for the generation of a binary decision tree. The first node of a CART tree is the root node, t_0. By definition, all examples belong to this node. The tree is then constructed using a divide-and-conquer strategy in which the attribute space is partitioned by several Boolean tests into a set of disjoint subregions, in each of which the decision problem is simpler. Each of the tests corresponds to an internal node of the decision tree. This procedure can be repeated recursively until a stopping criterion is met. The CART prescription is to generate a maximally developed tree and then to perform cost-complexity pruning using 10-fold cross-validation.

In the original CART formulation, the prediction for the dependent variable in each region is a constant value which is equal to the average of the dependent variable in that region. A CART tree thus yields a piecewise constant model for the unknown relation between the independent and dependent variables. Piecewise Linear Model decision trees (PLM trees) differ from the original CART trees in that in each of these disjoint regions, a local linear model for the data is constructed [22]. This formulation allows for a more flexible representation of the unknown function at each of the terminal nodes. The coefficients of the attributes are then determined by minimizing the mean square error over the training set. The predictions of the leaves (x) are linear models

$$\bar{y}_l(\mathbf{x}) = \beta_{l0} + \beta_{l1}x_1 + \ldots + \beta_{lD}x_D. \tag{1}$$

The tendency to overfitting may be partially avoided by selecting which attributes of the linear models at each of the leaf nodes have to remain. This is achieved using an algorithm designed by Jennrich [13]. According to this algorithm, a series of regressions is constructed, starting from a linear model that includes all variables. The attributes are then added or removed from the linear model according to some statistically meaningful criteria. The PLM trees generated are more flexible than traditional trees and are also smaller. The increased complexity introduced when linear models are generated at the leaves is balanced with the decrease of the number of subdivisions of the attribute space.

In a CART tree, each internal node corresponds to a test on the attributes and splits the data into two disjoint regions by means of a question. This question can be stated in terms of only one attribute (univariate splits) or of linear combinations of several attributes (multivariate splits),

$$Q_i = \mathbf{c}_i \cdot \mathbf{x} > a_i, \tag{2}$$

where the vector c_i contains the coefficients that define a variable which is a linear combination of the original variables. The parameter a_i is the threshold value of the split.

The parameters (c_i, a_i) are determined by the local optimization of a cost function, which in regression is taken to be the mean square error over the examples of the training set,

$$R_{train} = \frac{1}{N_{train}} \sum_{n=1}^{N_{train}} (y_n - \bar{y}(x_n))^2, \tag{3}$$

where $\bar{y}(x_n)$ is the prediction of the tree for example x_n.

The Boolean test (2) can be reinterpreted in terms of membership functions. Each node t_i is characterized by an absolute membership function $\mu_i(x)$ which is equal to one for those examples that satisfy the conjunction of Boolean tests leading to the node and zero otherwise. The relative degree of membership of example x in node $t_{i\alpha}$, a child node of t_i, is a Boolean function that is equal to 1 if the example satisfies test on node t_i (2) and equal to zero otherwise, independent of the value of $\mu_i(x)$. For the t_{iL} left child node of t_i,

$$\mu_L^{(i)}(x) = \theta(c_i \cdot x - a_i), \tag{4}$$

where $\theta(x)$ is the Heavyside step function. For the right child node,

$$\mu_R^{(i)}(x) = \theta(a_i - c_i \cdot x). \tag{5}$$

The absolute degree of membership is given by

$$\mu_{i\alpha}(x) = \mu_i(x)\mu_\alpha^{(i)}(x), \quad \alpha = L, R, \tag{6}$$

where $\mu_i(x)$ is the absolute degree of membership for the parent node t_i, which can be recursively calculated using (6) until the root node is reached. By definition, all points belong to the root node, so that $\mu_0(x) = 1; \ \forall x$.

Given a vector of attributes x, the value predicted by the for the dependent variable is

$$\bar{y}(x) = \sum_{t_l \in \tilde{T}} \mu_l(x)\bar{y}_l(x), \tag{7}$$

where $\bar{y}_l(x)$ is the linear predictor associated to the terminal node t_l given by (1). The set of terminal nodes is denoted by $\tilde{T}$.

Note that Equation (7) remains valid with real-valued degrees of membership. It is therefore possible to replace the Boolean test (2) by a fuzzy test, characterized by a real-valued membership function. A natural choice for fuzzification is to use sigmoidal functions of inverse width b_i. In this way, the membership functions (4) and (5) are replaced by

$$\mu_L^{(i)}(x) = \frac{1}{1 + exp[-b_i(c_i \cdot x - a_i)]}, \qquad \mu_R^{(i)}(x) = 1 - \mu_L^{(i)}(x). \tag{8}$$

The splitting threshold of a standard crisp tree is broadened into a splitting band. Outside this band, examples are assigned to one of the child nodes with degree of membership very close to one. It is for the examples that fall within this band that the fuzzy character of the tree becomes important: examples are assigned to both child nodes with relevant degrees of membership. A crisp split can be seen as the limiting case of a fuzzy split when $b_i \to \infty$.

Once the fuzzy structure of the tree has been fixed, the parameters of the splits are adjusted by minimization of a global cost function. In a fuzzy regression tree, the cost function is the mean squared error of the tree predictions in the training set. The optimization problem is similar to that encountered in neural networks, where the problem is solved by the backpropagation algorithm. Here the problem is solved by a similar algorithm in which the estimations at the leaves are propagated from the leaves upwards to the root node.

It is important to notice that a fuzzy tree assigns each example to every leaf node with some degree of membership, which depends on the conjunction of tests leading to the leaf node and which can be calculated by iteration of (6) until the root node is reached. For a leaf node, the prediction for a given vector of attributes $\boldsymbol{x}$ is a linear model given by (1). For an inner node, t_i, it can be defined as the prediction of the subtree $T(t_i)$ (the tree composed of t_i as the root node and all of its descendants) and can be calculated using the recursion

$$\bar{y}_i(\boldsymbol{x}) = \mu_L^{(i)}(\boldsymbol{x})\bar{y}_{iL}(\boldsymbol{x}) + \mu_R^{(i)}(\boldsymbol{x})\bar{y}_{iR}(\boldsymbol{x}). \tag{9}$$

The value predicted by the regression tree for the dependent variable can be obtained by iterating (9) from the predictions at the leaves to the root node, in a manner similar to the backpropagation algorithm in neural networks. This algorithm fixes the structural parameters of the tree by minimizing a global cost function, thus avoiding the greedy approach of traditional crisp trees.

The optimization of the cost function (3) with respect to the parameter α_j of node t_j yields

$$\frac{\partial R_{train}(T)}{\partial \alpha_j} = \frac{1}{N_{train}} \sum_{n=1}^{N_{train}} -2(y_n - \bar{y}(\boldsymbol{x}_n))\frac{\partial \bar{y}(\boldsymbol{x}_n)}{\partial \alpha_j} = 0. \tag{10}$$

For a leaf node t_l, the parameters α_j are the coefficients in the linear fit β_l. Using the expression

$$\frac{\partial \bar{y}(\boldsymbol{x})}{\partial \beta_l} = \mu_l(\boldsymbol{x})\tilde{\boldsymbol{x}}, \tag{11}$$

where $\tilde{\boldsymbol{x}} = \{1, x_1, \ldots, x_D\}$, equation (10) becomes

$$\sum_{n=1}^{N_{train}} (y_n - \bar{y}(\boldsymbol{x}_n))\mu_l(\boldsymbol{x}_n)\tilde{\boldsymbol{x}}_n = 0, \tag{12}$$

thus resulting in $D+1$ equations. For an inner node, t_i, the results are analogous to those in [21]

$$\sum_{n=1}^{N_{train}} (y_n - \bar{y}(\boldsymbol{x}_n))\mu_i(\boldsymbol{x}_n)(\bar{y}_{iL}(\boldsymbol{x}_n) - \bar{y}_{iR}(\boldsymbol{x}_n))\frac{\partial \mu_L^{(i)}(\boldsymbol{x}_n)}{\partial \boldsymbol{\xi}_i} = 0, \qquad (13)$$

where $\boldsymbol{\xi}_i = \{-b_i a_i, b_i c_i\}$ are the parameters of the membership function (8), and

$$\frac{\partial \mu_L^{(i)}(\boldsymbol{x}_n)}{\partial \boldsymbol{\xi}_i} = \tilde{\mathbf{x}}\,\mu_L^{(i)}(\boldsymbol{x})\mu_R^{(i)}(\boldsymbol{x}). \qquad (14)$$

The solutions to the system of equations (12) and (13) are the parameters that characterize the optimized PLM tree. In this work, the optimization problem is solved by a quasi-Newton method (the Broyden-Fletcher-Goldfarb-Shanno algorithm [17]). Because the prediction of the tree for any example is given by the combination of the predictions at each of the leaves and not by the individual predictions themselves, the estimations of the parameters of the linear models at the leaves are propagated upwards to the root node in order to obtain the values of $\bar{y}_i(\boldsymbol{x}_n)$ that are needed in the computation of (3) and its derivatives.

4 Experiments

The objective of this section is to show how the design of a global optimization algorithm leads to an improvement in the performance of a regression tree. The algorithm was tested on a variety of data sets, both synthetic and real world data sets. The Housing and Servo are real-world data sets and were obtained from the UCI repository (ftp ics.uci.edu/pub/machine-learning-databases). The synthetic data sets focus on several regression problems in the presence of noise and/or irrelevant data. These data sets have been suggested by Cherkassky and Mulier (see Table 1) [7] and by Friedman [9]. The sets suggested by Friedman are

- Friedman #1: There are ten independent predictor variables $x_1, \ldots, x_{10}$ each of which is uniformly distributed over $[0, 1]$. The response is given by

$$y = 10 sin(\pi x_1 x_2) + 20(x_3 - 0.5)^3 + 10 x_4 + 5 x_5 + N(0, 1). \qquad (15)$$

- Friedman #2, #3: They are both 4-variable data sets with

$$y = (x_1^2 + (x_2 x_3 - (1/x_2 x_4))^2)^{1/2} + \epsilon_2$$
$$y = tan^{-1}\left(\frac{x_2 x_3 - (1/x_2 x_4)}{x_1}\right) + \epsilon_3, \qquad (16)$$

where the variables are uniformly distributed over the ranges

$$0 \le x_1 \le 100, \quad 20 \le (x_2/2\pi) \le 280, \quad 0 \le x_3 \le 1, \quad 1 \le x_4 \le 11. \qquad (17)$$

The noise variables ϵ_2, ϵ_3 are distributed as $N(0, \sigma_2^2), N(0, \sigma_3^2)$ with σ_2, σ_3 selected to give 3:1 signal/noise ratios.

Table 1. Data set summaries for the first experiment (from Ref. [7]).

Set	Attributes $\mathbf{x}$	Function $f(\mathbf{x})$	Range	σ_{noise}
1	$x_1 = a^2$, $x_2 = b^2$, $x_3 = \cos(a^2 + b^2)$	$a + b$	$a, b \in [0, 1]$	0.1
2	$x_1 = a^2$, $x_2 = \sin b$, $x_3 = \cos(a^2 + b^2)$	$a\,b$	$a, b \in [0, 1]$	0.1
3	$x_1 = a^2$, $x_2 = (a^2 - 0.5)^2$, $x_3 = \cos(a^2 + b^2)$	a	$a, b \in [0, 1]$	0.1
4	$x_1 = \sin 2\pi a$, $x_2 = \cos 2\pi a$	a	$a \in [0, 1]$	0.1
5	$x_1 = a$, $x_2 = \sin a$	$\cos a$	$a \in [-1, 1]$	0.05
6	$x_1 = a$, $x_2 = a^2$	$(1 - 0.5(a^2 + a^4))^{\frac{1}{2}}$	$a \in [-1, 1]$	0.05
7	$x_1 = x_2 = x_3 = a$	$(1 - a^2)^{\frac{1}{2}}$	$a \in [-1, 1]$	0.05
8	$x_1 = x_3 = a$, $x_2 = \cos a$, $x_4 = a^2$, $x_5 = a^3$	$\sin a$	$a \in [-1, 1]$	0.05
9	$x_1 = a$, $x_2 = \sin 2\pi a$	$\cos 2\pi a$	$a \in [-1, 1]$	0.05

Table 2. Data set summaries for the second experiment.

Set	Size	No. Inputs	N_{train}	N_{test}
Housing	506	13	455	51
Servo	167	4	150	17
Friedman #1	1200	10	200	1000
Friedman #2	1200	4	200	1000
Friedman #3	1200	4	200	1000

Both CART and the stepwise algorithm used to select the number of PLM variables have a tendency to prefer simple hypotheses. Following this philosophy, the global optimization algorithm only tunes the parameters corresponding to those variables that appear in the tree in the splits or in the linear models at the leaves. However, other possibilities are being considered.

Table 3 summarizes experiments with data sets with ($N_{train} = N_{test} = 300$) where the performance of the algorithm designed in this work is compared to different extensions of CART. The values reported are the root mean square errors normalized by the standard deviation of the realization of the noise. With this normalization, a perfect predictor would achieve a value of one. We observe that our algorithm gives very similar predictions than fuzzy CART, though for 7 of the data sets the predictions of our algorithm are better than the other extensions to CART. For the other two data sets (4 and 9), the results are within one standard deviation of the best result.

The decrease in size is remarkable. This is a consequence of the stepwise PLM character of the tree. The increased complexity of the predictions at the leaves is compensated with a reduction in the decision nodes, which implies a reduction in size. The size for the fuzzy versions is the same than for the non-fuzzy ones and is indicated in the third and sixth columns of Table 3.

The prediction quality is much better in the fuzzy versions of the CART algorithm. This is due to several advantages, namely:

Table 3. Results with $N_{train} = N_{test} = 300$.

Set	CART	Fuzzy CART	Size	CART+PLM	Fuzzy CART+PLM	Size
1	1.48 (0.06)	1.09 (0.03)	9.6 (1.8)	1.13 (0.03)	1.09 (0.06)	2.9 (0.3)
2	1.28 (0.07)	1.06 (0.03)	7.9 (1.1)	1.09 (0.04)	1.04 (0.01)	2.4 (0.7)
3	1.11 (0.04)	1.03 (0.03)	8.2 (0.9)	1.03 (0.02)	1.03 (0.02)	2.0 (0.0)
4	1.31 (0.13)	1.11 (0.08)	6.1 (2.0)	1.18 (0.14)	1.13 (0.09)	2.0 (0.0)
5	1.21 (0.07)	1.02 (0.02)	8.1 (1.3)	1.03 (0.02)	1.01 (0.01)	2.0 (0.0)
6	1.29 (0.08)	1.03 (0.02)	6.5 (0.7)	1.09 (0.04)	1.02 (0.01)	2.3 (0.5)
7	1.54 (0.11)	1.03 (0.02)	8.4 (1.1)	1.14 (0.05)	1.03 (0.02)	5.5 (1.3)
8	1.42 (0.11)	1.05 (0.04)	11.3 (0.9)	1.05 (0.03)	1.02 (0.01)	3.1 (1.7)
9	3.84 (0.30)	1.06 (0.03)	12.3 (0.8)	1.90 (1.25)	1.11 (0.09)	9.0 (4.0)

- The tree parameters are found through the optimization of a global cost function, in contrast to the greedy strategy used in the construction of standard decision trees.
- The functions are approximated continuously. The CART/PLM tree tries to adjust a linear model to the function in each region. There are no constraints between the boundaries of the different regions, thus yielding a discontinuous representation. This is not the case now. This also limits the tendency to overfitting.
- The notion of locality is recovered. Due to the introduction of smooth splits, data points very close to each other in the attribute space will have similar degrees of membership for each leaf.

In a second group of experiments, the performance of globally optimal CART regression trees is compared to ensemble algorithms, such as bagging [2] and smearing [5]. The data sets used in the second experiment are described briefly in Table 2, together with the training and test sizes for each of them. The numbers reported in Table 4 are averages over 10 independent runs of the algorithm and show the mean generalization error with its standard deviation between parentheses. The algorithm designed in this work is significantly better than bagging for all the data sets considered and better than smearing for 4 datasets, being second only in Friedman #1, but within one standard deviation from the best result. For the Servo dataset, the results from [5] are not shown due to unresolved discrepancies in the values [6].

The performance of Fuzzy CART trees with Linear Models at the leaves trees (Fuzzy CART+PLM) is systematically better than a Fuzzy CART tree alone (Fuzzy CART), although in some cases the results are not statistically significant. The reduced size of the trees generated and thus the interpretability of the predictions is also a factor to take into account.

Table 4. Root mean-square error estimates.

Data set	Fuzzy CART	Fuzzy CART+PLM	Bagging	Smearing
Housing	3.4 (0.3)	3.1 (0.3)	3.26	3.21
Servo	0.6 (0.2)	0.4 (0.2)	-	-
Friedman #1	2.5 (0.2)	2.30 (0.09)	2.50	2.24
Friedman #2	136 (9)	134 (7)	146	149
Friedman #3	0.15 (0.02)	0.149 (0.002)	0.158	0.153

5   Summary and Conclusions

A backpropagation algorithm to generate decision trees optimized with a global cost function has been applied to the problem of approximating an unknown real-valued function from data. The method takes as a starting point a CART regression tree extended with linear models at the leaves. In order to make optimization by analytic methods possible, the standard crisp splits of a CART tree are replaced by sigmoidal continuous splits. The predictions of the model are propagated from the leaves upward towards the root node in order to the calculate the derivatives of the global cost function used in the optimization procedure. This backpropagation algorithm makes it possible to adjust the parameters of the tree so that, given the fixed tree structure, a minimum of the cost function is reached.

The introduction of continuous splits can be seen as giving the tree a fuzzy character. In regression problems, fuzzification has the advantage of yielding a continuous approximation to the unknown function recovering the notion of locality lost in the traditional decision-tree approximation. It also enlarges the expressive capabilities of the tree incorporating in the construction of symbolic learners the robustness and flexibility of connectionist ones. However, some interpretability is lost with respect to the clarity of a single tree.

The experiments carried out both in synthetic and real-world datasets show that the algorithm designed leads to a significant improvements with respect to the performance of standard CART trees, remaining robust to noise and irrelevant attributes. Its performance is also better than methods that involve a much greater number of parameters such as bagging and smearing.

References

1. Breiman, L., Friedman, J.H., Olshen, R.A. and Stone, C.J.: Classification and Regression Trees. Chapman & Hall, New York (1984).
2. Breiman, L., Bagging Predictors: Machine Learning, **24** (1996) 123-140.
3. Breiman, L.: Bias, Variance and Arcing Classifiers. Technical Report 460, Statistics Department, University of California, (1996).
4. Breiman, L.: Arcing Classifiers (with Discussion). The Annals of Statistics, **24** (1998) 2350-2383.

5. Breiman, L.: Randomizing Outputs to Increase Prediction Accuracy. Machine Learning, **40** (2000) 229-242.
6. Breiman, L.: Private Communication.
7. Cherkassky, V. and Muller, F.: Statistical and Neural Network Techniques for Nonparametric Regression. In: Cheeseman, P.W. and Oldford, R.W. (eds.): Selecting Models from Data. Springer-Verlag, New York (1994) 383-392..
8. Freund, Y. and Schapire, R.E.: Experiments with a New Boosting Algorithm. In Machine Learning: Proc. 13th International Conference. Morgan-Kaufmann, San Francisco (1996) 148-156.
9. Friedman, J.H.: Multivariate Adaptive Regression Splines (with Discussion). The Annals of Statistics, **19** (1991) 1-141.
10. Gelfand, S.B., Ravishankar, C.S. and Delp, E.J.: An Iterative Growing and Pruning Algorithm for Classification Tree Design. IEEE Trans. Pattern Analysis and Machine Intelligence, **13**, 2 (1991) 163-174.
11. Geman, S., Bienenstock, E. and Doursat, R.: Neural Networks and the Bias/Variance Dilemma. Neural Computation, **4** (1992) 1-58.
12. Quinlan, J. R. Learning with continuous classes, Proceedings of the Australian Joint Conference on Artificial Intelligence (1992) 343-348.
13. Jennrich, R.E.: Stepwise Regression. In: Statistical Methods for Digital Computers. Wiley, New York (1977) 58-75.
14. Jordan, M.I. and Jacobs, R.A.: Hierarchical Mixtures of Experts and the EM algorithm. Neural Computation, **6** (1994) 181-214.
15. Kohavi, R. and Wolpert, D.H.: Bias Plus Variance Decomposition for Zero-one Loss Functions. In Machine Learning, Proc. 13th International Conference. Morgan-Kaufmann, San Francisco (1996) 275-283.
16. Kong, E.B. and Dietterich, T.G.: Error-correcting Output Coding Corrects Bias and Variance. In Proc. 12th International Conference on Machine Learning. Morgan-Kaufmann, San Francisco (1995) 313-321.
17. Press, W. Teukolsky, W.T., Vetterling, S.A. and Flannery, B.: Numerical Recipes in C: The Art of Scientific Computing. Cambridge Univ. Press, Cambridge (1993).
18. Quinlan, J.R.: C4.5: Programs for Machine Learning. Morgan Kaufmann, San Mateo (1993).
19. Quinlan, J.R.: Induction of Decision Trees. Machine Learning **1**, 1 (1986) 81-106.
20. Schapire, R.E., Freund, Y. Bartlett, P. and Lee, W.S.: Boosting the Margin: a New Explanation for the Effectiveness of Voting Methods. The Annals of Statistics **26** 5 (1998) 1651-1686.
21. Suárez, A. and Lutsko, J.F.: Globally Optimal Fuzzy Decision Trees for Classification and Regression. IEEE Trans. Pattern Analysis and Machine Intelligence **21** 12 (1999) 1297-1311.
22. Suárez, A. and Lutsko, J.F.: Automatic Induction of Piecewise Linear Models with Decision Trees. In Proc. International Conference on Artificial Intelligence, Vol 2. H.R. Arabnia ed. Las Vegas, (2000) 1025-1031.

Comparing the Bayes and Typicalness Frameworks

Thomas Melluish, Craig Saunders, Ilia Nouretdinov, and Volodya Vovk

Computer Science, Royal Holloway, University of London, Egham, Surrey, TW20
0EX {T.Melluish, C.Saunders, I.Nouretdinov, V.Vovk}@cs.rhul.ac.uk

Abstract. When correct priors are known, Bayesian algorithms give
optimal decisions, and accurate confidence values for predictions can be
obtained. If the prior is incorrect however, these confidence values have
no theoretical base – even though the algorithms' predictive performance
may be good. There also exist many successful learning algorithms which
only depend on the iid assumption. Often however they produce no confidence values for their predictions. Bayesian frameworks are often applied
to these algorithms in order to obtain such values, however they can rely
on unjustified priors.

In this paper we outline the typicalness framework which can be used in
conjunction with many other machine learning algorithms. The framework provides confidence information based only on the standard iid
assumption and so is much more robust to different underlying data
distributions. We show how the framework can be applied to existing
algorithms. We also present experimental results which show that the
typicalness approach performs close to Bayes when the prior is known to
be correct. Unlike Bayes however, the method still gives accurate confidence values even when different data distributions are considered.

1 Introduction

In many real-world applications (such as risk-sensitive applications or those
which rely on human-computer interaction) it is desirable to obtain confidence
values for any predictions that are given. In most cases these confidence values
are used as a filter mechanism, whereby only those predictions in which the algorithm has a certain confidence are predicted; other examples are rejected or
possibly simply abstained from and passed on to a human for judgement. Many
machine learning algorithms for the problems of both pattern recognition and
regression estimation give confidence levels, and the Bayesian framework is often
used to obtain such values. When applying the Bayesian framework one has to
assume the existence of a (often strong) prior, which for real-world data sets is
often chosen arbitrarily. If an incorrect prior is assumed an algorithm may give
'incorrect' confidence levels; for example, 95% predictive intervals can contain
the true label with in much less than 95% of the time. For real-world applications
this is a major failure, as one would wish confidence levels to bound the number
of expected errors.

L. De Raedt and P. Flach (Eds.): ECML 2001, LNAI 2167, pp. 360–371, 2001.
© Springer-Verlag Berlin Heidelberg 2001

We therefore desire confidence values to be valid in the following sense. Given some possible label space $\mathcal{Y}$, if an algorithm predicts some set of labels $R \subseteq \mathcal{Y}$ with confidence t for a new example which is truly labelled $y \in \mathcal{Y}$, then we would expect the following to hold over randomisations of the training set and the new example:

$$P(y \notin R) \leq 1 - t \tag{1}$$

Moreover, we prefer algorithms which give 'nearly precise' confidence values, that is values such that (1) approaches equality.

In this paper we outline the typicalness framework which can produce nearly precise confidence values for data which is independently and identically distributed. We compare methods within this framework to their Bayesian counterparts and show experimentally that when the correct prior is known the difference in performance of the two approaches is negligible; when an incorrect prior is given (or benchmark data is used) however, the Bayesian algorithms give inaccurate confidences, whereas those using typicalness remain valid and even nearly precise.

The rest of this paper is laid out as follows. In Section 2 we describe the typicalness framework. Sections 3, 4, 5 and 6 sketch algorithms for regression estimation and pattern recognition in both the Bayesian and typicalness frameworks. A more comprehensive treatment is given in [4]. In Section 7 we present some experimental results and our conclusions are in Section 8.

2   The Typicalness Framework

Here we give a brief outline of the typicalness framework. For more details, see [7,5,12]. Consider a sequence of examples $(z_1, \ldots, z_l) = ((\mathbf{x}_1, y_1), \ldots, (\mathbf{x}_l, y_l))$ drawn independently from the same distribution over $\mathcal{Z} = \mathcal{X} \times \mathcal{Y}$ where $\mathcal{Y}$ is some label space. We can use the typicalness framework to gain confidence information for possible labelings for a new example $\mathbf{x}_{l+1}$. The idea is that we postulate some labels $\tilde{y}_{l+1}$ and for each one we examine how likely it is that all elements of the extended sequence $((\mathbf{x}_1, y_1), \ldots, (\mathbf{x}_l, y_l), (\mathbf{x}_{l+1}, \tilde{y}_{l+1}))$ might have been drawn independently from the same distribution, or how typically iid the sequence is. The more typical the sequence, the more confident we are in $\tilde{y}_{l+1}$.

To measure the typicalness of sequences, we define, for every $n = 1, 2, \ldots$, a function $t : \mathcal{Z}^n \to [0, 1]$ which has the property

$$P((z_1, \ldots, z_n) : t((z_1, \ldots, z_n)) \leq r) \leq r \tag{2}$$

If such a function returns 0.1 or less for a particular sequence, we know that the sequence is unusual because such values will be produced at most 10% of the time by any iid process. This means that we can exclude labels that we consider to be 'unlikely' at some particular significance level, e.g. we can exclude all labels for the new example which would occur only 10% of the time or less.

It turns out that we can construct such functions by considering the 'strangeness' of individual examples. If we have some family of functions f :

$\mathcal{Z}^n \times \{1, 2, \dots, n\} \to \mathbb{R}$, $n = 1, 2, \dots$, then we can associate some strangeness value α_i

$$\alpha_i = f(\{z_1, \dots, z_n\}, i) \quad i = 1, \dots, n \tag{3}$$

with each example and define the following typicalness function

$$t((z_1, \dots, z_n)) = \frac{\#\{\alpha_i : \alpha_i \geq \alpha_n\}}{n} \tag{4}$$

which can be proven to satisfy (2), provided that the strangeness function returns the same value for each example regardless of the order in which they are presented [9,12].

3 Regression Estimation

We will now consider some algorithms for regression estimation in the context of the Bayesian and typicalness frameworks before moving on to the pattern recognition setting.

Given a training sequence $(\mathbf{x}_1, y_1), \dots, (\mathbf{x}_l, y_l)$ where $\mathbf{x}_i \in \mathbb{R}^d$ and $y_i \in \mathbb{R}$ we choose to model the dependency $y_i = f(\mathbf{x}_i)$ as $y_i = \mathbf{x}_i \cdot \mathbf{w}$ where $\mathbf{w} \in \mathbb{R}^d$. The well known ridge regression procedure [3] recommends choosing $\mathbf{w}$ to achieve

$$a||\mathbf{w}||^2 + \sum_{i=1}^{l} (y_i - \mathbf{w} \cdot \mathbf{x}_i)^2 \to \min$$

where a is a positive constant (the ridge factor).

The method has a natural matrix representation: let Y be the vector of labels $Y = (y_1, \dots, y_l)'$ and X be the matrix formed from the training examples $X = (\mathbf{x}_1, \dots, \mathbf{x}_l)'$. We now wish to find $\mathbf{w}$ such that

$$a||\mathbf{w}||^2 + ||Y - X\mathbf{w}||^2 \to \min$$

Taking derivatives in $\mathbf{w}$ and rearranging we find this is achieved when

$$\mathbf{w} = (X'X + aI)^{-1}X'Y \tag{5}$$

so our ridge regression estimate of the label for some new point $\mathbf{x}_{l+1}$ is

$$\tilde{y}_{l+1} = \mathbf{x}'_{l+1}(X'X + aI)^{-1}X'Y$$

4 Bayesian Ridge Regression

We now give a Bayesian derivation of the ridge regression estimator. Suppose we have some data points $(\mathbf{x}_1, y_1), \dots, (\mathbf{x}_l, y_l)$ and an unlabeled example $\mathbf{x}_{l+1}$. We assume that the unlabelled examples $x_1, \dots, x_{l+1}$ are fixed (deterministic) and the labels $y_1, \dots, y_l$ were generated by the rule

$$y_i = \mathbf{w} \cdot \mathbf{x}_i + \xi_i \tag{6}$$

where $\mathbf{w} \sim N(0, \frac{1}{a}I)$ and each $\xi_i \sim N(0,1)$. We would like to predict y_{l+1} under these assumptions. We should therefore predict

$$y_{l+1} = \mathbf{x}_{l+1} \cdot \mathbf{w}_{\text{post}} + N(0,1)$$

where $\mathbf{w}_{\text{post}}$ is chosen according to the distribution $P(\mathbf{w}|(\mathbf{x}_1, y_1), \dots, (\mathbf{x}_l, y_l))$. Bayes rule gives us

$$P(\mathbf{w}|(\mathbf{x}_1, y_1), \dots, (\mathbf{x}_l, y_l)) \propto P(\mathbf{w})P((\mathbf{x}_1, y_1), \dots, (\mathbf{x}_l, y_l)|\mathbf{w}) \qquad (7)$$

Recalling that the Normal distribution's density is

$$\frac{1}{\sigma\sqrt{2\pi}}e^{\frac{(x-m)^2}{2\sigma^2}} \qquad (8)$$

equations (6), (7) and the multivariate form of (8) give us

$$P(\mathbf{w}|(\mathbf{x}_1, y_1), \dots, (\mathbf{x}_l, y_l)) \propto e^{-\frac{1}{2}a||\mathbf{w}||^2} \prod_{i=1}^{l} e^{-\frac{1}{2}(y_i - \mathbf{x}_i \cdot \mathbf{w})^2}$$

$$\propto e^{-\frac{1}{2}(a||\mathbf{w}||^2 + \sum_{i=1}^{l}(y_i - \mathbf{x}_i \cdot \mathbf{w})^2)} \qquad (9)$$

If we choose $\mathbf{w}$ to maximise (9), which is equivalent to choosing $\mathbf{w}$ such that

$$a||\mathbf{w}||^2 + \sum_{i=1}^{l}(y_i - \mathbf{x}_i \cdot \mathbf{w})^2) \to \min$$

we obtain exactly the same ridge regression estimator as in section 3.

Formula (9) can be written as

$$e^{-\frac{1}{2}(\mathbf{w}'(X'X+aI)\mathbf{w} - 2Y'X\mathbf{w}+Y'Y)} \propto e^{-\frac{1}{2}(\mathbf{w}-\mu)'(X'X+aI)(\mathbf{w}-\mu)} \qquad (10)$$

where μ is given by the right-hand side of (5), and the probability distribution of the multivariate Normal distribution is

$$P(\mathbf{x}) \propto e^{-\frac{1}{2}(\mathbf{x}-\mu)'\Lambda^{-1}(\mathbf{x}-\mu)}$$

where μ is the mean of the distribution and Λ is the covariance matrix. Therefore the weight vector's posterior distribution is

$$P(\mathbf{w}|(\mathbf{x}_1, y_1), \dots, (\mathbf{x}_l, y_l)) \sim N((X'X + aI)^{-1}X'Y, (XX' + aI)^{-1}) \qquad (11)$$

and so the predictive distribution for a new example's label y_{l+1} is

$$y_{l+1} \sim N(\mathbf{x}'_{l+1}(X'X + aI)^{-1}X'Y, \mathbf{x}'_{l+1}(XX' + aI)^{-1}\mathbf{x}_{l+1} + 1)$$

Ridge Regression has a well known dual formulation [6], also known as Kriging, which allows the 'kernel trick' to be applied to find non-linear decision rules. The posterior for a new label's classification in the dual form is

$$\hat{y}_{l+1} \sim N(Y'(K + aI)^{-1}\mathbf{k}, \mathbf{b}(K + aI)^{-1}\mathbf{k} + 1)$$

K is the kernel matrix defined by $K_{i,j} = \mathcal{K}(\mathbf{x}_i, \mathbf{x}_j)$, $i, j = 1 \dots l + 1$ where $\mathcal{K}$ is some kernel function [10], $\mathbf{k}$ is the vector defined by $\mathbf{k}_i = \mathcal{K}(\mathbf{x}_i, \mathbf{x}_{l+1})$ and $\mathbf{b}$ is the $l + 1$-vector $(0, \dots, 0, 1)'$. A $t\%$ confidence tolerance region for a label will lie between the $\frac{1-t}{2}\%$ and $\frac{1+t}{2}\%$ quantiles of the label's posterior distribution.

5   Typicalness Tests for Regression Estimation

Now we consider applying the typicalness framework to the particular case of regression estimation. In this case our sample space is $\mathcal{Z} = \mathbb{R}^d \times \mathbb{R}$. If we have some training sequence $((\mathbf{x}_1, y_1), \dots, (\mathbf{x}_l, y_l))$ and a new example $\mathbf{x}_{l+1}$ it is easy to find the typicalness of any postulated label $\hat{y}_{l+1}$. We use some regression algorithm whose predictions are independent of the order of training examples (e.g. ridge regression) to make predictions $\tilde{y}_1, \dots, \tilde{y}_l, \tilde{y}_{l+1}$ on the basis of the training sequence extended with the new example and its postulated label $((\mathbf{x}_1, y_1), \dots, (\mathbf{x}_l, y_l), (\mathbf{x}_{l+1}, \hat{y}_{l+1}))$. We use the residuals to those predictions to find strangeness values:

$$\alpha_i = |y_i - \tilde{y}_i| \tag{12}$$

and then use equation (4) (with $n = l + 1$) to find the typicalness of $\hat{y}_{l+1}$.

In regression however, we are not interested in the typicalness of a single label, our confidence information should take the form of a set of possible labels admissible at some confidence level. That is, we consider a set of labels $R \subseteq \mathcal{Y}$ such that

$$t((\mathbf{x}_1, y_1), \dots, (\mathbf{x}_l, y_l), (\mathbf{x}_{l+1}, \hat{y})) \leq r \ \ \forall \hat{y} \notin R, r \in [0, 1] \tag{13}$$

and return our confidence in the set as being at least $100(1 - r)\%$. In statistics such a set is often called a tolerance region. Probably we will most often have some particular confidence level in mind (e.g. 95%) and will wish to predict some tolerance region in which we have at least that much confidence. Obviously, in order to find such a region we cannot consider all possible $\hat{y}$.

5.1   Ridge Regression Confidence Machine

There exists an efficient application of the typicalness framework to ridge regression, the Ridge Regression Confidence Machine (RRCM), which allows tolerance regions to be found for any particular confidence level without considering all possible labelings of the new example. For details of the algorithm see [5].

The algorithm works by partitioning the real line into a set of intervals, each of which has uniform typicalness. This avoids the problem of having to explicitly consider all possible values for $\hat{y}$. For any particular confidence level $r\%$, the algorithm returns a union of these intervals that have typicalness $> 1 - \frac{r}{100}$.

6   Pattern Recognition

In this section we briefly describe two algorithms which provide confidence values for pattern recognition tasks. One is Bayesian Transduction [1] which can be shown to approximate the Bayes optimal decision; the other uses the typicalness framework in conjunction with a kernel perceptron (which is equivalent to a Support Vector Machine with no threshold).

6.1   Bayesian Transduction

The Bayesian Transduction (BT) algorithm [1] is a transductive algorithm which uses Bayes Point Machines [2] as a basis. The idea behind the algorithm is as follows. Suppose we have a training sequence $S = (\mathbf{x}_1, y_1), \ldots, (\mathbf{x}_l, y_l)$ where $\mathbf{x}_i \in \mathbb{R}^d$ and $y_i \in \{\pm 1\}$. Assume that our hypothesis space $\mathcal{H}$ is the class of kernel perceptrons, where decision functions are given by

$$f_\mathbf{w}(\mathbf{x}) = \text{sign}(\mathbf{w} \cdot \phi(\mathbf{x})) = \text{sign}\left(\sum_{i=1}^{l} \alpha_i \mathcal{K}(\mathbf{x}_i, \mathbf{x})\right) \qquad (14)$$

where $\mathbf{w} = (\alpha_1, \ldots, \alpha_l)'$, $\phi(\mathbf{x}) = (\mathcal{K}(\mathbf{x}_1, \mathbf{x}), \ldots, \mathcal{K}(\mathbf{x}_l, \mathbf{x}))'$, and $\mathcal{K}$ is a kernel function. We define the so-called *version space* as the set of all $\mathbf{w}$ which are consistent with the training sample

$$V(S) = \{\mathbf{w} | f_\mathbf{w}(\mathbf{x}_i) = y_i; (\mathbf{x}_i, y_i) \in S; i = 1, \ldots, l\}^1 \qquad (15)$$

Restricting $\|\mathbf{w}\| = 1$ ensures uniqueness of index $\mathbf{w}$ for every $f = f_\mathbf{w} \in \mathcal{H}$. Note that the introduction of a test point $\mathbf{x}_{l+1}$ may bisect the volume V of version space into two sub volumes V^+ and V^-, where V^+ is the volume of version space in which any perceptron would classify the test point as $+1$, and V^- is the volume where perceptrons predict a negative classification. When assuming a uniform prior over $\mathbf{w}$ and the class of perceptrons it is clear that the ratio $p^+ = V^+/(V^+ + V^-)$ is the posterior probability of labelling the test point as $+1$. An ergodic billiard can be used to obtain estimates for the volumes of version space which produce posteriors p^+ (p^-) which do not deviate significantly from the true expectation of p^+ (p^-).

For this paper we followed the algorithm given in [1] and used $n = 1000$ bounces for the billard, which bounds the deviation from the true posterior at $e < 0.05$ with a probability of 99%. If the prior assumptions are satisfied, then we would expect the predictions and confidence values assigned by the algorithm to be approximately Bayes-optimal.

6.2   Perceptron with Typicalness

The typicalness framework has recently been successfully applied to pattern-recognition Support Vector Machines [11,8]. As a comparison with BT, we will use the typicalness framework in conjunction with a kernel perceptron.

In order to obtain our confidences and predictions for a test example $\mathbf{x}_{l+1}$, we do the following:

1. Add $(\mathbf{x}_{l+1}, 1)$ to our training sequence and run the kernel perceptron algorithm [2].
2. Use the resulting α_i values (from the expansion of $\mathbf{w}$) as the strangeness values, and use eq (4) to obtain t^+.

---

[1] It is assumed that there is a function f^* in the space $\mathcal{H}$ such that for all $(\mathbf{x}, y) \in S$, $y = f^*(\mathbf{x})$.

3. Repeat the above steps, but add $(\mathbf{x}_{l+1}, -1)$ to the training sequence instead, and use (4) to obtain t^-.

Once we have values for t^+ and t^- we use the following: for every confidence level $1 - r$, output as the prediction region

$$R = \begin{cases} \{-1, 1\} & \text{if } t^+ > r \text{ and } t^- > r \\ \{1\} & \text{if } t^+ > r \text{ and } t^- \le r \text{ (and vice versa)} \\ \emptyset & \text{if } t^+ \le r \text{ and } t^- \le r \end{cases}$$

7   Experimental Comparisons

In order to compare the Bayesian and typicalness frameworks' performance, we generated artificial datasets from the prior distributions assumed by the Bayesian algorithms. We then generated a similar data set, using a different (incorrect) prior, and compared the results. We also include some results on benchmark data sets which are taken from the UCI machine learning repository.

The general experimental set-up was as follows. For all experiments, 100 training and 100 test points were randomly selected a total of 10 times. For the benchmark data sets, the training and testing examples were randomly drawn from the set of all data points.

7.1   Regression Estimation Experiments

For the toy dataset we generated data points drawn from a uniform distribution over $[-10, 10]^5$ and for each of the 10 datasets drew a vector $\mathbf{w}$ from a five-dimensional normal distribution $N(0, I)$. That vector was then used to generate labels using the equation $y_i = \mathbf{w} \cdot \mathbf{x}_i + N(0, 1)$. MATLAB implementations of both algorithms take about 15 minutes to run all 10 splits on a 600Mhz DEC Alpha processor. However more efficient implementations might show a gap in performance between the algorithms.

This data precisely meets the prior for Bayesian ridge regression with the ridge factor $a = 1$. We also experimented on two benchmark datasets, the auto-mpg dataset and the Boston housing dataset. For each experiment, we show the percentage confidence against the percentage of labels outside the tolerance region predicted for that confidence level. The percentage outside the tolerance region should never exceed 100 minus the percentage confidence, up to statistical fluctuations. If we have two valid algorithms, we need some qualitative measure with which to compare them. One natural comparison for regression estimation is the width of tolerance regions. We also therefore plot the percentage confidence against the mean width of the tolerance regions predicted for that confidence level. We say that algorithms giving narrower tolerance regions are more accurate. Figure 1 shows results on the artificial data which was generated to meet Bayesian ridge regression's prior. The top left graph shows that when Bayesian RR is run with $a = 1$, fitting the prior, it generates valid tolerance regions. If we increase a however, a greater number of labels fall outside the tolerance regions. With a set to 10000, only about 15% of labels fall within a 90% tolerance region.

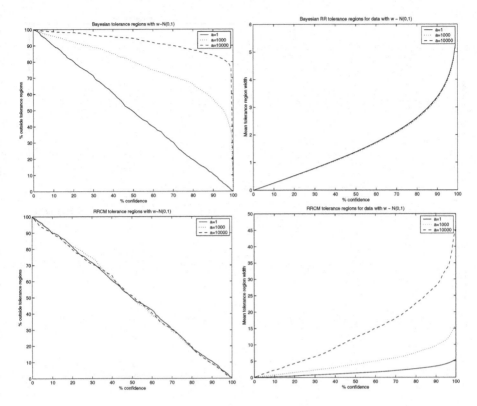

Fig. 1. Bayesian RR and RRCM on data generated with $\mathbf{w} \sim N(0, 1)$

Looking at the top right graph one can see that the tolerance region width is almost identical no matter how a is set. This causes more and more errors to be made as the regularisation is increased. If we instead look at the RRCM's performance (bottom graphs in Figure 1) we can see that the tolerance regions contain almost precisely $r\%$ of the labels for every confidence level r, independent of the setting of a.

These results show that the Bayesian algorithm only predicts tolerance regions valid in the sense of (1) when using the correct prior. As we change a we are effectively changing the prior, and the tolerance regions degrade in terms of validity. The typicalness algorithm however makes no assumptions about the value of the ridge parameter and so makes valid (and indeed 'nearly precise') predictions independent of its value.

Figure 2 shows results from applying the algorithms to two real world datasets, with the ridge coefficient a chosen so that a reasonable mean square error is obtained. The top graphs in the figure show that Bayesian ridge regression is overconfident on the auto-mpg dataset, predicting tolerance regions that are too narrow. The RRCM predicts valid tolerance regions, the top right graph shows that to do so it gives wider tolerance regions than Bayesian ridge regression. On the Boston housing dataset, Bayesian ridge regression is too con-

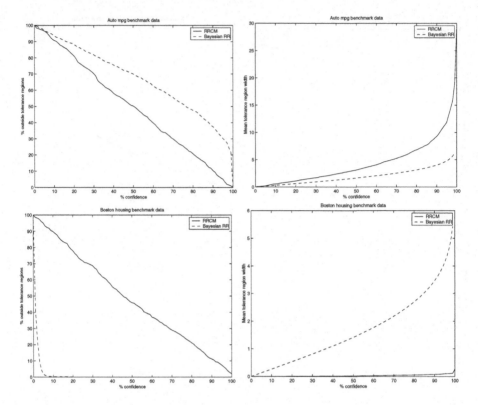

Fig. 2. Bayesian RR and RRCM applied to Auto mpg and Boston housing benchmarks

servative. The bottom left graph shows that its predicted tolerance regions are always valid, however it also shows that they are much wider than those given by the RRCM. As the RRCM's tolerance regions are also valid, we prefer the more accurate RRCM's predictions.

7.2   Pattern Recognition Experiments

In this section we compare the Bayesian-Transduction (BT) algorithm and the kernel perceptron when used within the typicalness framework. We ran experiments on two toy datasets, and the well-known heart data set.

For the artificial data, one dataset was created using a uniform prior over $\mathbf{w}$ such that $\|\mathbf{w}\| = 1$ (this is the correct prior for BT). We generated 100 train and 100 test points uniformly in the range $[-10, 10]^5$ and then labeled all points with a $\mathbf{w}$ selected from the uniform prior, and repeated this process 10 times. For the second artificial data set we used a similar set-up to the one above, except that we added noise to our data from a normal distribution, and the experiments were run using an RBF kernel with $\sigma = 0.2$ (so the prior was no longer satisfied). To get an idea of the timings involved, all 10 splits took a total of 13 minutes when using BT (implemented in C++) and the typicalness method took just over 7 minutes (in MATLAB). All experiments were run on a 233Mhz Dec Alpha. Both algorithms however have a naive implementation, and improvements in performance could be made.

In the case of pattern recognition our aim is once again to exclude labels which do not meet our confidence threshold. For a two class problem this means that we have four possible predictions; the label $+1$, the label -1, both labels $\{+1, -1\}$ and the empty set $\{\emptyset\}$. Hopefully our algorithm will only give one prediction for an example, however the other two cases also provide us with important information. Predicting the empty set indicates that we cannot make a prediction at the required confidence level and this can be used as a filter mechanism to perhaps indicate that a human should classify this example. Similarly predicting both labels indicates that it is not possible to reject a classification with that confidence level, and this could also be used as a filter. It is interesting to note that for confidence thresholds below 50%, the Bayesian method is always forced to make a non-empty prediction, whereas the typicalness method is not.

As in the regression case we plot two graphs; the first shows the percentage error achieved on the test set, and the second shows the number of 'dual predictions' made for each confidence level. We want our algorithms to be valid in the sense of (1) so we would not expect any points to lie above the $y = x$ line in the first graph, again up to statistical fluctuations. Of course an algorithm can be trivially made valid by always predicting both labels (this corresponds to an infinitely wide tolerance region in the regression case), however we wish our algorithms not only to be valid but also to be more accurate (have narrower tolerance regions). The second graph therefore shows the number of dual predictions made for each confidence level and the lower this value the better. We are less interested in empty predictions, since there cannot be many of them (at most $100r\%$ at any confidence level $100(1 - r)\%$, up to statistical fluctuations).

The top graphs in Figure 3 show results for data generated by a correct prior. Both algorithms give valid results for this data set. The bottom two graphs show the setting when an incorrect prior is used. In this case BT is over confident and produces too many errors for many confidence levels; whereas the values given by typicalness are valid.

Figure 4 presents results on the heart data set. Once again BT is over confident and produces a higher error rate than would be expected by the confidence rejection threshold. This is certainly not desirable in a real-world application, for a 95% threshold you would not expect the error rate to be much above 5% of errors. Notice how once again the typicalness method gives valid confidence values, with error rates at certain thresholds never in great excess of the values expected.

8   Conclusions

In this paper we presented a comparison of the Bayesian and typicalness frameworks. We highlighted the need for algorithms to produce valid (and ideally 'nearly precise') confidence values and outlined the typicalness framework which can be used in conjunction with many machine learning algorithms to achieve this goal. We have shown that the typicalness framework can be easily applied

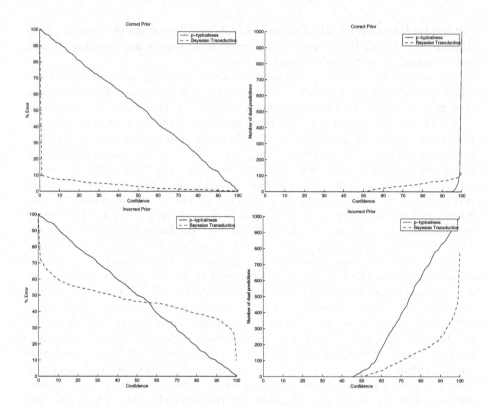

Fig. 3. Bayesian Transduction (BT) and typicalness perceptron on data with a uniform prior (top), and a non-uniform prior (bottom).

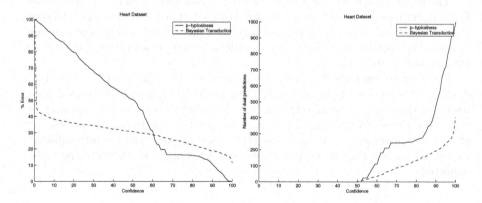

Fig. 4. Bayesian transduction and typicalness perceptron on the heart benchmark

to existing well-known algorithms for both regression and classification problems. In our experimental results we have shown that when the prior is correct Bayesian methods perform well (as expected), however the difference in performance to the methods using the typicalness framework (which does not rely on such priors) is negligible. When incorrect priors or real-world datasets are used, then Bayesian methods can be shown to produce 'incorrect' confidence values for their predictions, whereas the typicalness methods still produce valid and nearly precise confidence levels. Indeed, in almost all our experiments typicalness methods outperform their Bayesian counterparts in either validity or tightness of confidence intervals.

References

1. Thore Graepel, Ralf Herbrich, and Klaus Obermayer. Bayesian Transduction. In Sara A. Solla, Todd K. Leen, and Klaus-Robert Müller, editors, *Advances in Neural Information Processing Systems 12: Proceedings of the 1999 Conference*, pages 456–462. The MIT Press, 1999.
2. Ralf Herbrich, Thore Graepel, and Colin Campbell. Bayesian Learning in Reproducing Kernel Hilbert Spaces. Technical report, Technical University of Berlin, Franklinstr. 28/29, 10587 Berlin, 1999.
3. A. Hoerl and R.W. Kennard. Ridge regression: Biased estimation for nonorthogonal problems. *Technometrics*, 12(1):55–67, 1970.
4. T. Melluish, C. Saunders, I. Nouretdinov, and V Vovk. The typicalness framework: a comparison with the Bayesian approach. Technical Report CLRC-TR-01-05, Royal Holloway University of London, 2001.
5. Ilia Nouretdinov, Tom Melluish, and Volodya Vovk. Ridge Regression Confidence Machine. In *Accepted for ICML*, 2001.
6. C. Saunders, A. Gammerman, and V. Vovk. Ridge regression learning algorithm in dual variables. In *Proceedings of the 15th International Conference on Machine Learning*, 1998.
7. C. Saunders, A. Gammerman, and V. Vovk. Transduction with Confidence and Credibility. In *Proceedings of IJCAI '99*, volume 2, 1999.
8. C. Saunders, A. Gammerman, and V. Vovk. Computationally Efficient Transductive Machines. In *Proceedings of the Eleventh International Conference on Algorithmic Learning Theory 2000 (ALT '00)*, Lecture Notes in Artificial Intelligenece. Springer-Verlag, 2000.
9. Craig Saunders. *Efficient Implementation and Experimental Testing of Transductive Algorithms for Predicting with Confidence*. PhD thesis, Royal Holloway and Bedford New College, University of London, 2000.
10. Vladimir Vapnik. *The Nature of Statistical Learning Theory*. Springer, 1995.
11. V. Vovk, A. Gammerman, and C. Saunders. Machine-learning applications of algorithmic randomness. In *Machine Learning, Proceedings of the Sixteenth International Conference (ICML'99)*, 1999.
12. Volodya Vovk and Alex Gammerman. *Algorithmic theory of randomness and its applications in computer learning*. Unpublished manuscript, 2000.

Symbolic Discriminant Analysis for Mining Gene Expression Patterns

Jason H. Moore, Joel S. Parker, and Lance W. Hahn

Program in Human Genetics, Department of Molecular Physiology and Biophysics,
519 Light Hall, Vanderbilt University, Nashville, TN, USA 37232-0700
moore, parker, hahn@phg.mc.Vanderbilt.edu

Abstract. New laboratory technologies have made it possible to measure the expression levels of thousands of genes simultaneously in a particular cell or tissue. The challenge for computational biologists will be to develop methods that are able to identify subsets of gene expression variables that classify cells and tissues into meaningful clinical groups. Linear discriminant analysis is a popular multivariate statistical approach for classification of observations into groups. This is because the theory is well described and the method is easy to implement and interpret. However, an important limitation is that linear discriminant functions need to be pre-specified. To address this limitation and the limitation of linearity, we developed symbolic discriminant analysis (SDA) for the automatic selection of gene expression variables and discriminant functions that can take any form. We have implemented the genetic programming machine learning methodology for optimizing SDA in parallel on a Beowulf-style computer cluster.

1 Introduction

New laboratory technologies such as DNA microarrays [1], the serial analysis of gene expression (SAGE) [2], and protein mass spectrometry [3] have made it cost-effective and efficient to measure the relative expression levels of thousands of different genes in cells and tissues. The availability of massive amounts of gene expression information afforded by such technologies presents certain statistical and computational challenges to those hoping to use this information to improve our understanding of the initiation, progression, and severity of human diseases. Current statistical and computational methods such as linear discriminant analysis are simplistic and inadequate. Linear discriminant analysis [4] is a multivariate statistical classification procedure that linearly combines measurements on multiple explanatory variables into a single value or discriminant score that can be used to classify observations. This method is popular because there is a solid theoretical foundation [5] and it is easy to implement and interpret [6]. However, an important limitation is that the linear discriminant functions need to be pre-specified and only the coefficients for each linear predictor are estimated from the data. This limitation is not unique to linear discriminant

L. De Raedt and P. Flach (Eds.): ECML 2001, LNAI 2167, pp. 372–381, 2001.
© Springer-Verlag Berlin Heidelberg 2001

analysis. Linear, polynomial, and logistic regression also require a pre-specified model [7].

Symbolic regression was developed by Koza [8] as a means of identifying regression equations that do not need to be pre-specified. Identification of optimal symbolic regression models is accomplished using the genetic programming machine learning methodology, an approach that is capable of generating creative solutions to a particular problem because it is not limited by human preconceptions about what the solution should look like [9]. Symbolic regression applications have included the discovery of trigonometric identities [8], econometric modeling [8], forecasting power demand [10], and modeling chemical process systems [11,12].

The goal of the present study was to develop a symbolic discriminant analysis approach by extending symbolic regression and parallel genetic programming to identify optimal linear or nonlinear discriminant functions and coefficients. We applied this new supervised classification method to identifying combinations of gene expression variables that differentiate acute myeloid leukemia (AML) from acute lymphoblastic leukemia (ALL) using the data collected and analyzed by Golub et al. [13].

2   A Review of Linear Discriminant Analysis

Sir Ronald Fisher developed linear discriminant analysis (LDA) as tool for classifying observations using information about multiple variables [4]. Consider the case in which there are two groups with n1 and n2 observations and k variables measured per observation. Fisher suggested forming linear combinations of measurements from multiple variables to generate a linear discriminant score (1) that takes the form

$$l_{ij} = \alpha_1 x_{ij1} + \alpha_2 x_{ij2} + \ldots + \alpha_k x_{ijk} \tag{1}$$

for the ith group and the jth observation in that group where each α is a coefficient and each x is an explanatory variable (e.g. gene expression variable). The goal of LDA is to find a linear combination of explanatory variables and coefficient estimates such that the difference between the distributions of linear discriminant scores for each group is maximized.

Classification of observations into one of the two groups requires a decision rule that is based on the linear discriminant score. For example, if $l_{ij} ¿ l_o$ then assign the observation to one group and if $l_{ij} \leq l_o$ then assign the observation to the other group. When the prior probability that an observation belongs to one group is equal to the probability that it belongs to the other group, l_o can be defined as the median of the linear discriminant scores for both groups. When the prior probabilities are not equal, l_o is adjusted appropriately. Using this decision rule, the classification error for a particular discriminant function can be estimated from the observed data. When combined with cross-validation or independent data, the prediction error can be estimated as well.

3 Symbolic Discriminant Analysis

An obvious limitation of LDA is the need to pre-specify the linear discriminant function. Additionally, optimal classification of observations into groups may not be possible with a linear combination of explanatory variables. To address these limitations, we developed a method called symbolic discriminant analysis (SDA) that is able to identify the optimal functional form and coefficients of the discriminant function that may be linear or nonlinear. The SDA approach is inspired by the symbolic regression approach of Koza [8].

The goal of Koza's symbolic regression [8] is to identify a mathematical function or equation, in symbolic form, that fits a set of numerical data. Functionally, symbolic regression equations take the form of a computer program that accepts input values from one or more independent or explanatory variables and produces predictions for the dependent variable as output. These symbolic regression equations are represented as binary expression trees. Each binary expression tree is rooted with a mathematical function called a node. Each node or tree branch is connected to another node or ends with a connection to a terminal representing one of the independent variables. The number of vertical levels in the tree that contain at least one node is referred to as the tree depth. In general, increasing the number of levels in the tree increases the size and complexity of the symbolic regression equations.

The first step in implementing symbolic regression is to decide which mathematical functions (e.g. +, -, /, *, log, etc.) will comprise the function set. Additionally, the list of predictor or explanatory variables (e.g. X_1, X_2, X_3, etc.) that will comprise the terminal set must also be established. Random constants can be added to the terminal set to allow coefficients to be estimated. Once the function and terminal sets are defined, the next step is to identify the combination of functions and explanatory variables that minimize the sum of the squared differences between the output or predicted values and the observed values of the dependent variable. When the number of potential symbolic regression models is effectively infinite, machine learning methods must be employed (see Section 4).

With SDA, the binary expression tree or symbolic equation is used to generate symbolic discriminant scores for each observation in each group. Once the symbolic discriminant scores are generated, the classification error can be estimated as described in Section 2. In this study, the function set consisted of addition, subtraction, division (protected from division by zero), and multiplication. The terminal set consisted of approximately 7100 gene expression variables from the human leukemia dataset [13]. This number of explanatory variables presents an extraordinarily large search space.

4 Parallel Genetic Programming

Genetic or evolutionary algorithms, neural networks, case-based learning, rule induction, and analytic learning are some of the more popular paradigms in machine learning [14]. Genetic algorithms perform a beam or parallel search of the solution space that is analogous to the problem solving abilities of biological populations undergoing evolution by natural selection [15,16]. With this procedure, a randomly generated 'population' of solutions to a particular problem are generated and then evaluated for their 'fitness' or ability to solve the problem. The highest fit individuals or models in the population are selected and then undergo 'recombination' or exchanges of model pieces. Recombination generates variability among the solutions and is the key to the success of the beam search just as it is a key mechanism of evolution by natural selection. Following recombination, the models are reevaluated and the cycle of selection, recombination, and evaluation continues until an optimal solution is identified. A limitation of genetic algorithms is that the solutions or models must be represented by one-dimensional binary arrays or 'chromosomes'. Thus, these algorithms lack some flexibility. Koza [8] has addressed this by developing genetic programming which operates on computer programs rather than binary arrays. This advance opened the door for the optimization of problems ranging from robotics to electronic circuit discovery [9].

As with any machine learning methodology [14], genetic programming is not immune to stalling on local optima [17]. To address this issue, distributed or parallel approaches to genetic programming have been implemented [8,17,18]. Here, multiple genetic programming populations are generated each evolving semi-independently. At regular iterative intervals, the best solution obtained by each population is migrated to all other populations. Thus, if one population stalls on a local optimum, its search can be rekindled by the immigration of good solutions from other regions of the search space. Parallel genetic programs are conveniently implemented on parallel computer clusters where each population evolves on a single node or processor with migration occurring to other nodes via message-passing [19].

We used parallel genetic programming in the present study to optimize the selection of symbolic discriminant functions and gene expression variables. We implemented the parallel genetic programming by integrating the lil-gp software package [20] with the parallel virtual machine (PVM) message-passing library [19]. The parallel genetic program was run on two nodes of the VAnderbilt Multi-Processor Integrated Research Engine or VAMPIRE, a 55 node Beowulf-style parallel computer system running the Linux operating system. Each node has two Pentium III 600Mhz processors, 256 Mb RAM, a network card, and a 10 Gb hard drive. A total of two populations were used each consisting of 200 individuals. We allowed the genetic programs to run a total of 100 iterations with migration between each population every 25 iterations. A recombination frequency of 0.6 was used along with a mutation frequency of 0.02. We limited all binary expression trees to a node depth of six to prevent symbolic discriminant functions from becoming too large to interpret.

5   Data Analysis

Two independent human leukemia datasets were available for analysis [13]. We selected this dataset because previous class prediction methods have been applied with marginal success [13]. The first dataset consists of 38 acute myeloid leukemia (AML) and acute lymphoblastic leukemia (ALL) samples and was used to develop symbolic discriminant functions of the gene expression variables. We used a leave-one-out cross validation strategy with the parallel genetic programming to select symbolic discriminant functions with low classification and prediction errors. For each 37/38 of the data, we ran the parallel genetic program and selected the resulting model that minimized the misclassification rate and correctly predicted the class membership of the single observation left out of the training step. Optimal symbolic discriminant functions were then evaluated for their predictive ability using the independent dataset consisting of 34 AML and ALL samples. All of the approximately 7100 gene expression variables were available for possible inclusion in a model.

6   Results

We identified two 'near-perfect' symbolic discriminant functions that correctly classified 38 out of 38 (100%) leukemia samples in the training dataset and correctly predicted 33 out of 34 (97.1%) leukemia samples in the independent second dataset. Additionally, we identified 16 'very good' models that correctly classified 38 out of 38 (100%) in the training dataset and correctly predicted 32 out of 34 (94.1%) in the independent dataset. The first near-perfect symbolic discriminant function had four different gene expression variables while the second had just two. Each had different combinations of gene expression variables and different mathematical functions suggesting that there may be many subsets of gene expression variables that define leukemia type. For example, the first discriminant function had the form

$$X_{2555} * (X_{1153} + X_{2289} + X_{3193}) \tag{2}$$

while the second had the form

$$X_{1835} + X_{2546} \tag{3}$$

The binary expression trees for these two symbolic discriminant functions are illustrated in Figure 1 while boxplots of the discriminant scores are illustrated in Figure 2. For the first model (2), the genes identified were a testis-specific cDNA on chromosome 17q (X_{2555}), erythroid beta-spectrin (X_{1153}), adipsin (X_{2289}), and nucleoporin 98 (X_{3193}). For the second model (3), the genes identified were CD33 (X_{1835}) and Rho-E (X_{2546}). Most of these genes are biologically related to leukemia or leukemia progenitor cells. For example, the erythroid beta-spectrin protein is a major component of red blood cell membranes and is expressed during normal erythropoiesis. The adipsin gene is part of a chromosomal cluster

of genes that is expressed during myeloid cell differentiation and the nucleoporin
98 gene is located at a chromosomal breakpoint that is associated with AML.
The CD33 gene encodes a differentiation antigen of AML progenitor cells and
is a very well-know pathological marker of AML. Thus, from approximately
7100 different gene expression variables, SDA identified several genes with direct
biological relevance to human leukemia. Further, the level of prediction accuracy
obtained with these two symbolic discriminant functions was nearly perfect and
significantly better than the class prediction methods of Golub et al. [13].

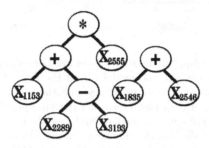

Fig. 1. Binary expression trees for model (1) on the left and model (2) on the right.
Note that the nodes are arithmetic functions and the terminals are gene expression
variables.

7   Discussion

This paper has presented symbolic discriminant analysis (SDA) for the identification and modeling of gene expression variables that can classify observations
and predict clinical outcomes. This new approach to linear and nonlinear discriminant analysis is based on the building block idea of symbolic regression [8].
That is, we formed discriminant functions by selecting gene expression variables
and mathematical functions of the gene expression variables. We implemented
the genetic programming machine learning methodology [8,9,17] in parallel [18]
to optimize selection of symbolic discriminant functions. Application of SDA
to the problem of identifying symbolic discriminant functions of gene expression variables that classify and predict human leukemia types demonstrates the
utility of this approach for both variable or feature selection and statistical modeling. This is particularly important for gene expression monitoring because as
many as 10,000 or 15,000 gene expression variables are routinely being measured.
Further, the relationship between different combinations of gene expression variables and clinical endpoints such as cancer type may be part of a very rugged
fitness landscape.

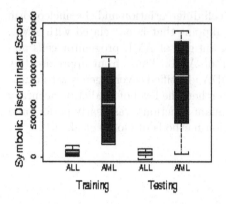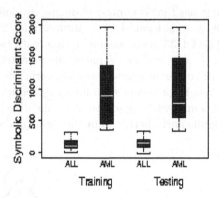

Fig. 2. Boxplots representing the distributions of symbolic discriminant scores generated using model (1) on the left and model (2) on the right. Boxplots are presented for the training or classification dataset (n=38) and the testing or prediction dataset (n=34). The shaded box of each plot represents the interquartile range of the distribution, the white line represents the median, and the whiskers or brackets above and below each box represent the maximum and minimum values, respectively. Note that for the training datasets, the whiskers of the ALL and AML scores do not overlap. This reflects the correct classification of every observation.

7.1   What Are the Advantages of SDA?

There are two important advantages of SDA over traditional multivariate methods such as linear discriminant analysis [4,5,6] and multiple logistic regression [21]. First, SDA does not pre-specify the functional form of the model. For example, with linear discriminant analysis, the discriminant function must take the form of equation (1). This limits the models to linear additive functions of the explanatory variables. With SDA, the basic mathematical building blocks are defined and then flexibly combined with explanatory variables to derive the best discriminant function. In this study, we used the four basic arithmetic functions as building blocks. However, other functions such as square root, logarithm, exponential, and absolute value could have been used. In fact, virtually any function can be added to the list with little modification of the code. We selected the basic arithmetic function in this study to help facilitate interpretation of discriminant functions. Additionally, combining multiple arithmetic functions can approximate many other mathematical functions such as square root and logarithm.

The second advantage of SDA is the automatic selection of variables from a list of thousands. Traditional model fitting involves stepwise procedures that enter a variable into the model and then keep it in the model if it has statistically significant marginal or independent main effect [7,21]. Interaction terms are only evaluated for those variables that are already in the model. This deals with the combinatorial problem of selecting variables, however, variables whose effects are mostly through interactions with other variables will be missed. This may be an unreasonable assumption for most complex biological systems. The SDA approach employs a parallel machine learning approach to selecting variables that permits interactions to be modeled in the absence of marginal effects. For example, the first 'near-perfect' model (2) identified from the leukemia dataset is a linear combination of interaction terms. No one variable contributes to the discriminant function independently of the others.

7.2   What Are the Disadvantages of SDA?

Although SDA has several important advantages over traditional multivariate statistical methods, there are several disadvantages. First, there is no guarantee that the genetic programming machine learning methodology will find the optimal solution. Heuristic searches tend to sacrifice finding an optimal solution in favor of tractability [14]. Implementing evolutionary-type machine learning algorithms in parallel certainly improves the chances of finding an optimal solution [8,17,18], but it is not a certainty. This is due to the stochastic nature of how genetic programming operates. The initial populations of solutions are randomly generated and the recombination and mutation occurs at random positions in the binary expression trees. Further, there may be a stochastic component to how the highest fit individuals are selected. For these reasons, evolutionary-type algorithms should be run multiple times with multiple parallel populations.

A second disadvantage of this approach is the computational requirement. Linear discriminant analysis can be performed on a standard desktop workstation while SDA requires a parallel computer cluster for optimal performance. When the number of genes to be evaluated is large (e.g. n=5,000 or n=10,000), the power of a parallel computer is required. Although such systems are fairly inexpensive to build, the time investment to establish and manage a parallel computing farm may be prohibitive to some.

A third disadvantage is the complexity of the symbolic discriminant functions obtained. An attractive feature of linear discriminant analysis is the simplicity of the models, which facilitates interpretation. Although the two near-perfect models obtained using SDA in the present study were fairly simple, SDA has the potential to generate rather large complex models. If so desired, this can be handled in several ways. One solution is to limit the size of the binary expression trees that the genetic program can build and manipulate. In this study, we limited the size of the symbolic discriminant functions by limiting the depth of the binary expression trees to a maximum of six. An alternative solution is to simplify the mathematical functions used. For example, by limiting the functions to addition and subtraction, SDA becomes linear discriminant analysis with heuristic variable selection.

7.3   Other Machine Learning Approaches to SDA

We selected parallel genetic programming as a machine learning methodology for optimizing SDA for several reasons. Most importantly, genetic programming provided the necessary flexibility to use binary expression tree representation of symbolic discriminant functions. Additionally, given the size and complexity of the solution space, performing multiple hill-climbing-type searches in parallel (i.e. a beam search) has a higher likelihood of success than a single hill-climbing search [14]. However, with this in mind, genetic programming is not the only option for optimizing SDA. For example, it might be advisable to carry out a limited exhaustive search as an initial step. The second near-perfect symbolic discriminant function (3) obtained during the analysis of the leukemia data was a simple additive linear function of two variables with no corresponding coefficients. This function could have been identified by carrying out an exhaustive search of the 25,201,450 possible pairwise combinations of gene expression variables. However, the first symbolic discriminant function (2), which contained a completely different set of genes with multiplicative effects, would have been missed.

Perhaps a more promising approach would be to combine the general search features of parallel genetic programming with the local search features of simulated annealing [22] or a stochastic search. For example, Krasnogor and Smith [23] employed a stochastic search once the genetic algorithm had reached a convergence state. Application of this new hybrid genetic algorithm seemed to improve optimization of the traveling salesman problem and a protein folding problem. We will explore the use of a combined local search for optimizing SDA in future studies.

8   Conclusions

We conclude from this study that the SDA approach provides a powerful alternative to traditional multivariate statistical methods for identifying gene expression patterns that are predictive of a clinical endpoint. The advantages of SDA include the ability to automatically identify important subsets of gene expression variables from among thousands of candidates and the ability to automatically identify the most appropriate mathematical functions relating the gene expression variables to a clinical endpoint. We anticipate this will be an important methodology to add to the repertoire of supervised pattern recognition and machine learning approaches for mining gene expression patterns.

References

1. Schena, M., Shalon, D., Davis, R.W., Brown, P.O.: Quantitative monitoring of gene expression patterns with a complementary DNA microarray. Science **270** (1995) 467–470
2. Velculesco, V.E., Zhang, L., Vogelstein, B., Kinzler, K.W.: Serial analysis of gene expression. Science **270** (1995) 484–487
3. Caprioli, R.M., Farmer, T.B., Gile, J.: Molecular imaging of biological samples: Localization of peptides and proteins using MALDI–TOF MS. Analyt. Chem. **69** (1997) 4751–4760
4. Fisher, R.A.: The Use of Multiple Measurements in Taxonomic Problems. Ann. Eugen. **7** (1936) 179–188

5. Johnson, R.A., Wichern, D.W.: Applied Multivariate Statistical Analysis. Prentice Hall, Upper Saddle River (1998)
6. Huberty, C.J.: Applied Discriminant Analysis. John Wiley & Sons, Inc., New York Chichester Bisbane Toronto Singapore (1994)
7. Neter, J., Wasserman, W., Kutner, M.H.: Applied Linear Statistical Models, Regression, Analysis of Variance, and Experimental Designs. 3rd edn. Irwin, Homewood (1990)
8. Koza, J.R.: Genetic Programming: On the Programming of Computers by Means of Natural Selection. The MIT Press, Cambridge London (1992).
9. Koza, J.R., Bennett III, F.H., Andre, D., Keane, M.A.: Genetic Programming III: Darwinian Invention and Problem Solving. Morgan Kaufmann Publishers, San Francisco (1999).
10. Lee, D.G., Lee, B.W., Chang, S.H.: Genetic Programming Model for Long–Term Forecasting of Electric Power Demand. Elec. Power Syst. Res. **40** (1997) 17–22
11. McKay, B., Willis, M., Barton, G.: Steady–State Modelling of Chemical Process Systems using Genetic Programming. Computers Chem. Engng. **21** (1997) 981–996
12. Willis, M., Hiden, H., Hinchliffe, M., McKay, B., Barton, G.W.: Systems Modelling using Genetic Programming. Computers Chem. Engng. **21** Suppl. (1997) S1161–S1166
13. Golub, T.R., Slonim, D.K., Tamayo, P., Huard, C., Gaasenbeek, M., Mesirov, J.P., Coller, H., Loh, M.L., Downing, J.R., Caligiuri, M.A., Bloomfield, C.D., Lander, E.S.: Molecular Classification of Cancer: Class Discovery and Class Prediction by Gene Expression Monitoring. Science **286** (1999) 531–537
14. Langley, P.: Elements of Machine Learning. Morgan Kaufmann Publishers, Inc., San Francisco (1996)
15. Holland, J.H.: Adaptation in Natural and Artificial Systems. University of Michigan Press, Ann Arbor (1975)
16. Goldberg, D.E.: Genetic Algorithms in Search, Optimization, and Machine Learning. Addison–Wesley, Reading (1989)
17. Banzhaf, W., Nordin, P., Keller, R.E., Francone, F.D.: Genetic Programming: An Introduction. Morgan Kaufmann Publishers, San Francisco (1998)
18. Cantu–Paz, E.: Efficient and Accurate Parallel Genetic Algorithms. Kluwer Academic Publishers, Boston (2000)
19. Leopold, C.: Parallel and Distributed Computing: A Survey of Models, Paradigms, and Approaches. John Wiley & Sons, Inc., New York (2001)
20. http://garage.cps.msu.edu/software/software–index.html
21. Hosmer, D.W., Lemeshow, S.: Applied Logistic Regression. John Wiley & Sons, Inc., New York (2000)
22. Kirkpatrick, S., Gelatt, C., and Vecchi, M.: Optimization by simulated annealing. Science **220** (1983) 671–680
23. Krasnogor, N., Smith, J.: A memetic algorithm with self–adaptive local search: TSP as a case study. In: Whitley, D., Goldberg, D., Cantu–Paz, E., Spector, L., Parmee, I., Beyer, H–G. (eds.): Proceedings of the Genetic and Evolutionary Computation Conference. Morgan Kaufmann Publishers, Inc., San Francisco (2000)

Social Agents Playing a Periodical Policy

Ann Nowé, Johan Parent, and Katja Verbeeck

Vrije Universiteit Brussel, Belgium
Computational Modeling Lab
asnowe@info.vub.ac.be, johan@info.vub.ac.be, kaverbee@vub.ac.be

Abstract. Coordination is an important issue in multiagent systems. Within the stochastic game framework this problem translates to policy learning in a joint action space. This technique however suffers some important drawbacks like the assumption of the existence of a unique Nash equilibrium and synchronicity, the need for central control, the cost of communication, etc. Moreover in general sum games it is not always clear which policies should be learned. Playing pure Nash equilibria is often unfair to at least one of the players, while playing a mixed strategy doesn't give any guarantee for coordination and usually results in a sub-optimal payoff for all agents. In this work we show the usefulness of periodical policies, which arise as a side effect of the fairness conditions used by the agents. We are interested in games which assume competition between the players, but where the overall performance can only be as good as the performance of the poorest player. Players are social distributed reinforcement learners, who have to learn to equalize their payoff. Our approach is illustrated on synchronous one-step games as well as on asynchronous job scheduling games.

1 Introduction

In multiagent systems the feedback experienced by an agent is usually influenced by the actions taken by the other agents present in the same system. Therefore modeling the other agents seems a natural thing to do. This leads to what is called the joint action space approach. As we will discuss below this approach suffers from some important drawbacks. On the other hand neglecting the presence of the other agents very often yields a suboptimal behavior of the global system. This is for instance the case in systems where resources are limited, such as job scheduling, routing and so on. In such systems agents should make agreements on how to share the resources to obtain a global optimal behavior, see [9]. Since communication has its price, we are interested in finding an approach where the communication between the agents can be kept low, yet yielding a fair solution to all agents. In this paper we present an approach inspired by the Homo egualis society described in sociology. The policy learned by the agents is a periodical policy, meaning that agents learn to play a repetitive combination of actions.

In many decision-making and strategy-settings people do not behave like the self-interested "rational" actors depicted in neoclassical economics and classical

---

L. De Raedt and P. Flach (Eds.): ECML 2001, LNAI 2167, pp. 382–393, 2001.
© Springer-Verlag Berlin Heidelberg 2001

game theory [2]. In a Homo egualis society, individuals have an inequality aversion. As a result altruism appear in ultimatum and public good games. As Gintis states in [2] support for Homo egualis comes from the anthropological literature, describing how Homo sapiens evolved in small hunter-gatherer groups. Such societies had no centralized structure of governance, so the enforcement of norms depends on the voluntary participation of peers.

In section 5 we will show how the objective of equalizing the utility can be incorporated into distributed reinforcement learning agents with only limited communication.

The rest of the paper is organized as follows. In section 2 we discuss the join action space approach and why we believe this is not a solution to learning in multi agent systems. In section 3 we briefly look at the special case of dominance solvable games. Section 4, deals with general sum games and why mixed policies are not the solution we are looking for. Section 5 introduces our approach of learning periodical policies, section 6 reports some experiments. Section 7 gives some ideas for future work and we conclude with section 8.

2   The Joint Action Space Approach

For learning in a multiagent system, two extreme approaches can be recognized. On the one hand, the presence of other agents, who are possibly influencing the effects a single agent experiences, can be completely ignored. Thus a single agent is learning as if the other agents are not around.

On the other hand, the presence of other agents can be modeled explicitly. This results in a joint action space approach which recently received quite a lot of attention [1,5,6].

2.1   What Is the Joint Action Space Approach

In the joint action space technique, learning happens in the product space of the set of states S, and the collections of action sets $A_1, ... A_n$ (one set for every agent). The state transition function $T : S \times A_1 \times ... \times A_n \to P(S)$ maps a state and an action from every agent onto a probability distribution on S and each agent receives an associated reward, defined by the reward function $R_i : S \times A_1 \times ... \times A_n \to P(\Re)$. This is the underlying model for the stochastic games, also referred to as Markov games in [5,6].

2.2   Drawbacks of the Joint Action Space Approach

The joint action space, is a safe technique in the sense that the influence of an agent on every other agent can be modeled. However the joint action space approach violates the basic principles of multi-agent systems : distributed control, asynchronous actions, incomplete information, cost of communication etc.

3   Learning Dominance Solvable Games

For some classes of games, the joint action space approach is complete overkill. Any game which is dominance solvable[1] can be tackled successfully by distributed, asynchronous reinforcement learning agents. A successful learning scheme in this situation is the reward-inaction scheme, where actions are selected probabilistically and actions which return high payoffs are positively reinforced, [8]. In fact what happens is an asynchronous, stochastic approximation of the well known iterated elimination of dominated strategies technique to obtain a Nash equilibrium strategy. In [7] a class of games which are called maximum games are proven to be dominance solvable. For an example see Figure 1 (left). However what happens when there isn't a Pareto dominant Nash equilibrium as in the Bach/Stravinsky game depicted in Figure 1 (middle). In the next section we discuss the use of a mixed policy for this case.

$$\begin{pmatrix} (9,11) & (5,6) & (1,0) \\ (5,6) & (5,6) & (5,6) \\ (1,0) & (5,6) & (1,0) \end{pmatrix}, \begin{pmatrix} (2,1) & (0,0) \\ (0,0) & (1,2) \end{pmatrix}, \begin{pmatrix} (10,1) & (0,0) \\ (0,0) & (1,2) \end{pmatrix}$$

Fig. 1. Left: A maximum game of common interest. Middle: The Bach/Stravinsky game. Right: Variant of the Bach/Stravinsky game.

4   Mixed Policies for General Sum Games

An example of a game with more than one Nash equilibrium is the Bach-Stravinsky game in Figure 1 (middle). There are two Nash equilibria (2,1) and (1,2). None of the Nash equilibria is Pareto dominant since they represent conflicting objectives for the two agents. If in this case the distributed, non-communicating reinforcement learning approach should be applied, the strategy learned by the agents would converge to either of the Nash equilibria, see [8]. If the strategy to which the agents converge is the first one then agent 1 has his maximal possible payoff, and agent 2 is left with a suboptimal payoff, and visa versa for the other Nash equilibrium.

For the Bach-Stravinsky game, there is also a unique mixed Nash equilibrium, which is, agent one playing Bach with probability 2/3 and Stravinsky with probability 1/3, and agent 2 playing Bach with probability 1/3 and Stravinsky with probability 2/3. The question is however, why should we like agents to learn this mixed strategy? If we compute the expected payoffs both agents receive in

---

[1] A strategic game is dominance solvable if all players are indifferent to all outcomes that survive the iterative procedure in which all the weakly dominated actions of each player are eliminated, see [11]

this case, we get a payoff of 2/3 for both agents, so both get less than what they get in the pure Nash equilibria. So on the one hand mixed strategies are not necessarily better than pure strategies, on the other hand playing pure Nash equilibria is often unfair to one of the agents. This brings us to the next section where we introduce the notion of a periodical policy.

5 Learning Fair Periodical Policies

As already mentioned in the introduction the idea of learning periodical policies is inspired by the Homo egualis society from sociology. In a Homo egualis system, agents do not only care about their own payoff, but also about how it compares to the payoff of others. A Homo egualis agent may be willing to reduce his own payoff to increase the degree of equality in the group. On the other hand he is also displeased when receiving a lower payoff than the other group members. A Homo egualis society can be modeled following [3] where the utility function of player i, u_i in an n-player game is:

$$u_i(x) = x_i - \frac{\alpha_i}{n-1}\Sigma_{x_j > x_i}(x_j - x_i) - \frac{\beta_i}{n-1}\Sigma_{x_j < x_i}(x_i - x_j) \qquad (1)$$

Where $x = (x_i, \ldots, x_j)$ are the cumulative payoffs for each player respectively and $0 \le \beta_i < \alpha_i \le 1$. $\beta_i < \alpha_i$ reflects the fact that Homo egualis exhibits a weak urge to inequality when doing better than the others and a strong urge to reduce reduce inequality when doing worse than the others.

This idea can be translated into distributed reinforcement learning agents with limited communication. First we concentrate on the second term in formula (1), i.e. the term expressing that agents with a higher payoff than other group members are willing to share some of their payoff with the less fortunate agents. This is realized as follows in the learning algorithm. Agents are distributed Q-learners who learn a stateless action function which is updated every game iteration[2] with the immediate payoff they receive in the previous game. Without communication they start exploring their action space and as the agents are selfish utility optimizing reinforcement learners, the group will converge to a Nash equilibrium, [8]. After a given period of time a communication phase will take place in which all agents send their cumulative payoff as well as their average payoff collected in the last non-communication period, to each other. The agent who experiences the highest cumulative payoff and the highest average payoff in the last period will exclude the action he is currently playing so as to give the other agents the opportunity to converge to a more rewarding situation. In more formal terms, after convergence to one of the Nash equilibria, the hyperplane containing the action of the best performing agent is removed from the joint action space, and a new learning period is stared in which the resulting subspace is explored. During this new exploration phase there is again

---

[2] One time unit corresponds to one game iteration.

no communication between the agents. After a while the group will converge to another Nash equilibrium and one of the other agents might have caught up with the former best agent. Again communication takes place and the currently "best" agent can be identified. If this is still the previous best agent nothing will happen[3]. However if another agent has outperformed the previous best one, the latter will release again his excluded action. As a result another subspace is explored, and the group will seek for yet another Nash equilibrium. As a result agents play a periodical policy, they alternate between the different Nash equilibria of the game. Even in games were the different Nash equilibria do not give the same best payoff as in Figure 1 (right) the algorithm is able to alternate between the Nash equilibria such that the average payoff for all players is equalized[4]. In Figure 2 the above described algorithm for learning fair periodical policies, is given in pseudo code.

6   Some Experiments

In this section we test the previous described algorithm on both synchronous and asynchronous games. Some preliminary results were already reported in [10]. To test the scalability of our approach in more complex action spaces, we also experimented with 3 to 5 player games with action spaces of 3 and 5 actions respectively.

The representatives of the synchronous type of games we tested are the Bach/Stravinsky game of Figure 1 (middle) and a variant shown in Figure 1 (right). In the variant game the Nash equilibrium (1,1) gives 5 times more payoff to player 1, than the Nash equilibrium (2,2) gives to player 2.

The asynchronous games we played are asynchronous network games of the common pool resource type [4] which were simulated in the QNAP2 network modeling language [14] . The simplest game being the job scheduling game depicted in Figure 3. This job scheduling game has two pure Nash equilibria: one player always chooses the common resource and the other one uses the private resource and vice versa. Note that the payoff should be minimized here. Although the common resource looks more interesting to use from an agents' point of view (because it can handle the jobs more quickly on average), the benefit disappears when there is an overconsumption of the common good by all the agents.

6.1   Results on Symmetric Games

When the players use a Q-learning algorithm [13], they find in both games one of the Nash equilibria as is shown in the payoff each players receives, see Figure 4

---

[3] The agent needs the average payoff over the previous period to determine whether he was playing his best Nash equilibrium in the last period or if someone else was trying to catch up, but actually needs more time to do so. In this case the social agent will keep his excluded action excluded.

[4] This because the average payoff of the last period is also communicated. This prevents a player to free an excluded action when another agent who is currently playing his best Nash equilibrium needs more time to catch up.

```
## INITIALIZATION
qValues := initialize_qValues ( );
payoff_all := initialize_payoffs ( );
last_payoff := initialize_payoff();
last_payoff_all := initialize_payoffs();
```

```
loop {

  ## NON-COMMUNICATION PHASE
  action := select/explore ( qValues, actionSet);
  immediate_payoff := environment ( actions );
  cumulative_payoff := cumulate ( cumulative_payoff, immediate_payoff );
  last_period_payoff := cumulate( last_period_payoff, immediate_payoff );
  qValues := update ( qValues, immediate_payoff );

  ## COMMUNICATION PHASE
  if (time_to_communicate) {
  communicate_to_all ( cumulative_payoff , last_payoff );
  payoff_all := receive_from_all ( cumulative_payoff );
  last_period_payoff_all := receive_from_all ( last_period_payoff );
  if (not_equal_payoffs ( payoff_all ) ) {
    if (and (has_best_payoff ( payoff_all ))
        (has_best_payoff ( last_period_payoff_all)))
      actionSet := actionSet - best_action;
    else
      if ( not (has_best_payoff ( payoff_all )))
        actionSet := original_actionSet;

    INITIALIZATION ;
  }
}
}
```

Fig. 2. Pseudo code of the algorithm executed by each Homo egualis Q-learning player.

(top). The left column gives the result for the Bach Stravinsky game, the right column gives the results for the variant of the Bach/Stravinsky game. One of the players seems to win the game, while the other one performs sub-optimally. In both cases the learning rate α is 0.1.

When the Q-learning players use a Homo egualis argument, by setting up a communication channel between them, a periodic policy is learned which alternates between the different pure Nash equilibria of the game. See Figure 4 (left-middle) and Figure 4 (right-middle) for the equalization of the payoff. The average payoff to which they converge goes to the optimal, which is 1.5 for the standard Bach/Stravinsky game and 1.9 for the variant. For the Bach/Stravinsky game this proofs that both equilibria are played equally. While in the variant of this game, the Nash equilibrium $(2, 2)$ is played 9 times for every period

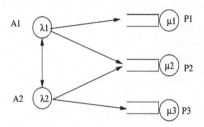

Fig. 3. A simple job scheduling game. Two agents can use either their private processor or a common processor. The agents generate jobs according to an exponential law with a mean value of 1.5 time units. Both the private processors handle the jobs with a time consumption chosen from an exponential distribution with mean value of 1 time unit, while the common processor works with a mean of 0.7 time units.

of play of the other Nash equilibrium $(1, 1)$. Figure 4 (right-middle)shows that the period in which player 1 climbs is $1/9$ of the period in which it drops. In the Bach/Stravinsky game communication was done every 50 time units, in the variant of the game communication size was every 100 time units.

Finally Figure 4 (left-bottom) and Figure 4 (right-bottom) gives the payoffs of the players when both players play their mixed Nash equilibrium strategy for the two symmetric games respectively. For both games the average payoff isn't as good as for the periodical policy, and in the variant of the Bach/Stravinsky game the payoffs aren't equalized at all.

6.2   Results on Asymmetric Games

In the asymmetric games, agents keep generating jobs independently of one another and feedback from the processors only arrives at certain time intervals. So the action selection isn't synchronous anymore as in the previous games and reinforcement is delayed. Using synchronous communication and social rules as described by the Homo equalis condition, periodical policies equalizing the job turn around time can still be found.

Figure 5 shows the payoff for the agents in the job scheduling game of Figure 3 for respectively 2 Q-learners, 2 Homo egualis Q learners and 2 players playing their mixed Nash equilibrium. As in the synchronous games, 2 Q-learners converge to one of the Nash equilibria, meaning here one player can use the common processor while the other has to use his own. Two Homo egualis players however alternate between using the common and private processor separately. Remarkable to note is that while playing the periodic policy the players implicitly learn the policy for playing the mixed Nash equilibria off-line. When the mixed Nash equilibrium is played the payoff also has the tendency to be equalized, however the average payoff isn't that good and in real-world situations where jobs may be relatively large, the discrete game may be approximated and the periodic policy may give more security for the players. Communication between 2 Homo egualis players is done every 2000 time units.

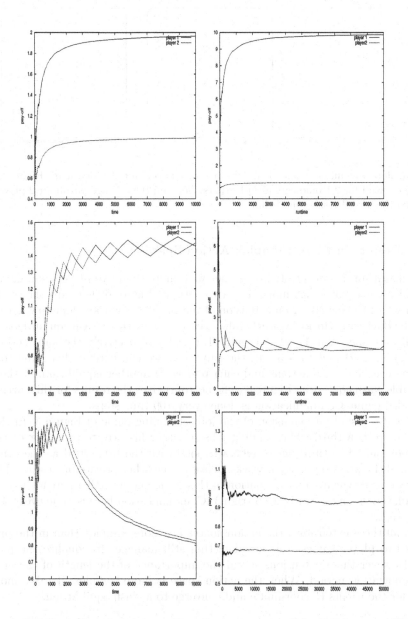

Fig. 4. Left:Bach/Stravinsky game. Top: the average payoff for 2 Q-learners, Middle: the average payoff for 2 Homo egualis Q-learners, Bottom: the average payoff for 2 players playing the mixed Nash equilibrium.
Right: Variant of the Bach/Stravinsky game. Top: the average payoff for 2 Q-learners, Middle: the average payoff for 2 Homo egualis Q-learners, Bottom: the average payoff for 2 players playing the mixed Nash equilibrium

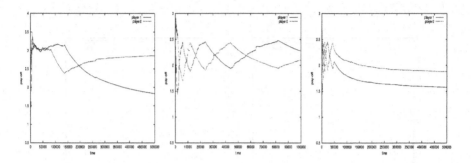

Fig. 5. Job scheduling game. Left: the average payoff for 2 Q-learners, Right: the average payoff for 2 Homo egualis Q-learners, Bottom: the average payoff for 2 players playing the mixed Nash equilibrium.

6.3   Results in More Complex Action Spaces

Our algorithm was also tested on games with more than two players and games in which each player has more than two actions. Figure 6 (left, up) shows the evolution of the payoff for an extension of the Bach/Stravinsky game to what we call the Bach/Stravinsky/Mozart game. There are now three Nash equilibria with payoff outcomes $(2, 1, 1)$, $(1, 2, 1)$ and $(1, 1, 2)$ for respectively the joint actions $(1, 1, 1)$, $(2, 2, 2)$ and $(3, 3, 3)$. In the same way we can extend this game to 5 players each having 5 actions and each preferring another equilibrium of the 5 available Nash equilibria. Figure 6 (left, bottom) gives the results for this further extended game. Communication is done every 100 time steps.

We also tested an extension of the job scheduling game of Figure 3. In this game there is a third agent sending jobs to either his private processor or the common one. The third agent generates jobs with the same load as the other ones and the private processor works as fast as the other private processors. The results of the synchronous simulation of this game and a further extended game to 5 players is found in Figure 6 (right). Communication here is done every 300 time steps.

In all these extensions, the action spaces are more complex than in the previous two player games, yet our algorithm still manages to equalize the payoffs. However these extensions reveal the importance of the length of the non-communication period. When the action space is more complex, it takes more time for the agents to coordinate and converge to a Nash equilibrium.

7   Future Work

At this point the Homo equalis player is implemented so that only when an agent receives a higher payoff than the other group members an effort is made to share some of their payoff with the less fortunate agents. The Homo equalis player described in [2] also has a strong urge to equalize the payoffs when being

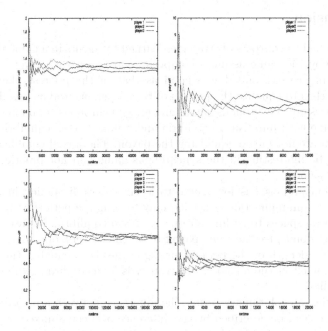

Fig. 6. Left: The average payoff for 3 (up) / 5 (bottom) Homo equalis players in the extended Bach/Stravinsky game. Right: The average payoff for 3 (up) / 5 (bottom) Homo-equalis players in a synchronous version of the Job Scheduling game with 3 / 5 agents, 3 / 5 private processors and one common processor. A payoff of 10 is collected when using the common processor alone, while a payoff of 3 is collected while using the private processor.

on the bottom. This is reflected in the third term of equation (1). This term can be incorporated in the learning system by increasing the learning rate of agents who have a low accumulated utility compared to the others. This will give these poor agents a higher probability to pull the group towards their favorite Nash equilibrium. This has not been implemented yet, but we believe that this idea might be a solution to games where some Nash equilibria are found faster than others. Especially when concerned with games in complex action spaces and multiple players, convergence to a Nash equilibrium may take a while. Exploration should be done carefully and the non-communication part should be long enough for the equilibrium to be found and played. Here also the adaptation of the learning rate of the agents might speed up convergence. Maybe after a while the agent can learn the sequence of Nash equilibria to play.

We also assumed that the games we played had some pure Nash equilibria with conflicting concerns. Of course when this is not the case and a player feels that even when he is forced to a new Nash equilibrium which still favors the previous best player, a periodical policy is not the answer.

8   Conclusion

This work studied the fairness of strategies learned by agents in a game theoretic setting, whereby the game assumes competition between the players, but the overall performance can only be as good as that of the poorest player. The global goal is thus to equalize the payoffs of the players as well as possible. The chosen test cases are synchronous games and an asynchronous common good job scheduling game with pure Nash equilibria and a mixed Nash equilibrium. The pure equilibria are not fair in equalizing the payoff. The mixed equilibrium was shown not to be interesting in the synchronous game and not practical in the asynchronous game.

The solution proposed is for agents to learn a periodic policy in a Homo egualis society. Communication is needed only to compare performances and to reduce the action spaces to go find alternative Nash equilibria. In case the pure Nash equilibria don't give the same payoff to all the players, our algorithm was able to learn the length of the period each agent needs to equalize the average payoff. As a side-effect the mixed Nash strategy is learned off-line while playing the period policy.

To conclude, in evolutionary terms, the difference between a periodic policy and a mixed one can be described by the difference between a mixed population of entities playing pure strategies and a population of entities playing mixed strategies, see [12].

References

1. Claus C., Boutilier C.,: The dynamics of reinforcement learning in cooperative multi-agent systems. Proceedings of the fifteenth National Conference on Artificial Intelligence,(1998) p 746 - 752.
2. Gintis H.,: Game Theory Evolving: A Problem-Centered Introduction to Modeling Strategic Behavior. Princeton University Press, 2000.
3. Fehr E., Schmidt K.M.,: A Theory of Fairness, Competition, and Cooperation. Quarterly Journal of Economics, 114 (1999) p 817 - 868.
4. Hardin G.,: The tragedy of the commons. Science 162 (1968) p1243-1248.
5. Hu J., Wellman M. P.,: Multi Agent Reinforcement Learning in Stochastic Games. Submitted, 1999.
6. Litmann M.L.,: Markov games as a framework for multi-agent reinforcement learning. Proceedings of the Eleventh International Conference on Machine Learning, (1994) p 157 - 163.
7. Mariotti M.,: Maximum Games, Dominance Solvability, and Coordination. Games and Economic Behavior 31, (2000) p 97 - 105.
8. Narendra K., Thathachar M., : Learning Automata: An Introduction. Prentice-Hall (1989).
9. Nowé, A., Verbeeck, K.,: Distributed Reinforcement learning, Loadbased Routing a case study. Proceedings of the Neural, Symbolic and Reinforcement Methods for sequence Learning Workshop at ijcai99.
10. Nowé, A., Verbeeck, K., Lenaerts T.,: Learning Agents in a Homo Egualis Society Technical report Computational Modeling Lab. Maart 2001. Vrije Uniuversiteit Brussel (2001).

11. Osborne J.O.,Rubinstein A., :A course in game theory. Cambridge, MA: MIT Press (1994).
12. Smith J.M.,: Evolution and the Theory of Games. Cambridge University Press (1982).
13. Sutton, R.S., Barto, A.G. : Reinforcement Learning: An introduction. Cambridge, MA: MIT Press (1998).
14. QNAP2 reference manual, SIMULOG 1996.

Learning When to Collaborate
among Learning Agents

Santiago Ontañón and Enric Plaza

IIIA, Artificial Intelligence Research Institute
CSIC, Spanish Council for Scientific Research
Campus UAB, 08193 Bellaterra, Catalonia (Spain).
{santi,enric}@iiia.csic.es, http://www.iiia.csic.es

Abstract. Multiagent systems offer a new paradigm where learning techniques can be useful. We focus on the application of lazy learning to multiagent systems where each agents learns individually and also learns when to cooperate in order to improve its performance. We show some experiments in which CBR agents use an adapted version of LID (Lazy Induction of Descriptions), a CBR method for classification. We discuss a collaboration policy (called Bounded Counsel) among agents that improves the agents' performance with respect to their isolated performance. Later, we use decision tree induction and discretization techniques to learn how to tune the Bounded Counsel policy to a specific multiagent system—preserving always the individual autonomy of agents and the privacy of their case-bases. Empirical results concerning accuracy, cost, and robustness with respect to number of agents and case base size are presented. Moreover, comparisons with the Committee collaboration policy (where all agents collaborate always) are also presented.

1   Introduction

Multiagent systems offer a new paradigm to organize AI applications. Our goal is to develop techniques to integrate lazy learning into applications that are developed as multiagent systems. Learning is a capability that together with autonomy is always defined as a feature needed for full-fledged agents. Lazy learning offers the multiagent systems paradigm the capability of autonomously learning from experience. In this paper we present a framework for collaboration among agents that use CBR and some experiments illustrating the framework.

A distributed approach for lazy learning in agents that use CBR (case-based reasoning) makes sense in different scenarios. Our purpose in this paper is to present a multiagent system approach for distributed case bases that can support these different scenarios. A first scenario is one where cases themselves are owned by different partners or organizations. These organizations can consider their cases as assets and they may not be willing to give them to a centralized "case repository" where CBR can be used. In our approach each organization keeps their private cases while providing a CBR agent that works with them. Moreover, the agents can collaborate with other agents if they keep the case

L. De Raedt and P. Flach (Eds.): ECML 2001, LNAI 2167, pp. 394–405, 2001.
© Springer-Verlag Berlin Heidelberg 2001

privacy intact and they can improve their performance by cooperating. Another scenario involves scalability: it might be impractical to have a centralized case base when the data is too big.

Our research focuses on the scenario of separate case bases that we want to use in a decentralized fashion by means of a multiagent system, that is to say a collection of CBR agents that manage individual case bases and can communicate (and collaborate) with other CBR agents. In this paper we focus on a collaboration policy (*Bounded Counsel* policy) that improve the individual performance of CBR agents without compromising the agent's autonomy and the privacy of the case bases. We also present later the *Committee* policy for comparison purposes. These collaboration policies are a refinement of the general multiagent scenario of *Cooperative CBR* proposed in [10]. The collaboration policies presented here are strategies that CBR agents can follow to improve their individual performance in this framework.

The structure of the paper is as follows. Section 2 presents the collaboration policies the CBR agents can follow to improve their performance cooperating with other agents in a multiagent system. Then, section 3 presents the CBR method that the agents use in our current experiments. Section 4 presents the proactive learning process that allows the agents to generate the examples that characterize the collaboration states in the multiagent system and then learn to tune their individual collaboration policies. The experiments themselves are explained in section 5. The paper closes with related work and conclusion sections.

2   Policies for Cooperative CBR

A multiagent CBR ($\mathcal{MAC}$) system $\mathcal{M} = \{(A_i, C_i)\}_{i=1...n}$ is composed on n agents, where each agent A_i has a case base C_i. In the experiments reported here we assume the case bases are disjunct ($\forall A_i, A_j \in \mathcal{MAC} : C_i \cap C_j = \emptyset$), i.e. there is no case shared by two agent's case bases. This is just an experimental option and not a restriction on our model. In this framework we restrict ourselves to analytical tasks, i.e. tasks (like classification) where the solution is achieved by selecting from an enumerated set of solutions $K = \{S_1 \ldots S_K\}$. A case base $C_i = \{(P_j, S_k)\}_{j=1...N}$ is a collection of pairs problem/solution.

When an agent A_i asks another agent A_j help to solve a problem the interaction protocol is as follows. First, A_i sends a problem description P to A_j. Second, after A_j has tried to solve P using its case base C_j, it sends back a message that is either :sorry (if it cannot solve P) or a solution endorsement record (SER). A SER has the form $\langle \{(S_k, E_k^j)\}, P, A_j \rangle$, where the collection of *endorsing pairs* (S_k, E_k^j) mean that the agent A_j has found E_k^j cases in case base C_j endorsing solution S_k—i.e. there are a number E_k^j of cases that are relevant (similar) for endorsing S_k as a solution for P. Each agent A_j is free to send one or more endorsing pairs in a SER record.

Before presenting the two policies for cooperative CBR, *Committee* and *Bounded Counsel* policies, we will introduce the voting mechanism.

2.1 Voting Scheme

The voting scheme defines the mechanism by which an agent reaches an aggregate solution from a collection of SERs coming from other agents. The principle behind the voting scheme is that the agents vote for solution classes depending on the number of cases they found endorsing those classes. However, we want to prevent an agent having an unbounded number of votes. Thus, we will define a normalization function so that each agent has one vote that can be for a unique solution class or fractionally assigned to a number of classes depending on the number of endorsing cases.

Formally, let $\mathcal{A}^t$ the set of agents that have submitted their SERs to agent A_i for problem P. We will consider that $A_i \in \mathcal{A}^t$ and the result of A_i trying to solve P is also reified as a SER. The vote of an agent $A_j \in \mathcal{A}^t$ for class S_k is

$$Vote(S_k, A_j) = \frac{E_k^j}{c + \sum_{r=1...K} E_r^j}$$

where c is a constant that on our experiments is set to 1. It is easy to see that an agent can cast a fractional vote that is always less than 1. Aggregating the votes from different agents for a class S_k we have ballot

$$Ballot^t(S_k, \mathcal{A}^t) = \sum_{A_j \in \mathcal{A}^t} Vote(S_k, A_j)$$

and therefore the winning solution class is the class with more votes in total, i.e.

$$Sol^t(P, \mathcal{A}^t) = arg \max_{k=1...K} Ballot(S_k, \mathcal{A}^t)$$

. We will show now two collaboration policies that use this voting scheme.

2.2 Committee Policy

In this collaboration policy the agents member of a $\mathcal{MAC}$ system $\mathcal{M}$ are viewed as a committee. An agent A_i that has to solve a problem P, sends it to all the other agents in $\mathcal{M}$. Each agent A_j that has received P sends a solution endorsement record $\langle \{(S_k, E_k^j)\}, P, A_j \rangle$ to A_i. The initiating agent A_i uses the voting scheme above upon all SERs, i.e. its own SER and the SERs of all the other agents in the multiagent system. The final solution is the class with maximum number of votes.

2.3 Bounded Counsel Policy

In this policy the agents member of a $\mathcal{MAC}$ system $\mathcal{M}$ try first to solve the problems they receive by themselves. Thus, if agent A_i receives a problem P and finds a solution that is satisfactory according to a *termination check* predicate, the solution found is the final solution. However, when an agent A_i assesses that its own solution is not reliable, the Bounded Counsel Policy tries to minimize the number of questions asked to other agents in $\mathcal{M}$. Specifically, agent A_i asks counsel only to one agent, say agent A_j. When the answer of A_j arrives the agent A_i uses the termination check. If the termination check is true the result of the voting scheme is the global result, otherwise A_i asks counsel to another agent—if there is one left to ask, if not the process terminates and the voting scheme determines the global solution.

The termination check works, at any point in time t of the Bounded Counsel Policy process, upon the collection of solution endorsement records (SER) received by the initiating agent A_i at time t. Using the same voting scheme as before, agent A_i has at any point in time t a plausible solution given by the winner class of the votes cast so far. Let V_{max}^t be the votes cast for the current plausible solution, $V_{max}^t = Ballot^t(Sol^t(P, \mathcal{A}^t), \mathcal{A}^t)$ and $V_r^t = \left(\sum_{S_k \in K} Ballot(S_k, \mathcal{A}^t)\right) - V_{max}^t$. The termination check is a boolean function $TermCheck(P, \mathcal{A}^t)$ that determines whether there is enough difference between the majority votes and the rest to stop and obtain a final solution. In the experiments reported here the termination check function (applied when there are votes for more than one solution class) is the following

$$TermCheck(P, \mathcal{A}^t) = \frac{V_{max}^t}{V_r^t} \geq \eta$$

i.e. it checks whether the majority vote V_{max}^t is η times bigger than the rest of the ballots. After termination the global solution is the class with maximum number of votes at that time.

Later in §4 we will show how the *TermCheck* predicate can be learnt by each individual agent. The results of using this "fixed" *TermCheck* predicate (with value $\eta = 3$) will be compared with the results of the learnt predicate in §5.

The collaboration policies described here have been implemented on the Noos Agent Platform [8]. NAP consists of Noos, a representation language with support for case management and retrieval [1], and FIPA-compliant utilities for agent interaction. A multiagent system in NAP consists on the individual agents capabilities (like CBR) plus a specification of the agent roles and interaction protocols in the framework of agent-mediated institutions [8]. Cases are represented as feature terms in Noos and the next section introduces the CBR method used in our CBR agents.

3   Case-Based Reasoning Agents

In this section we present LID, the CBR method used by agents. LID (Lazy Induction of Descriptions) builds a symbolic description $\mathcal{D}_P$ for a problem P to one or more cases in the case base [3]. In this framework, cases are structured and they are represented in the formalism of feature terms and symbolic descriptions are also built as generalizations [2]. We can consider $\mathcal{D}_P$ as a *similitude term* [9], i.e. a symbolic description of the similarities between a problem P and the retrieved cases $\mathcal{S}_{\mathcal{D}_P}$. Also notice that a new similitude term is generated for each new problem.

An agent has a case base $C_i = \{(P_j, S_k)\}_{j=1...N_i}$ of classified cases that is used by LID. In order to classify a problem P in one of those classes, LID builds a description $\mathcal{D}_P$ such that

- $\mathcal{D}_P$ is a partial description of P, i.e. $\mathcal{D}_P \sqsubseteq P$ ($\mathcal{D}_P$ subsumes P).
- $\mathcal{D}_P$ contains the most relevant features of P.
- $\mathcal{D}_P$ induces a subset of the case base that satisfies that description: $\mathcal{S}_{\mathcal{D}_P} = \{(P_j, S_k) \in C_i | \mathcal{D}_P \sqsubseteq P_j\}$; we call $\mathcal{S}_{\mathcal{D}_P}$ the *discriminatory set* of $\mathcal{D}_P$.

LID uses a top-down heuristic strategy to build the description $\mathcal{D}_P$. LID uses an heuristic to determine which of the features present in P are more relevant for the purpose of classifying P correctly into a solution class in K. LID uses an heuristic[1] that determines which feature f is more discriminating with respect to the solution classes K. Then it adds f to $\mathcal{D}_P$ with the value $P.f = v$ (the value that P has in feature f). Then LID only considers the subset of the case base defined by the discriminatory set $\mathcal{S}_{\mathcal{D}_P}$ —the other cases are discarded. Using the new case base $\mathcal{S}_{\mathcal{D}_P}$ LID uses the heuristic to determine which of the remaining features present in P is most discriminatory and adds it to $\mathcal{D}_P$. This process continues adding features to $\mathcal{D}_P$ until the termination criterion is met.

The termination criterion is met a) if all cases in $\mathcal{S}_{\mathcal{D}_P}$ are classified into a unique solution class S_k or b) adding further features of P into $\mathcal{D}_P$ does not reduce the discriminatory set $\mathcal{S}_{\mathcal{D}_P}$ to a set that has a unique solution class S_k.

When the termination is due to the second condition it means that the retrieved cases belong to more than one solution class, say problem P may belong to a subset of solution classes ($S_P \subset K$). The answer of LID is the following:

- the solution to problem P is one of the classes $S_k \in S_P$,
- the explanation of solution classes S_P is that problem P satisfies the description $\mathcal{D}_P$,
- there are a number of cases endorsing each solution class $S_k \in S_P$ —namely the cases in $\mathcal{S}_{\mathcal{D}_P}$ with solution S_k. All this cases have description $\mathcal{D}_P$, in common with P.

In the framework of a single agent the multiplicity solutions can be resolved by adopting a majority criterion and then the CBR system gives as solution the solution class $S_k \in K$ with more number of endorsing cases. In the framework of multiagent CBR system the multiplicity solutions is managed by the cooperation policies explained in §2.

4   Proactive Learning

We have seen that in the Bounded Counsel policy the agents need a definition for the termination check predicate. In the section 2.3 we have defined the *Term-*

---

[1] See [3] for a full explanation and evaluation of LID. The heuristic used is the RLM distance [6], also used in [2] as a heuristic to select the most discriminatory features.

Check predicate with a user defined parameter η, but probably a better approach is to let each agent to learn its own termination check predicates.

We are going to present an approach where each agent will take actions in order to obtain examples from which to learn its individual *TermCheck* predicate. A new stage is needed before the agents are ready to cooperate. In this stage, called the *proactive learning stage*, the agents will actively obtain the experience they need (a training set) through sending problems to some other agents and evaluating their results. From this experience each agent will learn a concrete definition of *TermCheck* (each agent learning it from its own training set). Specifically, each agent will learn a decision tree that will be used to assess when to terminate.

4.1 Defining the Examples

In order to learn the *TermCheck* predicate the agents need experience on the situations where *TermCheck* would be applicable. That is to say, each agent wants to learn when the result of the voting scheme will lead to the correct solution depending on the collection of SERs (solution endorsement records) that take part in the voting process.

Let's define the situations where *TermCheck* is applicable: Given an agent A_i that wants to solve a problem P, and at a time t has asked counsel to a subset of agents $\mathcal{A}^t$. A_i will have a set R_P^t of known SERs for the problem P at time t, that includes all the SERs received from the agents in $\mathcal{A}^t$ and the SER obtained by trying to solve the problem by A_i. The agent A_i can obtain a winning class with the voting scheme of section 2.1. The termination check has to predict if $Sol^t(P, \mathcal{A}^t)$ is the correct solution (and thus A_i won't need the counsel of more agents) or not.

We will call this a *voting situation*, and it is defined by the set of endorsing pairs $E_P^t = \{(S_k, E_k^j)\}$ that take part in the voting process. We will characterize a voting situation E_P^t by several attributes: V_{max}^t, the votes for the most voted solution, V_r^t, the votes for the rest of solutions, and $\rho = V_{max}^t / (V_{max}^t + V_r^t)$, the ratio between the most voted solution and the total number of votes.

We will use these three attributes to define our examples. Specifically, a v-example is defined by the three attributes above $v = \langle V_{max}^t, V_r^t, \rho \rangle$. Each v-example belongs to the positive class $(+)$ when $Sol^t(P, \mathcal{A}^t)$, the most voted solution, is equal to the correct solution —otherwise it belongs to the negative class $(-)$. In this way we have a classification problem with two classes: $(+, \langle V_{max}^t, V_r^t, \rho \rangle)$ and $(-, \langle V_{max}^t, V_r^t, \rho \rangle)$. In other words, a positive v-example characterizes a voting situation where there is no need of asking counsel to more agents and a negative v-example characterizes a voting situation where the agent do need the counsel of more agents.

4.2 Obtaining the Training Examples

Since every A_i has a case-base (collection of problems with known solution), A_i can obtain v-examples of voting situations from which to learn the termination check. Sending those problems to the other agents an agent A_i can then assess the correctness of the voting processes derived from the SERs received from those agents. Thus, an agent A_i obtains a training set for *TermCheck* as follows:

1. Choose a subset B_i of cases from its own case-base $B_i \subseteq C_i$.
2. For each problem P in B_i
3. A_i sends P to a subset $\mathcal{A}^S$ of the other agents.
4. A_i solves P by itself by a *leave-one-out* method, i.e. it solves P using $C_i - P$ as case-base.
5. With the set R_P^S of SERs obtained in steps 3 and 4, A_i builds v-examples of voting situations.

Note that from the collection R_P^S of SERs obtained in step 5 we can build more than one v-example. In fact we can build a v-example for any possible non empty subset $R_P^E \subseteq R_P^S$. Thus, step 5 is decomposed in 3 substeps:

1. Choose a collection $\mathcal{R}$ of non empty subsets of R_P^S, i.e. $\mathcal{R} \subseteq \mathbb{P}(R_P^S)$
2. For each voting situation $R_P^x \in \mathcal{R}$ let $v^x = \langle V_{max}^x, V_r^x, \rho \rangle$ be the example characterizing that situation.
3. If the most voted solution class is the correct class, build a positive example $(+, \langle V_{max}^x, V_r^x, \rho \rangle)$ otherwise build a negative example $(-, \langle V_{max}^x, V_r^x, \rho \rangle)$.

The collection $\mathcal{R}$ chosen in step 1 depends on the number of agents involved. In our experiments we have chosen collections that amount to generate a number of approximately 5,000 v-examples. The result of this process on all $P \in B_i$ is a collection of examples that form the training set Υ_i for learning *TermCheck*.

4.3 Learning the Termination Check

Once an agent A_i has enough v-examples, it can learn a good *TermCheck* predicate. In our experiments we have used all cases $B_i = C_i$ and all agents $\mathcal{A}^S = \{A_1, \ldots A_n\}$. The agents learn *TermCheck* using a decision tree algorithm with a discretization technique for the numeric attributes.

To build the decision tree T_i, each agent A_i does the following with its own training set Υ_i:

1. For each attribute $a \in \{V_c, V_r, \rho\}$ find the best cut point κ (in the sense of maximizing the information gain) that divides Υ_i in two subsets, one with the examples that have $Value(a) < \kappa$ and another with the examples that have $Value(a) \geq \kappa$.
2. Select the attribute a that has obtained the best information gain, and repeat the process for each one of the two resulting subsets of examples and the remaining attributes.

Note that with only three attributes characterizing the examples the tree will have at most depth 3. In this condition it is unavoidable to have a mix of positive and negative examples in each leaf. In the Figure 1.a shows a decision

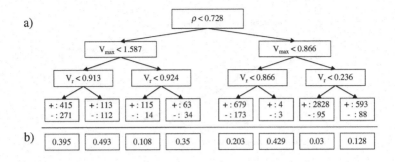

Fig. 1. Example of a learned tree for the termination check predicate.

tree where each leaf l has a number of positive and negative examples belonging to l, e.g. first leaf on the left has 415 positive and 271 negative examples.

In order to use the T_i, each agent A_i transforms the leaves of T_i into leaves that contain the probability for an example to be in the negative class. Let p_l be the number of positive examples and n_l negative examples belonging to leaf l, then probability of an example to be in the negative class is $N_l = \frac{n_l}{(n_l + p_l)}$. Figure 1.b shows the result of this transformation, e.g. first leaf on the left has $N_l = 0.395$.

4.4   Proactive Bounded Counsel

An agent A_i solving a problem P uses the decision tree T_i as *TermCheck* every time it asks the counsel to a new agent. If *TermCheck* returns true A_i terminates and yields as result the solution class with maximum votes in the current voting situation—otherwise A_i will ask a new agent for counsel. A_i assess every voting situation building its corresponding characterization $v^t = \langle V_{max}^t, V_r^t, \rho \rangle$ and then uses T_i to classify it. The result is that T_i will classify v^t in some leaf l with negative class probability N_l.

Now A_i would want to ask counsel of another agent if the probability of the current result of the voting process to be incorrect is high. Thus, each A_i has a threshold ν such that if $N_l \geq \nu$ it considers that the probability of being incorrect is too high and decides to ask counsel to another agent, and if $N_l < \nu$ it considers that the current solution is good enough and the process terminates. Thus, ν determines the degree of confidence that A_i wants to have about a solution before answering it without asking counsel to more agents. That is to say, we want at most a predicted probability of error of ν. Constant ν has been fixed to 0.05 for all the agents in our experiments. This means that *TermCheck* predicts that the solution given will be the correct with a probability of 0.95.

If we look at Figure 1 we can see that with $\nu = 0.05$ only one leaf has $N_l < \nu$ (the seventh leaf with $N_l = 0.03$). However, notice that most of the examples (2923 of the 5600, i.e. 52.2%) belong to that leaf.

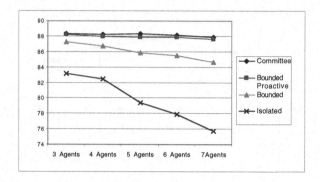

Fig. 2. Accuracy comparison between proactive bounded, bounded, and committee policies.

5 Experimental Results

In this section we want to analyze how the collaboration policies improve the agents performance with respect to the isolated agents scenario, where the agents do not cooperate and each agent tries to solve the problem by itself. We experiment with with multiagent systems composed of 3 to 7 agents. The purpose of varying the number of agents is to assess how well behave the collaboration policies when data is more fragmented.

We use the marine sponge identification (classification) problem as our test bed —this data set was also used to assess the relational inductive method INDIE in [2]. Sponge classification is interesting because the difficulties arise from the morphological plasticity of the species, and from the incomplete knowledge of many of their biological and cytological features. Moreover, benthology specialists are distributed around the world and they have experience different benthos that spawn species with different characteristics due to the local habitat conditions.

In order to compare the performance of the three policies, we have designed an experimental suite with a case base of 280 marine sponges pertaining to three different orders of the *Demospongiae* class (*Astrophorida*, *Hadromerida* and *Axinellida*). In an experimental run, training cases are randomly distributed to the agents (without repetitions, i.e. each case will belong to only one agent case base). In the training phase, problems arrive randomly to one of the agents. The goal of the agent receiving a problem is to identify the correct biological order given the description of a new sponge.

The experimental setting allows us to compare the collaboration policies behavior with different number of agents. For instance, in the 3 agents scenario, an agent has about 84 cases (about 28 cases per class)—while in the 7 agents scenario, an agent has about 36 cases (about 12 cases per class). The results presented here are the result of the average of 5 10-fold cross validation runs.

Figure 2 plots the accuracy of the three collaboration policies compared with respect to the accuracy of isolated agents. Clearly, any collaboration policy is

Table 1. Cost comparison of Bounded Counsel, Proactive Bounded Counsel, and Committee policies.

	3 Agents	4 Agents	5 Agents	6 Agents	7 Agents
Isolated Agents	1.00	1.00	1.00	1.00	1.00
Bounded	1.43	1.59	1.71	1.89	2.01
Proactive Bounded	2.11	2.66	3.41	4.11	4.80
Committee	3.00	4.00	5.00	6.00	7.00

more desirable for the agents than working alone with its own data. Let us consider the accuracies of *Proactive Bounded Counsel* and fixed *Bounded Counsel*. Figure 2 shows that the agents with proactive learning always have better accuracy. Moreover, *Proactive Bounded Counsel* is more robust when the number of agents is greater (i.e. the size of the case-bases is smaller) because they can learn an adequate *TermCheck* predicate for each situation.

Let us consider now the *Committee* policy. This collaboration policy has better accuracy than the fixed *Bounded Counsel* policy. However, *Proactive Bounded Counsel* is always very near to the *Committee* policy—and the difference is not statistically significant (99% confidence in a signed rank test).

The difference between the *Committee* and the *Proactive Bounded Counsel* policies is in terms of cost. The *Committee* policy always ask all agents while *Proactive Bounded Counsel* is intended to minimize those questions. Table 1 shows the costs involved in different policies for a situation where each time an agent asks counsel to another has a fixed cost, 1 euro in this example. The isolated agents never ask counsel so cost is constant, while the *Committee* policy always asks counsel to all agents and cost increases with the number of agents in the system. The cost of *Bounded Counsel* policies are between these two extremes. Notice that the *Proactive Bounded Counsel* policy is more expensive (asks more counsels) than the fixed *Bounded Counsel* policy. However, the accuracy results in Figure 2 shows that the Proactive Bounded policy asks for counsel when it's really needed, achieving an increased accuracy that matches that of the expensive Committee policy. Summarizing, the *Proactive Bounded Counsel* policy has the same accuracy that the *Committee* policy at a lower cost.

In order to assess that this results are not dependent on the assumption that case bases are disjunct we performed a specific experiment with overlapping cases. Specifically, each agent has a case base with a 10% of duplicated cases (in the sense that they are already present in another case base). The results are very close to the ones in Fig. 2, showing that the collaboration policies work well with some overlapping. Clearly, in a setting where overlapping grows to higher values the incentives for the agents to collaborate will diminish.

6 Related Work

A general result on multiple model learning [5] demonstrated that if uncorrelated classifiers with error rate lower than 0.5 are combined then the resulting error rate must be lower than the one made by the individual classifiers. The BEM (*Basic Ensemble Method*) is presented in [7] as a basic way to combine continuous estimators, and since then many other methods have been proposed: *Stacking generalization, Cascade generalization, Bagging* or *Boosting* are some examples. However, all these methods do not deal with the issue of "partitioned examples" among different classifiers as we do—they rely on aggregating results from multiple classifiers that have access to *all* data. Their goal is to use a multiplicity of classifiers to increase accuracy of existing classification methods. Our goal is to combine the decisions of autonomous classifiers (each one corresponding to one agent), and to see how can they cooperate to achieve a better behavior than when they work alone.

The meta-learning approach in [4] is applied to partitioned data. They experiment with a collection of classifiers which have only a subset of the whole case base and they learn new meta-classifiers whose training data are based on predictions of the collection of (base) classifiers. They compare their meta-learning approach results with weighted voting techniques. The final result is an *arbitrator tree*, a centralized and complex method whose goal is to improve classification accuracy. We also work on "partitioned examples" but we assume no central method that aggregates results; moreover we assume a multiagent approach where communication and cooperation may have a cost that has to be taken into account.

DRL [11] is a distributed technique that learns rules from partitioned data; DRL's goal is to achieve scalability for large data sets. Rule induction in a workstation follows a top-down strategy in each data set, finding rules that are *satisfactory* for a specific data set. These rules —termed *candidate rules*— are sent to an additional workstation reviewing them over the entire data set; when a rule is satisfactory for the entire data set it is *accepted* by the algorithm. We work on a multiagent setting instead of a distributed one, but it seems DRL could be easily adapted to a multiagent setting. The main differences are i) that DRL is an inductive learning technique (designed to speed up class descriptions) while we use lazy learning techniques and ii) DRL has a centralized stage where the entire data set is available to the algorithm.

7   Conclusions and Future Work

We have presented a framework for cooperative CBR in multiagent systems. The framework is cooperative in that the CBR agents help each other to improve their individual performance. Since the agents improve with respect to their performance as isolated individual, cooperating is also in their individual interest—specially since the framework allows them to keep confidential their own cases. A major theme in multiagent systems is the *autonomy* of the agents. In our framework the agent autonomy is mainly insured by two facts: i) the capability of each agent to determine whether or not itself is competent to solve a problem, and ii) the capability of each agent to integrate into a global solution for a problem the counsels given by other agents.

Another issue is the generality of the cooperation policies and their dependence upon the CBR agents using LID. The cooperation policies depend only on the CBR agents being able to provide SERs (Solution Endorsement Records), so any CBR method that can provide that is compatible.

Finally, we plan to lift the restriction of the case bases of the agents in a $\mathcal{M}$AC system being disjunct. Basically, our idea is that agents could incorporate in their case bases some cases originally owned by other agents. The interesting question here is this: what strategy of case sharing can improve the overall $\mathcal{M}$AC system performance —without every agent having in their case base every case known to the $\mathcal{M}$AC system.

Acknowledgements. The authors thank Josep-Lluís Arcos and Eva Armengol of the IIIA-CSIC for their support and for the development of the Noos agent platform and the LID CBR method respectively. Support for this work came from CIRIT FI/FAP 2001 grant and projects TIC2000-1414 "eInstitutor" and IST-1999-19005 "IBROW".

References

[1] J. L. Arcos and R. López de Mántaras. Perspectives: a declarative bias mechanism for case retrieval. In David Leake and Enric Plaza, editors, *Case-Based Reasoning. Research and Development*, number 1266 in Lecture Notes in Artificial Intelligence, pages 279–290. Springer-Verlag, 1997.

[2] E. Armengol and E. Plaza. Bottom-up induction of feature terms. *Machine Learning Journal*, 41(1):259–294, 2000.

[3] E. Armengol and E. Plaza. Lazy induction of descriptions for relational case-based learning. In *ECML-2001*, Lecture Notes in Artificial Intelligence, 2001.

[4] Philip K. Chan and Salvatore J. Stolfo. A comparative evaluation of voting and meta-learning on partitioned data. In *Proc. 12th International Conference on Machine Learning*, pages 90–98. Morgan Kaufmann, 1995.

[5] L. K. Hansen and P. Salamon. Neural networks ensembles. *IEEE Transactions on Pattern Analysis and Machine Intelligence*, 12(10):993–1001, 1990.

[6] Ramon López de Mántaras. A distance-based attribute selection measure for decision tree induction. *Machine Learning*, 6:81–92, 1991.

[7] M. P. Perrone and L. N. Cooper. When networks disagree: Ensemble methods for hybrid neural networks. In *Artificial Neural Networks for Speech and Vision*. Chapman-Hall, 1993.

[8] E. Plaza, J. L. Arcos, P. Noriega, and C. Sierra. Competing agents in agent-mediated institutions. *Journal of Personal Technologies*, 2:212–220, 1998.

[9] E. Plaza, R. López de Mántaras, and E. Armengol. On the importance of similitude: An entropy-based assessment. In I. Smith and B. Saltings, editors, *Advances in Case-Based Reasoning*, number 1168 in Lecture Notes in Artificial Intelligence, pages 324–338. Springer-Verlag, 1996.

[10] Enric Plaza, Josep Lluís Arcos, and Francisco Martín. Cooperative case-based reasoning. In Gerhard Weiss, editor, *Distributed Artificial Intelligence Meets Machine Learning. Learning in Multi-Agent Environments*, number 1221 in Lecture Notes in Artificial Intelligence, pages 180–201. Springer-Verlag, 1997.

[11] F. J. Provost and D. Hennessy. Scaling up: Distributed machine learning with cooperation. In *Proc. 13th AAAI Conference*, 1996.

Building Committees by Clustering Models Based on Pairwise Similarity Values

Thomas Ragg

Institut für Logik, Komplexität und Deduktionssysteme,
Universität Karlsruhe, D-76131 Karlsruhe
ragg@ira.uka.de http://i11www.ira.uka.de

Abstract. Forming a committee is an approach for integrating several opinions or functions instead of favouring a single one. Selecting and weighting the committee members is done in several ways by different algorithms. Possible solutions to this problem is still the topic of current research. Our starting point is the decomposition of the committee error into a bias- and variance-like term. Two requests can be derived from this equation: Models should on the one hand be regularized properly to reduce the average error. On the other hand they should be as independent as possible (in the mathematical sense) to decrease the committee error.

The first request of regularization can be handled by a Bayesian learning framework. For the second request I want to suggest a new selection method for committee members based on the pairwise stochastical dependence of their output functions, which maximizes the overall independence. Given these pairwise similarity values the models can be separated in classes by a hierarchical clustering algorithm. From the committee error decomposition I derive a criterion that allows to find the optimal number of classes, i.e. the optimal stop criteria for the clustering algorithm. The benefits of the approach are demonstrated on a noisy benchmark problems as well as on the prediction of newspaper sales rates for a large number of retail traders.

1   Introduction

If one wants to learn a functional relationship from empirical data, then the goal of training a model is to recognize a structure in the data or an underlying process and to generalize this knowledge to former unknown data points. When estimating a functional relationship we face three basic problems.

Noisy data and limited amount of data: Firstly we have to deal with noisy and finite-sized data sets which is usually done be regularization techniques and/or bootstrapping [Vapnik, 1995,Bishop, 1995,Efron & Tibshirani, 1993]. Vapnik states that the problem of density estimation based on empirical data is ill posed, i.e., small changes in the learning situation can result in a totally different model; for example little distortions in the target data. The theory of

L. De Raedt and P. Flach (Eds.): ECML 2001, LNAI 2167, pp. 406–418, 2001.
© Springer-Verlag Berlin Heidelberg 2001

regularization shows that instead of minimizing the difference between the target data and the output of the network, a regularized error function

$$E = E_D + \lambda E_R \tag{1}$$

should be minimized where E_D is the error on the data and λ is a weighting factor. E_R is an additional term that measures the complexity of the model; for example the often used weight decay regularizer in neural network training [Bishop, 1995]. Thus, regularization is not an optional possibility, but a fundamental technique [Ramsay & Silverman, 1997]. One crucial problem is to determine the weighting factor λ. In case of neural networks, its optimal value depends on the size of the network, i.e., the number of weights, the weight initialization, as well as the patterns used for training, and the noise in the data. Often this value is determined by cross-validation which is clearly suboptimal for the reasons just given. Adjusting this value properly has been solved for neural networks by using a Bayesian learning algorithm. It was introduced by MacKay and provides an elegant theory to prevent neural networks from overfitting by determining λ during the training process without the necessity of additional validation data [MacKay, 1992,Bishop, 1995]. Furthermore, the Bayesian framework provides an analytical criterion to compare different models, the so-called model evidence. A discussion of Bayesian learning for neural networks as used in this work can be found in [Ragg & Gutjahr, 1998] or more detailed in [Gutjahr, 1999,Ragg, 2000].

Curse of dimensionality: Secondly, for many applications we need to encode the problem by features and have to decide which and how many of them to use. Bearing in mind the empty space phenomenon, it is often an advantage to select few features and estimate a non-linear function in a low-dimensional space [Silverman, 1986,Bishop, 1995]. In practical applications only a limited amount of data is available for determining the parameters of a model. The dimensionality of the input vector must be in a sensible relation to the number of data points. By adding more features the information content of the input about the target increases, but at the same time the number of data points per dimension decreases in order to determine the parameters. Silverman gives some values for the number of data points needed to estimate a multivariate normal distribution up to a an error of 10% in the origin, which grow approximately like 4^d, when d is the number of dimensions [Silverman, 1986]. That means that the class of functions in which the solution is searched increases greatly with every additional component. This problem is called the *curse of dimensionality* [White, 1989,Bishop, 1995] or the *empty space phenomenon* [Scott & Thompson, 1983,Silverman, 1986]. A consequence is that renunciation of supplementary information leads to a more precise approximation of the underlying process in a low-dimensional input space. If one's problem solution is designed from the beginning as a committee, it is not necessary to discard input features and therefore all the information can be used for the overall solution. In this way one can train models which use different features, i.e., they have different viewpoints of the problem. Therefore, every individual model has a small input space, i.e., the problem caused by using many input features is avoided. However, the committee can utilize the information of the entire input space through the combination of its members.

Model selection: Thirdly, if we have trained several models, we are left with the problem of model selection. It is common practice to train several networks and then select the best one according to the performance on an independent validation set. This procedure has the disadvantage of introducing an additional dependency on a fixed sample of data bearing the danger of overfitting if it is used iteratively. Forming a committee of networks is a promising approach to overcome these drawbacks and to avoid favouring one model while discarding all others. This is sensible if one would like to minimize the insecurities during the learning process. This can be seen directly from the inequation

$$\frac{1}{L}E_{AV} \le E_{COM} \le E_{AV} \tag{2}$$

which says, that the committee error E_{COM} is always smaller than the average error E_{AV} of several networks y_i, when y_{COM} is defined as $y_{COM}(x) := \frac{1}{L}\sum_{i=1}^{L} y_i(x)$. E_{AV} is given by the average error of the single models, i.e. $E_{AV} := \frac{1}{L}\sum_{i=1}^{L} E(y_i(x))$. The right inequation follows directly by applying Jensen's inequality [Bishop, 1995,Henze, 1997] to a convex error function. The left inequation, i.e., the rather dramatic possibility of error reduction by a factor L follows under the assumption that the deviations $\epsilon_i(x)$ of the committee members $y_i(x)$ from the target function $h(x)$ are uncorrelated and have zero mean, and justifies the efforts invested in these kind of algorithms. Thus, several methods of forming committees were suggested in recent years. An overview is given in the book *Combining Artificial Neural Nets* [Sharkey, 1999]. These algorithms differ in the way how the committee members are selected or weighted within the committee.

Up to now, there is no algorithm which tries to minimize both the average model error and the independence of committee members systematically without resorting to cross-validation techniques or by neglecting the importance of regularization. It's is obvious that averaging reduces the generalization error, when arbitrary models can be in the committee, but does it also reduce the generalization error compared to a proper regularized model?

In the following I want to show that this is possible, and derive a method for selecting committee members to achieve a maximal performance under certain constraints, e.g. all models receive the same weight in the committee. For clarity I will not write the dependency on the input vector **x** in the following.

2   Committee Error Decomposition

The error of a committee can be decomposed into the sum of two terms similar to the bias-variance decomposition, which gives us a further insight into the reasons for better generalization capabilities. The equation provides a connection between the average error of the network and the error of the single networks through the expectation value of the committee error [Krogh & Vedelsby, 1995, Bishop, 1995]:

$$\mathcal{E}\left[(y_{COM} - h)^2\right] = \frac{1}{L}\sum_{i=1}^{L}\mathcal{E}\left[(y_i - h)^2\right] - \frac{1}{L}\sum_{i=1}^{L}\mathcal{E}\left[(y_i - y_{COM})^2\right]. \quad (3)$$

Since the first term depends on the generalization errors of the single networks we can conclude that the average value should be as small as possible, which can be ensured if the models are regularized. The second term measures the spread of predictions of the single networks to the committee prediction itself. If we have a set of trained networks we should prefer those networks to form a committee, which maximize the second term.

Bagging for example averages over all models and does not try to maximize the variance of the models [Breiman, 1996]. *Boosting* adapts the training set for each model depending on the error of the previously trained model [Freund & Schapire, 1996] and tends to overfit for noisy data as shown recently by [Rätsch et al., 1998]. Furthermore, neither boosting nor bagging expect the models to be regularized, which might cause the first term to be larger than necessary. Other methods make use of validation sets to select the committee members and determine the weights [Hashem, 1999] or optimize solely the second term of eq. (3) which allows the single models to overfit strongly [Rosen, 1996].

All considered, our goal must be to find a subset of networks, such that the first term does not increase while at the same time the second term is maximal large. We cannot measure the average generalization error without an additional validation set, but we can expect the value to stabilize if the number L of networks in our subset increases, and even more, if the models are regularized properly.

Committee member selection: To find a criterion that maximizes the second term of equation (3), we can resolve the quadratic form to

$$\frac{1}{L}\sum_{i=1}^{L}\mathcal{E}[y_i^2] - \frac{2}{L}\sum_{i=1}^{L}\mathcal{E}[y_{COM}y_i] + \frac{1}{L}\sum_{i=1}^{L}\mathcal{E}[y_{COM}^2] \quad (4)$$

and then further evaluate the second and third term. The second term becomes

$$-\frac{2}{L}\sum_{i=1}^{L}\mathcal{E}[y_{COM}y_i] = -\frac{2}{L}\sum_{i=1}^{L}\mathcal{E}\left[\frac{1}{L}\sum_{j=1}^{L}y_j y_i\right]$$

$$= -\frac{2}{L^2}\sum_{i=1}^{L}\sum_{j=1}^{L}\mathcal{E}[y_j y_i]$$

$$= -\frac{2}{L^2}\left(2\sum_{i=1}^{L-1}\sum_{j=i+1}^{L}\mathcal{E}[y_j y_i] + \sum_{i=1}^{L}\mathcal{E}[y_i^2]\right)$$

$$= -\frac{4}{L^2}\sum_{i=1}^{L-1}\sum_{j=i+1}^{L}\mathcal{E}[y_j y_i] - \frac{2}{L^2}\sum_{i=1}^{L}\mathcal{E}[y_i^2] \quad (5)$$

where we summarized over the diagonal elements and used $y_j y_i = y_i y_j$. Together with the definition of y_{COM} the third term can be transformed to

$$\mathcal{E}[y_{COM}^2] = \mathcal{E}\left[\left(\frac{1}{L}\sum_{i=1}^{L}y_i\right)\left(\frac{1}{L}\sum_{j=1}^{L}y_j\right)\right]$$

$$= \mathcal{E}\left[\frac{1}{L^2}\left(\sum_{i=1}^{L}y_i^2 + 2\sum_{i=1}^{L-1}\sum_{j=i+1}^{L}y_i y_j\right)\right]$$

$$= \frac{1}{L^2}\sum_{i=1}^{L}\mathcal{E}[y_i^2] + \frac{2}{L^2}\sum_{i=1}^{L-1}\sum_{j=i+1}^{L}\mathcal{E}[y_i y_j] \qquad (6)$$

Substituting these two expressions into equation (4) and taking $\mathcal{E}[XY] = \mathcal{E}[X]\mathcal{E}[X] + Cov(X,Y)$ into account, leaves us with

$$\frac{1}{L}\sum_{i=1}^{L}\mathcal{E}[y_i^2] - \frac{2}{L^2}\sum_{i=1}^{L-1}\sum_{j=i+1}^{L}\mathcal{E}[y_j y_i] - \frac{1}{L^2}\sum_{i=1}^{L}\mathcal{E}[y_i^2]$$

$$= \frac{L-1}{L^2}\sum_{i=1}^{L}\mathcal{E}[y_i^2] - \frac{2}{L^2}\sum_{i=1}^{L-1}\sum_{j=i+1}^{L}\mathcal{E}[y_j y_i]$$

$$= \frac{L-1}{L^2}\sum_{i=1}^{L}(\mathcal{E}[y_i])^2 + \frac{L-1}{L^2}\sum_{i=1}^{L}Cov(y_i, y_i) -$$

$$\frac{2}{L^2}\sum_{i=1}^{L-1}\sum_{j=i+1}^{L}\mathcal{E}[y_j]\mathcal{E}[y_i] - \frac{2}{L^2}\sum_{i=1}^{L-1}\sum_{j=i+1}^{L}Cov(y_i, y_j) \qquad (7)$$

The expectation values of y_i depend upon the data which was used to train the specific model, since the mean value $\bar{y}_i$ after training should be equal to the mean value of the target data [Bishop, 1995]. Thus, the first and third term will be nearly constant. Since $Cov(X, X) = V(X)$ the variance of the network output functions should be maximal, while the last term should be as small as possible. The value of $Cov(y_j, y_i)$ depends on the stochastical dependence of y_j and y_i. The covariance of two random variables, $Cov(X, Y)$, is 0 when they are independent and it is maximal if $X = Y$ [Berger, 1980,Henze, 1997]. Thus it is possible to optimize equation (7) by minimizing a sum over stochastical dependencies. A measure for the stochastical dependence between two variables is their mutual information $I(X, Y)$ [Cover & Thomas, 1991]. An estimation procedure for the mutual information will be defined below. Our goal is then to find a subset of networks such that

$$\frac{L-1}{L^2}\sum_{i=1}^{L}I(y_i, y_i) - \frac{2}{L^2}\sum_{i=1}^{L-1}\sum_{j=i+1}^{L}I(y_i, y_j) \longrightarrow \max \qquad (8)$$

The above formula (8) is referred to as *heterogeneity criterion* in the following. It is already for small L impossible to compute the value of the criterion for all $\binom{L}{k}$

combinations for all k. A straightforward possibility is to use a cluster algorithm to group the networks and choose from each cluster a representative, i.e., the network with the highest model evidence. Note that maximizing the term (8) can be done on arbitrary input data because no target data is necessary. Thus, if only a small amount of training data is available the suggested method has another important advantage.

Computation of pairwise similarity values: The mutual information $I(X;Y)$ of two random variables X, Y is defined as the Kullback-Leibler distance between the joint distribution $p(x, y)$ and the product $p(x)p(y)$.

$$I(X;Y) = \int \int p(x, y) \cdot \log \frac{p(x, y)}{p(x)p(y)} \tag{9}$$

and measures the degree of stochastic independence of X and Y. In order to calculate (9), we approximate the three probability distributions $p(x, y), p(x)$ and $p(y)$, where we use a nonparametric density function approximation with a Epanechnikov kernel function K [Silverman, 1986]. If $\mathbf{z}$ is a d-dimensional vector, then

$$K(\mathbf{z}) = (3/4)^d (1 - (z_1^2 + z_2^2 + \ldots + z_d^2)) \tag{10}$$

if $\|\mathbf{z}\|_2 < 1$ and 0 otherwise. The normalizing constant $(3/4)^d$ guarantees that $\int K(\mathbf{z})d\mathbf{z} = 1$. Finally, the probability density for a given data point k is estimated as

$$p(\mathbf{z}(k)) = \frac{1}{N \cdot h^d} \sum_{j=1}^{N} K\left(\frac{1}{h}(\mathbf{z}(k) - \mathbf{z}(j))\right) \tag{11}$$

where N is the number of training patterns and h is the spread of the kernel function. In case of the Epanechnikov kernel a sensible value for h can be determined

$$h_{opt} = \left(\frac{8}{c_d}(d + 4)(2\sqrt{\pi})^d\right)^{-(d+4)} \frac{1}{N^{1/d+4}} \tag{12}$$

where N is the number of data points, d the dimension of the vector and c_d is the volume of the unit d-dimensional sphere [Silverman, 1986]. By summarizing equation (11) over all data points we get the desired density estimations.

Algorithm for clustering models based on similarity values: If we compute the mutual information between pairs of network output functions we can derive a matrix of pairwise similarity values. It is not possible to define a metric based on the Kullback-Leibler divergence, since the triangle property does not hold [Cover & Thomas, 1991], but clustering of models based on the stochastic dependence can be done on basis of this matrix with a hierarchical agglomerative cluster method, e.g. the complete linkage algorithm, which generates homogenous classes [Kaufmann & Pape, 1996]. This is important, if we select a member as representative.

The algorithm starts by putting each network in an own class. In each step two classes are merged. They are determined by computing the minimal similarity between two elements for each pair of classes

$$Sim(G_1, G_2) := \min_{i,j} I(y_i, y_j) \quad \text{with } y_i \in G_1; y_j \in G_2$$

and then choose that pair of classes $\{G_1, G_2\}$ that has maximal similarity. This is done until only one cluster is left. In every step the heterogeneity criterion (8) is computed. According to this criterion, the committee error should be minimal if the value of the criterion is maximal large. Thus, after termination of the clustering procedure we can determine the optimal number of classes by selecting that number that corresponds to the maximal value of the heterogeneity criterion and use the corresponding committee as our final model. An example is shown in figure 3. Figure 2 plots the clusters for the benchmark problem from figure 1a in the test error/evidence space. From each of the corresponding clusters one network is selected as a committee member. If a Bayesian framework is used for training then it is sensible to pick the network with the highest evidence from each class [Ragg, 2000].

3 Experimental Results

At first, a noisy artificial regression problem serves as benchmark to explore the algorithm presented here in detail. The data for this benchmark was generated by adding Gaussian noise to a sinus function (Figure 1). The training data contains 40 points, which do not cover the complete domain. Note that because of the noise there are several sensible models for the data except the underlying process. Figure 1 shows 4 models, two of them are networks trained with Bayesian learning and give plausible explanations for the data. Thus, even proper regularization gives still a variety of different models. Our next goal is to demonstrate that forming a committee can further reduce this variance in performance, thus lowering the probability of choosing the 'wrong' model in a practical application. If we train 50 networks and apply then the cluster algorithm as described above we get 8 classes which are maximal independent. The result of this process is shown in figure 2. Visualization of the functions shows that the classes are sensibly chosen [Ragg, 2000]. Note that it is possible, that some networks with lower generalization performance will be part of the committee, as long as they are independent from others. This is sensible, since they were optimized with Bayesian learning and thus reflect the probability of this parameter vector to be a model for the given data. Committees integrate over the various posterior probabilities to form an overall solution [Bishop, 1995]. The committee error is smaller than the error of almost all of the single networks (dashed line). The test error was computed on 100 data points of the underlying process (without noise). Figure 3 shows the value of the heterogeneity criterion (8) and the committee error during the clustering process. For each step the members of the committee are determined and the corresponding error is plotted over the number of classes.

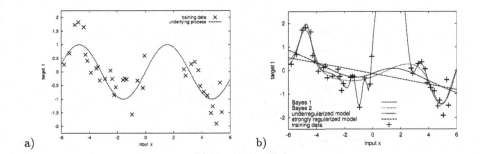

Fig. 1. The figure shows the data for the benchmark regression problem. a) The underlying process is just the sinus function $sin(x)$. The target data was generated by adding Gaussian noise with variance 0.4 and zero mean. Note that there is an interval, where no data is available. b) Output functions of 4 models are plotted: An overregularized network, an underregularized network and two proper regularized networks trained with Bayesian learning which still differ significantly.

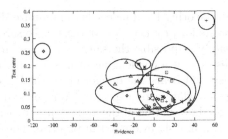

Fig. 2. The figure shows the result of the clustering process for 50 networks which were trained with the data from figure 1. The cluster, indicated by ellipses, are shown in the test error-evidence space. Note that this is always a slightly distorted illustration. Networks with similar output function will have a similar test error, but the evidence might vary because its value depends on the overall network complexity. Conversely, different network functions can still have a similar test error and a similar evidence. The dashed line at the bottom shows the error (for 100 test points) of the resulting committee, which is below the error of most of the single networks.

The committee error reaches its minimum (0.034) when the heterogeneity criterion is maximal as expected. In the first step the committee is just the average of all single networks with an error of 0.042. This corresponds to the *bagging* approach with the difference that the networks were regularized with Bayesian learning.

Predicting Sales Rates of newspapers for many retail traders serves as a real world application to evaluate the approach. Every newspaper publisher has to solve the problem of printing a large number of copies and distributing them to the retail traders trying to keep the return quote as low as possible. On the one hand the newspaper publisher wants to maximize his profit by selling as many

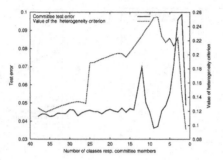

Fig. 3. The figure shows how the number of classes is determined for a given set of networks for the benchmark problem from figure 1. The heterogeneity criterion is a curve with a clear maximum, which is reached here for 8 classes. The committee error is relatively constant for a long time and decreases then strongly. Greater changes in one step indicate that two heterogenous classes were merged together.

copies as possible. On the other hand he needs to minimize the number of unsold copies to reduce his costs for production and logistic. To solve this task he needs to estimate as accurately as possible the sales rates for each retail trader.

Prediction of sales rates is a challenging task, since the underlying times series is extremely noisy and bears the danger of overfitting easily. At the same time the large number of data sets, e.g., data from several thousands of retail traders, allows for a good evaluation of the approach. Furthermore, the real time prediction system is continuously evaluated in practice. The 'BILD-Zeitung' is a

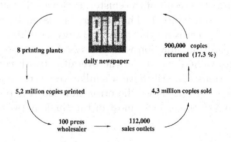

Fig. 4. The figures illustrates the problem of distributing newspapers: About 5,5 million copies of 'BILD' are printed each day, which have to be distributed to wholesalers and from there to retail traders. About 16.2% of the total number of copies is returned each day resulting in a loss of approximately 100.000 Euro.

german newspaper of the Axel Springer Verlag. More than 5,5 million copies are printed daily depending on the orders of 110 wholesalers (Fig.4). Each of them estimates the individual sales rates for all his retail traders based on the latest data. Before neural networks were used to perform this task, the estimation was based on a moving average model. The results of the individual predictions are combined with an extra charge to an overall prediction for the wholesaler. On average, 4,6 million copies are sold resulting in a return of 900,000 copies, i.e., 16.3% of the amount ordered, causing a loss of more than 25 million Euro each year. The sales department of the Axel Springer Verlag developed a prediction system based on neural network models for the time series of each retail trader and improved the return quota of several wholesalers by more than 5%. That is an average reduction of the percental return quota from 16.3% to about 15.5%. The system uses pre-processed input features over the time series (x_τ), e.g. differences like $(x_\tau - x_{\tau-1})$ or higher differences, long time history measures and general movement indicators. Predictions are made for one week ahead, i.e., always from Monday to Monday, Tuesday to Tuesday, etc. The target data is the difference of the sales rate of next week sale to a short term moving average. In this sense, the neural network is an error correction model for the linear moving average model. All in all, 47 input features were used, resulting in a large input space and a long training time for the single networks. A standard weight decay regularizer was used, where the weighting parameter λ was adjusted experimentally by a series of training runs for a few data sets such that the overfitting effect on a validation set was just suppressed and then fixed for all data sets which is clearly suboptimal. On the other hand is it impossible in practice to adjust this parameter manually for all time series, and this every time the model is retrained. This makes the task an interesting application for Bayesian learning algorithms because they compute the optimal weighting parameter λ without resorting to cross validation techniques. Finally, the fast learning algorithm *Rprop* was used to minimize the resulting error function [Riedmiller, 1994]. The data used for this research was gained in the area of Münster (a university city in north-west Germany), in the area of Freiburg (a university city in south-west Germany) and Hamburg (north Germany). In total, the time series from over 1000 retail traders were available for training and testing. Training data ranged over 4 years from 1993 to 1996 while the generalization performance was estimated based on the sales rates of 1997 and 1998. For every data set, 50 networks with different network initializations were trained with standard weight decay as well as Bayesian learning. The network topology had one hidden layer with 4 units.

Figure 5 shows clearly the improvement of the average error (over all models and data sets) of the Bayesian approach compared to optimizing the regularization weighting factor by cross validation. Selecting always a subset of networks to form a committee as proposed in this paper further reduces the generalization error. As in figure 2 we get the same result that the committee is almost always better than most single networks. Note also, that selecting for each time series the network with the highest evidence also improves the system performance significantly. Still, forming a committee leads to a lower prediction error. Furthermore the range from the committee with the best test error to that with the worst test error is smaller, e.g. the probability of choosing a suboptimal model is reduced.

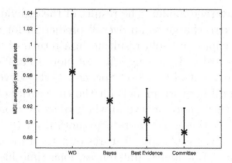

Fig. 5. Average error for different approaches. 'WD' stands for training with standard weight decay as previously done by the Axel-Springer-Verlag, 'Bayes' stands for training with a Bayesian learning rule and 'Committee' represents the clustering process to select maximal independent committee members. The bars represent the range for the model with the lowest test error to the model with the largest test error. That is, for each time series the model with the lowest test error is selected and the average over all time series is plotted (as the lower end of the vertical bar). The crosses mark the the average errors of the different approaches. The figure shows clearly the average reduction of the prediction error. Note also, that the spread between the best model and the worst model decreases from left to right.

4   Conclusions

In this paper an approach was presented that combines several important steps of neural network design into an optimization procedure. This method was primarily aimed at developing committees of neural networks for tasks where the data is noisy and limited and the optimal subset of features is not known. For example as for time series prediction tasks [Ragg *et al.*, 2000], which bear the danger of overfitting easily. The averaging process of forming a committee is always sensible, since it can be shown that the committee error is never larger than the average error of set of trained networks. On the other hand, the committee error can be drastically reduced if the network functions are uncorrelated. Based on the committee error decomposition we derived a criterion that allows us to select a subset of networks which form the best committee. This criterion measures the overall independence of the network functions. By applying a hierarchical cluster algorithm we can group the networks according to their similarities and determine the number of classes such that the criterion (8) reaches its maximal value. The benefits of the approach were demonstrated on a noisy benchmark problem and a prediction tasks consisting of several thousand time series of sales rates from retail traders.

The algorithm presented here can also be used with other function approximators, e.g., Support Vector Machines or Gaussian Processes, as long as they provide a possibility of model selection by some quality measure like the model evidence in the Bayesian framework.

Acknowledgments. This work was supported by the Deutsche Forschungsgemeinschaft (DFG), ME 672/10-1, 'Integrierte Entwicklung von Komitees neuronaler Netze'.

References

[Berger, 1980] Berger, J. O. *Statistical decision theory and Bayesian analysis.* Springer Verlag, 1980.

[Bishop, 1995] Bishop, C. M. *Neural Networks for Pattern Recognition.* Oxford Press, 1995.

[Breiman, 1996] Breiman, L. Bagging predictors. *Machine Learning,* 24:123–140, 1996.

[Cover & Thomas, 1991] Cover, T. and Thomas, J. *Elements of Information Theory.* Wiley Series in Telecommunications. John Wiley & Sons, 1991.

[Efron & Tibshirani, 1993] Efron, B. and Tibshirani, R. J. *An introduction to the bootstrap.* Chapman & Hall, 1993.

[Freund & Schapire, 1996] Freund, Y. and Schapire, R. E. Experiments with a new boosting algorithm. In *Proceedings of 13th International Conference on Machine Learning,* pages 148–156, 1996.

[Gutjahr, 1999] Gutjahr, S. *Optimierung Neuronaler Netze mit der Bayes'schen Methode.* Dissertation, Universität Karlsruhe, Institut für Logik, Komplexität und Deduktionssysteme, 1999.

[Hashem, 1999] Hashem, S. Treating Harmful Collinearity in Neural Network Ensembles. In Sharkey, A. J., editor, *Combining Artificial Neural Nets,* pages 101–125. Springer, 1999.

[Henze, 1997] Henze, N. *Stochastik für Einsteiger.* Vieweg, 1997.

[Kaufmann & Pape, 1996] Kaufmann, H. and Pape, H. Clusteranalyse. In Fahrmeir, L., Hamerle, A., and Tutz, G., editors, *Multivariate Statistische Verfahren.* de Gruyter, 1996.

[Krogh & Vedelsby, 1995] Krogh, A. and Vedelsby, J. Neural Network Ensembles, Cross Validation and Active Learning. In D.S. Touretzky, G. Tesauro, T. L., editor, *Advances in Neural Information Processing,* volume 7. MIT press, 1995.

[MacKay, 1992] MacKay, D. J. C. Bayesian interpolation. *Neural Computation,* 4(3):415–447, 1992.

[Ragg & Gutjahr, 1998] Ragg, T. and Gutjahr, S. Optimizing the Evidence – with an application to Time Series Prediction. In *Proceedings of the International Conference on Artificial Neural Networks 1998, Sweden,* Perspectives in Neural Computing, pages 275–280. Springer, 1998.

[Ragg et al., 2000] Ragg, T., Menzel, W., Baum, W., and Wigbers, M. Predicting Sales Rates for Thousands of Retail Traders. In Tsaptsinos, D., editor, *Proceedings of the International Conference on Engineering Applications of Neural Networks, Kingston, England,* pages 199–206, 2000.

[Ragg, 2000] Ragg, T. *Problemlösung durch Komitees neuronaler Netze.* Dissertation, Universität Karlsruhe, Institut für Logik, Komplexität und Deduktionssysteme, 2000.

[Ramsay & Silverman, 1997] Ramsay, J. O. and Silverman, B. *Functional data analysis.* Springer, 1997.

[Rätsch et al., 1998] Rätsch, G., Onoda, T., and Müller, K. Soft margins for adaboost. Technical Report NC-TR-1998-021, GMD, Berlin, 1998.

[Riedmiller, 1994] Riedmiller, M. Advanced supervised learning in multi-layer perceptrons - from backpropagation to adaptive learning algorithms. *Int. Journal of Computer Standards and Interfaces*, 16:265–278, 1994. Special Issue on Neural Networks.

[Rosen, 1996] Rosen, B. E. Ensemble Learning Using Decorrelated Neural Networks. *Connection Science*, 8:373–384, 1996.

[Scott & Thompson, 1983] Scott, D. and Thompson, J. Probability density estimation in higher dimensions. In Gentle, J., editor, *Computer Science and Statistics: Proceedings of the Fifteenth Symposium on the Interface*, pages 173–179. 1983.

[Sharkey, 1999] Sharkey, A. J. Multi-Net Systems. In Sharkey, A. J., editor, *Combining Artificial Neural Nets*, pages 1–30. Springer, 1999.

[Silverman, 1986] Silverman, B. *Density Estimation for Statistics and Data Analysis*. Chapman and Hall, 1986.

[Vapnik, 1995] Vapnik, V. *The Nature of Statistical Learning Theory*. Springer, 1995.

[White, 1989] White, H. Learning in artificial neural networks: a statistical perspective. *Neural Computation*, 1:425–464, 1989.

Second Order Features for Maximising Text Classification Performance

Bhavani Raskutti, Herman Ferrá, and Adam Kowalczyk

Telstra Corporation, 770 Blackburn Road, Clayton, Victoria 3168, Australia
{Bhavani.Raskutti, Herman.Ferra, Adam.Kowalczyk}@team.telstra.com

Abstract. The paper demonstrates that the addition of automatically selected word-pairs substantially increases the accuracy of text classification which is contrary to most previously reported research. The word-pairs are selected automatically using a technique based on frequencies of n-grams (sequences of characters), which takes into account both the frequencies of word-pairs as well as the context in which they occur.

These improvements are reported for two different classifiers, support vector machines (*SVM*) and k-nearest neighbours (*kNN*), and two different text corpora. For the first of them, a collection of articles from PC Week magazine, the addition of word-pairs increases micro-averaged breakeven accuracy by more than 6% point from a baseline accuracy (without pairs) of around 40%. For second one, the standard Reuters benchmark, SVM classifier using augmentation with pairs outperforms all previously reported results.

1 Introduction

Text classification is the problem of automatically assigning electronic text documents to pre-specified categories. In recent years, many statistical classification and machine learning techniques have been successfully applied to this problem [1,7,10,18,19]. Most of these systems use a simple "bag of words" representation of text in which each feature corresponds to a single word. Typically, this results in feature sets consisting of hundreds of thousands of features. Many learning algorithms such as decision trees, Bayes probabilistic models and neural networks have serious difficulty dealing with such large feature spaces. Hence, earlier research on feature extraction for text classification has primarily focussed on reducing dimensionality of input space [14,19].

In contrast, in this paper, we investigate the effect of increasing the size of the native input feature space by augmentation with headline features and second order features. In particular, we focus on the addition of word-pairs that are derived automatically using a technique based on frequencies of n-grams or sequences of characters, and investigating the effect of such addition on text classification performance. We note that the use of *linguistically* derived phrases have been found to be of limited utility in text classification [7,9,13,16], while *statistically* derived word sequences have been found to be useful in classification

L. De Raedt and P. Flach (Eds.): ECML 2001, LNAI 2167, pp. 419–430, 2001.
© Springer-Verlag Berlin Heidelberg 2001

of web pages and newsgroup data [15,8]. Our investigation into word-pairs selected on the basis of n-gram frequencies confirms that the addition of word pairs does give better accuracy, and moreover, the larger the proportion of word-pair features added, the larger the gain.

The paper is organised as follows. Section 2 describes the n-gram-based feature selection technique that is used to extract word-pairs. Section 3 discusses two classifiers that are used for categorisation: k-nearest-neighbour classifier and support vector machines. In Section 4, we describe the experimental setup: the document corpora used for empirical validation and the evaluation metrics. We then present the experiments and their results in Section 5, and discuss their implications in Section 6. Section 7 summarises our contributions.

2 n-Gram Method for Feature Selection

The aim of the feature selector introduced in this section is to select terms which are good discriminators of the categories of interest. Here the terms are either words or word pairs, and n-grams are only the means for the selection of these terms.

An n-gram is a sequence of n consecutive characters in a document generated by sliding a "window" n characters wide across the document text, moving it one character at a time. For example, the sequence of characters "to build" will give rise to the following 5-grams: "to bu", "o bui", " buil" and "build". Thus, n-grams may span across words.

The n-grams have several advantages over words as basic units for text processing. In particular, they are language-independent and hence, the same software can be used to process documents in any language. They also permit operation with degraded text - documents that contain typos and other transcription errors [11]. Due to these advantages, n-grams have been used for text indexing [2], for text filtering [3], text categorisation [4] and for index term extraction [6].

The idea of our approach to selecting discriminating features for a category is based on [6] and its main elements are as follows.

- First, the distribution of n-grams is computed by counting the occurrence of n-grams inside and outside the category. On the basis of this count, each n-gram is assigned a *novelty score* per category that indicates how novel or unique it is for the category.
- The novelty score of each n-gram is then apportioned across its characters, in a way that the middle character gets a higher score than the characters surrounding it, e.g., for $n = 5$, the score is distributed across the 5 characters in the ratio $0.05 : 0.15 : 0.60 : 0.15 : 0.05$, respectively. This apportioning allows each character in the documents in the category to be assigned a weight that is the sum of the contributions from all the n-grams that contain this character. For instance, the character "o" in the word "score" in the context "to score by", will have contributions from the 5-grams, "o scor", " scor", "score", "core ", and "ore b". The contributions depend both on the n-gram score as well as the position of that character in the n-gram.

- Next, each instance of a word or phrase is assigned a score which is the *average* of the component character weights. Thus, there is no bias towards longer or shorter words. Since the same word may occur in different contexts and thus have different contributing n-grams, different instances of the same words may have different scores. Hence, the final score of a feature for the category is computed as an *average* of the scores for different instances of the same feature in the category.
- Finally, these scores are used to rank the features and eliminate those with scores less than a *cut-off threshold* (= mean plus one standard deviation).

In our experiments we have used $n = 5$. The novelty score Ψ_i for the i-th n-gram is allocated according to the following developed in [6]:

$$
\Psi_i = \begin{cases} C_i \ln \frac{C_i}{C} + B_i \ln \frac{B_i}{B} - (C_i + B_i) \ln \frac{C_i + B_i}{C + B} & \text{if } \frac{C_i}{C} \geq \frac{B_i}{B}, \\ 0 & \text{otherwise,} \end{cases}
$$

where C_i and B_i are number of occurrences of the n-gram, and C and B are the total number of n-grams in the category and in the background, i.e. outside of it, respectively. The non-zero component in the above formula is the G^2 statistics, and has a large value only when $\frac{C_i}{C}$ is much greater than $\frac{B_i}{B}$, i.e., when the n-gram is much more likely to occur in the category than in the background.

3   Classifiers

In our experiments we have used *k-nearest-neighbour* classifier (kNN) and *support vector machines* (SVM). This choice was primarily due to the fact that both kNN and SVM scale well to large feature spaces (unlike, e.g., decision trees or back propagation neural networks)[1]. This is particularly important here since the feature space we are dealing with is large to start with and the addition of pairs will make it larger still. Other properties that make these two classifiers very suitable for this work are:

- Both kNN and SVM can naturally provide a score that indicates the likelihood that a document belongs to a given category. These scores may be used for ranking documents, and measuring precision at different recall levels.
- kNN and SVM differ statistically: kNN is a non-parametric[2] and non-linear classifier, while our SVM is a linear parametric model.
- kNN and SVM are both easy to implement.

For both classifiers, each document is represented as a sparse *binary* vector of feature presence, i.e. with entries indicating if a word or word-pair is present

---

[1] Our aim is not to find the ultimate accuracy, but to demonstrate the usefulness of addition of pairs. To that end, those two classifiers selected should provide an indicative sample.

[2] We mean non-parametric in the sense that no parameters are estimated from the training data.

or not. This representation was chosen due to its simplicity and due to the fact that, in preliminary tests with both classifiers, it performed on par with more complicated frequency counts representation (cf. similar observation in [7]).

We have used the linear kernel SVM in our experiments [5,17], with a separate machine trained for each category. The output for a category c is a ranked list of documents with scores allocated according to the following formula:

$$score_{SVM}(d) = w \cdot x + b,$$

where x is the vector of features for document d, "$\cdot$" denotes the dot product in features space and the vector w and bias b are determined by minimising the following functional:

$$\Phi(w, b) = \frac{1}{2}(\|w\|^2 + b^2) + C \sum_{i=1}^{n} \max\left(0, \ 1 - y_i(w \cdot x_i + b)\right)^2,$$

where $(x_i, y_i) \in R^m \times \{-1, 1\}$ are labelled training instances, i.e. the feature vector for document d_i and corresponding label, where 1 indicates membership of the category and -1 indicates non-membership, n is the number of training instances and $\xi \mapsto \max(0, \xi)^2$ is the error penalty function. The constant C controls the trade-off between the complexity of the solution and the error penalty. It has been set to $C = 0.850$ for all our tests (this value is not critical).

The score for kNN is based on the similarity between the test document d and the k nearest neighbours in the training document set, and whether these neighbours are in category or not. It is equal to:

$$score_{kNN}(d) = \sum_{i \in kNN(d)} y_i \frac{x \cdot x_i}{\|x\| \, \|x_i\|},$$

where $kNN(d)$ are indices of k nearest neighbours of the document d in terms of the "cosine" similarity, $Similarity(d, d_i) \to x \cdot x_i / (\|x\| \, \|x_i\|)$, and, as above, x_i and y_i are the ith training document feature vector and label, respectively. The value for k for our experiments was chosen to be 30 after careful experimentation.

4   Experimental Setup

In our experiments we first pre-process the data, determine the feature sets for different experimental settings, and then use the two selected classifiers to learn models of different categories. This is accomplished using the training set documents only. The created models are then evaluated on the test sets using micro-averaged breakeven point [12] that has been the benchmark measure for the Reuters data set.

4.1   Data Collections

Our first data corpus is the *Reuters*-21578 news-wires collection of documents. This is the most commonly used corpus in text classification research. In particular, the modApte split, available at http://www.research.att.com/lewis, has been used as a standard benchmark in [1,7,10,18]. This split has 9603 training documents and 3,299 test documents. We have used 115 categories, i.e. all those with at least one training case, while some researchers have used 95 categories, i.e. all those with at least two training cases. The categories cover topics such as commodities, interest rates and trade. The frequency of occurrence of categories varies greatly. For instance, roughly 30% of the documents appear in *earnings*, while *ringgit*, *rubber* and *rupiah* have only one training example each.

The second corpus used is *ComputerSelect* collection, consisting of a set of 6070 articles from *PC Week* magazine extracted from the ComputerSelect CD December 1996. These articles have manually assigned categories with many articles belonging to multiple categories. There are 840 categories, out of which the largest 128 were chosen for our tests. Only those articles that belonged to one of these 128 categories are included in the document set, which resulted in a total of 5257 articles. This set was then split into 2807 training articles and 2450 test articles such that all 128 categories contained at least 5 training articles. Again, as with the Reuters collection, the frequency of occurrence of categories varies greatly. For example *Software Product Introduction* appears in 10% of the documents while *Protocol Gateway Software* has only 20 documents assigned to it. This collection is more of a real-world example of classification since the manual assignments to categories have not been evaluated by multiple people, and not all categories are based on subject matter alone. Some categories indicate type of article, e.g., *Software Product Introduction*, while others indicate what the article is about, e.g., *Image Scanner*.

4.2   Pre-processing

First, all text is converted to a single case and non-alphabetic characters are turned into spaces, and then the sequences of consecutive blanks are compressed into a single space. Next, words that are in a standard stop list are removed, and the remaining words stemmed using the standard rule-based Porter stemmer. For instance, the text "for building, Permits" will be converted to "build permit". The text is then processed to yield different feature sets for different experiments.

4.3   Performance Measure

The standard evaluation criterion for the Reuters benchmark is the *breakeven point*, the point at which precision equals recall. Since this is different for different categories, the standard evaluation figure is the *micro-averaged breakeven point* (μBP) [12]. Micro-averaging gives each category-document assignment decision equal weight. We have some concerns over the use of this single figure of merit, particularly since the micro-averaging step can obscure many subtle performance details. However, this figure has been widely reported by a number of researchers, and hence we report the same for the sake of comparison.

5   Experiments

In this paper, we focus on the investigation of the effect of augmentation of input feature space with word-pairs. Hence, in each of the following settings, we first learn models using a baseline feature set. Then the accuracy of each model is compared with the performance of models learnt by augmenting this baseline feature set with the set of word-pairs extracted using the n-gram feature selector.

Two set of experiments have been conducted, one with universal dictionaries, i.e. with all categories using the same feature set, and the other with category specific dictionaries, "optimised", i.e. selected, for each category separately.

5.1   Experiments with Universal Feature Sets

The following four baseline feature sets are considered for augmentation with word-pairs.

1. All words: The data collection is pre-processed, and all words from the training set documents are used as baseline features. This gives 20197 words for Reuters and 20572 words for ComputerSelect.
2. Selected words: We first create category-specific word sets as follows. For each category, up to 300 words describing "in-category" documents are selected using the n-gram feature selector (cf. Section 2). Then the same number of words describing "out-of-category" documents are added. In general, for most categories, this results in far fewer than 300 "in-category" words (since many words do not have a score larger than our cut-off threshold see Section 2). There is also an overlap between "in-category" and "out-of-category" words. All this results in the largest category-specific word set having 176 items for Reuters and 359 for ComputerSelect.
   The universal word sets are created by pooling all the category-specific word sets together. For Reuters, this results in a baseline feature set of 1375 words, while the ComputerSelect collection consists of 2552 words. These consist of 6.8% and 12.4% of the total word sets, respectively.
3. All words + headlines: In this setting, the baseline feature set in the first setting is augmented with words extracted from headlines in the training set. All words other than those in a standard stop list are retained. The number of such headline words for Reuters set is 8179 while the ComputerSelect set contains 3403 headline words.
4. Selected words + headlines: In this setting, the same headline words extracted in the previous setting are used to augment the features in the "selected words" setting as above.

The universal word-pair set is selected using the n-gram feature selector in the same manner as the universal word set. For Reuters, we selected 2714 pairs from the total set of 303086, while for ComputerSelect we obtained 4050 pairs from the total of 413572 word-pairs in the training set. Thus, less than 1% of the word-pair feature space is selected by the n-gram feature selector.

Table 1. Micro-averaged breakeven point (μBP %) for the *universal feature* sets experiments illustrating the impact of addition of pairs

Experimental Setting	Number Baseline Features	μBP % for **SVM**			μBP % for **kNN**		
			Sel. Method			Sel. Method	
			n-gram	χ^2		n-gram	χ^2
Reuters		**Base.**	**+2714 Pairs**		**Base.**	**+2714 Pairs**	
All words	20197	85.6	86.3	85.8	75.6	76.3	75.8
Selected words	1375	85.6	86.2	85.7	77.1	78.3	77.5
All words + headlines	28376	86.8	87.3	87.0	77.2	77.9	77.3
Sel. words + headlines	9554	87.0	87.5	87.1	78.2	79.3	78.4
ComputerSelect		**Base.**	**+4050 Pairs**		**Base.**	**+4050 Pairs**	
All words	20572	39.6	45.6	45.8	28.4	32.9	32.5
Selected words	2552	38.6	45.9	45.8	30.5	35.0	35.1
All words + headlines	23124	40.6	45.9	46.3	29.1	33.5	33.2
Sel. words + headlines	5595	40.1	46.2	46.0	31.0	35.2	35.3

Table 1 lists the micro-averaged breakeven point for the different experiments conducted for the two classifiers for the 115 Reuters categories and 128 ComputerSelect categories. For the purpose of comparison with other feature selection techniques, results are also reported for the situation where the same number of word-pairs are selected using maximum of χ^2 statistics, which was the best word selector in [19].

As expected, the breakeven points for the real world collection of ComputerSelect articles are much lower than that for Reuters. As evident from Table 1 both classifiers show improvement in their performance once selected word pairs are added (cf. Section 6 for further discussion). The accuracy for kNN is lower than that for SVM for both collections

5.2   Category Specific Feature Sets

Another approach to feature selection for text classification is the use of small category-specific feature sets, which has been found to increase accuracy [7]. In this context, it is useful to investigate the effect of the addition of category-specific word pairs to category-specific word sets. The feature sets for this investigation are created as described in Section 5.1. The average size of the word set for Reuters and ComputerSelect is 55.4 words and 107.2 respectively. However, there is a large variation in the size of the word sets, e.g. category *"earnings"* in Reuters with the largest number of training examples has a feature set with 176 words, while some categories (with one training example) have an empty word set. For ComputerSelect, the feature set size varies between 25 to 359. Classification performances are compared by adding category-specific pair sets which are generated as described in Section 5.1. These sets also show enormous variation for different categories. For Reuters the average, maximum and minimum sizes of the pair set are 55.4, 352 and 0 respectively, while for ComputerSelect the average is 88.2 pairs and the sizes vary from 6 to 257.

Table 2. Micro-averaged breakeven point (μBP %) for the *category-specific* feature sets experiments illustrating the impact of addition of pairs

Base Data	No. of Base Feat.	μBP % for **SVM**		μBP % for **kNN**	
Reuters	Min–Max	Base-line	+ 0–352 Pairs	Base-line	+ 0–352 Pairs
Word sub-sets	0–176	84.3	85.4	78.6	79.4
Word sub-sets + headlines	8179–8355	87.9	88.8	80.3	80.4
ComputerSelect	Min–Max	Base-line	+ 6–257 Pairs	Base-line	+ 6–257 Pairs
Word sub-sets	6–257	39.6	46.8	33.1	38.3
Word sub-sets + headlines	3409–3660	41.2	48.1	29.9	35.5

Table 2 shows the micro-averaged breakeven point for experiments with category specific word sets. As before the addition of pairs does indeed improve the categorisation performance in all cases. Comparing these results with the results for the selected word set in Table 1, we see that the use of category specific word and pair sets instead of the larger pooled sets does not substantially decrease performance, and in many cases it actually improves it.

6   Discussion

As shown in Tables 1 and 2, the statistically-derived word pairs, in general, increase the categorisation performance for both classifiers and corpora. Below we analyse the significance of observed improvements and different contributing factors.

Differences in baseline precisions: Baseline precisions obtained for ComputerSelect are much lower than for Reuters (e.g. $\tilde{4}0\%$ vs. $\tilde{8}5\%$ for SVM classifier, respectively). This can be attributed to qualitative differences in the documents in the two collections: Reuters articles are written by journalists to disseminate information and hence contain precise words that are useful for classification, e.g., "grain" and "acquisition", whereas ComputerSelect articles are written as advertisements and contain words, such as, "software" and "system", which are useful only in context, e.g., "network software" and "array system".

Gain relative to ideal classifier: In the universal set situation, for ComputerSelect we observe over 6% point improvement from a low base (40% for SVM), while the increase in precision for Reuters is less than 1% point from a high starting base (85% for SVM). A fairer comparison which takes into account the different baselines can be made by calculating relative gain, $\frac{\mu BP(new) - \mu BP(old)}{100 - \mu BP(old)}$, which compares the observed improvement to the ultimate improvement possible for the ideal classifier. When measured this way, the improvement for both Reuters (4% on average) and ComputerSelect (10% for SVM and 6% for kNN) is of similar, substantial size.

Significance test: We have performed a matched pairs t-test, where for each setting of document collection, classifier and baseline feature set, we paired the breakeven point for each category using just the baseline set with the corresponding breakeven point after the addition of pairs. In each case our conjecture is that the use of pairs provides an improvement in performance, hence the alternative hypothesis (H_1) is that the mean breakeven point for feature sets with pair features is greater than that for the corresponding set without pair features, i.e., $\mu_p > \mu_b$, where μ_b and μ_p are the mean breakeven points for the baseline feature set and for the baseline set plus pairs, respectively. The null hypothesis (H_0) is that there is no difference in the mean breakeven point between the baseline feature set and the set with pair features, i.e. $\mu_p = \mu_b$. Using a one tailed t-test, in all except one case (Reuters, SVM, selected set + headlines) we can reject the null hypothesis with a significance level of 1%.

Note that the t-test performed gives equal importance to all categories, independent of their sizes. In contrast, the improvements measured relative to the ideal classifier based on μBP gives each category the importance proportional to its size. This also shows substantial improvements, as discussed above.

Larger proportion of pairs, larger accuracy improvements: In order to analyse which categories are helped by the addition of pairs, Figure 1 plots the difference between micro-averaged breakeven points with pairs and without pairs for the universal dictionaries as the number of categories is increased. The categories are ordered in the descending order of their training set sizes.

Referring to Figures 1(b) and 1(c), which show the strongest difference in performance for different baseline sets, the order of the curves suggests that the increase in performance due to pairs increases as the size of baseline set decreases. For instance, the lowest curve in Figures 1(b) and 1(c) belongs to the largest baseline feature set, namely, all words + headlines, while the highest curve belongs to smallest baseline set, namely, selected word set. This observation may explain why earlier experiments using a small number of linguistically derived phrases produced little improvement [7,9,13,16].

In fact, a closer analysis of Reuters results shows that n-gram selected pairs provide non-positive gains in breakeven point if the ratio of the number of the (category-specific) selected word-pairs to selected words is $< 70\%$ and non-negative gains if otherwise (with only 3 exceptions!).

Significant improvement for medium size categories: The curves in Figure 1(a) and (b) indicate that pairs provide greatest improvement in classification accuracy for medium sized categories for Reuters. The larger ComputerSelect categories are similar in size to the medium sized categories for Reuters given that the largest category for the ComputerSelect document set is only 10% of the data and consists of 287 examples while the largest category in Reuters contains nearly 30% of the data ($\sim$3000 training examples). Not surprisingly, the performance on the ComputerSelect collection improves for all categories when pairs are taken into account (cf. Figure 1(c) and (d)), unlike the Reuters case where the difference is small and sometimes negative for the larger categories.

In fact, for the medium size Reuters categories (numbered 12 to 45 in the decreasing order) the ratio of pairs to selected words is $> 100\%$ (with 2 exception),

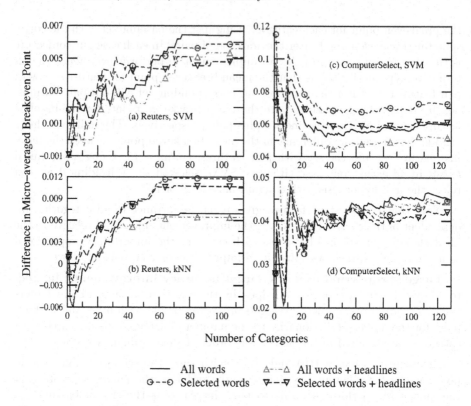

Fig. 1. Influence of Pairs on Classification Performance. The figures show the difference between micro-averaged breakeven accuracy with pairs and without pairs as a function of the number of categories included. Here the categories are ordered in the descending order of their training set sizes.

and the gain in breakeven point is ≥ 0, with very solid positive improvements noted for the (majority of) categories numbered 14 to 28.

Comparisons of n-gram and χ^2 word-pair selectors: Addition of pairs selected by either method shows improvements (cf. Table 1). For Reuters, using SVM, just 2714 selected pairs with 7% of words produces better μBP than all 20197 words. For ComputerSelect using SVM, just 4050 pairs more than compensates for the 87.5% of the words that were discarded. However, the improvement for pairs selected by χ^2 statistics is smaller in most cases than for n-gram method.

The n-gram method has other important advantages. For instance, this method produces word sequences of any length m with just two passes over the input, while other methods based on direct, explicit ranking of features, need m passes in such a case [15,8]. Further, for large document corpora, the number of n-grams is smaller than the number of word-pairs (in the two collections considered, the number of word-pairs is more than double the number of n-grams), and hence, n-gram method is also more memory efficient. Finally, although we used language-dependent techniques such as stemming, the n-gram method itself is designed to be language-independent since the basic unit for measuring novelty is just sequences of characters.

Use of category-specific feature sets: The use of small category-specific feature sets has been investigated by Dumais et. al [7]. They use 300 category-specific features with SVM classifier and obtained high classification accuracy. Our experiments show that category-specific word sets combined with category-specific pair sets can lead to higher accuracy than using universal sets with or without pairs. The result on the Reuters set for the SVM classifier using category specific word and pair sets on all 115 categories outperforms all previously reported results on this benchmark. The best earlier performance on the same data set is 87.8% for the top 95 categories and is obtained using a very complex classifier consisting of an ensemble of decision trees [18] and uses words and headline features. This figure is less than our figure of 88.78% for all 115 categories. Our best performance for the top 95 categories is 88.9%. This translates to the gain of 9% relative to the hypothetical ideal classifier.

7 Conclusion

We have presented a method (n-grams) for automatically selecting phrases that can take into account both the co-occurrent frequencies as well as the context in which the pairs occur. We have shown that addition of such pairs to the input feature space substantially improves performance of classifiers (kNN and SVM in our experiments). This is valid for at least two different collections examined in this research with very different properties and very differing baseline precisions (40% for ComputerSelect and 85% for Reuters). The improvements translate to 4-10% gain of relative to the hypothetical ideal classifier. In particular, for the standard Reuters benchmark we obtained SVM classifiers (using augmentation with selected pairs) outperforming all previously reported results.

Our results show significant improvements occurring mainly for medium size categories. We found that in general the larger the proportion of pairs added to word sets the larger the improvement in performance suggesting the usage of small baseline sets augmented with pairs for compact accurate classifiers.

Our future work will focus on investigation of the effect of the relative sizes of the baseline and augmenting set on the classification accuracy, and evaluation of the usefulness of pairs for automatic email and news categorisation.

Acknowledgements. The permission of the Chief Technology Officer, Technology Strategy and Research, Telstra Corporation, to publish this paper is gratefully acknowledged.

References

1. C. Apte, F. Damerau, and S. M. Weiss. Text Mining with Decision Trees and Decision Rules . In *Conference on Automated Learning and Discovery*, 1998.

2. J. E. Burnett, D. Cooper, M. F. Lynch, P. Willett, and M. Wycherley. Document Retrieval Experiments Using Indexing Vocabularies of Varying Size. I. Variety Generation Symbols Assigned to the Fronts of Index Terms . *Journal of Documentation*, **35**(3):197–206, (1979).
3. W. B. Cavnar. N-gram-based text filtering for TREC-2 . In *Proceedings for Second Text Retrieval Conference (TREC-2)*, pages 200–215. NIST Special Publication, 1993.
4. W. B. Cavnar and J. M. Trenkle. N-gram-based text Categorization . In *Proceedings of Third Annual Symposium on Document Analysis and Information Retrieval*, 1994.
5. N. Christianini and J. Shawe-Taylor. *Support Vector Machines and other Kernel Based Methods* . Cambridge University Press, 2000.
6. J. D. Cohen. Highlights: Language- and domain-independent automatic indexing terms for abstracting . *Journal of the American Society for Information Science*, **46**(3):162–174, (1995).
7. S. Dumais, J. Platt, D. Heckerman, and M. Sahami. Inductive Learning Algorithms and Representations for Text Categorization . In *Seventh International Conference on Information and Knowledge Management*, 1998.
8. J. Furnkranz. A Study Using n-gram Features for Text Categorization . Technical report, Austrian Reserach Institute for Artificial Intelligence, 1998.
9. J. Furnkranz, T. Mitchell, and E. Riloff. A Case Study in Using Linguistic Phrases for Text Categorization on the WWW . In *In AAAI-98 Workshop on Learning for Text Categorization*, 1998.
10. T. Joachims. Text Categorization with Support Vector Machines: Learning with Many Relevant Features . In *Proceedings of the Tenth European Conference on Machine Learning ECML98*, 1998.
11. K. Kukich. Technique for automatically correcting words in text . *ACM Computing Surveys*, **24**:377–439, (1992).
12. D. Lewis. Evaluating Text Categorization . In *Proceedings of the Speech and Natural Language Workshop*, 1991.
13. D. Lewis. An Evaluation of Phrasal and Clustered Representations on a Text Categorization Task . In *Proceedings of the Fifteenth International ACM SIGIR Conference on Research and Development in Information Retrieval*, 1992.
14. D. Lewis. Feature selection and feature extraction for text categorization . In *Proceedings of the Speech and Natural Language Workshop*. Defense Advanced Research Projects Agency, 1992.
15. D. Mladenic and M. Grobelnik. Word Sequences as Features in Text Learning . In *In Seventeenth Electrotechnical and Computer Science Conference*, 1998.
16. S. Scott and S. Matwin. Feature Engineering for Text Classification . In *Proceedings of the Sixteenth International Conference on Machine Learning*, 1999.
17. V. Vapnik. *Statistical Learning theory* . Wiley, 1998.
18. S. M. Weiss, C. Apte, F. Damerau, D.E. Johnson, F. J. Oles, T. Goetz, and T. Hampp. Maximizing Text-Mining Performance . *IEEE Intelligent Systems*, **14**(4), (1999).
19. Y. Yang and J. O. Pedersen. A Comparative Study on Feature Selection in Text Categorization . In *Proceedings of the Fourteenth International Conference on Machine Learning*, 1997.

Importance Sampling Techniques in Neural Detector Training

José L. Sanz-González and Diego Andina

Universidad Politécnica de Madrid (Dpto. SSR), ETSI de Telecomunicación-UPM,
Ciudad Universitaria, 28040 Madrid, Spain
{jlsanz, andina}@gc.ssr.upm.es

Abstract. Importance Sampling is a modified Monte Carlo technique applied to the estimation of rare event probabilities (very low probabilities). In this paper, we propose and develop the use of Importance Sampling (IS) techniques in neural network training, for applications to detection in communication systems. Some key topics are introduced, such as modifications of the error probability objective function, optimal and suboptimal IS probability density functions (biasing density functions), and experimental results of training with a genetic algorithm. Also, it is shown that the genetic algorithm with the IS technique attains quasi-optimum training in the sense of minimum error probability (or minimum misclassification probability).

1   Introduction and Preliminaries

Importance Sampling is a modified Monte Carlo technique [1] commonly applied to the performance analysis of radar and communication detectors [2-9]. In communications detectors, the error probability (P_e) is estimated by Importance Sampling (IS) techniques for very low P_e (e.g. $P_e<10^{-5}$). In radar detectors, the very low false-alarm probabilities are also estimated by IS techniques. In paper [10] we have applied IS techniques to neural network detectors for testing performances, where the first part of [10] presents IS as a Monte Carlo technique for computer simulations, and the second part presents false-alarm probability estimations of neural detectors (in the testing phase) applied to radar.

Now, in this paper we propose as a novelty the application of IS techniques in the training phase of neural network detectors. For this purpose, we have to modify adequately the objective functions of our neural networks, as we shall explain in Section 2. Some computer results are presented in Section 3, and conclusions are summarized in Section 4.

Throughout the paper, we shall refer to Fig. 1, where $\mathbf{x}= (x_1, x_2, ..., x_n)$ is the input vector of the R^n-space, $y=g(\mathbf{x})$ is the scalar output, $g(\cdot)$ is a nonlinear system (e. g. a neural network), T_0 is the detection threshold, and $z=u(g(\mathbf{x})-T_0)$ is the detector output, where $u(\cdot)$ is the unit-step function (i.e. $u(t)=1$ if $t>0$ and $u(t)=0$ if $t<0$). We denote $\mathbf{X}=(X_1, X_2, ..., X_n)$ as a random vector and $f_{\mathbf{X}}(\mathbf{x} \mid H_i)$ as the probability density function (pdf) of $\mathbf{X}$ under a hypothesis H_i, $i=1, 0$ (binary hypotheses), where H_0 is the null hypothesis or symbol "0" and H_1 is the alternative hypothesis or symbol "1". $P(H_i)$ is

L. De Raedt and P. Flach (Eds.): ECML 2001, LNAI 2167, pp. 431–441, 2001.
© Springer-Verlag Berlin Heidelberg 2001

the "a priori" probability of the hypothesis H_i, $i=1, 0$, and $P(D_j|H_i)$ is the conditional probability of deciding H_j, $j=1, 0$, under the true hypothesis H_i, $i=1, 0$. If $g(\mathbf{x}) > T_0$ (or $z=1$), the decision is H_1; if $g(\mathbf{x}) < T_0$ (or $z=0$), the decision is H_0. Finally, $\mathscr{E}\{Z \mid H_i\}$ is the expectation of the random variable Z conditioned by H_i, $i=1, 0$, and $\mathscr{E}\{g(\mathbf{X})\}$ is the expectation of $g(\cdot)$ with respect to the pdf of $\mathbf{X}$ (i.e. $f_\mathbf{X}(\mathbf{x})$).

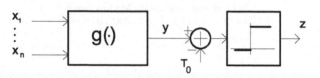

Fig. 1. Binary detector structure

2   Error Probability as Objective Function for Training

To supervise neural network (NN) training, estimations of an objective function (or risk function) have to be performed. The value of this function decreases as the training progresses; then, the number of test patterns required for an accurate estimation has to be increased. Consequently, the training computational cost is unaffordable for very low objective function values, and the use of Importance Sampling (IS) techniques becomes indispensable.

To illustrate the use of IS techniques in the training phase of a NN, let us consider the misclassification probability as an objective function for applications in classifications (or the error probability for detection in communications [11-13]). According to the notation given above, the error probability (P_e) can be expressed as follows

$$P_e = P(H_0)P(D_1 \mid H_0) + P(H_1)P(D_0 \mid H_1) \tag{1}$$

where

$$P(D_1 \mid H_0) = \int_{g(\mathbf{x})>T_0} f_\mathbf{X}(\mathbf{x} \mid H_0)d\mathbf{x} \quad \text{and} \quad P(D_0 \mid H_1) = \int_{g(\mathbf{x})<T_0} f_\mathbf{X}(\mathbf{x} \mid H_1)d\mathbf{x} \tag{2}$$

Also, in order to save space, let us define

$$h(\mathbf{x}) = P(H_0)f_\mathbf{X}(\mathbf{x} \mid H_0)u(g(\mathbf{x}) - T_0) + P(H_1)f_\mathbf{X}(\mathbf{x} \mid H_1)u(T_0 - g(\mathbf{x})), \quad \mathbf{x} \in R^n \tag{3}$$

where all items have been defined above.

Now, if we consider a new probability density function (pdf) $f_\mathbf{X}^*(\mathbf{x})$, such that $f_\mathbf{X}^*(\mathbf{x}) \neq 0$ wherever $h(\mathbf{x}) \neq 0$, then from (1), (2) and (3) we have

$$P_e = \int_{R^n} h(\mathbf{x}) d\mathbf{x} = \int_{R^n} \frac{h(\mathbf{x})}{f_\mathbf{X}^*(\mathbf{x})} f_\mathbf{X}^*(\mathbf{x}) d\mathbf{x} = \mathscr{E}^* \left\{ \frac{h(\mathbf{X})}{f_\mathbf{X}^*(\mathbf{X})} \right\} \tag{4}$$

where $\mathcal{E}^*\{\cdot\}$ means expectation with respect to $f_X^*(x)$ (known as the Importance Sampling pdf).

The last equality in (4) is the key of the Importance Sampling technique. From the statistical inference theory applied to (4), an estimator of P_e is given by

$$P_e^* = \frac{1}{N} \sum_{k=1}^{N} \frac{h(x_k^*)}{f_X^*(x_k^*)} \tag{5}$$

where x_k^*, $k=1, 2, ..., N$, are independent sample vectors whose pdf is $f_X^*(x)$. Estimator P_e^*, given in (5), must be computed in order to perform the neural network training (i.e. to find g($\cdot$) for minimum P_e^*).

The mean $\mu_{P_e^*} = \mathcal{E}^*\{P_e^*\} = P_e$ and the variance $\sigma_{P_e^*}^2$ of the estimator P_e^* is given by

$$\sigma_{P_e^*}^2 = \mathcal{E}^*\{(P_e^* - \mu_{P_e^*})^2\} = \frac{1}{N}\left[\mathcal{E}^*\left\{\left(\frac{h(X_k^*)}{f_X^*(X_k^*)}\right)^2\right\} - P_e^2\right] \tag{6}$$

Then, P_e^* is an unbiased and consistent estimator of P_e (i.e. $P_e^* \to P_e$ as $N \to \infty$).

The estimation error $\varepsilon_{P_e^*}$ of the estimator P_e^* is defined by

$$\varepsilon_{P_e^*} = \frac{\sigma_{P_e^*}}{\mu_{P_e^*}} = \sqrt{\frac{1}{N}\left(\frac{\mathcal{E}^*\left\{\left(\frac{h(X_k^*)}{f_X^*(X_k^*)}\right)^2\right\}}{\left(P_e\right)^2} - 1\right)} \tag{7}$$

Because the variance is not a negative number, from (6) we have

$$\mathcal{E}^*\left\{\left(\frac{h(X_k^*)}{f_X^*(X_k^*)}\right)^2\right\} \geq P_e^2 \tag{8}$$

The equality case in (8) is satisfied if

$$f_X^*(x) = \frac{1}{P_e}h(x), \quad x \in R^n \tag{9}$$

that it can be proved by taking (9) into (8); then, the estimator variance in (6) is zero for any value of N, i.e. only one sample vector ($N=1$) is required for estimating P_e without error (estimation error (7) is zero). Expression (9) is the unconstrained optimal solution for $f_X^*(x)$. Note that $h(x) \geq 0$, $x \in R^n$ (from definition (3)), then expression (9) is a pdf because of (4).

By taking (3) into (9), the unconstrained optimal solution for $f_X^*(x)$ can be expressed for future references as follows

$$f_{\mathbf{X}}^*(\mathbf{x}) = \frac{1}{P_e}\left[P(H_0)f_{\mathbf{X}}(\mathbf{x}\,|\,H_0)u(g(\mathbf{x})-T_0) + P(H_1)f_{\mathbf{X}}(\mathbf{x}\,|\,H_1)u(T_0-g(\mathbf{x}))\right], \mathbf{x} \in R^n \quad (10)$$

The optimal solution for $f_{\mathbf{X}}^*(\mathbf{x})$ given in (10) is not realistic, because P_e is not known "a priori" (it has to be estimated by (5)). Furthermore, in the training phase, $g(\cdot)$ is changing from one iteration to the other.

A suboptimal solution for $f_{\mathbf{X}}^*(\mathbf{x})$ is obtained in a way similar to that done in [10]. Usually $f_{\mathbf{X}}(\mathbf{x}\,|\,H_i)$, $i = 1,0$, depends on a parameter θ (e.g. the signal-to-noise ratio) [12,13] and we can write $f_{\mathbf{X}}(\mathbf{x};\theta\,|\,H_i)$, $i = 1,0$; if $\theta=0$ there is only noise (both pdf's are identical to the noise pdf); if θ is too large, both hypotheses are highly separate (and corresponding to very low error probability). Now, we consider the following (suboptimal) density function as the Importance Sampling pdf

$$f_{\mathbf{X}}^*(\mathbf{x}) = P(H_0)f_{\mathbf{X}}(\mathbf{x};\theta^*\,|\,H_0) + P(H_1)f_{\mathbf{X}}(\mathbf{x};\theta^*\,|\,H_1), \quad \mathbf{x} \in R^n \quad (11)$$

where θ^* is the θ-value that minimizes the variance (6) of the estimator P_e^*. Note that (11) satisfies the necessary condition for the unbiasedness of P_e^*, i.e. $f_{\mathbf{X}}^*(\mathbf{x}) \neq 0$ as $h(\mathbf{x})\neq0$, $\mathbf{x}\in R^n$, where $h(\mathbf{x})$ is given by (3).

The optimal θ^*-value is obtained experimentally by computing an estimator of (6). An estimator of (6) is given by

$$\hat{\sigma}_{P_e^*}^2 = \frac{1}{N}\left[\frac{1}{N}\sum_{k=1}^{N}\left(\frac{h(\mathbf{x}_k^*)}{f_{\mathbf{X}}^*(\mathbf{x}_k^*)}\right)^2 - \left(P_e^*\right)^2\right] \quad (12)$$

where P_e^* is given by (5) and $h(\mathbf{x})$ is given by (3). Then, θ^* can be estimated experimentally and corresponds to the θ-value that minimizes (12). However, a better statistical parameter for this purpose is the relative error of P_e^* given by (7). An estimator of the relative error (7) (denoted as $\hat{\varepsilon}_{P_e^*}$) is

$$\hat{\varepsilon}_{P_e^*} = \frac{\hat{\sigma}_{P_e^*}}{\hat{\mu}_{P_e^*}} = \sqrt{\frac{1}{N}\left(\frac{\dfrac{1}{N}\displaystyle\sum_{k=1}^{N}\left(\dfrac{h(\mathbf{x}_k^*)}{f_{\mathbf{X}}^*(\mathbf{x}_k^*)}\right)^2}{\left(P_e^*\right)^2} - 1\right)} \quad (13)$$

where $h(\mathbf{x})$, $f_{\mathbf{X}}^*(\mathbf{x})$ and P_e^* are given by (3), (11) and (5), respectively.

Expressions (5) and (13) are computed at the same time for a given θ (fixed during the training), N (that can be adjusted in each iteration), and $g(\cdot)$ which changes as the training progresses. At the end of the training, P_e^* and $\hat{\varepsilon}_{P_e^*}$ are good estimations of P_e and $\varepsilon_{P_e^*}$, respectively. After some computer runs with different θ-values, the optimal θ^* of minimum $\hat{\varepsilon}_{P_e^*}$ can be obtained by inspection.

In a general application, where parameter θ can be a vector, the minimization of (13) have to be performed by an adequate optimization algorithm like stochastic gradient descent algorithms [4,5] or, alternatively, by genetic algorithms. Nowadays, this subject is under consideration by our research group.

Finally, we have to point out that (11) is a suboptimal solution of $f_{\mathbf{X}}^{*}(\mathbf{x})$ (optimum expressed by (10)), if the neural network is already trained (or quasi-trained), as is stated and fulfilled in [10], because Importance Sampling was applied there for testing performances. Nevertheless, (11) can be used also in the first iterations of the training because the error probability (P_e) is high and the error probability estimation (P_e^{*}) is also high (although inaccurate). In the last iterations of the training (network quasi-trained), both P_e and P_e^{*} are low (or very low) and close each other. These facts were also tested by means of computer simulations.

3   Computer Simulations

In order to show how Importance Sampling works in neural detectors, consider a detection of binary symbols in Gaussian noise. The hypotheses are $H_1 : \mathbf{x} = \mathbf{\eta} + \mathbf{a}$ and $H_0 : \mathbf{x} = \mathbf{\eta} - \mathbf{a}$, where $\mathbf{a} = (a_1, a_2, ..., a_n)$, $a_i = \mu$, $i = 1, 2, ..., n$ and μ is a real constant (for simulations $\mu = 2$), $\mathbf{\eta} = (\eta_1, \eta_2, ..., \eta_n)$ is a Gaussian noise vector of independent and identically distributed zero-mean components of unit variance. Then, the pdf's under each hypothesis are normal distributed with means $\mathbf{a}$ and $-\mathbf{a}$, respectively, i.e.

$$f_{\mathbf{X}}(\mathbf{x} \mid H_1) = (2\pi)^{-n/2} \exp\left(-\frac{1}{2} \sum_{i=1}^{n} (x_i - \mu)^2\right)$$

$$f_{\mathbf{X}}(\mathbf{x} \mid H_0) = (2\pi)^{-n/2} \exp\left(-\frac{1}{2} \sum_{i=1}^{n} (x_i + \mu)^2\right)$$

(14)

Also, we suppose for simulations that $P(H_1) = P(H_0) = 1/2$ (the symbols are equally likely).

Referring to Fig. 1, a Multi-Layer Perceptron (MLP) is the NN used as nonlinear system $g(\mathbf{x})$. The parameters for the MLP are 5×5×1 (i.e. number of input nodes: $n=5$, number of hidden-layer nodes: 5, number of outputs: 1) and the threshold $T_0=0.5$. A genetic algorithm [14] is used for training the MLP. Genetic algorithms for optimization are very close to Monte Carlo techniques, so Importance Sampling is well tailored for training neural networks by genetic algorithms. Computer programs for implementing both genetic algorithm and Importance Sampling are independent, and a main program calls each one. Although our genetic algorithm (with elitism) is not the subject of this paper (in fact, here it is only considered as a tool), we give the parameters used in our training. These are the following: number of MLP's in genetic set: 20; mutation probability: 0.1; crossover probability: 0.1; fitness function: $-\log(P_e^{*})$; number of iterations (generations): 100. The number of patterns (input sample vectors) for estimating P_e^{*} by IS technique is N ($10^2 < N < 10^3$); in fact, it is required $N>200$ for efficient training. Finally, for this application, back-propagation training does not work well because the objective function (5) is discontinuous (due to the unit-step function in (3)).

In this example, after numerical computations of (13) with $\theta=\mu$, we obtain the solution $\theta^*=0$ which minimizes expression (13); consequently, from (11) we have that the noise pdf is the suboptimal solution for the IS pdf, i.e.

$$f_{\mathbf{X}}^*(\mathbf{x}) = (2\pi)^{-n/2} \exp\left(-\frac{1}{2}\sum_{i=1}^{n} x_i^2\right) \tag{15}$$

In Fig. 2, we show the results of the error probability estimations (P_e^*) versus iteration number. Also, for $\theta^*=0$ in (11), we have (15) as our IS pdf to generate patterns for training. We have used a number of patterns $N=200$ in the first iterations of the training process, and $N=10^3$ in the last ones (N increases from 200 to 10^3, following a cubic parabola as the training progresses). So, N increases slowly at the beginning of the training, and very fast at the end. In Fig. 3, we present the relative error $\hat{\varepsilon}_{P_e^*}$ computed from (13) at the same time that P_e^* is computed from (5). In the first iterations of the training, both P_e^* and $\hat{\varepsilon}_{P_e^*}$ are high, and inaccurate estimations of P_e and $\varepsilon_{P_e^*}$, respectively, because of two reasons. The first reason is the low number of vector samples ($N=200$) in the computations of P_e^* and $\hat{\varepsilon}_{P_e^*}$; the second reason is that $f_{\mathbf{X}}^*(\mathbf{x})$ (corresponding to $\theta^*=0$) departs from the optimum one. In the last iterations of the training, $N=10^3$ and $f_{\mathbf{X}}^*(\mathbf{x})$ corresponds to the optimum ($\theta^*=0$), then both P_e^* and $\hat{\varepsilon}_{P_e^*}$ are highly accurate ($P_e^* \approx 4\cdot10^{-6}$ with an error $\hat{\varepsilon}_{P_e^*}\approx 5\%$ from Figs. 2 and 3, respectively, and the iteration number equals 100).

We can see a quick convergence of the training (less than 60 iterations) and the quasi-optimality of the resultant neural detector with $P_e^* \approx 4\cdot10^{-6}$, which is close to the optimal Bayes' detector (linear detector) with $(P_e)_{\mathrm{Bayes}} = 3.87\cdot10^{-6}$. On the other hand, if we use a standard Monte Carlo simulation for estimating P_e (denoted as $\hat{P}_e$), we need more than $N=10^7$ patterns (compare with $N=10^3$ of the Importance Sampling). For the case of a Monte-Carlo simulation with $N=10^7$ we have obtained an error probability estimation $\hat{P}_e = 4.8\cdot10^{-6} \approx P_e^*$ (within a precision of 15%).

In Figs. 4 and 5 we have considered the same conditions and parameters to those of Figs. 2 and 3, except for the number of patterns (N). Now, $N=10^3$ for each iteration number (the same number of patterns in the first iterations and in the last ones). As it can be seen, Figs. 2 and 3 are noisier than Figs. 4 and 5, respectively; however, Figs. 2 and 4 converge to the same value ($\approx 4\cdot10^{-6}$) with the same precision (5% of precision from Figs. 3 and 5), whenever the 80th iteration is reached. On the other hand, the time required for Figs. 2 and 3 was 3 minutes in a Pentium III-PC at 800 Mhz, and 9 minutes for Figs. 4 and 5 (programs were written in Matlab). Consequently, it is better to use: $200<N<10^3$ in an adjustable way, depending on the training iteration number.

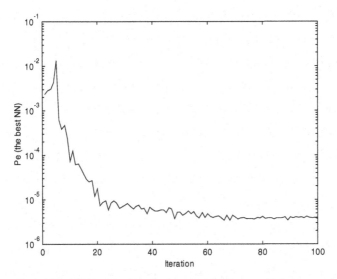

Fig. 2. Error Probability (*Pe*) versus iteration number for the neural detector training, using the Importance Sampling technique. An MLP of 5×5×1 nodes, and a genetic algorithm for training with 200 patterns (input sample vectors) in the first iterations and 1000 patterns in the last ones. The IS parameter $\theta^*=0$ (optimum for the IS pdf).

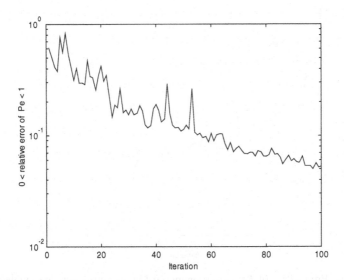

Fig. 3. Relative Error ($\hat{\varepsilon}_{P_e}$) of *Pe* (corresponding to Fig. 2) versus iteration number for the neural detector training, using the Importance Sampling technique. An MLP of 5×5×1 nodes, and a genetic algorithm for training under the conditions of Fig. 2.

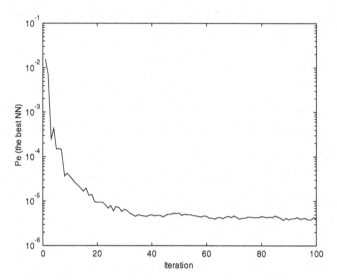

Fig. 4. Error Probability (*Pe*) versus iteration number for the neural detector training, using the Importance Sampling technique. An MLP of 5×5×1 nodes, and a genetic algorithm for training with 1000 patterns (input sample vectors) in each iteration. The IS parameter $\theta^*=0$ (optimum).

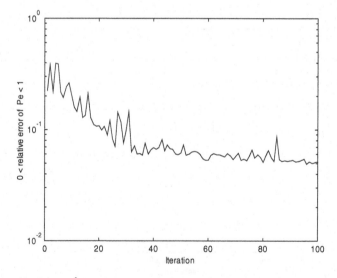

Fig. 5. Relative Error ($\hat{\varepsilon}_{p_e}$) of *Pe* (corresponding to Fig. 4) versus iteration number for the neural detector training, using the Importance Sampling technique. An MLP of 5×5×1 nodes, and a genetic algorithm for training under the conditions of Fig. 4.

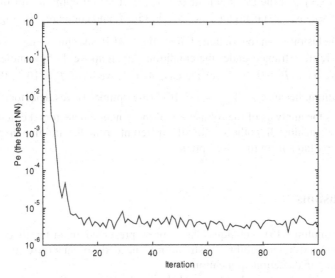

Fig. 6. Error Probability (*Pe*) versus iteration number for the neural detector training, using the Importance Sampling technique. An MLP of 5×5×1 nodes, and a genetic algorithm for training with 1000 patterns (input sample vectors) in each iteration. The IS parameter θ=1 (which is non-optimum for IS pdf).

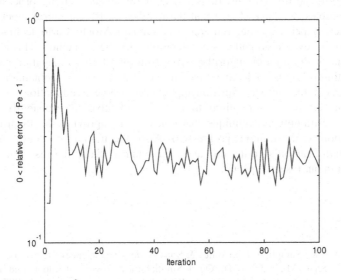

Fig. 7. Relative Error ($\hat{\varepsilon}_{P_e}$) of *Pe* (corresponding to Fig. 6) versus iteration number for the neural detector training, using the Importance Sampling technique. An MLP of 5×5×1 nodes, and a genetic algorithm for training under the conditions of Fig. 6.

In Figs. 6 and 7 we have considered the same conditions and parameters to those of Figs. 4 and 5, except for the IS parameter θ. Now, $\theta = 1$ is non-optimum for the IS pdf given by (11), because (13) is high ($\hat{\varepsilon}_{P_e^*} \approx 25\%$ in Fig. 7, and compare with Fig. 5).

Similar conclusions can be obtained for other MLP structures (e.g. 8×8×1 or 8×4×1, 10×5×1, etc.), trained under the conditions given above. For example, for the case 8×8×1, we have $P_e^* \approx 9 \cdot 10^{-9}$; for the case 8×4×1, we have $P_e^* \approx 10^{-8}$; then both are quasi-optimum, because $(P_e)_{\text{Bayes}} = 7.7 \cdot 10^{-9}$ (the optimal Bayes detector). Finally, another issue is the analysis of the robustness of these neural detectors, i.e. testing our neural detectors against hypotheses slightly different from the training hypotheses (analysis of departures from the assumptions).

4   Conclusions

Importance Sampling (IS) techniques have been presented in order to drastically accelerate "low error probability" estimations, needed to supervise the Neural Network training in detection applications.

Adequate modifications on the error probability objective function were realized in order to use standard training algorithms for neural detector training. This approach is useful in communications systems, where very low error probabilities are concerned. Also, generalizations to other types of objective functions are straightforward.

The suboptimal IS probability density function (biasing density function) corresponding to the trained conditions is useful for all the training process. From empirical examples, we have shown that the number of 10^7 (or more) input sample vectors (patterns) per iteration, required by standard Monte Carlo techniques, is reduced to 10^3 (or even less) patterns per iteration with the IS method. This reduction is independent of the training algorithm type. Note that back-propagation algorithm requires continuity of the objective function, so that its use is problematic in our application (due to the unit-step function appears in our objective function).

Finally, further work is required to consider adaptive IS probability density functions in the training (a technique that consists of improving the IS probability density function as the training progresses). Also, the training of neural detectors under Neyman-Pearson's criterion and Importance Sampling is now under consideration in our research group.

References

1.   Thompson, S.K.: Sampling. John Wiley & Sons (Wiley-Interscience), New York (1992).
2.   Smith, P.J., Shafi, M., and Gao, H.: Quick Simulation: A Review of Importance Sampling Techniques in Communications Systems. IEEE J. Select. Areas Commun., 1997, 15, (4), pp. 597-613.
3.   Chen, J.-C., Lu, D., Sadowsky, J.S., and Yao, K.: On Importance Sampling in Digital Communications—Part I: Fundamentals. IEEE J. Select. Areas Commun., 1993, 11, (3), pp. 289-299.

4. Al-Qaq, W.A., Devetsikiotis, M., and Townsend, J.K.: Stochastic Gradient Optimization of Importance Sampling for the Efficient Simulation of Digital Communication Systems. IEEE Trans. Commun., 1995, 43, (12), pp. 2975-2985.

5. Al-Qaq, W.A., and Townsend, J.K.: A Stochastic Importance Sampling Methodology for the Efficient Simulation of Adaptive Systems in Frequency Nonselective Rayleigh Fading Channels. IEEE J. Select. Areas Commun., 1997, 15, (4), pp. 614-625.

6. Gerlach, K.: New Results in Importance Sampling. IEEE Trans. Aerosp. Electron. Syst., 1999, 35, (3), pp. 917-925.

7. Orsak, G.C.: A Note on Estimating False Alarm Rates via Importance Sampling. IEEE Trans. Commun., 1993, 41, (9), pp. 1275-1277.

8. Orsak, G.C., and Aazhang, B.: Constrained Solutions in Importance Sampling via Robust Statistics. IEEE Trans. Inform. Theory, 1991, 37, (2), pp. 307-316.

9. Sadowsky, J.S., and Bucklew, J.A.: On Large Deviation Theory and Asymptotically Efficient Monte Carlo Estimation. IEEE Trans. Inform. Theory, 1990, 36, (3), pp. 579-588.

10. Sanz-González, J.L., and Andina, D.: Performance Analysis of Neural Network Detectors by Importance Sampling Techniques. Neural Processing Letters, 1999, 9, (3), pp. 257-269.

11. Andina, D., Sanz-González, J.L., and Jiménez-Pajares, A.: A Comparison of Criterion Functions for a Neural Network Applied to Binary Detection. Proc. of IEEE Int. Conf. on Neural Networks (ICNN'95), 1995, Vol. 1, pp. 329-333.

12. Poor, H.V.: An Introduction to Signal Detection and Estimation, (Second Edition) Springer-Verlag, Berlin (1994).

13. Van Trees, H.L.: Detection, Estimation, and Modulation Theory. Part. I. John Wiley & Sons, New York (1968).

14. Seijas, J. and Sanz-González, J.L.: Basic-Evolutive Algorithms for Neural Networks Architecture Configuration and Training. Proc. IEEE Int. Symp. Circuits Syst. (ISCAS'95), 1995, Vol. 1, pp. 125-130.

Induction of Qualitative Trees

Dorian Šuc[1] and Ivan Bratko[1]

Faculty of Computer and Information Science, University of Ljubljana,
Tržaška 25, 1000 Ljubljana, Slovenia
{dorian.suc, ivan.bratko}@fri.uni-lj.si

Abstract. We consider the problem of automatic construction of qualitative models by inductive learning from quantitative examples. We present an algorithm QUIN (QUalitative INduction) that learns *qualitative trees* from a set of examples described with numerical attributes. At difference with decision trees, the leaves of qualitative trees contain qualitative functional constraints as used in qualitative reasoning. A qualitative tree defines a partition of the attribute space into the areas with common qualitative behaviour of the chosen class variable.
We describe a basic algorithm for induction of qualitative trees, improve it to the heuristic QUIN algorithm, and give experimental evaluation of the algorithms on a set of artificial domains. QUIN has already been used to induce qualitative control strategies in dynamic domains such as controlling a crane or riding a bicycle (described elsewhere) and can be applied to other domains as a general tool for qualitative system identification.

1 Introduction

Various studies in recent years showed that for some tasks qualitative models are more suitable than classical quantitative (numerical) models. These tasks include diagnosis [1], generating explanation of the system's behaviour [7] and designing novel devices from first principles [17]. Qualitative reasoning about processes (QPT-Qualitative Process Theory) [8] and qualitative simulation (QSIM) [9] with Qualitative Differential Equations enable a kind of commonsense reasoning by abstracting numerical values into qualitative values and real functions into qualitative constraints.

Besides qualitative reasoning and qualitative simulation, qualitative models can also be used to guide machine learning [3] and offer a space for solution optimization [16,12]. However, building a qualitative model for a complex system requires significant knowledge and is a time-consuming process. For this reason, many researchers are addressing the problem of automatic generation of qualitative models. One approach is to build models from existing libraries of model fragments [8]. Another approach is to learn a model of a physical system from behaviours using existing knowledge of processes and mechanisms commonly found in physical systems [5]. Less knowledge-intensive approaches [4,2,6,10] use inductive learning of qualitative differential equations from a set of qualitative behaviours.

L. De Raedt and P. Flach (Eds.): ECML 2001, LNAI 2167, pp. 442–453, 2001.
© Springer-Verlag Berlin Heidelberg 2001

In this paper we present algorithm QUIN for induction of qualitative constraint trees from examples described with numerical attributes. At difference with decision trees, the leaves of qualitative trees contain qualitative functional constraints that are inspired by qualitative proportionality predicates Q_+ and Q_- as defined by Forbus [8]. This is a novel approach to automatic generation of qualitative models. To our knowledge, no study has yet addressed the induction of similar tree-structured qualitative constraints from numerical examples.

The motivation for learning of qualitative trees came from applications in reconstruction of human skill to control dynamic systems, such as a plane or a crane. Our experiments in controlling a crane [12] and double pendulum called acrobot [13], showed that qualitative strategies are suitable as explanatory models of human control skill and can be used as spaces for controller optimization. These qualitative strategies were obtained as abstractions of quantitative control strategies induced from the logged data from skilled human operators. The learning of qualitative trees *directly* from numerical examples is a natural extension of that approach.

The structure of the paper is as follows. First we give the learning problem description for induction of qualitative trees and define monotonicity constraints, called qualitatively constrained functions. Then we describe how qualitatively constrained functions are learned from a set of numeric examples. This provides the basis for induction of qualitative trees in Section 4. Finally, we give experimental evaluation of the algorithms on a set of artificial domains and conclude.

2   Learning Problem Description

2.1   Qualitative Trees

We consider the usual setting of classification learning, but in our case the hypothesis language involves *qualitative constraints*. Let there be N learning examples. Each example is described by $n + 1$ continuous variables $X_1, \ldots, X_{n+1}$. The variable X_{n+1} is called the *class*, and the others are called *attributes*.

Given the learning examples, our problem is to learn a hypothesis that separates the areas of attribute space which share a common qualitative behaviour of the class variable. We learn such hypotheses in the form of *qualitative trees*. A qualitative tree is a binary tree with internal nodes called splits and *qualitatively constrained functions* in the leaves. The splits define a partition of the state space into areas with common qualitative behaviour of the class variable. A split consists of a split attribute and a split value. Qualitatively constrained functions (abbreviated QCFs) in leaves define qualitative constraints on the class variable.

Fig. 1 shows an example of qualitative tree induced from a set of example points for the function $z = x^2 - y^2$.

2.2   Qualitatively Constrained Functions

Qualitatively constrained functions are inspired by the qualitative proportionality predicates Q_+ and Q_- as defined by Forbus [8] and are also a generalization

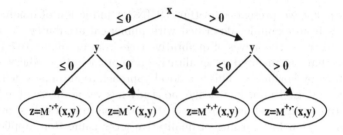

Fig. 1. A qualitative tree induced from a set of examples for the function $z = x^2 - y^2$. The rightmost leaf, applying when attributes x and y are positive, says that z is strictly increasing in its dependence on x and strictly decreasing in its dependence on y.

of the qualitative constraint M^+, as used in [9]. We use QCFs to define qualitative constraints on the class variable. A QCF constrains the qualitative change of the class variable in response to the qualitative changes of the attributes.

A *qualitatively constrained function* $M^{s_1,\ldots,s_m}: \Re^m \mapsto \Re$, $s_i \in \{+,-\}$ represents an arbitrary function with $m \leq n$ continuous attributes that respect the qualitative constraints given by signs s_i. The qualitative constraint given by sign $s_i = +$ ($s_i = -$) requires that the function is strictly increasing (decreasing) in its dependence on the i-th attribute. We say that the function is *positively related* (negatively related) to the i-th attribute. $M^{s_1,\ldots,s_m}$ represents any function which is, for all $i = 1,\ldots,m$ positively (negatively) related to the i-th argument, if $s_i = +$ ($s_i = -$).

Note that the qualitative constraint given by sign $s_i = +$ only states that when the i-th attribute increases, the QCF will also increase, *barring other changes*. It can happen that a QCF with the constraint $s_i = +$ decreases even if the i-th attribute increases, because of a change in another attribute. For example, consider the behaviour of gas pressure in a container: $Pres \times Vol/Temp = const$. We can express the qualitative behaviour of gas by QCF $Pres = M^{+,-}(Temp, Vol)$. This constraint allows that the pressure decreases even if the temperature increases, because of a change in the volume. Note however, that gas qualitative behaviour is not consistent with $Pres = M^+(Temp)$.

QCFs are concerned with qualitative changes and qualitative change vectors. *Qualitative change* q_j is the sign of change in continuous variable X_j, where $q_j \in \{pos, neg, zero\}$, corresponding to *positive, negative* or *zero* change. A *qualitative change vector* is a vector of qualitative changes of the variables. We define *QCF-prediction* $P(s_i, q_i)$ as:

$$P(s_i, q_i) = \begin{cases} \text{pos, if } (s_i = + \land q_i = pos) \lor (s_i = - \land q_i = neg) \\ \text{neg, if } (s_i = + \land q_i = neg) \lor (s_i = - \land q_i = pos) \\ \text{zero, otherwise} \end{cases}$$

A qualitative change vector $q = (q_1,\ldots,q_{n+1})$ is *consistent* with a given QCF $M^{s_1,\ldots,s_m}$, if the QCF does not reject the qualitative change of the class variable, that is, if either (a) class qualitative change is zero, (b) all attribute's QCF-predictions are zero, or (c) there exists an attribute whose QCF-prediction is equal to the class's qualitative change.

A QCF does not always uniquely predict the class's qualitative change given the qualitative changes of the attributes. *Qualitative ambiguity*, i.e. ambiguity in the class's qualitative change appears whenever there exist both positive and negative QCF-predictions or whenever all QCF-predictions are zero. In this case any qualitative class change is consistent with the QCF.

3   Learning Qualitatively Constrained Functions

When learning a QCF from a set of numerical examples we are interested in a QCF that is consistent with most of the examples, i.e. in the *"minimal cost"* QCF. For this reason we define *error-cost* $E(g)$ of a QCF g (defined later in Eq. 3) that penalizes g with inconsistent and ambiguous qualitative change vectors at every example. The "minimal cost" QCF is learned from a set of numerical examples by first forming qualitative change vectors from examples and then minimizing error-cost of a QCF over all possible QCFs.

First, every pair of examples e and $f \neq e$ is used to form a qualitative change vector with qualitative changes $q_{(e,f),j} \in \{pos, neg, zero\}$, $j = 1, \ldots, n+1$ defined as:

$$q_{(e,f),j} = \begin{cases} \text{pos, if } x_{f,j} > x_{e,j} + Tzero_j \\ \text{neg, if } x_{f,j} < x_{e,j} - Tzero_j \\ \text{zero, otherwise} \end{cases} \quad (1)$$

where $Tzero_j$ denotes a user-defined steady threshold defining negligible changes of j-th attribute. The default value of $Tzero_j$ is 1% of the difference between maximal and minimal value of j-th attribute. Typically, many pairs of examples map into the same qualitative change vector. A qualitative change vector is either consistent or not consistent with a given QCF. Note that a consistent qualitative change vector can also be ambiguous for a given QCF.

We illustrate the method to find the "minimal cost" QCF by an example of gas in the container. Fig. 2 gives five numerical examples described with attributes $Temp$ and Vol and class $Pres$, giving gas temperature, volume and pressure according to equation $Pres = 2\, Temp/Vol$. There are five numerical points, each with four qualitative change vectors with respect to other points. Fig. 2 illustrates qualitative change vectors q_1, q_2, q_3 and q_4 at the circled point $e=(Temp{=}315, Vol{=}56, Pres{=}11.25)$. To find the "minimal cost" QCF at point e, qualitative change vectors that are inconsistent and ambiguous with each possible QCF are counted. Consider for example QCF $Pres = M^+(Temp)$. Qualitative change vector $q_3=(q_{Temp}{=}neg, q_{Vol}{=}neg, q_{Pres}{=}pos)$ is not consistent with this QCF since the QCF-prediction of the only attribute $(P(+, q_{Temp}){=}neg)$ is different than the qualitative class change $q_{Pres}{=}pos$. Qualitative change vector $q_1=(q_{Temp}{=}zero, q_{Vol}{=}pos, q_{Pres}{=}neg)$ is ambiguous with respect to this QCF.

The table in Fig. 2 gives qualitative change vectors at point e that are inconsistent with and ambiguous for each possible QCF. QCF $M^{+,-}(Temp, Vol)$ is

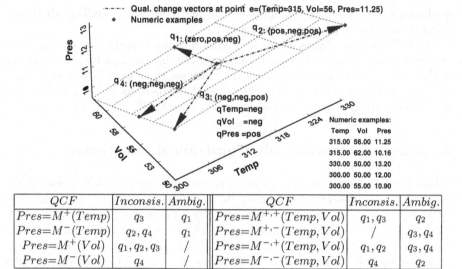

Fig. 2. Gas in the container example: five numerical examples are represented as points in the attribute space. The arrows denote the qualitative change vectors at the circled point e. For example, the point ($Temp$=300, Vol=50, $Pres$=12) gives qualitative change vector q_3=(q_{Temp}=neg, q_{Vol}=neg, q_{Pres}=pos) with point e. The table bellow gives qual. change vectors that are inconsistent and ambiguous for each possible QCF.

the only QCF consistent with all qualitative change vectors and is the "minimal cost" QCF. It also minimizes the error-cost (defined below) over all QCFs.

The error-cost of a QCF is based on the minimum description length principle [11]. Basically it is defined as the number of bits needed to code the QCF plus the number of bits to code the inconsistent and ambiguous qualitative change vectors as follows. Let $\mathcal{C}_e(q)$ and $n_e(q)$ denote respectively the set and the number of all examples f that form, with e, qualitative change vector q (with qualitative changes q_j):

$$\mathcal{C}_e(q) = \{f | \forall j = 1, \ldots, n+1 : q_{(e,f),j} = q_j\}, \quad n_e(q) = |\mathcal{C}_e(q)| \qquad (2)$$

In the above gas in the container example, the circled point e and qualitative change vector q_3 give $\mathcal{C}_e(q_3) = \{(Temp=300, Vol=50, Pres=12)\}$ and $n_e(q_3)=1$. The *error-cost* $E(g)$ of a QCF g that mentions m out of all n attributes is:

$$E(g) = \log_2 n + m(\log_2 n + 1) +$$
$$\log_2 N_{nonamb} + N_{reject}(\log_2 N_{nonamb}) + \log_2 N_{amb} + N_{amb} \qquad (3)$$

Here N_{reject} denotes the number of example pairs (e,f), $f \neq e$, that form a qualitative change vector that is not consistent with QCF g and is computed as the sum of $n_e(q)$ over all examples e and over all qualitative change vectors q that are not consistent with g. Similarly, N_{amb} and N_{nonamb} denote the sum of $n_e(q)$

of vectors q that are respectively ambiguous and not ambiguous for g. This error-cost is based on the following encoding: we code the QCF, the indexes of N_{reject} inconsistent qualitative change vectors (each index requires $\log_2 N_{nonamb}$ bits since ambiguous qualitative change vectors are always consistent) and one bit for each ambiguous qualitative change vector. Note that we specify just the signs of class changes for ambiguous qualitative change vectors and we do not need to specify which qualitative change vectors are ambiguous, since all qualitative change vectors of particular forms are ambiguous for a given QCF.

The given error-cost penalizes inconsistent and ambiguous qualitative change vectors formed from every pair of examples. We later define (Eq. 7) a different error-cost and refer to here defined error-cost also as *ep-QUIN error-cost* (ep standing for every pair).

4   Learning Qualitative Trees

Here we describe how a qualitative tree is learned from a set of numeric examples. The algorithm uses top-down greedy approach and is guided by error-cost of a QCF. We define two learning algorithms that use different error-costs. First we give ep-QUIN algorithm that uses error-cost defined in Section 3. Then we present an example showing the myopia of ep-QUIN algorithm and (in Section 4.3) give an improvement of ep-QUIN, i.e. QUIN algorithm.

4.1   Algorithm ep-QUIN

Algorithm ep-QUIN uses top-down greedy approach similar to the ID3 algorithm. Given the examples, ep-QUIN chooses the best split by comparing the partitions of the examples they generate: for every possible split, it splits the examples into two subsets, finds the "minimal cost" QCF in both subsets, and selects the split which minimizes the *tree error-cost* (defined below). It puts the best split in the root of the tree and recursively finds subtrees for the corresponding example subsets, until the best split does not improve the tree error-cost.

The *tree error-cost* of a leaf is the error-cost $E(g)$ (Eq. 3) of the QCF g that is induced from the examples in the leaf. The tree error-cost of an internal node is the sum of error-costs of both subsets plus the cost of the split, i.e. the number of bits needed to encode the split:

$$E_{tree} = E_{left} + E_{right} + SplitCost$$
$$SplitCost = \log_2 n + \log_2(Splits_i - 1)$$

$$(4)$$

Here E_{left} and E_{right} denote the error-costs in both subsets, n is the number of variables and $Splits_i$ is the number of possible splits for the split variable, i.e. the number of different values of the variable X_i.

4.2   An Example

Here we give a simple example showing the myopia of ep-QUIN's error-cost. Fig. 3 shows the learning dataset consisting of 12 learning examples with one

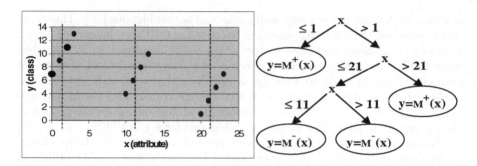

Fig. 3. Example partition and a qualitative tree induced by ep-QUIN. The points on the left figure give 12 learning examples with attribute x and class y. The vertical lines correspond to the example partition from the qualitative tree on the right.

attribute x and class y. The examples correspond to 3 linear functions that are increasing in its argument x:

$$y = \begin{cases} 2x + 7, & x = 0, 1, 2, 3 \\ 2x - 16, & x = 10, 11, 12, 13 \\ 2x - 39, & x = 20, 21, 22, 23 \end{cases} \quad (5)$$

Given these examples ep-QUIN algorithm proceeds as follows. It first finds the "most-consistent" QCF for the whole attribute space and then tries to reduce the error-cost by splitting the attribute space into subregions. There are 12 examples, therefore ep-QUIN forms $12 \times (12-1) = 132$ qualitative change vectors. With x as the only attribute there are only two possible QCFs: QCF $y = M^+(x)$ that is consistent with 50 (out of 132) qual. change vectors and $y = M^-(x)$ that is consistent with 82 qual. change vectors. Split minimizing ep-QUIN error-cost is $x \leq 1$, splitting the examples into two subsets. In the first subset ($x \leq 1$) there are only two examples, forming two qualitative change vectors, both consistent with $y = M^+(x)$. The second subset ($x > 1$) is then further divided, resulting in the qualitative tree given in Fig. 3. Note that the split at $x = 11$ splits the examples into two leaves with the same QCF $y = M^-(x)$. A split giving *the same leaves* would be unusual for decision trees, but is correct for qualitative trees since the split divides the examples into monotonic areas.

Clearly the induced qualitative tree is not optimal. We would prefer a qualitative tree with 3 leaves (each with QCF $y=M^+(x)$), that would divide the attribute space into 3 regions corresponding to definition areas of 3 linear functions. One reason is that ep-QUIN does not consider the *locality* of qualitative changes. A human observing Fig. 3 might notice 3 groups of near-by example points and consider the proximity of examples when estimating qualitative changes at a particular example point. In this way a qual. change of nearby points ($x=1$ and $x=2$ for example) would be weighted more than a qual. change of far-away points ($x=1$ and $x=13$). One might also consider the *consistency* of qualitative class change for a particular vector of qualitative attributes changes. One way to asses the consistency of qual. class change for a particular vector of qual. attributes changes q_x is to consider 3 nearest neighbors (ignoring the class distance) of a given point that form q_x with this point. Then the confidence in the positive class change (q_y=pos) for vector of qual. attributes changes q_x=pos at the point at x=0 would be higher than at the point at x=2 since all three corresponding neighbors (with q_x=pos) of the first point give positive class change, whereas the second point has one neighbor giving positive class change (point at x=3) and two neighbors giving negative class change (points at x=10,11). Here only neighbors giving q_x=pos with the reference point are considered since this is confidence for vector of qualitative attributes changes q_x=pos.

An improvement of ep-QUIN, algorithm QUIN follows this idea, i.e. it considers also the locality and consistency of qualitative change vectors. Note that QUIN algorithm, from this learning dataset, induces the above mentioned qualitative tree with 3 leaves, each with QCF y=$M^+(x)$.

4.3   Algorithm QUIN

QUIN is an improvement of the ep-QUIN algorithm that follows the ideas described in the example above. The algorithms differ in their error-cost. ep-QUIN's error-cost (Eq. 3) uses only counts of inconsistent and ambiguous qualitative change vectors. QUIN's error-cost (defined later in Eq. 7) uses heuristic confidence estimates of qualitative change vectors that take into account the proximity of examples and the consistency of qualitative change vectors.

The proximity of the examples e and f is evaluated by Gaussian weight $w(e, f) = e^{\frac{-d(e,f)}{2K^2}}$, where $d(e, f)$ is the normalized Euclidean distance of the examples that considers only the attributes of the two examples and K is a user-defined parameter with the default value computed as 10 % of maximal Euclidean distance of two examples from the learning dataset. By changing K, more (smaller K) or less importance is assigned to the distance between examples and therefore more local (smaller K) or more global estimates are used.

We say that example f is a q-$neighbor$ of example e if the qualitative change vector $q_{(e,f)}$ is equal to q in all the qualitative attribute changes (but not necessarily in the qualitative class change). Let $\mathcal{N}_e(q)$ denote the set of all q-neighbors of e and $\mathcal{N}_e^k(q)$ the set of k nearest q-neighbors of example e. The confidence estimate $w_e(q)$ of the qualitative change vector q at example e takes into account the proximity of the k nearest q-neighbors and the consistency of qualitative class change w.r.t. the k nearest q-neighbors. The intuition in estimates $w_e(q)$ is in modelling the local probability of qualitative class change q_{n+1} given the attribute's changes $q_i, i = 1, \ldots, n$:

$$\mathcal{N}_e(q) = \{f | \forall j = 1, \ldots, n : q_{(e,f),j} = q_j\}$$
$$\mathcal{N}_e^k(q) = \text{set of } k \text{ examples } f \in \mathcal{N}_e(q) \text{ minimizing } d(e, f)$$
$$\mathcal{C}_e^k(q) = \{f \in \mathcal{N}_e^k(q) | q_{(e,f),n+1} = q_{n+1}\} \tag{6}$$
$$w_e(q) = \frac{1}{|\mathcal{N}_e^k(q)|} \sum_{f \in \mathcal{C}_e^k(q)} w(e, f)$$

Here $\mathcal{C}_e^k(q)$ denotes the set of k nearest q-neighbors of e with the qualitative class change equal as in q and k is a user-defined parameter with the default value 5. Note that using $\left|\mathcal{N}_e^k(q)\right|$ in denominator penalizes estimate $w_e(q)$ if nearest q-neighbors of e differ in qualitative class change.

Lets consider the example in Fig. 3. Suppose that e_0 and e_2 are respectively the points at $x=0$ and $x=2$. Then for qualitative change vector $q=(pos, pos)$ the set $\mathcal{N}_{e_2}^3(q)$ are the examples at $x=3,10,11$ and $\mathcal{C}_{e_2}^3(q)$ is the example at $x=3$. The confidence estimate $w_{e_2}(q)$ is one third $(1/\left|\mathcal{N}_{e_2}^3(q)\right|)$ of the Gaussian weight $w(e_2, f)$ that evaluates the proximity of examples e_2 and the example at $x=3$. The sets $\mathcal{N}_{e_0}^3(q)$ and $\mathcal{C}_{e_0}^3(q)$ are the examples at $x=1,2,3$. Therefore qualitative change vector $q=(pos, pos)$ has higher confidence estimate at e_0 than at e_2.

QUIN's error-cost is similar to ep-QUIN's error-cost, but with QUIN's error-cost the qualitative change vectors q are weighted according to their confidence estimates $w_e(q)$ (Eq. 6). Because of this weighting QUIN's error-cost is heuristic and does not correspond to a particular coding of examples. The error-cost $E(g)$ of a QCF g that mentions m out of all n attributes is:

$$E(g) = \log_2 n + m(\log_2 n + 1) + \\ \log_2 W_{nonamb} + W_{reject}(\log_2 W_{nonamb}) + \log_2 W_{amb} + W_{amb} \tag{7}$$

Here W_{reject} denotes the sum (over all examples e) of estimates $w_e(q)$ of qualitative change vectors q that are not consistent with g. Similarly W_{amb} and W_{nonamb} denote the sum of estimates $w_e(q)$ of vectors q that are respectively ambiguous and not ambiguous for g.

Besides the improved error-cost, QUIN uses also a more efficient algorithm for selecting the "minimal cost" QCF. ep-QUIN finds the "minimal cost" QCF by a simple exhaustive search algorithm that forms all possible QCFs and selects the one with the smallest error-cost. This requires the number of error-cost computations that is exponential in the number of attributes. Instead of the exhaustive search, QUIN uses a greedy heuristic algorithm that requires the number of error-cost computations that is quadratic in the number of attributes, but does not guarantee the "minimal cost" QCF. The idea is to start with the QCF that minimizes error-cost over all QCFs that use only one attribute, and then use error-cost to refine the current QCF with another attribute.

5   Experimental Evaluation of QUIN Algorithm

Here we experimentally evaluate learning qualitative trees from numerical examples on a set of artificial domains. Since the usual error measures, such as accuracy or mean squared error, are not suitable for qualitative models, we define *qualitative tree performance* as a measure of qualitative tree prediction error. Then we describe the details of our experiments and give results.

We define *qualitative tree performance* as a pair of *qualitative consistency* and *qualitative ambiguity*, that are the percentages of qualitative change vectors that are respectively consistent with, and ambiguous for a qualitative tree. The examples are partitioned according to the splits of the tree and for each example

Table 1. Experimental results: the second column gives the description of the domains, i.e. the class variables c as the function of uniformly distributed attributes. The third column gives qualitative performance of the optimal qualitative tree. The fourth and the fifth column give qualitative performance of trees induced by ep-QUIN and QUIN.

Domain	Class variable	Optimal	ep-QUIN	QUIN
Sin	$c = \sin(\pi \times \frac{x}{10})$	100/6	100.0/6.4	100.0/5.8
$SinLn$	$c = \frac{x}{10} + sign(x) \times \sin(\pi \times \frac{x}{10}))$	100/4	96.2/11.8	**98.7/3.1**
$Poli$	$c = \ln(10^4 + |(x+16)(x+5)(x-5)(x-16)|)$	100/10	96.9/27.4	**96.4/6.3**
$Signs$	$c = \begin{cases} sign(u+0.5)(x-10)^2, & \text{if } v \geq 0 \\ sign(u-0.5)(y+10)^2, & \text{otherwise} \end{cases}$	100/2	93.2/19.4	**97.4/8.1**
$QuadA$	$c = x^2 - y^2$	100/44	99.0/27.1	**99.7/33.9**
$QuadB$	$c = (x-5)^2 - (y-10)^2$	100/44	98.3/17.4	99.7/27.2
$SQuadB$	$c = sign(u)((x-5)^2 - (y-10)^2)$	100/38	96.6/32.7	98.0/31.1
$YSinX$	$c = y\sin(\pi \times \frac{x}{10})$	100/39	94.0/62.0	**81.6/12.4**

partition the qualitative change vectors are formed. Consistency is the percentage of qualitative change vectors that are consistent with QCFs in the corresponding leaves. Ambiguity is the percentage of qualitative change vectors which give ambiguous QCF-prediction in the corresponding leaves.

When giving the qualitative tree performance we use the notation c/a, where c denote the consistency and a ambiguity of a qual. tree on the example set. We prefer a qual. tree with high consistency and low ambiguity. However, low ambiguity is not possible when many attributes are used in the same QCF.

Ambiguity is used in qualitative tree performance since consistency of the qualitative tree does not give full information about the qualitative tree prediction strength. Consider for example a dataset with two attributes x_1 and x_2 that are pairwise equal for all the examples. Then QCF $M^{+,-}(x_1, x_2)$ is consistent with all the examples, but is not useful in predicting qualitative class change, since it is also ambiguous for any qualitative change vector from the dataset. The qualitative tree performance would in this case be 100%/100%.

The learning algorithms were evaluated on a set of artificial domains with uniformly distributed attributes $x, y \in [-20, 20]$ and $u, v \in [-1, 1]$. The class variables c, i.e. the variables to be predicted by a qualitative trees were computed as given in Table 1. For learning we used just the relevant attributes plus 2 uniformly distributed (noise) attributes that do not affect the class value.

To compare qualitative performance of the trees produced by the two algorithms we used learning sets consisting of 200 examples and a separate test set consisting of 500 examples. The results in Table 1 are averages of 10 runs. The table also gives the qualitative performance of the *optimal qualitative trees*, i.e. the smallest trees with 100% consistency. An example of such optimal qualitative tree for the domain $QuadA$ is given on Fig. 1. Note that the ambiguity of the optimal trees is not zero. This is either because QCFs in leaves use more than one attribute or because of zero change of all the attributes used in a QCF.

On most of the domains, QUIN has better qualitative performance, i.e. higher qualitative consistency and lower ambiguity. Usually QUIN induces a "near-optimal" tree, i.e. small tree with consistency over 96%. The exception is the domain $YSinX$ where the optimal tree has 16 leaves. ep-QUIN and QUIN fail to find a "near-optimal" tree in this domain.

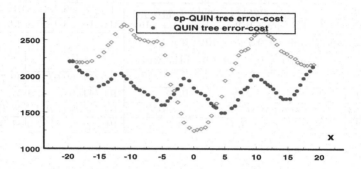

Fig. 4. ep-QUIN's and QUIN's criterion of split goodness (i.e. tree error-cost) for attribute x in domain Sin. Note that x values with minima of QUIN's error cost (x=5,-5,-15, 15) correspond to points dividing $sin(\pi x/10)$ into monotonic areas.

When we compared the trees induced by ep-QUIN and QUIN, we observed that QUIN trees are usually smaller and better correspond to the human intuition. An example is the domain Sin where QUIN usually induces optimal tree with 5 leaves, whereas ep-QUIN induces larger tree. Fig. 4 gives ep-QUIN's and QUIN's tree error-cost for the only relevant attribute x in the domain Sin. Both algorithms put the split that minimizes the tree error-cost in the root of the qualitative tree. Minima of QUIN tree error-cost (x=5,-5,-15, 15) correspond to splits dividing $sin(\pi x/10)$ into monotonic areas, whereas minimum of ep-QUIN tree error-cost (x=0) is not a good split since it splits a monotonic area $x \in [-5, 5]$. QUIN puts the split $x \leq 5$ in the root of the qualitative tree, whereas ep-QUIN chooses a suboptimal split $x \leq 0$ as the topmost split.

6   Conclusions

We presented the QUIN algorithm for induction of qualitative trees and evaluated it on a set of artificial domains. To our knowledge, no study has yet addressed the induction of similar tree-structured qualitative constraints from numerical examples. QUIN, a heuristic improvement of the basic ep-QUIN algorithm, usually produces preferable qualitative trees and is more time-efficient. Our experiments described here and in [14] show that QUIN can handle noisy data, and, at least in simple domains, produces qualitative trees that correspond to human intuition.

In [14,15] QUIN has already been used to induce qualitative control strategies in dynamic domains such as controlling a crane or riding a bicycle. In both domains some surprising and non-trivial aspects of human control skill have been induced. QUIN can be applied to other domains as a general tool for qualitative system identification.

Acknowledgements. The work reported in this paper was partially supported by the European Fifth Framework project Clockwork and the Slovenian Ministry of Education, Science and Sport.

References

1. Bratko, I., Mozetič, I., Lavrač, N.: *KARDIO: a Study in Deep and Qualitative Knowledge for Expert Systems.* MIT Press (1989).
2. Bratko, I., Muggleton, S., Varšek, A.: Learning qualitative models of dynamic systems. In *Proc. of the 8th Int. Conf. on Machine Learning* (1991).
3. Clark, P., Matwin, S.: Using qualitative models to guide inductive learning. In *Proc. 10th Int. Conf. on Machine Learning*, 49–56. Morgan Kaufmann (1993).
4. Coiera, E.: Generating qualitative models from example behaviours. *Technical Report Technical report 8901*, University of New South Wales (1989).
5. Doyle, R.: *Hypothesizing Device Mechanisms: Opening Up the Black Box.* Ph.D. Dissertation, Massachusetts Institute of Technology (1988).
6. Džeroski, S., Todorovski, L.: Discovering dynamics. In *Proceedings of the 10th International Conference on Machine Learning* 97–103. Morgan Kaufmann (1993).
7. Falkenhainer, B., Forbus, K.: Self explananatory simulations: an integration of qualitative and quantitative knowledge. In *Proceedings of the 4th International Workshop on Qualitative Physics* (1990).
8. Forbus, K.: Qualitative process theory. *Artificial Intelligence* (1984) 24:85–168.
9. Kuipers, B. J.: Qualitative simulation. *Artificial Intelligence* (1986) 29:289–338.
10. Richards, B., Kraan, I., Kuipers, B: Automatic abduction of qualitative models. In *Proc. of the National Conf. on Artificial Inteligence.* AAAI/MIT Press (1992).
11. Rissanen, J.: Modelling by shortest data description. *Automatica* (1978) 14:465–471.
12. Šuc, D., Bratko, I.: Symbolic and qualitative reconstruction of control skill. *Electronic Transactions on Artificial Intelligence, Section B* (1999) 3:1–22. http://www.ep.liu.se/ej/etai/1999/002/.
13. Šuc, D., Bratko, I.: Skill modelling through symbolic reconstruction of operator's trajectories. *IEEE Transaction on Systems, Man and Cybernetics, Part A* (2000), 30(06):617–624.
14. Šuc, D: *Machine reconstruction of human control strategies.* Ph.D. Dissertation, Faculty of Computer and Information Sc., University of Ljubljana, Slovenia (2001). http://ai.fri.uni-lj.si/dorian/MLControl/MLControl.htm.
15. Šuc, D., Bratko, I: Qualitative induction. In *Proceedings of the 15th International Workshop on Qualitative Reasoning* (2001). Accepted for publishing.
16. Varšek, A., Urbančič, T., Filipič, B.: Genetic algorithms in controller design and tuning. *IEEE Trans. on Systems, Man and Cybernetics* (1993), 23(6):1330–1339.
17. Williams, B.: Interaction-based invention: designing devices from first principles. In *Proceedings of the 4th International Workshop on Qualitative Physics* (1990).

Text Categorization Using Transductive Boosting

Hirotoshi Taira[1] and Masahiko Haruno[2]

[1] NTT Communication Science Laboratories
2-4, Hikaridai, Seika-cho, Soraku-gun
Kyoto 619-0237, Japan
`taira@cslab.kecl.ntt.co.jp`
[2] Advanced Telecommunications Research Institute International
2-2, Hikaridai, Seika-cho, Soraku-gun
Kyoto 619-0288, Japan
`mharuno@isd.atr.co.jp`

Abstract. In natural language tasks like text categorization, we usually have an enormous amount of unlabeled data in addition to a small amount of labeled data. We present here a transductive boosting method for text categorization in order to make use of the large amount of unlabeled data efficiently. Our experiments show that the transductive method outperforms conventional boosting techniques that employ only labeled data.

1 Introduction

We can easily access vast quantities of online information with the rapid growth of the Internet and the increase in computing power. However, the more information we can access, the more difficult it becomes to get necessary and sufficient information. Automatic *text categorization* has attracted a lot of attention among researchers and companies as a measure to extract the necessary and sufficient information efficiently.

The approach of machine learning has recently become popular for text categorization since it can create text classifiers with a high accuracy and without difficulty even if the target text is large and updated frequently. In this approach, inductive methods have played a central role in discriminating unlabeled test data with classifiers constructed from a priori labeled training data. For instance, k-nearest-neighbor [17], Rocchio [12], decision trees [7], Naive-Bayes [7], and SVM [5,1,15] have been applied to text categorization and have achieved remarkable success.

However, the inductive approach can not guarantee a high enough accuracy when there is a great difference between the training and test data distributions. The problem becomes extremely serious if the amount of training data is small. This is often the case under many practical conditions such as the classification of online Internet texts. Therefore, it is reasonable to utilize the unlabeled test data distribution for training as well as the distribution of a small number of

L. De Raedt and P. Flach (Eds.): ECML 2001, LNAI 2167, pp. 454–465, 2001.
© Springer-Verlag Berlin Heidelberg 2001

labeled training data. Nigam et al. proposed an EM-based method with Naive-Bayes to take account of the distribution of test data under the situation of a small amount of training data [11]. Although the method shows substantial improvements over the performance of the standard Naive Bayes classifier, one of its limitations is the nature that it sometimes obtains a local optimum.

In contrast, Joachims adapted a transductive method to Support Vector Machines (SVM) [6] and obtained significant improvements in the classification performance. Transduction is a general learning framework that minimizes classification errors only for the test data, while induction tries to minimize classification errors for both the training and test data [16]. Transductive SVM (TSVM) achieves a high performance by assuming that the portion of unlabeled examples to be classified into the positive class is determined by the ratio of positive and negative examples in the training data. Accordingly, the possibility of a performance decrease remains under different but typical conditions when the ratio of positive and negative examples in the training data is very different from that in the test data, e.g., a classifier learned by articles in 1995, classifies articles related to the Internet in 2000.

Like SVM, AdaBoost [3,2] is an alternative large margin classifier recently noted for its high generalization ability in NLP applications [4,13]. It produces highly accurate classification rules by combining a number of weak hypotheses, each of which is only moderately accurate. The advantage of AdaBoost over SVM is that we can choose any classifier suitable for our own classification applications. Since the original AdaBoost is an inductive learning method, we propose here a novel transductive boosting algorithm to cope with a small number of training data; in particular, the condition where the ratio of positive and negative examples greatly differs between the training and test data. Our experimental results demonstrate that the proposed algorithm not only outperforms SVM and AdaBoost but is also comparative and sometimes superior to TSVM. The advantage of the method is significant when the number of training data is small and the ratio of positive examples to negative ones in the training data is different from that in the test data. These results confirm that the usefulness of the transductive approach is not limited to SVM but is also effective for a variety of learning methods.

The remainder of the paper is organized as follows. The next section introduces AdaBoost and its global error analysis. After briefly describing how boosting can be regarded as a gradient descent method in a function space, we show how a transductive method can be adapted to AdaBoost. We then report our experimental results on a text categorization task using Japanese newspaper articles and discuss these results. The last section concludes the paper.

2   Boosting

2.1   AdaBoost Algorithm

Boosting became popular for practical use after Freund and Schapire proposed the AdaBoost algorithm [2]. We briefly introduce AdaBoost here.

(step 1) Given m training samples $(\boldsymbol{x}_1, y_1), ..., (\boldsymbol{x}_m, y_m)$ with feature vectors $\boldsymbol{x}_1, ..., \boldsymbol{x}_m$ and classification classes $y_1, ..., y_m$ (+1 for positive, −1 for negative).

Initialize the weights for training data $D_1(i) = \frac{1}{m}$, where $i = 1, ..., m$

(step 2) For $t = 1, ..., T$, repeat (step 3)-(step 5).

(step 3) A weak learner learns the training data under weight D_t, and we get weak hypothesis $h_t(\boldsymbol{x})$, which outputs +1 for a positive evaluation for $\boldsymbol{x} = \boldsymbol{x}_i$; −1 for a negative evaluation.

(step 4) Calculate parameter α_t based on $\alpha_t = \frac{1}{2} \ln(\frac{1-\epsilon_t}{\epsilon_t})$, where ϵ_t denotes weighted error rates calculated based on $\epsilon_t = \sum_{i:h_t(\boldsymbol{x}_i) \neq y_i} D_t(i)$.

(step 5) Update every weight of the training data based on the following,

$$D_{t+1}(i) = \frac{D_t(i) \exp(-\alpha_t y_i h_t(\boldsymbol{x}_i))}{Z_t}$$

where Z_t, the normalized factor for $\sum_{i=1}^{m} D_{t+1}$, equals 1.

(step 6) Return the final hypothesis, merging weak hypotheses linearly as,

$$H(\boldsymbol{x}) = \sum_{t=1}^{T} \alpha_t h_t(\boldsymbol{x}) \quad .$$

AdaBoost produces a weak hypothesis for a round and updates weights for the training data T times ($t = 1, ..., T$). As we can see based on (step 5), weight $D_t(i)$ is multiplied by $\exp(-\alpha_t)$ when data i is classified correctly by the weak hypothesis (that is, when $h_t(\boldsymbol{x}_i) = y_i$); it is multiplied by $\exp(\alpha_t)$ when data i is classified incorrectly (that is, when $h_t(\boldsymbol{x}_i) \neq y_i$). When error rates ϵ_t are less than 50%, parameter α_t takes a positive value based on (step 4). The weights of the data learned incorrectly are multiplied by a number larger than one and the learners learn weak hypotheses to focus on their data in the next round. Finally, in (step 6), the learners combine all of the weak learners weighted by parameter α_t, and the final classifier $H(\boldsymbol{x})$ is obtained.

Schapire et al. introduced the idea of "margin" and analyzed global errors of AdaBoost (that is, classification errors for unlabeled test data) [14]. The margin for training data in boosting is determined as $y \sum_t \alpha_t h_t(\boldsymbol{x}) / \sum_t \alpha_t$. When α_t is normalized as $\sum_t \alpha_t = 1$, the margin equals $yH(\boldsymbol{x})$. If we can take larger margins, the global errors become smaller [14].

3   Transductive Methods and Text Categorization

3.1   The Transductive Method Used in TSVM

We illustrate the transductive SVM (TSVM) and the novel transductive boosting in Figure 1. The circles, crosses, and triangles denote positive training data, negative training data, and unlabeled test data, respectively. TSVM produces separated hyperplanes by finding the positive examples closest to the negative side and the negative examples closest to the positive side. The "margin" of

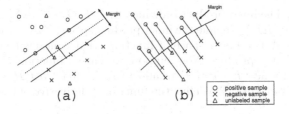

Fig. 1. TSVM (a) and Transductive Boosting (b).

TSVM is defined as the distance between two separated hyperplanes. TSVM chooses separated hyperplanes such that they maximize the margins while allowing classification errors below some fixed rate.

TSVM first produces a classifier using only the training data by SVM. All of the test data are given temporary classes by the classifier. The classifiers, after that, are iteratively constructed by focusing only on the temporary labeled data. As the figure shows, if they can find a pair of positive and negative examples near the classification boundary such that an exchange of their temporary classes decreases the classification errors, they exchange their classes and re-learn the classifier by SVM. They repeat the exchange of classes and re-learning until there is no pair of test data for which labels have to be exchanged, and they finally obtain a hyperplane fitting the distribution of the test data.

On the other hand, the margin in boosting is the sum of the distances between every training data and optimal classification bound, such as the right side of Figure 1. Boosting tries to maximize the average of all margins. Our transductive method labels the one most reliable example at every round as described in the following sections.

3.2   Explanation of Boosting Using Gradient Descent Methods

Recently, it has become clear that boosting can be regarded as an algorithm that chooses a weak hypothesis in the direction of the gradient descent of cost functions in a function space [9].

Mason et al. stated that the AdaBoost algorithm corresponds to an algorithm that minimizes a cost function of the $\exp(-M)$ type in MarginBoost, where M is the margin. The cost function of the AdaBoost algorithm is

$$Cost(H(\boldsymbol{x})) = \frac{1}{m} \sum_{i=1}^{m} \exp(-y_i H(\boldsymbol{x}_i)).$$

The cost is taken as an average of margins for a power function measure. As a result, a larger cost is evaluated for classification errors for example. Minimizing the value of this cost function corresponds to maximizing the margins and also corresponds to minimizing the global errors as mentioned in the previous section.

Let us consider a class $\mathcal{H}$ of weak classifiers $h : X \to \{+1, -1\}$ (where X is the space of feature vectors). $lin(\mathcal{H})$ is the set of all linear combinations of the functions in $\mathcal{H}$. The inner product is defined by $< F, G >\overset{\text{def}}{=} \frac{1}{m} \sum_{i=1}^{m} F(\boldsymbol{x}_i)G(\boldsymbol{x}_i)$ for all $F, G \in lin(\mathcal{H})$. We define the inner product space $(\mathcal{X}, <, >)$ using the inner product, where $\mathcal{X}$ is a linear space of functions that contains $lin(\mathcal{H})$, and $<, >$ stands for the inner product. Now suppose we have a function $H \in lin(\mathcal{H})$ and we wish to find a new $h \in lin(\mathcal{H})$ to add to H so that $Cost(H + \epsilon h)$ decreases for some small value of ϵ. We define the functional derivative of the cost function of H as

$$\nabla Cost(H)(\boldsymbol{x}) \overset{\text{def}}{=} \left. \frac{\partial Cost(H + \alpha 1_x)}{\partial \alpha} \right|_{\alpha=0}$$

where 1_x is the indicator function of $\boldsymbol{x}$. The cost function can be expanded to the first order in ϵ,

$$Cost(H + \epsilon h) = Cost(H) + \epsilon < \nabla Cost(H), h > .$$

Here, we can use the gradient descent method. That is, the greatest reduction in cost will occur for the h maximizing $- < \nabla Cost(H), h >$. After all, we wish to find h_{t+1}, α_{t+1} to minimize

$$\sum_{i=1}^{m} Cost(y_i H_t(\boldsymbol{x}_i) + y_i \alpha_{t+1} h_{t+1}(\boldsymbol{x}_i))$$

in the function space to get the weak hypothesis h_{t+1} at round t.

3.3   The Transductive Boosting Method

Let us consider the minimization of the cost function mentioned in the former section in the framework of transductive methods. The cost function, including n test examples $\boldsymbol{x}_{m+1}, ..., \boldsymbol{x}_{m+n}$, is described as

$$Cost(H(\boldsymbol{x})) = \frac{1}{m + n} \{ \sum_{i=1}^{m} \exp(-y_i H(\boldsymbol{x}_i))$$

$$+ \sum_{j=m+1}^{m+n} \exp(-y_j^* H(\boldsymbol{x}_j)) \}$$

where y_j^* is a temporary class label for $\boldsymbol{x}_j$. y_j^* is unknown, and the initial value of y_j^* is stored with 0. This algorithm aims to label +1(positive) or −1(negative) correctly for y_j^*. In the early rounds, the accuracy of the classifiers combining linearly weak learners is low because the learning is not sufficient unlike in SVM. If we label the classes for y_j^* based on these classifiers, incorrect labels are labeled to the data at a high ratio. Then, if boosting is performed with this large amount of wrongly labeled test data, an incorrect gradient descent is obtained, and moreover, the accuracy of the final classifier is low. We should perform labeling for the test data at a high accuracy.

Therefore, in every round, we label the class for only the most reliable test data. We label this class supposing that the ratio of positive and negative examples is the same as the ratio of positive and negative examples in the training data. For the test data, we add (step 2) and (step 7) to the AdaBoost algorithm in section 2.1 as follows.

(**step 1**) Given m training samples $(\boldsymbol{x}_1, y_1), ..., (\boldsymbol{x}_m, y_m)$ with feature vectors $\boldsymbol{x}_1, ..., \boldsymbol{x}_m$ and classification classes $y_1, ..., y_m$ (+1 for positive, -1 for negative).
Initialize the weights for training data $D_1(i) = \frac{1}{m}$, where $i = 1, ..., m$.

(**step 2**) Given n test samples $(\boldsymbol{x}_{m+1}, y^*_{m+1}), ..., (\boldsymbol{x}_{m+n}, y^*_{m+n})$ with feature vectors $\boldsymbol{x}_{m+1}, ..., \boldsymbol{x}_{m+n}$ and classification classes $y^*_{m+1}, ..., y^*_{m+n}$ whose initial values are 0.
Initialize the weights for test data $D_1(j) = 0$ $(j = m + 1, ..., m + n)$.

(**step 3**) For $t = 1, ..., T$, repeat (step 4)-(step 7)

(**step 4**) A weak learner learns labeled data (that is, $y_i \neq 0$) under weight D_t, and we get weak hypothesis $h_t(\boldsymbol{x})$, which outputs $+1$ for a positive evaluation for $\boldsymbol{x} = \boldsymbol{x}_i$; -1 for a negative evaluation.

(**step 5**) Calculate parameter α_t based on $\alpha_t = \frac{1}{2}\ln(\frac{1-\epsilon_t}{\epsilon_t})$, where ϵ_t denotes weighted error rates calculated based on $\epsilon_t = \sum_{i:h_t(\boldsymbol{x}_i) \neq y_i} D_t(i)$.

(**step 6**) Update every weight of the training data based on the following,

$$D_{t+1}(i) = \frac{D_t(i)\exp(-\alpha_t y_i h_t(\boldsymbol{x}_i))}{Z_t}$$

where Z_t, the normalized factor for $\sum_{i=1}^{m} D_{t+1}$, equals 1.

(**step 7**) Let m^+ be the number of training data with a positive class, $n_{labeled}$ be the number of test data with an already labeled class, and $n^+_{labeled}$ be the number of test data with an already labeled positive class.

(i) If $n_{labeled} = 0$ or $m^+/m \geq n^+_{labeled}/n_{labeled}$, then we choose the test sample j that maximizes

$$H(\boldsymbol{x}_j) = \sum_{k=1}^{t} \alpha_k h_k(\boldsymbol{x}_j)$$

in the test data such that $y_j = 0$, and give $y_j = +1$ and $D_{t+1}(j) = \epsilon$ (ϵ is a small value, for example, $\epsilon = 0.01$). Then, we update the weight of the data already labeled as follows,

$$D_{t+1}(i) = \frac{D_t(i)}{Z'_t}.$$

Here, Z'_t is the normalizing factor such that the sum of the data without j equals $1 - \epsilon$.

(ii) If $n_{labeled} \neq 0$ and $m^+/m < n^+_{labeled}/n_{labeled}$, then we choose the test sample j that minimizes

$$H(\boldsymbol{x}_j) = \sum_{k=1}^{t} \alpha_k h_k(\boldsymbol{x}_j)$$

in the test data such that $y_j = 0$, and give $y_j = -1$ and $D_{t+1}(j) = \epsilon$. Then, we update the weight of the data already labeled as follows,

$$D_{t+1}(i) = \frac{D_t(i)}{Z'_t}.$$

Here, Z'_t is the normalizing factor such that the sum of the data without j equals $1 - \epsilon$.

(**step 8**) Return the final hypothesis, merging weak hypotheses linearly as,

$$H(\boldsymbol{x}) = \sum_{t=1}^{T} \alpha_t h_t(\boldsymbol{x}) \quad .$$

(step 2) is for initializing the labels and weights of the test samples. (step 7) is for performing labeling such that the ratio of positive and negative test samples always equals that of the training data. A small value is given for the weight to test samples selected at this step, because the reliability of the labels is lower than that of the training samples.

Taking these steps can produce classifiers minimizing the value of the cost function because we can select data to lower the probability of labeling y_j^* wrongly and can choose data to maximize $y_j^* H(\boldsymbol{x}_j)$ at a round in the hill-climbing way with the term of $\exp(-y_j^* H(\boldsymbol{x}_j))$ in the cost function (Figure 2).

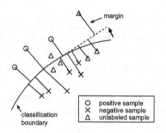

Fig. 2. The effect of unlabeled samples.

As another option of our algorithm, we can use the algorithm after weak learners are produced using only labeled data several times. We can also choose to label several test examples per round by executing (step 7) several times per round, although the algorithm would need more iterations than the number of test examples.

4   Experimental Results

4.1   Experimental Settings

Our experiments were conducted using the RWCP corpus, which contains 30,207 newspaper articles taken from the Mainichi Shinbun Newspaper published in 1994 [8]. Each article was assigned multiple UDC (Universal Decimal Classification) codes, each of which represented a category of the articles. UDC is a hierarchical classification system and has about 60,000 main categories. The text collection has a total of 97,095 categories among which there are 14,407 different categories, i.e., 3.2 categories per article.

In the remainder of this paper, we focus on the ten categories that appeared most often in the corpus: [1] sports, criminal law, government, education, traffic, military affairs, international relations, communications, theater, and agriculture. We made binary classifiers for each of the categories whether a sample belonged to the category or not. The total number of articles used for both the training and the test was 1,000. Table 1 summarizes the numbers of training and test articles in each category. These articles were word-segmented and part

Table 1. RWCP corpus for training and test.

Category	training articles	test articles
sports	161	147
criminal law	156	148
government	135	142
educational system	110	124
traffic	112	103
military affairs	110	118
international relations	96	97
communications	76	83
theater	86	95
agriculture	78	72

of speech tagged by the Japanese morphological analyzing system Chasen [10]. This process generated 20,490 different words. Throughout our experiments, 1000 words with high mutual information were used as the input feature space because they were keywords sufficient enough to characterize the classes.

The mutual infomation (MI) between a word t and a category c is defined as follows,

$$MI(t, c) = \sum_{t \in \{0,1\}} \sum_{c} P(t, c) \log \frac{P(t, c)}{P(t)P(c)}.$$

MI becomes large when the occurrence of t is biased to one side between category c and other categories. Consequently, the words with high mutual information in category c can be considered as keywords in the category.

The iteration T was 1000 in all of our experiments. The value of 0.01 was used for ϵ in transductive AdaBoost. The value for each feature was a binary value, which indicated whether the word appeared in a document or not. This binary value was employed to study the pure effects of each word.

4.2   The Evaluation Method

The F-measure was used for the evaluation measure. For every classification, we can calculate

---

[1] The results for other categories were very similar to these 10 categories.

a = (the number of data the classifier evaluates positive for positive data),
b = (the number of data the classifier evaluates positive for negative data),
c = (the number of data the classifier evaluates negative for positive data).
Then, we can calculate the precision (P) and recall (R) as

$$P = \frac{a}{a+b}, \quad R = \frac{a}{a+c}.$$

By combining the precision and recall, the F-measure is defined as follows:

$$F = \frac{1 + \beta^2}{\frac{1}{P} + \beta^2 \frac{1}{R}}.$$

The F-measure varies between 0 and 1. The larger the F-measure becomes, the higher the classification accuracy gets. β is a weight parameter and we set $\beta = 1$.

4.3   Relation between the Number of Training Data and the Accuracy

First, when the ratio of positive to negative examples in the training data was the same as that in the test data, we carried out experiments on text classification using the transductive AdaBoost algorithm with a one-depth decision tree as a weak learner. For comparison, we also performed experiments using the standard AdaBoost with a one-depth decision tree (BoosTexter) [13], SVM, and TSVM. We increased the number of training data from 75 to 1000, and we classified the 1000 test data. Figure 3 shows the results (F-measure) of the average among ten categories.

The accuracy increases significantly using the transductive method considering the distribution of 1000 test data. In particular, when there is a small number of training data, the growth of the classification accuracy becomes dramatically large. When the number of training data is 75, the F-measure for boosting is 0.438 and that for transductive boosting is 0.569; the difference is 0.131. The accuracy of the classification using only 75 training data in the transductive method almost equals the accuracy of that using 200 training data in the inductive method. This indicates that the transductive method is useful for improving the classification accuracy for a small number of training examples. Compared with SVM and TSVM with a linear kernel function, the classification using transductive boosting is slightly weaker than TSVM but exceeds SVM. The increase in the accuracy from the boosting to the transductive boosting decreases, while the classification accuracy increases monotonically without 1000 training data in the boosting. This might be because when the number of training data is 1000, the distribution of the test data is similar to that of the training data.

We show the details of the results for every category in Table 2 and Table 3. The bold face numbers denote the best accuracies for every category.   The categories with high classification accuracies sometimes show decreases using the transductive method, e.g., 0.750 to 0.723 for criminal law using 1000 training data. However, the categories of education system, military affairs, international relations, and communications, which have low classification accuracies using the inductive method, show dramatically increases using the transductive method.

Table 2. F-measure for the number of training data (Transductive Boosting).

Category \ # of training data	75	100	200	500	750	1000
sports	0.642	0.726	0.766	0.875	0.901	**0.903**
criminal law	0.600	0.571	0.663	0.656	0.743	**0.750**
government	0.723	0.560	0.622	0.689	**0.727**	0.722
educational system	0.459	0.624	0.661	0.675	0.762	**0.778**
traffic	0.495	0.493	0.500	0.638	0.680	**0.698**
military affairs	0.507	0.561	0.688	0.748	0.754	**0.781**
international relations	0.429	0.396	0.363	0.558	0.508	**0.560**
communications	0.493	0.523	0.641	0.612	**0.703**	0.692
theater	0.583	0.749	0.756	0.795	0.857	**0.862**
agriculture	0.750	0.817	0.831	0.805	0.761	**0.853**
avg.	0.569	0.602	0.649	0.705	0.740	**0.760**

Table 3. F-measure for the number of training data (Boosting).

Category \ # of training data	75	100	200	500	750	1000
sports	0.675	0.681	0.826	0.867	0.891	**0.912**
criminal law	0.561	0.402	0.649	0.664	0.681	**0.723**
government	0.607	0.524	0.580	0.683	**0.692**	0.670
educational system	0.287	0.525	0.563	0.646	0.667	**0.714**
traffic	0.514	0.510	0.493	0.647	**0.658**	0.579
military affairs	0.216	0.321	0.550	**0.728**	0.686	0.628
international relations	0.324	0.317	0.233	0.428	**0.490**	0.329
communications	0.119	0.220	0.528	**0.576**	0.561	0.559
theater	0.385	0.645	0.767	0.693	0.800	**0.813**
agriculture	0.690	0.643	0.734	0.855	**0.864**	0.850
avg.	0.438	0.479	0.592	0.679	**0.699**	0.678

Let us move on to the second experimental condition. We changed the ratio of positive to negative examples in the training data from 1:1 to 1:4 (the original data distribution depicted in Figure 3 is 1:9). The total number of training examples was changed from 20 to 150. The results (the averages of ten categories) are shown in Figure 4. The performance of the transductive boosting is almost the same as that of TSVM and sometimes outperforms TSVM when the training and test distributions are significantly distinct, for example, $N_p : N_n = 1 : 1$ and 150 training samples. This indicates that the good performance of TSVM is largely dependent on the ratio of positive and negative examples.

5   Conclusion

We have proposed a transductive boosting method for text classification problems. We carried out experiments in which we varied the number of training

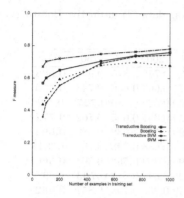
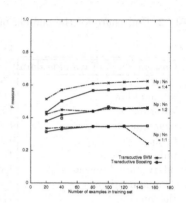

Fig. 3. F-measure and the number of training data.

Fig. 4. F-measure and the ratio of positive and negative examples in the training data.

data, and compared the transductive method to the standard AdaBoost, SVM, and TSVM. The results indicated that the transductive boosting method can improve the performance of text categorization in situations where we have an enormous number of unlabeled data in addition to a small number of labeled training data. When the ratio of positive to negative examples in the training data differs from that in the test data, the advantage of our transductive boosting method in terms of performance is significant. This suggests that our transductive boosting method might be appropriate particularly when we do not know the ratio of positive and negative examples in the test data. Overall, our results show that the transductive approach is effective for a variety of learning methods and potentially promising for other applications.

References

1. S. Dumais, J. Platt, D. Heckerman, and M. Sahami. Inductive learning algorithms and representations for text categorization. In *Proc. of 7th International Conference on Information and Knowledge Management*, 1998.
2. Y. Freund and R. Schapire. A decision-theoretic generalization of on-line learning and an application to boosting. *Journal of Computer and System Sciences*, 55(1):119–139, 1997.
3. Y. Freund. Boosting a weak learning algorithm by majority. *Information and Computation*, 121(2):256–285, 1995.
4. M. Haruno, S. Shirai, and Y. Ooyama. Using decision trees to construct a practical parser. *Machine Learning*, 34:131–149, 1999.
5. T. Joachims. Text categorization with support vector machines. In *Proc. of European Conference on Machine Learning(ECML)*, 1998.
6. T. Joachims. Transductive inference for text classification using support vector machines. In *Proc. of the 16th International Conference on Machine Learning (ICML'99)*, 1999.

7. D.D. Lewis and M. Ringuette. A comparison of two learning algorithms for text categorization. In *Proc. of Third Annual Symposium on Document Analysis and Information Retrieval*, pages 81–93, 1994.
8. Mainichi. *CD Mainichi Shinbun 94*. Nichigai Associates Co., 1995.
9. L. Mason, J. Baxter, P. Bartlett, and M. Frean. Boosting algorithms as gradient descent. In *Proc. of Neural Information Processing Systems 1999 (NIPS-99)*, 1999.
10. Y. Matsumoto, A Kitauchi, T. Yamashita, Y. Hirano, O. Imaichi, and T. Imamura. *Japanese Morphological Analysis System Chasen Manual*, 1997. NAIST Technical Report NAIST-IS-TR97007.
11. K. Nigam, A. McCallum, S. Thrun, and T. Mitchell. Text classification from labeled and unlabeled documents using EM. *Machine Learning*, 39:103–134, 2000.
12. G. Salton (Ed.). *The Smart Retrieval System-experiments in Automatic Document Processing*. Prentice-Hall, 1971.
13. R. E. Schapire and Y. Singer. Boostexter: A boosting-based system for text categorization. *Machine Learning*, 39:135–168, 2000.
14. R. E. Schapire, Y. Freund, P. Bartlett, and W. S. Lee. Boosting the margin: A new explanation for the effectiveness of voting methods. *The Annals of Statistics*, 26(5):1651–1686, 1998.
15. H. Taira and M. Haruno. Feature selection in SVM text categorization. In *Proc. of the 16th National Conference on Artificial Intelligence (AAAI-99)*, pages 480–486, 1999.
16. V. Vapnik. *Statistical Learning Theory*. John Wiley & Sons, 1998.
17. Y. Yang. Expert network: Effective and efficient learning from human decisions in text categorization and retrieval. In *Proc. of the 17th Annual International ACM SIGIR Conference on Research and Development in Information Retrieval*, pages 13–22, 1994.

Using Multiple Clause Constructors in Inductive Logic Programming for Semantic Parsing

Lappoon R. Tang and Raymond J. Mooney

Department of Computer Sciences
University of Texas
2.124 Taylor Hall
Austin, TX 78712
{rupert, mooney}@cs.utexas.edu

Abstract. In this paper, we explored a learning approach which combines different learning methods in inductive logic programming (ILP) to allow a learner to produce more expressive hypotheses than that of each individual learner. Such a learning approach may be useful when the performance of the task depends on solving a large amount of classification problems and each has its own characteristics which may or may not fit a particular learning method. The task of semantic parser acquisition in two different domains was attempted and preliminary results demonstrated that such an approach is promising.

1 Motivation

While a significant portion of machine learning research has devoted to tackling tasks that involve solving a single classification problem, some domains require solving a large sequence of classification problems in order to perform the task successfully. For instance, in learning control rules for semantic parsing using inductive logic programming [1], one needs to specialize a parser by inducing control rules for a large set of parsing operators. However, each induction problem has its own characteristics. The performance hit on the task could be significant if a single (ILP) learner performs poorly on some of these problems because its language bias is "inappropriate" for them. Therefore, using a mixture of language biases might be beneficial (if not sacrificing too much computational efficiency).

A typical ILP algorithm can be viewed as a loop in which a certain *clause constructor* is embedded. A clause constructor is formally defined here as a function $f : T \times B \times E \rightarrow S$ such that given the current building theory T, a set of training examples E, and the set of background knowledge B, it produces a set of clauses S. For example, to construct a clause using FOIL [2] given an existing partial theory T_p (which is initially empty) and a set of training examples $\xi^+ \cup \xi^-$ (positive and negative), one uses all the positive examples not covered by T_p to learn a single clause C. So, we have $f_{Foil}(T_p, B, \xi^+ \cup \xi^-) = f_{Foil}(T_p, B, \{e \in \xi^+ \mid T_p \not\models e\} \cup \xi^-) = \{C\}$. Notice that f_{Foil} always produces a singleton set. Since different constructors create

L. De Raedt and P. Flach (Eds.): ECML 2001, LNAI 2167, pp. 466–477, 2001.
© Springer-Verlag Berlin Heidelberg 2001

clauses of different characteristics (like syntax and accuracy), a learner using multiple clause constructors could exploit the various language biases available to produce more expressive hypotheses. We want to examine the potential benefit of this approach on learning semantic parsers.

Section 2 reviews two ILP algorithms we used in our new approach which is described in Section 3. Section 4 presents the task of learning semantic parsers as our experimental domain. Experimental results are presented in Section 5 followed by conlusions in Section 6.

2 Background

2.1 An Overview of CHILLIN

CHILLIN [3] was the first ILP algorithm that has been applied to the task of learning control rules for a semantic parser in a system called CHILL [1]. It has a compaction outer loop that builds a more general hypothesis with each iteration. In each iteration, a clause is built by finding the least general generalization (LGG) under θ-subsumption of a random pair of *clauses* in the building definition DEF and is specialized by adding literals to its body like FOIL. The clause with the most compaction is returned. The compaction loop is as follows:

$DEF := \{e \leftarrow true \mid e \in \xi^+\}$
Repeat
    $PAIRS :=$ a sampling of pairs of clauses from DEF
    $GENS := \{G \mid G = Find\_A\_Clause(C_i, C_j, DEF, \xi^+, \xi^-)$ for $\langle C_i, C_j \rangle \in PAIRS \}$
    $G :=$ the clause in $GENS$ yielding most compaction
    $DEF := (DEF - (\text{clauses empirically subsumed by } G)) \cup \{G\}$
Until no-further-compaction
Return DEF

Once a clause is found, it is added to the current theory DEF. Any other clause *empirically* subsumed by it will be removed. A clause C empirically subsumes D if all (finitely many) positive examples covered by D are covered by C given the same set of background knowledge. If a clause cannot be refined using the given set of background knowledge, it will attempt to invent a predicate using a method similar to CHAMP [4]. Now, let's define the clause constructor $f_{Chillin}$ for CHILLIN. (Strictly speaking, $f_{Chillin}$ is not a function because of algorithmic randomness. To make it a function, one has to include an additional argument specifying the state of the system. For simplicity, we just omit it here and assume it behaves like a function.) Given a current partial theory T_p (initially empty), background knowledge B, and $\xi^+ \cup \xi^-$ as inputs, $f_{Chillin}$ takes $T_p \cup \{e \in \xi^+ \mid T_p \not\models e\}$ to form the initial DEF. A clause G with the best coverage is then learned by going through the compaction loop for one step. So, $f_{Chillin}(T_p, B, \xi^+ \cup \xi^-) = \{G\}$. However, we are going to allow $f_{Chillin}$ to return the best n clauses in $GENS$ by coverage instead and use this more relaxed version of $f_{Chillin}$ in our algorithm.

2.2   An Overview of mFoil

Like Foil, mFoil is a top-down ILP algorithm. However, it uses a more direct accuracy estimate, the m-estimate [5], to measure the expected accuracy of a clause which is defined as

$$accuracy(C) = \frac{s + m \cdot p^+}{n + m} \tag{1}$$

where C is a clause, s is the number of positive examples covered by the clause, n is the total number of examples covered, p^+ is the prior probability of the class $\oplus$, and m is a parameter.

mFoil was designed with handling imperfect data in mind. It uses a pre-pruning algorithm which checks if a refinement of a clause can be *possibly* significant. If so, it is retained in the search. The significant test is based on the likelihood ratio statistic. Suppose a clause covers n examples and s of which are positive examples, the value of the statistic is calculated as follows:

$$Likelihood\ Ratio = 2n(q^+ \log \frac{q^+}{p^+} + q^- \log \frac{q^-}{p^-}) \tag{2}$$

where p^+ and p^- are the prior probabilities of the class $\oplus$ and $\ominus$ respectively, $q^+ = \frac{s}{n}$, and $q^- = 1 - q^+$. This is distributed approximately as χ^2 with 1 degree of freedom. If the estimated value of a clause is above a particular threshold, it is considered significant. A clause, therefore, cannot be possibly significant if the upper bound $-2s \log p^+$ is already less than the threshold and will not be further refined.

The search starts with the most general clause. Literals are added successively to the body of a clause. A beam of promising clauses are maintained, however, to partially overcome local minima. The search stops when no clauses in the beam can be significantly refined and the most significant one is returned. So, given the current building theory T_p, background knowledge B, training examples $\xi^+ \cup \xi^-$, $f_{mFoil}(T_p, B, \xi^+ \cup \xi^-) = \{C\}$ where C is the most significant clause found in the search beam. Again, we use a modified version of f_{mFoil} which returns the entire beam of promising clauses when none of them can be significantly refined.

3   Using Multiple Clause Constructors in Cocktail

The use of multi-strategy learning to exploit diversity in hypothesis space and search strategy is not novel [15]. However, our focus here is applying a similar idea specifically in ILP where different learning strategies are integrated in a unifying hypothesis evaluation framework.

A set of clause constructors (like Foil's or Golem's) have to be chosen in advance. The decision of what constitutes a sufficiently rich set of constructors depends on the application one needs to build. Although an arbitrary number of clause constructors is permitted (in principle), in practice one should use only a handful of useful constructors to reduce the complexity of the search as much as

Procedure COCKTAIL
Input:

ξ^+, ξ^-:	the $\oplus$ and $\ominus$ examples respectively
F:	a set of clause constructors
B:	a set of sets of background knowledge for each clause constructor in F
M:	the metric for evaluating a theory

Output:

T:	the learned theory

$T := \{\}$
Repeat
    $Clauses := \bigcup_{f_i \in F, B_i \in B} f_i(T, B_i, \xi^+ \cup \xi^-)$
    Choose $C \in Clauses$ such that $M(T - \{$clauses empirically subsumed by $C\} \cup \{C\}$,
       $\xi^+ \cup \xi^-)$ is the best
    $T := T - \{$clauses empirically subsumed by $C\} \cup \{C\}$
Until $M(T, \xi^+ \cup \xi^-)$ does not improve
Return T
End Procedure

Fig. 1. Outline of the COCKTAIL Algorithm

possible. We have chosen mFOIL's and CHILLIN's clause constructors primarily because of their inherent differences in language bias and the relative ease to modify them to return a set of clauses of a given size.

The search of the hypothesis space starts with the empty theory. At each step, a set of potential clauses is produced by collecting all the clauses constructed using the different clause constructors available. Each clause found is then used to *compact* the current building theory to produce a set of new theories; existing clauses in the theory that are empirically subsumed by the new clause are removed. The best one is then chosen according to the given theory evaluation metric and the search stops when the metric score does not improve. The algorithm is outlined in Figure 1.

As the "ideal" solution to an induction problem is the hypothesis that has the minimum size and the most predictive power, some form of bias leading the search to discover such hypotheses would be desirable. It has been formulated in the *Minimum Description Length (MDL) principle* [6] that the most probable hypothesis H given the evidence (training data) D is the one that minimizes the complexity of H given D which is defined as

$$K(H \mid D) = K(H) + K(D \mid H) - K(D) + c \qquad (3)$$

where $K(\cdot)$ is the Kolmogorov complexity function and c is a constant. This is also called the *ideal* form of the MDL principle. In practice, one would instead find an H of some set of hypotheses that minimizes $L(H) + L(D \mid H)$ where $L(x) = -\log_2 Pr(x)$ and interpret $L(x)$ as the corresponding Shannon-Fano (or Huffman) codeword length of x. However, if one is concerned with just the *ordering* of hypotheses but not *coding* or *decoding* them, it seems reasonable to use a metric that gives a rough estimate instead of computing the complexity directly using the encoding itself as it would be computationally more efficient.

Now, let $S(H \mid D)$ be our estimation of the complexity of H given D which is defined as

$$S(H \mid D) = S(H) + S(D \mid H) - S(D) \tag{4}$$

where $S(H)$ is the estimated prior complexity of H and

$$S(D \mid H) = S(\{e \leftarrow true \mid e \in \xi^+ \text{ and } H \not\models e\}) + \tag{5}$$
$$S(\{false \leftarrow e \mid e \in \xi^- \text{ and } H \models e\})$$

is the estimated complexity of D given H. This is rougly a worst case estimate of the complexity of a program that computes the set D given H. A much better scheme would be to compute $S(H_1 \cup \{T \leftarrow T', not\ T''\} \cup H_2)$ instead where H_1 and H_2 are some (compressive) hypotheses consistent with the uncovered positive examples of H and covered negative examples of H respectively, T is the target concept $t(R_1, \cdots, R_k)$ that we need to learn, $T' = t'(R_1, \cdots, R_k)$ and $T'' = t''(R_1, \cdots, R_k)$ are the renaming of the target concept. (All predicates t/k appearing in any clause in H and H_2 have to be renamed to t'/k and t''/k respectively.) Computing H_1 and H_2 could be problematic, however, and thus we simply take the worst case assuming the discrepancy between H and D is not compressible. A very simple measure is employed here as our complexity estimate [8]. The size S of a set of *Clauses* (or a hypothesis) where each clause C with a *Head* and a *Body* is defined as follows:

$$S(Clauses) = \sum_{C \in Clauses} 1 + termsize(Head) + termsize(Body) \tag{6}$$

where

$$termsize(T) = \begin{cases} 1 & \text{if } T \text{ is a variable} \\ 2 & \text{if } T \text{ is a constant} \\ 2 + \sum_{i=1}^{arity(T)} termsize(arg_i(T)) & otherwise. \end{cases} \tag{7}$$

The size of a hypothesis can be viewed as a sum of the average number of bits required to encode a symbol appearing in it which can be a variable, a constant, a function symbol, or a predicate symbol, plus one bit of encoding each clause terminator. (Note that this particular scheme gives less weight to variable encoding.) Finally, our theory evaluation metric is defined as

$$M(H, D) = S(H) + S(D \mid H). \tag{8}$$

The goal of the search is to find the H that minimizes the metric M. The metric is purely syntactic; it does not take into account the complexity of proving an instance [14]. However, we are relying on the assumption that syntactic complexity implies computational complexity although this and the reverse are not true in general. So, the current metric does not gaurantee finding the hypothesis with the shortest proof of the instances.

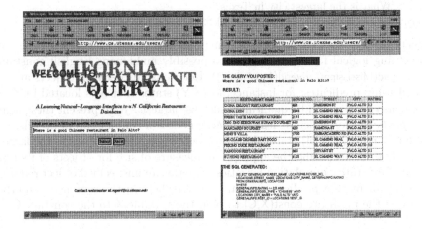

Fig. 2. Screenshots of a Learned Web-based NL Database Interface

4   Learning to Parse Questions into Logical Queries

Being able to query a database using natural languages has been an interesting task since the 60's as most users of the database may not know the underlying database access language. The need for such applications is even more pronounced with the rapid development of the Internet which has become an important channel for information delivery. Screenshots of a natural language interface (NLI) we developed are shown in Figure 2.

Traditional (*rationalist*) approaches to constructing database interfaces require an expert to hand-craft an appropriate semantic parser [9]. However, such hand-crafted parsers are time consuming to develop and suffer from problems with robustness and incompleteness. Nevertheless, very little research in empirical NLP has explored the task of automatically acquiring such interfaces from annotated training examples. The only exceptions of which we are aware are a statistical approach to mapping airline-information queries into SQL presented in [10], a probabilistic decision-tree method for the same task described in [11], and an approach using inductive logic programming to learn a logic-based semantic parser described in [1].

We are going to briefly review our overall approach using an interface developed for a U.S. Geography database (Geoquery) as a sample application [1] which is available on the Web at http://www.cs.utexas.edu/users/ml/geo.html.

4.1   Semantic Representation

First-order logic is used as a semantic representation language. CHILL has also been applied to a restaurant database in which the logical form resembles SQL, and is translated automatically into SQL (see Figure 2). We explain the features of the Geoquery representation language through a sample query:

Input: "What is the largest city in Texas?"
Query: answer(C,largest(C,(city(C),loc(C,S),const(S,stateid(texas))))).

Objects are represented as logical terms and are typed with a semantic category using logical functions applied to possibly ambiguous English constants (e.g. stateid(Mississippi), riverid(Mississippi)). Relationships between objects are expressed using predicates; for instance, loc(X,Y) states that X is located in Y.

We also need to handle quantifiers such as 'largest'. We represent these using *meta-predicates* for which at least one argument is a conjunction of literals. For example, largest(X, Goal) states that the object X satisfies Goal and is the largest object that does so, using the appropriate measure of size for objects of its type (e.g. area for states, population for cities). Finally, an unspecified object required as an argument to a predicate can appear elsewhere in the sentence, requiring the use of the predicate const(X,C) to bind the variable X to the constant C.

4.2   Parsing Actions

Our semantic parser employs a shift-reduce architecture that maintains a stack of previously built semantic constituents and a buffer of remaining words in the input. The parsing actions are automatically generated from templates given the training data. The templates are INTRODUCE, COREF_VARS, DROP_CONJ, LIFT_CONJ, and SHIFT. INTRODUCE pushes a predicate onto the stack based on a word appearing in the input and information about its possible meanings in the lexicon. COREF_VARS binds two arguments of two different predicates on the stack. DROP_CONJ (or LIFT_CONJ) takes a predicate on the stack and puts it into one of the arguments of a meta-predicate on the stack. SHIFT simply pushes a word from the input buffer onto the stack. The parsing actions are tried in exactly this order. The parser also requires a lexicon to map phrases in the input into specific predicates. This lexicon can also be learned automatically from the training data [12].

Let's go through a simple trace of parsing the request "What is the capital of Texas?" A lexicon that maps 'capital' to 'capital(_)', 'of' to 'loc(_,_)', and 'Texas' to 'const(_,stateid(texas))' suffices here. Interrogatives like "what" may be mapped to predicates in the lexicon if necessary. The parser begins with an initial stack and a buffer holding the input sentence. Each predicate on the parse stack has an attached buffer to hold the context in which it was introduced; words from the input sentence are shifted onto this buffer during parsing. The initial parse state is shown below:

Parse Stack: [answer(_,_):[]]
Input Buffer: [what,is,the,capital,of,texas,?]

Since the first three words in the input buffer do not map to any predicates, three SHIFT actions are performed. The next is an INTRODUCE as 'capital' is at the head of the input buffer:

Parse Stack: [capital(_):[], answer(_,_):[the,is,what]]
Input Buffer: [capital,of,texas,?]

The next action is a COREF_VARS that binds the argument of capital(_) with the first argument of answer(_,_).

Parse Stack: [capital(C):[], answer(C,_):[the,is,what]]
Input Buffer: [capital,of,texas,?]

The next sequence of steps are a SHIFT followed by an INTRODUCE

Parse Stack: [loc(_,_):[], capital(C):[capital], answer(C,_):[the,is,what]]
Input Buffer: [of,texas,?]

The next sequence of steps are a COREF_VARS, a SHIFT, an INTRODUCE, and then a COREF_VARS:

Parse Stack: [const(S,stateid(texas)):[], loc(C,S):[of],capital(C):[capital],
              answer(C,_):[the,is,what]]
Input Buffer: [texas,?]

The last four steps are three DROP_CONJ's followed by two SHIFT's:

Parse Stack: [answer(C, (capital(C),loc(C,S),const(S,stateid(texas))))):[the,is,what]]
Input Buffer: []

This is the final state and the logical query is extracted from the stack.

4.3 Learning Control Rules

The initially constructed parser has no constraints on when to apply actions, and is therefore overly general and generates numerous spurious parses. Positive and negative examples are collected for each action by parsing each training example and recording the parse states encountered. Parse states to which an action *should* be applied (i.e. the action leads to building the correct semantic representation) are labeled positive examples for that action. Otherwise, a parse state is labeled a negative example for an action if it is a positive example for another action below the current one in the *ordered* list of actions. Control conditions which decide the correct action for a given parse state are learned for each action from these positive and negative examples.

5 Experimental Results

5.1 The Domains

Two different domains are used for experimentation here. The first one is the United States Geography domain. The database contains about 800 facts implemented in Prolog as relational tables containing basic information about the U.S. states like population, area, capital city, neighboring states, and so on. The second domain consists of a set of 1000 computer-related job postings, such as job announcements, from the USENET newsgroup austin.jobs. Information from these job postings are extracted to create a database which contains the following types of information: 1) the job title, 2) the company, 3) the recruiter, 4) the location, 5) the salary, 6) the languages and platforms used, and 7) required or desired years of experience and degrees [13].

Table 1. Results on all the experiments performed. Geo1000 consists of 1000 sentences from the U.S. Geography domain. Jobs640 consists of 640 sentences from the job postings domain. R = recall, P = precision, S = average size of a hypothesis found for each induction problem when learning a parser using the entire corpus, and T = average training time in mins.

Parsers learned with \ Corpora	Geo1000				Jobs640			
	R	P	S	T	R	P	S	T
COCKTAIL ($f_{mFoil}+f_{Chillin}$)	79.40	89.92	64.79	62.88	79.84	93.25	105.77	68.10
COCKTAIL (f_{mFoil} only)	75.10	88.98	127.61	76.67	63.75	82.26	427.02	66.64
COCKTAIL ($f_{Chillin}$ only)	70.80	91.38	150.69	41.24	72.50	86.24	177.99	43.81
CHILLIN	71.00	90.79	142.41	38.24	74.22	87.48	175.94	45.31
mFOIL	67.50	87.10	204.62	65.17	58.91	82.68	561.34	69.08

5.2   Experimental Design

The U.S. Geography domain has a corpus of 1000 sentences collected from undergraduate students in our department and from real users of our Web interface. The job database information system has a corpus of 640 sentences; 400 of which are artificially made using a simple grammar that generates certain obvious types of questions people may ask and the other 240 are questions obtained from real users of our interface. Both corpora are available at ftp://ftp.cs.utexas.edu/pub/mooney/nl-ilp-data/.

The experiments were conducted using 10-fold cross validation. In each test, the recall (a.k.a. accuracy) and the precision of the parser are reported. Recall and precision are defined as

$$Recall = \frac{\text{\# of correct queries produced}}{\text{\# of sentences}} \tag{9}$$

$$Precision = \frac{\text{\# of correct queries produced}}{\text{\# of successful parses}}. \tag{10}$$

The recall is the number of correct queries produced divided by the total number of sentences in the test set. The precision is the number of correct queries produced divided by the number of sentences in the test set from which the parser produced a query (i.e. a successful parse). A query is considered correct if it produces the same answer set as that of the correct logical query.

5.3   Discussion of Results

For all the experiments performed, we used a beam size of four for mFOIL (and therefore for f_{mFoil}), a significant threshold of 6.64 (i.e. 99% level of significance), and a parameter $m = 10$. We took the best four clauses (by coverage) found by CHILLIN. COCKTAIL using both the mFOIL's and CHILLIN's clause constructors performed the best; it outperformed all other learners by at least 4% in recall in either domains. In addition, COCKTAIL using only f_{mFoil} performed better than using only $f_{Chillin}$ in the Geography domain while the latter performed better in the job postings domain. This indicates that there are some inherent differences between the two domains as far as language bias is concerned. This will be further explained below. Notice that CHILLIN alone performed slightly better than COCKTAIL using only $f_{Chillin}$. There must be other factors in the picture we were not aware of as using a hill-climbing search actually performed better in this case. One possibility might be that the current MDL metric has problems handling complicated terms with lots of constants which could result in choosing overly specific clauses (if they are in the beam) and therefore learning a larger number of clauses for the building theory. Perhaps somewhat surprising is the result obtained from using the original mFOIL algorithm; the poor results seem to suggest that choosing the most statistically significant clause (in the search beam) does not necessarily produce the most compressive hypothesis. Apparently, this is due to the fact that some compressive clauses were wrongly rejected by a statistical based measure [14].

COCKTAIL found the most compressive hypothesis on average for an induction problem when learning a parser using the entire corpus. (There were 138 induction problems for Geo1000 and 87 for Jobs640.) Before we proceed to explain the results, let's go through an example to see how f_{mFoil} and $f_{Chillin}$ construct clauses of very different language biases which are good for expressing different types of features present in a set of training examples. Suppose we want to learn a concept class of lists of atoms and tuples of atoms and we have positive examples $\xi^+ = \{t([a, [e, c], b]), t([c, [a, b], a])\}$ and negative examples $\xi^- = \{t([[e, c], b]), t([b, c, [a, b]]), t([c, b, c]), t([d, [e, c], b, b])\}$. One possible hypothesis H_1 consistent with the data would be

$$t(X) \leftarrow member(a, X). \tag{11}$$

which states that any list containing the constant a is in the concept. Another possible hypothesis H_2 would be

$$t([W, [X, Y], Z]) \leftarrow true. \tag{12}$$

which asserts that the concept class contains lists of three elements and the second element has to be a tuple. Both H_1 and H_2 are qualitatively different in the sense that they look for different *types* of features for classification; the former looks for the presence of a certain specific *element* that might appear anywhere in a given list while the latter looks for a specific *structure* of a list.

This is exactly what is happening here. mFOIL and CHILLIN learn very different features for classification; mFOIL is given background predicates which check the presence (or absence) of a particular element in a given parse state (e.g. a certain predicate or a certain word phrase) while CHILLIN is not given any such background predicates but it learns the structural features of a parse state through finding $LGGs$ with good coverage (and inventing predicates if necessary). Each learner is effective in expressing each type of feature using its own language bias; if one were to learn structural features of a parse state using mFOIL's language bias (e.g. not allowing function terms), the hypothesis thus expressed would have a very high complexity and vice versa.

When inspecting the set of control rules learned by COCKTAIL, we discovered that on small induction problems involving only a few training examples, only one type (either mFOIL's or CHILLIN's) of clause constructors was sufficient; the resulting hypothesis contained clauses built only by one of them. However, different (similarly small) problems require different constructors. On larger induction problems involving a few hundred examples, COCKTAIL learned hypotheses with clauses constructed by both f_{mFoil} and $f_{Chillin}$. This suggests that some problems do require inspecting structural features of a parse state and examining its elements; using a variety of language biases allows the learner to discover and effectively express these different features in a problem which is illustrated by the fact that the average size of a hypothesis found is minimal (as irrelevant features tend to make complicated hypotheses), at least in the domains attempted. The training time of COCKTAIL using all the given clause constructors in each domain was much less than the sum of using each of them alone (unlike what one might expect) and in fact in some case closer to the average time.

6   Conclusion

An ILP learning approach which employs different clause constructors from different ILP learners is discussed. It was applied to the task of semantic parser acquisition and was demonstrated to perform better than using a single learner. Future work could explore using a larger set of clause constructors and examine their effects on language learning problems. Since problems that require solving a large sequence of induction problems do not seem to occur very often, we would like to see if the existing approach is applicable to domains where only a single or a relatively small number of classification prolems are involved. It is also interesting to use a more precise theory evaluation metric like the one described by Srinivasan et. al. [7].

Acknowledgements. This research was supported by the National Science Foundation under grant IRI-9704943. Special thanks go to Sugato Basu for proof-reading an earlier draft of this paper.

References

1. John M. Zelle and Raymond J. Mooney: Learning to Parse Database Queries Using Inductive Logic Programming. Proceedings of the Thirteenth National Conference on Artificial Intelligence (1996) 1050–1055
2. J. Ross Quinlan: Learning Logical Definitions from Relations. Machine Learning **5** (1990) 239–266
3. John M. Zelle and Raymond J. Mooney: Combining Top-Down and Bottom-Up Methods in Inductive Logic Programming. Proceedings of the Eleventh International Conference on Machine Learning (1994) 343–351

4. Boonserm Kijsirikul and Masayuki Numao and Masamichi Shimura: Discrimination-Based Constructive Induction of Logic Programs. Proceedings of the Tenth National Conference on Artificial Intelligence (1992) 44–49
5. Bojan Cestnik: Estimating probabilities: A crucial task in machine learning. Proceedings of the Ninth European Conference on Artificial Intelligence (1990) 147–149
6. Jorma Rissanen: Modeling by Shortest Data Description. Automatica **14** (1978) 465–471
7. Ashwin Srinivasan, Stephen Muggleton, Michael Bain: The Justification of Logical Theories based on Data Compression. Machine Intelligence **13** (1994) 87–121
8. Stephen Muggleton and W. Buntine: Machine Invention of First-order Predicates by Inverting Resolution. Proceedings of the Fifth International Conference on Machine Learning (1988) 339-352
9. G. G. Hendrix and E. Sacerdoti and D. Sagalowicz and J. Slocum: Developing a Natural Language Interface to Complex Data. ACM Transactions on Database Systems **3** (1978) 105–147
10. Scott Miller and David Stallard and Robert Bobrow and Richard Schwartz: A Fully Statistical Approach to Natural Language Interfaces. Proceedings of the 34th Annual Meeting of the Association for Computational Linguistics (1996) 55–61
11. Roland Kuhn and Renato De Mori: The Application of Semantic Classification Trees to Natural Language Understanding. IEEE Transactions on Pattern Analysis and Machine Intelligence **17** (1995) 449–460
12. Cynthia A. Thompson and Raymond J. Mooney: Automatic Construction of Semantic Lexicons for Learning Natural Language Interfaces. Proceedings of the Sixteenth National Conference on Artificial Intelligence (1999) 487–493
13. Mary Elaine Califf and Raymond J. Mooney: Relational Learning of Pattern-Match Rules for Information Extraction. Proceedings of the Sixteenth National Conference on Artificial Intelligence (1999) 328–334
14. S. Muggleton, A. Srinivasan, and M. Bain: Compression, significance and accuracy. Proceedings of the Ninth International Machine Learning Conference (1992) 338-347
15. Attilio Giordana, Filippo Neri, Lorenza Saitta, and Marco Botta: Integrating Multiple Learning Strategies in First Order Logics. Machine Learning **27**(3): 209-240 (1997)

Using Domain Knowledge on Population Dynamics Modeling for Equation Discovery

Ljupčo Todorovski and Sašo Džeroski

Department of Intelligent Systems, Jožef Stefan Institute
Jamova 39, SI-1000 Ljubljana, Slovenia
Ljupco.Todorovski@ijs.si, Saso.Dzeroski@ijs.si

Abstract. State of the art equation discovery systems are concerned with the empirical approach to modeling of physical systems, where none or a very limited portion of the expert knowledge about the observed system is used in the modeling process. In this paper, we propose a formalism for integration of the population dynamics modeling knowledge into the process of equation discovery. The formalism allows the encoding of a high-level domain knowledge accessible to human experts. The encoded knowledge can be automatically transformed into the operational form of context dependent grammars. We present an extended version of the equation discovery system LAGRAMGE that can use these context free grammars. Experimental evaluation shows that the integration of domain knowledge in the process of equation discovery considerably improves the efficiency and noise robustness of LAGRAMGE.

1 Introduction

Most of the work in scientific discovery [4] is concerned with assisting the empirical approach to modeling of physical systems. Following this approach, the observed system is modeled on a trial-and-error basis to fit observed data. None or a very limited portion of the available domain background knowledge about the observed system is used in the modeling process. This is especially the case in domains where a limited amount of knowledge is expressed in the form of mathematical laws, such as biology, medicine and other life sciences. The empirical approach is in contrast to the theoretical approach to modeling, where the basic physical processes involved in the observed system are first identified. Then, the human expert uses the domain knowledge about the identified processes to write down a proper structure of the model in the form of differential equations. Finally, the values of the constant parameters of these equations are fitted against the observed data using system identification methods [5].

The focus of this paper is on integrating expert theoretical knowledge about the domain of interest within the process of automated modeling of population dynamics. The equation discovery system LAGRAMGE [7] has made initial steps toward this integration. It allows the user to define the space of possible equations using a context free grammar, written on the basis of the user background

L. De Raedt and P. Flach (Eds.): ECML 2001, LNAI 2167, pp. 478–490, 2001.
© Springer-Verlag Berlin Heidelberg 2001

knowledge about the domain at hand. However, one can argue that it is difficult to encode a context free grammar from the expert domain knowledge. In this paper, we propose a formalism for encoding population dynamics modeling knowledge that is more accessible to human experts. It allows an automated generation of a grammar for equation discovery. The generated grammar is context dependent (and not context free as in LAGRAMGE), so LAGRAMGE 2.0 was developed that, among other improvements, allows the use of context dependent constraints in the grammar specifying the space of possible equations. The experimental evaluation of the proposed framework shows that integrating expert knowledge within the process of equation discovery considerably improves the efficiency and noise robustness of LAGRAMGE.

The paper is organized as follows. Section 2 gives a brief introduction to equation discovery. The basics of population dynamics modeling are introduced in Section 3. The formalism for encoding the population dynamics modeling knowledge and the process of its transformation into a grammar for equation discovery are presented in Section 3. The necessary improvements of LAGRAMGE are presented in Section 4. The experimental evaluation of LAGRAMGE 2.0 is given in Section 5. The last Section 6 summarizes the paper and gives directions for further work.

2   Equation Discovery

Equation discovery is the area of machine learning that develops methods for automated discovery of quantitative laws, expressed in the form of equations, in collections of measured data [4]. It is related to the area of system identification. However, mainstream system identification methods work under the assumption that the structure of the model, i.e., the form of the equations, is known and are concerned with determining the values of the constant parameters in the model [5]. Equation discovery systems, on the other hand, aim at identifying both an adequate structure of the equations and appropriate values of the constant parameters.

2.1   Background Knowledge and Language Bias

Equation discovery systems search through the space of possible equation structures. Most of the equation discovery systems emulate the empirical approach to scientific discovery: different equation structures are generated and fitted against measured data. However, some of the possible equation structures may be inappropriate for modeling the observed system. For example, consider the case where the measured variables of the observed system are not dimensionless. In that case some algebraic combinations of the system variables, such as addition (or subtraction) of mass and energy, are not valid. Beyond this simple example, there are also more sophisticated inconsistencies of equation structures with a background knowledge from the domain of the observed system.

Different equation discovery systems explore different spaces of possible equation structures, or in other words they use different language biases. One possibility is to use some pre-defined (built-in) language bias that restricts the space of possible equation structures to some reasonably small class, such as polynomials or trigonometric functions, like in LAGRANGE [2]. In this case, the user can not influence the space of possible equations or use domain specific knowledge in the process of equation discovery. It is much better to use a declarative bias approach, where the user is allowed to influence or directly specify the space of possible equations. This approach provides users with a tool for incorporating their background knowledge about the domain at hand in the process of equation discovery. The use of background knowledge in the sense of a declarative language bias can avoid the problems of inconsistency of the discovered equations with the knowledge about the domain of the observed system, mentioned above.

Several equation discovery systems make use of domain specific knowledge. In equation discovery systems that are based on genetic programming, the user is allowed to specify a set of algebraic operators that can be used. A similar approach has been used in the EF [10] equation discovery system. The equation discovery system SDS [8] effectively uses scale-type information about the dimensions of the system variables and is capable of discovering complex equations from noisy data.

However, expert users can usually provide much more modeling knowledge about the domain at hand than merely enumerating the algebraic operators to be used or (the scale-type of) dimensions of the measured system variables. In order to incorporate this knowledge in the process of equation discovery, we should provide the user with a more sophisticated declarative bias formalism. In LAGRAMGE [7], the formalism of context free grammars has been used to specify the space of possible equations. Note here that context free grammars are a far more general and powerful mechanism for incorporating domain specific knowledge than the ones used in SDS [8] and EF [10].

The use of declarative bias in the form of context free grammar was crucial for modeling the phytoplankton growth in Lake Glumsoe in Denmark from real-world sparse noisy measurements [3]. However, one can argue that it is difficult for the users of LAGRAMGE to express their knowledge about the domain in the form of a context free grammar. In this paper, we present a formalism for encoding the domain knowledge at a higher, more user-friendly level, which can be automatically transformed to the operational form of grammars for equation discovery.

2.2 Discovery of Differential Equations

In this paper, we consider the problem of modeling dynamic systems, i.e. systems that change their state over time. Differential equations are the most common tool for modeling dynamic systems. LAGRANGE [2] was the first equation discovery system that extended the scope of equation discovery systems to ordinary differential equations. The basic idea was to introduce the time derivatives of the systems variables through numerical differentiation and then search for algebraic equations. This simple approach has a major drawback: large errors are introduced by numerical differentiation.

The problem was partly resolved in LAGRAMGE, where numerical integration is used instead of differentiation for the highest-order derivatives [7]. However, LAGRAMGE is only capable of discovering a differential equation for a single user specified system variable. In order to discover a system of simultaneous differential equations, LAGRAMGE has to be invoked once for each system variable.

3   Population Dynamics Modeling

Population ecology studies the structure and dynamics of populations, where each population is a group of individuals of the same species inhabiting the same area. In this paper we consider modeling the dynamics of populations, especially the dynamics of change of their density. We consider models of predator-prey population dynamics, where the interaction between predator and prey is antagonistic in the sense that it causes increase of the predator population and decrease of the prey population. The models are systems of differential equations [6].

3.1   Generalized Volterra-Lotka Model of Population Dynamics

Consider a simple model based on two populations, foxes and rabbits. The latter are grazing on grass and the foxes are carnivores that hunt rabbits. We assume that rabbits are the only food of foxes, rabbits have unlimited supply of grass and seasonal changes are ignored. Under these assumptions, if the rabbit population is large, the fox population grows rapidly. However, this causes many rabbits to be eaten, thus diminishing the rabbit population to the point where the food for foxes is not sufficient. Consequently, the fox population decreases, which causes faster growth of the rabbit population.

The oscillatory behavior of the two population densities can be modeled using the Volterra-Lotka population dynamics model [6]. It can be generalized using the following schema:

$$\dot{N} = growth\_rate(N) - feeds\_on(P, N)$$
$$\dot{P} = feeds\_on(P, N) - decay\_rate(P),$$

where N is the prey (rabbit) population density and P is the predator (fox) population density.

Using this model schema, we can build models of predator-prey population dynamics with different complexity. The term $growth\_rate(N)$ defines the model of the prey population growth in absence of predation. Two models of single population growth are usually used [6]: $(a)\, aN$; and $(b)\, aN(1 - N/K)$. The first model (a) assumes that the population growth is exponential and unlimited. However, there are real-world environments that have some carrying capacity for the population, which limits the density of the population. In such cases, an alternative logistic growth model (b) can be used, where K is a constant, determining the carrying capacity of the environment.

The second assumption made in simple population models is that the predation rate is proportional to the densities of predator and prey populations ($feeds\_on(N, P) = bPN$). As for population growth, this means that the predation growth is exponential and unlimited. Again, in some cases the predators have limited predation capacity. When the prey population density is small the predation rate is proportional to it, but when the prey population becomes abundant, the predation capacity saturates to some limit value ($feeds\_on(N, P) = bPs(N)$). Three different terms are often used to model the predator saturation response to the increase of the prey density $(a) AN/(N + B)$, $(b) AN^2/(N^2 + B)$ and $(c) A(1 - e^{-BN})$, where A is the limit value of the predation capacity saturation, and B is the constant, which determines the saturation rate [6].

The modeling knowledge about population growth and saturation presented here can be very useful as a background knowledge for automated modeling of ecological systems with equation discovery.

3.2   Encoding of Domain and Modeling Knowledge

The knowledge about modeling population dynamics can be divided in two types. The first type is domain specific knowledge about the populations and their role in the food-chain. In the Volterra-Lotka model of population dynamics, this knowledge is represented by the single fact that foxes feed on rabbits. This type of knowledge can be expect from a biologist without any experience in mathematical modeling of population dynamics.

The second type of knowledge is domain independent knowledge about population dynamics modeling, presented in the Section 3.1. This type of knowledge can be provided by, say a mathematician with modeling experience, who is not necessary familiar with the biological ecosystem structure and the interactions involved.

Domain Specific Knowledge. We first provide a specification of the food-chain in the domain: for our example rabbits and foxes domain it is given in Table 1. We use three first-order predicates: the domain(domain_name) predicate is used to specify the name of the domain at hand; each population in the domain is specified using the predicate population(domain_name, population_name); finally, we use the predicate feeds_on(domain_name, predator_population, prey_population) to specify each interaction between two populations. For now, only predator-prey interactions can be specified. However, the formalism can be easily generalized to allow the specification of other types of interactions between populations, such as parasytism, competitive exclusion and symbiosis [6].

Note that by using the predicates population and feeds_on, the user is allowed to specify an arbitrary number of populations and predator-prey interactions between them.

Table 1. Description of a simple Volterra-Lotka population dynamics domain consisting of two populations of foxes (predators) and rabbits (preys).

```
domain(vl).
population(vl, fox).
population(vl, rabbit).    feeds_on(vl, fox, rabbit).
```

Domain Independent Modeling Knowledge. The second part of the modeling knowledge, which is domain independent, is given in Table 2. We use the predicate `template` to specify a set of alternative models for population dynamics processes like population growth and saturation, described in Section 3. Note that the symbol `const` is used to specify a constant parameter, whose value has to be fitted against measured data. A constraint of the form [L:U] can be assigned to each constant parameter specifying that the value v of the constant parameter should be within the interval $L \leq v \leq U$. Omitting the U (L) value in this constraint means that there is no upper (lower) bound on the constant parameter value. For example, the symbol `const[0:]` means that the constant parameter should be non-negative.

Table 2. Templates with alternative sub-expressions used for modeling the processes of saturation and population growth.

```
template(saturation, X, (X)).
template(saturation, X, (X / (X + const[0:]))).
template(saturation, X, (X * X / (X * X + const[0:]))).
template(saturation, X, (1 - exp(-const[0:] * X))).
template(growth, X, (const * X)).
template(growth, X, (const * X * (1 - X / const[0:]))).
```

Transforming the Background Knowledge into a Grammar. Using the definitions of the background knowledge from Tables 1 and 2, a grammar for equation discovery can be automatically generated. The process of transformation of the knowledge into grammar is automated using the predator-prey model schema presented in Section 3. The grammar for the example population dynamics domain, consisting of rabbits and foxes, is given in Table 3.

The starting non-terminal symbol in the grammar `vl` is used to generate the system of two differential equations of the population dynamics model, using the schema from Section 3. The growth of the rabbit population in the absence of predation is modeled using the non-terminal symbol `growth(rabbit)` with two alternative productions, reflecting the two `template` predicates for growth from Table 2. The third non-terminal symbol `feeds_on(fox,rabbit)` models the predation of foxes on rabbits. The predation rate is always proportional to the density of the fox population and the non-terminal `nutrient(rabbit)`

Table 3. A grammar for equation discovery constructed from the background knowledge in Tables 1 and 2.

```
vl -> time_deriv(rabbit) = growth(rabbit) - feeds_on(fox,rabbit);
      time_deriv(fox) = feeds_on(fox,rabbit) - const * fox
feeds_on(fox,rabbit) -> const * fox * nutrient(rabbit)
nutrient(rabbit) -> rabbit
nutrient(rabbit) -> rabbit / (rabbit + const[0:])
nutrient(rabbit) -> rabbit * rabbit / (rabbit * rabbit + const[0:])
nutrient(rabbit) -> 1 - exp(-const[0:] * rabbit)
growth(rabbit) -> const * rabbit
growth(rabbit) -> const * rabbit * (1 - rabbit / const[0:])
```

is used to introduce the model of predator response to the increase of rabbit population density (the productions reflect the templates from Table 2). The terminal symbols fox and rabbit are used to introduce the measured system variables of the population densities.

Strictly speaking, the grammar in Table 3 is not context free. Namely, the production for the starting symbol vl generates two feeds_on(fox,rabbit) symbols, one in the first and another one in the second equation. In context free grammar, these two non-terminal symbols can generate two different expressions. In population dynamics models, however, these two expressions have to be the same. The use of context dependent constraints can overcome this limitation of the context free grammars.

4   LAGRAMGE 2.0

In order to use grammars like the one from Table 3 for equation discovery, we developed LAGRAMGE 2.0, an improved version of LAGRAMGE 1.0 [7]. Improvements were made in three directions. First, the context dependent constraints have to be checked for each expression. Second, the grammar in Table 3 generates all model equations at once, therefore a system of simultaneous equations has to be discovered, instead of a single equation for each system variable separately. Third, the constraints on the lower and upper bound of the values of the constant parameters have to be considered. The top-level algorithm of the LAGRAMGE 2.0 exhaustive search procedure is presented in Table 4.

The search procedure of LAGRAMGE 2.0 takes as an input a set of variables V, a (sub)set of dependent variables $V_d \subseteq V$, a data set *Data* with measured time behaviors of the variables in V, a (context dependent) grammar G, and a parameter b that determines the number of best models (systems of equations) returned as output of LAGRAMGE.

The search space of LAGRAMGE is the set of parse trees that can be derived with the user provided grammar G. The search space is ordered according to the height of the parse trees using the refinement operator defined in [7]. Starting with an empty parse tree, it can be repeatedly used to generate all parse trees.

Table 4. Exhaustive search procedure of LAGRAMGE 2.0.

	procedure LagramgeSearch(V, V_d, *Data*, G, b)
1	$Q \leftarrow \{\}$
2	$S \leftarrow$ enumerate all derivation trees in G
3	**foreach** T **in** S **do**
4	**if** CheckConstraints(T, G) **then**
5	T.error $\leftarrow 0.0$
6	**foreach** v **in** V_d
7	T.error $\leftarrow T$.error $+$ Fit($\hat{v} = T.v$, *Data*)
8	**endfor**
9	**endif**
10	$Q \leftarrow Q \cup T$
12	**endwhile**
11	**return** the b best parse trees in Q

Context Dependent Constraints. Each generated parse tree is first checked to see if it satisfies the context dependent constraints in G (line 4 of the algorithm in Table 4). The user is allowed to specify an arbitrary number of context dependent constraints for each production in the grammar. Examples of productions with context dependent constraints are presented in Table 5.

Table 5. Examples of grammar productions with context dependent constraints.

E -> A + B, B - A { A.1 == A.2; }
E -> A + B, B - A { A.1 == A.2; B.1 == B.2; }
E -> A * E { A <= E; }

In the first production, a single constraint A.1 == A.2 specifies that the first (A.1) and the second (A.2) occurrence of the symbol A on the right hand side of the production should generate the same sub-expression. For example, the expression a1 + b1, b2 - a2 can not be derived using that production (A.1 -> a1 is different from A.2 -> a2), whereas the expression a1 + b1, b2 - a1 can. However, the latter expression can not be derived using the second production due to the second constraint B.1 == B.2. a1 + b1, b1 - a1 is an example of an expression that can be derived using both productions.

The third production illustrates the use of a context dependent constraint to avoid redundant generation of expressions that are equivalent due to the commutativity of multiplication. The context free production E -> A * E can generate both a * b and b * a. On the other hand, using the context dependent constraint A <= E (where the operator <= stands for lexicographic comparison), the second expression b * a can not be derived.

Simultaneous Equations. In order to evaluate a system of simultaneous equations for the user provided set of dependent variables V_d, the sub-trees T_v of the generated tree T are identified for each dependent variable $v \in V_d$. Then the error of each equation of the form $\dot{v} = T.v$ is evaluated (using the Fit function in line 7 of the algorithm in Table 4), where $T.v$ here denotes the expression derived by the sub-tree T_v. The errors of the equations for all dependent variables are added together to obtain the error of the whole parse tree T (lines 5-8).

Constraints on the Values of the Constant Parameters. The function Fit(*equation*, *Data*) is used to fit the values of the constant parameters of the equation to the given data set *Data*. The discrepancy between the measured data *Data* and the data obtained by simulating the equation is used to evaluate the error of the equation. The nonlinear regression algorithm used in LAGRAMGE 1.0 can not impose any constraints on parameter values. Because of this, we replaced replaced it with the nonlinear regression algorithm proposed in [1]. The latter allows the use of simple constraints specifying the lower and upper bounds on the values of the constant parameters.

5   Experiments

The goal of the experiments with LAGRAMGE, presented in this section, is to evaluate the effect of using the new type of background knowledge in the process of equation discovery. For that purpose, we compared the performance of LAGRAMGE 2.0 with the performance of LAGRAMGE 1.0 on a task of reconstructing different models of a simple aquatic ecosystem consisting of three populations of inorganic nutrient, phytoplankton and zooplankton. The food-chain in the ecosystem contains two predator-prey interactions: zooplankton feeds on phytoplankton and phytoplankton feeds on inorganic nutrient.

5.1   Experimental Setup

Using the food-chain description along with the domain independent modeling templates from Table 2, the context dependent grammar presented in Table 6 has been built using the algorithm described in Section 3.2. The grammar in Table 6 generates thirty-two different models, i.e. systems of three simultaneous equations, which are used in the experiments. The experimental evaluation of LAGRAMGE 2.0 consisted of attempting to reconstruct each of these 32 models from simulated data.

Using the grammar, we generated all thirty-two different model structures. In order to obtain simulation models, the values of the constant parameters have to be set. We used randomly generated values uniformly distributed on the $[0, 1]$ interval. We simulated each of the thirty-two obtained models from ten different randomly selected initial states (initial values of nut, phyto and zoo) for 100 time steps of 1. Thus, ten different behaviors were obtained of each of the thirty-two models.

Table 6. A grammar for equation discovery in the aquatic ecosystem domain constructed from the food chain description and modeling knowledge from Table 2.

```
aquatic -> time_deriv(nut) = - feeds_on(phyto,nut);
      time_deriv(phyto) = growth(phyto) + feeds_on(phyto,nut)
                          - feeds_on(zoo,phyto);
      time_deriv(zoo) = const * zoo + feeds_on(zoo,phyto)
  feeds_on(phyto,nut) -> const[0:] * phyto * nutrient(nut)
  feeds_on(zoo,phyto) -> const[0:] * zoo * nutrient(phyto)
  nutrient(nut) -> nut
  nutrient(nut) -> nut / (nut + const[0:])
  nutrient(nut) -> nut * nut / (nut * nut + const[0:])
  nutrient(nut) -> 1 - exp(-const[0:] * nut)
  nutrient(phyto) -> phyto
  nutrient(phyto) -> phyto / (phyto + const[0:])
  nutrient(phyto) -> phyto * phyto / (phyto * phyto + const[0:])
  nutrient(phyto) -> 1 - exp(-const[0:] * phyto)
  growth(phyto) -> const * phyto
  growth(phyto) -> const * phyto * (1 - phyto / const[0:])
```

In order to test the robustness of the approach to noise in the data, we added artificially generated random Gaussian noise to the behaviors. The noise was added at four different relative noise levels: 1%, 5% and 10%. The relative noise level of $l\%$ means that we multiplied the original value x with $(1+l*G/100)$ to obtain a noisy value, where G is a normally distributed random variable with mean equal to 0 and standard deviation equal to 1.

Two evaluation criteria were used for evaluating the performance of the equation (re)discovery. First, the leave-one-out procedure was applied in order to estimate the error of discovered equations on test data, unseen during the discovery process. In each iteration of the leave-one-out procedure, nine out of ten behaviors were used to discover a system of differential equations with LAGRAMGE. The obtained differential equations were then simulated using the initial state of the remaining (test) behavior. The simulation error was measured as a sum of squared differences between the simulated behavior and the test behavior. Second, the structure of the best model discovered by LAGRAMGE, was matched against the structure of the original model equations. The structure of the equations is obtained by abstracting the values of the constant parameters in them and replacing them with the generic symbol const.

5.2 Experimental Results

We compared the performance of (1) LAGRAMGE 2.0 using the context dependent grammar with the performance of (2) LAGRAMGE 2.0 using the grammar without constraints on the values of the constant parameters, and (3) LAGRAMGE 1.0 (where no context dependent constraints, and no constraints on the values of the constant parameters can be used). The results of the comparison are summarized in Tables 7 and 8.

Before we discuss the experimental results, we should note here that the using the context dependent constraints in the grammar reduces the space of possible models. The grammar in Table 6 generates thirty-two models when interpreted as a context dependent grammar. On the other hand, when interpreted as a context free grammar (as interpreted by LAGRAMGE 1.0) this grammar generates 512 possible models. Therefore, using context dependent constraints reduces the search space of LAGRAMGE by a factor of sixteen.

Table 7. Performance of LAGRAMGE 2.0 (L2.0), LAGRAMGE 2.0 without applying constraints on constant parameters (L2.0-NCC) and LAGRAMGE 1.0 (L1.0). Left hand side: average sum of squared errors on the test behavior. Right hand side: number of successfully reconstructed original model structures.

NOISE LEVEL	AVERAGE TEST ERROR			STRUCTURE RECONSTRUCTION		
	L2.0	L2.0-NCC	L1.0	L2.0	L2.0-NCC	L1.0
0%	0.0031	0.0020	0.0006	29	28	5
1%	0.0083	*(1)	*(10)	8	6	0
5%	0.1490	*(6)	*(13)	3	5	1
10%	0.6187	*(6)	*(13)	4	5	2

In the left hand side of Table 7 the average leave-one-out testing error of the thirty-two (re)discovered models is given. Note that the symbol *(N) means that N out of thirty-two (re)discovered models could not be simulated (and therefore the average error could not be properly evaluated) due to the singularities, such as division by zero or unstable behavior of the discovered system of differential equations. Some of the singularities were caused by inappropriate values of the constant parameters (e.g., negative saturation limit or carrying capacity): these are the reasons for the failure of LAGRAMGE 2.0 without applying the constraints on the values of the constant parameters to discover a valid model. In models discovered by LAGRAMGE 1.0, some of the simulation failures are also caused by inappropriate model structure, due to the lack of context dependent constraints.

These results shows one important aspect of the noise robustness of LA-GRAMGE 2.0: at all noise levels it discovers models that can be simulated and have stable behaviors. This is due both to the context dependent constraints and the constraints on the values of the constant parameters. This is very important: in our earlier experiments on modeling phytoplankton growth in Lake Glumsoe, we had to manually filter out models, discovered by LAGRAMGE 1.0 with inappropriate values of the constant parameters [3].

In Table 8, the win-loss-tie counts for the comparison of the test error is presented. We counted the number of wins, losses and ties in the following manner. For each of the thirty-two experiments, we compared the simulation error e_1 of LAGRAMGE 2.0 with the simulation error e_2 of the other two algorithms (L2.0-NCC and L1.0 in Table 8). Comparisons where the relative difference of the simulation errors is less than 10% ($0.9 < e_2/e_1 < 1.1$) are considered ties.

Table 8. Win-loss-tie counts for comparison of the test error of (L2.0) with the test errors of L2.0-NCC and L1.0 (see caption of Table 7).

NOISE LEVEL	L2.0 VS. L2.0-NCC	L2.0 VS. L1.0
0%	10-9-13	26-2-4
1%	4-5-23	18-2-12
5%	7-12-13	16-6-10
10%	6-16-10	14-10-8

The comparison of simulation errors shows clear performance improvement of LAGRAMGE 2.0 over LAGRAMGE 1.0 for all noise levels. On the other hand, models discovered by LAGRAMGE 2.0 without applying the constraints on the values of the constant parameters better fits noisy data than the ones generated with LAGRAMGE 2.0. This observation shows that models with inappropriate values of the constant parameters (or inappropriate structure for models discovered by LAGRAMGE 1.0) can sometimes fit the observed data better. However, these models do not make sense from biological point of view.

6   Discussion

In the paper, a new approach to representing and using background knowledge for equation discovery is presented. The formalism for encoding knowledge about population dynamics, allows encoding two types of knowledge. The first type is domain specific knowledge about predator-prey food chain in the domain and can be provided by a biologist without any experience in mathematical modeling. The second type of knowledge is modeling knowledge in form of typical models used for modeling different population dynamic processes, such as growth of a population and saturation of predation. The modeling knowledge is provided by a population modeling expert, not necessary familiar with the domain at hand. This is high-level knowledge represented in first-order logic, which can be automatically transformed to the operational form of grammars used to guide the search for models in the process of equation discovery. This can be done for arbitrarily complex predator-prey models consisting of any number of populations and interactions between them. The proposed formalism can be easily extended with predicates for specifying other types of interactions between populations, such as parasytism, competitive exclusion and symbiosis.

The grammars generated using the presented approach are context dependent and generate context dependent and generate whole models, i.e., systems of simultaneous equations. The equation discovery system LAGRAMGE 2.0 was developed that accept such grammars. Using context dependent constraints reduces the space of possible models as compared to purely context free grammars used in LAGRAMGE 1.0. Therefore, context dependent constraints improve the efficiency of LAGRAMGE.

Experimental evaluation of LAGRAMGE 2.0 shows that both context dependent constraints and constraints on the values of the constant parameters improves noise robustness of LAGRAMGE in several ways. First, all the models (re)discovered by LAGRAMGE 2.0 at different noise levels can be simulated and generate stable behaviors. Second, all the models have clear interpretations from biological point of view. Finally, LAGRAMGE 2.0 (re)discovers the original model structure more often than LAGRAMGE 1.0. The experimental results should be further confirmed with experiments on the real-world observational data. These include modeling phytoplankton growth in Danish lake Glumsoe, predicting algae blooms in Lagoon of Venice [3] and modeling plankton population dynamics in Japanese lake Kasumigaura [9].

Currently, the presented formalism focuses on representing background knowledge for population dynamics modeling. However, the presented formalism can be extended so knowledge about dynamic processes from other areas can be encoded and used for equation discovery. The knowledge should include ontology of typical processes in the area (such as predator-prey interaction and population growth in population dynamics) and templates of models typically used for modeling these processes. Finally, knowledge from different areas can be organized in the form of libraries of background knowledge for equation discovery.

References

1. D. S. Bunch, D. M. Gay, and R. E. Welsch. Algorithm 717; subroutines for maximum likelihood and quasi-likelihood estimation of parameters in nonlinear regression models. *ACM Transactions on Mathematical Software*, 19:109–130, 1993.
2. S. Džeroski and L. Todorovski. Discovering dynamics: from inductive logic programming to machine discovery. *Journal of Intelligent Information Systems*, 4:89–108, 1995.
3. S. Džeroski, L. Todorovski, I. Bratko, B. Kompare, and V. Križman. Equation discovery with ecological applications. In A. H. Fielding, editor, *Machine learning methods for ecological applications*, pages 185–207. Kluwer Academic Publishers, 1999.
4. P. Langley, H. A. Simon, G. L. Bradshaw, and J. M. Żythow. *Scientific Discovery*. MIT Press, 1987.
5. L. Ljung. Modelling of industrial systems. In *Proc. of Seventh International Symposium on Methodologies for Intelligent Systems*, pages 338–349. Springer, 1993.
6. J. D. Murray. *Mathematical biology*. Springer, 1993. Second, Corrected Edition.
7. L. Todorovski and S. Džeroski. Declarative bias in equation discovery. In *Proc. of the Fourteenth International Conference on Machine Learning*, pages 376–384. Morgan Kaufmann, 1997.
8. T. Washio and H. Motoda. Discovering admissible models of complex systems based on scale-types and identity constraints. In *Proc. of the Fifteenth International Joint Conference on Artificial Intelligence*, volume 2, pages 810–817. Morgan Kaufmann, 1997.
9. P. A. Whigham. An inductive approach to ecological time series modelling by evolutionary computation. In *Abstract Book of the Second International Conference on Applications of Machine Learning to Ecological Modelling*, page 35. Adelaide University, 2000.
10. R. Zembowicz and J. M. Żytkow. Discovery of equations: Experimental evaluation of convergence. In *Proc. of the Tenth National Conference on Artificial Intelligence*, pages 70–75. Morgan Kaufmann, 1992.

Mining the Web for Synonyms:
PMI-IR versus LSA on TOEFL

Peter D. Turney

Institute for Information Technology, National Research Council of Canada,
M-50 Montreal Road, Ottawa, Ontario, Canada, K1A 0R6
peter.turney@nrc.ca

Abstract. This paper presents a simple unsupervised learning algorithm for recognizing synonyms, based on statistical data acquired by querying a Web search engine. The algorithm, called PMI-IR, uses Pointwise Mutual Information (PMI) and Information Retrieval (IR) to measure the similarity of pairs of words. PMI-IR is empirically evaluated using 80 synonym test questions from the Test of English as a Foreign Language (TOEFL) and 50 synonym test questions from a collection of tests for students of English as a Second Language (ESL). On both tests, the algorithm obtains a score of 74%. PMI-IR is contrasted with Latent Semantic Analysis (LSA), which achieves a score of 64% on the same 80 TOEFL questions. The paper discusses potential applications of the new unsupervised learning algorithm and some implications of the results for LSA and LSI (Latent Semantic Indexing).

1 Introduction

This paper introduces a simple unsupervised learning algorithm for recognizing synonyms. The task of recognizing synonyms is, given a problem word and a set of alternative words, choose the member from the set of alternative words that is most similar in meaning to the problem word. The unsupervised learning algorithm performs this task by issuing queries to a search engine and analyzing the replies to the queries. The algorithm, called PMI-IR, uses Pointwise Mutual Information (PMI) [1, 2] to analyze statistical data collected by Information Retrieval (IR). The quality of the algorithm's performance depends on the size of the document collection that is indexed by the search engine and the expressive power of the search engine's query language. The results presented here are based on queries to the AltaVista search engine [3].

Recognizing synonyms is often used as a test to measure a (human) student's mastery of a language. I evaluate the performance of PMI-IR using 80 synonym test questions from the Test of English as a Foreign Language (TOEFL) [4] and 50 synonym test questions from a collection of tests for students of English as a Second Language (ESL) [5]. PMI-IR obtains a score of 73.75% on the 80 TOEFL questions (59/80) and 74% on the 50 ESL questions (37/50). By comparison, the average score on the 80 TOEFL questions, for a large sample of applicants to US colleges from non-English

L. De Raedt and P. Flach (Eds.): ECML 2001, LNAI 2167, pp. 491-502, 2001.
© Springer-Verlag Berlin Heidelberg 2001

speaking countries, was 64.5% (51.6/80) [6]. Landauer and Dumais [6] note that, "… we have been told that the average score is adequate for admission to many universities."

Latent Semantic Analysis (LSA) is another unsupervised learning algorithm that has been applied to the task of recognizing synonyms. LSA achieves a score of 64.4% (51.5/80) on the 80 TOEFL questions [6]. Landauer and Dumais [6] write, regarding this score for LSA, "We know of no other fully automatic application of a knowledge acquisition and representation model, one that does not depend on knowledge being entered by a human but only on its acquisition from the kinds of experience on which a human relies, that has been capable of performing well on a full scale test used for adults." It is interesting that PMI-IR, which is conceptually simpler than LSA, scores almost 10% higher on the TOEFL questions.

LSA is a statistical algorithm based on Singular Value Decomposition (SVD). A variation on this algorithm has been applied to information retrieval, where it is known as Latent Semantic Indexing (LSI) [7]. The performance of LSA on the TOEFL test has been widely cited as evidence for the value of LSA and (by relation) LSI. In this paper, I discuss the implications of the new unsupervised learning algorithm and the synonym test results for LSA and LSI.

In the next section, I describe the PMI-IR algorithm. I then discuss related work on synonym recognition in Section 3. I briefly explain LSA in the following section. The experiments with the TOEFL questions and the ESL questions are presented in Sections 5 and 6, respectively. In Section 7, I discuss the interpretation of the results and their significance for LSA and LSI. The next section discusses potential applications of PMI-IR and the final section gives the conclusions.

2   PMI-IR

Consider the following synonym test question, one of the 80 TOEFL questions. Given the problem word *levied* and the four alternative words *imposed, believed, requested, correlated*, which of the alternatives is most similar in meaning to the problem word [8]? Let *problem* represent the problem word and $\{choice_1, choice_2, ..., choice_n\}$ represent the alternatives. The PMI-IR algorithm assigns a score to each choice, $score(choice_i)$, and selects the choice that maximizes the score.

The PMI-IR algorithm, like LSA, is based on co-occurrence [9]. The core idea is that "a word is characterized by the company it keeps" [10]. There are many different measures of the degree to which two words co-occur [9]. PMI-IR uses Pointwise Mutual Information (PMI) [1, 2], as follows:

$$score(choice_i) = \log_2(p(problem \ \& \ choice_i) / (p(problem)p(choice_i))) \quad (1)$$

Here, $p(problem \ \& \ choice_i)$ is the probability that *problem* and $choice_i$ co-occur. If *problem* and $choice_i$ are statistically independent, then the probability that they co-occur is given by the product $p(problem)p(choice_i)$. If they are not independent, and they have a tendency to co-occur, then $p(problem \ \& \ choice_i)$ will be greater than p(*problem*)p(*choice*$_i$). Therefore the ratio between p(*problem & choice*$_i$) and p(*problem*)p(*choice*$_i$) is a measure of the degree of statistical dependence between *problem* and *choice*$_i$. The log of this ratio is the amount of information that we acquire about the presence of *problem* when we observe *choice*$_i$. Since the equation is symmetrical, it is also the amount of information that we acquire about the presence of *choice*$_i$ when we observe *problem*, which explains the term *mutual information*.[1]

Since we are looking for the maximum score, we can drop $\log_2$ (because it is monotonically increasing) and p(*problem*) (because it has the same value for all choices, for a given problem word). Thus (1) simplifies to:

$$\text{score}(choice_i) = p(problem \ \& \ choice_i) \ / \ p(choice_i) \tag{2}$$

In other words, each choice is simply scored by the conditional probability of the problem word, given the choice word, p(*problem* | *choice*$_i$).

PMI-IR uses Information Retrieval (IR) to calculate the probabilities in (2). In this paper, I evaluate four different versions of PMI-IR, using four different kinds of queries. The following description of these four different methods for calculating (2) uses the AltaVista Advanced Search query syntax [11]. Let hits(*query*) be the number of hits (the number of documents retrieved) when the query *query* is given to AltaVista. The four scores are presented in order of increasing sophistication. They can be seen as increasingly refined interpretations of what it means for two words to co-occur, or increasingly refined interpretations of equation (2).

Score 1: In the simplest case, we say that two words co-occur when they appear in the same document:

$$\text{score}_1(choice_i) = \text{hits}(problem \ \text{AND} \ choice_i) \ / \ \text{hits}(choice_i) \tag{3}$$

We ask AltaVista how many documents contain both *problem* and *choice*$_i$, and then we ask how many documents contain *choice*$_i$ alone. The ratio of these two numbers is the score for *choice*$_i$.

Score 2: Instead of asking how many documents contain both *problem* and *choice*$_i$, we can ask how many documents contain the two words close together:

$$\text{score}_2(choice_i) = \text{hits}(problem \ \text{NEAR} \ choice_i) \ / \ \text{hits}(choice_i) \tag{4}$$

The AltaVista NEAR operator constrains the search to documents that contain *problem* and *choice*$_i$ within ten words of one another, in either order.

Score 3: The first two scores tend to score antonyms as highly as synonyms. For example, *big* and *small* may get the same score as *big* and *large*. The following score tends to reduce this effect, resulting in lower scores for antonyms:

---

[1] For an explanation of the term *pointwise* mutual information, see [9].

$$\text{score}_3(\text{choice}_i) =$$

$$\frac{\text{hits}((\text{problem NEAR } \text{choice}_i) \text{ AND NOT } ((\text{problem OR } \text{choice}_i) \text{ NEAR "not"}))}{\text{hits}(\text{choice}_i \text{ AND NOT } (\text{choice}_i \text{ NEAR "not"}))} \qquad (5)$$

Score 4: The fourth score takes context into account. There is no context for the TOEFL questions, but the ESL questions involve context. For example [5], "Every year in the early spring farmers [tap] maple syrup from their trees (drain; boil; knock; rap)." The problem word *tap*, out of context, might seem to best match the choice words *knock* or *rap*, but the context *maple syrup* makes *drain* a better match for *tap*. In general, in addition to the problem word *problem* and the alternatives {*choice_1*, *choice_2*, ..., *choice_n*}, we may have context words {*context_1*, *context_2*, ..., *context_m*}. The following score includes a context word:

$$\text{score}_4(\text{choice}_i) =$$

$$\frac{\text{hits}((\text{problem NEAR } \text{choice}_i) \text{ AND } \text{context AND NOT } ((\text{problem OR } \text{choice}_i) \text{ NEAR "not"}))}{\text{hits}(\text{choice}_i \text{ AND } \text{context AND NOT } (\text{choice}_i \text{ NEAR "not"}))} \qquad (6)$$

This equation easily generalizes to multiple context words, using AND, but each additional context word narrows the sample size, which might make the score more sensitive to noise (and could also reduce the sample size to zero). To address this issue, I chose only one context word from each ESL question. For a given ESL question, I automatically selected the context word by first eliminating the problem word (*tap*), the alternatives (*drain, boil, knock, rap*), and stop words (*in, the, from, their*). The remaining words (*every, year, early, spring, farmers, maple, syrup, trees*) were context words. I then used $p(\text{problem} \mid \text{context}_i)$, as calculated by $\text{score}_3(\text{context}_i)$, to evaluate each context word. In this example, *syrup* had the highest score (*maple* was second highest; that is, *maple* and *syrup* have the highest semantic similarity to *tap*, according to score_3), so *syrup* was selected as the context word *context* for calculating $\text{score}_4(\text{choice}_i)$.

3   Related Work

There are several well-known lexical database systems that include synonym information, such as WordNet [12], BRICO [13], and EuroWordNet [14]. These systems were constructed by hand, without machine learning, which ensures a certain level of quality, at the cost of a substantial amount of human labour. A major limitation of such hand-generated lexicons is the relatively poor coverage of technical and scientific terms. For example, I am interested in applying synonym recognition algorithms to the automatic extraction of keywords from documents [15]. In a large collection of scientific and technical journals, I found that only about 70% of the authors' keywords were in WordNet. (On the other hand, 100% were indexed by AltaVista.) This is a strong motivation for automating aspects of the construction of lexical databases. Another motivation is that the labour involved must be repeated for each new language and must be repeated regularly as new terms are added to a language.

Statistical approaches to synonym recognition are based on co-occurrence [9]. Manning and Schütze distinguish between co-occurrence (or association) and collocation: *collocation* refers to "grammatically bound elements that occur in a particular order", but *co-occurrence* and *association* refer to "the more general phenomenon of words that are likely to be used in the same context" [9]. Order does not matter for synonyms, so we say that they co-occur, rather than saying that they are collocated. Pointwise Mutual Information (PMI) has primarily been applied to analysis of collocation, but there have been some applications to co-occurrence analysis [1, 2]. I believe that the novelty in PMI-IR is mainly the observation that PMI can exploit IR. Instead of analyzing a document collection from scratch, specifically for co-occurrence information, we can take advantage of the huge document collections that have been indexed by modern Web search engines.

Various measures of semantic similarity between word pairs have been proposed, some using statistical (unsupervised learning from text) techniques [16, 17, 18], some using lexical databases (hand-built) [19, 20], and some hybrid approaches, combining statistics and lexical information [21, 22]. Statistical techniques typically suffer from the *sparse data problem*: they perform poorly when the words are relatively rare, due to the scarcity of data. Hybrid approaches attempt to address this problem by supplementing sparse data with information from a lexical database [21, 22]. PMI-IR addresses the sparse data problem by using a huge data source: the Web. As far as I know, no previous work in the statistical approach to semantic similarity has been able to exploit such a large body of text.

Another popular statistical approach to measuring semantic similarity is Latent Semantic Analysis (LSA) [6, 7, 8]. I will discuss this approach in the next section.

The work described in this paper is also related to the literature on data mining and text mining, in that it presents a method for extracting interesting relational information from a very large database (AltaVista). The most closely related work is the use of *interest* to discover interesting associations in large databases [23]. The *interest* of an association A & B is defined as $p(A$ & $B) / (p(A)p(B))$. This is clearly equivalent to PMI without the log function (see equation (1) above). As far as I know, *interest* has been applied to data mining, but not to text mining.

4   Latent Semantic Analysis

LSA uses the Singular Value Decomposition (SVD) to analyze the statistical relationships among words in a collection of text [6, 7, 8]. The first step is to use the text to construct a matrix X, in which the row vectors represent words and the column vectors represent chunks of text (e.g., sentences, paragraphs, documents). Each cell represents the *weight* of the corresponding word in the corresponding chunk of text. The *weight* is typically the TF.IDF score (Term Frequency times Inverse Document Frequency) for the word in the chunk. (TF.IDF is a standard tool in Information Retrieval.) The next step is to apply SVD to $\mathbf{X}$, to decompose $\mathbf{X}$ into a product of three matrices $\mathbf{ULA}^T$, where $\mathbf{U}$ and $\mathbf{A}$ are in column orthonormal form (i.e., the columns are orthogonal and have unit length) and $\mathbf{L}$ is a diagonal matrix of *singular values* (hence SVD). If $\mathbf{X}$ is of rank r, then $\mathbf{L}$ is also of rank r. Let $\mathbf{L}_k$, where $k < r$, be the matrix produced by removing from $\mathbf{L}$ the $r - k$ columns and rows with the smallest singular values, and let $\mathbf{U}_k$ and $\mathbf{A}_k$ be the matrices produced by removing the corresponding columns from $\mathbf{U}$ and $\mathbf{A}$. The matrix $\mathbf{U}_k\mathbf{L}_k\mathbf{A}_k^T$ is the matrix of rank k that best approximates the original matrix $\mathbf{X}$, in the sense that it minimizes the sum of the squares of the approximation errors. We may think of this matrix $\mathbf{U}_k\mathbf{L}_k\mathbf{A}_k^T$ as a "smoothed" or "compressed" version of the original matrix $\mathbf{X}$. SVD may be viewed as a form of *principal components* analysis. LSA works by measuring the similarity of words using this compressed matrix, instead of the original matrix. The similarity of two words is measured by the cosine of the angle between their corresponding compressed row vectors.

When they applied LSA to the TOEFL questions, Landauer and Dumais used an encyclopedia as the text source, to build a matrix $\mathbf{X}$ with 61,000 rows (words) and 30,473 columns (chunks of text; each chunk was one article from the encyclopedia) [6, 8]. They used SVD to generate a reduced matrix of rank 300. When they measured the similarity of the words (row vectors) in the original matrix $\mathbf{X}$, only 36.8% of the TOEFL questions were answered correctly (15.8% when corrected for guessing, using a penalty of 1/3 for each incorrect answer), but using the reduced matrix of rank 300 improves the performance to 64.4% (52.5% corrected for guessing). They claim that the score of 36.8%, using the original matrix, "... is similar to what would be obtained by a mutual information analysis..." (see footnote 5 in [6]).

5   TOEFL Experiments

Recall the sample TOEFL question: Given the problem word *levied* and the four alternative words *imposed, believed, requested, correlated*, which of the alternatives is most similar in meaning to the problem word [8]? Table 1 shows in detail how score$_3$ is calculated for this example. In this case, PMI-IR selects *imposed* as the answer.

Table 2 shows the scores calculated by LSA for the same example [8]. Note that LSA and AltaVista are using quite different document collections for their calculations. AltaVista indexes 350 million web pages [24] (but only a fraction of them are in English). To apply LSA to the TOEFL questions, an encyclopedia was used to create a matrix of 61,000 words by 30,473 articles [8]. However, it is interesting that the two techniques produce identical rankings for this example.

Table 3 shows the results for PMI-IR, for the first three scores, on the 80 TOEFL questions. (The fourth score is not applicable, because there is no context for the questions.) The results for LSA and humans are also presented, for comparison.

Table 1. Details of the calculation of score$_3$ for a sample TOEFL question.

Query	Hits
imposed AND NOT (imposed NEAR "not")	1,147,535
believed AND NOT (believed NEAR "not")	2,246,982
requested AND NOT (requested NEAR "not")	7,457,552
correlated AND NOT (correlated NEAR "not")	296,631
(levied NEAR imposed) AND NOT ((levied OR imposed) NEAR "not")	2,299
(levied NEAR believed) AND NOT ((levied OR believed) NEAR "not")	80
(levied NEAR requested) AND NOT ((levied OR requested) NEAR "not")	216
(levied NEAR correlated) AND NOT ((levied OR correlated) NEAR "not")	3

Choice		Score$_3$
p(levied | imposed)	2,299 / 1,147,535	0.0020034
p(levied | believed)	80 / 2,246,982	0.0000356
p(levied | requested)	216 / 7,457,552	0.0000290
p(levied | correlated)	3 / 296,631	0.0000101

Table 2. LSA scores for a sample TOEFL question.

Choice	LSA Score
imposed	0.70
believed	0.09
requested	0.05
correlated	-0.03

Table 3. Results of the TOEFL experiments, including LSA results from [6].

Interpretation of p(*problem* | *choice*$_i$)	Description of Interpretation	Number of Correct Test Answers	Percentage of Correct Answers
score$_1$	co-occurrence using AND operator	50/80	62.5%
score$_2$	co-occurrence using NEAR	58/80	72.5%
score$_3$	co-occurrence using NEAR and NOT	59/80	73.75%
Latent Semantic Analysis		51.5/80	64.4%
Average Non-English US College Applicant		51.6/80	64.5%

6   ESL Experiments

To validate the performance of PMI-IR on the TOEFL questions, I obtained another set of 50 synonym test questions [5]. Table 4 shows the results of PMI-IR using all four of the different interpretations of p(*problem* | *choice*$_i$).

Table 4. Results of the ESL experiments.

Interpretation of p(*problem* | *choice*$_i$)	Description of Interpretation	Number of Correct Test Answers	Percentage of Correct Answers
score$_1$	co-occurrence using AND operator	24/50	48%
score$_2$	co-occurrence using NEAR	31/50	62%
score$_3$	co-occurrence using NEAR and NOT	33/50	66%
score$_4$	co-occurrence using NEAR, NOT, and context	37/50	74%

7   Discussion of Results

The results with the TOEFL questions show that PMI-IR (in particular, score$_3$) can score almost 10% higher than LSA. The results with the ESL questions support the view that this performance is not a chance occurrence. However, the interpretation of the results is difficult, due to two factors: (1) PMI-IR is using a much larger data source than LSA. (2) PMI-IR (in the case of all of the scores except for score$_1$) is using a much smaller chunk size than LSA.

PMI-IR was implemented as a simple, short Perl program. One TOEFL question requires eight queries to AltaVista (Table 1).[2] Each query takes about two seconds, for a total of about sixteen seconds per TOEFL question. Almost all of the time is spent on network traffic between the computer that hosts PMI-IR and the computer(s) that host(s) AltaVista. If PMI-IR were multi-threaded, the eight queries could be issued simultaneously, cutting the total time to about two seconds per TOEFL question. If PMI-IR and AltaVista were hosted on the same computer, the time per TOEFL question would likely be a small fraction of a second. Clearly, the hard work here is done by AltaVista, not by the Perl program.

---

[2] For the ESL questions, score$_4$ requires extra queries to select the context word.

The majority of the time required for LSA is the time spent on the SVD. To compress the 61,000 by 30,473 matrix used for the TOEFL questions to a matrix of rank 300 required about three hours of computation on a Unix workstation [6]. A fast SVD algorithm can find a rank k approximation to an m by n matrix X in time $O(mk^2)$ [25]. Recall that m is the number of words and n is the number of chunks of text. If we suppose that there are about one million English words, then to go from $m \approx 50,000$ to $m \approx 1,000,000$ is an increase by a factor of 20, so it seems possible for SVD to be applied to the same corpus as AltaVista, 350 million web pages [24]. For future work, it would be interesting to see how LSA performs with such a large collection of text.

Several authors have observed that PMI is especially sensitive to the sparse data problem [9]. Landauer and Dumais claim that mutual information analysis would obtain a score of about 37% on the TOEFL questions, given the same source text and chunk size as they used for LSA (footnote 5 in [6]). Although it appears that they have not tested this conjecture, it seems plausible to me. It seems likely that PMI-IR achieves high performance by "brute force", through the sheer size of the corpus of text that is indexed by AltaVista. It would be interesting to test this hypothesis. Although it might be a challenge to scale LSA up to this volume of text, PMI can easily be scaled down to the encyclopedia text that is used by Landauer and Dumais [6]. This is another possibility for future work. Perhaps the strength of LSA is that it can achieve relatively good performance with relatively little text. This is what we would expect from the "smoothing" or "compression" produced by SVD. However, if you have access to huge volumes of data, there is much less need for smoothing.

It is interesting that the TOEFL performance for $score_1$ (62.5%) is approximately the same as the performance for LSA (64.4%) (Table 3). Much of the difference in performance between LSA and PMI-IR comes from using the NEAR operator instead of the AND operator. This suggests that perhaps much of the difference between LSA and PMI-IR is due to the smaller chunk size of PMI-IR (for the scores other than $score_1$). To test this hypothesis, the LSA experiment with TOEFL could be repeated using the same source text (an encyclopedia), but a smaller chunk size. This is another possibility for future work.

Latent Semantic Indexing (LSI) applies LSA to Information Retrieval. The hope is that LSI can improve the performance of IR by, in essence, automatically expanding a query with synonyms [7]. Then a search for (say) *cars* may be able to return a document that contains *automobiles*, but not *cars*. Although there have been some positive results using LSI for IR [8], the results from TREC2 and TREC3 (Text Retrieval Conferences 2 and 3) did not show an advantage to LSI over other leading IR techniques [26]. It has been conjectured that the TREC queries are unusually long and detailed, so there is little room for improvement by LSI [8]. The results reported here for PMI-IR suggest an alternative hypothesis. Most of the TREC systems use a technique called *query expansion* [27]. This technique involves searching with the original query, extracting terms from the top retrieved documents, adding these terms to the original query, and then repeating the search with the new, expanded query. I hypothesize that this query expansion achieves essentially the same effect as LSI, so there is no apparent advantage to LSI when it is compared to an IR system that uses query expansion.

If (say) *cars* and *automobiles* have a high semantic similarity, then we can expect p(*automobiles* | *cars*) to be relatively high (see equation (2)). Thus, the query *cars* is likely to retrieve a document containing the word *automobiles*. This means that there is a good chance that query expansion will expand the query *cars* to a new query that contains *automobiles*. Testing this hypothesis is another area for future work. The hypothesis implies that LSI will tend to perform better than an IR system without query expansion, but there will be no significant difference between an IR system with LSI and an IR system with query expansion (assuming all other factors are equal).

8   Applications

A limitation of PMI-IR is that the network access time for querying a large Web search engine may be prohibitive for certain applications, for those of us who do not have very high-speed, high-priority access to such a search engine. However, it is possible that PMI-IR may achieve good results with a significantly smaller document collection. One possibility is a hybrid system, which uses a small, local search engine for high-frequency words, but resorts to a large, distant search engine for rare words.

PMI-IR may be suitable as a tool to aid in the construction of lexical databases. It might also be useful for improving IR systems. For example, an IR system with query expansion might use $score_4$ to screen candidate terms for expanding a query. The candidates would be extracted from the top retrieved documents, as with current query expansion techniques. However, current query expansion techniques may suggest sub-optimal expansion terms, because the top retrieved documents constitute a relatively small, noisy sample. Thus there could be some benefit to validating the suggested expansions using PMI-IR, which would draw on larger sample sizes.

I am particularly interested in applying PMI-IR to automatic keyword extraction [15]. One of the most helpful clues that a word (or phrase) is a keyword in a given document is the frequency of the word. However, authors often use synonyms, in order to avoid boring the reader with repetition. This is courteous for human readers, but it complicates automatic keyword extraction. I am hoping that PMI-IR will help me to cluster synonyms together, so that I can aggregate their frequency counts, resulting in better keyword extraction.

9   Conclusions

This paper has introduced a simple unsupervised learning algorithm for recognizing synonyms. The algorithm uses a well-known measure of semantic similarity (PMI). The new contribution is the observation that PMI can exploit the huge document collections that are indexed by modern Web search engines. The algorithm is evaluated using the Test of English as a Foreign Language. The algorithm is compared with Latent Semantic Analysis, which has also been evaluated using TOEFL. The comparison sheds new light on LSA, suggesting several new hypotheses that are worth investigating.

Acknowledgements. Thanks to Joel Martin for many helpful suggestions and general encouragement. Thanks to Eibe Frank, Gordon Paynter, Alain Désilets, Alan Barton, Arnold Smith, and Martin Brooks for their comments on an earlier version of this paper. The 80 TOEFL questions were kindly provided by Thomas K. Landauer, Department of Psychology, University of Colorado.

References

1. Church, K.W., Hanks, P.: Word Association Norms, Mutual Information and Lexicography. In: Proceedings of the 27th Annual Conference of the Association of Computational Linguistics, (1989) 76-83.
2. Church, K.W., Gale, W., Hanks, P., Hindle, D.: Using Statistics in Lexical Analysis. In: Uri Zernik (ed.), Lexical Acquisition: Exploiting On-Line Resources to Build a Lexicon. New Jersey: Lawrence Erlbaum (1991) 115-164.
3. AltaVista, AltaVista Company, Palo Alto, California, http://www.altavista.com/.
4. Test of English as a Foreign Language (TOEFL), Educational Testing Service, Princeton, New Jersey, http://www.ets.org/.
5. Tatsuki, D.: Basic 2000 Words - Synonym Match 1. In: Interactive JavaScript Quizzes for ESL Students, http://www.aitech.ac.jp/~iteslj/quizzes/js/dt/mc-2000-01syn.html (1998).
6. Landauer, T.K., Dumais, S.T.: A Solution to Plato's Problem: The Latent Semantic Analysis Theory of the Acquisition, Induction, and Representation of Knowledge. Psychological Review, 104 (1997) 211-240.
7. Deerwester, S., Dumais, S.T., Furnas, G.W., Landauer, T.K., Harshman, R.: Indexing by Latent Semantic Analysis. Journal of the American Society for Information Science, 41 (1990) 391-407.
8. Berry, M.W., Dumais, S.T., Letsche, T.A.: Computational Methods for Intelligent Information Access. Proceedings of Supercomputing '95, San Diego, California, (1995).
9. Manning, C.D., Schütze, H.: Foundations of Statistical Natural Language Processing. Cambridge, Massachusetts: MIT Press (1999).
10. Firth, J.R.: A Synopsis of Linguistic Theory 1930-1955. In Studies in Linguistic Analysis, pp. 1-32. Oxford: Philological Society (1957). Reprinted in F.R. Palmer (ed.), Selected Papers of J.R. Firth 1952-1959, London: Longman (1968).
11. AltaVista: AltaVista Advanced Search Cheat Sheet, AltaVista Company, Palo Alto, California, http://doc.altavista.com/adv_search/syntax.html (2001).
12. Fellbaum, C. (ed.): WordNet: An Electronic Lexical Database. Cambridge, Massachusetts: MIT Press (1998). For more information: http://www.cogsci.princeton.edu/~wn/.
13. Haase, K.: Interlingual BRICO. IBM Systems Journal, 39 (2000) 589-596. For more information: http://www.framerd.org/brico/.
14. Vossen, P. (ed.): EuroWordNet: A Multilingual Database with Lexical Semantic Networks. Dordrecht, Netherlands: Kluwer (1998). See: http://www.hum.uva.nl/~ewn/.
15. Turney, P.D.: Learning Algorithms for Keyphrase Extraction. Information Retrieval, 2 (2000) 303-336.
16. Grefenstette, G.: Finding Semantic Similarity in Raw Text: The Deese Antonyms. In: R. Goldman, P. Norvig, E. Charniak and B. Gale (eds.), Working Notes of the AAAI Fall Symposium on Probabilistic Approaches to Natural Language. AAAI Press (1992) 61-65.

17. Schütze, H.: Word Space. In: S.J. Hanson, J.D. Cowan, and C.L. Giles (eds.), Advances in Neural Information Processing Systems 5, San Mateo California: Morgan Kaufmann (1993) 895-902.
18. Lin, D.: Automatic Retrieval and Clustering of Similar Words. In: Proceedings of the 17th International Conference on Computational Linguistics and 36th Annual Meeting of the Association for Computational Linguistics, Montreal (1998) 768-773.
19. Richardson, R., Smeaton, A., Murphy, J.: Using WordNet as a Knowledge Base for Measuring Semantic Similarity between Words. In Proceedings of AICS Conference. Trinity College, Dublin (1994).
20. Lee, J.H., Kim, M.H., Lee, Y.J.: Information Retrieval Based on Conceptual Distance in IS-A Hierarchies. Journal of Documentation, 49 (1993) 188-207.
21. Resnik, P.: Semantic Similarity in a Taxonomy: An Information-Based Measure and its Application to Problems of Ambiguity in Natural Language. Journal of Artificial Intelligence Research, 11 (1998) 95-130.
22. Jiang, J., Conrath, D.: Semantic Similarity Based on Corpus Statistics and Lexical Taxonomy. In: Proceedings of the 10th International Conference on Research on Computational Linguistics, Taiwan, (1997).
23. Brin, S., Motwani, R., Ullman, J., Tsur, S.: Dynamic Itemset Counting and Implication Rules for Market Basket Data. In: Proceedings of the 1997 ACM-SIGMOD International Conference on the Management of Data (1997) 255-264.
24. Sullivan, D.: Search Engine Sizes. SearchEngineWatch.com, internet.com Corporation, Darien, Connecticut, http://searchenginewatch.com/reports/sizes.html (2000).
25. Papadimitriou, C.H., Raghavan, P., Tamaki, H., Vempala, S.: Latent Semantic Indexing: A Probabilistic Analysis. In: Proceedings of the Seventeenth ACM-SIGACT-SIGMOD-SIGART Symposium on Principles of Database Systems, Seattle, Washington (1998) 159-168.
26. Sparck Jones, K.: Comparison Between TREC2 and TREC3. In: D. Harman (ed.), The Third Text REtrieval Conference (TREC3), National Institute of Standards and Technology Special Publication 500-226, Gaithersburg, Maryland (1994) C1-C4.
27. Buckley, C., Salton, G., Allan, J., Singhal, A.: Automatic Query Expansion Using SMART: TREC 3. In: The Third Text REtrieval Conference (TREC3), D. Harman (ed.), National Institute of Standards and Technology Special Publication 500-226, Gaithersburg, Maryland (1994) 69-80.

A Unified Framework for Evaluation Metrics in Classification Using Decision Trees

Ricardo Vilalta, Mark Brodie,
Daniel Oblinger, and Irina Rish

IBM T.J. Watson Research Center,
30 Saw Mill River Rd., Hawthorne N.Y., 10532 USA
vilalta,brodie,oblinger,rish@us.ibm.com

Abstract. Most evaluation metrics in classification are designed to reward class uniformity in the example subsets induced by a feature (e.g., Information Gain). Other metrics are designed to reward discrimination power in the context of feature selection as a means to combat the feature-interaction problem (e.g., Relief, Contextual Merit). We define a new framework that combines the strengths of both kinds of metrics. Our framework enriches the available information when considering which feature to use to partition the training set. Since most metrics rely on only a small fraction of this information, this framework enlarges the space of possible metrics. Experiments on real-world domains in the context of decision-tree learning show how a simple setting for our framework compares well with standard metrics.

1 Introduction

Evaluation metrics play a critical role in the operation of decision-tree learning algorithms and other symbolic methods for classification, such as rule-based learning and decision lists. An evaluation metric measures the quality in the partitions induced by each of the available features (or functions of features) on a set of training examples; a decision tree is constructed by choosing the highest-quality feature at each tree node. Selecting the right features has strong impact on the final decision tree [8,14,6], contrary to results on earlier studies [9].

Evaluation metrics can be divided in two kinds. The most common kind, *traditional* or *purity-based*, use the proportion of classes on the example subsets induced by each feature; the best result is attained if each example subset is class uniform (i.e., comprises examples of the same class). Examples of traditional or purity-based evaluation metrics are Information Gain and Gain Ratio [11,12], G statistic [9], χ^2 [9,14], Laplace [13], Gini Index [1]. A different class of metrics, *discrimination-based*, quantifies the ability of a feature to separate examples of different class [3,4,7]; most research in this area is found in the context of feature selection as a pre-processing step to classification. Discrimination-based metrics deserve particular attention because of their ability to address the high interaction problem, in which the relevance of a feature can be observed only in combination with other features.

L. De Raedt and P. Flach (Eds.): ECML 2001, LNAI 2167, pp. 503–514, 2001.
© Springer-Verlag Berlin Heidelberg 2001

This paper introduces a unified framework for evaluation metrics in classification. Our framework is based on a set of parameters and a function of the distance between examples. We show how varying the choice of parameters and distance function allows more emphasis to be placed on either the class uniformity or the discrimination power of the induced example subsets. Our framework, therefore, enables us to combine the strengths of both traditional (or purity-based) and discrimination-based metrics. Furthermore, we show how existing metrics can be defined as instances of this unified framework.

The unification of evaluation metrics in a single framework unveils a space with more metrics than those currently known. This richer characterization of metrics opens the gates to a further understanding of the effects that different splitting functions have during decision-tree learning. Experiments in real-world domains show that the unified framework produces results comparable to using the best of a set of standard evaluation metrics.

The organization of the paper follows. Section 2 provides background information on classification and decision-tree learning. Section 3 reviews the differences between purity and discrimination-based metrics. Section 4 describes our unified framework for evaluation metrics. Section 5 shows experiments on real-world domains using decision trees. Finally, Section 6 presents our conclusions and future work.

2 Preliminaries

A classifier receives as input a set of training examples T_{train} : $\{(\tilde{\mathbf{X}}_{\mathbf{i}}, c_i)\}$. $\tilde{\mathbf{X}}$ is a feature vector characterized as a point in an n-dimensional feature space, $\tilde{\mathbf{X}} = (X_1, X_2, \cdots, X_n)$. Each feature X_k can take on a different number of values $\{V_m\}$. We refer to the value of feature X_k on vector $\tilde{\mathbf{X}}_{\mathbf{i}}$ as x_k^i, $\tilde{\mathbf{X}}_{\mathbf{i}} = (x_1^i, x_2^i, \cdots, x_n^i)$. $\tilde{\mathbf{X}}_{\mathbf{i}}$ is labeled with class c_i according to an unknown target function or concept C, $C(\tilde{\mathbf{X}}_{\mathbf{i}}) = c_i$ (we assume a deterministic target function, i.e., zero-bayes risk). T_{train} consists of independently and identically distributed (i.i.d.) examples obtained according to a fixed but unknown joint probability distribution Φ in the space of possible feature-vectors $\mathcal{X}$. The goal of the classifier is to produce a hypothesis h that best approximates C, i.e., that minimizes a loss function (e.g., zero-one loss) in the input-output space $\mathcal{X} \times \mathcal{C}$ according to distribution Φ.

In decision-tree learning, each hypothesis takes the form of a tree graph. In its most simple form, the algorithm proceeds top-down; the root of a decision tree is formed by selecting the feature X_k with highest score on T_{train} according to an evaluation metric $\mathcal{M}$. The selected feature splits the training set T_{train} into mutually exclusive subsets $\{T_m\}$, one for each possible feature value. The same methodology is recursively applied to each induced subset, resulting in new subtrees. A node is terminal (i.e., a leaf) if the set of examples T covered by that node are all of the same class, or if the number of examples in T is less than a (user-defined) threshold. A new vector $\tilde{\mathbf{X}}_{\mathbf{i}}$ is classified by starting at the root of the tree and following the branches which match the feature values of $\tilde{\mathbf{X}}_{\mathbf{i}}$ until a leaf is reached.

3   A Review of Evaluation Metrics

3.1   Traditional Metrics

An evaluation metric $\mathcal{M}$ quantifies the quality of the partitions induced by a feature X_k over a set of training examples T. Traditional or purity-based metrics define $\mathcal{M}$ by measuring the amount of class uniformity gained by decomposing T into the set of example subsets $\{T_m\}$ induced by X_k. Let $\tilde{\mathbf{P}}$ be the vector of class probabilities estimated from the data in the complete set T, let $\tilde{\mathbf{P}}_{\mathbf{m}}$ be the corresponding vector of class probabilities estimated from the data in the induced subset T_m, and let I be a measure of the impurity of a class probability vector. $\mathcal{M}$ is typically defined as follows:

$$\mathcal{M}(X_k) = I(\tilde{\mathbf{P}}) - \frac{|T_m|}{|T|} \sum_m I(\tilde{\mathbf{P}}_{\mathbf{m}}) \tag{1}$$

Different variations of $\mathcal{M}$ can be obtained by changing the impurity function I. For example, for Information Gain [11,12], impurity is defined in terms of entropy:

$$I_{\text{entropy}}(\tilde{\mathbf{P}}) = - \sum_i p_i \log_2 p_i \tag{2}$$

Another example is Gini Index [1], where impurity is defined as follows:

$$I_{\text{gini}}(\tilde{\mathbf{P}}) = 1 - \sum_i p_i^2 \tag{3}$$

Equation 1 covers most traditional metrics. Other metrics exist in which the class probability vectors are compared with each other, rather than assessed in isolation (e.g., to maximize their degree of orthogonality [2]). Thus, in a general sense, a characterization of traditional metrics can only be obtained by defining $\mathcal{M}$ as an arbitrary function over the class probability vectors[1]:

$$\mathcal{M}(X_k) = F(\tilde{\mathbf{P}}, \{\tilde{\mathbf{P}}_{\mathbf{m}}\}) \tag{4}$$

Traditional metrics exhibit two major limitations. First is a tendency to favor features with many values. Inducing many example subsets increases the probability of finding class-uniform subsets, but at the expense of overfitting. Several solutions have already been proposed for this problem [14,6].

We focus on a second limitation - the inability to detect the relevance of a feature when its contribution to the target concept is hidden by combinations with other features, also known as the feature-interaction problem [3,10]. As an illustration, Figure 1 shows a three-dimensional boolean space where each example can take one of two classes, $\{+, -\}$. The target concept is the Exclusive-OR $X_1 \oplus X_2$, and X_3 is irrelevant (the double arrows will be explained in the next section). Features X_1 and X_2 exhibit high interaction because the class label of an example can be determined only if both features are known.

---

[1] Strictly speaking $\mathcal{M}$ is also dependent on the size of the example set T, $|T|$. For example both the G and χ^2 statistics depend on $|T|$ in addition to the class probability vectors.

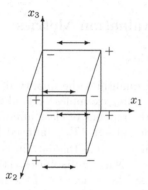

Fig. 1. A 3-dimensional boolean space for target concept $F = X_1 \oplus X_2$, feature X_3 is irrelevant. Features X_1 and X_2 exhibit high interaction: both features are always needed to determine the class label of an example.

In the example above, purity-based metrics fail to give more merit to X_1 and X_2 as compared with X_3, because the class probability vectors are the same for each feature ($\tilde{\mathbf{P}} = \tilde{\mathbf{P}}_{\mathbf{m}} = (0.5, 0.5)$). To attack the feature-interaction problem additional information besides class probabilities is required.

3.2   Discrimination-Based Metrics

A different kind of evaluation metric considers the discrimination power of each feature, i.e., the ability of a feature to separate examples of different class. Let $\tilde{\mathbf{X}}_{\mathbf{i}}$ and $\tilde{\mathbf{X}}_{\mathbf{j}}$ be two examples lying close to each other according to some distance measure D. Feature X_k is awarded some amount of discrimination power if it takes on different values when the class values of $\tilde{\mathbf{X}}_{\mathbf{i}}$ and $\tilde{\mathbf{X}}_{\mathbf{j}}$ differ, i.e., when $x_k^i \neq x_k^j$ and $C(\tilde{\mathbf{X}}_{\mathbf{i}}) \neq C(\tilde{\mathbf{X}}_{\mathbf{j}})$. The more often this condition is true for pairs of nearby examples, the higher the quality of feature X_k.

Let us illustrate how this works for the example in Figure 1. Assume that a feature scores a unit amount whenever the condition $x_k^i \neq x_k^j$ and $C(\tilde{\mathbf{X}}_{\mathbf{i}}) \neq C(\tilde{\mathbf{X}}_{\mathbf{j}})$ is true. As a further simplification, consider only pairs of examples at unit Hamming distance. The double arrows in Figure 1 indicate pairs of neighboring examples where feature X_1 differs in value. Since every time this happens the class of the examples differs, feature X_1 scores a total value of 4. Feature X_2 gets the same score as X_1, whereas X_3 scores a value of 0. Thus discrimination-based metrics take advantage of the distribution of examples in the training set to handle the feature-interaction problem.

Two representative examples of discrimination-based metrics are Contextual Merit [3] and Relief [4,5]. Before describing them, we define the distance between two examples as follows:

$$D(\tilde{\mathbf{X}}_{\mathbf{i}}, \tilde{\mathbf{X}}_{\mathbf{j}}) = \sum_{k=1}^{n} d(x_k^i, x_k^j) \tag{5}$$

For nominal features $d(x_k^i, x_k^j)$ is defined as

$$d(x_k^i, x_k^j) = \begin{cases} 1 & \text{if } x_k^i \neq x_k^j \\ 0 & \text{if } x_k^i = x_k^j \end{cases} \tag{6}$$

For numeric features $d(x_k^i, x_k^j)$ is defined as

$$d(x_k^i, x_k^j) = \frac{|x_k^i - x_k^j|}{\text{TH}(x_k^i, x_k^j)} \tag{7}$$

where TH is a normalization factor, e.g., $\text{MAX}(X_k) - \text{MIN}(X_k)$ (difference between the maximum and minimum values observed for feature X_k in T).

Figure 2 describes the logic behind discrimination-based metrics in a single framework[2]. The algorithm returns a vector of feature scores $\tilde{Q} = (q_1, q_2, \cdots, q_n)$. For every pair of nearby examples, q_k, the score for feature X_k, is updated as a function of $D(\tilde{X}_i, \tilde{X}_j)$ (equation 5) and $d(x_k^i, x_k^j)$ (equations 6 and 7). Different metrics are obtained by varying the update function (lines 5–6). The Relief algorithm, for example, updates score q_k as follows[3]:

$$q_k = \begin{cases} q_k + d(x_k^i, x_k^j) & \text{if } C(\tilde{X}_i) \neq C(\tilde{X}_j) \\ q_k - d(x_k^i, x_k^j) & \text{if } C(\tilde{X}_i) = C(\tilde{X}_j) \end{cases} \tag{8}$$

Thus Relief updates q_k whenever the feature values of two neighbor examples differ; the score increases if their class values differ and decreases if they are the same. Contextual Merit updates q_k when both feature values and class values differ; it uses the update function:

$$q_k = q_k + \frac{d(x_k^i, x_k^j)}{D(\tilde{X}_i, \tilde{X}_j)^2} \text{ if } C(\tilde{X}_i) \neq C(\tilde{X}_j) \tag{9}$$

In this case the score of a feature decreases quadratically with the distance between two examples.

Discrimination-based metrics have proved effective in the context of feature selection as a pre-processing step to classification. Their design is particularly suitable for domains exhibiting high degree of feature interaction such as protein-folding prediction, board games, parity, etc. These type of metrics, however, ignore the degree of class uniformity of the examples subsets induced by a feature; discrimination power is the only criterion used. We now propose a framework that combines the strengths of both traditional and discrimination-based metrics *during* classification.

---

[2] We encourage reviewing the references on Relief and Contextual Merit for a detailed understanding of their mechanism. Our description is over-simplified.

[3] The original description of Relief uses the update function $d(x_k^i, x_k^j)/l$ where l is the number of neighbor examples. Since l is a constant we can dispense with it without affecting the final feature ranking.

Algorithm 1: Discrimination-Based Metric
Input: Example set T
Output: Vector of feature scores $\tilde{\mathbf{Q}}$
COUNT-DISCRIMINATION-POWER(T)
(1)   Initialize $\tilde{\mathbf{Q}} = (q_1, q_2, \cdots, q_k)$
(2)   **foreach** example $\tilde{\mathbf{X}}_\mathbf{i} \in T$
(3)   **foreach** example $\tilde{\mathbf{X}}_\mathbf{j}$ close to $\tilde{\mathbf{X}}_\mathbf{i}$
(4)   **foreach** feature X_k
(5)   Update q_k as a function of
(6) $D(\tilde{\mathbf{X}}_\mathbf{i}, \tilde{\mathbf{X}}_\mathbf{j})$ and $d(x_k^i, x_k^j)$
(7)   **return** $\tilde{\mathbf{Q}}$

Fig. 2. A general algorithm describing the logic behind discrimination-based metrics.

4   A Unified Framework

To evaluate the quality of feature X_k in our unified framework we extend the strategy of discrimination-based metrics by exploiting additional information between any pair of examples. Recall that feature X_k divides the training set T into a set of subsets $\{T_m\}$, one for each feature value. Figure 3(a) illustrates the possible scenarios in terms of the class agreement between any pair of examples $\tilde{\mathbf{X}}_\mathbf{i}$ and $\tilde{\mathbf{X}}_\mathbf{j}$. The two examples may fall in the same subset (e.g., T_1) and either agree in their class values or not (cases 1 and 2 respectively), or the examples may belong to different subsets (e.g., T_1 and T_2) and either agree in their class values or not (cases 3 and 4 respectively). Although Figure 3(a) shows two classes only, we assume any number of possible classes. Our general approach consists of storing counts for each of these four possible cases separately. Ideally we would like to see high scores for cases 1 and 4, and low scores for cases 2 and 3, since case 1 ($x_k^i = x_k^j$ and $C(\tilde{\mathbf{X}}_\mathbf{i}) = C(\tilde{\mathbf{X}}_\mathbf{j})$) and case 4 ($x_k^i \neq x_k^j$ and $C(\tilde{\mathbf{X}}_\mathbf{i}) \neq C(\tilde{\mathbf{X}}_\mathbf{j})$) ensure the properties of class uniformity and discrimination power respectively, whereas case 2 ($x_k^i = x_k^j$ and $C(\tilde{\mathbf{X}}_\mathbf{i}) \neq C(\tilde{\mathbf{X}}_\mathbf{j})$) and case 3 ($x_k^i \neq x_k^j$ and $C(\tilde{\mathbf{X}}_\mathbf{i}) = C(\tilde{\mathbf{X}}_\mathbf{j})$) work against them.

Our approach works as follows. For each induced example subset T_m, we associate a count matrix R_m. If p is the number of possible class values, each T_m is characterized by a matrix R_m of size $p \times 4$, where row r is a count vector $\tilde{\mathbf{Z}}_\mathbf{r} = (z_{r1}, z_{r2}, z_{r3}, z_{r4})$ which stores the counts for each of the four cases involving examples in class r, as shown in Figure 3(b). In addition we define a weight vector $\tilde{\theta} = (\theta_1, \theta_2, \theta_3, \theta_4)$, $\theta_i \in [0, 1]$, that modulates the contribution of the four counts.

We now explain how to update $\tilde{\mathbf{Z}}_\mathbf{r}$. Given an example $\tilde{\mathbf{X}}_\mathbf{i}$ in class r, for every other example $\tilde{\mathbf{X}}_\mathbf{j}$, exactly one of the four counts z_{ri} is updated, depending on which of the four cases applies to that pair of examples. The appropriate z_{ri} is updated as follows. Given the vector $\tilde{\theta}$ and the function f_α explained below:

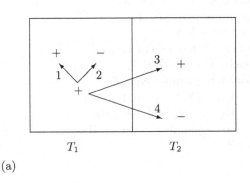

(a)

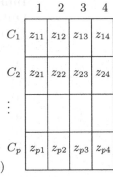

(b)

Fig. 3. (a) All four possible scenarios in terms of class agreement for a pair of examples $(\tilde{X}_i, \tilde{X}_j)$. (b) Each count matrix has 4 columns corresponding to the four cases in (a); each row corresponds to a different class.

$$z_{ri} = z_{ri} + \theta_i \cdot f_\alpha(x) \qquad (10)$$

where $x = D(\tilde{X}_i, \tilde{X}_j)$ is the distance between the two examples. We assume all features are nominal such that the distance between two feature values may be either zero or one (equation 6). The function f_α decreases with x and may have one of several forms [3]:

$$f_\alpha(x) = \frac{1}{x^\alpha} \quad \text{or} \quad f_\alpha(x) = \frac{1}{2^{\alpha \cdot x}} \qquad (11)$$

Large values for α narrow our attention to only the closest neighboring examples. Small values for α extend our attention to examples lying far apart. In the extreme case where $\alpha = 0$ all examples are considered equally, irrespective of distance. Thus α enables us to vary the relative importance of the distance between any two examples.

The vector $\tilde{\theta}$ modulates the degree of contribution of each of the four cases in Figure 3. In particular, setting θ_i to zero nullifies the contribution of the ith case. We will show how varying the values of $\tilde{\theta}$ allows us to put more weight on either class uniformity or discrimination power.

Figure 4 describes the computation of the set of matrices $\{R_m\}$. In essence, every example is compared against all other examples in T, while the counts for each matrix R_m are updated. For simplicity the algorithm is described for a single feature X_k, but the double loop in lines $2-3$ can be done over all features. We select a matrix R_m according to the value of feature X_k in $\tilde{X}_i$. The row index corresponds to the class value of $\tilde{X}_i$, $C(\tilde{X}_i)$. The column index corresponds to the case to which $\tilde{X}_i$ and $\tilde{X}_j$ belong (Figure 3(a)). Once the matrix entry is located, the corresponding z_i is updated according to equation 10.

Lines $2-3$ in Figure 4 cycle through all examples in T. There is no need to limit the second loop to the closest examples (as in Algorithm 1) because

Algorithm 2: Unified Framework
Input: Example set T, Feature X_k
Output: Set of matrices $\{R_m\}$
UPDATE-MATRICES(T,X_k)
(1)   Initialize all matrices in $\{R_m\}$
(2)   **foreach** example $\tilde{\mathbf{X}}_\mathbf{i} \in T$
(3)   **foreach** example $\tilde{\mathbf{X}}_\mathbf{j} \in T$
(4)   Let $C(\tilde{\mathbf{X}}_\mathbf{i}) = c_r$ and $x_k^i = V_m$
(5)   Update $R_m[r, \cdot]$ using the
(6)   corresponding z_r. in eq. 10
(7) **return** $\{R_m\}$

Fig. 4. Logic describing how to compute the set of count matrices for feature vector X_k on example set T.

the update function depends on distance and is regulated by parameter α (we explain later why we allow comparison of pairs of identical examples).

The training set T also gives rise to a matrix R, as a function of the set $\{R_m\}$, but because examples in T cannot be compared to different example sets all columns in R corresponding to cases 3 and 4 must equal zero. Our evaluation metric evaluates the quality of a feature X_k as a function of the matrix R for the training set T and the matrix R_m for each of the induced subsets $\{T_m\}$ (computed as shown in Figure 4):

$$\mathcal{M}(X_k) = F(R, \{R_m\}) \qquad (12)$$

Finally, our unified framework for evaluation metrics Π is a 4-tuple containing all the parameters necessary to define a metric of the form defined in equation 12:

$$\Pi = (F, \tilde{\theta}, \alpha, f_\alpha) \qquad (13)$$

Complexity Analysis. The algorithm in Figure 4 runs in time $O(n\, t^2)$, where n is the number of features and $t = |T_{\text{train}}|$ is the size of the training set. If the algorithm is used at every node of a decision tree, the complexity is $O(l\, n\, t^2)$ where l is the number of nodes in the tree. This contrasts with traditional metrics where the complexity is usually $O(l\, n\, t)$. One natural extension is to pre-compute, for each example, an ordered list of examples based on distance, with a complexity of $O(t^2\, log\, t)$. Then, during decision-tree learning, one can find the (fixed) k closest examples to each example within the induced partition in time $O(l\, n\, t\sqrt{t})$. The solution[4] is feasible only for small k. Another solution for large datasets ($t \sim 10^3 - 10^4$), is to use only a sample S of the training set to compute the count matrices. Let $s = |S|$, the complexity is reduced to $O(l\, n\, s^2)$.

---

[4] The $\sqrt{t}$ term is derived from a worst case analysis (using the best of two different methods) for obtaining the k closest examples.

4.1   Instances of the Unified Framework

We now show how our unified framework for evaluation metrics covers traditional, or purity-based metrics (Section 3.1), and also discrimination-based metrics (Section 3.2).

Proposition 1. For a specific setting on the parameters of framework Π, it is possible to derive all traditional metrics.

Proof. Function F in equation 4 is left undefined; F defines how to measure the quality of a feature based on class proportions. We simply show that for a specific setting of Π we can derive all class proportions. Consider the result of running Algorithm 2 with $\tilde{\theta} = (1, 0, 0, 0)$. Since we care about class uniformity only (Figure 3, Case 1), we consider only pairs of examples with the same class value and the same feature value. Assume $f_\alpha(x = 0) = 1$ and $f_\alpha(x \neq 0) = 0$ (x is the distance $D(\tilde{\mathbf{X}}_i, \tilde{\mathbf{X}}_j)$ between the two examples). Since $f_\alpha(x) = 1$ only when the distance between examples is zero, our comparisons are limited to pairs of identical examples. Therefore, the counts on each matrix R_m are zero in columns $2 - 4$, and column 1 reflects the number of examples of each class when the feature value is fixed. These counts are sufficient to compute F: class counts can be easily converted into class proportions by dividing over the sum of all entries in column 1, i.e., by dividing over $\sum_i R_m[i, 1]$. This completes the proof.

Proposition 2. Both Relief and Contextual Merit can be defined as instances of framework Π.

Proof. We begin with Contextual Merit. Consider the result of running Algorithm 2 with $\tilde{\theta} = (0, 0, 0, 1)$, $\alpha = 2$, and $f_\alpha = \frac{1}{x^\alpha} = \frac{1}{x^2}$. We now care about discrimination power exclusively (Figure 3, Case 4), and compare examples with different class value and different feature value. The counts on each matrix R_m are zero on columns $1 - 3$; the sum of the values along column 4 over all $\{R_m\}$, $\sum_m (\sum_i (R_m[i, 1]))$, is exactly the output produced by Contextual Merit when each example in T is compared against all other examples (i.e., when lines 2-3 in Algorithm 1 run over all examples).

We now look into Relief. Consider the result of running Algorithm 2 with $\tilde{\theta} = (0, 0, 1, 1)$ and $f_\alpha(x) = 1$ if $x < \alpha$ and 0 otherwise; α takes the role of defining a threshold that allows comparison of only the α-nearest neighbors. Since $\tilde{\theta} = (0, 0, 1, 1)$, we favor discrimination power but penalize working against it. We compare examples with different feature value irrespective of class value. The counts on each matrix R_m are zero in columns $1 - 2$; the sum of the values along column 4 over all $\{R_m\}$ minus the respective sum along column 3, $\sum_m (\sum_i (R_m[i, 4] - R_m[i, 3]))$, is the output produced by Relief for the appropriate value of α. This completes the proof.

The unified framework Π adds versatility to our new family of metrics by enabling us to modulate how much emphasis should be placed on class uniformity (or lack thereof) and discrimination power (or lack thereof). We now measure empirically the effects of a simple settings for Π in decision-tree learning.

5   Experiments

Our experiments measure the performance accuracy for a simple setting of Π and compare it to the performance of a set of standard evaluation metrics. We adopt a simple model for F by adding the values, over all matrices in $\{R_m\}$, in columns 1 and 4, and subtracting the values in columns 2 and 3. We do this for each feature value and then take the weighted average according to the number of examples in each example subset:

$$F = \frac{|T_m|}{|T|} \sum_m G(R_m) \tag{14}$$

$G(R_m)$ is defined as follows:

$$G(R_m) = \sum_{i=1}^{p} (R_m[i,1] + R_m[i,4] - R_m[i,2] - R_m[i,3] \tag{15}$$

where p is the number of classes. The definition for $G(R_m)$ corresponds to $\tilde{\theta} = (1,1,1,1)$, which can be regarded as a compromise between class purity and discrimination power. For the update function, we consider $f_\alpha = \frac{1}{2^{\alpha \cdot x}}$ and $\alpha = 0.1$.

5.1   Methodology

We test our model using a decision-tree learning algorithm. An initial discretization step on all numeric features divides each feature domain into ten equally-sized intervals. We stop growing a tree if the number of examples on a node is less than $\beta = 3$ or if all examples are class uniform. The final tree is pruned using a pessimistic-pruning method [12].

All experiments use real-world domains extracted from the UCI repository. Predictive accuracy is estimated by averaging over five repetitions using 10-fold cross validation. Tests of significance use a two-sided Student-t distribution at the $p = 0.05$ level.

5.2   Results on Real-World Domains

Our experimental results are depicted in Table 1 (numbers enclosed in parentheses represent standard deviations). For each row, the best score is highlighted in bold style; an asterisk on the left implies a significant difference. Among the set of standard metrics, the subset corresponding to purity-based metrics (Gini and Information Gain; columns 2 and 3 respectively) tend to perform, on average (last row), slightly better than the subset corresponding to discrimination-based metrics (Contextual Merit and Relief; columns 4 and 5 respectively). This may simply indicate that most domains in the UCI repository exhibit a low degree of feature interaction. Our framework scores best on eight of the eighteen domains, outperforming the second-best metric significantly on 4 of these. Performance is, on average, better than other metrics (not significantly).

Table 1. A comparison of decision-tree accuracy using different evaluation metrics. Numbers enclosed in parentheses represent standard deviations.

Domain	Gini	Info Gain	C. Merit	Relief	Instance of Π
bupa	57.86 (0.31)	58.54 (2.78)	57.40 (0.65)	58.50 (1.80)	***62.32** (1.29)
cancer	93.64 (0.30)	**95.02** (0.15)	95.00 (0.25)	93.10 (0.27)	92.56 (0.38)
credit	72.80 (1.35)	67.80 (2.57)	66.56 (1.03)	70.82 (1.89)	***74.74** (0.67)
heart	***78.62** (1.48)	76.06 (1.52)	66.14 (1.18)	71.74 (2.48)	75.68 (1.26)
hepatitis	81.82 (1.41)	81.90 (1.36)	82.66 (0.45)	83.04 (2.23)	**83.26** (0.61)
ionosphere	90.32 (0.75)	**90.46** (0.48)	78.90 (0.50)	81.64 (1.05)	86.62 (0.56)
chess-end	98.14 (0.52)	**98.42** (0.50)	97.38 (0.47)	88.74 (1.48)	94.96 (0.72)
lymphography2	79.28 (1.69)	**81.88** (1.82)	74.02 (2.13)	74.44 (3.00)	81.50 (1.89)
lymphography3	77.64 (2.03)	**78.90** (2.13)	73.30 (2.10)	77.54 (3.02)	77.02 (1.31)
mushroom	98.36 (0.63)	98.84 (0.27)	98.64 (0.16)	99.50 (0.36)	**99.52** (0.48)
thyroid-hyper	89.22 (0.30)	94.34 (0.33)	93.24 (0.77)	92.96 (0.88)	**94.44** (0.29)
thyroid-hypo	86.08 (0.04)	92.36 (0.48)	86.44 (0.69)	89.68 (1.48)	***93.70** (0.35)
diabetes	64.68 (0.30)	73.42 (0.25)	***74.28** (0.48)	66.38 (0.66)	68.84 (0.73)
promoters	74.36 (2.15)	74.94 (4.64)	73.20 (3.80)	**76.36** (2.68)	81.36 (3.29)
star-cluster	80.64 (0.46)	80.64 (0.46)	80.64 (0.46)	78.32 (2.75)	**81.36** (0.82)
tic-tac-toe	82.96 (0.69)	85.62 (1.26)	83.06 (1.07)	79.42 (1.47)	***87.94** (0.23)
voting	95.20 (0.13)	94.78 (0.31)	***95.44** (0.15)	93.38 (0.88)	95.16 (0.08)
zoo	94.76 (0.78)	**95.16** (0.08)	95.16 (0.08)	94.76 (0.78)	94.76 (0.78)
Average	**83.13**	**84.39**	**81.75**	**81.68**	**84.47**

Other empirical tests (not shown here for space considerations) illustrate the effect of varying $\tilde{\theta}$ (Section 4). Results show significant differences in accuracy, but no single setting for $\tilde{\theta}$ outperforms other settings consistently. In addition, our framework is sensitive to function $f_\alpha(x)$. Varying $f_\alpha(x)$ while keeping other parameters fixed results in significant differences in accuracy but to a lesser degree than varying $\tilde{\theta}$.

6 Conclusions and Future Work

We have defined a novel framework for evaluation metrics in classification. Our framework enriches the information derived when a feature is used to partition the training set T by capturing all possible scenarios in terms of class agreement (or disagreement) between pairs of examples in T. Most metrics utilize only a small fraction of the information contained in Π; our framework, therefore, provides a broader view of the space of possible metrics. A limitation of our approach is the complexity of the algorithm that generates count matrices (Figure 4); proposed solutions include a pre-processing step, or using a sample of the training set (for large datasets). Experiments using real-world domains show our unified framework compares well in performance with the best of a set of standard metrics in the context of decision-tree learning. Our results imply that the best metric for any given problem may not be one of the few instances previously studied. Placing them in a parameterized framework is important–it delineates a much larger and richer space of alternatives.

A line of future research is to explore whether there exists generally useful instances in the new space of metrics that could be applied to a wider class of learning tasks. Another line of research consists of trying to match domain characteristics with the appropriate parameter settings in Π (equation 13). The flexibility inherent in our unified framework in finding a balance among several criteria suggests guiding the parameter settings according to the characteristics (i.e., meta-features) of the domain under analysis. For example, meta-features could be functions of the counts in the matrix R over the set T, where T corresponds to the whole training set T_{train} (Section 4). Those counts provide information about the domain itself and relate directly to Π.

Acknowledgments. We are grateful to Vittorio Castelli for his valuable help and suggestions. This work was supported by IBM T.J. Watson Research Center.

References

1. Breiman, L., Friedman, J. H., Olshen, R. A., Stone, C. J.: Classification and Regression Trees. Wadsworth, Belmont, CA (1984).
2. Fayyad, U., Irani, K. The Attribute Selection Problem in Decision Tree Generation. Conference of the American Association for Artificial Intelligence (1992), 104–110.
3. Hong, S. J.: Use of Contextual Information for Feature Ranking and Discretization. IEEE Transactions of Knowledge and Data Engineering (1997).
4. Kira, K., Rendell, L.: A practical approach to feature selection. Ninth International Workshop on Machine Learning. Morgan Kaufmann Publishers (1992), 249-256.
5. Kononenko, I.: Estimating attributes: analysis and extensions of RELIEF. European Conference on Machine Learning. Springer Verlag (1994), 171-182.
6. Kononenko, I: On Biases in Estimating Multi-Valued Attributes. International Joint Conference on Artificial Intelligence (1995), 1034-1040.
7. Kononenko, I, Hong, S.J.: Attribute Selection for Modeling. Future Generation Computer Systems (1997).
8. Liu, W.Z., White, A.P.: The Importance of Attribute Selection Measures in Decision Tree Induction. Machine Learning (1994), 15, 25-41.
9. Mingers, J.: An Empirical Comparison of Selection Measures for Decision-Tree Induction. Machine Learning (1989), 3, 319–342.
10. Pérez, E., Rendell, L. A.: Using Multidimensional Projection to Find Relations, Twelfth International Conference on Machine Learning (1995), 447-455.
11. Quinlan, J. R.: Induction of Decision Trees. Machine Learning (1986), 1, 81-106.
12. Quinlan, J. R.: C4.5: Programs for Machine Learning. Morgan Kaufmann (1994).
13. Quinlan, J. R.: OverSearching and Layered Search in Empirical Learning. International Joint Conference on Artificial Intelligence. Morgan Kaufmann (1995), 1019-1024.
14. White, A.P., Liu, W.Z.: Bias in Information-Based Measures in Decision Tree Induction. Machine Learning (1994), 15, 321-329.

Improving Term Extraction by System Combination Using Boosting

Jordi Vivaldi[1], Lluís Màrquez[2], and Horacio Rodríguez[2]

[1]Institut Universitari de Lingüística Aplicada, Universitat Pompeu Fabra
La Rambla, 30–32. E-08002, Barcelona, Catalonia
`jorge.vivaldi@info.upf.es`
[2]TALP Research Center, Universitat Politècnica de Catalunya
Jordi Girona Salgado 1–3. E-08034, Barcelona, Catalonia
{`lluism,horacio`}`@lsi.upc.es`

Abstract. Term extraction is the task of automatically detecting, from textual corpora, lexical units that designate concepts in thematically restricted domains (e.g. medicine). Current systems for term extraction integrate linguistic and statistical cues to perform the detection of terms. The best results have been obtained when some kind of combination of simple base term extractors is performed [14]. In this paper it is shown that this combination can be further improved by posing an additional learning problem of how to find the best combination of base term extractors. Empirical results, using AdaBoost in the metalearning step, show that the ensemble constructed surpasses the performance of all individual extractors and simple voting schemes, obtaining significantly better accuracy figures at all levels of recall.

1 Introduction

As most scientific disciplines evolve in an increasingly faster manner, the creation of new terms grows continuously and their timelife decreases. This context can explain the growing interest in Automatic Term Extraction (TE) Systems. Terms, like words, are lexical units that designate concepts in a thematically constrained domain. Terms cannot be distinguished from general language words just by looking at their forms. It has been empirically shown (see [15]) that term structure coincides with that of words and, often, terms take complex forms, i.e., they are made up of more than one lexical unit. Both terms and words are created and manipulated according to the same linguistic rules. Sometimes, however, a word can be considered a term only in some of its forms.

Usually, the construction of large term repositories has been carried out by terminologists. This task demands a massive manual intervention, which is unfeasible in accordance with today's requirements. Hence, there is a strong need to react quickly (and in a standardized way) so as to comply with current requirements of information. Many techniques have been applied to TE but none of them has proved to be fully successful in isolation. Differences in source texts,

L. De Raedt and P. Flach (Eds.): ECML 2001, LNAI 2167, pp. 515–526, 2001.
© Springer-Verlag Berlin Heidelberg 2001

text specialization levels, end-user profiles and purposes, and level of automation account for this fact.

Current Status. Most current TE systems follow either a statistical or a linguistic approach [8]. Recently, however (as discussed below) some hybrid approaches are trying to overcome the limitations of those purely one-sided approaches and have included both linguistic and statistical elements.

Linguistics based approaches are mainly based on syntactic patterns. Usually, terms are described by a regular expression based on the Part-of-Speech of the sequence of words found in the text under analysis. TERMS [7] is a prototypical system following this approach. The approach followed by LEXTER [3], a well-known TE system, is quite similar but uses knowledge of what is known not to be a term. In spite of their linguistic approach, both systems include some basic statistical information. A different linguistic approach, shown in [1], benefits from the decomposition of term candidates in their Greek and Latin forms.

Statistical based systems range from the simplicity of frequency counts to the calculation of complex statistical indicators for measuring the collocational strength of the words occurring in the term candidates. The main problems found by these approaches are that frequent words or high-scored collocational pairs are not limited to terms but may occur with general language. Other approaches include some linguistic data to overcome these limitations. This information may be used a priori, as in ACABIT [5], or a posteriori. TRUCKS, a modern hybrid system [11], provides a more balanced use of these kinds of information.

The main shortcomings encountered in most term extractors are[1]: 1) *Noise.* Many of the candidates are not real terms and have to be rejected by a manual post-process. This problem is mainly posed by linguistic systems and has to do with the inadequacy of purely syntactic patterns for isolating and detecting terms. 2) *Silence.* Some of the actual terms are not detected by the TE system. This problem usually affects systems including some kind of statistical knowledge. Often, these limitations are related to the difficulty in dealing with mono–lexeme or coordinated terms.

Term extraction provides an appropriate framework for combining some of the techniques typically used for this task. In fact, the combination of multiple classifiers is a technique that has been successfully applied in several NLP tasks, e.g., tagging, parsing, or text classification and filtering, leading to significant improvement on the results obtained by individual methods. Recently, a TE system has been proposed based on combining the results obtained from different individual term extractors (TE) and applying different kinds of voting [14]. Since those TE's are based on very different Knowledge Sources, a further attempt can be made. This would imply using a metalearning approach to learn to combine such TE's in a way that each TE would be chosen in the situation it performs best. In this paper we follow this approach using a boosting algorithm.

---

[1] *Noise* and *silence* are commonly used in the terminology domain as complementary of the terms *precision* and *recall*, respectively.

Overview. The paper is organized as follows: Section 2 is devoted to briefly explain the overall organization of the system and the individual TE's. Section 3 describes the experiments carried out to evaluate the individual TE's and the basic way of combination. In section 4 the boosting approach is presented and tested. Finally, section 5 summarizes some qualitative conclusions.

2   A System Proposal for Term Extraction

The aim of our TE system is to analyze a set of textual documents in the medical domain and produce a list of term candidates (tc) ordered by their *termhood*. In order to achieve this objective the following is proposed: 1) Building a number of individual TE's where each of them is based on a different kind of information; and 2) Combining the results (i.e., the set of candidates and the certainty factor of each candidate) of each TE. Once obtained, the list of tc can be processed in several ways depending on the intended use of the extracted terms, ranking from automatic acceptance of those tc's having a termhood over a certain threshold to manual checking of best scored tc by a terminologist.

The architecture of the system is depicted in figure 1. There are three main modules,which take part after a linguistic pre-processing:

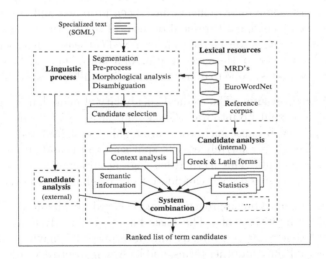

Fig. 1. Architecture of the system proposed

1. *Candidate Selection.* It consists of the selection of the sequences of units that can be potentially terminological.
2. *Candidate Analysis.* It consists of a number of TE's that have to score the term candidates with a termhood measure.
3. *System Combination.* The results of the different extractors are combined in order to produce the final set of candidates. This is mainly the issue that will be addressed in this paper.

2.1   Individual Term Extraction Systems

Four families of TE's, corresponding to four different kinds of sources, have been implemented. We include below a short description of each TE.

Semantic content extractor. This module is based on the idea that the more likely it is that the components of the tc belong to the domain the more likely it is that the tc will be a real term (i.e. medicalhood is a good indicator of termhood). The module uses EuroWordNet (EWN)[2] to determine whether a given word belongs to the medical domain or not. EWN presents some important limitations: It is a general purpose (not restricted to medical domain) ontology and it lacks domain information. It was chosen, however, because it has a relatively high coverage of medical domain entries and a good coverage of Spanish language.

The lack of domain information was tackled by identifying and marking about 30 medical borders (mb) and assuming that all hyponyms that fall under these borders belong to the medical domain. Thus, we may say that "disease" constitutes a mb as all diseases registered in EWN are hyponyms of this synset.

To cope with polysemy a "medical coefficient" (mc) was defined to measure the termhood of each tc. This coefficient can be computed straightforwardly as the ratio between the number of medical senses and the total number of senses registered in EWN. Despite its simplicity, this way of computing mc's works fairly well. In [15] some improvements have been proposed and evaluated. This coefficient is used to define a threshold of medical sense. Any noun with an mc higher than such value is considered to have a medical sense. This coefficient can be considered a measure of the specialization of a word. Due to EWN particular features, this method is prone to detect monosemic non-highly specialized words.

Greek and Latin forms. The medical vocabulary of many languages includes words that can be split up into their Greek and Latin (G&L) word forms. This feature is important because such words are highly specialized and do not occur in standard lexica. It is relatively easy to split such words and obtain the meaning of their components. This method has high accuracy although very limited coverage. Therefore, it is a good candidate to be combined with other TE's.

Context analyzer. Our approach is mainly based on Maynard's TE system [11] with minor improvements. The basis for context analysis are: a) Words surrounding "prime" tc's, (i.e, already known terms or tc's having a high score) can become useful clues for other terms, and b) Among context words, those that are "prime" tc's and semantically similar to the tc under evaluation provide additional information. Thus, our context factor (cf) has two components: a lexical context factor and a semantic context factor. The "lexical cf" is based on words that surround "prime" candidates while the "semantic cf" depends on the conceptual distance between the tc and the "prime" terms that appear in their context. Three choices have to be made: 1) The selection of the "prime" tc,

---

[2] EWN [16] is a general-purpose multilingual lexical DB based on Princeton WordNet and covering Spanish and other european languages. WordNet's are structured in lexical-semantic units linked by basic semantic relations.

2) The selection of the context window, and 3) The definition of an appropriate similarity measure. We have considered "prime" term candidates those having a maximal mc (a bootstrapping approach could have been followed instead, starting with an initial list of true tc's). We have experimented with several context window sizes and different relative weighting of lexical and semantic factors. The semantic distance was computed on the EWN hierarchy (see [15]).

Collocational analysis. We have also used some traditional statistical methods to rank candidates. Several techniques involving different association measures between the words included in poly-lexeme terms, e.g. noun–adjective (NJ) and noun–preposition–noun (NPN), have been tried. Our intuition is that two components having a high association in a medical domain are more likely to form a term. Three association criteria (loglike, mutual information, and cubed mutual information, MI^3 [5]) have been considered. Most of these methods have been previously used for the related task of detecting collocations.

Note that neither the context analyzer extractor nor the G&L extractor impose constraints on the length and composition of the tc. Therefore, both methods can be applied to any pattern accepted by the Candidate Selection Module. The association measures involved in the collocational analysis extractor have been calculated only between the two main words appearing in the pattern (i.e., noun–adjective in the NJ pattern and $noun_1$–$noun_2$ in the NPN pattern). Finally, the semantic content extractor can be applied to any pattern having at least one component with a mc above the threshold. In practice, however, the results were satisfactory only for noun (N) and NJ patterns.

3 System Evaluation

The system was trained and tuned using a Spanish corpus (henceforth corpus#1) taken from the IULA LSP corpus[3]. It consists of a number of abstracts of medical reports on asthma that amount to 100,000 words, manually annotated. A shorter (10,000 words) corpus (henceforth corpus#2), was used for testing.

As previously said, the system can be applied to any pattern accepted by the Candidate Selection Module (214 different patterns were detected in corpus#1, see [15]) although not all TE's work on all patterns. However, the distribution of real terms is highly biased and only three patterns actually occur on our corpora: 696 N terms, 664 NJ terms, and 86 NPN terms were manually detected in corpus#1. All along the paper, we will present the average results over the three patterns (ALL). Additionally, the results on the most frequent pattern (N) will be presented separately.

Results. Individual methods present different recall/precision behaviours, reflecting the differences of the involved knowledge sources. The results for N and

---

[3] This corpus has been collected at the Institute for Applied Linguistics of the Universitat Pompeu Fabra. See http://www.iula.upf.es/corpus/corpubca.htm.

the other patterns present high differences as well. We summarize next the results of individual methods (see [14] or [15] for details).

The Semantic Content TE has a limited coverage (due to its dependence on
EWN). For the N pattern the precision achieved was 96.3% with a recall of 30%.
For the whole problem, the precision and recall values are 97.2% and 23.6%,
respectively. Figures obtained for the G&L forms were 90% in precision and 8%
in recall. Best results for the Context analyzer (cf) were 81.6% and 19.2% in
recall for the N pattern (64%–21% on the whole problem) although in this case
still accurate results can be obtained at higher recall levels, as shown in figure 2.
Best results for collocational methods were obtained using MI^3: 50.3%–15.1%.

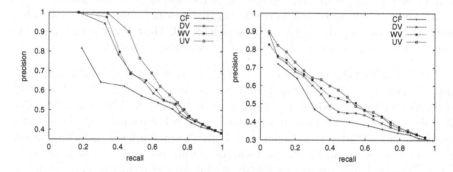

Fig. 2. Precision–recall curves obtained by the individual cf extractor and the combination schemes DV, UV, WV on the N (left) and ALL (right) patterns

Regarding the combination of methods, several voting schemes were tried,
following [9]: a) Simple voting, i.e., each method reports a term/no term status
from each single term extractor. It allows two variations: democratic (DV) and
non–democratic voting (UV) according to whether all the TE's have the same
weight or not. b) Numeric voting, i.e, each tc is considered according to its
termhood value provided by each TE. We experimented with several forms of
combination: maximum, minimum, median and weighted (WV). In the UV voting
scheme, several TE's are considered with priority in some cases, e.g., G&L forms,
Semantic Content with mc=1, etc. In WV, the results of each extractor are
normalized according to the maximum score of the corresponding TE.

All combination methods were systematically better at all recall levels, as
shown in figure 2, where the best individual method, context factor (cf), is compared with three forms of combination, i.e. DV, UV, WV. For instance, in the
case of nouns, the best recall for a simple method is 19.1% (precision 81,6%); for
combined methods recall increases up to 32% (precision 99.1%). The results are
clearly better for nouns than for the poly–lexeme patterns. This may be due to
the fact that NJ and NPN patterns are much more sensitive to the EWN missing
data and so the treatment of some kind of adjectives should be improved. We
also found that about 15% of terms were not detected due to tagging mistakes,
term variation and missing dictionary entries.

4   Using Boosting to Combine Basic Term Extractors

In the previous section we have shown how the voting combination of several TE's leads to a significant performance improvement, comparing to the individual results. In this section, we will see how this combination step can be further improved by considering the new learning problem of "how to find the best combination of individual term extractors on the training examples", which will be addressed by means of a boosting–based learning algorithm.

In machine learning approaches, the combination of a set of heterogeneous classifiers is usually performed by defining a metalearning step in which a meta–level classifier is trained to characterize the situations in which each of the base classifiers is able to make correct predictions. *Stacked generalization* [17] is probably the most popular exemplar among the existing approaches for metalearning.

In our situation, the approach can be simpler since the base TE's perform their predictions based on some external linguistic knowledge sources, and do not perform a real training process. Thus, the problem of learning how to combine them can be directly posed as a learning problem in which the predictions of the base TE's are codified as regular features in order to complete the descriptions of training examples. See section 4.2 for details about the features used.

4.1   AdaBoost Algorithm

In this section the generalized AdaBoost algorithm with confidence–rated predictions is briefly sketched. We assume that the reader is familiar with the related concepts (see [12] otherwise). It has to be noted that this algorithm has been applied, with significant success, to a number of NLP disambiguation tasks, such as: Part–of–speech tagging and PP–attachment [2], text categorization [13], and word sense disambiguation [6].

The purpose of boosting is to find a highly accurate classification rule by combining many *weak classifiers* (or weak hypotheses), each of which may be only moderately accurate. The weak hypotheses are learned sequentially, one at a time, and, conceptually, at each iteration the weak hypothesis is biased to classify the examples which were most difficult to classify by the preceding weak hypotheses. The final weak hypotheses are linearly combined into a single rule called the *combined hypothesis*.

Let $S = \{(x_1, y_1), \ldots, (x_m, y_m)\}$ be the set of m training examples, where each instance x_i belongs to an instance space $\mathcal{X}$ and $y_i \in \{-1, +1\}$ is the class or label associated to x_i (which, in this case, stand for *non-term* and *term*). The AdaBoost algorithm maintains a vector of weights as a distribution D_t over examples. At round t, the goal of the weak learner algorithm is to find a weak hypothesis $h_t : \mathcal{X} \to \mathbb{R}$ with moderately low error with respect to the weights D_t. In this setting, weak hypotheses $h_t(x)$ make real–valued confidence–rated predictions. Initially, the distribution D_1 is uniform, but after each iteration, the boosting algorithm increases (or decreases) the weights $D_t(i)$ for which $h_t(x_i)$ makes a bad (or good) prediction, with a variation proportional to the confidence $|h_t(x_i)|$. The final hypothesis, $f : \mathcal{X} \to \mathbb{R}$, computes its predictions using a weighted vote of the weak hypotheses $f(x) = \sum_{t=1}^{T} \alpha_t h_t(x)$. For each example x, the sign of $f(x)$ is interpreted as the predicted class (-1 or $+1$), and the magnitude $|f(x)|$ is interpreted as a measure of confidence in the prediction. Such a function can be used either for classifying new unseen examples or for ranking them according to the confidence degree. The latter is the goal in the problem of term extraction.

Weak Rules. In this work we have used weak hypotheses which are simple rules with real–valued predictions. Such simple rules test the value of a boolean predicate and make a prediction based on that value. The predicates used refer to the attributes that describe the training examples (e.g. "the word *health* appears in the context of the term candidate", or to the predictions given by the individual term extractors (e.g. "cf's confidence is *high*"). Formally, based on a given predicate p, weak hypotheses h are considered that make predictions of the form: $h(x) = c_0$ if p holds in x, and c_1 otherwise. Where the c_0 and c_1 are real numbers. See [12] for the details about how to calculate the c_i values given a certain predicate p in the AdaBoost framework.

This type of weak rules can be seen as extremely simple decision trees with one internal node and two leaves, which are sometimes called *decision stumps*. Furthermore, the criterion for finding the best weak rule can be seen as a natural splitting criterion and used for performing decision–tree induction [12]. In this way, we can consider an additional parameter in the learning algorithm that accounts for the depth of the decision trees induced at each iteration.

4.2   Feature Representation

All tc's have been considered training examples, and, thus, all three patterns have been treated simultaneously. Each example consists of the set of occurrences of the corresponding tc in corpus#1 (although, for practical reasons, we have limited the number of occurrences to 10). The number of examples in the corpus is 4,693, from which 1,446 are N, NJ, or NPN terms (the exact proportions are presented in section 3). The set of features used for training purposes includes the results of several variants of the individual TE's together with some of the data used by such TE's. They are the following:

1. The medical coefficient (mc).
2. "G&L form prediction", which is 1 when the tc has been recognized by the corresponding TE, and 0 otherwise.
3. Context factors, which include the output of the Context Analysis method in its basic form and some variations. It also includes the lexical and semantic components separately.
4. Medical borders (mb) of the tc.
5. Number of occurrences of the tc in the training set.

Since the version of AdaBoost used works only with binary features, a discretizing process has been performed on all non–binary attributes. In particular, we have considered equal width intervals of 3 and 10 parts in the domain range of these attributes. The redundancy of this representation is not a problem for the AdaBoost learning algorithm. As we will see later, no overfitting is produced, and it seems that it is able to select the appropriate granularity level.

It has to be said that a number of experiments have been carried out in order to select an appropriate feature set for the task. In particular, we have considered the context words, collected from a window of 10 words to the left and to the right of the different occurrences of each tc. The results obtained using these new features were slightly worse, probably due to the small size of the learning corpus, which is unable to provide reliable estimates of word frequency counts. In the same way, the Collocational analysis extractor was finally excluded from the feature set since it was very irregular in its predictions and contributed negatively to the final performance. See [15] for a detailed description of the whole experimental setting developed for the task. Finally, observe that the final set of predictors used does not perform any learning process on the training corpus, and, therefore, they can be considered directly as regular features, contributing to ease the meta–learning process.

4.3   Evaluation

We have tested the approach proposed using corpus#1, with the standard 10-fold cross validation technique. Consequently, the results presented in this section are the average figures among the ten folds. AdaBoost was run using decision stumps as default weak learners.

Figure 3 shows the precision–recall curves obtained by the algorithm on the N and ALL patterns at different number of learning rounds ($T = 10, 50, 100, 150, 200$). It can be observed that above a minimum number of rounds ($T = 50$), the system performance remains stable and that no overfitting is produced.

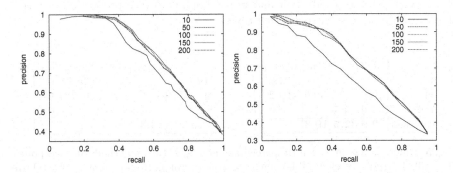

Fig. 3. AdaBoost precision–recall curves for N (left) and ALL (right) patterns varying the number of rounds

In order to determine whether the already presented curves are good or not, we compare these results with those obtained using the best individual term extractors (cf and mc) and the best voting method (UV). Figure 4 contains such comparison (AdaBoost results correspond to a training process of 50 rounds).

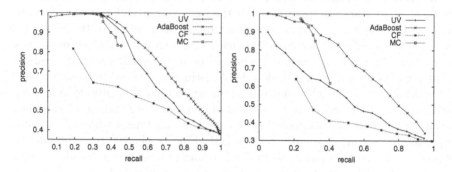

Fig. 4. Precision–recall curves obtained by AdaBoost, the individual cf and mc term extractors, and the best voting approach UV, for N (left) and ALL (right) patterns

It can be observed that in the whole problem, AdaBoost performs systematically better than the other methods at all levels of recall, achieving significantly higher precision values (the maximum difference against the UV voting scheme is almost 30 points). In the particular case of N pattern, AdaBoost achieves again the best curve, with significantly better precision results for recall values over 45–50%. At lower recall levels (specially for values lower than 30%), the differences in precision are not significant due to the extremely high precision obtained by the individual mc extractor. In order to complete the information of figure 4 with some numerical results, we present in figure 5 the differences in precision between all methods, achieved at two fixed recall levels of 30% and 50% (which are the usual lower and upper bounds for the proportion of terms that naturally appear in specialized texts).

	UV	cf	mc	AdaBoost
UV		19.5	0.0	**0.0**
cf	-29.6		-19.6	**-19.2**
mc	-7.9	21.7		**0.0**
AdaBoost	**2.9**	**32.5**	**10.8**	

	UV	cf	mc	AdaBoost
UV		15.0	-25.2	**-28.0**
cf	-13.5		-40.0	**-44.5**
mc	—	—		**-4.0**
AdaBoost	**23.3**	**36.5**	—	

Fig. 5. Differences in precision (in percentage points) between methods at fixed points of recall. Patterns: N (left table) and ALL (right table). Recall points: 30% (above diagonal) and 45% (below diagonal)

We also performed some experiments by boosting deeper decision trees (in the same way as it is done [4] for constructing a high precision clause identifier), but the results obtained were systematically slightly worse comparing to the basic model of decision stumps. In this case, we guess that maybe we are working with a learning problem that can be (almost) explained by a linear combination of functions of a single variable (feature). But another explanation could be that the richer learning representations are more prone to overfit the training corpus (specially when it is not very large).

Assessment of TE systems is a very difficult task. On the one hand, there is very limited agreement between human experts on deciding whether a tc is a real term or not (in [15], an evaluation of this agreement rate using the Kappa statistic is presented). On the other hand, direct comparisons between TE systems are not possible due to the language and domain dependencies of most systems and the lack of benchmark collections. Therefore, the only way of performing a comparison of the TE presented in this paper is to apply a state-of-the-art TE system to our corpus. The only well known system publicly available is FASTR. We have used it in a series of limited experiments but a complete comparison is not fair because the "english" FASTR uses a meta–grammar not available for Spanish. Another possibility is using Maynard's TRUCKS system as a referent for comparison. As explained before, our Context Analyzer extractor is heavily based on TRUCKS. The main differences between our adaptation and the original are: 1) The replacement of UMLS by EWN as the lexical source; and 2) The way of selecting the "prime" tc's. These issues are discussed in detail in [15]. Briefly, the first change is due to the problems of coverage and presentation of Spanish terms in UMLS, while the second tries to perform a more accurate selection of "almost sure" tc's. As a result of such improvements, our Context Analyzer extractor outperforms Maynard's (for Spanish and in our domain) and it could be considered a valid baseline when compared to AdaBoost.

5   Conclusions

In this paper it has been presented a general system for term extraction in the medical domain, which is based on the combination of several simple and independent TE's. It has been shown that in this domain even a simple combination scheme based on voting is able to consistently improve the results of the individual TE's, and that using a more sophisticated learning algorithm for performing an additional metalearning step leads to further improvements. We have empirically shown that the improvements achieved by AdaBoost in this second approach are quite significant and very relevant to the task.

Moving to different domains or including additional individual TE's does not imply important problems. The only resource used by the system that needs some tuning is EWN (corpora and dictionaries need no changes). Furthermore, EWN is a general language resource and the customization task is reduced to identify the concepts equivalent to our *medical borders*. This task has to be carried out carefully and some knowledge about the domain and the organization of EWN is required, but this is not a labour intensive task. For instance, only 30 mb were detected in the medical domain. An alternative and not already explored possibility could be the use of existing domain codes (as those proposed by [10]).

Acknowledgments. This research has been partially funded by the European Commission (IST-1999-12392 project) and the Spanish Research Department (PB-96-0293 and TIC2000-0335-C03-02 projects).

References

1. Ananiadou, S.: A Methodology for Automatic Term Recognition. In *Proceedings of the 15th International Conference on Computational Linguistics, COLING*, pages 1034–1038, Kyoto, Japan, 1994.
2. Abney, S., Schapire, R.E. and Singer, Y.: Boosting Applied to Tagging and PP–attachment. In *Proceedings of the Joint SIGDAT Conference on Empirical Methods in Natural Language Processing and Very Large Corpora, EMNLP-VLC*, pages 38–45, College Park, MD, 1999.
3. Bourigault, D.: *LEXTER, un Logiciel d'EXtraction de TERminologie. Application à l'acquisition des connaissances à partir de textes.* Phd. Thesis, École des Hautes Études en Sciences Sociales, Paris, 1994.
4. Carreras, X. and Màrquez, L.: Boosting Trees for Clause Splitting. To appear in *Proceedings of the 5th Conference on Computational Natural Language Learning, CoNLL'01*, Tolouse, France, 2001.
5. Daille, B.: *Approche mixte pour l'extraction de terminologie: statistique lexicale et filtres linguistiques.* Phd. Thesis, Université Paris VII, 1994.
6. Escudero, G; Màrquez, L. and Rigau, G.: Boosting Applied to Word Sense Disambiguation. In *Proceedings of the 12th European Conference on Machine Learning, ECML*, Barcelona, Spain, 2000.
7. Justeson, J. and Katz, S.: Technical Terminology: Some Linguistic Properties and an Algorithm for Identification in Text. *Natural Language Engineering*,1(1),1994.
8. Kageura, K. and Umino, B.: Methods for Automatic Term Recognition: A Review. *Terminology*, 3(2):259–289, 1996.
9. Kittler, J.; Hatef, M.; Duin, R. and Matas, J.: On Combining Classifiers. *IEEE Transations on Pattern Analysis and Machine Intelligence*, 20(3):226–238, 1998.
10. Magnini, B. and Cavaglia, G.: Integrating Subject Field Codes into WordNet. *Proceedings of the 2nd International Conference on Language resources and Evaluation, LREC2000*, Atenas .
11. Maynard, D.: *Term Recognition Using Combined Knowledge Sources.* Phd. Thesis, Manchester Metropolitan Univ., Faculty of Science and Engineering, 1999.
12. Schapire, R.E. and Singer, Y.: Improved Boosting Algorithms Using Confidence-rated Predictions. *Machine Learning*, 37(3):297–336, 1999.
13. Schapire, R.E. and Singer, Y.: BoosTexter: A Boosting-based System for Text Categorization. *Machine Learning*, 39(2/3):135–168, 2000.
14. Vivaldi, J. and Rodríguez, H.: Improving Term Extraction by Combining Different Techniques. In *Proceedings of the Workshop on Computational Terminology for Medical and Biological Applications*, pages 61–68, Patras, Greece, 2000.
15. Vivaldi, J.: *A Multistrategy Approach to Term Candidate Extraction.* Phd. Thesis (forthcoming). Dep. LSI, Technical University of Catalonia, Barcelona, 2001
16. Vossen, P. (ed.): *EuroWordNet: A Multilingual Database with Lexical Semantic Networks.* Kluwer Academic Publishers, Dordrecht, 1998.
17. Wolpert, D. H.: Stacked Generalization. *Neural Networks, Pergamon Press*, 5:241-259, 1992.

Classification on Data with Biased Class Distribution

Slobodan Vucetic[1] and Zoran Obradovic[2]

[1] School of Electrical Engineering and Computer Science, Washington State University,
Pullman, 99164 WA, USA
svucetic@eecs.wsu.edu

[2] Center for Information Science and Technology, Temple University,
Philadelphia, PA 19122, USA
zoran@ist.temple.edu

Abstract. Labeled data for classification could often be obtained by sampling that restricts or favors choice of certain classes. A classifier trained using such data will be biased, resulting in wrong inference and sub-optimal classification on new data. Given an unlabeled new data set we propose a bootstrap method to estimate its class probabilities by using an estimate of the classifier's accuracy on training data and an estimate of probabilities of classifier's predictions on new data. Then, we propose two methods to improve classification accuracy on new data. The first method can be applied only if a classifier was designed to predict posterior class probabilities where predictions of an existing classifier are adjusted according to the estimated class probabilities of new data. The second method can be applied to an arbitrary classification algorithm, but it requires retraining on the properly resampled data. The proposed bootstrap algorithm was validated through experiments with 500 replicates calculated on 1,000 realizations for each of 16 choices of data set size, number of classes, prior class probabilities and conditional probabilities describing a classifier's performance. Applications of the proposed methodology to a benchmark data set with various class probabilities on unlabeled data and balanced class probabilities on the training data provided strong evidence that the proposed methodology can be successfully used to significantly improve classification on unlabeled data.

1 Introduction

A common assumption made in machine learning is that labeled data used for training a classifier and unlabeled new data can be considered as samples from the same underlying distribution. In such a case one could apply standard machine learning procedures to learn a classifier from labeled data (e.g., logistic regression, decision trees, neural networks), estimate its accuracy (e.g., directly from training set, using cross-validation), and apply it on unlabeled examples in a straightforward manner. However, this assumption is often violated with labeled and/or unlabeled data obtained by biased sampling from an underlying distribution. While inference and learning in such a general setup is an open machine learning problem, in this paper we propose a methodology for solving an important special case where class distributions

L. De Raedt and P. Flach (Eds.): ECML 2001, LNAI 2167, pp. 527–538, 2001.
© Springer-Verlag Berlin Heidelberg 2001

in labeled and/or unlabeled data are biased. To simplify the presentation it will be assumed that unlabeled data is a sample from an underlying distribution. This corresponds to the goal of constructing a classifier optimized for successful predictions on an unlabeled data set.

A familiar example that involves biased class distribution is classification of a rare medical condition where false negative predictions can have high costs. A common approach is to intentionally provide a biased training set with a disproportionally large number of examples from the rare condition in order to produce a successful classifier with a small fraction of false negative predictions. Another example is the case where costs of obtaining labeled examples are class-dependent and where the resulting labeled data set is biased towards examples from less expensive classes.

An interesting example that motivated this work is the problem of predicting protein disorder from its amino-acid sequence [11,13]. Protein disorder is a biological concept that refers to proteins that do not crystallize into a unique 3D structure [7]. To obtain training set for prediction of protein disorder one should collect representative examples of ordered and disordered proteins. However, since protein disorder is an insufficiently explored phenomenon, accurate estimates of its commonness in nature do not exist. Additionally, current databases of proteins with known structure are highly biased towards ordered proteins. The explanation is that crystallographers are reluctant to publish structural results for disordered proteins since there is always a risk that some procedural error prevented proper protein crystallization. The proposed methodology could lead to a successful predictor of protein disorder and provide confident estimates of protein disorder commonness.

The learning problem considered in this paper can be defined as construction of a classifier using labeled data of size n_L with class probabilities $P_L(i)$, $i = 1, \ldots c$, where c is the number of classes, for accurate prediction on unlabeled data of size n_U with unknown class probabilities $P_U(i)$. This problem can be solved by (step1) estimating the class distribution $P_U(i)$, followed by (step2) using this estimate to construct a desired classifier. We propose a bootstrap methodology [8] to estimate distribution of $P_U(i)$ based on (step1.a) an estimate of classifier's accuracy obtained on labeled data, and (step1.b) an estimate of classifier's class predictions on unlabeled data.

To construct a successful classifier (step2) we propose two approaches depending on the type of classification algorithm and available computational resources. If a classifier was trained to estimate posterior class probabilities (e.g., logistic regression, neural networks) it is possible to use the existing classifier on an unlabeled data set by adjusting its outputs according to estimated $P_U(i)$. If computational resources allow, or if a classifier represents a nonlinear discriminant function that directly provides classification (e.g., decision trees) we propose a procedure for retraining of classifier using resampled labeled data according to estimated $P_U(i)$.

In real-life applications of classification different costs are often associated with different types of errors. Misclassification costs are usually described by cost matrix C with elements $C(j, i)$ representing the costs of predicting class j when the true class is i. Unless explicitly mentioning otherwise, in this paper we assume 0/1 loss, where $C(j, i) = 1$ if $i \neq j$ and $C(i, i) = 0$, to simplify presentation. However, it is important to note that the proposed methodology is not restricted to the choice of cost matrix so that it can be generalized to an arbitrary cost matrix.

2   Estimation of the Class Distribution on an Unlabeled Data Set

Let us assume that a labeled data set S_L with n_L examples is available to learn a classifier and to estimate its accuracy, while the constructed classifier should be applied to a new unlabeled data set S_U with n_U examples. Classification accuracy is completely determined by (i) conditional probabilities $p(j|i)$ of predicting a class j if the true class is i, and (ii) prior probabilities p_i (shorthand for $P_U(i)$) of class i on S_U, where $i, j = \{1, ..., c\}$, and c represents the number of classes. The 0/1 loss or error rate can then be calculated as

$$error\_rate = \sum_j \sum_i p(j|i) \cdot p_i \cdot (1 - \delta_{ji}) \cdot 100 \, [\%], \qquad (1)$$

where δ_{ij} is the Kronecker's delta with $\delta_{ij} = 1$ for $i = j$ and zero otherwise.

Calculating Class Probabilities from Very Large Data Sets
Class probabilities p_i on S_U are not known in advance, so they should be estimated using an available classifier with known conditional probabilities $p(j|i)$. Note that the only information that could be obtained using the classifier on unlabeled data S_U are its predictions. From these predictions we can estimate the probability of predicting class j on S_U denoted as q_j. The connection between p_i and q_j can be expressed as

$$q_j = \sum_i p(j|i) p_i, \qquad (2)$$

or as $\mathbf{q} = \mathbf{P} \cdot \mathbf{p}$ in the matrix form, where $\mathbf{q} = \{q_j\}$, $\mathbf{P} = \{p(j|i)\}$, $\mathbf{p} = \{p_i\}$. From (2) and assuming an invertible matrix $\mathbf{P}$, one can easily estimate true class probabilities as

$$\mathbf{p} = \mathbf{P}^{-1} \cdot \mathbf{q}. \qquad (3)$$

Equation (3) is correct under assumption that values of q_j and $p(j|i)$ are known with certainty. This can occur only if available training and new data sets are very large. However, for majority of real-life applications, the size of available data sets is limited and q_j and $p(j|i)$ can be considered as random variables whose properties should be estimated first.

A Bootstrap Method for Estimating p_i from S_L and S_U
Statistical inference using S_L and S_U can lead to the proper estimation of multinomial distributions q_j and $p(j|i)$. However, it can be difficult to obtain the distribution of p_i expressed with (3) in a closed form. In this study we are primarily interested in estimating the expected values of class probabilities p_i on S_U. Although distributions of q_j and $p(j|i)$ alone might be estimated in a straightforward manner, even the estimation of the expected value of p_i could not be done directly. Although $\mathbf{P}$ and $\mathbf{q}$ are independent, such an estimation is difficult since $E[\mathbf{P}^{-1}] \neq E[\mathbf{P}]^{-1}$. Therefore, we use the idea of bootstrap [8], which is a powerful simulation methodology for statistical inference suitable for estimating the distribution of p_i. We first describe the basic idea of bootstrap.

Given an original sample X with n examples *the bootstrap sample X^** is obtained by randomly sampling n examples from X with replacement. Bootstrap algorithm generates a large number B of bootstrap samples X^{*1}, X^{*2} ..., X^{*B} and calculates desired statistics $s^{*b} = s(X^{*b})$ from each of them. Statistics $s(\cdot)$, for example, can represent the sample mean, but it can be an almost arbitrarily complex function such as the one expressed by (3). Properties of the statistics $s(\cdot)$ such as mean, variance or confidence intervals can be estimated from B obtained values s^{*b} that are called *the bootstrap replicates of s*.

In our problem two independent samples S_L and S_U are available for separately estimating q_j and $p(j|i)$. Given a labeled set S_L, one should properly use this set both for training a classifier and for estimating conditional probabilities $p(j|i)$. If n_L is large, the usual practice is to reserve a test set S_{test} of size n_{test} for estimating $p(j|i)$, and to train a classifier on the remaining data $S_{train} = S_L - S_{test}$. If n_L is relatively small, cross-validation [e.g., 8] is usually employed where, effectively, $n_L = n_{train} = n_{test}$ and all n_L examples are used both for training and for estimating $p(j|i)$, at the cost of a larger computational effort needed to learn a number of cross-validation classifiers. On the other side, all n_U examples from S_U can be directly used to estimate q_j.

In Table 1 we present a bootstrap algorithm for estimating class probabilities p_i. With $n_{test}^*(j, i)$ we denoted the number of examples in a bootstrap sample S_{test}^* that are predicted to be of class j when their true class is i. Similarly, with $n_U^*(j)$ we denoted the number of examples in a bootstrap sample S_U^* predicted to be of class j. The idea of the algorithm is clearly to generate two bootstrap samples, calculate the corresponding bootstrap replicates of q_j and $p(j|i)$ and then use equation (3) to determine bootstrap replicate of p_i. Finally, the estimate Ep_i of class probability p_i on S_U can be calculated as $Ep_i = (1/B)\Sigma_b p_i^{*b}$. According to [8], 100 – 200 bootstrap iterations are needed if we are interested only in Ep_i, and 500 – 1000 bootstrap iterations are needed if we are interested in the two-tailed confidence intervals of p_i.

Table 1. A bootstrap algorithm for estimating class probabilities p_j in unlabeled data

---

Given B, S_{test}, S_U and a classifier
$b = 0$
repeat
    Generate a bootstrap sample from n_{test} examples of S_{test} and calculate

$$p^*(j|i) = n_{test}^*(j,i) \Big/ \sum_j n_{test}^*(j,i) \text{ for } i, j = 1, ..., c.$$

    Generate a bootstrap sample from n_U examples of S_U and calculate

$$q_j^* = n_U^*(j) \Big/ n_U \text{ for } j = 1, ..., c.$$

    Use (3) to calculate bootstrap replicate p_i^{*b} for $i = 1, ..., c.$
    if all p_i^{*b} are within interval $[0, 1]$
        $b = b + 1$
    end
until $b = B$

It is important to observe that for small S_L and S_U some bootstrap samples can result in infeasible replicates p_i^*, but the proposed algorithm discards all such infeasible replicates. For explanation, let us consider an example of two-class classification problem with an iteration of the bootstrap algorithm resulting in replicates $p^*(1|1) =$ $p^*(0|0) = 0.8$ and $q_1^* = 0.9$. Clearly, assuming the conditional probabilities are true, even for the extreme case with all examples from S_U being from class 1, q_1 could not be larger then 0.8. As a consequence, applying (3) on a given example would result in infeasible replicates $p_1^* = 1.17$ and $p_0^* = -0.17$. Therefore, in the algorithm from Table 1 all such replicates are discarded.

Modifications of the Bootstrap Algorithm from Table 1
We propose two modifications of the algorithm from Table 1 in order to improve its speed and to obtain better estimates of class probabilities. Obtaining B bootstrap samples can become computationally expensive if data sets S_L and S_U are large. For sufficiently large data sets estimates of q_j and $p(j|i)$ become very close to their true values and the algorithm from Table 1 might not be necessary to estimate p_i. However, in practice it is often not clear how large data set is large enough and, therefore, we use a simple procedure to provide bootstrap replicates q_j^* and $p^*(j|i)$ computationally fast when S_L and S_U are large.

Let us assume a sample X contains discrete random variables $x_i \in \{1, ..., c\}$, $i = 1,$ ..., n, such that f_j represents the fraction of examples with value j. Since vector f with elements $\{f_j\}$ is a sufficient statistics of X, replicate f^* of a bootstrap sample with elements $\{f_j^*\}$ has distribution $f^* \sim Mult(n,f)/n$, where $Mult$ denotes multinomial distribution with $E[f_j^*]=f_j$, $Var[f_j^*]=f_j(1-f_j)/n$. If n is large f_j^* can be approximated by a normal distribution $N(f_j, f_j(1-f_j)/n)$. In Table 2 we describe a procedure for random generation of f^* without the need for bootstrap sampling, where by $norm\_rnd(\mu, \sigma^2)$ we denoted a random generator of a normal distribution with mean μ and variance σ^2.

Table 2. A fast procedure for estimating frequencies from large bootstrap samples

> **Given** n, f, c. (c is the number of classes)
> $f_1^* = norm\_rnd(f_1, f_1(1-f_1)/n)$
> **if** $c = 2$
> $f_2^* = 1 - f_1^*$
> **else**
>   **for** $i = 2: c - 1$
> $$f = f_i \Big/ \sum\nolimits_{j=i}^{c} f_j \; , \; n^* = n(1 - \sum\nolimits_{j=1}^{i-1} f_j^*)$$
> $$f_i^* = norm\_rnd(f, f(1-f)/n^*) \cdot n^*/n$$
>   **end**
> $$f_c^* = 1 - \sum\nolimits_{i=1}^{c-1} f_i^*$$
> **end**

For large S_{test} and S_U the algorithm from Table 1 can be modified so that replicates q_j^* and $p^*(j|i)$ are calculated directly by using the procedure from Table 2 instead of taking actual bootstrap samples. To perform this one should only calculate $\hat{q}_j$ from S_U or $\hat{p}(j|i)$ from S_{test} and use these values as the corresponding sufficient statistics f.

The second modification to the algorithm from Table 1 is using Laplace corrections [4] to improve bootstrap replicates q_j^* and $p^*(j|i)$ when S_L and S_U are small. Let us assume that probability that example of class i occurs in a sample is small. If the sample size n is also small, there is a considerable probability that the fraction f_i of examples from the rare class in the sample will be zero. In such a case, all the bootstrap samples will also have zero examples of class i, resulting in $f_i^* = 0$. As already shown [9], for certain cost matrices this can result in very poor predictions of classifier's loss. The idea of Laplace correction is to bias the fractions f_i^* towards uniform distribution. To achieve this, a simple adjustment of frequency f_i from the original sample is performed as

$$f_i = \frac{n_i + \lambda}{n + c\lambda} \tag{4}$$

where n_i is the number of examples from class i within a sample of size n, and λ is the Laplace coefficient. Laplace correction with $\lambda = 1$ is a very suitable choice that can be validated in the following way. If $n_i = 0$ it can be assumed that the true frequency f_i of class i is at one standard deviation from zero, i.e., $f_i = sqrt\{f_i(1-f_i)/n\}$. From there it follows that $f_i = 1/(n+1)$, which after replacing in (4) results in $\lambda = n/(n-c+1) \approx 1$. Finally, it should be noted that Laplace correction can be easily incorporated in both procedures from Table 1 and Table 2.

3   Improving Classification Based on Class Probability Estimates

Once class probabilities on S_{new} are estimated it should be possible to improve the initial classifier. We analyze two distinct cases depending on the type of classifier and on the available computational resources.

Improving a Classifier That Estimates Posterior Class Probabilities

If a classifier was trained to estimate posterior class probabilities $p(i|\mathbf{x})$ when presented with a new example $\mathbf{x}$, then it can be directly adjusted without the need for retraining according to estimated class probabilities p_i on S_U. For example, a neural network with a hidden layer and c outputs (representing each of the c classes) trained by minimizing the mean squared error is known to approximate posterior class probabilities [1]. Denoting class frequencies in training set S_{train} as $f_{i,train}$, and predictions of a classifier as $p(i|\mathbf{x})$, adjusted predictions $p_{adjust}(i|\mathbf{x})$ can be calculated as [1]

$$p_{adjust}(i|\mathbf{x}) = \frac{p(i|\mathbf{x})\,Ep_i/f_{i,train}}{\sum_j p(j|\mathbf{x})\,Ep_j/f_{j,train}} \tag{5}$$

If computational resources permit one could try to produce a number of predictions for any given input $\mathbf{x}$ using different bootstrap replicates of p_i, $i = 1, ..., c$ and average the obtained values to the final prediction. However, this approach will not be considered further in this paper. If an arbitrary cost matrix C is assumed, one can further modify the existing classifier $p_{adjust}(i|\mathbf{x})$ to provide classifications that minimize the conditional classification risk [6].

Retraining a Classifier According to Estimated Class Probabilities

Retraining a classifier on $S_{retrain}$ resampled from S_{train} so that $f_{i,retrain} = Ep_i$ should lead to better accuracy on S_U regardless of the type of classification algorithm. Moreover, if a classifier represents a nonlinear discriminant function that directly provides classification such a retraining might represent the only viable choice to improve the classification accuracy. Therefore, in Table 3 we describe a simple iterative procedure for retraining of classifier that starts by training a classifier based on the original class probabilities from S_{train}. As seen from the Table 3, in the following iterations $S_{retrain}$ is resampled according to bootstrap estimate Ep_i.

Table 3. A procedure for retraining classifier using estimates of class probabilities Ep_i

---

Given $S_{train} = \{(\mathbf{x}_k, y_k)\}$, $k = 1, ..., n_{train}$, $y_k \in \{1, ... c\}$ and S_U
Assign $f_{i,retrain} = f_{i,train}$, ($f_{i,train}$ is the frequency of class i in S_{train})
repeat
  For each k, $d_k = f_{i,retrain} / f_{i,train}$, where i is label of example $(\mathbf{x}_k, y_k)$
  Normalize d_k such that $\Sigma_k d_k = 1$
  Resample n_{train} examples $S_{retrain}$ from S_{train} according to d_k
  Train a classifier on $S_{retrain}$
  Produce bootstrap estimates p_i^{*b} on S_U
  For each $i = 1, ..., c$, assign $f_{i,retrain} = (1/B)\Sigma_b p_i^{*b}$
until stopping criterion

Termination of the retraining procedure depends on the available computational resources. In the simplest, just one retraining might be needed to produce a satisfactory classifier adjusted for prediction on S_U. Also, if $f_{i,retrain}$ is very similar to $f_{i,train}$, it might be decided that retraining is not necessary. For example, if $f_{i,train}$ is within certain confidence interval of bootstrap estimate of p_i it can be claimed that, statistically, class probabilities in S_L and S_U are identical. Finally, if possible, the procedure should be repeated until convergence of estimated class probabilities is observed between consecutive iterations.

Few of the many modifications of the proposed procedure that can depend on an application include:

- If training set S_{train} is large the size of resampled data can be made smaller than n_{train} to speed-up the retraining without much loss of accuracy [12];
- For neural network classifiers, retaining on S_{train} and adjusting the weighting cost function according to estimated class probabilities could lead to a better accuracy then when resampling S_{train} [1];
- Using the similar reasoning as in section 2, Laplace correction can be used on $f_{i,retrain}$ to adjust it towards uniform distribution;
- If computational resources allow, instead of training a single classifier, bagging [3] can be used to train an ensemble of classifiers to improve both the classification accuracy and the estimate of class probabilities on S_U;
- Some of known methods [2,5] can be coupled with the procedure from Table 3 in a straightforward manner to produce classifiers that are optimized to an arbitrary cost matrix.

4   Experimental Results

We performed two groups of experiments to validate the proposed procedures for improving classifiers trained on data with biased class distribution. In the first group, we validated bootstrap methodology proposed in Section 2, while in the second group we applied the proposed methodology to the benchmark Waveform data set [2].

4.1.   Validation of the Proposed Bootstrap Algorithm

The proposed bootstrap algorithm was examined across a wide range of possible scenarios including different choices of data sizes n_{test}, n_U, number of classes c, prior class probabilities $p_{i,train}$ on S_{train} and p_i on S_U, and conditional probabilities $p(j|\,i)$ describing classifier's performance. In our experiments we have first chosen several sets of parameters $\{c,\ \lambda,\ n_{test},\ n_U\}$ as shown in Table 4. Then, for each such set of parameters we randomly generated 1000 probabilities $p_{i,train}$, p_i, and $p(j|\,i)$ to obtain 1000 7-tuples $\{c,\ \lambda,\ n_{test},\ n_U,\ p_{i,train},\ p_i,\ p(j|\,i)\}$. To examine a large range of possible choices we used the following random generators (by $rand$ we denote a uniform random number from $[0,1]$): (a) $p_{i,train} = r_i/\Sigma r_i$, where $r_i = rand + 0.05$; (b) $p_i = r_i/\Sigma r_i$, where $r_i = rand + 0.05$; and (c) $p(j|\,i) = r_{ji}/\Sigma_j r_{ji}$, where $r_{ji} = rand + \delta_{ji}$. The reason for adding 0.05 in (a) and (b) was to avoid examination of extremely rare classes in training or in unlabeled data, while adding Kronecker's delta promoted higher probabilities at $i = j$ which is behavior expected of any classifier.

In our methodology for bootstrap validation, starting from a given 7-tuple $\{c,\ \lambda,\ n_{test},\ n_U,\ p_{i,train},\ p_i,\ p(j|\,i)\}$, we use $\{n_{test},\ p_{i,train},\ p(j|\,i)\}$ to randomly generate a realization $\hat{p}(j|\,i)$, and $\{n_U,\ p_i,\ p(j|\,i)\}$ to randomly generate a realization $\hat{q}_j$ by the procedure described in Table 2. Therefore, for the each given 7-tuple we generate a pair $\{\hat{p}(j|\,i),\ \hat{q}_j\}$. Then, from $\{\hat{p}(j|\,i),\ \hat{q}_j\}$ we generate 500 bootstrap replicates of $\hat{p}(j|\,i)$ and $\hat{q}_j$, and apply (3) to calculate 500 bootstrap replicates p_i^*. Using 500 replicates p_i^* we calculate 90% confidence intervals for bootstrap estimates of p_i, and measure if all actual values p_i, $i = 1, \ldots, c$, belong to the estimated confidence intervals. If the proposed bootstrap algorithm is well designed, in about 90% of experiments the true values of p_i will belong to the estimated 90% confidence intervals.

In Table 4, for 16 different sets of parameters $\{c,\ \lambda,\ n_{test},\ n_U\}$, we report $B90$ values showing the fractions of the 1000 90% confidence intervals that contained the true p_i values. As could be seen, $B90$ values were between 0.83-0.92 in different experiments, they were slightly larger for $\lambda = 1$, and did not depend much on the choice of data size and the number of classes. Slightly lower $B90$ means that the estimated confidence intervals for the proposed bootstrap method are slightly shorter then their true value, but the difference is small enough to conclude that the evaluated bootstrap method gives satisfactory estimates. We also report the average number of bootstrap iterations $total\_b$ needed to obtain 500 feasible bootstrap replicates of p_i. As seen, for $c = 5$ and $n_{test} = 250$, the number of infeasible solutions was very large. In other cases $total\_b$ was acceptably small.

Table 4. For each of 16 tuples $\{c, \lambda, n_{test}, n_U\}$, 1000 7-tuples tuples $\{c, \lambda, n_{test}, n_U, p_{i,train}, p_i, p(j| i)\}$ were generated and for each of them 500 bootstrap replicates of p_i were calculated. The fraction of the 90% confidence interval that contained the true p_i values is denoted as *B90*.

Classes	λ	n_{test}	n_U	total_b	B90
		100	100	657	0.87
	0	100	1000	603	0.83
		1000	100	526	0.84
2		1000	1000	510	0.83
		100	100	638	0.89
	1	100	1000	579	0.86
		1000	100	527	0.86
		1000	1000	507	0.85
		250	250	2240	0.87
	0	250	5000	2110	0.85
		5000	250	976	0.84
5		5000	5000	621	0.85
		250	250	2210	0.87
	1	250	5000	2070	0.92
		5000	250	936	0.87
		5000	5000	612	0.84

4.2. Experiments on Waveform Data Set

As proposed by Breiman [2] we generated waveform data sets with arbitrary number of examples with 21 continuous attributes from each of the 3 classes, where each class represents a certain combination of 2 "base" waves chosen from the 3 available "base" waves. The concept to be learned is highly nonlinear and noisy and its Bayes error is known to be 13.2% [2] if all 3 classes have the same probability in training and in test data. The fact that we were able to generate an arbitrary number of examples allowed us to perform a range of experiments with different data sizes and different class probabilities.

In the performed experiments we first defined a set of two parameters $\{n_{test}, \mathbf{p}\}$, where elements of $\mathbf{p}$, p_i, represented the class probabilities on the unlabeled data. We assumed that the class probabilities on labeled data were the same, $p_{i,train} = 1/3$. For simplicity, we also assumed a labeled data set is composed of separate training set S_{train} and test set S_{test} with the same numbers of examples n_{test}. We could as well decided to apply a more data-efficient cross-validation approach by using S_{train} both for training and test, but the choice of the separate test set allowed us to perform a larger set of experiments.

Based on the given values $\{n_{test}, \mathbf{p}\}$ we first generated balanced sets S_{train} and S_{test} with the same number of examples n_{test}. Then, we generated $n_U = n_{test}$ (again, for convenience) examples according to class probabilities $\mathbf{p}$. Note that the exact fractions of classes within S_U can be considered as random numbers from $Mult(n_u, \mathbf{p})/n_u$ distribution. We also generated another large data set S_{large} with 30,000 examples from each of the 3 classes to be able to precisely measure the accuracy of each constructed classifier.

All combinations $\{n_{test}, \mathbf{p}\}$ used in our experiments are shown in Table 5. For each combination $\{n_{test}, \mathbf{p}\}$ we performed 30 experiments using neural networks with 21 inputs, 5 hidden nodes and 3 sigmoid outputs, trained by resilient backpropagation algorithm [10] on S_{train}. Then, we tested neural network performance on S_{test} to estimate matrix $\mathbf{P}$ with elements $p(j| i)$, and on S_U to estimate vector $\mathbf{q}$ with elements q_j. Then, we applied the proposed bootstrap method with 200 iterations to estimate vector $\mathbf{p}$ with elements p_i.

In Table 5 we report the average bootstrap estimate Ep_i and +/- one standard deviation over 30 experiments and, in the parentheses, the average length of 90% confidence intervals of p_i over 30 experiments. We also report on the average accuracy +/- one standard deviation of the original neural classifier, of the adjusted neural network using (5), and of the neural network retrained according to estimated class probabilities of unlabeled data. We were able to use (5) since described neural networks were trained to approximate posterior class probabilities $p(i| x)$. Note that all accuracies were measured on S_{large} by accounting for the true class probabilities of the unlabeled data $\mathbf{p}$.

Table 5. Accuracy and class probability estimates over different combinations $\{n_{test}, \mathbf{p}\}$

$\mathbf{p}$	n_{test}	Bootstrap estimates of class frequencies on unlabeled data [%]			Accuracy [%]		
		Class1	Class2	Class3	Original	Adjusted	Retrain
$\frac{1}{3},\frac{1}{3},\frac{1}{3}$	500	34±3 (12)	33±3 (11)	33±3 (11)	**83.2±1.2**	**83.0±1.2**	81.1±0.9
	2000	33±2 (6)	34±2 (5)	33±2 (5)	**85.1±0.7**	**85.1±0.7**	84.8±0.5
$\frac{1}{2},\frac{1}{3},\frac{1}{6}$	500	49±4 (13)	33±3 (11)	18±3 (10)	82.7±1.6	**84.1±1.4**	82.4±1.5
	2000	49±2 (6)	34±2 (6)	17±2 (5)	84.1±0.8	**85.6±0.8**	85.5±1.1
$\frac{2}{3},\frac{1}{3},\frac{1}{6}$	500	66±5 (14)	17±3 (11)	17±4 (11)	81.1±2.3	**85.0±2.0**	83.9±1.8
	2000	67±2 (7)	17±3 (5)	17±4 (5)	83.2±1.3	86.7±1.3	**87.5±1.0**
$\frac{3}{4},\frac{1}{6},\frac{1}{12}$	500	75±4 (15)	17±4 (12)	9±2 (10)	80.0±2.5	**87.4±2.0**	86.0±1.6
	1000	75±3 (10)	17±2 (8)	8±2 (7)	81.5±1.8	**88.1±1.2**	88.2±1.1
	2000	75±2 (7)	17±1 (5)	8±1 (5)	81.3±1.8	88.2±1.4	**89.1±1.0**
	5000	75±1 (4)	17±1 (3)	9±1 (3)	82.4±1.7	88.9±1.2	**90.0±0.9**

As expected, for $\mathbf{p} = [1/3, 1/3, 1/3]$ an original neural network had the highest accuracy for n_{test}=500, while for n_{test}=2000 all 3 strategies gave similar accuracy. For small data sets the estimates of $\mathbf{p}$ can be slightly off which can cause slight decrease in the accuracy of adjusted classifier. If another classifier is trained on resampled data using inaccurate estimate of $\mathbf{p}$ this difference can be even higher. For other 3 examined vectors $\mathbf{p}$ ([1/2,1/3,1/6], [2/3.1/3,1/6], [3/4,1/6,1/12]) adjusted classifiers and retrained classifiers were clear winners over original classifiers. Also, for large data sets retrained classifiers were superior to adjusted ones, while adjusted classifiers were better with smaller samples. Observe also that the classification accuracy was increasing with the size of the data sets for all 3 scenarios (Original, Adjusted, and Retrain). Looking at the estimated class probabilities of $\mathbf{p}$ expressed as $100p_i$ %, it can be seen that these estimates were consistent with the true class probability on unlabeled data, while the confidence intervals of these estimates decreased as the data size increased.

5   Conclusions

If class distribution on labeled data is different from that of unlabeled data, a classifier trained on labeled data can cause wrong inference and produce sub-optimal classification on unlabeled data. In this paper we proposed a bootstrap algorithm to estimate class probabilities of unlabeled data and used these estimates to improve classification on unlabeled data. It was shown experimentally that this approach can be successfully applied to improve classifiers trained on data with biased class distribution. It is worth noting that the proposed bootstrap methodology alone could be very useful in estimating the confidence intervals for class probabilities in important real-life problems such as determining the commonness of protein disorder in nature.

Although bootstraping is known as a computer intensive methodology, it is computationally fairly cheap in the framework of classification. The proposed algorithm uses an existing classifier and the estimate of its accuracy that should both be products of a standard process of classifier construction. The proposed bootstrap algorithm requires only an additional pass through unlabeled data to estimate the probability of predicting each of the classes. Based on these estimates, the bootstrap estimation of the true class probabilities on unlabeled data could be done in seconds regardless of the sizes of labeled and unlabeled data. Even when retraining a classifier to improve the prediction accuracy, the overall computational effort is just twice more costly as compared to training a single classifier.

However, it should be remembered that the proposed methodology is applicable only to the sampling bias in class distribution. Therefore, some theoretical or empirical evidence about sampling bias in labeled and unlabeled data should validate the methodology application. The goal of our work in progress is to derive statistical tests that could determine: (i) if class distribution is biased, and (ii) if there are other types of sampling bias in data. If such tests were derived, the proposed methodology could become a standard off-the-shelf procedure for machine learning and knowledge discovery.

References

1. Bishop, C.: Neural Networks for Pattern Recognition. Clarendon Press, Oxford (1995)
2. Breiman, L., Friedman, J., Olshen, R., Stone, C.: Classification and Regression Trees. The Wadsworth International Group (1984)
3. Breiman, L.: Bagging predictors. Machine Learning. **24** (1996) 123-140
4. Cestnik, B.: Estimating Probabilities: A Crucial Task in Machine Learning. Proceedings of the 9th ECAI. Stockholm, Sweden (1990) 147-149
5. Domingos, P.: MetaCost: A General Method for Making Classifiers Cost-Sensitive. Proceedings of the 5th International Conference on Knowledge Discovery and Data Mining. San Diego, ACM Press (1999) 155-164
6. Duda, R.O., Hart, P.E.: Pattern Classification and Scene Analysis. John Wiley & Sons, New York, US (1973)
7. Dunker A.K., Lawson J.D., Brown C.J., Romero P., Oh J.,Oldfield C.J., Campen A.M., Ratlif, Hipps K.W., Ausio J., Nissen M.S., Reeves R., Kang C.H., Kissinger C.R., Bailey R.W., Griswold M.D., Chiu W., Garner E.C. and Obradovic Z.: Intrinsically Disordered Proteins. Journal of Molecular Graphics and Modeling, **19** (2001) 28-61

8. Efron, B., and Tibshirani, R. J.: An Introduction to the Bootstrap. New York: Chapman & Hall (1993)
9. Margineantu, D.D., Dietterich, T.G.: Bootstrap Methods for the Cost-Sensitive Evaluation of Classifiers. Proceedings of the 17th International Conference on Machine Learning, (2000) 582-590
10. Riedmiller, M., Braun, H.: A direct adaptive method for faster backpropagation learning: the RPROP algorithm. Proceedings of the IEEE International Conference on Neural Networks. (1993) 586-591
11. Romero, P., Obradovic, Z., Li, X., Garner, E., Brown, C.J., Dunker, A.K.: Sequence Complexity and Disordered Protein. Proteins: Structure, Function and Genetics. **42** (2001) 38-48
12. Vucetic, S., Obradovic, Z.: Performance Controlled Data Reduction for Knowledge Discovery in Distributed Databases. Proceedings of the 4th Pacific-Asia Conference on Knowledge Discovery and Data Mining. Computer Science Editorial 3, Springer-Verlag, Kyoto, Japan (2000) 29-39
13. Vucetic, S., Radivojac, P., Dunker, K., Brown, C., Obradovic, Z.: Methods for Improving Protein Disorder Prediction. Proceedings of the IEEE/INNS International Conference on Neural Networks. Washington D.C. (2001, in press)

Discovering Admissible Simultaneous Equation Models from Observed Data

Takashi Washio[1], Hiroshi Motoda[1], and Yuji Niwa[2]

[1] Institute for Scientific and Industrial Research, Osaka University,
8-1, Mihogaoka, Ibarakishi, Osaka, 567-0047, Japan
{washio, motoda}@sanken.osaka-u.ac.jp
[2] Institute of Nuclear Safety System, Inc.,
64 Sada, Mihamacho, Mikatagun, Fukui, 919-1205, Japan
niwa@inss.co.jp

Abstract. Conventional work on scientific discovery such as BACON derives empirical law equations from experimental data. In recent years, SDS introducing mathematical admissibility constraints has been proposed to discover first principle based law equations, and it has been further extended to discover law equations from passively observed data. Furthermore, SSF has been proposed to discover the structure of a simultaneous equation model representing an objective process through experiments. In this paper, SSF is extended to discover the structure of a simultaneous equation model from passively observed data, and is combined with the extended SDS to discover a quantitative simultaneous equation model reflecting the first principle.

1 Introduction

Langley and others' BACON [6] is the most well known pioneering work to discover a complete equation representing scientific laws governing an objective process under experimental observations. FAHRENHEIT [4], ABACUS [3], etc. are the successors of BACON that use basically similar algorithms. However, a drawback of the BACON family, that is their low likelihood to discover the equations representing the first principle underlying the objective process, is reported. To alleviate the drawback, some systems, *e.g.*, ABACUS and COPER [5], utilize the information of the unit dimensions of quantities to prune the meaningless terms. However, many of these conventional scientific equation discovery systems have the following limitations.

(1) The information of the unit dimension of each quantity in the data is needed to discover the first principle based equation.
(2) The data must be acquired under *"active observations"* where the values of some quantities representing the objective process are observed for various process states by controlling the values of the other relevant quantities.
(3) A complex equation model, especially a *"simultaneous equation model"*, to represent the process consisting of multiple mechanisms is hardly discovered due to the complexity of the search space.

L. De Raedt and P. Flach (Eds.): ECML 2001, LNAI 2167, pp. 539–551, 2001.
© Springer-Verlag Berlin Heidelberg 2001

To alleviate the first limitation, a law equation discovery system named SDS based on the mathematical constraints of "*scale-type*" and "*identity*" is proposed for the active observations [10]. Since the knowledge of scale-types of quantities is widely obtained in various domains, SDS is applicable to non-physics domains. The equations discovered by SDS are highly likely to represent the first principle underlying the objective process. To address the second limitation, SDS has been further extended by introducing a novel principle named "*quasi-bi-variate fitting*" [12] for the application to the "*passive observations*" where the quantities of the objective process can only be partially or even hardly controlled. Moreover, to overcome the third limitation, a simultaneous structure finding system named SSF has been proposed to discover a valid simultaneous equation structure under the active observations [11]. SSF identifies the number of equations needed to represent the objective process, and further identifies the sets of quantities to appear in the respective equations of the model while excluding quantities irrelevant to the equations. The combination of SDS and SSF enables the discovery of the first principle based simultaneous equation model for the objective process under active observations.

One of the important unexplored studies of the scientific law equation discovery is to propose a practical framework to discover a simultaneous equation model reflecting the first principles from passively observed data. This study tries to address all aforementioned limitations at once. If SSF can be extended to be applicable to the passively observed data, the second and the third limitations in the discovery of the structure of the simultaneous equation model are removed. Once the sets of quantities appearing in respective equations are derived, the aforementioned extended SDS which addresses the first and the second limitations is applicable to figure out the equation formula governing each quantity set. Accordingly, the extension of the applicability of SSF to the passive observations is the main issue in this study. The objectives of this paper are (i) to propose a practical principle to discover the first principle based simultaneous equation structure from passively observed data, (ii) to provide an algorithm of the "*extended SSF*" based on the principle, (iii) to evaluate the basic performance of the combination of the extended SSF and the extended SDS through simulations and (iv) to demonstrate its practicality through a real application.

The main technical contribution of this study is to propose a principle named "*quasi-experiment on dependency*" which checks the dependency among quantities in the passively observed data without performing actual experiment. The quasi-experiment probes the influence propagation from a quantity to some other quantities while virtually fixing the values of some extra quantities by a data sampling technique. The repetitions of this probing figure out the entire dependency structure among quantities in form of a simultaneous equation model. The quasi-experiment on dependency is different from the quasi-bi-variate fitting used in the extended SDS since the latter assumes that the quantities under consideration are governed by a complete equation, and focuses only on the binary relation between every pair of quantities. The approach to combine the extended SSF and the extended SDS requires three assumptions, which are

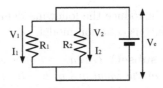

Fig. 1. An circuit of parallel resistances.

allowable in many practical applications. One is that the scale-types of all observed quantities are known. The scale-types of the measurement quantities are widely known based on the measurement theory [10]. The second assumption is that the observed data are uniformly distributed over the possible states of the objective system [12]. The lack of the uniform distribution of the data over a certain value range of a quantity implies the low observability of the quantity [7]. Any approaches such as the linear system identification and the neural network do not derive valid models under low observability. This limitation is generic, and further discussion on this issue is out of scope of this paper. The third assumption is that the simultaneous equation model under consideration is not over-constrained where the number of the equation is not more than the number of quantities in the model. This assumption always holds for the models in scientific and engineering domains, since the over-constrained state does not exist in any real world process.

2   Structure of a Simultaneous Equation Model

The principle to discover the simultaneous equation structure from passively observed data is based on some fundamental and generic characteristics of simultaneous equation models presented in the past work [11]. These characteristics are briefly explained though an example electric circuit depicted in Fig. 1. This can be represented by the following simultaneous equation model.

$$V_1 = I_1 R_1 \ \#1, \ V_2 = I_2 R_2 \ \#2, \ V_e = V_1 \ \#3 \ \text{and} \ V_e = V_2 \ \#4, \tag{1}$$

where R_1, R_2: two resistances, V_1, V_2: voltage differences across resistances, I_1, I_2: electric current going through resistances and V_e: voltage of a battery. We consider a thought experiment to externally control some values of the quantities in this model. For example, the quantities R_1 and V_e can be externally controlled by the specification of the resistance and the battery. If we specify these values in Eq.(1), the values of the other quantities, V_1, V_2 and I_1, that are involved in the first, the third and the forth equations, #1, #3 and #4, are determined since the number of the quantities which are not externally specified is equal to the number of the equations. But, this external control does not determine the values of R_2 and I_2 through the equation #2. Thus, the equation set $\{\#1, \#3, \#4\}$ is considered to represent a mechanism which determines the state of a part of the objective process. We introduce the following definition to characterize this mechanism in the simultaneous equation model.

Definition 1 (complete subset) *Given a set of equations, E, let the set of all quantities be Q appearing in the equations in E. Given a quantity set $RQ(\subset Q)$ for external specification, when the values of all quantities in $NQ = CQ - RQ$ are determined where CQ ($RQ \subset CQ \subset Q$) is a set of all quantities appearing in a set of equations $CE(\subseteq E)$, CE is called a "complete subset". The cardinality $|CE| = |NQ|$ is called the "order" of the complete subset.*

The equation set $\{\#1, \#3, \#4\}$ is a complete subset of the order 3. Under any external control of two quantities among R_1, V_e, V_1, V_2 and I_1, $\{\#1, \#3, \#4\}$ always determines the values of the remained three quantities. Thus, the complete subset is "*invariant*" for the selection of the externally controlled quantities.

The complete subset gives an important foundation to discover the structure of the simultaneous equation model which appropriately reflects the dependency embedded in the observation of quantities. For example, the circuit in Fig. 1 can be represented by the following different simultaneous equation formula.

$$I_1 R_1 = I_2 R_2 \ \#1', \ V_2 = I_2 R_2 \ \#2, \ V_e = V_1 \ \#3 \text{ and } V_e = V_2 \ \#4. \tag{2}$$

If the same specification on V_e and R_1 is made in Eq.(2), a different complete subset $\{\#3, \#4\}$ is obtained, and any complete subset to determine the value of I_1 does not exist since the equation $\#1'$ cannot determine the value of I_1 without the constraint of $\#2$. $\#1'$ and $\#2$ that include the undetermined quantities I_2 and R_2 do not satisfy Definition 1. In the real observation on the electric circuit, the value of I_1 is physically determined, and this fact contradicts the consequence derived by the analysis on Eq.(2). In contrast, the model of Eq.(1) always gives correct answers on the determination of quantities for any external specifications of quantities. The model having the complete subsets which are isomorphic with the actual dependency among quantities is named a "*structural form*".

Conversely, if we identify all complete subsets from the observation of quantities in the objective process, and compose a simultaneous equation model consisting of these complete subsets, the model is ensured to be the structural form. The following theorem provides a basis for the composition [11].

Theorem 1 (modular lattice theorem) *Given a model of an objective process consisting of equations E, the set of all complete subsets of the model, i.e., $L = \{\forall CE_i \subseteq E\}$, forms a modular lattice of the sets for the order of the complete subsets, i.e., $\forall CE_i, CE_j \in L$, $CE_i \cup CE_j \in L$, $CE_i \cap CE_j \in L$ and $n(CE_i \cup CE_j) = n(CE_i) + n(CE_j) - n(CE_i \cap CE_j)$ where n is the order of a given complete subset.*

For instance, the following four complete subsets having the modular lattice structure can be found in the example of Eq.(1).

$$\{\#3, \#4\}(n = 2), \ \{\#1, \#3, \#4\}(n = 3),$$
$$\{\#2, \#3, \#4\}(n = 3), \ \{\#1, \#2, \#3, \#4\}(n = 4). \tag{3}$$

Because the complete subsets of an objective process mutually overlap in the modular lattice, the redundant overlaps must be removed in the model composition by introducing the following definition of independent component.

Definition 2 (independent component of a complete subset) *The independent component DE_i of the complete subset CE_i is defined as*

$$DE_i = CE_i - \bigcup_{\forall CE_j \subset CE_i \, and \, CE_j \in L} CE_j,$$

where L is the set of all complete subsets of the model. The set of essential quantities DQ_i of CE_i which do not belong to any other complete subsets but are involved only in CE_i is also defined as

$$DQ_i = CQ_i - \bigcup_{\forall CE_j \subset CE_i \, and \, CE_j \in L} CQ_j,$$

where CQ_i is the set of all quantities in CE_i. The order δn_i and the freedom δm_i of DE_i are defined as

$$\delta n_i = |DE_i| \text{ and } \delta m_i = |DQ_i| - |DE_i|.$$

For instance, the following independent components can be found for Eq.(1).

$$
\begin{aligned}
DE_1 &= \{\#3, \#4\} - \phi = \{\#3, \#4\}, \ \delta n_1 = 2 - 0 = 2, \\
DE_2 &= \{\#1, \#3, \#4\} - \{\#3, \#4\} = \{\#1\}, \ \delta n_2 = 3 - 2 = 1, \qquad (4) \\
DE_3 &= \{\#2, \#3, \#4\} - \{\#3, \#4\} = \{\#2\}, \ \delta n_3 = 3 - 2 = 1.
\end{aligned}
$$

Because the independent components do not overlap, their collection represents the structure of the simultaneous equation model.

However, the issue on the ambiguity of the representation of the structural form still remains. For example, the set of equations $\{V_1 = I_1 R_1 \#1, V_e = V_1 \#3, V_e = V_2 \#4\}$ in Eq.(1) which is a complete subset of order 3 can be transformed by the linear transformation as follows.

$$
\begin{aligned}
2V_e + V_1 + V_2 &= 4I_1 R_1 \ \#1, \ 2V_e = 2V_1 - V_2 + I_1 R_1 \ \#3, \\
\text{and } 3V_e &= -V_1 + 2V_2 + 2I_1 R_1 \ \#4. \qquad (5)
\end{aligned}
$$

This transformation preserves the complete subset, and the model remains as a structural form. This ambiguity of the equation representation in a complete subset can cause combinatorial explosion in the enumeration of the structural forms. As indicated in the above example, if the set of all quantities, CQ, appearing in a complete subset CE is preserved through some transformation maintaining quantitative equivalence, the complete subset is also preserved [11]. Accordingly, only the following formulae of a complete subset is focused in the search.

Definition 3 (canonical form of a complete subset) *Given a complete subset CE, the "canonical form" of CE is the form where all quantities in CQ appears in each equation in CE.*

An example of the canonical form is Eq.(5). Based on this definition, the structural canonical form of a simultaneous equation model is further defined.

Definition 4 (structural canonical form of simultaneous equations)
The "canonical form" of a simultaneous equation consists of the equations in $\cup_{i=1}^{b} DE_i$ where each equation in DE_i is represented by the canonical form in the complete subset CE_i, and b is the total number of DE_i. If the canonical form of a simultaneous equation is derived to be a "structural form", then the form is named "structural canonical form".

The structural form of Eq.(1) is shown as follows.

$$DE_1 = \{f_{11}(V_e, V_1, V_2) = 0 \ \#3, \quad f_{12}(V_e, V_1, V_2) = 0 \ \#4\},$$
$$DE_2 = \{f_2(V_e, V_1, V_2, I_1, R_1) = 0 \ \#1\}, \ DE_3 = \{f_3(V_e, V_1, V_2, I_2, R_2) = 0 \ \#2\}, \ (6)$$

where $f(\bullet) = 0$ is an arbitrary formula to represent a quantitative relation. Because Eq.(1) is a structural form, Eq.(6) is the structural canonical form.

3   Principle and Algorithm

3.1   Quasi-Experiment on Dependency

If actual experiments are applicable, the algorithm of SSF can search the complete subsets in which quantities are mutually constrained through the control to fix the values of the other quantities. However, when only the passively observed data are available, a novel principle, *"quasi-experiment on dependency,"* proposed in this study is needed to enable virtual experiments under the aforementioned assumption that the observed data are uniformly distributed over the possible states of the objective process. Given a set of quantities representing the objective process, $Q = \{q_1, ..., q_w\}$, and the set of their passively observed data, $OBS = \{X_1, ..., X_t\}$ where X_i is the i-th observation of Q, we consider to virtually control each quantity q_k in a subset $Q_c (\subset Q)$. As depicted in Fig. 2, a datum $X_g (\in OBS)$ is chosen, and the data of OBS involved in the vicinity of X_g in the subspace defined by Q_c are sampled as OBS_{cg}. The vicinity is defined as follows for every $q_k (\in Q_c)$.

$$\Delta q_k = |q_k - q_{kg}| < \epsilon_k, \tag{7}$$

where ϵ_k is a parameter to define the size of the vicinity. ϵ_k is determined as 5% of the total value range of q_k upon an extensive parameter survey in this paper. This vicinity is shown as a rectangular parallelepiped in Fig. 2 (a). This operation is called *"quasi-control"* and Q_c *"quasi-controlled quantity set"*.

Furthermore, for a quantity q_m in $Q - Q_c$, the following correlation coefficient between q_m and each $q_d (\in Q - Q_c - \{q_m\})$ is calculated within the data of OBS_{cg}.

$$r_{md} = \frac{S_{md}}{\sqrt{S_{mm}}\sqrt{S_{dd}}}, \tag{8}$$

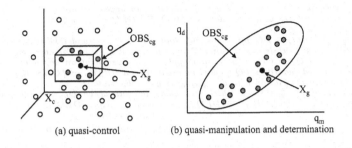

Fig. 2. Quasi-experiment on dependency

where

$$S_{md} = \sum_{OBS_{cg}} q_m q_d - (\sum_{OBS_{cg}} q_m \sum_{OBS_{cg}} q_d)/|OBS_{cg}|,$$

$$S_{mm} = \sum_{OBS_{cg}} q_m^2 - (\sum_{OBS_{cg}} q_m)^2/|OBS_{cg}|, \quad S_{dd} = \sum_{OBS_{cg}} q_d^2 - (\sum_{OBS_{cg}} q_d)^2/|OBS_{cg}|.$$

If r_{md} shows significant correlation as depicted in Fig. 2 (b), q_m and q_d may be mutually constrained under the quasi-control of Q_c in the equation structure embedded in the given data. This process is considered to virtually manipulate the value of q_m by using the scatter of q_m's values in OBS_{cg} and to check if the value of q_d is determined. The operation on q_m is called "*quasi-manipulation*" and q_m "*quasi-manipulated quantity*". The determination of q_d is called "*quasi-determination*" and q_d "*quasi-determined quantity*".

The significance of r_{md} must be tested by the following index and criterion based on the one-sided interval of t-distribution, $t(|OBS_{cg}| - 2, \alpha)$, under the freedom $|OBS_{cg}| - 2$ and a significance level $\alpha(= 0.05)$,

$$r(|OBS_{cg}| - 2, \alpha) = \frac{t(|OBS_{cg}| - 2, \alpha)}{\sqrt{|OBS_{cg}| - 2 + \{t(|OBS_{cg}| - 2, \alpha)\}^2}},$$

$$|r_{md}| \geq r(|OBS_{cg}| - 2, \alpha) \Rightarrow r_{md} \text{ is significant.} \tag{9}$$

The test may fail when the relation between q_m and q_d has strong non-monotonicity. However, this possibility is not very problematic, since the first principle law equations do not contain very strong nonlinearity in most of cases [6,10]. Furthermore, this test is repeated for multiple OBS_{cg}s defined by p different X_gs to confirm the stability of the t-test consequences. p is set to be 10 in this work which is sufficient to check the stability. Let s be the number of the test satisfying the condition Eq.(9). Because s follows the binomial distribution $B(p, 1 - \alpha)$, the following condition should be met, if q_m and q_d is mutually constrained.

$$s/p \geq (1 - \alpha) - 2\sqrt{\alpha(1 - \alpha)/p} \ (\simeq 0.8). \tag{10}$$

The principle of the quasi-experiment on dependency seems similar to the quasi-bi-variate test of the extended SDS. However, the latter assumes that

(S1) Let $Q = \{q_k | k = 1, ..., w\}$ be a set of quantities to appear in the model of an objective process, and let OBS be a given data set for Q. Set $DEQ = \phi$, $DQ = \phi$, $N = \phi$, $M = \phi$, $h = 1$ and $i = 1$.

(S2) Choose $C_j \subset DQ_j \in DQ$ for some DQ_j and also $C_q \subseteq Q$, and take their union $C_{hi} = ... \cup C_j \cup ... \cup C_q$, while maintaining $|C_j| \leq \delta m_j$ and $|C_{hi}| = h$. For every $q_m \in C_{hi}, m = 1, ..., |C_{hi}|$, let $Q_c = C_{hi} - \{q_m\}$, and apply quasi-experiment on dependency under the quasi-controlled quantity set Q_c, quasi-manipulated quantity q_m and OBS. If $q_d (\in Q - C_{hi})$ has significant correlation with any q_m, q_d is quasi-determined.

(S3) Let a set of all quantities which are quasi-determined be $D_{hi} \subseteq (Q - C_{hi})$. Set $DEQ_{hi} = C_{hi} + D_{hi}$, $DQ_{hi} = DEQ_{hi} - \cup_{\forall DEQ_{h'i'} \subset DEQ_{hi} \atop DEQ_{h'i'} \in DEQ} DEQ_{h'i'}$, $\delta n_{hi} = |D_{hi}| -$

$\sum_{\forall DEQ_{h'i'} \subset DEQ_{hi} \atop DEQ_{h'i'} \in DEQ} \delta n_{h'i'}$, and $\delta m_{hi} = |DQ_{hi}| - \delta n_{hi}$. If $\delta n_{hi} > 0$, then add DEQ_{hi} to the list DEQ, DQ_{hi} to the list DQ, δn_{hi} to the list N, δm_{hi} to the list M and $Q = Q - DQ_{hi}$.

(S4) If all quantities are quasi-determined, i.e., $D_{hi} = Q - C_{hi}$, then go to (S5), else if any more C_{hi} where $|C_{hi}| = h$ does not exist, $h = h + 1, i = 1$ and go to (S2), else $i = i + 1$ and go to (S2).

(S5) The contents of the lists DEQ, DQ, N and M represent the sets of quantities involved in independent components, the sets of essential quantities of independent components, their orders and their degrees of freedom respectively. SCF is a list of all $f_{jr}(q_k \in DEQ_j) = 0$ $(r = 1, ..., \delta n_j)$ for every $DEQ_j (\in DEQ)$ and its order $\delta n_j (\in N)$.

Fig. 3. Algorithm for structural canonical form

the set of quantities $Q = \{q_1, ..., q_w\}$ are governed by a complete equation $f(q_1, ..., q_w) = 0$, and searches feasible binary quantitative relations on some pairs of quantities $\{q_i, q_j\} \in Q$ while quasi-controling the rest of the quantities, i.e., $Q_c = Q - \{q_i, q_j\}$, for each pair. On the other hand, the quasi-experiment on dependency searches a simultaneous equation structure not limiting to a complete equation. The quasi-controlled quantity set Q_c can be an arbitrary subset of Q not limiting to $Q - \{q_i, q_j\}$, and multiple pairs of quantities $\{q_m, q_d\} \in Q - Q_c$ can be found under the unique Q_c.

3.2   Algorithm for Structural Canonical Form

Based on the theory described in section 2 and the quasi-experiment on dependency in subsection 3.1, we propose a novel algorithm shown in Fig. 3 to discover the structure of a simultaneous equation from passively observed data. The notations in Fig. 3 follows Definition 2. It takes a list of quantities Q and their observed data OBS, and outputs the structural canonical form SCF. Starting from the small set C_{hi} which is a union of Q_c and $\{q_m\}$, q_d for the q_m is searched. Though the quasi-experiment on dependency for a q_m can derive all elements of D_{hi} in principle, the experiment is repeated while selecting every quantity in C_{hi} as q_m. This is because some quantity q_m may not have enough sensitivity to change the value of its q_d, and does not show the significant correlation even if they are mutually constrained. The resultant D_{hi} together with $C_{hi} = Q_c + \{q_m\}$ forms a set DEQ_{hi} of quantities belonging to the independent component of a complete subset. Then its set of the essential quantities DQ_{hi}, its order δn_{hi} and its freedom δm_{hi} are derived. Based on the modular lattice structure of a simultaneous equation, the $|C_{hi}|(= h)$ quantities for quasi-control and quasi-manipulation are taken from the union of δm_j quantities in each independent component DQ_j and the quantities not included in any independent components. The constraint of DQ_j does not miss any complete subset in the search due to the monotonic lattice structure among complete subsets. By repeating this procedure, all independent components are found and stored in the list DEQ. Though the complexity of this algorithm is non-polynomial in the worst case, the search space is significantly reduced by DQ_j. At the final step, the formulae where each indicates the quantities to appear in an equation included in the structural canonical form are listed in SCF.

The law discovery systems such as the extended SDS [12] for passively observed data cannot directly accept SCF. The values of the quantities within an independent component are simultaneously constrained in the order δn_i, and the constraints disable the quasi-bi-variate fitting, if the order δn_i is larger than one. To remove this difficulty, the $(\delta n_i - 1)$ quantities are eliminated by the substitution of the other $(\delta n_i - 1)$ equations within the independent component, and the "*maximally eliminated structural canonical form*" $MESCF$ is derived. The algorithm to obtain $MESCF$ has already been reported [11]. Using the resultant $MESCF$, the extended SDS determines the quantitative formula of each equation reflecting the first principle underlying the objective process.

4   Performance Evaluation

The extended SSF has been developed and combined with the extended SDS on a numerical processing shell named MATLAB in a PC of PentiumIII 666MHz and 128MB RAM. The performance has been evaluated through the following artificial examples for certain combinations of data sizes and noise levels.

1) **Two parallel resistances and a battery**: This has been explained in Fig. 1. Its model consists of 4 equations and 7 quantities as shown in Eq.(1).

2) **Two parallel resistances and a battery**: The objective process is identical with the first example except that an extra equation $R_1 = R_2$ is added. Its model consists of 5 equations and 7 quantities.

3) **Heat transfer at walls of holes**: A large solid material having two vertical holes is considered. Gas goes into these holes, and condenses to its liquid phase by providing its heat energy to the walls while flowing in the holes. The heat transfer process is represented by the 8 equations involving 17 quantities.

4) **A circuit of photometer**: An electric circuit of photometer to measure the rate of increase of photo intensity within a certain time period is considered. It consists of 3 transistors, 3 resistance, 1 light Csd sensor, 1 capacitor and 1 current meter. This system is represented by 14 equations involving 22 quantities.

Table 1 is the summary of problem size, required computation time and error rate for each example for the given OBS consisting of 1000 observed data which contain 5% Gaussian noise relative to the absolute value of each quantity in Q. T_{ssf} is the time to derive the $MESCF$. T_{sds} and T_{av} are the total time and the average time per equation required by the extended SDS. T_{ssf} shows strong dependency on the parameter m and n, *i.e.*, the size of the problem, since the algorithm to derive a structural canonical form requires non-polynomial time

Table 1. Computation time and failure rate

Ex.	m	n	av	T_{ssf}	T_{sds}	T_{av}	FR
1)	4	7	2.5	18	37	9	0.0
2)	5	7	2.4	15	46	9	0.0
3)	8	17	3.9	2,936	147	18	0.18
4)	14	22	2.6	13,992	142	10	0.16

m, n: numbers of equations and quantities, av: average number of quantities per equation, T_{ssf}, T_{sds}: CPU time (sec) required by the extended SSF and the extended SDS, T_{av}: average CPU time (sec) per equation required by the extended SDS, FR: failure rate in the discovery of correct simultaneous equation in 100 trials.

Table 2. Failure rate for noise levels

	failure rate (FR)			
Ex.	0%	5%	10%	20%
1)	0.00	0.00	0.00	0.00
2)	0.00	0.05	0.10	0.83
3)	0.13	0.18	0.23	1.00
4)	0.11	0.16	0.24	1.00

Table 3. Computation time and failure rate

Data Num.	T_{ssf}	T_{sds}	FR
100	2,583	79	0.96
1000	2,936	147	0.18
10000	3,288	207	0.11

to the size. T_{ssf} also moderately depends on $n - m$, because the large number of $n - m$ represents the high degree of freedom of the objective simultaneous equation model which exponentially increases the search space. T_{sds} does not seem to very strongly depend on the size of the problem. Because the extended SDS handles each equation independently in $MESCF$, the required time is proportional to the number of equations in the model. The complexity of the extended SDS is known to be around $O(av^2)$ [12]. This is almost consistent with the relation between T_{av} and av. Thus, T_{sds} may vary approximately in $O(mav^2)$. Except the examples 1) and 2), we observed certain level of failure rates FRs in the discovery. Especially when m and/or av are large, the extended SSF tends to become erroneous. This is because the coupling of many quantities though the equations increases the dependency among the quantities in the observation data, and the required assumption that the observed data are uniformly distributed over the possible states of the objective process becomes no more valid.

Table 2 shows FRs of each example under $0\% - 20\%$ relative noise levels and OBS consisting of 1000 data. When the coupling of quantities is stronger, the larger FR is observed. This tendency is significant in the difference of FRs between the examples 1) and 2). In the example 2), the coupling effect of the extra equation $R_1 = R_2$ significantly increases FR. In addition, the examples containing tight coupling show high sensitivity to the increase of the noise level. Table 3 shows the required computation time and the failure rates of the example

3) for OBS of $100 - 10000$ data and 5% relative noise level. T_{ssf} and T_{sds} seem to be almost $O(\log |OBS|)$. This is because only a limited number of the data sampled by Eq.(7) are used for the discovery even for the large amount of data. FR shows the significant increase for small data size, because the statistical stability is not ensured. In short summary, the computational complexity of the extended SSF seems to be crucial for a very large-scale problem but not for the large data size. The upper limit of the noise contained in the data is considered to be 10% for the extended SSF. The performance of the combined use of the extended SSF and SDS seems to work well for numbers of engineering problems.

5   Application to Practical Problem

The proposed method has been applied to a real world problem to discover a simultaneous equation model consisting of generic law formulae governing the mental preference of people for social infrastructures based on their subjective impressions. We designed a questionnaire sheet to ask the subjective evaluation on the five infrastructures of aviation transport facilities, waste disposal facilities, nuclear power plants, automobile transport facilities and oil power plants from the viewpoints of affinity q_1, unsafety q_2, scale of facility q_3, frequency of daily contacts q_4, benefit q_5, availability of alternative measure q_6 and genetic influence q_7. The last viewpoint may be meaningful only for the infrastructures producing radio-active and/or chemical wastes, and may be evaluated as negligible for the others. The former four viewpoints are asked in form of pair wise comparisons, and the obtained categorical data are transformed to ratio scale quantities by using the constant-sum method which is widely used in the experimental psychology [9]. The latter three are asked in form of the choice from categorical degrees, and the data are transformed to interval scale quantities by following the method of successive categories which is also widely used [1]. We distributed this questionnaire sheet to 482 persons living in a district of a country where the aforementioned facilities are located within a certain distance, and all of the answer sheets have been collected back. Hence, $OBS = \{X_1, X_2, ..., X_{482}\}$ was obtained where $X_i = [q_{1i}, q_{2i}, ..., q_{7i}]$.

The extended SSF was applied to OBS, and the following structural canonical form SCF and maximally eliminated structural form $MESCF$ were obtained.

$$SCF = \{f_{11}(q_1, q_4, q_5, q_6) = 0, \ f_{12}(q_1, q_4, q_5, q_6) = 0, \ f_{13}(q_1, q_4, q_5, q_6) = 0,$$
$$f_{21}(q_2, q_3, q_7) = 0, \ f_{21}(q_2, q_3, q_7) = 0\} \tag{11}$$
$$MESCF = \{f'_{11}(q_1, q_6) = 0, \ f'_{12}(q_4, q_6) = 0, \ f'_{13}(q_5, q_6) = 0,$$
$$f'_{21}(q_2, q_7) = 0, \ f'_{21}(q_3, q_7) = 0\} \tag{12}$$

Subsequently, the extended SDS was applied to OBS based on $MESCF$ and the scale-type information, and it derived the following model.

$$q_6 = -0.59 \log q_1 - 1.09, \ q_6 = 1.04 \log q_4 + 1.34, \ q_6 = 0.69 q_5 + 0.57,$$
$$q_7 = -0.90 \log q_2 - 1.00, q_7 = -0.47 \log q_3 - 1.00. \tag{13}$$

The statistical tests on the goodness of fitting [12] indicated the sufficient accuracy of this model. The former three equations relate affinity, frequency of daily contacts, benefit and availability of alternative measure, and can be interpreted to represent a psychological mechanism developing the affinity on a social facility based on its benefit and necessity in people's daily life. The latter two relate unsafety, scale of facility and genetic influence. They seem to represent another psychological mechanism developing the sense of danger on a social facility.

6   Discussion and Conclusion

Dzeroski and Todorovski developed LAGRANGE which discovers simultaneous equation models from observed data [2]. However, the mathematical admissibility is not considered in the discovery process, and many redundant representations of simultaneous equations can be derived at an expense of high computational complexity. They recently extended it to LAGRAMGE which allows the user to explicitly define the space of possible equations [8]. But, it does not provide definitions to efficiently prune the search space within the admissible equation formulae. In contrast, COPER, which also discovers simultaneous equations, uses very strong mathematical constraints based on the unit dimensions to prune the meaningless terms [5]. However, it essentially requires the unit information which is not frequently obtained in non-physical domains. The major advantages of our proposing method in comparison with the past approaches are the efficiency of the equation search, the soundness of the discovery in terms of the first principle and the wide applicability not limited to the physical domain. These are achieved by introducing the criteria of generic mathematical admissibility.

In this paper, we proposed the principle and the algorithm of a practical method to discover the first principle based simultaneous equations from passively observed data. The satisfactory performance of the method has been confirmed through simulations. Moreover, its high practicality has been demonstrated through a real application in socio-psychology. The application of the proposed method to a real-world research project collaborated with socio-psychologists is currently underway.

References

[1]   Comrey, A. L.: A proposed method for absolute ratio scaling. In *Psychometrika*, Vol.15 (1950) 317–325

[2]   Dzeroski, S. and Todorovski, L.: Discovering Dynamics: From Inductive Logic Programming to Machine Discovery. In *Journal of Intelligent Information Systems*, Boston, Kluwer Academic Publishers (1994) 1–20

[3]   Falkenhainer, Br. C. and Michalski, R. S.: Integrating Quantitative and Qualitative Discovery: The ABACUS System. In *Machine Learning*, Boston, Kluwer Academic Publishers (1986) 367–401

[4]   Koehn, B. and Zytkow, J. M.: Experimenting and theorizing in theory formation. In *Proceedings of the International Symposium on Methodologies for Intelligent Systems*, ACM SIGART Press (1986) 296–307

[5] Kokar, M. M.: Determining Arguments of Invariant Functional Descriptions. In *Machine Learning*, Boston, Kluwer Academic Publishers (1986) 403–422

[6] Langley, P. W., Simon, H. A., Bradshaw, G. L. and Zytkow, J. M.: *Scientific Discovery; Computational Explorations of the Creative Process*, MIT Press, Cambridge, Massachusetts (1987)

[7] Ljung, L.: *System Identification*, P T R Prentice-Hall (1987)

[8] Todorovski, L. and Dzeroski, S.: Declarative Bias in Equation Discovery, In *Proceeding of the fourteenth International Conference on Machine Learning*, San Mateo, CA, Morgan Kaufmann (1997) 376–384

[9] Torgerson, W. S.: In *Theory and Methods of Scaling*, N.Y.: J. Wiley (1958)

[10] Washio, T. and Motoda, H.: Discovering Admissible Models of Complex Systems Based on Scale-Types and Identity Constraints, In *Proceedings of IJCAI'97*, Vol.2, Nagoya (1997) 810–817

[11] Washio T. and Motoda, H.: Discovering Admissible Simultaneous Equations of Large Scale Systems, In *Proceedings of AAAI'98*, Madison (1998) 189–196

[12] Washio, T., Motoda, H. and Niwa, Y.: Discovering admissible model equations from observed data based on scale-types and identity constraints. In *Proceedings of IJCAI'99*, Vol.2 (1999) 772–779

Discovering Strong Principles of Expressive Music Performance with the PLCG Rule Learning Strategy

Gerhard Widmer

Dept. of Medical Cybernetics and Artificial Intelligence, University of Vienna, and
Austrian Research Institute for Artificial Intelligence, Vienna
gerhard@ai.univie.ac.at

Abstract. We present a new rule learning algorithm named PLCG — a kind of ensemble learning method — that can find simple, robust partial theories (sets of classification rules) in complex data where neither high coverage nor high precision can be expected. The motivating application problem comes from an interdisciplinary research project that aims at discovering fundamental principles of expressive music performance from large amounts of complex real-world data (measurements of actual performances by concert pianists). It is shown that PLCG succeeds in finding some surprisingly simple and robust performance principles, some of which represent truly novel and musically meaningful discoveries. A more systematic experiment shows that PLCG learns significantly simpler theories than more direct approaches to rule learning, while striking a compromise between coverage and precision.

1 Introduction

The research described in the present paper is part of a large, long-term interdisciplinary research project situated at the intersection of the scientific disciplines of Musicology and AI [12]. The goal is to use intelligent data analysis methods to study the complex phenomenon of *expressive music performance*. We want to understand what great musicians do when they interpret and play a piece of music, and to what extent an artist's musical choices are constrained or 'explained' by (a) the structure of the music, (b) common performance practices, and (c) cognitive aspects of music perception and comprehension. Formulating formal, quantitative models of expressive performance is one of the big open research problems in contemporary empirical musicology. Our project develops a new direction in this field: we use *inductive machine learning* to discover general and valid expression principles from (large amounts of) real performance data.

The purpose of this research is *knowledge discovery*. We search for simple, general, interpretable models of aspects of expressive music performance (such as tempo and expressive timing, dynamics, articulation). To that end, we have compiled what is most probably the largest set of performance data (precise measurements of timing, dynamics, etc. of real musical performances) ever collected in empirical performance research. Specifically, we are analyzing large

L. De Raedt and P. Flach (Eds.): ECML 2001, LNAI 2167, pp. 552–563, 2001.
© Springer-Verlag Berlin Heidelberg 2001

sets of recordings by highly skilled concert pianists, with the goal of discovering explainable patterns in the way the music is played.

The work described in this paper represents a first major step towards this goal. In section 2, we first explain basic concepts of expressive music performance, and then report on some problems encountered when some standard machine learning algorithms were applied in a straightforward way. These experiences prompted us to develop a new, general-purpose rule learning algorithm called PLCG, which is described in section 3. The main purpose of PLCG is to find simple, robust theories (sets of classification rules) in complex data where neither high coverage nor high precision can be expected. PLCG achieves this by learning multiple theories via some standard rule learning algorithm, and then combining these theories into one final rule set via clustering, generalization, and heuristic rule selection. Section 4 demonstrates the potential of the approach by describing some extremely simple and general performance principles and rule sets discovered by PLCG — some of the learned rules represent truly novel and musically meaningful discoveries. Then, a systematic experiment is described that compares PLCG's performance to two more 'direct' rule learning methods. The results indicate that PLCG finds more compact theories than the simpler rule learners, while striking a compromise between generality and precision.

2   The Target: Expressive Music Performance

Expressive music performance is the art of shaping a musical piece by continuously varying important parameters like tempo, dynamics, etc. Human musicians do not play a piece of music mechanically, with constant tempo or loudness. Rather, they speed up at some places, slow down at others, stress certain notes or passages by various means, and so on. The expressive nuances added by an artist are what makes a piece of music come alive. The most important dimensions available to a performer (a pianist, in particular) are tempo, dynamics (loudness variations), and articulation (the way successive notes are connected).

Expressive variation is more than just a 'distortion' of the original (notated) piece of music. In fact, the opposite is the case: the notated music score is but a small part of the actual music. Not every intended nuance can be captured in a limited formalism such as common music notation, and the composers were and are well aware of this. The performing artist is an indispensable part of the system, and expressive music performance plays a central role in our musical culture. That is what makes it a central object of study in the field of musicology.

Our approach to studying this complex phenomenon is to collect large corpora of performance data (i.e., exact measurements of onset and offset times and loudness of each note as played in a performance), and to apply inductive learning algorithms to find models that compactly characterize various classes of situations that are treated in a similar way by the performer (such as 'situations where the performer slows down' vs. 'situations where s/he speeds up'). At the moment, we limit ourselves to classical piano music.

In a first major study, we investigated the feasibility of inducing performance rules at the most basic musical level: the level of individual notes. The goal was to discover rules that predict how individual notes will most likely be played by a pianist (e.g., louder or softer than their predecessor). In a first suite of experiments [11], we succeeded in showing that even at that low level, there is structure in the data; learning algorithms like C4.5 [8] were able to find rule sets that predict the performer's choices with better than chance probability.

However, the improvement over the baseline accuracy was generally rather small (though statistically significant), which indicates that there are severe limits as to how much of a performer's behaviour can be explained at the note level. Moreover, the learned models were extremely complex. For instance, a decision tree discriminating between *accelerando* (speeding up) and *ritardando* (slowing down) with 58.09% accuracy had 3037 leaves (after pruning)! This is clearly not desirable if our goal is knowledge discovery.

There are good musical reasons for these difficulties; we cannot go into these here. From a machine learning perspective, the main insight is that looking for a model that completely describes the target categories is futile. Decision tree learners attempt to build a global model that fully discriminates between the members of the various classes. What we need to do instead is search for *partial* models that only explain what *can* be explained, and simply ignore those parts of the instance space where no compact characterization of the target classes seems possible. Moreover, given the nature of our data and target phenomena, we cannot expect very high levels of discriminative accuracy — we cannot assume the artist to be perfectly consistent and predictable.

In the following, we describe a rule learning algorithm named PLCG that was developed for this purpose. It will be shown that PLCG can find very simple partial models that still characterize a number of interesting subclasses of expressive performance behaviour. (Indeed, we will show that 4 simple rules are sufficient to predict 22.89% of the instances of note lengthening in our large data set, which contrasts nicely with the decision tree with 3037 leaves mentioned above.)

3   The PLCG Rule Learning Algorithm

Given the goal of learning partial models, an obvious choice is to apply rule learning algorithms of the *set covering* variety (also known as *separate-and-conquer* learners [5]), such as FOIL [7] or RIPPER [1]. These algorithms learn theories one rule at a time, in each rule refinement step selecting a literal that maximizes some measure of discrimination (e.g., information gain). A rule is specialized until a given stopping criterion (typically based on the rule's purity or precision) is satisfied, and the overall learning process stops when no more rules can be found that satisfy this purity criterion. The stopping criterion is thus the natural entry point for the user to influence the generality and precision of the induced rules. In the context of our problem, we would require rather low levels of precision. The degree of coverage of the resulting rules would then follow automatically, dictated by the data.

After some experimentation, we have chosen to pursue a more complex approach. The basic idea is to learn several models in parallel (from subsets of the data), search for groups of similar rules in these models, generalize these into summarizing rules (of varying degrees of generality), and then select those generalizations for the final model that optimize some (possibly global) user-defined criterion (which will typically be a trade-off function between coverage and precision). This strategy gives us more direct control over the overall coverage and precision of the induced models, and at the same time helps ameliorate one of the major problems of the greedy literal selection strategy of the underlying rule learner: the danger of selecting sub-optimal conditions due to the local maximization of a given discrimination measure. In this sense, our approach — let us call it the PLCG (**P**artition+**L**earn+**C**luster+**G**eneralize) strategy — is inspired by the success of *ensemble methods* in machine learning (see [2] for a good overview). The corresponding algorithm is given in more detail in figure 1.

PLCG is really a *meta-algorithm* that can be wrapped around any algorithm that learns classification rules. We are using our own implementation of a propositional FOIL-type [7] learner, with the standard information gain heuristic and with a parameterizable stopping criterion based on rule purity and mininum required rule coverage. More precisely: a single rule is grown by adding conditions until its *purity* (or *precision*) $P = p/(p + n)$ reaches or surpasses a given *minimum precision* MP_{RL}, where p and n are the numbers of positive and negative examples, respectively, covered by the rule. The outer loop of the algorithm ter-

---

Given:

- a set of training instances D
- a target concept (class) c
- a rule learning algorithm L
- a rule selection criterion C

Algorithm:

1. Separate the training examples D into n subsets D_i, $i = 1 \ldots n$ (randomly or according to a particular scheme);
2. Learn partial rule models $R_i = \{r_{ij}\}$ for class c from each of these subsets D_i separately, using the learning algorithm L.
3. Merge the rule sets R_i into one large set R: $R = \bigcup R_i$.
4. Perform a hierarchical clustering of the rules in R into a tree of clusters C_i, $i = 1 \ldots k$, of similar rules, using some hierarchical clustering algorithm and an appropriate syntactic/semantic rule similarity measure.
5. For each cluster C_i, compute the *least general generalization* of all the rules in C_i: $\hat{r}_i = lgg(\{r_{ij}|r_{ij} \in C_i\})$. The resulting tree T of rules $\hat{r}_i$ represents generalizations of various degrees of the original rules.
6. From this generalization tree T, select those rules r_i that optimize the given selection criterion C.

Fig. 1. The PLCG (**P**artition+**L**earn+**C**luster+**G**eneralize) rule learning strategy.

minates when no more rule can be found with $P \geq MP_{RL}$ and positive coverage p greater than some user-defined minimum coverage MC_{RL}.

For *rule clustering*, we use a standard bottom-up hierarchical agglomerative clustering algorithm [6] that produces a binary cluster tree, with the individual rules forming the leaves of the tree, and the root containing all the rules. The *rule similarity measure* used for clustering is simply the inverse of the number of generalization operations needed to compute the *least general generalization (lgg)* of two rules. Given our standard proposititional representation of instances and rules (see 4.2 below for an example), the definition of the *lgg* is obvious.

As for the *rule selection criterion* (step 6 of the PLCG algorithm), we currently use another greedy set-covering algorithm that starts with the empty rule set and always adds the rule that has maximum purity on the as yet uncovered instances. (In fact, we use the *Laplace estimate* $L = (p+1)/(p+n+2)$, which is related to purity, but gives higher weight to rules that cover a higher number of positive examples.) Again, the selection is terminated when no rule with purity (Laplace) greater than some user-defined MP_{PLCG} and coverage greater than some minimum required coverage MC_{PLCG} can be found.

This is just one of many possible rule selection strategies. Many others are conceivable that could use different criteria for trading coverage against precision, or that might aim at optimizing other aspects of the evolving rule set (e.g., minimum overlap or a minimum number of contradictions between rules).

4   Experimental Results

4.1   Data and Target Concepts

The data used in our first experimental investigation consists of recordings of 13 complete piano sonatas by W.A. Mozart (K.279–284, 330–333, 457, 475, and 533), performed by a Viennese concert pianist on a Bösendorfer SE290 computer-monitored grand piano. The Bösendorfer SE290 is a full concert grand piano with a special mechanism that measures and records every key and pedal movement with high precision. These measurements, together with the notated score in machine-readable form, provide us with all the information needed to compute expressive variations (e.g., tempo fluctuations). The resulting dataset consists of more than 106,000 performed notes and represents some four hours of music.

The experiments described here were performed on the melodies (usually the soprano parts) only, which gives an effective training set of 41,116 notes. Each note is described by 29 attributes (10 numeric, 19 discrete) that represent both intrinsic properties (such as scale degree, duration, metrical position) and some aspects of the local context (e.g., melodic properties like the size and direction of the intervals between the note and its predecessor and successor notes, and rhythmic properties like the durations of surrounding notes etc.).

In terms of performance parameters, we are looking at (local) tempo or timing, dynamics, and articulation. We defined the following discrete target classes:

1. in the tempo dimension, a note N is assigned to class *ritardando* if the local tempo at that point is significantly ($> 2\%$) slower than the tempo at the previous note; the opposite class *accelerando* contains all cases of local speeding up;
2. in dynamics, a note N is considered an example of class *crescendo* if it was played louder than its predecessor, and also louder than the average level of the piece; class *diminuendo* (growing softer) is defined analogously;
3. in articulation, three classes were defined: *staccato* if a note was sounded for less than 80% of its nominal duration, *legato* if the proportion is greater than 1.0 (i.e., the note overlaps the following one), and *portato* otherwise; we will only try to learn rules for the classes staccato and legato.

A performed note is considered a counter-example to a given class if it belongs to one of the competing classes. (Note that due to some details of our class definitions, there will be some notes that are neither examples nor counter-examples of some concept.)

4.2   Musical Discoveries

Let us first look at some of PLCG's discoveries from a musical perspective. When run on the complete Mozart performance data set (41,116 notes) for each of the six target concepts defined above,[1] PLCG (with parameter settings $MP_{PLCG} = .7$, $MC_{PLCG} = .02$, $MP_{RL} = .9$, $MC_{RL} = .01$) selected a final set of 17 performance rules (from a total of 383 specialized rules) — 6 rules for tempo changes, 6 rules for local dynamics, and 5 rules for articulation. (Two rules were selected manually for musical interest, although they did not quite reach the required coverage and precision, respectively.) Some of these rules turn out to be discoveries of significant musicological interest. We lack the space to list all of them here (see [13]). Let us illustrate the types of patterns found by looking at just one of the learned rules:

RULE TL2:
`abstract_duration_context = equal-longer`
`& metr_strength ≤ 1`
`⇒ ritardando`

"Given two notes of equal duration followed by a longer note, lengthen the note (i.e., play it more slowly) that precedes the final, longer one, if this note is in a metrically weak position ('metrical strength' ≤ 1)."

---

[1] In this experiment, the data were not split into subsets randomly; rather, 10 subsets were created according to global tempo (fast or slow) and time signature (3/4, 4/4, etc.) of the sonata sections the notes belonged to. We chose these two dimensions for splitting because it is known (and has been proved experimentally [11]) that global tempo and time signature strongly affect expressive performance patterns. As a result, we can expect models that tightly fit (overfit?) these data partitions to be quite different, and diversity should be beneficial to an ensemble method like PLCG.

Table 1. Fit of rule sets on training data (13 Mozart sonatas); True Positives (*TP*) = correct predictions; False Positives (*FP*) = incorrect predictions (relative to total number of positive and negative instances, respectively); Precision = $TP/(TP + FP)$.

Category	#rules	True Positives	False Positives	Precision
ritardando	4	3069/13410 (22.89 %)	1234/20551 (6.00 %)	.713
accelerando	2	397/13307 (2.98 %)	179/20550 (0.87 %)	.689
crescendo	3	1318/11629 (11.33 %)	591/18260 (3.24 %)	.690
diminuendo	3	625/9429 (6.63 %)	230/20113 (1.14 %)	.731
staccato	4	6916/22132 (31.25 %)	1089/18984 (5.74 %)	.864
legato	1	687/9256 (7.42 %)	592/31860 (1.86 %)	.537

This is an extremely simple principle that turns out to be surprisingly general and precise: rule TL2 correctly predicts 1,894 cases of local note lengthening, which is 14.12% of all the instances of significant lengthening observed in the training data. The number of incorrect predictions is 588 (2.86% of all the counterexamples). Together with a second, similar rule relating to the same type of phenomenon, TL2 covers 2,964 of the positive examples of note lengthening in our performance data set, which is more than one fifth (22.11%)! It is highly remarkable that one simple principle like this is sufficient to predict such a large proportion of observed note lengthenings in a complex corpus such as Mozart sonatas. This is a truly novel (and surprising) discovery; none of the existing theories of expressive performance were aware of this simple pattern.

A few other interesting rules were discovered, such as two pairs of timing and articulation rules that nicely characterize the pianist's consistent treatment of certain types of melodic leaps and rhythmic patterns. These discoveries and their relation to other theories of expressive performance in the musicological literature are discussed in [13].

4.3   Fit and Generality of Discovered Principles

As our primary goal is knowledge discovery, we are first of all interested in how much of the given (training) data is explained by the learned model — in other words, how well the induced models capture the pianist's performance style. Thus, contrary to more 'standard' machine learning applications, the degree of *fit* on the training set is relevant. (Of course, we will also be looking at *generalization accuracy* on unseen data — see below). As a quantification of fit, we measure the *coverage* (i.e., the number of positive examples correctly predicted) and the *precision* (the proportion of predictions that are correct) of the rule sets on the training data, separately for each prediction category. Table 1 gives the results.

A detailed discussion of the results and their musical interpretation is beyond the scope of this paper. Generally, it turns out that certain sub-classes of note lengthening (local *ritardando*), *staccato*, and to a lesser extent the local dynamics variations (*crescendo* and *diminuendo*) are surprisingly well predictable, and with extremely few (and simple) rules. On the other hand, categories like *accelerando*

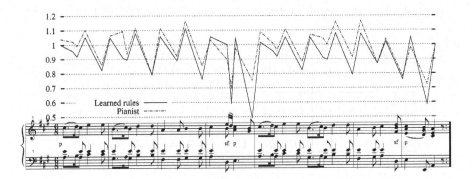

Fig. 2. Mozart Sonata K.331, 1st movement, 1st part, as played by pianist and learner. The curve plots the relative tempo at each note — notes above the 1.0 line are shortened relative to the tempo of the piece, notes below 1.0 are lengthened. A perfectly regular performance with no timing deviations would correspond to a straight line at $y = 1.0$

and *legato* seem more difficult to predict — at least at the level of individual notes. Uncovering the reasons for this will require more specialized investigations.

To give the reader an impression of just how effective a few simple rules can be in predicting a pianist's behaviour in certain cases, Figure 2 compares the tempo variations predicted by our rules to the pianist's actual timing in a performance of the well-known Mozart Sonata K.331 in A major (first movement, first section). In fact, it is just two simple rules (one for note lengthening (*ritardando*), one for shortening (*accelerando*)) that produce the system's timing curve.[2]

The next question concerns the *generality* of the discovered rules. How well do they transfer to other pieces and other performers? To assess the degree of *performer-specificity* of the rules, we tested them on performances of the same pieces, but by a different artist.[3] The test pieces in this case were the Mozart sonatas K.282, K283 (complete) and K.279, K.280, K.281, K.284, and K.333 (second movements), performed by the renowned conductor and pianist Philippe Entremont, again on a Bösendorfer SE290. The results are given in Table 2.

Comparing this to Table 1, we find no significant degradation in coverage and precision (except in category *diminuendo*). On the contrary, for some categories (*ritardando, crescendo, staccato*) the coverage is higher than on the original training set. The discriminative power of the rules — the precision — remains roughly at the same level. This (surprising?) result testifies to the generality of the discovered principles (and the merits of the PLCG rule discovery method).

---

[2] To be more precise: the rules predict whether a note should be lengthened or shortened; the *precise numeric amount* of lengthening/shortening is predicted by a *k-nearest-neighbor* algorithm (with $k = 3$) that uses only instances for prediction that are covered by the matching rule, as proposed in [9] and [10].

[3] The true *generalization accuracy* of the rules on music of the same style will be tested on recordings of *additional* Mozart sonatas by P.Entremont (i.e., pieces not used in training). At the time of writing, the performance measurements are still being prepared for analysis (unfortunately, that takes several person weeks!).

Table 2. Prediction results on test data (Mozart performances by P.Entremont).

Category	#rules	True Positives	False Positives	Precision
ritardando	4	596/2036 (29.27 %)	242/3175 (7.62 %)	.711
accelerando	2	90/2193 (4.10 %)	45/3013 (1.49 %)	.667
crescendo	3	210/1601 (13.12 %)	87/3055 (2.85 %)	.707
diminuendo	3	53/1598 (3.32 %)	45/2725 (1.65 %)	.541
staccato	4	861/2192 (39.28 %)	228/3996 (5.71 %)	.791
legato	1	131/2827 (4.63 %)	57/3361 (1.70 %)	.697

Table 3. Prediction results on test data (Chopin performances by 22 pianists).

Category	#rules	True Positives	False Positives	Precision
ritardando	4	1752/2537 (69.06 %)	327/2988 (10.94 %)	.843
accelerando	2	1472/2767 (53.20 %)	110/2746 (4.01 %)	.930
crescendo	3	601/2392 (25.13 %)	285/2578 (11.06 %)	.678
diminuendo	3	0/2249 (0.00 %)	0/2784 (0.00 %)	—
staccato	4	950/2932 (32.40 %)	166/2802 (5.92 %)	.851
legato	1	17/2011 (0.85 %)	27/3723 (0.73 %)	.386

Another experiment tested the generality of the discovered rules with respect to *musical style*. They were applied to pieces of a very different style (Romantic piano music), namely, the Etude Op.10, No.3 in E major (first 20 bars) and the Ballade Op.38, F major (first 45 bars) by *Frédéric Chopin*, and the results were compared to performances of these pieces by 22 Viennese pianists. The melodies of these 44 performances amount to 6,088 notes. Table 3 gives the results.

This result is even more surprising. *Diminuendo* and *legato* turn out to be basically unpredictable, and the rules for *crescendo* are rather imprecise. But the results for the other classes are extremely good, better in fact than on the original (Mozart) data which the rules had been learned from! The high coverage values, especially of the tempo rules, are remarkable. Remember also that the data represent a mixture of 22 different pianists. When looking at how well the rules fit individual pianists, we find that some of them are predicted extremely well (e.g., pianist #15: ritardando: $TP = 89/122$ (72.95%), $FP = 4/129$ (3.10%), $\pi = .957$; accelerando: $TP = 71/120$ (59.17%), $FP = 3/132$ (2.27%), $\pi = .959$). We are currently preparing recordings of a larger variety of Chopin pieces, which will permit more extensive investigations into the rules' general validity.

4.4   PLCG vs. Direct Rule Learning: A First Systematic Study

The above results show that PLCG can discover general and robust rules in complex data. To establish its advantages, if any, over the underlying rule learning algorithm, more systematic comparative experiments are needed. A first step in this direction is described here. PLCG, with parameter settings $MP_{RL} = .9$,

Table 4. Summary of 60 cross-validation results; NR = total number of rules (summed over all 60 data sets × 5 folds) and average number of rules per learning run ($NR/60/5$); TP = true positives, FP = false positives; π = precision.

	RL0.9	RL0.7	PLCG0.9/0.7
TP	12731/62017 (20.53 %)	28358/62017 (45.73 %)	18767/62017 (30.26 %)
FP	2180/102136 (2.13 %)	11710/102136 (11.47 %)	6551/102136 (6.41 %)
π	0.854	0.708	0.741
NR	2475 (8.25)	4094 (13.65)	1707 (5.69)

MC_{RL} = .01 for the rule learner and MP_{PLCG} = .7, MC_{PLCG} = .04 for rule selection, was compared to two versions of the base-level separate-and-conquer learner in a set of 60 cross-validation experiments: learner RL0.9 learns rules directly from the data with a required purity level of $RP = 0.9$ (i.e., RL0.9 is exactly the same algorithm as the one used within PLCG's inner loop); RL0.7 uses the more relaxed minimum purity threshold $RP = 0.7$, which corresponds to the precision level used by PLCG in its rule selection phase. The purpose of the experiment was to study whether PLCG's multiple rule learning + generalization + selection approach yields any advantage over learning rules directly from the data with the corresponding parameter settings.

60 different experimental data sets were produced by partitioning our 41,116 performed and classified notes according to the general *tempo* (slow vs. fast) and the *time signature* (3/4, 4/4, etc.) of the Mozart sonata segments they belong to. This resulted in 10 training sets each for the 6 target concepts *accelerando*, *ritardando*, *crescendo*, *diminuendo*, *staccato*, and *legato*.

On each of these 60 data sets, the three learning algorithms were compared via a 5-fold (paired) cross-validation. Within each CV run, RL0.9 and RL0.7 were applied to the combined data from the four training folds, while PLCG used the four folds to learn four separate rule sets (via RL0.9) that were then combined, generalized, and selected from. We lack the space to present the full results table with 60 × 18 entries here. Table 4 gives a summary of the results.

The results clearly reflect the expected trade-off: learning with a tighter precision threshold for individual rules (RL0.9) yields theories with higher precision, but lower coverage than learning with a lower required precision (RL0.7). PLCG, with its mixture of precision thresholds (high in the individual rule learning runs, lower in the rule selection phase) figures somewhere in between: its coverage is higher than RL0.9's and lower than RL0.7's. Conversely, it reaches a precision lower than RL0.9's and higher than RL0.7's.

The interesting result is that PLCG achieves this with significantly *fewer rules* than *either* of the two base-level learners, RL0.9 and RL0.7. In other words, PLCG covers more instances than RL0.9 with fewer (more general) rules, while still retaining a higher precision than RL0.7, which used the same precision threshold MP in its search for rules. That is indeed the desired kind of behaviour for our application, where the goal is to discover simple, general, robust (partial) theories that can be presented to and discussed with musicologists.

In general, how much precision one is willing to sacrifice for how much coverage and theory simplicity, and vice versa, will depend on the particular application. The important advantage of the PLCG approach is that it makes it easy to explore and control this trade-off via different *rule selection strategies*. In fact, one can perform the rule learning and clustering steps once and then apply any number of different rule selection algorithms on the resulting rule cluster tree.

5   Discussion

To summarize, we have presented a rule (meta-)learner that learns simple theories from complex data and offers a natural mechanism for exploring the coverage/precision/complexity tradeoff, and we have shown that PLCG is able to make interesting and surprising discoveries in a complex real-world domain.

PLCG's bottom-up generalization of classification rules is reminiscent of Domingos' RISE algorithm [3], which performs a bottom-up generalization into more and more general rules, starting from the individual training instances. What the two have in common is the idea to learn rules only for those parts of the instance space where the concepts can be easily characterized. RISE caters for the remaining space with instance-based learning, while PLCG simply ignores it (because its focus is on finding comprehensible characterizations of sub-classes of the target). On the other hand, PLCG makes it easy to explore alternative (and arbitrarily complex) strategies for rule combination and selection, which is possible because it constructs an explicit tree of rules of varying generality. Another significant difference is PLCG's use of multiple models to arrive at a more stable theory.

More directly related to PLCG are the so-called *ensemble methods* [2], which learn multiple models from subsets or modified versions of the training data, with one or several learning algorithms, and combine the resulting classifiers in some way. While the majority of known ensemble methods like bagging, boosting, stacking, etc. only combine the *predictions* of the classifiers, there are a few algorithms that try to combine the resulting multiple *models* into one coherent, comprehensible model. A prime example of this is CMM [4], a meta-learner that combines multiple models into a single theory by applying a learning algorithm to (artificially generated) training examples labeled by the n learned base models. According to the reported experimental results, CMM usually achieves higher accuracy than the base learner (C4.5RULES), but the models produced by CMM are typically 2-6 times more complex than the base learner's. In [4], it is also suggested that the accuracy/complexity tradeoff could be handled via the meta-learner's pruning parameters; again, we think PLCG's way of explicitly addressing this tradeoff via a selection procedure that can select from a set of alternative rules (of various degrees of generality) is preferable.

So far, we have compared PLCG only to one rather simple rule learner. Of course, it should be systematically compared also to more sophisticated learners like RIPPER [1]. It will be interesting to see if PLCG's ability to find simple theories matches the effect of RIPPER's complex pruning strategy. On the other hand, whether or not PLCG is better is the wrong question to ask. PLCG is a meta-learner; it could equally well be wrapped around RIPPER, thus potentially combining the advantages of the two.

Future research will focus on trying to get a better understanding of PLCG's characteristics through systematic experiments with different underlying rule learners, and different application domains.

Acknowledgements. This research is made possible by a very generous START Research Prize (project no. Y99-INF) by the Austrian Federal Government, administered by the Austrian *Fonds zur Förderung der Wissenschaftlichen Forschung (FWF)*. The Austrian Research Institute for Artificial Intelligence acknowledges basic financial support by the Austrian Federal Ministry for Education, Science, and Culture. We are particularly grateful to the pianists Roland Batik nd Philippe Entremont for allowing us to use their performances for our investigations.

References

1. Cohen, W. (1995). Fast Effective Rule Induction. In *Proceedings of the 12th International Conference on Machine Learning*. San Francisco, CA: Morgan Kaufmann.
2. Dietterich, T. G. (2000). Ensemble Methods in Machine Learning. In J. Kittler and F. Roli (Ed.), *First International Workshop on Multiple Classifier Systems*. New York: Springer Verlag.
3. Domingos, P. (1996). Unifying Instance-Based and Rule-Based Induction. *Machine Learning* 24, 141–168.
4. Domingos, P. (1998). Knowledge Discovery via Multiple Models. *Intelligent Data Analysis* 2, 187–202.
5. Fürnkranz, J. (1999). Separate-and-Conquer Rule Learning. *Artificial Intelligence Review* 13(1), 3–54.
6. Hartigan, J. (1975). *Clustering Algorithms*. Chichester, UK: John Wiley & Sons.
7. Quinlan, J.R. (1990). Learning Logical Definitions from Relations. *Machine Learning* 5, 239–266.
8. Quinlan, J.R. (1993). *C4.5: Programs for Machine Learning*. San Francisco, CA: Morgan Kaufmann.
9. Weiss, S. and Indurkhya, N. (1995). Rule-based Machine Learning Methods for Functional Prediction. *Journal of Artificial Intelligence Research* 3, 383–403.
10. Widmer, G. (1993). Combining Knowledge-based and Instance-based Learning to Exploit Qualitative Knowledge. *Informatica* 17, 371–385.
11. Widmer, G. (2000). Large-scale Induction of Expressive Performance Rules: First Quantitative Results. In *Proceedings of the International Computer Music Conference (ICMC'2000)*. San Francisco, CA: International Computer Music Association.
12. Widmer, G. (2001). Using AI and Machine Learning to Study Expressive Music Performance: Project Survey and First Report. *AI Communications* 14 (in press).
13. Widmer, G. (2001). *Machine Discoveries: Some Simple, Robust Local Expression Principles*. Submitted.

Proportional k-Interval Discretization for Naive-Bayes Classifiers

Ying Yang and Geoffrey I. Webb

School of Computing and Mathematics, Deakin University, Vic3217, Australia

Abstract. This paper argues that two commonly-used discretization approaches, fixed k-interval discretization and entropy-based discretization have sub-optimal characteristics for naive-Bayes classification. This analysis leads to a new discretization method, Proportional k-Interval Discretization (PKID), which adjusts the number and size of discretized intervals to the number of training instances, thus seeks an appropriate trade-off between the bias and variance of the probability estimation for naive-Bayes classifiers. We justify PKID in theory, as well as test it on a wide cross-section of datasets. Our experimental results suggest that in comparison to its alternatives, PKID provides naive-Bayes classifiers competitive classification performance for smaller datasets and better classification performance for larger datasets.

1 Introduction

Many real-world classification tasks involve numeric attributes. Consequently, appropriate handling of numeric attributes is an important issue in machine learning. For naive-Bayes classifiers, numeric attributes are often processed by discretization. For each numeric attribute A, a new nominal attribute A^* is created. Each value of A^* corresponds to an interval of the numeric values of A. When training a classifier, the learning process uses the nominal A^* instead of the original numeric A.

A number of discretization methods have been developed. One common approach is fixed k-interval discretization [1,2,3,4,5]. It directly discretizes values of a numeric attribute into k equal-width intervals. Another approach uses information measures to discretize a numeric attribute into intervals. For example, Fayyad & Irani's entropy minimization heuristic [6] is extensively employed. Each of these strategies has advantages and disadvantages. Fixed k-interval discretization is easy to implement. But it does not adjust its behavior to the specific characteristics of the training data. Fayyad & Irani's heuristic approach was developed in the context of decision tree learning. It seeks to identify a small number of intervals, each dominated by a single class. However, for naive-Bayes classification, in contrast to decision tree learning, it is plausible that it is less important to minimize the number of intervals or to form intervals dominated by a single class.

In this paper, we introduce a new approach for discretizing numeric attributes. We focus our attention on classification tasks using naive-Bayes classifiers. We seek to balance two conflicting objectives. On one hand, we prefer

L. De Raedt and P. Flach (Eds.): ECML 2001, LNAI 2167, pp. 564–575, 2001.
© Springer-Verlag Berlin Heidelberg 2001

forming as many intervals as possible. This increases the representation power of the new nominal attribute. That is, the more intervals formed, the more distinct values the classifier can distinguish between. On the other hand, we should ensure that there are enough training instances in each interval, so that we have enough information to accurately estimate the probabilities required by Bayes' theorem. But when we are training a classifier, we usually have a fixed number of training instances. The number of intervals will decrease when the size of intervals (the number of instances in each interval) increases and vice versa. This can be viewed as a bias-variance [7] trade-off. Increasing the number of intervals will decrease bias and increase variance and vice versa. Allowing for this, we propose Proportional k-Interval Discretization (PKID). This strategy adjusts the number and size of discretized intervals proportional to the number of training instances, seeking an appropriate trade-off between the granularity of the intervals and the expected accuracy of probability estimation. Currently we adopt a compromise: given a numeric attribute A for which the number of instances that have a known value is N, we take the proportional coefficient as $\sqrt{N}$. We discretize A into $\sqrt{N}$ intervals, with $\sqrt{N}$ instances in each interval. Thus, both objectives receive the same weight. As N increases, both the number and size of discretized intervals increase. These are very desirable characteristics that we will discuss in more detail later.

To evaluate this new technique, we separately implement PKID, Fayyad & Irani's discretization (FID), and fixed k-interval discretization (FKID) with k=5,10 to train naive-Bayes classifiers. We compare the classification errors of the resulting classifiers. Our hypothesis is that naive-Bayes classifiers trained on data formed by PKID will have competitive classification error to those trained on data formed by alternative discretization approaches for smaller datasets, and that PKID will be able to utilize the incremental information in larger datasets to achieve lower classification error.

The rest of this paper is organized as follows. We give an overview of naive-Bayes classifiers and discretization in Section 2 and 3 respectively. In Section 4, we discuss Proportional k-Interval Discretization in detail. We compare the algorithm complexities in Section 5. Experimental results are presented in Section 6. Section 7 provides a conclusion and suggests research directions that are worth further exploration.

2 Naive-Bayes Classifiers

Naive-Bayes classifiers are simple, efficient and robust to noise and irrelevant attributes. One defect, however, is that naive-Bayes classifiers utilize an assumption that the attributes are conditionally independent of each other given the class. Although this assumption is often violated in the real world, the classification performance of naive-Bayes classifiers is still surprisingly good for many classification tasks, compared with other more complex classifiers. According to [8], this is explained by the fact that classification estimation is only a function of the sign (in binary cases) of the function estimation; the classification accuracy can remain high even while function approximation is poor.

We briefly introduce the main idea of naive-Bayes classifiers as follows. In classification learning, each instance is described by a vector of attribute values and its class can take any value from some predefined set of values. A set of training instances with their class labels, the training dataset, is provided, and a new instance is presented. The learner is asked to predict the class for this new instance according to the evidence provided by the training dataset. We define:

- C as the random variable denoting the class of an instance,
- $X < X_1, X_2, \cdots, X_k >$ as a vector of random variables denoting the observed attribute values (an instance),
- c as a particular class label,
- $x < x_1, x_2, \cdots, x_k >$ as a particular observed attribute value vector (a particular instance),
- $X = x$ as shorthand for $X_1 = x_1 \wedge X_2 = x_2 \wedge \cdots \wedge X_k = x_k$.

Bayes' theorem can be used to calculate the probability of each class given the instance x:

$$p(C = c \mid X = x) = \frac{p(C = c)\, p(X = x \mid C = c)}{p(X = x)}. \tag{1}$$

Expected error can be minimized by choosing the class with the highest probability as the class of the instance x. Because the probabilities needed by the calculation are not known, it is necessary to estimate them from the training dataset. Unfortunately, since x is usually an unseen instance which does not appear in the training dataset, it may not be possible to directly estimate $p(X = x \mid C = c)$. So a simplification is made: if each attribute $X_1, X_2, \cdots, X_k$ is conditionally independent of each other given the class, then:

$$p(X = x \mid C = c) = p(\wedge X_i = x_i \mid C = c)$$
$$= \prod p(X_i = x_i \mid C = c). \tag{2}$$

Since the denominator in formula 1, $p(X = x)$, is invariant across classes, it does not affect the final choice and can be dropped. Thus one can further estimate the most probable class using:

$$p(C = c \mid X = x) \propto p(C = c) \prod p(X_i = x_i \mid C = c). \tag{3}$$

Classifiers using the independence assumption embodied in formula 2 are called naive-Bayes classifiers. The independence assumption makes the computation of naive-Bayes classifiers more efficient than the exponential complexity of non-naive Bayes approaches because it does not use attribute combinations as predictors [9].

3   Discretize Numeric Attributes

An attribute is either nominal or numeric. Values of a nominal attribute are discrete. Values of a numeric attribute are either discrete or continuous [10].

For each attribute X_i with value x_i, $p(X_i = x_i | C = c)$ in formula 2 is often modeled by a single real number between 0 and 1, denoting the probability that the attribute X_i will take the particular value x_i when the class is c. This assumes that attribute values are discrete with a finite number, as it may not be possible to assign a probability to any single value of an attribute with an infinite number of values. Even for discrete valued attributes that have a finite but large number of values, as there will be very few training instances for any one value, it is often advisable to aggregate a range of values into a single value for the purpose of estimating the probabilities in formula 3. In keeping with normal terminology for this research area, we call the conversion of a numeric attribute to a nominal attribute, *discretization*, irrespective of whether this numeric attribute is discrete or continuous.

A nominal attribute usually takes only a small number of values. The probabilities $p(X_i = x_i | C = c)$ and $p(C = c)$ can be estimated from the frequencies of $X_i = x_i \wedge C = c$ and $C = c$ in the training dataset. In our experiment, when $p(X_i = x_i | C = c)$ was estimated, the M-estimate [11] with m=2 was used. When $p(C = c)$ was estimated, the Laplace-estimate [11] was used.

- M-estimate: $\frac{n_{ci}+mp}{n_c+m}$, where n_{ci} is the number of instances that satisfy $X_i = x_i \wedge C = c$, n_c is the number of instances who satisfy $C = c$, p is the prior estimate of $X_i = x_i$, $p(X_i = x_i)$ (estimated by Laplace-estimate), and m is a constant (2 in our research).
- Laplace-estimate: $\frac{n_c+k}{N+n*k}$, where n_c is the number of instances that satisfy $C = c$, n is the number of classes, N is the number of training instances, and k is normally 1.

A continuous numeric attribute has an infinite number of values, as do many discrete numeric attributes. The values are generated according to some probability distribution. Since classification tasks are normally carried out for real-world data, whose real probability distribution is unknown, a difficulty in naive-Bayes classification is how to estimate $p(X_i = x_i | C = c)$ when X_i is numeric. A common solution is discretization [12]. Discretization transforms numeric attributes into nominal attributes before they are used to train classifiers. In consequence, they are not bound by some specific distribution assumption. But since we do not know the real relationship underlying different values of a numeric attribute, discretization may suffer from loss of information.

One common discretization approach is fixed k-interval discretization (FKID). It divides a numeric attribute into k intervals, where (given n observed instances) each interval contains n/k (possibly duplicated) adjacent values. Here k is determined without reference to the properties of the training data[1]. A problem of this method is that it ignores relationships among different values, thus

---

[1] In practice, k is often set as 5 or 10.

potentially suffering much attribute information loss. But although it may be deemed inelegant, this simple discretization technique works surprisingly well for naive-Bayes classifiers. Hsu, Huang and Wong [13] provided an interesting analysis of the reason why fixed k-interval discretization works for naive-Bayes classifiers. They suggested that discretization approaches usually assume that discretized attributes have Dirichlet priors. "Perfect Aggregation" of Dirichlets can ensure that naive-Bayes with discretization appropriately approximates the distribution of a numeric attribute.

Another popular discretization approach is Fayyad & Irani's entropy minimization heuristic discretization (FID) [6]. They first suggested binary discretization, which discretizes values of a numeric attribute into two intervals. The training instances are first sorted by increasing values of the numeric attribute, and the midpoint between each successive pair of attribute values in the sorted sequence is evaluated as a potential cut point. FID selects the "best" cut point from the range of values by evaluating every candidate cut point. For each evaluation of a candidate cut point, the data are discretized into two intervals and the class information entropy of the resulting discretization is computed. A binary discretization is determined by selecting the cut point for which the entropy is minimal amongst all candidate cut points. Later, they generalized the algorithm to multi-interval discretization. The training instances are sorted once, then the binary discretization is applied recursively, always selecting the best cut point. A minimum description length criterion is applied to decide when to refrain from applying further binary discretization to a given interval.

FID was presented in the particular context of top-down induction of decision trees. It tends to form nominal attributes with few values. For decision tree learning, it is important to minimize the number of values of an attribute, so as to avoid the fragmentation problem [14]. If an attribute has many values, a split on this attribute will result in many branches, each of which receives relatively few training instances, making it difficult to select appropriate subsequent tests. Naive Bayes considers attributes independent of one another given the class, hence is not subject to the same fragmentation problem as experienced in decision tree learning if there are many values for a single attribute. So aiming at minimizing the number of discretized intervals for naive-Bayes classifiers may not be as well justified as for decision trees.

4   Proportional k-Interval Discretization

The conditional probabilities in formula 3 of a numeric attribute x will be drawn from an unknown probability density function $f(x|y)$. If we form a discretized value x_i^* corresponding to the interval $(a, b]$ of x, then

$$p(x_i^*|y) = \int_a^b f(x|y) \, dx. \tag{4}$$

We wish to estimate $p(x_i^*|y)$ from data. The larger the interval $(a, b]$, the more instances will be contained in it, and the lower the variance of the probability estimation. Conversely, however, the larger the interval, the less distinguishing information is obtained about each particular value of x, and hence the higher the bias of the probability estimation. So, on one hand we wish to increase the range of values in each interval in order to decrease variance, and on the other hand we wish to decrease the range of values to decrease bias.

We suggest Proportional k-Interval Discretization (PKID). This strategy seeks an appropriate trade-off between the bias and variance of the probability estimation by adjusting the number and size of intervals to the number of training instances. Currently we adopt a compromise: given a numeric attribute, supposing we have N training instances with known values for the attribute, we discretize it into $\sqrt{N}$ intervals, with $\sqrt{N}$ instances in each interval[2]. Thus we give equal weight to both bias and variance management. Further, with N increasing, both the number and size of intervals increase correspondingly, which means discretization can decrease both the bias and variance of the probability estimation. This is very desirable, because if a numeric attribute has more instances available, there is more information about it. A good discretization scheme should respond to this increase in information accordingly. But fixed k-interval discretization is fixed in the number of intervals and does not react to the above-mentioned information increase. Fayyad & Irani's discretization tends to minimize the number of resulting intervals, as is appropriate in order to avoid the fragmentation problem in decision tree learning, and does not tend to increase the number of intervals accordingly.

When implementing PKID, we follow rules listed below:

- Discretization is limited to known values of a numeric attribute. We ignore any unknown values. When applying formula 3 for a testing instance, we drop any attributes with an unknown value for this instance from the right-hand side.
- For some attributes, different training instances may hold identical values. We always keep the identical values in a single interval. Thus although ideally each interval should include exactly $\sqrt{N}$ instances, the actual size of each interval may vary.
- Given N training instances with known values of a numeric attribute, we hold $\lfloor \sqrt{N} \rfloor$ as the standard size of the discretized interval (the number of instances in an interval should be an integer). We do not allow smaller size. We allow larger size only when it is because of the presence of identical values or to accommodate the last interval when its size is between $\lfloor \sqrt{N} \rfloor$ and $\lfloor \sqrt{N} \rfloor \times 2$.

---

[2] We do not form intervals based on the number of values, such as, creating intervals with m values each. As Catlett [2] pointed out, this type of discretization is vulnerable to outliers that may drastically skew the range.

5 Algorithm Complexity Comparison

Each of the discretization algorithms, PKID, FID, and FKID can be considered to be composed of two stages. The first stage is to sort a numeric attribute by increasing values. The second stage is to discretize the sorted values into intervals. Suppose the number of training instances with known values of the attribute is n, and the number of classes is m. The complexity of each algorithm is as follows.

- PKID and FKID are dominated by sorting values of an attribute. So their complexities are all $O(n \log n)$.
- FID also does sorting first, resulting in $O(n \log n)$. It then goes through all the training instances a maximum of $\log n$ times, recursively applying "binary division" to find out at most $n - 1$ cut points. Each time, it will estimate $n - 1$ candidate cut points. For each candidate point, probabilities of each of m classes are estimated. Thus finding the cut points is an operation with maximum complexity $O(mn \log n)$. So FID's maximum complexity is $O(mn \log n)$.

This means that PKID has the same order of complexity as FKID, and lower than FID.

6 Experiments

We want to evaluate whether or not PKID can better reduce the classification error of naive-Bayes classifiers, compared with 5D, 10D (FKID with k=5, 10) and FID.

6.1 Experimental Design

We ran our experiments on 31 natural datasets from the UCI machine learning repository [15] and KDD archive [16], listed in Table 2. They exhibit a range of different sizes. This experimental suite comprises 3 parts. The first part is composed of all the UCI datasets used by [6] when publishing the entropy minimization heuristic for discretization. The second part is composed of all the UCI datasets with numeric attributes used by [17] for studying naive-Bayes classification. In addition, as PKID responds to dataset size, and the first two parts contain mainly datasets with relatively few instances, we further augmented this collection with datasets that we could identify containing numeric attributes, with emphasis on those having more than 5000 instances. The performance of PKID will differ most substantially from those of the alternatives when there are many instances in the training dataset and hence many intervals are formed. Therefore, if the technique is successful, we can expect PKID to demonstrate the greatest advantage for larger datasets.

Table 2 lists an index[3], as well as the number of instances (Size), numeric attributes (Num.), nominal attributes (Nom.) and classes (Class) for each dataset.

---

[3] For reference from Fig. 1.

For each dataset, a 10-trial, 3-fold cross validation is used to train and test a naive-Bayes classifier. In each fold, the dataset was discretized separately by the above-mentioned four approaches. Thus we obtained four versions of the original dataset. For each version, a naive-Bayes classifier was learned. We evaluated its classification performance in terms of average error (the percentage of incorrect classifications) in the testing data across trials. The testing data was not available to the discretization algorithm during discretization. Discretization was performed only by reference to the training data for a given cross validation fold.

The classification errors of PKID, FID, 10D and 5D on each dataset are also listed in Table 2. The records are sorted in ascending order of the datasets' sizes, so that we can track the effect of dataset size on PKID's performance. In each record, **boldface** font indicates the algorithm achieving the best classification performance for this dataset.

6.2 Experimental Statistics

We employed three statistics to evaluate the experimental results in Table 2.

Mean error. This is the mean of errors across all datasets. It provides a gross indication of relative performance. It is debatable whether errors in different datasets are commensurable, and hence whether averaging errors across datasets is very meaningful. Nonetheless, a low average error is indicative of a tendency toward low errors for individual datasets. The mean error for each algorithm is presented in the "Mean Error" row of Table 2.

Geometric mean error ratio. This method has been explained in detail by [18]. It allows for the relative difficulty of error reduction in different datasets and can be more reliable than the mean ratio of errors across datasets. The geometric mean error ratio of algorithm X against algorithm Y, $GM(X, Y)$, is calculated as

$$GM(X, Y) = \sqrt[n]{\prod_{i=1}^{n} \frac{x_i}{y_i}} ,$$

where x_i and y_i are respectively the errors of algorithm X and algorithm Y for the ith dataset, and n is the number of the employed datasets. The last row of Table 2 lists out the geometric mean error ratios of PKID against FID, 10D and 5D.

Win/Lose/Tie record. The three values are, respectively, the number of datasets for which PKID obtained better, worse or equal performance outcomes, compared with the alternative algorithms on a given measure. A sign test can be applied to these summaries. If the sign test result is significantly low (here we use the 0.05 critical level), it is reasonable to conclude that it is unlikely that the outcome is obtained by chance and hence that the record of wins to losses represents a systematic underlying advantage to one of the algorithms with respect to the type of datasets on which they have been tested. These win/lose/tie records and the sign test results are summarized in Table 1.

Table 1. Win/Lose/Tie

-	FID	10D	5D
PKID Win	21	21	23
PKID Lose	7	7	7
PKID Tie	3	3	1
Sign Test	≤ 0.0063	≤ 0.0063	≤ 0.0026

6.3   Experimental Evaluations

Utilizing the above statistics, we have the following evaluations:

- PKID achieves the lowest mean error among the four discretization approaches.
- The geometric mean error ratios of PKID against FID, 10D and 5D are all less than 1. This suggests that PKID enjoys an advantage in terms of error reduction over the type of datasets studied in this research.
- With respect to the win/lose/tie records, PKID is significantly better than all of FID, 10D and 5D in terms of reducing classification errors.
- PKID demonstrates advantage more apparently as datasets become larger. For datasets containing more than 1000 instances, it is only outperformed in Hypothyroid. For datasets containing fewer than 1000 instances, the win/lose/tie records of PKID against FID, 10D and 5D are respectively 10/6/2, 8/7/3, and 10/7/1, suggesting that PKID has at worst comparable performance to these alternatives. This tendency, which is also illustrated

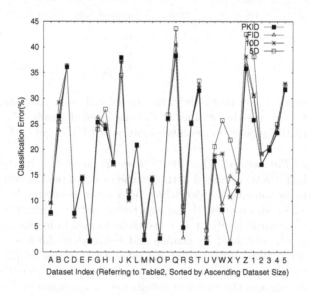

Fig. 1. PKID Responds to Dataset Size

in Figure 1, results from the ability of PKID to take advantage of training information increase by adjusting the size and number of discretized intervals to the number of training instances, thus achieves better classification performance among larger datasets.

– We suggest that PKID can adjust the number of discretized intervals to the number of training instances. To show a gross profile, the last two columns of Table 2 list the mean number of intervals produced by PKID and FID for each dataset, averaged on all the numeric attributes across 10 trials × 3 folds. Apparently, PKID is more sensitive to the increase of training instances than FID.

Table 2. Experimental Datasets and Results

Index	Dataset	Size	Num.	Nom.	Class	Error (%)				Inter. No.	
						PKID	FID	10D	5D	PKID	FID
A	Labor Negotiations	57	8	8	2	7.7	9.5	9.6	**7.5**	2	2
B	Echocardiogram	74	5	1	2	26.5	**23.8**	29.2	25.4	5	2
C	Postoperative Patient	90	1	7	3	**36.1**	36.3	**36.1**	36.3	2	2
D	Iris	150	4	0	3	7.5	**6.8**	7.5	7.6	7	4
E	Hepatitis	155	6	13	2	14.4	14.5	14.7	**14.3**	7	2
F	Wine Recognition	178	13	0	3	**2.1**	2.6	**2.1**	2.2	9	4
G	Sonar	208	60	0	2	25.4	26.3	25.2	**24.0**	10	2
H	Glass Identification	214	9	0	3	**24.1**	24.9	24.8	27.9	8	3
I	Heart Disease (Cleveland)	270	7	6	2	17.5	17.5	**17.1**	17.2	8	2
J	Liver Disorders	345	6	0	2	38.0	37.4	37.1	**34.5**	10	2
K	Ionosphere	351	34	0	2	10.6	11.1	**10.1**	11.9	12	4
L	Horse Colic	368	8	13	2	20.9	**20.6**	20.8	20.9	7	2
M	Synthetic Control Chart	600	60	0	6	**2.4**	2.8	3.4	5.3	19	5
N	Credit Screening (Australia)	690	6	9	2	14.2	14.5	14.5	**14.1**	15	3
O	Breast Cancer (Wisconsin)	699	9	0	2	2.7	2.7	**2.6**	3.2	6	4
P	Pima Indians Diabetes	768	8	0	2	26.1	26.0	**25.9**	26.8	16	3
Q	Vehicle	846	18	0	4	**38.3**	38.9	40.5	43.6	16	5
R	Annealing	898	6	32	6	4.8	**2.8**	7.7	8.9	5	3
S	German	1000	7	13	2	**25.1**	**25.1**	25.4	25.2	9	2
T	Multiple Features	2000	3	3	10	**31.5**	32.6	31.9	33.4	35	6
U	Hypothyroid	3163	7	18	2	1.8	**1.7**	2.8	4.3	27	4
V	Satimage	6435	36	0	6	**17.8**	18.1	18.9	20.6	34	6
W	Musk	6598	166	0	2	**8.3**	9.4	19.2	25.7	47	5
X	Pioneer-1 Mobile Robot	9150	29	7	57	**1.7**	14.8	10.8	21.9	37	5
Y	Handwritten Digits	10992	16	0	10	**12.0**	13.5	13.2	15.9	47	5
Z	Australian Sign Language	12546	8	0	3	**35.8**	36.5	38.2	42.5	19	4
1	Letter Recognition	20000	16	0	26	**25.8**	30.4	30.7	38.2	11	5
2	Adult	48842	6	8	2	**17.1**	17.2	19.2	19.2	49	5
3	Ipums.la.99	88443	20	40	13	**19.9**	20.1	20.5	20.4	29	4
4	Census Income	299285	8	33	2	**23.3**	23.6	24.5	25.0	80	5
5	Covertype	581012	10	44	7	**31.7**	32.1	32.9	32.6	264	6
-	**Mean Error**	-	-	-	-	18.4	19.2	19.9	21.2	-	-
-	**Geometric Mean Error Ratio**	-	-	-	-	1.00	0.92	0.85	0.78	-	-

7 Conclusions and Further Research

In this paper, we reviewed two common-used discretization approaches for naive-Bayes classifiers, FKID and FID. We then proposed a new discretization method, Proportional k-Interval Discretization (PKID). We argue PKID is more appropriate than FKID and FID for naive-Bayes classifiers. It attaches importance to both the number and size of discretized intervals, and adjusts them in response to the quantity of training data provided.

In our research, we have used $\sqrt{N}$ as the size of intervals to be formed. This was selected as a means to provide equal weight to both bias and variance managements. A promising direction for further research is to investigate alternative approaches to adjust interval size to training dataset size. It is plausible that selection of interval size should be responsive to some other attributes of the training dataset. For example, it might be that the more classes a dataset contains, the larger the optimal interval size, as more data is required for accurate conditional probability estimation. It may also be that as dataset size increases, there is greater potential for gains through one rather than the other of the two objectives, bias reduction and variance reduction, and hence the interval size should be weighted to favor one over the other.

Our experiments with an extensive selection of UCI and KDD datasets suggest that in comparison to its alternatives, PKID provides naive-Bayes classifiers competitive classification performance for smaller datasets and better classification performance for larger datasets.

References

[1] Wong, A. K. C., Chiu, D. K. Y.: Synthesizing Statistical Knowledge from Incomplete Mixedmode Data, IEEE Transaction on Pattern Analysis and Machine Intelligence 9, 796-805, 1987

[2] Catlett, Jason: Megainduction: Machine Learning on Very Large Databases, University of Sydney, Australia, 1991

[3] Catlett, Jason: On Changing Continuous Attributes into Ordered Discrete Attributes, Proceedings of the European Working Session on Learning, 164-178, 1991

[4] Chmielewski, M. R., Grzymala-Busse, J. W.: Global Discretization of Continuous Attributes as Preprocessing for Machine Learning, Third International Workshop on Rough Sets and Soft Computing, 294-301, 1994

[5] Pfahringer, Bernhard: Compression-Based Discretization of Continuous Attributes, Proceedings of the Twelfth International Conference on Machine Learning, 1995

[6] Fayyad, Usama M., Irani, Keki B.: Multi-Interval Discretization of Continuous-Valued Attributes for Classification Learning, Proceedings of the 13th International Joint Conference on Artificial Intelligence, 1022-1027, 1993

[7] Kohavi, R., Wolpert, D.: Bias Plus Variance Decomposition for Zero-One Loss Functions, Proceedings of the 13th International Conference on Machine Learning, 275-283, 1996

[8] Domingos, Pedro, Pazzani, Michael: On the Optimality of the Simple Bayesian Classifier under Zero-One Loss, Machine Learning 29, 103-130, 1997

[9] Yang, Yiming, Liu, Xin: A Re-examination of Text Categorization Methods, Proceedings of ACM SIGIR Conference on Research and Development in Information Retrieval, 42-49, 1999

[10] Johnson, Richard, Bhattacharyya, Gouri: Statistics: Principles and Methods, 12-13, 1985

[11] Cestnik, B.: Estimating Probabilities: A Crucial Task in Machine Learning, Proceedings of the European Conference on Artificial Intelligence, 147-149, 1990

[12] Dougherty, James, Kohavi, Ron, Sahami, Mehran: Supervised and Unsupervised Discretization of Continuous Features, Proceedings of the Twelfth International Conference on Machine Learning, 194-202, 1995

[13] Hsu, Chun-Nan, Huang, Hung-Ju, Wong, Tzu-Tsung: Why Discretization works for Naive Bayesian Classifiers, Machine Learning, Proceedings of the Seventeenth International Conference, 309-406, 2000

[14] Quinlan, J. Ross: C4.5: Programs for Machine Learning, 1993

[15] Blake, C. L., Merz, C. J.: UCI Repository of Machine Learning Databases [http://www.ics.uci.edu/~mlearn/MLRepository.html], Department of Information and Computer Science, University of California, Irvine, 1998

[16] Bay, S. D.: The UCI KDD Archive [http://kdd.ics.uci.edu], Department of Information and Computer Science, University of California, Irvine, 1999

[17] Domingos, Pedro, Pazzani, Michael: Beyond Independence: Conditions for the Optimality of the Simple Bayesian Classifier, Proceedings of the Thirteenth International Conference on Machine Learning, 105-112, 1996

[18] Webb, Geoffrey I.: MultiBoosting: A Technique for Combining Boosting and Wagging, Machine Learning, 40-2, 159-196, 2000

Using Diversity in Preparing Ensembles of Classifiers Based on Different Feature Subsets to Minimize Generalization Error

Gabriele Zenobi and Pádraig Cunningham

Department of Computer Science
Trinity College Dublin
Gabriele.Zenobi@cs.tcd.ie
Padraig.Cunningham@cs.tcd.ie

Abstract. It is well known that ensembles of predictors produce better accuracy than a single predictor provided there is diversity in the ensemble. This diversity manifests itself as disagreement or ambiguity among the ensemble members. In this paper we focus on ensembles of classifiers based on different feature subsets and we present a process for producing such ensembles that emphasizes diversity (ambiguity) in the ensemble members. This emphasis on diversity produces ensembles with low generalization errors from ensemble members with comparatively high generalization error. We compare this with ensembles produced focusing only on the error of the ensemble members (without regard to overall diversity) and find that the ensembles based on ambiguity have lower generalization error. Further, we find that the ensemble members produced focusing on ambiguity have less features on average that those based on error only. We suggest that this indicates that these ensemble members are *local* learners.

1.   Introduction

Ensembles of classifiers have recently emerged as a robust technique to improve the performance of a single classifier. Several ways to define an ensemble have been explored, from training each classifier in a subpart of the training set, to giving each classifier a subset of the features available.

When selecting an ensemble of classifiers a very simple approach consists of two separate steps: first a group of independently "good" classifiers is selected, then they are aggregated to form an ensemble. Such an approach has the advantage of simplicity, both conceptually and computationally, but the main disadvantage is that the classifiers are selected for the results they obtain singly and not for their contribution in the context of the ensemble. Following the work of Krogh and Vedelsby (1995), which demonstrated the crucial role played by the disagreement (ambiguity) in the final prediction of an ensemble, other less straightforward approaches have been proposed to build an ensemble of good predictors that have a high degree of disagreement. Among them the most relevant results were obtained by Liu (1999), who introduced a negative correlation penalty term to train ensembles of

L. De Raedt and P. Flach (Eds.): ECML 2001, LNAI 2167, pp. 576-587, 2001.
© Springer-Verlag Berlin Heidelberg 2001

neural networks, and that by Optiz and Shavlik (1996), who used the notion of ambiguity to find a diverse ensemble of neural networks using a genetic algorithm.

In this paper we focus on ensembles of classifiers based on different feature subsets and describe an algorithm that selects the different feature subsets (and thus the ensemble members) not just to minimize individual error but also to maximize ambiguity. This is compared with the default alternative of selecting the ensemble members based on error only without consideration for their contribution within the ensemble. In both scenarios the process of selecting the feature subsets is a "wrapper-like" search process (Kohavi & John, 1998) where Hill Climbing search is used to find a feature subset that minimizes error. In the default alternative (Cunningham & Carney, 2000) the search is guided by the error associated with the different feature subsets only. That research shows that the improvement due to the ensemble of nearest neighbour classifiers is correlated with the diversity in an ensemble. However, the diversity in the ensemble was determined after the ensemble was trained. Whereas, in the improvement presented here, the contribution of the ensemble member to the diversity of the ensemble is considered in the training process in order to ensure an ensemble of diverse members.

We present a study on ensembles of k-Nearest Neighbour (k-NN) classifiers that are trained on three different datasets with the two Hill Climbing approaches. The results show that the technique emphasizing ambiguity outperforms the strategy considering error only. Furthermore, we will see that forcing the classifiers to disagree leads to classifiers with a smaller number of features. This, as argued in (Cunningham & Zenobi, 2001) can be interpreted as an aggregation of several *local* specialists.

2.   Ensembles and Diversity

The key idea in ensemble research is; if a classifier or predictor is unstable then an ensemble of such classifiers voting on the outcome will produce better results – better in terms of stability and accuracy. While the use of ensembles in Machine Learning (ML) research is fairly new, the idea that aggregating the opinions of a committee of experts will increase accuracy is not new. The Codorcet Jury Theorem states that:

> *If each voter has a probability p of being correct and the probability of a majority of voters being correct is M, then p > 0.5 implies M > p. In the limit, M approaches 1, for all p > 0.5, as the number of voters approaches infinity.*

This theorem was proposed by the Marquis of Condorcet in 1784 (Condorcet, 1784) – a more accessible reference is (Nitzan & Paroush, 1985). We now know that M will be greater that p only if there is diversity in the pool of voters. And we know that the probability of the ensemble being correct will only increase as the ensemble grows if the diversity in the ensemble continues to grow as well. Typically the diversity of the ensemble will plateau as will the accuracy of the ensemble at some size between 10 and 50 members.

In ML research it is well known that ensembling will improve the performance of unstable learners. Unstable learners are learners where small changes in the training data can produce quite different models and thus different predictions.

2.1 Diversity Based on Different Feature Subsets

The most common means of producing diversity in an ensemble is by training the different ensemble members with different subset of the training data (Hansen & Salamon, 1992; Breiman, 1996). This does not work for k-Nearest Neighbour (k-NN) classifiers (Breiman, 1996) so instead we focus on ensembles based on different feature subsets.

A few studies have been done on the use of feature subset selection to create an ensemble of classifiers; among them those ones made by Cherkauer (1995), Ho (1998a, 1998b), Guerra-Salcedo and Whitney (1999a, 1999b) Tumer and Ghosh (1996) and Cunningham and Carney (2000) give the most promising results. However, if the use of ensembles improves the performance from one side, from another it reduces the other benefits of feature selection. It is clear that an ensemble of feature subsets affects the goal of economy of representation and also dramatically worsens the knowledge discovery (Cunningham & Zenobi, 2001), mainly because we cannot say anymore that the outcome of a phenomenon depends on a particular subset of features. In the last section of this paper we propose that the lack of interpretability associated with ensembles may be recoverable if the ensemble members prove to be *local* learners.

2.2 Different Measures of Diversity

There are a variety of ways to quantify ensemble diversity – usually associated with a particular error measure. In a regression problem (continuous output problem) it is normal to measure accuracy by the squared error so, as suggested by (Krogh & Vedelsby, 1995), a diversity measure can be variance, defined as:

$$a_i(x_k) = [V_i(x_k) - \overline{V}(x_k)]^2 \qquad (1)$$

where a_i is the ambiguity of the ith classifier on example x_k, randomly drawn from an unknown distribution, while V_i and $\overline{V}$ are, respectively the ith classifier and the ensemble predictions. In this scenario the error from the ensemble is: $E = \overline{E} - \overline{A}$, where $\overline{E}$ is the average of the single classifier errors and $\overline{A}$ is the ambiguity of the ensemble. The equation also holds for classification, provided that the loss function used is the squared error function and that the ensemble prediction is still given as the weighted average of the single classifier predictions. Provided also, that we are happy to deal with real-valued class membership figures (see example below).

However, for classification the most commonly used error measure is a simple 0/1 loss function, so a measure of ambiguity in this case is:

$$a_i(x_k) = \begin{cases} 0 \text{ if } classV_i(x_k) = class\overline{V}(x_k) \\ 1 \text{ otherwise.} \end{cases} \qquad (2)$$

where this time the classifier and ensemble outputs for the case labeled as x_k are classes instead of real numbers.

An Example

Our objective here is to identify an ambiguity measure that will help us determine the contribution of an individual ensemble member to diversity. The two above can quantify the contribution of an individual member to ensemble diversity and the variance based measure has the advantage that it directly quantifies the improvement due to the ensemble. To see how these would be applied in practice a simple example is shown in Table 1 and Table 2. In order to use squared error and variance it is necessary that the outputs of the ensemble members are real valued. This is achievable in a variety of ways with nearest neighbour classifiers where a degree of class membership can be aggregated from the similarity to nearest neighbours.

Table 1. An example with 3 classifiers and 5 data points. The top half of the table shows ensembled predictions allowing continuous values and the bottom half shows 0/1 predictions

Value	1	0	1	1	0	E_i
Cl 1:pred	1	0.33	1	0.33	0.67	1
Cl 2:pred	0	0	0.33	0.67	0.33	1.67
Cl 3:pred	0.33	0.67	0.67	1	0	1
Ensemb.	**0.44**	**0.33**	**0.67**	**0.67**	**0.33**	**0.75**
Cl 1: 0/1	1	0	1	0	1	0.4
Cl 2: 0/1	0	0	0	1	0	0.4
Cl 3: 0/1	0	1	1	1	0	0.4
Ensemb.	**0**	**0**	**1**	**1**	**0**	**0.2**

Table 2. Error and ambiguity measures for the scenario shown in Table 2.

	E	$\overline{E}$	$\overline{A}$	$\overline{E} - \overline{A}$
Squared Err.	0.75	1.22	0.47	0.75
0/1 Loss	0.2	0.4	0.33	0.07

In the first scenario the outputs from the individual classifiers are real valued and we can see in Table 2 that the Ambiguity measure directly determines the improvement due to the ensemble as Krogh and Vedelsby predict. Using 0/1 loss and the ambiguity measure proposed above the ensemble still produces an improvement but it is not directly related to the ambiguity figure.

While the squared error and variance figures have this very elegant relationship these real valued class membership figures are not particularly meaningful so we will proceed using the 0/1 loss error measure and the ambiguity metric proposed in (2).

3.   Using Ambiguity to Select Ensembles of Classifiers

The aim of this study is to show how using ambiguity to select ensembles of classifiers will improve performance. One thing that appears to be clear is that to obtain good results an ensemble must include classifiers with a high degree of disagreement. It is this disagreement that gives the potential to correct the errors made by a single classifier. In the extreme case that all the classifiers are good but make mistakes over the same subset of data, the ensemble will not give a better performance than any single classifier.

To compare the default selection strategy, that doesn't take into account diversity, and ours, which makes use of diversity (ambiguity), we will use Hill-Climbing search for a couple of reasons. First, we have a way to compare two ensembles performances that is not affected by any random event, once we state the same starting point (i.e. an initial set of feature masks). If we used for example a genetic algorithm it would be more difficult to make a direct comparison, due to its random nature. Second, a hill-climbing strategy is computationally less expensive then alternative stochastic search techniques. After all, we are interested in evaluating the heuristic to guide the search rather than the comprehensiveness of the search strategy.

3.1. The Default Search Strategy

In a classic hill climbing strategy *(HC)* that performs feature selection (Cunningham & Carney, 2000) a "good" classifier is selected by flipping each bit of the feature mask and accepting this flip if the classifier error E_i decreases. (A feature subset is a mask on the full feature set.) This process is repeated until no further improvements are possible – i.e. a local minimum in the feature set space is reached. The error is measured using leave-one-out testing. To produce an ensemble this process is repeated for each classifier and at the end all the classifiers are aggregated to form the ensemble. This approach is illustrated in Figure 1.

```
generate a random ensemble of feature subsets;

for every classifier i  in the ensemble {
      calculate initial error Eᵢ;
      do {
            for every bit j of the mask {
              flip jᵗʰ bit of iᵗʰ mask;
              calculate new Eᵢ′;
              if Eᵢ<= Eᵢ′
                    flip back jᵗʰ bit of iᵗʰ mask; //flip rejected
              else Eᵢ= Eᵢ′; //flip accepted
            }
      } while there are changes in the mask AND not   maximum number of
iterations;
}

aggregate classifiers to obtain ensemble prediction;
```

Fig. 1. *HC:* the default selection strategy for generating ensembles using error only.

Clearly, from what we have said about the importance of diversity, this approach has the disadvantage that the improvement due to the ensemble may not be great because there is no means of promoting diversity in the ensemble.

3.2. *AmbHC:* A Hill-Climbing Algorithm Using Ambiguity

The dominant loss function used in classification is 0/1 loss and it is difficult if not impossible to derive a simple and linear equation that relates E to $\overline{E}$ and $\overline{A}$. However it is still clear that the *uplift* due to the ensemble depends on the diversity in the ensemble members (Cunningham & Carney, 2000). In the evaluation that follows we will use 0/1 loss and the associated ambiguity introduced in equation (2).

Assuming a homogeneous distribution of the instances (so that the average is simply obtained by dividing by N, the number of training samples) and equal weights in the ensemble, Ambiguity is defined as:

$$\overline{A} = \frac{1}{N}\sum_{k=1}^{N}\frac{1}{m}\sum_{i=1}^{m}a_i(x_k)$$

where $a_i(x_k)$ is given by equation (2). As the two summations are finite we can swap them, leading to the formula:

$$\overline{A} = \frac{1}{N}\sum_{k=1}^{N}\frac{1}{m}\sum_{i=1}^{m}a_i(x_k) = \frac{1}{m}\sum_{i=1}^{m}\frac{1}{N}\sum_{k=1}^{N}a_i(x_k) = \frac{1}{m}\sum_{i=1}^{m}A_i$$

where the ambiguity A_i of the ith classifier is defined as

$$A_i = \frac{1}{N}\sum_{k=1}^{N}a_i(x_k) \tag{3}$$

On the basis of these definitions we may think of a new algorithm *(AmbHC)* that, taking the hill-climbing strategy as a starting point, tries to build an ensemble of classifiers with a high degree of disagreement. This approach considers every classifier in the context of the ensemble, and at each step accepts or rejects the flip depending on two parameters: the classifier error E_i and the classifier ambiguity A_i, as defined in the equation (3). If the improvement of one of the two parameters leads to a "substantial" deterioration of the other, then the flip is rejected. With "substantial" here we mean that a threshold value *(Thresh)* is given for the highest acceptable deterioration (if we consider acceptable a deterioration of 5% then *Thresh* takes the real value 0.05). The condition to accept or reject the flip of a bit is the following: if the improvement of one of the two parameters is less than the threshold value, then the highest acceptable deterioration of the other parameter is given by the improvement of the first one; if the improvement of one of the two parameters is instead greater than the threshold value, then the highest acceptable deterioration is the threshold itself. This technique allows us to avoid the selection of a set of good classifiers that make mistakes over the same subspace of the instances; it is illustrated in Figure 2.

In settling on this means of combining error and ambiguity in determining ensemble members we considered several alternatives; an evaluation of some of these is shown in Table 3. This table shows four columns of results for ensembles of size 13, 17 and 21. For the first column (HC (E)) the ensemble members were selected using error only. For the second, the selection was based on error minus ambiguity in the manner of Krogh and Vedelsby's (1995) work. The third is the same as the algorithm described in Figure 2 but without the threshold conditions. The fourth column shows results for the algorithm shown in Figure 2. Clearly, the threshold approach work best. The E-A approach does not work so well because there is no basis for assuming that diversity has such a direct effect in classification. The technique without a threshold fails because sometimes improvements in ambiguity (or error) come at too high a cost in error (or ambiguity). Introducing the threshold overcomes this problem.

```
generate a random ensemble of feature subsets;
do {
  for every classifier i in the ensemble {
    calculate initial error Ei and contribution to ambiguity Ai ;
    for every bit j of the mask {
      flip jth bit of ith mask;
      calculate new Ei' and new Ai';
      if {   { [ Ei'< Ei ] AND
             [    [( Ei'≤(1-Thresh ) × Ei ) AND (Ai'≥(1-Thresh) × Ai)] OR
                  [( Ei' >(1-Thresh ) × Ei ) AND (Ai'≥ Ei'/Ei × Ai) ]     ] } OR
           { [Ai' >Ai ] AND
             [    [( Ai'≥ (1+Thresh )× Ai ) AND (Ei'≤(1+Thresh )×Ei )] OR
                  [( Ai' < (1+Thresh )× Ai) AND (Ei'≤Ai'/ Ai ×Ei ) ]     ] }     }
      Ei= Ei' ; Ai = Ai';  //flip accepted
      else flip back jth bit of ith mask; //flip rejected
    }
  }
} while there are changes in the masks AND not maximum number of iterations;
calculate final ensemble prediction;
```

Fig. 2. *AmbHC:* The algorithm for generating ensembles while emphasising diversity in ensemble members.

Table 3. Results of different alternatives for combining error and ambiguity in selecting ensemble members (the UCI Heart data was used).

	Ens Size	HC (E)	E-A	AmbHC (NoThresh)	AmbHC
Heart	13	17.7	18.8	17.8	17.2
	17	17.3	17.3	17.8	17.2
	21	17.7	18.1	19.7	16.9
Pima	13	25.0	25.7	26.0	24.5
	17	25.0	24.1	25.1	24.1
	21	24.6	24.7	25.8	23.8
Warfarin	13	7.8	7.9	8.1	7.8
	17	7.6	8.0	8.8	7.4
	21	8.0	7.4	8.0	7.3

We have run the algorithms on three datasets; two available from the UCI repository (Pima Indians, Heart Disease) and the Warfarin data-set described in (Byrne et al., 2000). These were chosen on the basis of the following criteria:
- we have restricted our experimental comparison to 2-class datasets, turning a problem into a 2-class classification task if necessary, and have left the n-classe case for further research;

- we have considered datasets which do not have a skewed class distribution, as simple 0/1 error measures are questionable for datasets with very unbalanced class distributions.

In the next section we present a complete comparison of the results obtained by two of these algorithms, the basic hill-climbing error-only algorithm *(HC)* and *AmbHC*; below we give some further details about the *AmbHC* algorithm.

4.   Evaluation and Discussion

We present in this section a complete comparison of the *HC* and *AmbHC* selection strategies. We show that if the ensemble members are forced to be diverse then a better ensemble accuracy can be achieved with ensemble members that have poor overall accuracy, provided we include a sufficiently high number of classifiers in the ensemble. Also, these diverse ensemble members prove to have fewer features than ensemble members selected without consideration for diversity.

For each dataset we have run the two algorithms described in the previous section *(HC & AmbHC)*, varying their initial ensemble size. For each ensemble size we have also repeated the process with 4 different starting points (initial sets of feature masks), averaging the results obtained, as the hill-climbing strategy is quite sensitive to the initial condition. The scoring of any ensemble is determined using a 5-fold cross validation; in the 5-fold cross validation the data is divided into 5 parts and the ensemble is tested on each part in turn having been trained on the other 4 parts. The training involves the search processes described in Figures 1 & 2 and the fitness is determined using leave-one-out testing. The results are then averaged over the 5 validation sets. The threshold used for the *AmbHC* algorithm was set for all the datasets at 2.5%.

The evaluation on the three datasets shows that the ensembles trained with the *AmbHC* algorithm (higher diversity) have lower generalization errors than those trained with the simple *HC*, provided the size of the ensemble is sufficiently large (see Figures 3. Because of the nature of the ensemble training process *HC* ensembles have corresponding *AmbHC* ensembles allowing us to use a paired *t*-test to test the hypothesis that the *AmbHC* ensembles have lower error. We have randomly selected 9 different ensembles in each of the three datasets and performed a paired *t*-test; the results gave a confidence of >80% for Warfarin, and >95% and >99% for Heart and Pima sespectively. These figures are very satisfactory - the weaker figure for Warfarin is probably accounted for by the small impact of the ensemble given the already low error of the individual classifiers. This is the first main result of our study: the algorithm that takes into account diversity while selecting ensemble outperforms the simply error-only strategy.

In the following two tables we focus on some other aspects of the comparison between classifiers trained with the two different algorithms. In Table 4 we show, for each dataset and for both the algorithms, respectively the error obtained by the best ensemble, the average error and the average ambiguity of the single classifiers in the ensembles.

In Table 5 we show instead, for each dataset, respectively the total number of features and the average number of features of the masks trained with *HC* and with *AmbHC*.

As we can see from Table 4, the classifiers in the ensemble selected with the *AmbHC* algorithm have a higher average error than those selected by the simple *HC* algorithm: the increase in ambiguity (diversity) comes at the cost of significantly higher errors in the ensemble members. It seems to us that the only way to account for the improvement in overall performance in the face of deterioration of the ensemble members is that the members are local specialists. In fact, the use of ambiguity in the *AmbHC* algorithm means that the ensemble selection is made by choosing classifiers that disagree on a higher number of elements compared to those ones selected without ambiguity. For the first ones, the higher average ambiguity seems to compensate their higher error by 'distributing' the prediction of the different individuals over more diverse regions of the space of the instances; as a result we get a lower ensemble error.

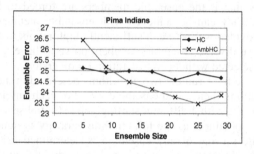

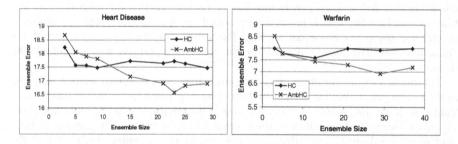

Fig. 3. Generalization error of different ensemble sizes on the Pima, Heart and Warfarin data.

This view is reinforced by another interesting result: the ensemble members produced using ambiguity have fewer features on average than the others (Table 5). It seems reasonable that fewer features are required to discriminate in these local regions. This observation also suggests a new perspective on the knowledge discovery aspect of feature selection. It may be useful to reconsider this as a process of finding the best ensemble of local feature subsets rather than a global feature subset. However, the problem remains that if the ensemble is performing a problem space decomposition then it is doing so implicitly and the decomposition is not accessible. An interesting avenue for future research will be to use clustering to see if meaningful regions of the problem space can be identified where ensemble members specialize.

Table 4. A summary of all the evaluations showing the best ensemble generated for each data set and showing the corresponding average member error and ambiguity.

Data	Algorithm	Best Ensemble	Average Error	Avg. Ambiguity
Pima	HC	24.6	27.0	13.7
	AmbHC	23.4	31.5	22.3
Heart	HC	17.4	21.8	12.2
	AmbHC	16.6	24.8	18.8
Warfarin	HC	7.6	8.6	3.3
	AmbHC	6.9	14.1	10.6

Table 5. The ensembles built using *AmbHC* have significantly less features on average that those built using the default search algorithm.

Data	Total	Average: HC	Average: AmbHC
Pima	8	4.8	3.5
Heart	13	7.4	6.0
Warfarin	22	12.9	10.7

The local learners hypothesis helps us also in explaining the behaviour shown in Figure 3, where, in each case, a minimum number of classifiers are needed for *AmbHC* to surpass *HC*. Since classifiers trained with the *AmbHC* algorithm have a higher average error than the ones trained with *HC* it is clear that each classifier will cover (i.e. predict correctly) a 'smaller' region of the problem space. So, to have the majority of the ensemble voting correctly we need a larger number of classifiers. Then, when the ensemble size is small (e.g. 5) even though we do not use diversity (in the *HC* algorithm) it is very probable that a set of classifiers randomly chosen has its own 'natural' diversity. As we increase the ensemble size, it becomes more probable that new members of *HC* ensembles will be similar to existing ones. While with the *AmbHC* algorithm diversity is still emphasized and variety is maintained. Thus, a diverse bunch of good classifiers outperforms a bunch of very good classifiers with less diversity.

However, as mentioned in section 2 when discussing the Condorcet Jury Theorem, this addition of new diverse members does not continue to deliver benefit indefinately. At best, it will not continue to be possible to find more diverse members and the reduction in error will bottom out. What is happening in the three examples here is actually slightly worse than that in that an overfitting effect is evident. Since the selection of the ensemble members is a training process there is the potential for the ensemble as a whole to overfit the training data and that is clearly evident in the three graphs shown here. So with this *AmbHC* approach there is an optimal ensemble size which apperars to be between 25 and 30 for these data sets. It seems that the best way to address this overfitting would be to use a cross validation process to determine a best ensemble size.

5.   Conclusions and Future Work

In this paper we have compared two approaches for selecting an ensemble of classifiers: a simple error-only strategy, where a group of independently 'good' classifiers is first selected and then aggregated, and a strategy which considers, during the training process, every classifier in the context of the ensemble and selects a group of classifiers with a high degree of diversity. We have focused our attention on ensembles of classifiers where diversity derives from different ensemble members using different feature sub-sets.

Since the objective of the evaluation has been to assess the feature selection strategies the comparison has been done using a simple hill-climbing search strategy. The strategies could be employed in a more comprehensive search algorithm such as a genetic algorithm or beam search.

Since there is a clear trade-off between diversity and error in the selection of the ensemble members the key question was; would diverse ensembles of (possibly) less accurate classifiers outperform ensembles of good classifiers with perhaps less diversity. The answer to this has proved to be 'yes' but it does depend on the careful management of the tradeoff between error and ambiguity that is implemented in the *AmbHC* algorithm as described in Figure 2.

This is interesting because it highlights something of a paradox associated with ensembles. It shows that it can be a good thing to have a committee of experts consistently voting 5 : 4 in favour of a prediction rather than 8 : 1. In fact, we are proposing selecting experts in a manner that will push down consensus in the committee. Intuitively, this is not what you want from a committee of physicians discussing your particular illness! You would like the committee of physicians to agree. A resolution of this paradox is as follows. If the committee members are very accurate there is little benefit in diversity; indeed there is little benefit in ensembles in classification tasks where accuracies of >93% (say) are achievable with a single classifier. However, ensembles make sense where individual classifiers have significant errors (say > 15%). In such cases, instead of adding a new very accurate committee member that makes the same errors as existing members in the ensemble it is sensible to add a member that makes different errors, one that has a different set of competences. There is no benefit in adding members that will change votes of 8:1 to 9:1.

Perhaps the most interesting finding of this research is the fact that the ambiguity-focused learners have less features and the implication that these ensemble members are local learners. This may prove useful in understanding the contribution of ensembles in reducing error and may lead to an increase in the interpretability of ensembles. This will be the subject of our future research.

References

Breiman, L., (1996) Bagging predictors. *Machine Learning*, 24:123-140.

Byrne, S., Cunningham, P., Barry, A., Graham, I., Delaney T., Corrigan, O.I., (2000) Using Neural Nets for Decision Support in Prescription and Outcome Prediction in Anticoagulation Drug Therapy, N. Lavrac, S. Miksch (eds.): *The Fifth Workshop on Intelligent Data Analysis in Medicine and Pharmacology (IDAMAP-2000)*.

Cherkauer, K.J. (1995) Stuffing Mind into Computer: Knowledge and Learning for Intelligent Systems. *Informatica* 19:4 (501-511) Nov. 1995

Condorcet, Marquis J. A. (1781) Sur les elections par scrutiny, *Histoire de l'Academie Royale des Sciences*, 31-34.

Cunningham, P., Carney, J., (2000) Diversity versus Quality in Classification Ensembles based on Feature Selection, *11th European Conference on Machine Learning (ECML 2000)*, Lecture Notes in Artificial Intelligence, R. López de Mántaras and E. Plaza, (eds) pp109-116, Springer Verlag.

Cunningham, P., & Zenobi, G., (2001) Case Representation Issues for Case-Based Reasoning from Ensemble Research, *to be presented at ICCBR 2001*.

Guerra-Salcedo, C., Whitley, D., (1999a). Genetic Approach for Feature Selection for Ensemble Creation. *in GECCO-99: Proceedings of the Genetic and Evolutionary Computation Conference*, Banzhaf, W., Daida, J., Eiben, A. E., Garzon, M. H., Honavar, V., Jakiela, M., & Smith, R. E. (eds.). Orlando, Florida USA, pp236-243, San Francisco, CA: Morgan Kaufmann.

Guerra-Salcedo, C., Whitley, D., (1999b). Feature Selection Mechanisms for Ensemble Creation: A Genetic Search Perspective, in *Data Mining with Evolutionary Algorithms: Research Directions. Papers from the AAAI Workshop*. Alex A. Freitas (Ed.) Technical Report WS-99-06. AAAI Press, 1999.

Hansen, L.K., Salamon, P., (1990) Neural Network Ensembles, *IEEE Pattern Analysis and Machine Intelligence*, 1990. **12**, 10, 993-1001.

Ho, T.K., (1998a) The Random Subspace Method for Constructing Decision Forests, *IEEE Transactions on Pattern Analysis and Machine Intelligence*, **20**, 8, 832-844.

Ho, T.K., (1998b) Nearest Neighbours in Random Subspaces, *Proc. Of 2nd International Workshop on Statistical Techniques in Pattern Recognition,* A. Amin, D. Dori, P. Puil, H. Freeman, (eds.) pp640-648, Springer Verlag LNCS 1451.

Kohavi, R. & John, G.H., (1998) The Wrapper Approach, in *Feature Selection for Knowledge Discovery and Data Mining*, H. Liu & H. Motoda (eds.), Kluwer Academic Publishers, pp33-50.

Krogh, A., Vedelsby, J., (1995) Neural Network Ensembles, Cross Validation and Active Learning, in *Advances in Neural Information Processing Systems 7*, G. Tesauro, D. S. Touretsky, T. K. Leen, eds., pp231-238, MIT Press, Cambridge MA.

Liu Y., Yao X. (1999) Ensemble learning via negative correlation, *Neural Networks* 12, 1999.

Nitzan, S.I., Paroush, J., (1985) *Collective Decision Making*. Cambridge: Cambridge University Press.

Opitz D., Shavlik J., (1996) Generating Accurate and diverse members of a Neural Network Ensemble, *Advances in Neural Information Processing Systems*, pp. 535-543, Denver, CO. MIT Press. 1996.

Tumer, K., and Ghosh, J., (1996) Error Correlation and Error Reduction in Ensemble Classifiers, *Connection Science,* , Vol. 8, No. 3 & 4, pp 385-404.

Geometric Properties of Naive Bayes in Nominal Domains

Huajie Zhang and Charles X. Ling

Department of Computer Science
The University of Western Ontario
London, Ontario, Canada   N6A 5B7
{hzhang, ling}@csd.uwo.ca

Abstract. It is well known that the naive Bayesian classifier is linear in binary domains. However, little work is done on the learnability of the naive Bayesian classifier in nominal domains, a general case of binary domains. This paper explores the geometric properties of the naive Bayesian classifier in nominal domains. First we propose a three-layer measure for the linearity of functions in nominal domains: hard linear, soft nonlinear, and hard nonlinear. We examine the learnability of the naive Bayesian classifier in terms of that linearity measure. We show that the naive Bayesian classifier can learn some hard linear and some soft nonlinear nominal functions, but still cannot learn any hard nonlinear functions.

1   Introduction

Learning classifiers from examples is an important issue in machine learning research. A classifier is a function that assigns a class label to an example. Assume A_1, A_2,$\cdots$, A_n are n attributes. An example E is represented by a vector $(a_1, a_2, \cdots, a_n)$, where a_i is the value of A_i. There are two types of attributes: nominal (taking values from a finite set) and numeric (taking values from a continuous range). We restrict our discussion to nominal attributes in this paper. Let C represent the classification variable, which takes values $+$ (positive class) or $-$ (negative class), and let c be the value that C takes.

Numerous approaches to learning classifiers, such as decision trees, neural networks, and instance-based learning, have been studied. In recent years, probability approaches to learning classifiers have been extensively investigated. According to Bayes Theorem, the probability of an example $E = (a_1, a_2, \cdots, a_n)$ being in class c is

$$p(c|E) = \frac{p(a_1, a_2, \cdots, a_n|c)p(c)}{p(a_1, a_2, \cdots, a_n)}.$$

E belongs to the class $C = +$ iff

$$g(E) = \frac{p(C = +)p(a_1, a_2, \cdots, a_n|C = +)}{p(C = -)p(a_1, a_2, \cdots, a_n|C = -)} \geq 1,$$

where $g(E)$ is called a Bayesian classifier.

L. De Raedt and P. Flach (Eds.): ECML 2001, LNAI 2167, pp. 588–599, 2001.
© Springer-Verlag Berlin Heidelberg 2001

Assume all attributes are independent given the class value (conditional independence), then

$$p(a_1, a_2, \cdots, a_n | c) = \prod_{i=1}^{n} p(a_i | c).$$

The corresponding Bayesian classifier $g(E)$ is then:

$$g(E) = \frac{p(C = +)}{p(C = -)} \prod_{i=1}^{n} \frac{p(a_i | C = +)}{p(a_i | C = -)},$$

where $g(E)$ is called a naive Bayesian classifier or, in short, Naive Bayes.

Naive Bayes is easy to construct simply by estimating the value of $p(a_i | c)$ from training examples. Intuitively this might be not accurate, because the conditional independence assumption rarely holds true. To some extent, however, this intuition is not correct. Many empirical comparisons between Naive Bayes and C4.5 [9] showed that Naive Bayes predicts just as well as C4.5 [7,6].

In recent years, researchers have attempted to uncover reasons for the good performance of Naive Bayes. Domingos and Pazzani [1] presented an explanation: even though Naive Bayes alters the probability distribution of a class, the class with the maximum probability may still be the same. This is verified by Frank's [3] work, which shows that the performance of Naive Bayes is much worse when it is used for regression (predicting a continuous value).

One interesting and fundamental question is the learnability of Naive Bayes. It is well-known that Naive Bayes can create only linear frontiers in binary domains [2]. That is, Naive Bayes can learn only linearly separable concepts in binary domains. For nominal domains, a general case of binary domains, there is no satisfying result. Attributes in nominal domains can have more than two values. Assume A_1, A_2, $\cdots$, A_n are n nominal attributes, each attribute A_i may have m values a_{i1}, a_{i2}, $\cdots$, and a_{im} ($m \geq 2$). Domingos and Pazzani [1] and Peot [8] introduced m new Boolean attributes B_{i1}, B_{i2}, $\cdots$, and B_{im} for each attribute A_i, and proved that Naive Bayes is linear over these new binary attributes. However, the linear separability on n original attributes is transformed to $m_1 \times m_2 \cdots \times m_n$ new attributes. To our knowledge, there is no general result for the linearity of Naive Bayes on original nominal attributes.

Given a function in nominal domains, however, how can we define linearity or linear separability? Typically, linearity is a geometric term on the Euclidean space $\mathcal{R}^n$ ($\mathcal{R}$ is the set of all real numbers), but nominal attributes do not have direct geometric meaning. We must map nominal attributes into numeric ones to discuss the linearity property of a function. The tricky issue is that different mappings may result in different results of linearity.

On the other hand, it is obvious that different functions in nominal domains may present different difficulties for Naive Bayes to learn. It is natural to ask the following questions: Can the complexity of a function be measured in terms of its geometric properties? Is there any relation between the geometric properties of a function and the learnability of Naive Bayes?

The motivation of this paper is to explore the learnability of Naive Bayes by answering the two questions above. The remainder of this paper is organized as follows. Section 2 introduces necessary definitions and briefly reviews the results in the upper bound on the learnability of Naive Bayes. Section 3 proposes a three-layer measure for the linearity of a function, and proves a sufficient and necessary condition for hard nonlinearity, and then examines the learnability of Naive Bayes in terms of that measure. In the conclusions, we summarize our results and outline our future work.

2   The Upper Bound on the Learnability of Naive Bayes

As mentioned above, Naive Bayes is a linear classifier in binary domains. Let us briefly review the relevant results [2].

Suppose that attributes A_1, A_2, $\cdots$, A_n are binary, taking value 0 or 1. Let p_i and q_i represent the probability $p(A_i = 1|C = +)$ and $p(A_i = 1|C = -)$ respectively, $E = (a_1, \cdots, a_n)$ be an example. Then the corresponding Naive Bayes $G(E)$ is:

$$G(E) = \frac{p(C = +)}{p(C = -)} \prod_{i=1}^{n} \frac{p_i{}^{a_i}(1 - p_i)^{1-a_i}}{q_i{}^{a_i}(1 - q_i)^{1-a_i}}. \tag{1}$$

It is straightforward to obtain a linear classifier by applying a logarithm to the above equation.

Two points should be noted here. First, we actually implicitly use a mapping from the two nominal values (such as *red* and *blue*) of a binary attribute to {0, 1}. Second, we cannot get a similar result when any of A_i has more than two values. Thus, we cannot simply extend the result in binary domains to nominal domains.

We begin our discussion on the linearity of Naive Bayes with a few definitions.

Definition 1 *Given n nominal attributes A_1, A_2, $\cdots$, A_n, and two classification labels {+, -}, a function f from $A_1 \times A_2 \cdots \times A_n$ to {+, -} is called an n-dimensional nominal function.*

Zhang and Ling [12] proved that if a nominal function f "contains" an XOR, then no Naive Bayes can represent it. So, roughly, XOR is the upper bound of Naive Bayes. We give detailed definitions of "contain" below, since we will use this term in the next section.

Definition 2 *Assume f is an n-dimensional nominal function on A_1, A_2, $\cdots$, A_n. An (n-1)-dimensional partial function f_p of f on A_1, $\cdots$, A_{i-1}, A_{i+1}, $\cdots$, A_n, and $A_i = a_{ij}$, is called an (n-1)-dimensional subfunction at $A_i = a_{ij}$, denoted by $f(a_{ij})$, where $1 \leq i \leq n$.*

To get a k-dimensional subfunction of f is straightforward, by fixing $n - k$ attributes, $2 \leq k \leq n - 1$.

Definition 3 *An n-dimensional nominal function f is said to contain a tangent XOR, if there is a 2-dimensional subfunction f_p on attributes A_i and A_j, and each of them has two distinct values a_i and $\bar{a}_i$, a_j and $\bar{a}_j$, respectively, such that a partial function $f_{p'}$ of f_p on $\{a_i, \bar{a}_i\} \times \{a_j, \bar{a}_j\}$ is an XOR function.*

Definition 4 *Assume f is an n-dimensional nominal function. f is said to contain a diagonal XOR if there are two attributes A_i and A_j, each of which has two distinct values, a_i, $\bar{a}_i$, and a_j, $\bar{a}_j$, respectively, such that:*

$$f(a_1, \cdots, a_i, \cdots, a_j, \cdots, a_n) = + \qquad (2)$$
$$f(a_1, \cdots, a_i, \cdots, \bar{a}_j, \cdots, a_n) = - \qquad (3)$$
$$f(\bar{a}_1, \cdots, \bar{a}_i, \cdots, a_j, \cdots, \bar{a}_n) = - \qquad (4)$$
$$f(\bar{a}_1, \cdots, \bar{a}_i, \cdots, \bar{a}_j, \cdots, \bar{a}_n) = + \qquad (5)$$

where a_l and $\bar{a}_l$ are two distinct values of A_l, $l \neq i$ and j.

Definition 5 *An n-dimensional nominal function f is said to contain an XOR if and only if f contains a tangent XOR or a diagonal XOR.*

3   Geometric Properties of Naive Bayes

Containing an XOR of a nominal function is a basic concept in this paper. It has been proved that Naive Bayes cannot learn any function containing XOR [12]. However, what is the relation between a function containing an XOR and its geometric linearity? We propose a measure for the geometric linearity of a function, and show that there is a close relation between a function's containing an XOR and its linear separability. Then we examine the learnability of Naive Bayes on functions with different linearity.

3.1   Measure for the Linearity of Nominal Functions

We have to map nominal attributes of a function into numeric ones in order to discuss its linearity. Since the values of a nominal attribute have no order, it is reasonable to map a nominal value into an arbitrary real number without conflicting with the mapping of another attribute value.

Definition 6 *Given n numeric attributes A_1, A_2, $\cdots$, A_n, and two classification labels $\{+, -\}$, a function f from $A_1 \times A_2 \cdots \times A_n$ to $\{+, -\}$ is called n-dimensional numeric function.*

Definition 7 *Given a nominal attribute $A = \{a_1, a_2, \cdots, a_m\}$, a numeric attribute mapping Γ is defined as a function from A to $\mathcal{R}$, such that for each a_i, $1 \leq i \leq m$, we have $\Gamma(a_i) = x_i$, $x_i \in \mathcal{R}$ and $x_i \neq x_j$ if $i \neq j$.*

Let us review the conclusion that Naive Bayes is a linear classifier in binary domains. As discussed in Section 2, this conclusion comes from an implicit assumption that the two values of each binary attribute are mapped into $\{0, 1\}$. Obviously, other reasonable mappings also exist, since we can map the two values of a binary attribute into any two different real numbers. Then we can no longer get Equation 1. Since the mapping affects the geometric properties of a nominal function, what we are interested in are the properties that are independent of mappings.

Definition 8 *Given a nominal function f on nominal attributes $A_1, A_2, \cdots, A_n$, an attribute mapping vector $\Omega = (\Gamma_1, \Gamma_2, \cdots, \Gamma_n)$ is called a numeric function mapping of f, where Γ_i is the numeric attribute mapping of A_i, $i = 1, 2, \cdots, n$. The resulting numeric function f_Ω is defined below:*

$$f_\Omega(\Gamma_1(A_1), \Gamma_2(A_2), \cdots, \Gamma_n(A_n)) = f(A_1, A_2, \cdots, A_n).$$

After f is mapped to f_Ω in the Euclidean space, geometrically, f_Ω corresponds to an n-dimensional hypercube, and each $(n-1)$-dimensional subfunction $f(a_{ij})$ corresponds to an $(n-1)$-dimensional surface of the hypercube, denoted by H_{ij}. Note that an $(n-1)$-dimensional surface is also an n-dimensional hyperplane. Each assignment of all attributes corresponds to a vertex of the hypercube with a class label. Let W^+ and W^- represent all positive and negative vertices respectively. Then we have the following definition.

Definition 9 *A numeric function f_Ω is linearly separable if there is a hyperplane H to separate W^+ from W^-, where $H = \sum_{i=1}^{n} w_i A_i + w_0$, $w_i \in \mathcal{R}$.*

Geometrically, if f_Ω is linearly separable, then there is an n-dimensional hyperplane slicing the hypercube of f_Ω, such that all positive vertices lie on the one side of the hyperplane and all negative vertices on its opposite side. Therefore, the problem of linear separability becomes the problem in which a hyperplane slices a hypercube [10]. As mentioned earlier, since we only care about the properties independent of mappings, we can freely move a surface H_{ij} of f_Ω (corresponding to an f's $(n-1)$-dimensional subfunction $f(a_{ij})$), which corresponds to assigning a different mapping value to a_{ij}; or we can freely exchange the positions of any two distinct surfaces H_{ij} and H_{ik}, which corresponds to exchanging the mapping values of a_{ij} and a_{ik}. Since moving a surface or exchanging two surfaces corresponds to a different mapping, we will use these two operations in the proof of theorems later.

Definition 10 *(1) A nominal function f is called hard linear, if for any numeric function mapping, the resulting numeric function is linearly separable.*

(2) A nominal function f is called soft nonlinear if it is not a hard linear function, and there exists a numeric function mapping such that the resulting numeric function is linearly separable.

(3) A nominal function f is called hard nonlinear if for any numeric function mapping, the resulting numeric function is not linearly separable.

Definition 10 proposes three layers to measure the linearity of nominal functions, independent of specific mappings. In binary domains, however, only two layers are needed, as given by the following Theorem.

Theorem 1. *There is no soft nonlinear Boolean function in binary domains.*

Proof: Suppose that f is a Boolean function on binary attributes $B_1, \cdots, B_n$, and there is a numeric function mapping $\Omega = (\Gamma_1, \cdots, \Gamma_n)$, where $\Gamma_i(b_{ij}) = x_{ij}$ (b_{ij} is the value of B_i, $i = 1, \cdots, n$, $j = 1, 2$), such that the resulting numeric function f_Ω is linearly separable. Then there is a hyperplane H to separate f_Ω. Assume $H = \sum_{i=1}^{n} w_i x_i + w_0$, $w_i \in \mathcal{R}$.

For any other mapping $\Omega' = (\Gamma_1', \cdots, \Gamma_n')$, where $\Gamma_i'(b_{ij}) = x_{ij}'$ ($i = 1, \cdots, n$, $j = 1, 2$), the following hyperplane

$$H' = \sum_{i=1}^{n} w_i \left(\frac{x_i - x_{i1}'}{x_{i2}' - x_{i1}'} (x_{i2} - x_{i1}) + x_{i1} \right) + w_0$$

will separate the resulting function $f_{\Omega'}$.

A straightforward result from Theorem 1 is that Naive Bayes is linear in binary domains regardless of mapping. That means that linearity in binary domains is simple. However, the linearity in nominal domains is more complex. As we will show in the following subsections, the learnability of Naive Bayes in the three layers of linearity is different.

3.2 Hard Linear Nominal Functions

Consider the m-of-n functions. An m-of-n function is a Boolean function that is true if m or more out of n Boolean variables are true. Clearly, if the two values of each Boolean variable are mapped into $\{0, 1\}$, an m-of-n function is linearly separable by the hyperplane $\sum_{i=1}^{n} x_i - m = 0$, where $x_i \in \{0, 1\}$. So it is hard linear by Theorem 1. It can be verified that some m-of-n functions are learnable to Naive Bayes, such as 13-of-25, 30-of-60, 31-of-60 [11]. However, not all m-of-n functions are learnable to Naive Bayes. Domingos and Pazzani [1] showed that for the concept 8-of-25, Naive Bayes gives an incorrect answer of 1 (instead of 0), when just six or seven input Boolean variables are true. This result is independent of mapping, since all variables are Boolean in an m-of-n function.

The above example shows that Naive Bayes can learn only a subset of hard linear nominal functions. Zhang and Ling [11] presented a sufficient and necessary condition for an m-of-n function to be learnable to Naive Bayes. But for an arbitrary linear function, such a condition is still unknown.

3.3 Soft Nonlinear Nominal Functions

Soft nonlinear nominal functions are those functions that are nonlinear under some mappings, but linear under others. The following is an example.

Let $A = \{a_1, a_2, a_3\}$, $B = \{b_1, b_2, b_3\}$, the nominal function f_1 is defined as follows: $f_1(a_1, b_1) = +$, $f_1(a_1, b_3) = +$, $f_1(a_3, b_1) = +$, $f_1(a_3, b_3) = +$, $f_1(a_2, *) = -$, $f_1(*, b_2) = -$, where $*$ means any valid values. Figure 1 (a) is the result of mapping a_i and b_i to i, $i = 1, 2, 3$. It is not linearly separable. However if we map a_1, b_1 to 1, and a_3, b_3 to 2, and a_2 to 5, b_2 to 4, the result, which is linearly separable, is shown in Figure 1 (b). Therefore, f_1 is soft nonlinear.

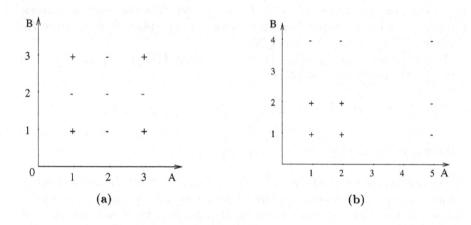

Fig. 1. (a) Nonlinear result of f_1 (b) linear result of f_1

Definition 11 *A numeric attribute mapping Γ on a nominal attribute $A = \{a_1, a_2, \cdots, a_m\}$ is called an integer mapping, if Γ is a one-to-one mapping from $\{a_1, a_2, \cdots, a_m\}$ to $\{1, 2, \cdots, m\}$, denoted by Γ_I.*

From Definition 7, we know that Γ_I is a special case of arbitrary Γ, since nominal attribute values are mapped one-to-one into a fixed set of integers. Indeed, application of Naive Bayes on real-world datasets often requires that all attributes be converted into nominal attributes, which are commonly represented internally by integers from 1 to k for k different values. Therefore, integer mapping is a typical and useful mapping in real applications.

Consider a Naive Bayes G on two specific nominal attributes A and B, where $A = \{a_1, a_2, a_3\}$, $B = \{b_1, b_2, b_3\}$, and Table 1 is the conditional probability table (CPT) for A, and B has the same CPT as A. Assume Γ_{IA} and Γ_{IB} are

Table 1. The conditional probability table for A.

	$A = a_1$	$A = a_2$	$A = a_3$
$C = -$	0.3	0.4	0.3
$C = +$	0.5	0	0.5

integer mappings from A and B to $\{1, 2, 3\}$ respectively, such that $\Gamma_{IA}(a_i) = i$, $\Gamma_{IB}(b_i) = i$, $i = 1, 2, 3$. It is easy to verify that the classifications of G are the same as in Figure 1 (a) after mapped to a two-dimensional Euclidean plane. So, f_1 is learnable to G.

Therefore, Naive Bayes can learn some soft nonlinear nominal functions. This conclusion is quite different from that in binary domains. As we have shown, there are no soft nonlinear functions in binary domains; a function is either hard linear, or hard nonlinear, and Naive Bayes can only learn some of hard linear functions. In nominal domains, however, there are soft nonlinear functions, which are nonlinear under some mappings, and Naive Bayes can actually learn some of them. This may explain why the performance of Naive Bayes is quite good in real-world datasets in which attributes are nominal (since continuous attributes are often discretized to nominal attributes).

3.4   Hard Nonlinear Nominal Functions

Consider the XOR function. Let $A = \{a, \bar{a}\}$, $B = \{b, \bar{b}\}$, the XOR function f_2 is defined as: $f_2(a, b) = +$, $f_2(a, \bar{b}) = -$, $f_2(\bar{a}, b) = -$, $f_2(\bar{a}, \bar{b}) = +$. It is easy to verify that f_2 is hard nonlinear.

We now establish a sufficient and necessary condition for the hard nonlinearity of a function.

Lemma 1. *If an n-dimensional nominal function f has an (n-1)-dimensional subfunction $f(a_{ij})$ with an identical class (called identical subfunction), where a_{ij} is a value of attribute A_i, then f is hard nonlinear if and only if f's partial function f_p on A_1, A_2, $\cdots$, $A_i - \{a_{ij}\}$, $\cdots$, A_n is hard nonlinear.*

Proof: It is obvious that if f_p is hard nonlinear, f is hard nonlinear too.

If f_p is not hard nonlinear, then there is a numeric function mapping Ω, such that after applying it on f_p, the resulting numeric function $f_{p\Omega}$ is linearly separable. Then there is a hyperplane H: $\sum_{j=1}^{n} w_j A_j + w_0 = 0$ to separate $f_{p\Omega}$.

Suppose that the vertices above H have class label $+$, and the vertices under H have class label $-$. Assume that H_{ik} is the surface corresponding to subfunction $f(a_{ik})$, $k = 1$, $\cdots$, m. We put H_{ij} on the side of H with the same class label and move it any distance from other surfaces H_{ik}, $k \neq j$. If H is exactly perpendicular to H_{ij}, we can adjust H slightly to make it not perpendicular to H_{ij}, while keeping the separation. This is possible since there are only finite vertices on the hypercube. Then it is obvious that if we move H_{ij} far enough, it will be totally on the one side of H, since H is not perpendicular to H_{ij}.

The current positions of H_{ik} for $k = 1$, $\cdots$, m, correspond to a numeric function transform of f. Applying this transform, the resulting numeric function f_Ω must be linearly separable by H. Therefore, f is not hard nonlinear too.

Lemma 1 shows that the identical surface has no influence on the linearity of a function, so it can be freely removed without affecting the linearity.

Now we begin to discuss the relation between a nominal function containing XOR and its nonlinearity.

Lemma 2. *Suppose f is a 2-dimensional nominal function. If f does not contain an XOR, then f is not hard nonlinear.*

Proof: Suppose that f is a 2-dimensional nominal function on attributes A and B and does not contain an XOR. After applying a numeric function mapping Ω, we get a corresponding numeric function f_Ω. f_Ω can be illustrated by a matrix M on $\mathcal{R}^2$ which consists of a set of vertices with class labels, as shown in Figure 1. Because f does not contain an XOR, it can be proved that M will be empty after successively removing the identical rows and columns of M. According to Lemma 1, f is not hard nonlinear.

Theorem 2 below establishes a close relation between a function containing an XOR and its nonlinearity.

Theorem 2. *An n-dimensional nominal function f is hard nonlinear if and only if it contains an XOR.*

See Appendix 1 for the proof of this theorem.

Interestingly enough, XOR is also related to the linearity of other classifiers. For example, the perceptron is linear since it cannot represent XOR.

Theorem 3. *Naive Bayes cannot learn any hard nonlinear nominal function.*

Proof: Since Naive Bayes cannot learn any nominal functions containing an XOR and, according to Theorem 2, a nominal function is hard nonlinear if and only if it contains an XOR, Naive Bayes cannot learn any hard nonlinear nominal function.

4   Empirical Experiment

In the above section, we proved that any hard nonlinear function is not learnable to Naive Bayes, and that a nominal function is hard nonlinear if and only if it contains an XOR. According to that result, it is intuitive that the more XORs contained in a nominal function, the more difficulty for it to be learnable to Naive Bayes. We have verified this statement by the empirical experiment below.

We randomly generate an augmented Naive Bayes (ANB) G [4], and count the number of XORs contained in G. Then we draw a dataset from G at random by logical sampling [5]. A Naive Bayes N_G is trained and applied to that dataset by 5-fold cross-validation . Then we can observe the relation between the number of XORs contained in G and the classification accuracy of N_G. We try different ANBs, and the results are similar. The following figure shows the results of two cases, in which the ANBs have six nodes and five edges, and eight nodes and seven edges respectively. We repeat the above process 10,000 times in both cases.

In Figure 2, the solid lines plot the classification accuracy of the target ANBs. Note that the accuracy is not 1, because not every example drawn by logical sampling is consistent to the classification of the target ANB. The dotted lines

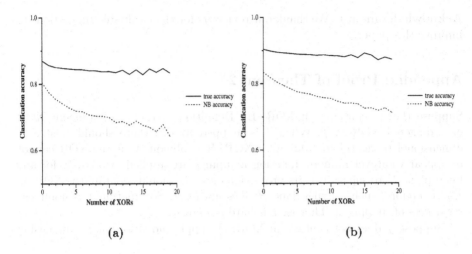

Fig. 2. (a) Target ANB with six nodes   (b) target ANB with eight nodes

are the classification accuracy of Naive Bayes. Clearly, the difference between the solid and dotted lines increases significantly in both cases, as the number of XORs contained in the target ANB increases. Approximately, the difference grows from six percent to nineteen percent.

The above experiment verifies our expectation that the more XORs contained in a nominal function, the more difficulty for it to be learnable to Naive Bayes. This provides us with the evidence that Naive Bayes cannot learn any hard nonlinear functions.

5   Conclusions

We investigated the linearity of nominal functions by introducing a three-layer measure: hard linear, soft nonlinear, and hard nonlinear. We discussed the learnability of Naive Bayes in term of the three layers of linearity. Our results showed that Naive Bayes can learn some hard linear and some soft nonlinear functions, but it cannot learn any hard nonlinear functions. Our experiment also verified that hard nonlinear functions are more difficult to be learned by Naive Bayes.

Our work establishes two fundamental facts. One is the limitation of Naive Bayes in terms of geometric properties of the nominal functions. The other is that linearity is an appropriate measure for the complexity of nominal functions in Bayesian learning.

From the theoretical results of our paper, Naive Bayes is quite limited in its learnability in nominal domains. A natural question is, what is the reachable upper bound on the learnability of Naive Bayes? That is, how well can Naive Bayes approximate a nonlinear function, even though it cannot represent it perfectly? This is one of our future research topics.

Acknowledgements. We thank our reviewers for their valuable suggestions to improve this paper.

Appendix: Proof of Theorem 2

Suppose that f contains an XOR. By Definition 5, there is a tangent XOR or a diagonal XOR in f. When f is mapped to $\mathcal{R}^n$, there should exist a 2-dimensional plane H_2 containing an XOR. It is obvious that the XOR cannot disappear whatever numeric function mappings are applied. Moreover, for any hyperplane H to separate f, its projection onto H_2 should separate the XOR on H_2. Therefore, such a hyperplane H does not exist. So function f is nonlinear regardless of mappings. That is, f is hard nonlinear.

Suppose f does not contain an XOR. We apply induction on f's dimension n.

Let $n = 2$. From Lemma 2, we know that f is not hard nonlinear.

Suppose when $n = m - 1$, all $(m\text{-}1)$-dimension nominal functions not containing an XOR are not hard nonlinear, where $m \geq 3$.

Consider $n = m$. Suppose f is an m-dimensional nominal function on attributes A_1, A_2, $\cdots$, A_m and does not contain an XOR. Applying a numeric function mapping Ω on f, the resulting numeric function is f_Ω and $f_\Omega(a_{m1})$, $\cdots$, $f_\Omega(a_{mk})$ correspond to all of f's $(m\text{-}1)$-dimensional subfunctions $f(a_{m1})$, $\cdots$, $f(a_{mk})$ on A_m. Suppose all $f(a_{m1})$, $\cdots$, $f(a_{mk})$ are not identical (otherwise we can delete it by Lemma 1).

Since none of $f(a_{m1})$, $\cdots$, $f(a_{mk})$ contains an XOR, $f_\Omega(a_{m1})$, $\cdots$, $f_\Omega(a_{mk})$ are all linearly separable. So there are k $(m\text{-}1)$-dimensional hyperplanes H_1, $\cdots$, H_k to separate $f_\Omega(a_{m1})$, $\cdots$, $f_\Omega(a_{mk})$ respectively.

When $k = 2$, if H_1 and H_2 are parallel, we can construct an m-dimensional hyperplane H from H_1 and H_2 to separate f_Ω. When H_1 and H_2 have the same orientation, [1] we can also construct an m-dimensional hyperplane H from H_1 and H_2 to separate f_Ω. When H_1 and H_2 have different orientation, f should contain an XOR.

If $k > 2$, H_1, H_2, $\cdots$, H_k should have the same orientation. Then we can sort H_1, H_2, $\cdots$, H_k in an decreasing order of the vertex number above each hyperplane. Suppose that the resulting sequence is H_{k1}, H_{k2}, $\cdots$, H_{kk}. We construct an m-dimensional hyperplane H from H_{k1}, H_{k2}. Then for each H_{ki} from $i = 3$ to k, since the number of vertices above H_{ki} is not greater than those above H_{k1}, $\cdots$, $H_{k(i-1)}$ and there are only finite vertices, it is easy to adjust the angle of H by moving H_{k1}, $\cdots$, $H_{k(i-1)}$ away from H_{ki} to separate $f_\Omega(a_{mk_i})$ while separating $f_\Omega(a_{mk_1})$, $\cdots$, $f_\Omega(a_{mk_{(i-1)}})$. Since k is finite, the hyperplane H constructed above will separate all H_{k1}, H_{k2}, $\cdots$, H_{kk}. So f_Ω is linearly separable. Therefore, f is not hard nonlinear.

---

[1] Here orientation is the angle of the intersection of H_i and the hyperplane perpendicular to $f_\Omega(a_{mi})$

References

1. Domingos P., Pazzani M.: Beyond Independence: Conditions for the Optimality of the Simple Bayesian Classifier. Machine Learning **29** (1997) 103-130
2. Duda R. O., Hart P. E.: Pattern Classification and Scene Analysis. A Wiley-Interscience Publication (1973)
3. Frank E., Trigg L., Holmes G., Witten I. H.: Naive Bayes for Regression. Machine Learning **41(1)** (2000) 5-15
4. Friedman N., Greiger D., Goldszmidt M.: Bayesian Network Classifiers. Machine Learning **29** (1997) 103–130
5. Henrion M.: Propagation of Uncertainty in Bayesian Networks by Probabilistic Logic Sampling. In Lemmer J. F. and Kanal L. N. (Eds): Uncertainty in Artificial Intelligence 2. Elsevier/North-Holland (1988) 149-163.
6. Kononenko I.: Comparison of Inductive and Naive Bayesian Learning Approaches to Automatic Knowledge Acquisition. Current Trends in Knowledge Acquisition. IOS Press (1990)
7. Langley P., Iba W., Thomas K.: An Analysis of Bayesian Classifiers. Proceedings of the Tenth National Conference of Artificial Intelligence. AAAI Press (1992) 223-228
8. Peot M. A.: Geometric Implications of the Naive Bayes Assumption. Proceedings of the 12th Conference on Uncertainty in Artificial Intelligence. Morgan Kaufmann (1996).
9. Quinlan J. R.: C4.5: Programs for Machine Learning. Morgan Kaufmann: San Mateo, CA (1993)
10. Saks M. E.: Slicing the Hypercube. Survey in Combinatorics 1993. Cambridge University Press (1993) 211-255
11. Zhang H., Ling, C. X., Zhao Z.: The Learnability of Naive Bayes. In Hamilton H. J. and Yang Q. (Eds.): Advances in Artificial Intelligence. Springer (2000) 432-441
12. Zhang H., Ling, C. X.: Learnability of Augmented Naive Bayes in Nominal Domains. Proceedings of the Eighteenth International Conference on Machine Learning (to appear). Morgan Kaufmann (2001)

Support Vectors for Reinforcement Learning

Thomas G. Dietterich and Xin Wang

Oregon State University, Corvallis, Oregon, USA,
tgd@cs.orst.edu,
WWW home page: http://www.cs.orst.edu/~tgd

Abstract. Support vector machines introduced three important inno-
vations to machine learning research: (a) the application of mathematical programming algorithms to solve optimization problems in machine
learning, (b) the control of overfitting by maximizing the margin, and (c)
the use of Mercer kernels to convert linear separators into non-linear decision boundaries in implicit spaces. Despite their attractiveness in classification and regression, support vector methods have not been applied to
the problem of value function approximation in reinforcement learning.
This paper presents three ways of combining linear programming with
kernel methods to find value function approximations for reinforcement
learning. One formulation is based on the standard approach to SVM regression; the second is based on the Bellman equation; and the third seeks
only to ensure that good actions have an advantage over bad actions. All
formulations attempt to minimize the norm of the weight vector while
fitting the data, which corresponds to maximizing the margin in standard
SVM classification. Experiments in a difficult, synthetic maze problem
show that all three formulations give excellent performance. However,
the third formulation is much more efficient to train and also converges
more reliably. Unlike policy gradient and temporal difference methods,
the kernel methods described here can easily adjust the complexity of
the function approximator to fit the complexity of the value function.

L. De Raedt and P. Flach (Eds.): ECML 2001, LNAI 2167, p. 600, 2001.
© Springer-Verlag Berlin Heidelberg 2001

Combining Discrete Algorithmic and Probabilistic Approaches in Data Mining

Heikki Mannila

Nokia Research Center and Helsinki University of Technology

Abstract. Data mining research has approached the problems of analyzing large data sets in two ways. Simplifying a lot, the approaches can be characterized as follows. The database approach has concentrated on figuring out what types of summaries can be computed fast, and then finding ways of using those summaries. The model-based approach has focused on first finding useful model classes and then fast ways of fitting those models. In this talk I discuss some examples of both and describe some recent developments which try to combine the two approaches.

L. De Raedt and P. Flach (Eds.): ECML 2001, LNAI 2167, p. 601, 2001.
© Springer-Verlag Berlin Heidelberg 2001

Statistification or Mystification? The Need for Statistical Thought in Visual Data Mining

Antony Unwin

Augsburg University

Abstract. Many graphics are used for decoration rather than for conveying information. Some purport to display information, but provide insufficient supporting evidence. Others are so laden with information that it is hard to see either the wood or the trees. Analysing large data sets is difficult and requires technically efficient procedures and statistically sound methods to generate informative visualisations. Results from big data sets are statistics and they should be statistically justified. Graphics on their own are indicative, but not substantive. They should inform and neither confuse nor mystify.

This paper will NOT introduce any new innovative graphics, but will discuss the statistification of graphics - why and how statistical content should be added to graphic displays of large data sets. (There will, however, be illustrations of the Ugly, the Bad and the possibly Good.)

L. De Raedt and P. Flach (Eds.): ECML 2001, LNAI 2167, p. 602, 2001.
© Springer-Verlag Berlin Heidelberg 2001

The Musical Expression Project: A Challenge for Machine Learning and Knowledge Discovery

Gerhard Widmer

Dept. of Medical Cybernetics and Artificial Intelligence, University of Vienna, and
Austrian Research Institute for Artificial Intelligence, Vienna
gerhard@ai.univie.ac.at

Abstract. This paper reports on a long-term inter-disciplinary research project that aims at analysing the complex phenomenon of *expressive music performance* with machine learning and data mining methods. The goals and general research framework of the project are briefly explained, and then a number of challenges to machine learning (and also to computational music analysis) are discussed that arise from the complexity and multi-dimensionality of the musical phenomenon being studied. We also briefly report on first experiments that address some of these issues.

1 Introduction

This paper presents a long-term inter-disciplinary research project situated at the intersection of musicology and Artificial Intelligence. The goal is to develop and use machine learning and data mining methods to study the complex phenomenon of *expressive music performance* (or *musical expression*, for short). Formulating formal, quantitative models of expressive performance is one of the big open research problems in contemporary (empirical and cognitive) musicology. Our project develops a new direction in this field: we use *inductive learning techniques* to discover general and valid expression principles from (large amounts of) real performance data. The project, financed by a generous research grant by the Austrian Federal Government, started in early 1999 and is intended to last at least six years. The research is truly inter-disciplinary, involving both musicologists and AI researchers. We also expect to contribute new results to both disciplines involved, and our first experimental results show that this is realistic — for instance, in [26] both a new, general rule learning algorithm and some interesting, novel musical discoveries are presented.

In recent years, there has been an increasing number of attempts, in the field of empirical musicology, to formulate quantitative, mathematical or computational models of (aspects of) expressive performance (e.g., [1,12,13,16,17,18,19, 20,21]). This work has produced a wealth of detailed hypotheses and insights, but has often been based on rather limited sets of performance data (which were sometimes also produced under 'laboratory conditions'). What distinguishes our project is the use of large amounts of 'real-world' data, and the application of inductive learning methods to discover interesting and possibly novel patterns and

L. De Raedt and P. Flach (Eds.): ECML 2001, LNAI 2167, pp. 603–614, 2001.
© Springer-Verlag Berlin Heidelberg 2001

regularities in the data. In short, we aim at performing the most data-intensive investigations ever done in musical expression research.

The purpose of the present paper is to give an overview of the project and its current state, and to discuss the challenges that this application problem presents to machine learning and knowledge discovery. In section 2, we explain the basic notions of expressive music performance. Section 3 sketches the general research framework of the project and briefly touches upon the enormous difficulties involved in data acquisition and preparation (an aspect often neglected in machine learning publications). Section 4 looks at the problem from a machine learning point of view and discusses some of the particular challenges posed by the complex nature of the target phenomenon. Section 5 briefly summarizes some interesting results obtained so far and talks about some of our ongoing research.

2   Expressive Music Performance

When played exactly as notated in the musical score, a piece of music would sound utterly mechanical and lifeless; it is both unmusical and physically impossible for a musician to perform a piece with perfectly constant tempo, even loudness, etc. What makes a piece of music come alive (and what makes some performers famous) is the art of *music interpretation*, that is, the artist's understanding of the structure and 'meaning' of a piece of music, and his/her (conscious or unconscious) expression of this understanding via *expressive performance*: a performer shapes a piece by continuously varying important parameters like tempo, dynamics (loudness), articulation, etc., speeding up at some places, slowing down at others, stressing certain notes or passages by various means, and so on. It is this shaping that can turn a lifeless piece of music into a moving experience, and that also makes both the composer's and the performer's ideas clear to the listener. What types of parameters are at a performer's disposal partly depends on the instrument being played, but the most important dimensions are *tempo* and *timing*, *dynamics* (variations in loudness), and *articulation* (basically, the way successive notes are connected).

Expressive music performance plays a central role in our current musical culture, and musicologists are showing increased interest in understanding exactly what it is that artists do when they play music. Are there explainable and quantifiable principles that govern expressive performance? To what extent and how are 'acceptable' performances determined by the (structure of the) music? What are the cognitive principles that govern the production (in the performer) and the perception (in the listener) of expressive performances? And what does this have to do with how we experience music?

Our project hopes to contribute to answering the first two of these questions. We collect precise measurements of performances by skilled musicians, and try to detect patterns and regularities (and intelligible characterizations of these) via inductive learning. As we also enable the computer to recognize structural aspects of the music, potential relationships between expressive patterns and musical structure should emerge naturally from these investigations.

This approach is based on earlier work by the author [23,24], where it was shown that given some knowledge about musical structure, a computer can indeed learn general performance rules that produce rather sensible 'interpretations' of musical pieces. The central problem with these early studies was a lack of real performance data (the investigations were based largely on performances by the author himself). In our current work, we go beyond this by working with large collections of performances by skilled musicians, recorded on special instruments (pianos) that precisely measure and record each action of the performer. Ideally, we would also like to study the performance style of famous artists, on the basis of, e.g., audio CDs, but that will depend on the availability of computational methods for precise musical information extraction from audio, which is still an open problem in signal processing.

3   The Project: A High-Level View

To give the reader an impression of the complexity of such a 'real-world' knowledge discovery project, Fig. 1 sketches the overall structure of our approach. As explained above, the basic goal is to take recordings of pieces as played by musicians, measure the 'expressive' aspects (e.g., tempo fluctuations) in these, and apply some machine learning algorithms to these measurements in order to induce general, predictive models of various aspects of expressive performance (e.g., a set of classification or regression rules that predict the tempo deviations a pianist is likely to apply to a given piece). These models must then be validated, e.g., by comparing them to theories in the musicological literature, by applying them to new pieces and analysing the musical quality of the resulting computer-generated performances, and, of course, by measuring their generalization accuracy on unseen data. All this is sketched in the lower half of Fig.1.

However, the story is much more complex. The problems involved in acquiring and pre-processing the data turned out to be formidable and forced us to develop a whole range of novel music analysis algorithms. And since we spent so much effort on these issues, I take the liberty of at least briefly mentioning them here.

3.1   Data Acquisition

The first problem was obtaining high-quality performances by human musicians (e.g., pianists) in machine-readable form. There are currently no signal processing algorithms that can extract the precise details of a performance from audio signals, so we cannot use sound recordings (e.g., audio CDs) as a data source. Our current source of information is the Boesendorfer SE290, a high-class concert grand piano that precisely measures every key, hammer, and pedal movement and records these measurements in a symbolic form similar to MIDI (though with higher precision). We did eventually manage to get large sets of performances that had been recorded on this instrument by a number of excellent pianists. For instance, we currently have performances of 17 complete piano sonatas by

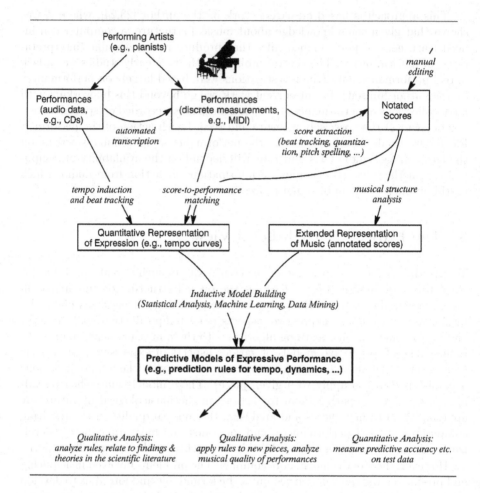

Fig. 1. The research framework: a sketch of data processing/analysis steps.

W.A. Mozart as played by a highly skilled concert pianist. This data set corresponds to some 5 1/2 hours of music and contains around 150.000 notes. We also have performances, by a famous Russian pianist, of essentially the entire piano works by Frédéric Chopin (more than 9 hours of music, 300.000 notes, 2 million pedal measurements). This is a huge amount of data indeed; in fact, it is by far the largest collection of detailed performance measurements that has ever been compiled and studied in expression research.

Another line of current research, which cannot be discussed here, concerns the extraction of performance information directly from *digital audio* data, e.g., audio CDs [9] (see top left corner in Fig. 1). This will eventually allow us to also study at least certain limited aspects of expression in arbitrary recordings by famous artists.

3.2   Data Preprocessing

Preprocessing these data to make them usable for analysis and machine learning is a formidable task. What we need is not only the performances (i.e., information about how the notes were played), but also the notated music score (i.e., information about how the notes 'should be' played) and the exact note-to-note correspondence between the two. Manually coding musical scores consisting of tens of thousands of notes is not feasible; in order to get at the scores, we had to develop computational methods for extracting (re-constructing) the score information from the expressive performances themselves. The result is a whole range of new algorithms for music analysis problems like *beat induction* and *tempo tracking* i.e., inferring the metrical structure of the piece in the face of (sometimes rather extreme) tempo changes [10,11], *quantization*, i.e., inferring the 'intended' onset times and durations of notes in the underlying score [2], and inducing the *correct enharmonic spelling* of notes (e.g., G♯ vs. A♭) [3], which is not merely an aesthetic issue, but absolutely vital for the correct interpretation of a musical passage.

The 'raw' score files extracted by these algorithms from the performance data (up to now, some 150.000 lines of text) still needed to be manually corrected and further annotated. And finally, the resulting score files were matched, in a semi-automatic process, with the performance files to establish the exact note-to-note correspondence; thousands of notes were manually identified and labelled as missing or extraneous (most of these are related to ornaments like trills etc.). From this information we could then finally compute all the detailed aspects of a performer's expressive playing (e.g., tempo changes, articulation details etc.) that serve as training data in the inductive learning process.

3.3   Enhancing the Data: Musical Structure Analysis

The next problem concerns the representation of the music. What we are searching for are systematic connections between the *structure* of the music (e.g., harmonic, metrical, and phrase structure) and patterns in the performances (e.g., a gradual rise in loudness (*crescendo*) over a given phrase). The representation of the musical pieces must therefore be extended with an explicit description of certain structural aspects. Again, a complete manual analysis of a large number of complex pieces is infeasible or at least highly impractical, so there is a need for computational methods. In the context of our project, we have developed a number of new music analysis algorithms that make explicit different structural aspects of a piece such as its segment structure [5], categories of melodic motifs and their recurrence [6], and various types of common melodic, harmonic, and rhythmic patterns, as postulated by music theorists [15]. These algorithms are of general interest to musicology, as they constitute formal computational models of aspects of musical structure understanding that had not hitherto been sufficiently formalized in music theory. The analyses computed by these tools can be used as additional descriptors in the representation of musical pieces.

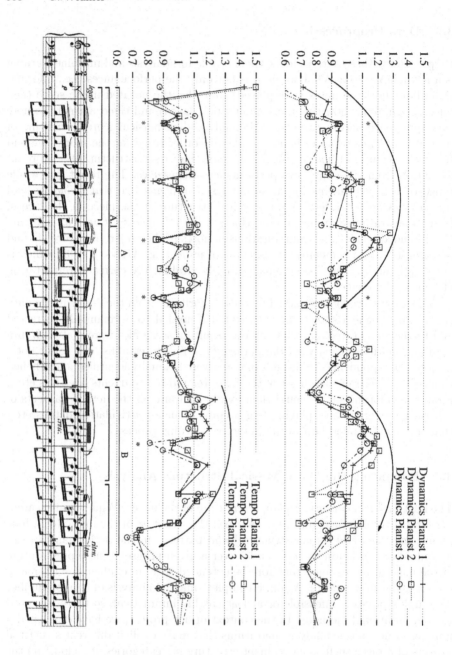

Fig. 2. Frédéric Chopin, Etude Op.10 No.3, mm.1–9, as played by three different pianists: dynamics (relative to average dynamics of entire piece) and tempo (relative to average tempo) of the melody.

4 Challenges to Machine Learning

The result of all these efforts are training data as exemplified in Fig. 2, which shows the dynamics and tempo deviations extracted from performances, by three different pianists, of a well-known piece by Frédéric Chopin. For the moment, we restrict our attention to how the *melodies* of the pieces are played (and neglect more complex aspects like interactions between different voices of a piece). All the three expression dimensions that we are currently studying — tempo/timing, dynamics, and articulation — can then be represented as curves that associate a particular tempo, loudness, or relative duration value with each melody note. Fig. 2 also contains a number of annotations added by the author to highlight different structural aspects of both the piece itself, and the performances. These will be of help in the following discussion.

The first question one might ask is: is there something to be learned at all? Isn't expressive performance something intangible, something that reflects the artistic uniqueness of a performer and thus necessarily escapes any attempt at formalisation or explanation? A look at Fig. 2 reassures us: there are, of course, individual differences in the interpretations by the three pianists, but there are also very clear commonalities in the three curves. In other words, there seem to be some strong common principles at work that lead performers to do things in a similar way. And these common performance patterns must somehow be determined by the structure of the music being played.

In fact, this situation affords opportunities for at least two different types of learning. The one that better fits the 'traditional' inductive learning setting is learning to characterise and predict the *commonalities* between performances. In the simplest case, a learner that is given different performances of the same piece can be expected to find descriptions of those patterns that are common to most of the performances, and treat those situations where the individual performers differ as *noise*.[1] Characterising common performance patterns that point to some fundamental underlying principles is indeed the primary goal of our project. But it would also be interesting to try to learn about characteristic *differences* between individual artists. Here, the problem is not to find out where two performers differ — that is directly obvious from the data — but to find classes of situations in which there is a *systematic* and *explicitly characteriseable* difference in behaviour. This might be a novel problem for machine learning.

A related question is *how much* we can expect to learn and formalise. Clearly, we cannot expect artists to be entirely predictable. We will have to make do with models that explain only a (possibly small) fraction of the observed phenomena. This requirement favours learners that, rather than trying to cover all of the instance space, can focus on those subspaces where something can be learned and produce models that clearly indicate when something is outside their area of expertise. Some interesting results along these lines are reported in [26].

---

[1] 'Real' noise (in the sense of mistakes or inaccuracies by the performer) is not much of a problem — high-class pianists are extremely precise, both in terms of motor control and in terms of their memory and capacity to reproduce particular expressive patterns over repeated performances.

Another fundamental question is: what are the target concepts? And that relates to a number of deep problems concerning representation, abstraction level, and context. At first sight, the curves in Fig. 2 are reminiscent of *time series*, which suggests the use of methods from time series analysis and forecasting. However, this is an inappropriate view. It is not so much the past states that determine how a curve is going to continue into the future; it is the structure of the underlying musical piece that partly determines what 'shapes' or 'envelopes' (in tempo, dynamics, etc.) a performer will apply to the music. The question then arises as to what exactly the scope of these 'shapes' is, and what the structural units in the music are to which these 'shapes' are applied — in other words, what is the appropriate *abstraction level*?

Actually, musical expression is a *multi-level phenomenon*. Good performances exhibit structure at several levels. Local deviations expressing detailed nuances (e.g., the stressing of a particular note) will be embedded in more extended, higher-level expressive shapes, such as a general *accelerando–ritardando* (speeding up – slowing down) over an entire phrase. For instance, the expression curves in Fig. 2 exhibit both local, note-level (see notes marked by asterisks) and more global structural patterns (e.g., a clear *crescendo–decrescendo* applied the medium-level phrase A.1 (dynamics curve), and an ever so slight *accelerando–ritardando* over phrase A in the tempo dimension). Thus, it will be necessary to learn models at different structural abstraction levels, which introduces the additional problems of discerning and separating multiple pattern levels in given training observations, and of combining learned models of different granularity at prediction time. Moreover, apart from the note and the phrase levels, there may be other, intermediate structural units relevant to explaining certain aspects of the curves. Discovering these is an intriguing musicological problem. One of our plans here is to study the utility of new *substructure discovery algorithms* [8].

Generally, the *representation* problem is a non-trivial one. There are many conceptual frameworks in which music can be described. Finding the most appropriate music-structural descriptors is a question of musicological interest. Systematic experimentation with different music-theoretic vocabularies will be necessary to identify these. In addition, the representation should capture the relevant *context* of notes and musical structures, which is a tricky issue not only because we do not know exactly how large this context should be, but also because there are also some highly *non-local* effects at work (e.g., when the recurrence of a melodic motif prompts the performer to 'fall back' into a previous pattern). As for the essentially *relational* nature of music, which would suggest the use of first-order logic for knowledge representation and Inductive Logic Programming for learning, it will be a matter of experimentation to study the trade-off between the increase in expressive power and the increase in search complexity implied by the use of ILP algorithms (see [14]).

Another interesting observation, which may be a source of new learning problems, is that the different target dimensions are very likely to *interact* or be *inter-dependent*. The performances in Fig.2 exhibit some clear parallels between dynamics and tempo, particularly in the case of some local deviations. For instance, there seems to be a strong correlation between dynamic emphasis and individual note lengthening (see the events marked by asterisks in Fig. 2). At a higher level, one could construe a certain parallelism between the dynamics and tempo shapes of the second of the high-level phrases (B) (see the arcs in the dynamics and tempo plots), which would confirm a general hypothesis by musicologists.[2] In general, performers have different means of stressing musical passages, by combining timing, dynamics, and articulation in certain ways. This suggests that expressive performance might be an ideal candidate domain for *multi-task learning* [7], where multiple learning tasks are pursued in parallel using a shared representation, which presumably enables the learner to transfer information between different related problems. Moreover, we would be interested in an explicit *characterisation* of the connection between, say, timing and dynamics, if there is one. This seems to be a new type of learning problem.

And finally, there is the *evaluation* problem. How is one to evaluate and quantify the validity of a given theory in a domain where there is no unique 'correct' solution (there are usually many 'acceptable' ways of performing a piece)? The empirical evaluation methods used in machine learning (measuring classification accuracy and prediction error on unseen data, estimating true error via cross-validation etc.) do have their place here, but they need to be complemented with more music-specific methods that, while avoiding to make judgments concerning the musical or aesthetic quality of a performance, do account for musical aspects of a model's predictions. This is a challenging research question for musicology and is beyond the scope of the present paper.

5   First Results and Ongoing Research

It is only rather recently that we have begun to perform systematic learning experiments with the huge data collections mentioned in section 3.1, so most of the above questions and challenges are still open. Our investigations so far have mostly concentrated on the *note level*, i.e., on describing and predicting how individual notes will be played, given various features of the notes and their immediate context. Here is a brief list of the most interesting results so far:

Basic learnability: In a first suite of experiments [25], we succeeded in showing that even at the level of individual notes, there is structure that can be learned. Standard inductive learners managed to predict the performer's choices with better than chance probability. Extented feature selection experiments showed that different sets of music-theoretic descriptors are relevant for different expressive dimensions (timing, dynamics, articulation).

New rule learning algorithm: Based on experiences gathered in these initial investigations, we developed a new rule learning algorithm named PLCG that can find simple partial theories in complex data where neither high coverage nor high precision can be expected. The PLCG algorithm and some experiments with it are described in more detail elsewhere in this volume [26].

---

[2] In fact, this parallelism becomes clearer once certain local distortions and artifacts in the expression curves (caused, e.g., by the grace notes in bars 7 and 8) are removed.

Partial note-level rule model: PLCG has discovered a number of surprisingly simple and surprisingly general and robust[3] note-level expression principles [27,28]. These rules are currently investigated more closely from a musicological perspective; some of them will probably form the nucleus of a quantitative rule-based model of note-level timing and articulation.

Learning at higher structural levels: In some limited earlier studies [23, 24], we had already found indications that learning at multiple structural levels does indeed improve the results (and the musical quality of the resulting computer-generated performances) considerably. However, the definitions of these higher musical levels and particularly the methods for combining learned theories of different granularity were very *ad hoc*, and the training material was extremely limited. We are currently developing a more principled approach.

Discovering stylistic differences: Regarding the possibility of discovering *stylistic differences* between different performers, we had obtained first indirect positive evidence in an early experiment that involved performances of the same piece by both the famous Vladimir Horowitz and a number of advanced piano students [22]. There it turned out that rules learned from Horowitz yielded a significantly higher predictive accuracy on other Horowitz data than on the student data, and vice versa. Recently, we have started new focussed investigations on this issue, with the aim of finding *characterisations* of these differences. This can be done with standard inductive rule learning algorithms, but requires the design of a different type of learning scenario. In a small initial experiment, several interesting rules were discovered that might describe characteristic differences in behaviour between the two great pianists Alfred Cortot and V. Horowitz. But the data were much too limited to permit general conclusions. We are now planning to repeat this type of experiments with a much more extended data set.

Machine learning for structural music analysis: And finally, computational music research offers many other opportunities for machine learning that are not necessarily related to the performance issue itself. There are many problems in *automated structural music analysis* for which there are as yet no reliable algorithms (e.g., harmonic analysis, phrase structure analysis, etc.) and which could benefit from inductive learning. For instance, we have developed an algorithm for finding classes of musical motifs and for elucidating the motivic structure of a piece, based on a new *clustering method*. This algorithm has been shown to be capable of reproducing motivic analyses by human musicologists of such complex pieces as Schumann's *Träumerei* and Debussy's *Syrinx* [6], and of predicting the categorizations made by human listeners [4].

Obviously, these are just first steps in a long research journey that should take us closer to our final goal — a quantitative, composite computational theory

---

[3] For instance, 4 simple timing rules turn out to be sufficient for correctly predicting more than 20% of a pianist's local *ritardandi*, and these rules seem to generalize well to music of different styles.

that explains as much as possible of the various dimensions of expressive music performance, and the interactions between them — and that will force us to address a number of novel machine learning problems on the way. This is a long-term undertaking, and we would like to extend an invitation to motivated young researchers to join our project team and work with us towards this goal.

Acknowledgements. The project is made possible by a very generous START Research Prize by the Austrian Federal Government, administered by the Austrian *Fonds zur Förderung der Wissenschaftlichen Forschung (FWF)* (project no. Y99-INF). Additional support for our research on machine learning and music is provided by the European project HPRN-CT-2000-00115 (MOSART). The Austrian Research Institute for Artificial Intelligence acknowledges basic financial support by the Austrian Federal Ministry for Education, Science, and Culture. I would like to thank my colleagues Emilios Cambouropoulos, Simon Dixon, and Werner Goebl for their cooperation and many fruitful and enjoyable discussions.

References

1. Bresin, R. (2000). *Virtual Virtuosity: Studies in Automatic Music Performance.* Doctoral Dissertation, Royal Institute of Technology (KTH), Stockholm, Sweden.
2. Cambouropoulos, E. (2000). From MIDI to Traditional Musical Notation. In *Proceedings of the AAAI'2000 Workshop on Artificial Intelligence and Music*, 17th National Conference on Artificial Intelligence (AAAI'2000), Austin, TX. Menlo Park, CA: AAAI Press.
3. Cambouropoulos, E. (2001). Automatic Pitch Spelling: From Numbers to Sharps and Flats. In *Proceedings of the 8th Brazilian Symposium on Computer Music*, Fortaleza, Brazil.
4. Cambouropoulos, E. (2001). Melodic Cue Abstraction, Similarity, and Category Formation: A Formal Model. *Music Perception*, 18(3) (in press).
5. Cambouropoulos, E. (2001). The Local Boundary Detection Model (LBDM) and its Application in the Study of Expressive Timing. In *Proceedings of the International Computer Music Conference (ICMC'2001)*. San Francisco, CA: International Computer Music Association.
6. Cambouropoulos, E. and Widmer, G. (2000). Automatic Motivic Analysis via Melodic Clustering. *Journal of New Music Research*, 29(4) (in press).
7. Caruana, R. (1997). Multitask Learning. *Machine Learning* 28(1), 41–75.
8. De Raedt, L. & Kramer, S. (2001). The Levelwise Versionspace Algorithm and its Application to Molecular Fragment Finding. In *Proceedings of the 17th International Joint Conference on Artificial Intelligence (IJCAI-01)*, Seattle, WA.
9. Dixon, S. (2000). Extraction of Musical Performance Parameters from Audio Data. In *Proceedings of the First IEEE Pacific-Rim Conference on Multimedia (PCM 2000)*, Sydney, Australia.
10. Dixon, S. (2001). Automatic Extraction of Tempo and Beat from Expressive Performances. *Journal of New Music Research* (in press).
11. Dixon, S. and Cambouropoulos, E. (2000). Beat Tracking with Musical Knowledge. In *Proceedings of the 14th European Conference on Artificial Intelligence (ECAI-2000)*, Berlin. IOS Press, Amsterdam.

12. Friberg, A. (1995). *A Quantitative Rule System for Musical Performance.* Ph.D. dissertation, Department of Speech Communication and Music Acoustics, Royal Institute of Technology (KTH), Stockholm.
13. Friberg, A., Bresin, R., Frydén, L., and Sundberg, J. (1998). Musical Punctuation on the Microlevel: Automatic Identification and Performance of Small Melodic Units. *Journal of New Music Research* 27(3), 271–292.
14. Kramer, S. (1999). *Relational Learning vs. Propositionalization. Investigations in Inductive Logic Programming and Propositional Machine Learning.* Ph.D. thesis, Technical University of Vienna.
15. Narmour, E. (1992). *The Analysis and Cognition of Melodic Complexity: The Implication-Realization Model.* Chicago, IL: University of Chicago Press.
16. Palmer, C. (1988). *Timing in Skilled Piano Performance.* Ph.D. Dissertation, Cornell University.
17. Repp, B. (1992). Diversity and Commonality in Music Performance: An Analysis of Timing Microstructure in Schumann's 'Träumerei'. *Journal of the Acoustical Society of America* 92(5), 2546–2568.
18. Shaffer, L.H. (1980). Analyzing Piano Performance: A Study of Concert Pianists. In G.Stelnmach and J. Requin (eds.), *Tutorials in Motor Behavior.* Amsterdam: North-Holland.
19. Sundberg, J., Friberg, A., and Frydén, L. (1991). Common Secrets of Musicians and Listeners: An Analysis-by-Synthesis Study of Musical Performance. In P. Howell, R. West & I. Cross (eds.), *Representing Musical Structure.* London: Academic Press.
20. Todd, N. (1989). Towards a Cognitive Theory of Expression: The Performance and Perception of Rubato. *Contemporary Music Review, vol. 4*, pp. 405–416.
21. Todd, N. (1992). The Dynamics of Dynamics: A Model of Musical Expression. *Journal of the Acoustical Society of America* 91, pp.3540–3550.
22. Widmer, G. (1996). What Is It That Makes It a Horowitz? Empirical Musicology via Machine Learning. In *Proceedings of the 12th European Conference on Artificial Intelligence (ECAI-96),* Budapest. Wiley & Sons, Chichester, UK.
23. Widmer, G. (1996). Learning Expressive Performance: The Structure-Level Approach. *Journal of New Music Research* 25(2), pp. 179-205.
24. Widmer, G. (1998). Applications of Machine Learning to Music Research: Empirical Investigations into the Phenomenon of Musical Expression. In R.S. Michalski, I. Bratko and M. Kubat (eds.), *Machine Learning, Data Mining and Knowledge Discovery: Methods and Applications.* Chichester, UK: Wiley & Sons.
25. Widmer, G. (2000). Large-scale Induction of Expressive Performance Rules: First Quantitative Results. In *Proceedings of the International Computer Music Conference (ICMC'2000).* San Francisco, CA: International Computer Music Association.
26. Widmer, G. (2001). Discovering Strong Principles of Expressive Music Performance with the PLCG Rule Learning Strategy. In *Proceedings of the 11th European Conference on Machine Learning (ECML'01),* Freiburg. Berlin: Springer Verlag.
27. Widmer, G. (2001). Inductive Learning of General and Robust Local Expression Principles. In *Proceedings of the International Computer Music Conference (ICMC'2001).* San Francisco, CA: International Computer Music Association.
28. Widmer, G. (2001). *Machine Discoveries: Some Simple, Robust Local Expression Principles.* Submitted.

Scalability, Search, and Sampling: From Smart Algorithms to Active Discovery

Stefan Wrobel

Otto-von-Guericke-Universität Magdeburg
School of Computer Science, IWS
Knowledge Discovery and Machine Learning Group
http://kd.cs.uni-magdeburg.de
P.O.Box 4120, Universitätsplatz 2
39016 Magdeburg, Germany
wrobel@iws.cs.uni-magdeburg.de

Abstract. The focus on *scalability* to very large datasets has been a distinguishing feature of the KDD endeavour right from the start of the area. In the present stage of its development, the field has begun to seriously approach the issue, and a number of different techniques for scaling up KDD algorithms have emerged. Traditionally, such techniques are concentrating on the *search* aspects of the problem, employing algorithmic techniques to avoid searching parts of the space or to speed up processing by exploiting properties of the underlying host systems. Such techniques guarantee perfect correctness of solutions, but can never reach sublinear complexity. In contrast, researchers have recently begun to take a fresh and principled look at stochastic *sampling* techniques which give only an approximate quality guarantee, but can make runtimes almost independent of the size of the database at hand. In the talk, we give an overview of both of these classes of approaches, focusing on individual examples from our own work for more detailed illustrations of how such techniques work. We briefly outline how *active learning* elements may enhance KDD approaches in the future.

L. De Raedt and P. Flach (Eds.): ECML 2001, LNAI 2167, p. 615, 2001.
© Springer-Verlag Berlin Heidelberg 2001

Author Index

Lecture Notes in Artificial Intelligence (LNAI)

Lecture Notes in Computer Science